Early Carolingian Warfare

THE MIDDLE AGES SERIES

Ruth Mazo Karras, Series Editor
Edward Peters, Founding Editor

A complete list of books in the series
is available from the publisher.

EARLY CAROLINGIAN WARFARE

Prelude to Empire

BERNARD S. BACHRACH

PENN

University of Pennsylvania Press

Philadelphia

10 9 8 7 6 5 4 3 2 1

Published by
University of Pennsylvania Press
Philadelphia, Pennsylvania 19104-4011

Library of Congress Cataloging-in-Publication Data
Bachrach, Bernard S., 1939–
  Early Carolingian warfare : prelude to empire / Bernard S. Bachrach.
    p.   cm. — (Middle Ages series)
  Includes bibliographical references and index.
  ISBN 0-8122-3533-9 (alk. paper)
  1. Europe—History, Military.   2. Military art and science—
History—Medieval, 500–1500.   I. Title.   II. Series.
D128 .B34   2000
355'.0094'0902—dc21   99-087239

To the Memory of
F. L. GANSHOF

Contents

Preface

In the West, military matters have consumed more material resources and lives than any other human endeavor over more than three thousand years. These unpleasant facts provide a dismal commentary that many people, including professional historians, would rather avoid than struggle to understand.[1] Sir Charles Oman, the erstwhile doyen of Anglophone military historians, observed: "Both the medieval monastic chroniclers and the modern liberal historiographers had often no closer notion of the meaning of war than that it involves various horrors and is attended by a lamentable loss of life. Both classes strove to disguise their personal ignorance or dislike of military matters by deprecating their importance and significance in history."[2] The famous line in the spiritual "I Ain't Gonna Study War No More" has been misunderstood by those who close their eyes to these bloody realities and urge others to do so as well. Historians, however, have an obligation to provide an understanding of war as one of Western civilization's dominant characteristics. In modern English usage, to "study" war does not mean eagerness (*studium*) for war.

This book is about war, preparation for war, and the aftermath of war in the early Middle Ages. Its aim is to understand how the early Carolingians—Pippin II (d. 714), Charles Martel (d. 741), and his sons, Carloman (d. 755) and Pippin (d. 768)—built a military machine that made it possible for Charlemagne (d. 814) to revive the Roman empire in the West. The society and particularly the government that made it possible emerge as both complex and sophisticated, running counter to the usual romantic fare purveyed in medieval textbooks and Hollywood films of warriors and their chiefs obsessed by the search for booty, the hunger for glory,[3] and other fantasies.

In this book, I discuss six principal aspects of early Carolingian warfare, each of which is the topic of a chapter. In Chapter 1, I examine the long-term strategy that the early Carolingians, who for the greater part of a century ruthlessly and single-mindedly pursued a diplomatic and military effort aimed at reconstructing the *regnum Francorum* under the rule of their dynasty. This chapter also provides a chronological examination of political events, as seen largely from the perspective of the winners, within which these efforts were executed. This chapter therefore provides the framework within which the study as a whole is set.

In the second chapter, I discuss the military organization of the Frankish kingdom when Pippin II came to power as Mayor of the Palace in Austrasia, the northeast quadrant of the *regnum Francorum* — specifically how troops were recruited and maintained. Special attention is given to the ongoing development of this organization by Pippin and his successors and its role in their long-term strategy to conquer regions that had escaped the control of the *rex Francorum*. An important goal in this connection was besieging and capturing the great fortress cities of Gaul built by the Romans and still the focus of wars of conquest in the eighth century. In the long view, Carolingian military organization was based primarily on that of their Merovingian predecessors, who had built on later Roman institutions.

Chapter 3 deals primarily with military training and equipment. Training was exceptionally well developed for fighting on foot and on horseback in the field. In addition, mounted troops were trained to dismount under battlefield conditions and to fight on foot. No less important than preparation for engaging the enemy in battle was the training of soldiers to undertake lengthy sieges of fortress cities. Troops were able to scale the walls in the most daunting circumstances. Undergirding this training was the technology needed for effective combat.

Chapter 4 examines the very broad subject of morale: in addition to thorough training and discipline, what makes good soldiers and results in successful armies. Under the rubric of morale also falls the value of large well-trained armies (now called the "doctrine of overwhelming force"). An army, however, travels on its stomach, and logistical support is crucial. The remuneration of the troops comes second only to their feeding. While fighting for good pay provides motivation, established goals of a "higher" nature, such as fighting for God or peace, also maintain high morale. In addition, the quality of commanders and their records of success are considered, as is spiritual help — the "no atheists in a foxhole" cliché. All of these morale factors help to bring about unit cohesion, without which a military force is unlikely to succeed in the short or long term.

Chapter 5 deals primarily with battlefield tactics. Fighting men in the fixed position of an infantry phalanx were used to turn back attacks by both enemy foot soldiers and mounted troops. These troops, however, also were deployed to charge enemy positions in an ordered and cohesive manner. Archers and slingers fighting on foot supported the battle line. On the march, foot soldiers mastered the military step which enabled them to deploy and redeploy from column to line and vice versa.

Some mounted troops, in addition to driving home a cavalry charge with swords, executed even more complicated maneuvers than foot soldiers. Some mastered the feigned retreat tactic, which was and remained the primary cavalry *ruse de guerre*. Horsemen also needed to remain tactically flexible so that they could fight on foot in the phalanx alongside men who had no horses.

Chapter 6 deals primarily with campaign strategy after an examination of the use of intelligence in military planning by government staff. King Pippin I's conquest of Aquitaine, which focused on the siege of an old Roman fortress city, illustrates early Carolingian campaign strategy and operations. I have therefore also integrated an examination of the tactics of siege warfare into this chapter. It is necessary to recognize that a long-term strategy, such as reconstituting the *regnum Francorum* under Carolingian rule, was composed of dozens of campaigns, each of which was carried out over a single season or several years and required detailed planning as to whether horsemen, artillery, and foot soldiers were to be mobilized and how large an army was to be mustered.

*   *   *

I decided rather early in writing this work that I would not use illustrations. This was a difficult decision because although many manuscript illustrations and a much smaller number of other artistic representations of various items that are of interest to the study of early Carolingian warfare have survived the ravages of time, Carolingian artists were not interested in providing a photograph-like record of military matters. As I have shown in previous publications, to explain what is useful and what is misleading requires digressions that are excessive in comparison to the value of such artistic representations. Many problems remain to be solved with regard to specific manuscript illustrations.[4]

Acknowledgments

As with all my other lengthy research projects, I have incurred many large and small debts in preparing *Early Carolingian Warfare*. First, I want to acknowledge the University of Minnesota for granting me a sabbatical leave for the academic year 1997–1998 during which the greater part of *Warfare* was written. However, the award of membership in the Institute for Advanced Study, Princeton, where the writing was done during this period, was no less important to the completion of this work. Indeed, the stimulating atmosphere of the Institute cannot be too strongly emphasized. I want to single out for attention Giles Constable, who not only read some parts of the manuscript but also and more important, provided for medievalists at the Institute a very special environment. Among others who have contributed in various ways, I want to recognize my former student Professor Steven Fanning of the University of Illinois, Chicago, and my present student and research assistant, Marguerite Ragnow, who saved me huge amounts of time and effort with her efficient and imaginative tracing of obscure material.

I will close with a few words regarding the dedication. I had the very great good fortune to study with Professor F. L. Ganshof during the academic year 1963–1964, where, in his seminar on Carolingian history, I learned the basic techniques for historical research in early medieval Europe. In addition, Professor Ganshof chaired my Ph.D. orals committee, read my dissertation, and advised me on numerous matters for the remainder of our acquaintance. In dedicating *Warfare* to Professor Ganshof, I am not repaying a debt, which, in fact, can never be repaid, but recognizing that debt in the hope that at least some of what I learned from him I have been able to pass on to my own students during the past thirty-five years.

Early Carolingian Warfare

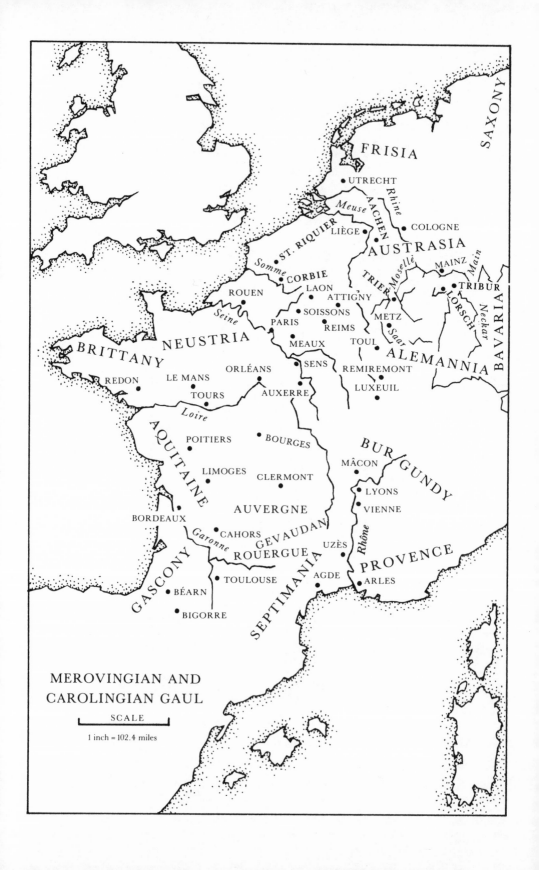

MEROVINGIAN AND
CAROLINGIAN GAUL

SCALE

1 inch = 102.4 miles

CHAPTER ONE

Long-Term Strategy

Modern scholars traditionally see strategy as having two components, grand strategy and campaign strategy.[1] Despite lengthy discussions by senior military officers and academics, however, no definition of grand strategy has been developed that satisfactorily approaches the epistemological criteria of both necessity and sufficiency. Indeed, there is no consensus even regarding what may be considered a flawed definition of grand strategy.[2] In addition, most historians who use the term *grand strategy* tend to avoid developing a formal definition[3] in favor of describing situations. Each reader then decides whether a grand strategy was in play.[4]

Both professional soldiers and academics agree, however, that some sort of "reality" underlies the term *grand strategy*, even if no valid definition has been formulated. However vague and putatively abused, the concept is widely viewed as having heuristic value even if only for the purpose of stimulating research and discussion.[5] Some rather broad areas have been accepted as useful in discussing this "elusive concept."[6] For example, it is now taken for granted that a grand strategy concerns the long term. However, there is no agreement on chronological thresholds, and so some commentators find that only a few years are sufficient, others think in terms of a few decades, and some consider the matter in terms of centuries.[7]

What is clear in this context is that a strategy that is limited to the short term—a year or so—is not to be considered grand strategy but is better considered campaign strategy. However, if a campaign lasts three or four years, then the question of labels becomes more controversial.[8] In addition, there now seems to be a tendency to discard or at least to replace the notion of campaign strategy, either wholly or in part, with the term *operations*. No definitions in a proper sense have been developed for operations; rather, scholars rely on catalogues of descriptive attributes, one of which reads: "Operational military activity involves the analysis, planning, preparation, and conduct of the various facets of a specific campaign."[9]

In another apparent area of agreement, grand strategy is generally regarded as transcending solely military matters and having an important political component. Thus, grand strategy is not primarily about winning battles or even about winning wars; rather, grand strategy is about how the polity develops the complex of its assets, including military resources, in order to define its place among its neighbors.[10]

This shaping process, which may be called long-term policy, brings together diverse military and nonmilitary elements. These include how the military is to be organized and the social basis for decisions regarding who shall serve and under what conditions. The government must have sufficient economic resources (i.e., *chremata* emphasized by Thucydides [I.12, 16] as vital to the pursuit of a successful military policy) to sustain its grand strategy. In addition, the support of the people — at least those in a position to make the policy work or to thwart it — is important. Thus, high morale, among both the soldiers and the rest of the society, is necessary. Basically, much of what is needed to win a war in the short term is required over time as an integral part of the society in order to have a long-term military policy.[11]

Although grand strategy remains an "elusive concept," some matters that have been raised in the discussion of this concept may well have heuristic value for the study of early Carolingian warfare. It seems worthwhile to ascertain whether the early Carolingians formulated and actively pursued a pattern of diplomatic and military behavior for the long term, perhaps even over two or three generations. Also, understanding how the early Carolingians mobilized their political, diplomatic, and economic resources allows the modern observer to ascertain whether these efforts were connected to military policy and followed a long-term pattern.

Carolingian Long-Term Strategy

The author of the *Annales mettenses priores*, writing ca. 805, takes as the theme of his work the idea that the early Carolingians — Pippin II (d. 714), Charles Martel (d. 741), and the latter's son Pippin (d. 768) — vindicated a long-term effort to reconstruct the *regnum Francorum* under the rule of their dynasty.[12] The Metz annalist emphasizes that the leaders, or *duces*, of the "Saxons, Frisians, Alamanni, Bavarians, Aquitanians, Gascons, and Bretons" had withdrawn from the *dominium* of the Merovingian *reges* because of their inaction (*desidia*). Therefore, the Carolingians from Pippin II onward had the task, given to them by God, to put the *regnum Francorum* back together.[13] Pursuant to this theme, the annalist sets out in a rather systematic manner a continuous history of Carolingian victories. These, he contends, were won with God's help, through a wide variety of diplomatic techniques and, when necessary, by the just use of military force.[14]

The conceptualization of such a pattern of action by the Metz annalist, not to mention the dogged pursuit and ultimate success of such an effort, over three generations, may well cast some light on early Carolingian long-term military thinking and planning. It seems likely that the Metz annalist and his patrons regarded Charlemagne (768–814) and his court as receptive to the idea that the Carolingian Mayor of the Palace, the emperor's great-grandfather Pippin II, along with his advisers, had developed such a long-term goal during the later seventh century. The Carolingians, as Pippin II's successors, seemed to see themselves as consistently pursuing with great success these efforts at reconstructing the *regnum Francorum*.

The Metz annalist, who had the benefit of hindsight, imposed an early Carolingian long-term strategy on the available facts. This does not prove that Pippin II or his successors had developed this long-term effort as a matter of considered foresight. No surviving documentation from either Pippin's court or the courts of his successors records or even refers to such a plan.

The Metz annalist may have worked backward from the fact that the *regnum Francorum* had been reconstructed under early Carolingian rule, sifting through a substantial body of written and oral information regarding a lengthy series of diplomatic and military victories which culminated in King Pippin I's conquest of Aquitaine in 768. The Metz annalist's identification of an early Carolingian long-term strategy from situations or events that may have developed more or less haphazardly during almost a century of diplomatic interaction and warfare permits the inference that he thought that such long-term military thinking was a possibility if not a *desideratum*. Whether he knew from some now lost document that Pippin II and his successors had a long-term military strategy cannot be ascertained.

Many written materials generated under the early Carolingians, however, have been lost. For example, it is very likely that a *vita*, written to glorify the career of Pippin II, was available to the Metz annalist but is now lost.[15] Thus, the Metz annalist or at least his source may have had information concerning Pippin II's thinking with regard to military matters in the long term. It is possible that Pippin and his son Charles Martel with the help of their advisers developed a pattern of diplomatic and military behavior that in the long term was intended to restore the *regnum Francorum* under Carolingian rule.

Modern scholars will probably never be able to demonstrate conclusively that the Metz annalist worked with now lost documents and oral traditions that in the aggregate could prove that the early Carolingians had some sort of long-term strategy. The Metz annalist probably imposed such a long-term plan upon the readily available facts of early Carolingian diplomatic and military behavior and presented these facts as God's plan.

To conclude, however, that the Metz annalist did not have access to an early

Carolingian plan is very different from saying that no such plan existed. By the early ninth century, the notion of conceptualizing a long-term strategy was alien neither to the Metz annalist nor to the Carolingian court. Indeed, by imposing a long-term plan for the future on the past, the Metz annalist relied on the receptivity of his audience in the present (ca. 805) to the notion that detailed planning for the future in the long term was an established norm. For example, the Metz annalist's awareness of various of Charlemagne's so-called programmatic capitularies makes it clear that long-term planning was a significant element of Carolingian governmental practice long before the acquisition of the imperial title.[16]

In the context of military planning, immense difficulties, due in large part to the primitive nature of transportation and communication technology, greatly hampered diplomatic and military operations throughout the history of the pre-modern West. Thus, detailed planning in the near term and the medium term was fundamental to military success, and even more so when a pattern of success over a substantial geographical area can be observed. Modern technology has in some ways made it easier for contemporary commanders to compensate for planning errors and other inadequacies than was the case during the Middle Ages.[17] With regard to the early Middle Ages, the realities of logistics, objectively understood, if nothing else, made detailed planning an ineluctable prerequisite for consistent military success.[18]

The development of plans to establish and sustain long-term diplomatic and military aims is quite another matter. For example, the Metz annalist would have his audience believe that Pippin II conceptualized the dual long-term goals of reconstructing the *regnum Francorum* and placing it under Carolingian rule. We may be skeptical of Pippin II's putative precociousness in both contexts. Nevertheless, when Pippin II's grandson, Pippin III, became King Pippin I, *rex Francorum*, after lengthy negotiations with various aristocratic factions and papal envoys, an important dynastic *desideratum* had been accomplished.[19] In addition, Pippin had legitimate warrant from his elevation to the kingship in 751 to reconstruct under his own rule whatever elements of the *regnum Francorum* that had escaped early Carolingian efforts. Modern scholars vary in their evaluation of how deliberate the early Carolingians were in pursuing this long-term goal and attaining the kingship prior to 751.[20] However, as will be seen below, once Pippin had acquired the kingship, he pursued the reconstruction energetically and consistently.

Like the Metz annalist, but in much greater detail, the modern scholar can catalogue the very frequent military campaigns of Pippin II, Charles Martel, and the latter's sons, Carloman and Pippin.[21] These military efforts were constrained by the available human and material resources, as well as formidable opposition from well-positioned adversaries. Nevertheless, Pippin II and his successors pursued their goal through an obvious pattern of diplomatic and military efforts which, as will be suggested below, betray the conscious imposition of a matrix of priorities rather than a mere haphazard response to opportunities for wealth and glory.

Political Geography of the *Regnum Francorum*

What was the extent of the *regnum Francorum* prior to the rather rapid fragmentation of direct royal power following the death of the last consistently effective Merovingian king, Dagobert I, in 639? And did Pippin II and his successors have sufficient information regarding its extent? Without such knowledge, the early Carolingians could not have developed a general plan for the political reconstruction of the *regnum Francorum* in the long term.

The historical works of Gregory of Tours, written during the later sixth century, were widely available and frequently copied during the later seventh and early eighth centuries in various versions and abridgments.[22] These books indicated both the peoples and the extent of the territory ruled by the Merovingian kings. The political geography of the *regnum Francorum* included not only the regions known to the early Carolingians as Austrasia, Neustria, Burgundy, and Aquitaine but also a considerable trans-Rhenish area.[23] For example, from Gregory's account, the region of the Rhine mouth was under the control of the Merovingians as early as ca. 520 when Theudebert, Clovis' grandson, defeated Danish raiders in the region.[24] The later poet Venantius Fortunatus makes clear that the Merovingians dominated Frisia,[25] which the early Carolingians knew had been a part of the *regnum Francorum*. Indeed, the English missionary Boniface, who received the patronage of Charles Martel and his sons Pippin and Carloman, was well aware that King Dagobert I had established a missionary operation based at Utrecht in order to convert the Frisians to Christianity.[26]

Gregory of Tours also notes that in 491, Clovis conquered a group of Thuringians.[27] This people was settled in the area that now is considered Hesse and which then was bounded on the north by Frisia, on the east by the Weser River (which constituted a frontier of sorts with the main region of Saxon settlement), and on the south by Alamannia.[28] Clovis conquered and absorbed Alamannia into the *regnum Francorum* in 496.[29] Gregory reports that the heartland of the Thuringian kingdom was conquered by Clovis' sons, Chlotar I and Theudebert I, in 531, and that the Thuringian princess Radegund was taken prisoner and subsequently made a Merovingian queen as the wife of Chlotar I.[30]

Bavaria, to the south of Thuringia, marked the southeastern limits of the

regnum Francorum. Gregory illustrates the subordination of its people, the Bai-
warii, to King Chlotar I (d. 561) by the fact that the *dux* Garibald was required
to marry a woman whom the Merovingian ruler chose for him. The Merovingian government considered Garibald the chief royal administrative officer in
the region.[31] In 631, Dagobert I seriously considered establishing a large military
colony of Bulgars in Bavaria, and some 9,000 fighting men and their families
were quartered for an entire winter on the Merovingian king's Bavarian subjects and at their expense. The Bavarians bore the economic and social costs of
the effort and played no role in the decision-making process, for Dagobert is
reported to have acted solely on the counsel of his Frankish advisers.[32]

The early Carolingians were well informed by Gregory's work and a variety
of other readily available sources that the peoples of the tran-Rhenish region
and the territory they inhabited had been integrated into the *regnum Francorum.* The process of integrating the people under the rule of the Merovingian
dynasty was substantially in accord with late Roman imperial traditions. For example, Merovingian coinage, which imitated imperial coinage, was used in the
trans-Rhenish areas. Control of coinage was a fundamental indicator of independence, and these people did not mint their own coins.[33] Second, troops from
the peoples who lived in these trans-Rhenish areas were commonly recruited
by the Merovingian kings for various types of military operations.[34] Third, the
Merovingians permitted these peoples to maintain the personality of the law
in the Roman peregrine tradition, although the Merovingian kings issued and
approved law codes for them. Those codes that survive for the Alamans and
Bavarians were written in Latin and were highly imitative of various Frankish
laws.[35]

In addition to information concerning peoples who were traditionally
ruled by the Merovingian kings and the geographical contours of the *regnum
Francorum*, the early Carolingians also knew that a great many other peoples
with whom the Merovingians had contact and the territories in which they lived
had not been a part of this domain: for example, the people of southern England
(Kent),[36] northern Spain,[37] northern Italy,[38] western Brittany,[39] and Saxony.[40]
The early Carolingians avoided campaigns aimed at the conquest of these territories outside what they understood to have been *regnum Francorum.*

Pippin II

Pippin II and his early Carolingian successors pursued a long-term goal of the
political reconstruction of the *regnum Francorum* under their dynastic control.
As early as 651, Grimoald, Pippin II's maternal uncle and Mayor of the Palace for

Austrasia, succeeded in placing his son, Childebert, on the throne of Austrasia. However, this effort at usurpation ended in 657 with Grimoald's execution, the disappearance of Childebert, and the temporary eclipse of the family in Austrasia.[41] Ansegisel, Grimoald's brother-in-law and the father of Pippin II, gradually rebuilt the position of the family during the next decade. Ansegisel was assassinated, however, before he could restore his family to the office of Mayor of the Palace in Austrasia.[42]

The death of Ansegisel freed Pippin and his brother Martin to depart radically from their father's ultimately unsuccessful diplomatic pursuit of the family's goals. Soon after Ansegisel's death, Wulfoald, the Austrasian Mayor of the Palace, and two successive Merovingian puppet kings, Chlotar III and Childeric II, all died (the latter monarch having been assassinated). Thus, Pippin and his brother Martin, in need of a puppet king of their own whose title and office would legitimize their actions, brought Dagobert II back to Gaul from his exile in Ireland.[43] Under Dagobert's nominal kingship, Pippin and Martin jointly assumed the office of *dux*, becoming the commanding generals of the Austrasian army.[44] The core of the latter force for deployment in major offensive campaigns aimed at territorial conquest was likely composed of expeditionary levies who, in principle, could be mobilized only at royal order. Along with their own military households, *obsequia*, and those of their aristocratic supporters, Pippin and Martin were able to mobilize an army of considerable size.[45]

By about 675, following the death of Wulfoald and the installation of Dagobert II as king, Pippin and Martin had secured military preeminence in the Austrasian kingdom. Both reasonably contemporary accounts of the state of affairs at this time indicate that they, in fact, ruled Austrasia.[46] In this context the brothers decided that they would abandon the diplomatic efforts their father had pursued and would lead their armies on the offensive in order to expand their domination beyond Austrasia. Three of the four traditional Merovingian *regna* that were located west of the Rhine — Neustria, Burgundy, and Aquitaine — were free of their control at this time.[47] They chose to attack Neustria, which remained the focus of Pippin's military operations in the west until it was absorbed in the wake of his victory at Tertry in 687.

Neustria
Pippin and Martin's campaign was one of territorial conquest rather than a mere raid for booty. The sources agree that the brothers mobilized a very large army, composed in great part of expeditionary levies.[48] However, at Lucofao, Bois-du-Fays near Rethel in the Ardennes, the Neustrian army under the command of Ebroin, the Mayor of the Palace, met the Austrasians in a great battle (*magnum certamen*) and decisively defeated the forces led by Pippin and Martin. The

Austrasians suffered massive casualties, and although he escaped the battlefield, Duke Martin was "murdered" in the wake of the encounter at Ebroin's orders and with the complicity of the archbishop of Rheims.[49]

Ebroin was able to enjoy the fruits of his success for only a few months. A band led by a certain Neustrian magnate named Ermenfrid attacked the victor of Lucofao at night in a raid on his home and killed him.[50] At first glance, it would seem obvious that Pippin orchestrated the assassination as a means of reversing the judgment that God had rendered on the field of battle. The only surprising thing is that Pippin, who had avenged his father's assassination in a night raid on the home of the perpetrator a few years earlier with a unit from his own military household (*cum satellitibus suis*), did not carry out this highly dangerous mission personally.[51] Nevertheless, Pippin had a sound political motive to conspire in the assassination. The death of Ebroin eliminated his major political adversary in Neustria.

Pippin also had a personal motive to see Ebroin dead: the Neustrian Mayor had ordered the execution of Duke Martin following the latter's capture in the wake of the defeat at Lucofao.[52] In this context, Pippin's desire for revenge complements his policy for the conquest of Neustria. Nevertheless, according to the sources, many men, including Ermenfrid, had strong personal motives to kill Ebroin.[53] If Pippin masterminded a conspiracy to have Ebroin assassinated, it would have made sense for him to have found an agent with a personal motive to do away with the target, such as Ermenfrid. Pippin then gave Ermenfrid safe haven in Austrasia.[54]

The Metz annalist makes every effort to justify Pippin's behavior with regard to his favorable treatment of Ermenfrid. The annalist emphasizes that "the omnipotent God had decreed that an end was to be put to his [Ebroin's] monstrous power." Then, the annalist indicates that Ermenfrid was *nobilis*, while Ebroin is described as an exceptionally savage tyrant (*immanissimus tirannus*). Following God's decree, the noble Ermenfrid strikes down the most savage tyrant and seeks protection (*fecit confugium*) with Pippin. From justifying the killing, the annalist makes clear that Pippin "understood" the reason for the killing (*homocidium*) of Ebroin. Pippin is then described as receiving Ermenfrid honorably (*cum honore*) after the assassination and with his accustomed gratitude (*solita pietate*). Indeed, Pippin, in giving refuge to Ermenfrid, is said to have treated him according to the *ius humanitatis*.[55] Pippin's motives, taken in connection with his very positive treatment of the assassin, amount to circumstantial evidence for his personal role in a conspiracy to have Ebroin eliminated. The treatment of the situation by the Metz annalist suggests that he was combating rumors, still current more than a century later, that Pippin had played more than a *post hoc* role.

Whether a conspirator, as I tend to believe, or merely a fortunate bystander who benefited greatly from the assassination and subsequently treated the perpetrator *cum honore*, Pippin was prepared for the new political reality in Neustria. Waratto, an important aristocrat from the region of Rouen on the lower Seine, replaced Ebroin as Mayor of the Palace. Almost immediately, Pippin and Waratto formed a personal alliance.[56] During the course of the later 670s, prior to Ebroin's death, Pippin had developed a strong aristocratic following in Neustria which had been attacked by Ebroin.[57] Indeed, Pippin's supporters in the West, who returned to Neustria after Ebroin's assassination, may well have helped in 680 to put Waratto in office.

Pippin, however, may have had an even deeper plan. In the early 680s Pippin was trying to arrange for the future marriage of his young son Drogo to Anstrudis, the young daughter of Waratto and his second (?) wife, Ansfledis.[58] This marriage, which finally took place toward the end of the decade, likely was visualized by Pippin as a means eventually of having his family, perhaps Drogo or the latter's offspring, inherit the position of Mayor of the Palace in Neustria. However, Ghislemar, Waratto's son, probably by a previous marriage, was a mature man of considerable military talent and political experience who understood that he might be cut out of the succession to the office of Mayor of the Palace in Neustria if the marriage of his putative half-sister, Anstrudis, to Drogo were to take place.[59] Ghislemar revolted against his father and took the office of Mayor for himself.[60]

Immediately upon expelling his father from the mayoral office, Ghislemar opened hostilities against the Austrasians, apparently to forestall any further efforts by Pippin in Neustria. Thus, following the maxim that the best defense is a good offense, Ghislemar soon mobilized a substantial army and laid siege to the Pippinid stronghold (*castrum*) at Namur.[61] After some initial success against Pippin's assets, including the capture of Namur (which earned him a reputation for the mistreatment of military prisoners, causing *bella civilia*, and rejecting the sound advice of the holy man, Bishop Audoin of Rouen d. 684), Ghislemar died or perhaps was killed. The surviving records do not indicate that his passing was much mourned.[62]

Following his son's death, however, Waratto repossessed the mayoral office but instead of arranging for Anstrudis to marry Drogo, he wed her to a magnate named Berchar.[63] Ansfledis seems to have preferred the connection with Pippin's family and opposed her husband's plan.[64] Waratto did not only make sure that the marriage took place, despite his wife's reservations. In addition, he arranged matters with a faction of great regional magnates so that upon his own death, Berchar would succeed him as Mayor of the Palace for Neustria.[65]

Why Waratto was willing to give up the alliance with Pippin and place Berchar in a position to succeed him must remain a matter for speculation. Berchar was a powerful magnate from the Champagne,[66] a region that was often a disputed frontier territory between Neustria and Austrasia. Thus, if Berchar's personal power base was localized in Champagne, perhaps Waratto understood the extent of Pippin's commitment to an expansionist policy that included the subjugation of Neustria. By his preferment of Berchar in the line of succession for the office of Mayor, Waratto was shoring up the defense of the Neustrian frontier with Austrasia and thus halting any further encroachment by Pippin and his allies.

After Berchar became Mayor following the death of his father-in-law, Waratto, he attacked Pippin's Neustrian supporters, confiscating their lands and forcing them into exile. These exiles sought refuge with Pippin and petitioned him to help repossess their unjustly seized property.[67] A large group of major magnates from Champagne, including Reolus, bishop of Rheims, also defected to Pippin.[68] Reolus had strongly opposed Pippin's invasion of Neustria in 675, and earlier was hardly guiltless in Duke Martin's capture or his execution.[69] Thus, Reolus' defection from the Neustrian side in 686 more than likely was the result of long-standing conflicts within Champagne that pitted him against Berchar, rather than any personal affinity for the Austrasians or Pippin II.[70]

By the end of 686 or early in 687, Pippin concluded that his diplomatic initiatives had been stymied and that he should attempt the domination of Neustria by military means. The Metz annalist suggests that Pippin was fighting a just war based on three imperatives: the enemy had illegally confiscated extensive goods belonging to the Neustrian church that the Austrasians were obligated to restore; the Austrasians were bound to help the numerous Neustrians who were being oppressed by their enemy Berchar; and the enemy Neustrians were planning to attack Austrasia under Berchar's leadership.[71] These reasons were, in part, a true representation of Berchar's behavior. However, Pippin's intention to conquer Neustria goes unmentioned by the Carolingian propagandist.

In 687, Pippin's army won a major military victory against the Neustrian army led by Berchar at Tertry, near Saint-Quentin. This success permitted Pippin to gain control of Neustria during the next few years through a rather transparent but effective series of diplomatic initiatives.[72] Indeed, Pippin moved events along rapidly in the wake of his victory at Tertry. Although the Neustrian Mayor, Berchar, fled from the battlefield and survived the defeat, he was assassinated shortly thereafter at the instigation of his mother-in-law, Ansfledis, and presumably with both the knowledge and support of Pippin.[73] Not long after Berchar's timely elimination, Ansfledis and Pippin arranged for the marriage of their respective offspring Anstrudis and Drogo.[74]

On a broader diplomatic level, Pippin's supporters, who had been driven from their homes into Austrasian exile by Berchar, returned to Neustria in triumph and their lands were restored.[75] In addition, through Drogo's marriage to Anstrudis, the Pippinid dynasty obtained access to significant landed assets in the Rouen area.[76] In fact, by 690–691, Pippin removed one of his most important Neustrian adversaries, Bishop Ansbert of Rouen. The prelate was sent into exile and jailed at the monastery of Hautmont, where he later died. Pippin installed his own relative, a certain Gripho, as bishop of Rouen.[77]

Despite the paucity of surviving documents for this period, there is sound evidence for two major confiscations of land from important Neustrian families during the early years following the victory at Tertry.[78] One confiscation, the expropriation of the Amalberti, who had been long-time enemies of the Pippinids, began shortly after the victory at Tertry and culminated in 692. What is important about these confiscations is Pippin's careful adherence to a lengthy and complicated judicial process. Numerous public court hearings (*plura placita*) were held regarding the charges against Amalbert. After the facts had been well aired in these *placita*, the case went to the royal court for a final judgment. There, the confiscations were upheld and more than fifty secular and ecclesiastical magnates played a juridical role in obvious support of the proceeding and Pippin's policy.[79] This elaborate process serves as a useful comparison to the summary judgments made by Berchar against Pippin's Neustrian friends which helped to bring down the Neustrian Mayor of the Palace.

Pippin's success in confiscating lands from his defeated enemies in Neustria, as well as his ability to oust influential church figures, gave him useful resources for rewarding selected Austrasian followers. For example, the Norberti were rewarded with lands in the valley of the Oise River as early as 688.[80] By settling Austrasians in Neustria, Pippin also altered the balance of power among the various aristocratic factions that he had to control if his *regnum* was to be successful in the region. At least a quarter of the magnates found to be active at the Neustrian court in the wake of Pippin's victory at Tertry were of Austrasian origins. However, there is no way to ascertain the pace of their settlement in the West. Of course, these very gross figures also indicate that about three-quarters of the magnates who were active at the court were native Neustrians,[81] some of whom undoubtedly had suffered under Berchar and thus owed the restoration of their lands to Pippin and his victory at Tertry.[82]

Exactly how early Pippin formally took the title Mayor of the Palace in Neustria is not clear.[83] However, it is generally accepted that not long after the victory at Tertry, Pippin personally took control of the Neustrian royal treasure and brought it back to Austrasia with him. Pippin then commissioned one of his trusted Austrasian supporters, Norbert, to serve as his surrogate in ruling Neustria.[84] The basic lines of Carolingian rule of Neustria were in place by about 692.

Gripho, Pippin's relative, had replaced Bishop Ansbert, and the "model" process for the expropriation of "enemy" lands had been established in the case of the Amalberti. Pippin's Neustrian friends had been given back their lands, Austrasian magnates had been settled in Neustria, Drogo's marriage to Anstrudis had been arranged, and Pippin was in possession of the Neustrian royal treasure.

The Austrasian victory at Tertry was sufficiently decisive that for the remaining twenty-seven years of his reign, Pippin did not mobilize his armies for military operations in Neustria. His diplomatic methods in dealing with the Neustrian magnates during the subsequent decades were so effective that he had no need to pursue diplomacy by other means.[85] Pippin's control of Neustria was so thoroughgoing that he selected his son Grimoald to succeed him as Mayor of the Palace. When the latter was assassinated, Pippin gave the office to his six-year-old grandson Theudoald.[86] For the remainder of his life, Pippin and more often than not his agents followed the diplomatic patterns that worked well in the wake of the victory at Tertry.[87] St. Augustine's view that success in war was the price of peace surely was borne out here.[88]

Frisia

By the early 690s, Pippin's diplomatic initiatives in Neustria were enjoying sufficient success to enable him to consider conquering yet another region of the *regnum Francorum*. He chose Frisia, or at least Frisia *citerior*, as his next target. Much of the putative Frankish heartland of Toxandria had been included in the territory of Pippin I's *principatus*, and this region had fallen under Frisian control during the decades following the death of Dagobert I in 639. The English historian Bede terms this region, which Pippin II ultimately conquered, *Fresia citerior*, and it comprised the greater part of Toxandria.[89] Indeed, the very contemplation by Pippin of engaging his armies in the trans-Rhenish area is prima facie evidence that he was satisfied with the situation in Neustria. Pippin, like the Merovingians, understood that it was very poor strategy to fight on two fronts at the same time.[90]

When Pippin selected Frisia as his second theater for offensive military operations, the situation in the region was ripe for exploitation. Since the 670s and perhaps a good deal earlier, the Frisians had acted independently of the rulers of the *regnum Francorum*. In 678, Frisia was ruled by a certain pagan magnate named Aldgisl, who appears to have styled himself *rex*, king of the Frisians.[91] In addition, during the second half of the seventh century the Frisians had been minting coins that were not a proper Merovingian issue. This coinage would appear to have been initiated in the context of the great commercial development of the emporium at Durstede on the Rhine. Although Durstede had minted Merovingian-type coins during the earliest period of its development,[92] this successful trading center, like the nearby old Roman fortress city of Utrecht, was controlled by the Frisians and was not subject to the ruler of the *regnum Francorum* during the 670s, 680s, and into the early 690s.[93]

Pippin had sound reasons to focus his military efforts on Frisia rather than on another trans-Rhenish region such as Alamannia or a western region such as Aquitaine. Indeed, Pippin's interest in reintegrating Durstede, if not all of Frisia, into the *regnum Francorum*, once he had concluded that his position in Neustria was not in danger, had a strong economic component. Pippin's seizure of the Neustrian royal treasury makes clear that he knew the importance of movable wealth in high-level diplomacy. Control of the emporium at Durstede brought with it access to the lucrative taxes and tolls collected there.[94]

Aldgisl, by usurping the title of *rex*, placed the Frisian people and the territory they inhabited in an overt secessionist posture, as compared, for example, to the more ambiguous situation that obtained in Burgundy.[95] This Frisian usurpation, therefore, made it possible to characterize Pippin's reassertion of Frankish authority through a military initiative as a just war, *de utilitate imperii* and against *rebelles*.[96] Not only did the Metz annalist structure the Carolingian success story as God's plan; he also diligently cast Pippin's military efforts as just wars.

There is no reason, however, to understand Pippin's motivation to control Frisia as focused solely on economic matters. Pippin's maternal grandfather, Pippin I of Landen (d. 640), had held the administrative responsibility (*principatus*) for governing the vast area of Austrasia between the Charbonnière forest and the Meuse River as far north and east as the border (*fines*) with the Frisians.[97] Thus, in deciding to initiate offensive military operations against Frisia, Pippin likely was motivated, at least in part, by the notion of reasserting control over a region that his maternal grandfather had governed.

Political changes in Frisia also played a role in Pippin's choice. King Aldgisl disappeared from the scene, and his replacement by Duke Radbod as the ruler in Frisia may have provided Pippin with the immediate context for his decision to act.[98] When an entrenched ruler is replaced by a new and untested successor, both outsiders and insiders may take advantage of a fluid political situation. Their titles — Aldgisl was styled *rex*, and Radbod apparently was recognized only as *dux*[99] — may have indicated a significant differential in their respective power and influence, which Pippin both understood and planned to exploit.[100]

Pippin undertook many military operations (*multa bella*) against the Frisians, and his particular adversary was Duke Radbod.[101] At the initiation of hostilities, however, Pippin's strategic position was not propitious for the conquest of Frisia. At least at the start of war with the Franks, the Frisians were well situated to thwart Pippin's aim of territorial conquest. The frontier between the Frisians and the Austrasians extended as far south as the line between Antwerp and Limburg, well into the northern hinterland of the diocese of Maastricht, on the left bank of the Maas.[102] Further to the east in the Rhineland, the frontier between the Frisian emporium at Durstede in the north, at the confluence of the Rhine and the Lek, and Pippin's major base at Cologne would appear to have been quite fluid.[103]

Pippin thus was faced with a difficult strategic question. One option was to lead his forces down the Rhine from Cologne, or perhaps from some forward base such as the old Roman fort at Xanten, in order to attack the emporium at Durstede and the stronghold (*castrum*) that protected it.[104] The risks inherent in such a strategy were high. This plan of attack required Pippin's army with his supplies and siege train to advance down the valley of the Rhine through hostile territory—both banks of the river were under Frisian control—for perhaps as long as a week, since the route from Cologne to Durstede was more than 150 kilometers. The advantage of such an attack route was that the expedition's commander had the capability to provide his forces with the necessary logistic support for a major campaign of territorial conquest, owing to the use of water transport. Such an operation might require that his army spend a lengthy amount of time in the field and/or maintain a lengthy siege of the *castrum* at Durstede.

A second option was for Pippin initially to assert his authority over *Fresia citerior*, Frisia south of the Lek and west of the Rhine, or at least the part of this region that included Toxandria. By controlling Toxandria and more particularly its northeastern reaches, Pippin could protect his left flank from an enemy attack while he was moving his army down the Rhine toward Durstede. This line of march would require the Frisians to cross the river in order to attack Pippin's forces or their encampments during their march north through the Rhine valley to attack Durstede.

It is traditionally argued, following Bede, that Pippin conquered Toxandria —indeed, all of *Fresia citerior*—in one or more decisive military campaigns.[105] These Pippinid operations are believed to have been vigorously opposed by the indigenous aristocracy of the region, who are thought to have loyally given their armed support to Duke Radbod. Pippin then followed up his victory in Toxandria against this resistance by dispossessing and probably disposing of these native magnates, whom he putatively had vanquished in battle, and replaced them en masse with men from the Mosel-Eifel district, his wife Plectrude's home region.[106]

Recently, it has been argued that the indigenous leaders of Toxandrian society were not replaced in the wake of a bloody conquest of the region by Pippin, although "Pippin brought them into the Frankish sphere through military action."[107] How many, if any, of the *multa bella* that Pippin is reported to have fought against Radbod were contested in Toxandria or by magnates from the region cannot be ascertained.[108] It is clear, however, that *Fresia citerior* was brought under Pippin's control and Toxandria was part of this larger region.[109] In addition, it seems possible that the indigenous magnates had not resisted Pippin II with sufficient vigor to be regarded as hostile enough to merit losing their possessions.[110]

It seems likely that Pippin began his military operations against Radbod and his supporters in 692 and won an impressive initial victory.[111] Although neither the location of this battle nor its exact date is known, Radbod reportedly had to flee the field and lost the greater part of his army. In the wake of this defeat, moreover, Radbod concluded that further resistance at this time to Pippin was not in his best interest and he sued for peace. As reported by the Metz annalist, Radbod placed himself and all of those whom he ruled under Pippin's authority (*ditio*), gave hostages to Pippin to ensure his adherence to the treaty, and he recognized himself to be a tribute payer (*tributarius*) or subject of the Austrasian Mayor of the Palace.[112]

Given the late date of the Metz account and the pro-Carolingian bias of its author, it would be incautious to conclude that all of the treaty details are accurate. If the part of the treaty that transfers Radbod's subjects into the *ditio* of Pippin is partially correct, however, then the Toxandrian magnates, who are unlikely to have been ethnic Frisians, may well have been subjected to a new regime. Insofar as Pippin's grandfather, Pippin I, had governed this *principatus* prior to 640, the Toxandrian magnates may have seen themselves as passing once again under the authority of a regime that had been familiar and apparently not excessively onerous to their parents or grandparents.

Some Toxandrian magnates may have developed a certain loyalty to the Frisian regime under which they had lived and presumably flourished for some two generations. Other Toxandrian magnates may have harbored long-term hostilities toward the Pippinids despite the passage of more than half a century. Nevertheless, it is likely that Pippin's decisive victory over Radbod on the field of battle convinced the native Toxandrian magnates (or at least those who subsequently flourished during the early eighth century under Pippin's rule) that the future lay with the Austrasian leader and political reintegration into the *regnum Francorum*. Pippin made the transfer of power less of a problem by promising *beneficia* to those who cooperated.[113]

Although Radbod may have agreed to give up control of Frisia as a whole (this is doubtful), he had no intention of honoring such a treaty. For the Frisian duke to defend Toxandria, especially if the magnates of the region were not fully committed to his *ditio*, was strategically difficult. Indeed, Pippin II now had key resources for military operations in Toxandria immediately to the north as a result of his second marriage to an aristocratic woman named Alpaida, whose family controlled extensive assets in the Maastricht-Liège region.[114] However, for a Frisian duke to defend the fluvial maze of the lower Rhine region and the islands to the north and east was another matter.[115]

Pippin quickly turned his attention to Durstede and moved directly against it with the intention of capturing the *castrum* that defended the emporium and taking control of the latter.[116] Pippin established his fortified camp (*castra*) next to the *castrum* of Durstede in order to establish a siege.[117] Radbod, however, concluded that the fortifications in and around Durstede would not be able to withstand a siege by Pippin's forces and thus advanced against the Austrasian invasion force with his army. The two forces met in the immediate environs of the *castrum*, and Pippin won a decisive victory.[118]

Not long after taking Durstede, Pippin advanced against the old Roman fortress city at Utrecht and took that as well. With the capture of Utrecht, Pippin controlled the southern access to the Vecht canal—the old *fossa Drusiana* built by the Romans and still in operating condition—and as a result entrance into the Ijselmer. Thus, Pippin could keep ships from going into the Rhine from the Ijselmer and vice versa. Also at Utrecht, ships could be monitored going to and from the emporium at Durstede. Pippin was the dominant figure in the region and henceforth had access to tolls and taxes from the merchants. Even the ships that traveled on the river could be commandeered by Pippin for military operations deep into the Frisian islands or southward along the middle Rhine.[119]

By the end of the campaigning season of 696, Pippin had recovered Toxandria and had captured both Durstede and Utrecht.[120] He had won at least two noteworthy victories in the field against Radbod. For all intents and purposes, Pippin had gained control of a large part of the Frisian *regnum* and, most important, he had secured possession of Durstede and Utrecht. However, Pippin envisioned establishing his control over all of Frisia and to that end, he deemed that diplomacy was sufficient. He negotiated an alliance with Radbod that was sealed by the marriage of Pippin's son Grimoald to Radbod's daughter Theudesinda.[121] The similarity of Pippin's Frisian policy to that of his Neustrian policy is noteworthy: in both cases, Pippin followed up military victories with an effective diplomatic treatment of important magnates and assured the transition of power at the top by having one of his sons married to the daughter of the dominant family in the newly acquired region.

One important difference between Neustria and Frisia during the later seventh century was that the Frisians were overwhelmingly pagan, whereas Neustria had been firmly Christian for several generations. In this context, Pippin would seem to have understood very clearly that the full integration of Frisia under his *ditio* would depend, in part at least, on converting not only the leaders but also a substantial portion if not a majority of the pagan Frisians to Christianity. From a diplomatic perspective, Pippin probably thought that Christianized Frisians, who were seriously committed to their newly acquired faith, would be more likely to make common cause with their coreligionists to the south than with the pagan Danes or Saxons who lived beyond the frontiers to the north and east.

Pippin decided to lend his full political and military support to a mission aimed at converting the Frisians to Christianity. He was fortunate insofar as certain Anglo-Saxon clerics during the later seventh and eighth centuries saw their vocation in terms of a personal dedication to converting various of the trans-Rhenish pagan peoples to Christianity.[122] Moreover, some of these missionaries were more amenable to secular direction than others, and Pippin selected a certain Willibrord to lead his mission to the Frisians.[123] Willibrord was sent to Rome for consecration as a bishop and to obtain a license to preach to the pagans. Not long after, Pippin sent Willibrord back to Rome to obtain consecration as the head of the Frisian church; this took place on 22 November 696. The missionary would appear to have been given Pippin's full economic, political, and military cooperation.[124]

Alamannia

During what was to be the latter part of his career, Pippin went on the military offensive for a third time. Now the target was the trans-Rhenish Alamannic duchy, which included a significant territory to the south and east of Austrasia.[125] Pippin's armies carried out a series of very successful military operations against the Alamanni from 709 through 712.[126] According to the Metz annalist, Pippin's efforts were aimed at the conquest of the entire Alamannic duchy, and it is reported that he succeeded.[127] The opening of a new theater of military operations with such ambitious aims surely is firm evidence that Pippin, who was over sixty at the time, judged that his position in Neustria and in Frisia, not to mention Austrasia, itself, was exceptionally solid. Pippin was not distracted from initiating this offensive strategy in Alamannia by the death of his son Drogo in 708 or by that fact that negotiations with the Frisian duke Radbod for the marriage alliance, discussed above, were not completed until 711.[128]

The immediate catalyst for Pippin's decision to take the offensive in Alamannia was the death of the ruling duke, Gotfrid, in the spring of 709.[129] The duke's successor, Willeharius, would seem to have been a usurper of sorts insofar as he displaced Gotfrid's sons, Lantfridus and Theodebaldus, the legitimate heirs.[130] In this fluid situation, Pippin personally led the Frankish invasion of the Alamannic duchy in 709.[131] As a result of this campaign, Willeharius recognized

Pippin's *ditio* over the entire region. However, Pippin returned home, where he celebrated a "triumph," but without either having fought and won a battle or having taken any booty.[132] This last point is important and lends some plausibility to the Metz annalist's account. The Alamannic region also had suffered crop failure during the spring of 709.[133] The Alamanni were in no position to offer serious opposition to Pippin's invasion force, and if the Alamanni had surrendered without opposition, Pippin would have had no excuse to loot a region that he now at least formally controlled.

In 710, however, the Alamanni "rebelled" against the Franks. Pippin mustered a large army and invaded Alamannia, which "he set aflame." In the process of ravaging the region, he took numerous prisoners and great masses of booty. Again, no battle was fought between the invading army and the Alamanni.[134] The account of the campaigns in 709 and 710 are noteworthy not only for the great differences between them, but also for the manner in which the Metz annalist structures the situation. Duke Willeharius, having recognized Pippin's *ditio* in 709, is therefore a "rebel" in 710 when he fails to act as a proper subject, making Pippin's invasion in 710 a just war. Austrasian ravishing of the land, taking large numbers of prisoners, and acquiring a great quantity of booty therefore may be regarded similarly as fully legitimate.

In 711, Pippin was occupied with the marriage of his son Grimoald to Radbod's daughter and with a plethora of other pressing diplomatic matters, which included the choice of a new king to be elevated to the Merovingian throne.[135] Thus, when the Alamanni "rebelled" again, a magnate named Walericus led the *exercitus* of the Franks into Alamannia.[136] In 712, there were two Frankish military expeditions into Alamannia. The first, led by a bishop whose name has not survived in the skimpy record, seems to have been unsuccessful; at the least, a second and major military expedition was required.[137] Later that year Pippin mobilized a large army and not only ranged vigorously over the entire region but also subjugated all of Alamannia to his *ditio* once again.[138]

Despite Pippin's deep military engagement in Alamannia between 709 and 712, neither the Frisians nor the Neustrians seem to have been restive during this four-year period. In 713, according to the Metz annalist, Pippin's entire *regnum* was at peace and it was not necessary to mobilize any Frankish armies for military operations.[139] So far as can be ascertained this report is accurate. At his death in 714, Pippin not only had regained the family's position as dominant in Austrasia but had extended the *regnum* of his dynasty to Neustria, Frisia, and to the northern reaches of Alamannia.

Pippin exercised great discipline in pursuing what would appear to be a long-term military strategy. He maintained his initial focus on Neustria despite military defeat and two major diplomatic setbacks. But he kept the pressure on and won a decisive military victory at Tertry which he followed up with effective diplomacy. Only after he regarded Neustria as secure did Pippin turn his attention to Frisia, and he did not alter his war aims in this regard until he had secured what he wanted in the region. Finally, in his sixties, he focused his military efforts on the conquest of Alamannia. Pippin finished his efforts in a particular area before moving on to a new target, and he did not become distracted by opportunity in Burgundy or Aquitaine and never sent military forces into Thuringia, Bavaria, or Saxony.

Charles Martel

When Pippin II died on 16 December 714, Charles Martel, his son and ultimate successor, was languishing in prison under the control of his stepmother, Plectrude. She was determined to support her young grandsons, Theudoald and Arnulf, who had been established as Mayors of the Palace in Neustria and Austrasia, respectively, and bar Charles from the Pippinid inheritance. Charles, however, escaped from captivity and began a civil war in order to succeed to his father's *regnum*, likely with the support of the aristocracy of the Maastricht-Liège region, which was dominated by the family of his mother, Alpaida.[140]

In a series of annual campaigns, Charles first gained control in Austrasia.[141] Then at the command of a substantial portion of the very effective army his father had developed, Charles defeated "rebel" Neustrian forces in a major battle at Vinchy on 21 March 717.[142] Even the Aquitanian duke Eudo, whose relations with Pippin had been peaceful, ventured to lend his support to Charles' Neustrian adversaries.[143] Any Burgundian magnates who saw the civil war as a means of asserting their independence gave up such notions after Charles' victory at Vinchy and lent him their support.[144] Interestingly, the Alamanni, whose duchy, as noted above, had probably not been thoroughly subjected to Pippinid rule, and the Thuringians, who had never broken with Pippin, did not rush to support Charles' adversaries. However, the situation in Hesse would appear to have become destabilized as Saxons living in the region began operations against Austrasian assets as early as 715.[145]

Austrasia
For more than five years following his victory at Vinchy, Charles cleaned up the mess that his father's death and stepmother's efforts to disinherit him had helped to create. Problems for the Pippinid *regnum* in Neustria began while Charles was still in prison. Ragamfred, a Neustrian magnate of considerable local influence in the west of the region, led an army against the child Theudo-

ald, Charles Martel's nephew. Theudoald's forces were decisively defeated in the region of Compiègne, and Ragamfred immediately seized the mayoral office for himself. The new mayor followed up this victory with a raid in force into the heartland of Austrasia, across the Charbonnière forest, and as far east as the valley of the Meuse.[146]

While Pippinid forces were involved in the west against Ragamfred, Duke Radbod of the Frisians retook both Utrecht and Durstede before launching a major naval attack on Austrasia.[147] Radbod transported a formidable army with equipment and supplies some 150 kilometers up the Rhine to Cologne. Not only was this old Roman fortress city serving as Plectrude's capital at the time of Radbod's invasion, but the Pippinid treasury was ensconced there, as well.[148]

In the wake of these victories, Ragamfred and Radbod entered into an alliance with the intention of dividing Austrasia between them.[149] With Austrasia facing attack on two fronts, Plectrude was unable to mobilize Pippin's erstwhile forces to defend the *patria*. Various magnates supported Charles, in the wake of Ragamfred's march to the Meuse.[150] Bishop Willibrord was especially important in this context as the dominant representative of Austrasian interests in Frisia.[151] Despite the fact that Plectrude had treated him well, he gave his support to Charles.

Ragamfred and Radbod's goal was the capture of Cologne. As the Neustrian Mayor of the Palace marched east toward the Meuse for a second time in two years, the Frisian duke invaded from the northeast.[152] Charles chose not to divide his army but rather to engage Radbod first in order to keep the two enemy invasion forces from linking up at Cologne. His attack on Radbod was unsuccessful, however, and he withdrew after his army suffered substantial casualties.[153] Meanwhile, Ragamfred's army crossed the Meuse and the Ardennes and encamped in the environs of Cologne. The joint force led by Ragamfred and Radbod apparently was not prepared to besiege the city, however. They likely feared that Charles, who still commanded a viable army in the field, would seriously harass their emplacements should they establish a formal siege. Plectrude, however, reportedly paid a ransom. The enemy departed in the direction of Malmédy in the Maastricht-Liège region, which prior to Pippin II's military successes against Radbod had been on the Austrasian frontier with *Fresia citerior*.[154]

Between his loss to Radbod somewhere north of Cologne and Plectrude's ransom of the city, Charles was able to strengthen his forces. As the joint force of Frisians and Neustrians led by Radbod and Ragamfred, respectively, advanced to Charles' power base, he was able to keep well informed of the enemy's movements. At Amblève not far from Malmédy, Charles' army attacked the enemy by surprise while the latter was resting at midday. He inflicted heavy casualties on both the Frisians and the Neustrians, who fled from the field in great confusion.

In the wake of this victory, Charles apparently recovered much of the movable wealth that Plectrude had paid in ransom for Cologne.[155]

Charles' victory over the combined armies of Radbod and Ragamfred at Amblève undermined the alliance between the Frisian duke and the Neustrian Mayor of the Palace. Consequently, early in March 717, Charles, apparently now without great fear of being attacked from Frisia, advanced westward to invade Neustria. At Vinchy near Cambrai, Charles met Ragamfred's army, and after trying to convince the latter to surrender (literally, to make peace), he won a decisive battle on 21 March.[156] Charles vigorously pursued the fleeing enemy force to the south-southwest for 150 kilometers until he approached the environs of Paris.[157]

On its return to the northeast from the Paris region, Charles' army reportedly ravished and looted the rich valley of the Oise as he led his forces toward the valley of the Sambre and on to Cologne.[158] At Cologne, Plectrude refused to surrender the city to him. Charles brought about a revolt (*seditio*) within the city, enabling him to enter the fortress with his troops. Plectrude surrendered the city and the Pippinid treasure to Charles only after forces loyal to each of them fought in the streets.[159]

Later in 717 — following the victory at Vinchy and the end of the Austrasian civil war — Duke Hedin II of Thuringia demonstrated his support for the early Carolingians by granting substantial resources to Bishop Willibrord, who had been charged with the Frisian mission.[160] In 704, the Thuringian duke had similarly supported Pippin II.[161] Despite these successes, however, Charles had to deal with the remnants of Frisian and Neustrian resistance. In 718, Charles led a force into Frisia and defeated Radbod decisively.[162] Indeed, the latter's death noted in the following year may have been the result of wounds suffered in combat against the Carolingians or the dissatisfaction of his followers, or natural causes.[163] Whatever the situation, Charles never again faced an offensive threat by the Frisians against *Fresia citerior* or Austrasia proper.[164] Charles regained control not only of Utrecht and Durstede but also all of *Fresia citerior*.[165]

It is not clear how Charles administered this region, which had the potential to contribute so much financially to his government. Willibrord, the archbishop for Frisia, is the only man of great stature associated with the region throughout Charles' reign who consistently received massive material support from the Mayor of the Palace and his supporters.[166] Willibrord may have been the early Carolingian official charged with administering Frisia.

In 715, while Charles was still in Plectrude's jail and affairs were nominally in the hands of his nephew Arnulf, a Saxon force raided the Chatuarian region of Austrasia.[167] These Saxons were probably part of a group that had long been settled in the eastern region of Hesse to the west of the Weser River in the area of the headwaters of the Lippe, which various sources call Saxe-Hesse and *Saxonia*.[168] However, these Saxons apparently broke their long-standing peace with the Pippinids in the hope of taking advantage of the fluid political situation obtaining in Austrasia. Pippin II had never mobilized his military forces against these Saxons. In any case, following his victory over Radbod in 718, Charles led his forces into *Saxonia*.[169] Charles' decision to wait more than two years after gaining his freedom to attack the Saxons indicates how firmly his attention was focused on gaining control of Austrasia and defeating the Neustrians and the Frisians.

If Charles believed that Neustrian opposition had been eliminated, however, he was greatly mistaken. Ragamfred, who had been soundly defeated at Vinchy, convinced Duke Eudo of Aquitaine to support him against Charles. This was a radical change of position for the Aquitanian duke, since neither he nor his predecessors had ever been hostile toward Pippin II.[170] It seems likely that the Saxons and the Aquitanians changed their policy because Charles was less strongly positioned than his father had been. The fluid political situation brought about by Pippin's death encouraged some former "neutrals" to risk becoming enemies of the Carolingians. It is noteworthy in this context that the Thuringians remained friendly and that the Alamanni did not seem inclined to take advantage of Charles' difficulties.

The Aquitanians and the Neustrians confirmed a treaty in 718 by which Duke Eudo would be given *regnum* in Neustria. In 719, the year Radbod died, Eudo crossed the Loire with a substantial force of Gascon mercenaries and advanced into Neustria to support Ragamfred against Charles. At the head of a formidable Austrasian army, which had been consistently successful over Neustrians, Frisians, and Saxons during the two and a half years since the victory at Amblève, Charles went out to meet the enemy coalition. Somewhere to the east of Paris, when the two armies began to maneuver for position, Eudo suddenly fled south with his mercenary force, King Chilperic, and the Neustrian royal treasure. Charles pursued the enemy to the region of Paris and again halted his army, as he had following his victory at Vinchy. Eudo crossed the Loire in the region of Orléans. Charles permitted Ragamfred to escape to the old Roman fortress city of Angers on the Breton frontier.[171]

The next year, Charles sent an embassy (*legatio*) to Eudo. The Aquitanian duke gave every appearance of feeling greatly threatened by the full force of Austrasian military might from which he had fled the previous year, and at Charles' "request," he surrendered the Neustrian "puppet king," Chilperic, along with the royal treasure. In addition, Eudo sent a great many gifts to the Austrasian Mayor of the Palace. However, most important, the Austrasian *missi* negotiated a treaty with Eudo so that an alliance (*amicitia*) was established between

Charles and the Aquitanian duke. In light of events a few years later, Charles may have promised to help Eudo against his Muslim enemies in the south should they come within striking distance of the Carolingian army. Reciprocally, Eudo may have promised to stay out of Neustrian affairs and perhaps even discourage any opposition to Charles that might arise in the lower Loire valley, west of Orléans.[172] In this Charles treated with Eudo as an equal and did not establish Carolingian *ditio* over the Aquitanians or their duke as part of the pact.

With the confirmation of this alliance, possession of the Neustrian royal treasure, and a Merovingian puppet king to parade for the magnates, Charles' position was comparable to that held by Pippin II at his death. Charles, however, recognized that a new force had complicated the diplomatic-military situation when the Saxons, who were settled in the Hesse region, had destabilized the situation east of the Rhine by attacking Frankish assets. After punishing them in 718 Charles was impelled to do so again in 720.[173] In order to bring about further stability, Charles pursued the diplomatic initiative of Christianizing the region, following a policy analogous to that of Pippin II in *Fresia citerior*.

In 722, an Anglo-Saxon monk named Boniface, who had helped Willibrord in Frisia between 719 and 721, was given permission by Charles Martel to preach in the region of Saxe-Hesse. Boniface formally had to recognize that he was subject to Charles' *dominium* and *patrocinium*.[174] Thus, he became Charles' *fidelis*, undoubtedly through an oath of faithfulness. Without the *patrocinium* of the Frankish *princeps*, the latter's *mandatum*, and the fear that the early Carolingian rulers inspired among potential adversaries, he could not govern the faithful of the church; protect priests, clerics, monks, and nuns; prohibit the practice of pagan ceremonies; or prohibit the worship of idols.[175] Boniface was, in fact, Charles' dependent, later the dependent of his sons, Pippin and Carloman, and his missionary activity from the perspective of the *princeps* was, at least in part, a government matter.[176]

With the help of Boniface and his disciples, both Anglo-Saxon and Frankish, the Hesse region was substantially Christianized during the following decades. Numerous monasteries were founded, including Fulda, Fritzlar, Hersfeld, and Amönenberg. These religious houses and others were provided with fortifications for defense against those Saxons of the region who ostensibly remained pagans.[177] The new episcopal seat, which Boniface established at Buraburg, was fortified, as well. Frankish settlement in Hesse also was actively encouraged and many new implantations were fortified, Christianberg being the most noteworthy example. With spiritual protection provided by Boniface's widespread ecclesiastical organization and military support provided by Charles Martel and his successors, the Carolingians gradually gained firm control of the region.[178]

Alamannia and Bavaria

In order to reclaim fully the Pippinid inheritance, Charles needed to test the strength of Carolingian *ditio* in Alamannia and Thuringia. In addition, Ragamfred, the erstwhile Neustrian Mayor of the Palace, was still ensconced in the fortress at Angers,[179] but his power had been broken in the course of two failed military campaigns and he was isolated diplomatically as a result of Charles' treaty with Eudo. Charles ultimately co-opted Ragamfred and permitted him to remain at Angers, presumably as count of Anjou with government responsibilities for protecting the Breton frontier.[180] Ragamfred remained loyal to Charles and died a natural death in 731.[181]

Before Charles turned to the exercise of Carolingian *ditio* over the Alamanni, he became seriously ill, and throughout 723 was unable to lead his armies into the field.[182] During this period, the Saxons of the Hesse region once again attacked Carolingian assets so that in 724, Charles (now recovered) took the field with a substantial army for the third time in six years and punished them severely.[183] Although potentially annoying, the Saxons were not a great hindrance to Charles' more major concerns, and he did not deal with them again until 738.

After punishing the Saxons in 724, Charles was ready to test his control in the Alamannic duchy.[184] Charles had intelligence that the Alamanni would not cause any problems and that he could easily go through the region to Bavaria. By adding to his strategic goals the domination of Bavaria through an Austrasian invasion of the region, Charles radically departed from the policy of noninterference in the southeast that Pippin II had pursued for some four decades. Pippin may have contemplated extending his power into Bavaria, as this region had been a part of the *regnum Francorum*, but death had deprived him of the opportunity. The Metz annalist credited Pippin with more than an abstract interest in pressing Carolingian domination of Bavaria.[185]

The chronicler known as Fredegar's Continuator, who was working under the patronage of Charles Martel's half-brother, Childebrand, indicates that the Mayor of the Palace mobilized a large army (*coacto agmine multitudine*) for his operations in Alamannia and projected invasion of Bavaria. Charles crossed the Rhine with his *multitudo*, without opposition from Duke Lantfrid in Alamannia.[186] Duke Lantfrid, the son of Duke Gotfrid, cooperated with Charles; at a joint court he reissued laws for the Alamanni under the aegis of his Frankish *princeps*.[187]

Indeed, Lantfrid's continued cooperation with Charles is evident as he accompanied the Mayor of the Palace south toward the Bavarian frontier. A second court was held at Richenau on Lake Constance where Count Bertoald, the local leader of the Alamannic people, also gave his support to Charles. Finally, a new monastery was founded at Richenau which was to serve as the base for the Christianization or "re-Christianization" of the region under the leadership of Pirmin, a cleric of Visigothic background. Thus, in the founding of Richenau, we see the familiar Carolingian policy of Christianizing regions over which they acquired control and recruiting non-Franks to play key roles in the process.[188]

Charles found that he was not undertaking a military invasion of Alamannia with his large army, but rather a kind of inspection tour through the duchy, similar perhaps to that which had been conducted by his ancestor, Arnulf of Metz, for young King Dagobert I in Thuringia. Charles may have been engaged in a more specific military review of Alamannic military assets.[189] Dagobert I had established Frankish military colonies in the southern reaches of Alamannia that were of considerable importance to Charles' designs on Bavaria, given their strategic position.[190] In any case, the Continuator's use of the richly connotative verb *lustro* to describe Charles' behavior in Alamannia permits the reader to see either a general survey (perhaps for tax purposes) or a specific military review.[191] The latter usage would seem more likely as both Cicero and Virgil (authors well known to the early Carolingians) use the verb in this way.[192]

Once Charles was satisfied with the situation in Alamannia, he led his large army across the Danube into the Bavarian duchy. This army ranged throughout the duchy and whatever opposition that appeared was of little or no consequence;[193] the Continuator reports that Charles imposed Frankish control over this region.[194] The stimulus for Charles' expedition and his subsequent easy victory would seem to have been the death of Duke Theodobert and the fact that Grimoald, Theodobert's brother and successor as duke, did not enjoy full support in Bavaria. Substantial backing, apparently in opposition to Grimoald, clustered about Hucbert, Theodobert's son. The latter, however, probably had not yet reached his majority and therefore was unable to look after his own interests in a vigorous manner.[195]

What the Carolingian court sources do not report, however, is that Charles was supported in his invasion of Bavaria by the Lombard king Liutprand, who "attacked . . . from the south while Charles attacked from the north."[196] This is the first surviving information concerning cooperation between the early Carolingians and the Lombards. Whether Charles or Liutprand took the initiative in the arrangement is unclear. Also about this time, Abbo, the rector of St. Maurienne and Susa, who controlled the pass at Mt. Cenis, saw the good sense of gaining Charles as an ally. In January 726, when Abbo formally founded the monastery of Novalesa, he observed that he was acting, in part, to assure *stabilitas* in the *regnum Francorum*.[197]

When Charles returned to Austrasia, he took a great part of the Bavarian ducal treasure with him. The Bavarian region, however, is not reported to have been looted by Charles' troops.[198] This benevolent treatment of a conquered region may be considered prima facie evidence that military opposition, if there was any, was of little consequence. Indeed, Charles' treatment of the Bavarians in this context is clearly analogous to Pippin II's treatment of the Alamanni, subsequent to his successful invasion of their duchy in 709. More important, Charles returned to Austrasia with two distinguished hostages from the Agilolfing ducal family: Peletrudis, the wife of Duke Grimoald, and the latter's niece, Sunnichildis, the sister of Hucbert.[199]

Poitiers and Aquitaine

During the half-decade following the imposition of Carolingian *ditio* over the Bavarians, 725–730, Charles found it necessary to mobilize his armies on only one occasion. This lengthy period of relative peace is rather unusual by comparison with the previous reign of Pippin II and the subsequent joint reign of Charles' sons, Pippin and Carloman. This calm illustrates the unwillingness or perhaps the practical incapacity of the great magnates, who possessed immense material assets and who had the potential to mobilize substantial military forces, to oppose Charles. The sources record no conspiracies at this time.

Perhaps even more important than evidence for the effectiveness of Charles' diplomacy in nullifying internal opposition to his reign, this period of peace casts substantial light on the character of his army. Charles' control of the army did not depend upon annual military campaigns that produced large amounts of booty to feed its supposedly insatiable appetite for glory and spoils.[200] As neither the "inspection tour" of the Alamannic duchy nor the invasion of the Bavarian duchy produced the *plurima spolia* frequently reported by the court chronicler, Charles' second invasion of Bavaria, in 728, merely demonstrated Carolingian overwhelming force to Hucbert, who had succeeded to the ducal office following his uncle Grimoald's death. No spoils were reported as having been taken in this expedition.[201] Similarly, Charles' minor incursion south of the Loire in 731, the purpose of which is unknown, did not produce noteworthy booty.[202] In short, between the ravaging of Saxon territory in the spring of 724 and the booty taken from the Muslims following the Carolingian victory at Poitiers in October 732, Charles' army was not fed on the spoils of war.[203]

During the normal campaigning season of 732, Charles did not mobilize his armies. He apparently was not yet ready to pursue a policy aimed at reducing his "ally" Duke Eudo of Aquitaine to Carolingian *ditio* or to attack those Provençal magnates who, in league with various Muslim princes, maintained their independence in the far south of the *regnum Francorum*. Charles was probably planning for the conquest of the northern and eastern parts of Frisia, what might perhaps be called *Fresia ulterior* in contrast with *Fresia citerior*, the region that he already controlled. These considerations, however, were interrupted by a panicked request from his ally Duke Eudo for help against the Muslims, who had invaded Aquitaine with great success under the leadership of Abd ar-Rachman, the governor of Spain.

Charles mobilized a formidable force and crushed the Muslims at Poitiers. Abd ar-Rachman was killed in battle and the Muslim position to the south was temporarily destabilized by his death and by the slaughter of a major Muslim field army.[204] Charles, however, did not follow up on this victory by leading his troops into Spain in order to plunder this rich region. Charles and his advisers undoubtedly were well aware that previous Frankish kings, such as Childebert I and Chlotar I, had operated with some considerable success on the Iberian peninsula. He also knew that this region had never been a part of the *regnum Francorum*.[205] Indeed, Charles' conservative behavior in this situation reveals his discipline in focusing on the strategic aim of asserting Carolingian control over the *regnum Francorum*. Charles avoided short-term opportunities for plunder and aggrandizement that might divert him from his long-term goal.

Charles' restraint following the victory at Poitiers is even more remarkable in regard to his treatment of Eudo. During the summer of 732, prior to Charles' intervention in Aquitaine and subsequent victory at Poitiers, Eudo's army had suffered several serious defeats at the hands of the Muslims. In addition, Charles, who among other things had saved the shrine of Saint Martin at Tours from the infidels "with God's help," was already in the heart of Aquitaine with a major army and was well positioned to demand concessions of various kinds from Duke Eudo. For example, the latter's quasi-independent status within the *regnum Francorum* may have been at risk in these circumstances and his personal relationship to Charles ripe for "renegotiation." However, Charles made no effort to capitalize on his overwhelming military force with which he had won the victory at Poitiers. Charles' troops were not permitted to loot the Aquitanian countryside and had to be satisfied with the booty taken from the Muslims.

Charles' restraint might seem curious to those who see early medieval military commanders as warrior chiefs leading poorly disciplined war bands driven by an insatiable lust for booty and glory.[206] However, avoiding military involvement in faraway Spain—the distance from Cologne to Saragossa over the old Roman roads is some 1,500 kilometers—surely provides evidence for sound early Carolingian strategic thinking. In addition, by maintaining his treaty with Eudo, Charles showed good diplomatic judgment. Violating the pact of *amicitia* with Eudo in the context of the Carolingian victory over the Muslims at Poitiers would have been unjust. In perhaps a more practical vein, a wise diplomatist would not want to create the impression that he could not be trusted and would exploit his friends.

In 732, however, Charles acted ruthlessly against Bishop Eucherius of Orléans and the latter's supporters in the Orléanais.[207] Charles had appointed Eucherius to this important episcopal office in the wake of the decisive Carolingian victory at Vinchy in March 717.[208] Not surprisingly in light of Charles' hostile actions in 732 with regard to Eucherius, the bishop's *Vita* characterizes the Carolingian Mayor as an "enemy of the human race" and claims that he was responsible for the saintly bishop's unjust deposition, expropriation, and exile. The putative reason for this behavior was Charles' capricious desire to satisfy the greed of his supporters (*satellites*). Indeed, this *Vita* was written two or three decades after Eucherius' death, in part at least to please the prelate's family, which still resented its loss of power, position, and property at Charles' hands.[209]

Efforts have been made to find deeper reasons for Charles' decision to dispossess and exile the bishop along with other powerful men of the region who were allied with the prelate. For example, it has recently been proposed that Eucherius and his supporters were punished for intriguing or conspiring against Charles with magnates from the southern parts of Burgundy.[210] However, the Burgundian magnates, whom Charles did punish, were from the Lyonnais.[211] These men were traditional enemies of Eucherius' family, that is, hardly likely allies for the bishop of Orléans. Indeed, Savaricus, Eucherius' uncle, died, probably in either 716 or 717, while trying to conquer the Lyonnais region. Moreover, Bishop Ainmar of Auxerre, Savaricus' son and Eucherius' cousin, was not punished by Charles following the Carolingian victory in 732. He is reported to have fought side by side with the *Franci* at the head of a Burgundian unit at the battle of Poitiers.[212] Finally, there is no evidence that Eucherius had any relation, either by blood or marriage, or, indeed, any contact with the magnates of the Lyonnais whom Charles punished or, for that matter, with Maurontus, who operated in the far south and whom the Mayor of the Palace punished later in the decade.[213]

Charles' displeasure with Eucherius and his men is explicitly seen in the *Vita* as very closely connected with the Carolingian campaign against the Muslims. The author of the *Vita* not only recognizes that in this campaign, the Frankish expeditionary forces were supported by Burgundian troops but, consistent with his hostility to Charles Martel, gives the latter group pride of place in the military operations. After the battle, however, Charles is depicted in the *Vita* as coming north from Aquitaine to Orléans, where he found Bishop Eucherius and is reported to have ordered the prelate to follow him to Paris. The author of the *Vita* makes it very clear that Eucherius expected serious trouble, indeed, ambushes (*insidiae*) to await him at the Carolingian court as a result of Charles' orders.[214] Charles probably took action because Eucherius and presumably the troops, normally mobilized by a very high ranking ecclesiastical official, had not been part of the Carolingian army that had campaigned against the Muslims. Given the strategic location of Orléans in the context of the Poitiers campaign of

732, it is unimaginable that Charles had not summoned the expeditionary levies of this region for active duty against the Muslims in the north of Aquitaine. Yet, as noted above, Charles found Eucherius and his supporters at Orléans when he returned from Poitiers.

The failure of the *Vita* to mention explicitly that the expeditionary levies of the Orléanais had participated in this celebrated campaign against the Muslims may be taken as prima facie evidence that these troops had not served. Indeed, the author of the *Vita* may well have been trying to obscure this crucial fact by highlighting the positive role of the "Burgundian forces," which did serve at Poitiers. Thus, the casual reader might not grasp immediately that it was Eucherius' failure to meet his military obligations that led to his downfall. In this context, Charles was not acting against Eucherius' family in a broad sense. It is clear that Ainmar, Eucherius' cousin, led the levies of the Auxerrois at the battle of Poitiers and that he was not punished by Charles at this time.

Charles had a record of punishing magnates, even ecclesiastical magnates, who did not cooperate with him fully in military matters. For example, when Bishop Rigobert of Rheims failed to obey Charles' orders during the latter's military operations against Ragamfred approximately a decade earlier, Charles responded vigorously to the prelate's dereliction of duty. He deposed Bishop Rigobert and sent him into exile in a manner that was similar to that suffered by Eucherius.[215] Pippin II's deposition and exile of Bishop Ansbert of Rouen, discussed earlier, may have also resulted from the latter's failure to provide military aid when required.

During the campaigning season following his punishment of Eucherius and his supporters in the Orléanais, likely for their failure to obey his military summons to fight against the Muslims in Aquitaine, Charles took strong action against a congeries of magnates in the Lyonnais. The court chronicler characterizes these men as "rebelles" and "infideles."[216] Obviously, men who had recognized Charles' *ditio* but who had failed to obey a military summons (*bannum*) that had been issued by the *princeps* to mobilize their troops for war could well be considered *rebelles*. Men who had given their personal oath of faithfulness to Charles but who subsequently failed to provide him with the military support that they owed him were no longer *fideles*, but *infideles*.[217]

Thus, Charles restored order, *pax*, by the effective deployment of his army in this region and eliminated the *rebelles* and *infideles* the same way he had dealt with Eucherius and his supporters. To stabilize the situation, Charles arranged for military settlements in the Lyonnais under the command of his most proven (*probatissimi*) and diligent (*industrii*) military commanders (*leudes*).[218] The court chronicler emphasizes that Charles handed over (*tradidit*) the region to these *fideles*. These matters were arranged according to written agreements that obligated Charles' *fideles* to provide military support (*firmata foedera*). The Continuator further emphasizes that these *foedera* or contracts for military service were legally binding (*judiciaria*).[219] The description of these arrangements by the Continuator in terms of late Roman military usage is thoroughly consistent with the broader institutional self-perception of the early Carolingian court — *imitatio imperii* — for which he was writing.[220]

As previously mentioned, this purge was limited to men in the Lyonnais, who apparently had not stood by their legally binding *foedera* with Charles, who then brought in new men under new but similar arrangements. The urban-based magnates, who controlled the great fortified bastion of Lyons, apparently were not included in this purge.[221] Thus, the *maiores natu*, who dominated the *urbs*, may have been among the many Burgundians who had served alongside the Franks at the battle of Poitiers.[222]

Frisia Ulterior

With the punishment of those officials and magnates who had not provided the required military support for the campaign against the Muslims, Charles was ready to turn to the final absorption of Frisia *ulterior* into the *regnum Francorum*. Thus, in the later part of the campaigning season of 733, Charles Martel successfully mobilized his forces in order to suppress a band of "rebels" based on the island of Westergo. The next year, however, a second "revolt" erupted, this one led by the apparent ruler of the *gens Frisionum*, Duke Bubo. Charles led a second expedition into the islands and won a decisive victory, and Bubo was killed in battle. The Frisians' remaining pagan shrines (*fana*) were destroyed, the region was looted, and the Frisians made no further trouble for the early Carolingians.[223]

Return to Aquitaine and Lyons

Prior to the beginning of the campaigning season of 735, Charles Martel learned that Duke Eudo of Aquitaine had died. He summoned a council of his great magnates (*proceres*), and after obtaining their advice, he mobilized a large army and invaded Aquitaine.[224] In a rapid march of seven or eight weeks — the distance from Cologne to Bordeaux is more that 1,000 kilometers — Charles crossed the breadth of Aquitaine from the Loire to the Atlantic coast.[225] In the course of this invasion, Charles is not recorded to have encountered any military opposition from the Aquitanians in general, nor from Eudo's sons, Hunoald and Hatto.[226]

Charles' aim appears not to have been the suppression and despoliation of this vast and wealthy region through a brutal military conquest. Rather, he apparently intended to alter the quasi-autonomous constitutional position of the

Aquitanian duchy in relation to the *regnum Francorum* that had developed during the preceding two generations.[227] Charles had convinced at least some of his magnates that Carolingian *regnum* could be imposed upon the region without great risk through a display of overwhelming force during a critical period of presumed political instability in Aquitaine, which had been caused by Eudo's recent death.

In the course of Charles' progress through Aquitaine, the Continuator reports that the Carolingian Mayor obtained the legal submission of the old Roman fortress cities as well as the fortified lesser administrative and population centers, *castra*. Charles also made a point of bringing under his *ditio* the generally unfortified settlements (*suburbia*), often composed in large part of merchants and their infrastructure of support groups, which had been established outside the walls of the fortified places.[228] It should be noted that Eudo had failed spectacularly to defend Aquitaine against the Muslims in the 730s.[229] Charles Martel, the hero of the Christian victory at Poitiers (unlike Eudo, who had been defeated by the Muslims), may have been considered a better protector of the region than Hunoald and Hatto, Eudo's untried sons and ostensible heirs.

In his brief account, the Carolingian court chronicler makes particular mention of the important old Roman fortress city (*urbs*) of Bordeaux and the *castrum* of Blaye on the Garonne as *exempla* of the places that submitted themselves to Charles' *ditio*.[230] The Bordeaux region had suffered greatly at the hands of the Muslims despite Eudo's efforts to defend it.[231] From an economic perspective, Bordeaux was of central importance to southern Aquitanian trade along the Atlantic coast. For example, Aquitanian oil traditionally was exported through Bordeaux to Rouen and probably then into the valley of the Seine.[232] Blaye was another important place by the early eighth century as it had progressed greatly since the late sixth century when it was characterized only as a *castellum* by contemporaries. Perhaps some reason for the success of Blaye lay in the fact that it dominated a critical crossing of the Garonne in the region of Bordeaux itself.[233]

The court chronicler's focus on fortified population centers when discussing the submission of Aquitaine to Charles reveals how contemporaries understood the strategic organization of the region. It recalls the pattern of warfare that prevailed in Merovingian Gaul, which was based upon laying siege to old Roman fortress cities and lesser strongholds.[234] Indeed, siege warfare dominated military operations in those regions of the West such as Gaul and Italy where the Romans had constructed massive urban fortifications during the later empire.[235] As will be seen below, this observation informs Charles Martel's military operation in both Provence and Septimania as well as the efforts of his son Pippin in Italy during the mid-750s and in Aquitaine during the 760s.

Charles' invasion of Aquitaine was not intended to exclude Eudo's sons,

Hunoald and Hatto, from the "office" of *dux* that their family had occupied for several generations. Rather, the Carolingian Mayor wanted to alter the constitutional relationship between himself and the *dux Aquitanorum*. The Metz annalist, who is never reticent to exaggerate Carolingian power and the thoroughness of their victories, emphasizes that Charles gave the *ducatus* to Hunoald. In addition, the annalist notes that Charles arranged that his own sons, Pippin and Carloman, were to receive from Hunoald a promise that he would be faithful (*promissio fidei*) to them.[236]

It is exceptional that Charles carried out these operations during the campaigning season of 735 in Aquitaine peacefully. He did not despoil this rich region so that he and his soldiers would return home with wagonloads of booty.[237] This absence of looting following the peaceful subjection of a once quasi-autonomous region was appropriate because the natives had offered no resistance. Such a policy had long been Frankish practice as they had inherited it from the Romans [238] and is reminiscent of Pippin II's success in Alamannia in 709 and Charles Martel's own success in Bavaria in 725. In both cases, moreover, offensive operations leading to the submission of the region were undertaken hard upon the death of the erstwhile ruler of the region.

However, in Alamannia, the year after Pippin II had peacefully subjected the region, rebel elements, as we have seen, sought to overturn the settlement. Consequently, the Franks had to fight another four years before fully subduing the region. Therefore, it should not have been surprising to Charles that in 736 Eudo's sons, Hunoald and Hatto, took up arms against the settlement that the Carolingians had imposed the previous year. Charles invaded Aquitaine once again and fought against the brothers with considerable success,[239] capturing Hatto during this campaign.[240]

Charles' line of march into Aquitaine in 732, 735, and 736, as well as his line of march into the Lyonnais in 733, brought him to and through the old Roman fortress city of Auxerre,[241] putting him in close contact on a regular basis with Ainmar, the bishop of Auxerre, who, as noted earlier, had strongly supported the Franks at Poitiers in 732. Charles handed Hatto over to Bishop Ainmar, probably in 736, to be held as a prisoner. However, Hatto escaped from captivity and Charles severely punished Ainmar, deposing and imprisoning him for this serious dereliction of duty. The bishop apparently was later killed by Charles' men while trying to escape from captivity.[242]

Following his escape, Hatto was not much more fortunate than Ainmar. Hunoald, who had been recognized as duke by Charles, tricked his brother, Hatto, into a meeting at Poitiers and had him blinded and imprisoned in a monastery.[243] Hunoald's rough handling of Charles' escaped captive may well have been the price that the Aquitanian *dux* was required to pay for peace with the

Carolingian Mayor of the Palace after the ill-fated rising in 736. No source indicates further hostilities between Charles and Hunoald and, as will be seen below, Charles maintained several successful military operations in Septimania. Thus, had Hunoald been hostile to Charles, both his Aquitanian and his Gascon forces were positioned to thwart the Carolingian line of march to the south through Aquitaine. Perhaps even more important and with considerable less risk or effort, Hunoald's troops could be positioned rather easily to cut the supply lines of the Carolingian army and make its operation in Septimania all but impossible. Hunoald's cooperative military posture lends support to a near contemporary local Aquitanian tradition that the duke served as Charles' *legatus* in the region.[244]

In 737, following his successful operations in Aquitaine against Hunoald and Hatto, Charles led his army to Lyons. His aim was to subject the magnates (*maiores natu*) of the city of Lyons to his domination, *ditio*.[245] This would seem a rather lenient treatment of these men if they are thought of as rebels. Rather, their likely defense was that they were subjects of the Merovingian king, Theuderic IV. However, following the death of this puppet king, Charles had not established a new monarch to replace him. Thus, the *maiores* of Lyons subsequently recognized Charles' *ditio* and therefore were neither expropriated nor exiled.[246] At this time, Charles probably established his brother Childebrand as *dux* of the Burgundian region with full responsibility for overseeing the mobilization of its expeditionary forces.[247]

Provence and Septimania

With Burgundy securely under Carolingian control, Charles turned his attention during the remainder of 737 to the far reaches of southern Gaul — Provence and Septimania. In Provence, two great magnate families apparently had struggled for decades to dominate the region. One family was led by Abbo, who, as noted above, controlled the Alpine passes, particularly Monte Cenis, and the old Roman fortress at Susa along with vast tracts of territory. His ancestors were previously important in Burgundy.[248] The other family was led by a certain Maurontus, who had his base in the region of Marseilles and likely could trace his roots, at least in part, back to some of the great families of the Neustrian aristocracy whose power had been broken several decades earlier by Pippin II.[249] In this struggle, Charles had Abbo as his ally.[250] When Charles finally subjugated the most southerly region of Provence, from Marseilles to the region around Arles and including the city, probably late in 736 or early in 737, his officials (*judices*) were put in place as administrators throughout the area. Maurontus was effectively dispossessed and forced into exile.[251]

However, Charles' control of the lower Rhône valley was not secure. Advance units of the armies of the new Muslim governor of Spain, Iussef ibn Abd ar-Rachman, were probing the region in search of opportunities to extend their power eastward from Septimania.[252] They managed to capture the old Roman fortress city of Avignon, perhaps with the help of Maurontus, who likely sought to reestablish a position of power and influence in the south of Provence with the help of the Muslims.[253] In response to this Muslim invasion, Charles mobilized an immense expeditionary force of not only Franks but also Burgundians and probably Alamanni and Bavarians.[254] The Carolingians drove the Muslims from Avignon. Charles' army crossed the Rhône, and, while besieging Narbonne, these forces defeated an enemy army sent by sea from Spain to raise the siege of this important fortress city, which had been in the hands of the Muslims since 719.[255] Charles captured Narbonne, as well.

While Charles was mopping up opposition in Burgundy during the latter part of 736 and planning to turn his full attention to the regions farther south, he learned that the Bavarian duke, Hucbert, had died.[256] Without being distracted from his operations in the south, Charles acted no later than early 737 to establish a certain Odilo as *dux* in Bavaria. As the situation developed, Charles did not need to send a military force to convince the Bavarian magnates that the selection of their duke was a Carolingian prerogative. Moreover, Odilo was probably not even a member of the core Bavarian Agilolfing family that had led the *ducatus* for several generations but a collateral relative from a Swabian branch of the family.[257] The successful reform efforts carried out by Boniface in Bavaria are a useful index of the dominant position exercised in that region by the Carolingians under Charles' leadership. By the autumn of 739, Boniface had divided Bavaria into four episcopal sees, consecrated numerous priests, and judged the worthiness of several local bishops.[258]

Saxon Hesse

With the exception of the latter part of 733 and the campaigning season of 734, Charles had spent the period from 731 to 737 leading military operations in Aquitaine, Burgundy, Provence, and Septimania. Before he had dealt more fully with the Muslims in the south, Charles turned his attentions once again to the neglected northeastern frontier of the *regnum Francorum*. It would seem that in 737, while Charles was besieging Narbonne in Septimania, the Saxons of eastern Hesse, who had not caused the Carolingians any noteworthy difficulties since being punished in 724, attacked Frankish assets west of the Rhine.[259]

Whether the relative quiescence of these Saxons vis-à-vis Frankish interests was the result solely of the earlier punishments that Charles had inflicted on them is problematic. There were many other places outside the *regnum Franco-*

rum where the Saxons could carry out military operations in search of booty. By 737, however, the Danes had completed a great earthen rampart to fortify their southern frontier against the Saxons. This defensive dike, the Danevirke, which effectively isolated the Jutland peninsula from the mainland, is described in the early Middle Ages as stretching from the eastern bay at Ostersalt as far as the western sea. It is reported to have followed along the northern or right bank of the Eider River.[260] The Danevirke cut off the Saxons from opportunities to raid in the north as they lacked the strategic naval assets with which to circumvent these new Danish defenses. Moreover, the decision to build the Danevirke may have been a response to Saxon military operations in "Danish" territory during the period between 724 and 737; the Danes were well aware of Saxon deficiencies in naval matters.[261]

Thus, the Saxons' renewed interest in raiding operations within the *regnum Francorum* perhaps was not primarily the result of Charles Martel's preoccupation with matters in the south. At this point in the Saxon decision-making process, however, Charles' apparent commitment to the southern theater of operations may have been a key factor in their determining to take action against Frankish assets west of the Rhine in 737. It was a costly error. Charles came north, mobilized a Frankish army, and quickly crossed the Rhine at its confluence with the Lippe near Wesel. He is reported by the court chronicler to have devastated the region of Saxon settlement, where the raiders dwelled. However, no enemy Saxon forces dared engage Charles' army in the field.[262]

Once the region had been thoroughly ravaged, Charles issued an order (*praecepit*) that the Saxons people (*gens*) from this region henceforth were to be taxpaying subjects (*tributaria*).[263] The court chronicler's use of this traditional if not overtly technical imperial language, in this context, may raise some suspicions regarding his subsequent use of the term *hospites*. The Continuator reports that Charles Martel received from the Saxons "plures hospitibus." [264] This, of course, may have been the author's ironic rendering for Charles taking Saxon hostages; he received "guests." Indeed, the Metz annalist, two generations later, interpreted the use of the term *hospites* by the Continuator thusly in this context.[265] However, the Continuator may have been alluding to Charles' use of some version of the erstwhile imperial *hospitalitas* agreement. If this is the case, then many of Charles' soldiers are to be seen as having been contracted to be treated as "guests" by the Saxons, settled in their territory and at their expense, to monitor the behavior of their Saxon hosts. As shown by the writings of Paul the Deacon, *hospitalitas* agreements were still known and in some manner understood at the Carolingian court where he flourished during the later eighth century.[266]

Return to the South

Following these successful operations in the northeastern parts of Saxon Hesse, Charles organized a massive military campaign in the south. An army that the Metz annalist refers to as an *exercitus* from "universali partibus" was mobilized. This force definitely included troops from Burgundian territory and troops seconded to the campaign from Italy under the direct command of the Lombard king Liutprand.[267] The initial goal of the operation was to retake Avignon, which apparently had fallen into Muslim hands while Charles was distracted by affairs in Saxe-Hesse. After recapturing Avignon, this army had as its secondary objective a march to the sea, to bring the old Roman fortress city of Marseilles and its surrounding territory under Carolingian control.[268] This operation is reported to have been successful on all counts, according to the contemporary court chronicler.[269] The Metz annalist emphasizes that Charles "subjugated the entire region to the *imperium* of the Franks."[270]

By 739, Charles Martel had asserted his *ditio* over virtually all of the *regnum Francorum* and the peoples living within its frontiers. Charles ruled an extent of territory comparable to that which had been ruled by King Dagobert I a century earlier, or by Chlotar I at the time of his death in 561. Austrasia, Neustria, Aquitaine, and Burgundy in the west, Frisia, Hesse, Alamannia, Thuringia, and Bavaria in the east all recognized Charles' *regnum*. Although the people of these regions recognized themselves to be subject to Charles, they all had not been integrated into his *principatus*. For example, Charles considered neither the duchy of Bavaria nor that of Aquitaine as part of his *principatus* which he could will to his heirs.[271]

Since the death of Theuderic IV in 737 there had been no Merovingian puppet king on the throne in whose name Charles acted. Charles' supremacy in the *regnum Francorum* was recognized in a practical sense by Pope Gregory III, who addressed him *subregulus*.[272] The pope, after consulting with the great magnates of the region around Rome, "proposed that an agreement (*pactus*) should be drawn up between himself and Charles." The pope indicated that "he would cease to belong to the imperial party" (*a partibus imperatoris recederet*) and that he would "irrevocably sanction" (*sanciret*) the adherence of Rome to the party of the *princeps* Charles.[273] In symbolic support of the transference of papal subjection from the emperor to Charles, Gregory sent to the Frankish *princeps* both the keys to the tomb of St. Peter and the chains that had held the first bishop of Rome.[274] In return for this offer to alter profoundly the political balance of power in the West, the pope required that Charles promise to protect the papacy and its assets from the Lombards with Carolingian military forces.[275] Despite two embassies from the pope and an amazingly attractive offer that likely held out the office of *patricius* to him, Charles diligently stayed out of Italian affairs.[276]

Carloman and Pippin

During the last year or so of his life, Charles Martel, who may have understood that he was terminally ill, arranged his affairs. The primary aspect of his testament was the disposition of his various *regna*. Following the imperial tradition, which the Franks seem to have adopted during Clovis' reign, Charles arranged for a *divisio* among his three sons: Pippin and Carloman (offspring of his first wife Crotrude), and Gripho (son of Charles' second wife, Sunnichildis, the Agilolfing hostage whom he married following the death of his first wife).[277] This *divisio regnum*, the contemporary court chronicler emphasized, was carried out with the advice (*consilium*) of Charles' magnates (*optimates*).[278]

It was Charles' will that each of his three sons was to be given an equal part (*aequa lanx*) of his *principatus*.[279] Gripho's share — the *terna portio* — constituted in the middle ("in medio") of Charles' *principatum* and composed from territory in Neustria, Austrasia, and Burgundy, was equal to that which had been designated for the shares that his half-brothers were to receive.[280] Pippin was to receive those parts of Burgundy, Neustria, and Provence that had not been willed to Gripho. Carloman was to get those parts of Austrasia not given to Gripho as well as Alamannia and Thuringia.[281] Frisia and Hesse were likely considered a part of the Austrasian *regnum* for purposes of this *divisio*.

Although no maps survive, the *portio* left to Gripho appears to have been smaller in geographic terms than those territories that were allotted to Carloman and Pippin. However, as subsequent *divisiones* of the Carolingian patrimony illustrate in an unambiguous manner, it was not the amount of land that constituted the *aequa lanx*. Rather, the aim of a *divisio* was to make equal resources available to each heir from the bequest. The emphasis therefore was not on territory alone, but upon a rough equality of *facultates* such as taxpaying population, economically productive lands, and elements or units of the fisc.[282]

In order to execute a *divisio* of the type indicated in 741 Charles needed vast amounts of information. Thus, a collection of *descriptiones* that listed Charles' assets in great detail was probably available to the early Carolingian court.[283] The availability of the bureaucratic assets necessary to carry out *descriptiones* of this type may be inferred from a variety of sources. It is well established, for example, that both the Merovingians and the early Carolingians habitually made all kinds of inventory lists, both public and private, for a wide variety of purposes. Lists of this type were an institutional commonplace in the empire's Romano-German successor states.[284] However, few of these documents have survived.[285] Nevertheless, shortly after the death of Charles Martel, a series of church councils reveals that Pippin and Carloman already had the bureaucratic assets at their command to ascertain which properties in their possession or in the possession of their men belonged to the church.[286] In 751, Pippin had a *descriptio* made of the *res ecclesiarum*; this was executed prior to a *divisio* of church resources.[287]

Soon after Charles Martel's death, according to the Metz annalist, the *Franci* were greatly depressed (*contristati erant*) by the prospect of Gripho's accession to power over a third of the *regnum*. This was because Gripho was *adolescens*. Thus, Carloman and Pippin, after having taken counsel with the magnates, decided to disinherit Gripho. The latter took refuge in Laon, probably part of his inheritance in Austrasia. However, after a short siege by an army led by his half-brothers, Gripho surrendered. Carloman and Pippin then had the youth imprisoned at the stronghold of Chèvremont near Liège, in Austrasia, and thus under Carloman's control. Gripho's mother, Sunnichildis, was shut up by her stepsons in the convent at Chelles in Neustria, and thus under Pippin's control. The entire process was completed between Charles Martel's death on 22 October 741 and the beginning of the campaigning season in 742.[288]

The saying "new wars always break out quickly against new rulers" held true following Charles Martel's death, as it had following the death of his father.[289] Over the course of the next six years, Carloman and Pippin operated in the field with major armies on a regular basis. These operations, which were ostensibly defensive efforts to restore the *status quo ante*, were executed not only during the normal campaigning season but at other times, as well. Carloman and Pippin carried out military operations from Gascony in the south to Angraria, as far east as the Saale River, in order to assert their *ditio* over some of their father's erstwhile subjects, who sought either autonomy or independence, and also to protect parts of the *regnum Francorum*, particularly Thuringia, from foreign invaders.

Observations that "pandemonium broke out" when Charles died and "peripheral regions" of the *regnum Francorum* demonstrated unified hostility to the brothers are exaggerations.[290] No hostile reaction is reported in Frisia, Hesse, Thuringia, or even in the recently subjected region of Provence. The Saxons, against whom Carloman and Pippin campaigned on two occasions, were not those of the Hesse region but troops raised in Angraria, east of the Weser, and thus outside the *regnum Francorum* (see below).[291] The Slavs, who supported Duke Odilo of Bavaria and against whom the brothers also engaged militarily, had never been part of the *regnum Francorum* or under Carolingian *ditio*. Indeed, the only region that rose in revolt against Charles' sons and that Charles, himself, had considered to have been a part of his *principatus* was the duchy of Alamannia.[292]

During this period, Pippin and Carloman campaigned in four theaters of operation: Bavaria, Aquitaine, southeastern Angraria on the northern borders of Thuringia, and Alamannia. Both Aquitaine and Bavaria had been subjected personally to Charles by oath, *promissio fidei*, which was made by the *dux* of each region on behalf of himself and his people. Indeed, Hunoald, duke of the Aquitanians, had made his *promissio* to Charles and to both Carloman and Pippin prior to their father's death. This *promissio* required that the duchy pay its taxes to Charles and his sons.[293] The relationship that Charles Martel created when he installed Odilo as duke in Bavaria in 737 likely was similar to the one that he had imposed upon Hunoald. One Carolingian court chronicler makes clear that the Bavarian ducal title was in the gift of Charles Martel and indicates that Odilo held his *ducatus* as a result of the largesse of the *princeps* ("largiente . . . Carollo principe"). Both Pippin and Carloman took the position that they exercised *dominatio* over Odilo from which he had no legitimate basis to withdraw.[294]

It would seem that following Charles Martel's death, the dukes who ruled the Bavarians, Aquitanians, and Alamanni arranged an alliance (*fedus*) intended to reject the *ditio* of Carloman and Pippin.[295] Indeed, Duke Hunoald is specifically said to have withdrawn his promise of faith and thereby his obedience to the law imposed on him by the Carolingians and that he had accepted.[296] Carloman and Pippin responded to Hunoald's rebellion by ravishing the northern reaches of Aquitaine, destroying numerous strongholds, taking whole garrisons as prisoners of war, and accumulating large amounts of booty.[297] After these operations, the brothers are reported to have met at Vieux-Poitiers, near the confluence of the Clain and the Vienne rivers, in order to carry out the *divisio* of Charles' *principatus*. Obviously, this new division was required by the brothers' need to share between them the *facultates* they had confiscated from Gripho.[298]

Before the year was out (the autumn of 742), however, Carloman led an army (*exercitus*) eastward across the Rhine and ravaged "with fire and sword" the breadth of the Alamannic duchy to the banks of the Danube. There, the Alamanni, with their backs against the river and in danger of being slaughtered, capitulated.[299] The Alamanni, in fact, consequently sought peace (*pax*). As terms for their surrender, Carloman imposed upon the Alamanni the constitutional situation prior to Charles' death and which was indicative of the fact that they were part of his *principatus*. The Alamanni promised to accept the laws (*jura*) that previously had been imposed upon them. In addition, they paid the taxes (*munera*) that they owed and recognized that they were Carloman's subjects (*se dicione submittunt*). To ensure compliance, Carloman took Alamannic hostages (*obsides*).[300]

The great military successes of Carloman's and Pippin's armies both jointly and singly in 742 were recapitulated over the next five years until all opposition was effectively crushed. In 743, Odilo refused to recognize Carolingian *ditio* and augmented his Bavarian army with Saxon and Slav mercenaries from beyond the frontiers of the *regnum Francorum* for resistence to Pippin and Carloman. In addition, Theudebald, duke of the Alamanni, despite the submission on the Danube during the previous year, joined with Odilo at this time. A very large Carolingian army crossed the Rhine and marched eastward toward the Lech where Odilo held a strongly fortified position. Several units of the Carolingian army commanded jointly by Pippin and Carloman engaged the combined forces of Odilo and his allies, which were slaughtered in great numbers. The Bavarian and Alamannic dukes barely escaped with their lives.[301]

In the autumn of the same year, Carloman, alone, led an army into south-eastern Saxony and captured the enemy stronghold (*castrum*) at Seeburg that had been used as a base for attacks on northern Thuringia. Finally, Theodoric, the Eastphalian Saxon leader, surrendered.[302] However, while the brothers were occupied in Bavaria, Duke Hunoald of the Aquitanians, pursuant to his alliance with Odilo, mobilized his army and crossed the Loire. He struck north as far as the city of Chartres, where he is reported to have sacked and burned the church of St. Mary. No local forces were mobilized in the West for the purpose of thwarting Hunoald's invasion, and sources do not mention local levies mustered by the counts or others responsible for raising troops, for example, immunists.[303]

By early 743, Carloman and Pippin decided to put a Merovingian puppet king on the throne. The constitutional benefit of this move in the context of their year-round military operations, both offensive and defensive, was a major consideration. The brothers needed large masses of troops on a regular basis in order to fight on several fronts at once. In addition, their army in the battle on the Lech against Odilo and his allies had suffered serious casualties.[304] From a constitutional perspective, the proclamation of the *bannum* for the mobilization of expeditionary levies in areas where neither of the brothers was personally involved would be facilitated if the operation were ordered in the king's name.[305] Thus, a key to the timing of the brothers' decision to make Childeric III *rex Francorum* likely was the recent failure of the counts in the West to mobilize an army to oppose Hunoald during the campaigning season of 743.

Following the establishment of Childeric as king, Carolingian armies battered the Alamanni in 744 and 746.[306] After the victory in 746, Carloman reluctantly drew the conclusion that the Carolingians' lenient treatment of the rebels — obtaining oaths and taking hostages — in 742 and 744 apparently only encouraged resistance. Thus, after having defeated them once again, Carloman brought a great crowd of rebel prisoners, put at many thousands by one source, to Cannstatt. There, Carloman held a court to decide the fate of these men who had proven on three separate occasions that they could not be relied upon to keep their oaths. The Metz annalist remarks particularly on the fact that Carloman was seriously disturbed by the *infidelitas* of the Alamanni. With no other choice apparently left open to him, Carloman, with a "heavy heart" — the prisoners, after all, were Christians — had the great majority of the rebels executed.[307] Subsequently, the Carolingians terminated the ducal status of the Alamannic region and placed the territory under the administration of two Frankish counts, Warin and Ruthard, whose families had been established in the Alamannic region earlier by Pippin II and Charles Martel.[308]

Pippin and Carloman may have been less thorough in their treatment of the Aquitanian duchy in 745. The brothers led a second expedition across the Loire River into Aquitaine and devastated the region. Duke Hunoald, who according to the Metz annalist, understood that he could not resist, therefore swore an oath (*sacramentum*) that he would obey all of the brothers' orders (*omnem voluntatem*). In addition, Hunoald gave Pippin and Carloman hostages (*obsides*), paid the "taxes" (*munera*) he owed, and begged them to withdraw their army to beyond the frontiers (*fines*) of Aquitaine.[309] Hunoald's defeats, both military and personal — he had transferred himself into the service of the brothers, a humiliation for a great magnate — led him to abdicate his ducal office and hurry off to a monastery on L'île de Ré. His son, Waiofar, replaced him as duke.[310]

In the course of a half-decade of constant warfare, Pippin and Carloman had been amazingly successful in their military operations. By 747, there was an obvious diminution of pressure for the defense of Carolingian dynastic interests. Carloman, who apparently had nurtured a desire for the cloistered life, left his family and entered the great Italian monastery of Monte Cassino.[311] Pippin was left as guardian of Carloman's young children and with full responsibility for completing the long-term strategy of assuring Carolingian rule of the *regnum Francorum*.

Pippin's initial act as sole ruler was to free his half-brother Gripho, who had reached adult status.[312] Pippin then gave Gripho responsibility for administering an important territory in the west of the *regnum Francorum* along with a great many royal fiscal installations (*fisci plurimi*).[313] This territory was, in fact, a duchy composed of the "twelve counties" which had as its capital the old Roman fortress city of le Mans.[314] This *ducatus* or march likely had been created by Dagobert I, and he probably had used as his model for its administration the territory that his father, Chlotar II, had controlled ca. 600. This march would appear to have encompassed the region between the Seine, the Loire, and the Breton frontier.[315] From this march and with locally based levies, military operations could be launched against the eastern frontiers of Brittany, perhaps as far west as Vannes, which had at one time been a part of the *regnum Francorum*. In addition, the extensive *pagi* of the le Mans *ducatus* had the potential to serve either as a defensive march to thwart military thrusts across the Loire from Aquitaine of the type that had been launched by Hunoald in 745, or as a base from which to prepare an invasion south of the river.[316] Pippin had not forgotten Hunoald's advance to Chartres and his subsequent replacement by the as yet unbloodied and very likely eager new duke, Waiofar.

Gripho, however, had no intention of serving as a high-ranking official in his half-brother's government as had, for example, Childebrand, the Continuator's patron, who loyally served Charles Martel and his sons. Rather, Gripho gathered a small military household and fled into southern Saxony, where he joined with the oft-defeated Eastphalian leader, Theodoric,[317] who had been captured twice, in 743 and 744.[318] Although on each occasion he had sworn to be a loyal supporter of the Carolingians, in 747 he was ready to go to war in violation of his oaths once again.[319]

In response to Gripho's provocation and Theodoric's apparent violation of his oath, Pippin mustered a large army and led an essentially Frankish force north through Thuringia into Saxony and toward the banks of the Oker, a tributary of the Aller that divided northern from southern Eastphalia.[320] Pippin wanted to catch Theodoric's forces in a tripartite pincer movement. Troops summoned from Frisia, on Saxony's northwestern frontier, marched south-southeast toward Eastphalia.[321] In addition, Pippin hired a force of Wends, probably mobilized from the region between the lower Saale and the upper Elbe which bordered on the eastern reaches of Eastphalia.[322]

Pippin's armies moved into Eastphalia and devastated the region from three directions. The court chronicler reports that a great many Saxons were killed and many others are described as having been sent into captivity in order to be used as slaves.[323] Theodoric concluded once again that there was little point in continuing to resist the might of the Carolingian armies and capitulated to overwhelming force along with those Saxon fighting men who had given their personal support to Gripho. Theodoric, therefore, once again found it necessary to surrender the fortress at Seeburg, which apparently he had repossessed and refurbished sometime after his defeat in 744.[324] Gripho, with his forces defeated, barely escaped with his life.[325]

The Carolingians, presumably having read their histories, reimposed upon these Eastphalian Saxons their erstwhile status as Frankish tributaries. This required them to live under the ancient custom (*antiquitus mos*) that had been imposed upon them by Chlotar I some two centuries earlier. They had to obey the laws (*jura*) that previously had been imposed upon them by the Franks and to pay the entire tax (*tributa*) — five hundred cows on an annual basis — that they had been assessed in the past. However, the tax could be commuted, as Dagobert I had done, if the Saxons effectively defended of the eastern frontier of Thuringia.[326]

Meanwhile, Gripho fled south to Bavaria. There, he not only found a safe haven but came to wield considerable political influence very quickly; some sources claim that he gained control of the Bavarian *ducatus*.[327] The circumstances were propitious for Gripho to gain power. His mother, Sunnichildis, was of Agilolfing noble stock. In addition, Gripho's half-sister, Childrudis, had married the Bavarian duke, Odilo, several years earlier, against the will of her brothers Carloman and Pippin but with the full support of her Bavarian stepmother, Sunnichildis.[328] Gripho also continued to have some political influence among the great men of the *regnum Francorum* simply because he was Charles Martel's son.[329] Finally, some important Franks were settled in the western parts of Bavaria and might be expected to give their support to Gripho because of his blood lines.[330]

When Gripho arrived in Bavaria toward the latter part of 748, he found that Duke Odilo had died earlier in the year (18 January). The latter's seven-year-old son, Tassilo, who was also Gripho's first cousin, was in no position to succeed to an active role in the rule of the duchy. Thus, Gripho, who was an Agilolfinger through his mother and Tassilo's uncle through his father, Charles Martel, rapidly seized the initiative in this very fluid political situation. He became the "guardian" for his sister, Odilo's widow, and her son, Tassilo.[331] Gripho also seems to have become somewhat of a magnet drawing to his side important men who were hostile to Pippin. In this respect, Lantfrid, the expropriated heir to the Alamannic ducal family, joined with Gripho,[332] as did Suidger, the count of Nordgau.[333]

After Gripho gained power in the *ducatus*, he convinced the Bavarian magnates that it was time to rise up against Pippin, as Odilo had in 743, in order to throw off Frankish *regnum*.[334] The Bavarians, who followed Gripho, had a rather poor understanding of the military situation, despite the devastating defeat they had suffered only five years earlier. When Pippin received intelligence regarding the revolt, he mobilized a formidable army and invaded the duchy. He quickly overcame all of those who opposed him in the field and captured both Gripho and Lantfrid.[335] Those Bavarians, who escaped, rapidly came to understand that they could not effectively oppose the Carolingian army in open battle. Thus, driven by terror (*terrore conpulsi*), they fled with their families (a contemporary report makes explicit mention of women and children) beyond the river Inn in search of refuge from Pippin's forces.[336]

After several weeks, the Bavarians grasped the fact that further resistance to Pippin's very large army (*maximus exercitus*) was hopeless, even with the river between their forces, and surrendered. The Bavarians sent legates to Pippin with many gifts and agreed to terms that reconstituted the situation as it had existed prior to Charles Martel's death. They recognized Pippin's *ditio* and took oaths of faithfulness to the Carolingian Mayor. Furthermore, the Franks received hostages (*obsides*) as guarantees that the Bavarians would not become rebels again.[337] Tassilo was placed under the close "protection" of Pippin. As the Carolingian court annals put it, Pippin established Tassilo in the *ducatus* as an act of kindness (*beneficium*).[338]

After crushing the Bavarians, Pippin enjoyed two years of peaceful diplomatic activity. In 747, Pope Zacharius (741–752) had approached Pippin, as Pope Gregory had approached Charles Martel less than eight years earlier, for the purpose of securing Frankish military support for the papacy against the Lombards.[339] Pippin, in turn, initiated negotiations with Rome for the purpose of gaining the support of the pope in helping the Carolingians to secure the title of *rex Francorum*.[340] This, as suggested above, was one of the early Carolingians' two primary long-term strategic goals. The success of these negotiations culminated in Pippin obtaining the position of *rex Francorum* in 751.[341] Rome's delegitimization of the Merovingian dynasty, however, did not absolve Pippin from undertaking a matrix of rituals within the *regnum Francorum* in order to legitimize his own elevation to the Frankish kingship.[342]

In addition to gaining the royal title, Pippin, as Mayor of the Palace, first in harness with his brother Carloman and then alone, had vigorously pursued the long-term diplomatic and military strategy of reconstructing the *regnum Francorum*. This strategy is perhaps best illustrated by their choices concerning where and when to fight. Pippin and Carloman, like their father, obviously had opportunities to expand Carolingian operations into Spain once opposition had been crushed in Aquitaine. Pippin had opportunities to advance further into the Eastphalian region of Saxony following the capture of Theodoric in 747. However, the brothers, in general, were so averse to becoming involved in Saxony that they captured and released the Eastphalian leader on three separate occasions. Finally, Pippin took no aggressive measures to become involved militarily in Italy between 747, when he was first approached by the pope, and 751, when he was elevated to the royal title. In short, the search for treasure in the especially rich territories beyond the southern frontiers of the *regnum Francorum* did not drive Pippin's military operations, and the viability of the early Carolingian army was not dependent on the consistent acquisition of large amounts of booty.

Pippin was king for seventeen years (751–768), and during that period the sources are in general agreement that he led military campaigns in three theaters of operation: Saxe-Hesse, Italy, and Aquitaine. Of these three, only those undertaken in Aquitaine, which was part of the *regnum Francorum*, were fundamentally offensive in nature.[343] Pippin had no intention of conquering Saxony nor in conquering the Lombard kingdom in northern Italy; both were beyond the frontiers of the *regnum Francorum*. In fact, Pippin's retaliatory expeditions in 753 and 758 were to punish raids within the Saxe-Hesse region that was a part of the *regnum Francorum*.[344]

Although Pippin's operations in Italy during the campaigning seasons of 754 and 755 were beyond the frontiers of the *regnum Francorum*, these expeditions were not offensive; Pippin did not intend to conquer and rule the region nor, indeed, was he even eager to become involved militarily in Italy. Pope Stephen II, who called on Pippin for aid in 753, very well understood Pippin's reluctance and spent a good part of the previous year trying to obtain military aid against the Lombards from the Byzantine emperor.[345] When the pope finally secured Pippin's support, the Frankish king made it very clear that he would go to Italy only if necessary. Thus, he sent envoys to the Lombard king, Aistulf, to solve the problem diplomatically.[346] When this embassy failed, but after mobilizing his troops, Pippin sent at least two and perhaps as many as four more embassies to Aistulf.[347] In the last of these efforts, Pippin offered Aistulf a bribe of 12,000 *solidi* to make peace with Rome.[348]

It seems that Pippin agreed to intervene militarily in Italy because he believed that he personally owed the papacy a debt for the pope's delegitimization of the Merovingian dynasty in 751. Whether Pippin had incurred an institutional debt to protect the Republic of St. Peter by accepting the title *Patricius Romanorum* is more problematic.[349] However, in two years of reluctant campaigning in Italy, Pippin defeated the armies of the Lombard king twice in the field. In addition, he captured and destroyed many small strongholds. Finally, Pippin's armies twice laid very close siege to the old Roman fortress city of Pavia, the Lombard capital, and in each instance, Aistulf surrendered. Pippin took large amounts of booty from the Lombards and extracted promises from Aistulf to the effect that the latter would not disturb papal assets. Both times, however, Pippin withdrew his forces as soon as he could.[350] Indeed, Einhard makes a point of noting that Pippin brought the war to a very rapid conclusion and, unlike Charlemagne, was not interested in conquering the region.[351]

Pippin was not alone among the Franks in not wanting to invade Italy. Many of his most important military advisers and supporters strongly opposed such a move,[352] undermining the romantic image of the Frankish magnate and his warrior following as greedy booty hunters and the notion that the army required a constant diet of loot to be maintained. Although the victories won by the Carolingian armies in northern Italy in both 754 and 755 indicate that the region was "easy pickings," Pippin's strategic agenda was focused on the *regnum Francorum* and the avoidance of military entanglements beyond its frontiers.

Pippin's agenda, which was vigorously supported by his advisers, may be surmised from his late operations in Aquitaine. He spent the last nine years of his reign (760–768) trying to reincorporate Aquitaine into the *regnum Franco-rum* in a unambiguous manner. I have reserved our discussion of this dogged effort by Pippin to provide a detailed illustration of early Carolingian campaign strategy and military operations in Chapter 6. However, in a larger sense, the early Carolingian long-term strategic agenda for the reconstruction of the *regnum Francorum* ostensibly was completed once full control had been gained in Aquitaine. Pippin's son Charlemagne thus was well positioned to go beyond the frontiers of the *regnum Francorum* in order to reconstitute the erstwhile western half of the Roman empire under his control; but that is another story.

Conclusion

The early Carolingians reconstructed the *regnum Francorum* under the rule of their dynasty during a short century that ostensibly ended in 768. Historians, of course, cannot take these simple facts as proof that Pippin II and his succes-sors conceived and sustained a long-term strategy to bring about these ends. Indeed, from a methodological perspective such an argument would assume the intentional nature of the process from its putative result and thus, in fact, would not be a proper proof. These days, it is not fashionable to think in terms of the intended efforts of a particular political leader even in a particular, rather short-term context, much less of a consistent and successful strategy pursued by a series of historical actors over the long term. Rather, in modern scholar-ship, there is a curious bias toward emphasizing the unintended consequences of largely unplanned and even putatively random or irrational acts. When strate-gies of some sort can be shown to have existed, there is a strong tendency to try to demonstrate either that they failed or, if success must be recognized, that it was due to forces beyond the control of the formulators.

In this climate of hyper-skepticism aimed essentially at cutting famous men down to size, it would be very helpful to have an early Carolingian ana-logue of the "Hosbach memorandum," in which Hitler set out his long-term goals for a greater Reich. Alas, however, Pippin II and his successors have not obliged us in this regard. In lieu of what is often referred to in popular terms as a "smoking gun," perhaps a pseudostatistical approach might have heuristic value. For example, it is clear that over the course of the period studied here, the early Carolingians made a myriad of decisions regarding whom to fight, when to fight, and where to fight. At the end of this process, they had reconstituted the *regnum Francorum* and acquired the royal office. In light of the sheer num-ber of all of these decisions, so such an argument goes, it is more likely that the early Carolingians found their way to the above-noted results because they were striving to reach these results rather than that things just worked out like that. Whether hyper-skeptical medievalists these days are likely to give serious consideration to a probabilistic model that suggests that there is a positive relation between planned behavior and results is doubtful. By contrast, our lawyering colleagues, when endeavoring to prove premeditation beyond reasonable doubt, might heighten the rhetoric with observations such as how could such a complex web be the result of a series of accidents or random occurrences?

Pre–World War II scholarship provided substantial support for the interpretation that the Carolingians likely did not need plans, much less a long-term strategy, to gain supremacy in the *regnum Francorum*. The early Carolingians were thought to have easily achieved their ends because of their inherent greatness. This of course was assumed from a reading backwards of a perhaps inflated view of the reign of Charlemagne. The putative early Carolingian "walkover" was symbolized for many scholars by the notion that after Pippin II's victory at the battle of Tertry in 687, the ultimate Carolingian victory was inevitable.[353] However, the most recent generation of historians has effectively demonstrated the great strength of the Frankish aristocracy, the presumed natural adversaries of the early Carolingian will to dominance, during this very period. Indeed, it is clear that Pippin II and his successors found it necessary to struggle against a wide variety of aristocratic groups, often broadly based and widely settled throughout the *regnum Francorum*, before attaining ultimate victory.[354] In light of this new appreciation of the great opposition faced by the early Carolingians, is it reasonable to conclude that Pippin II and his successors had no long-term strategy that they doggedly pursued to final success?

Of course, it will not do simply to cite the views of the Metz annalist as evidence that early Carolingians pursued the long-term strategy suggested here. When he wrote his *Annales*, ca. 805, the deeds had been already done by Pippin II and his successors. Thus, it could be argued that, despite the putatively primitive nature of the early medieval world—a natural corollary for those skeptical of a long-term strategy—the Metz annalist created this view of the past rather than reporting what the early Carolingians had done. This act of precocious creativity is perhaps to be explained by the annalist's desire to give his patrons credit for what was merely the result of good luck.

One might perhaps counter this deep skepticism with the hypothesis that the Metz annalist had sources going as far back as the reign of Charles Martel. Various men may well have told the annalist, when he was a younger man, about early Carolingian long-term strategic goals. The annalist is even likely, as most scholars agree, to have had some kind of written account of Pippin II's reign available to him, but which is now lost. Thus, it may perhaps be asked, is it more likely that the Metz annalist learned about a long-term early Carolingian strategy from written and/or oral sources than to assume that he made up the idea himself?

In asking, ostensibly, where the burden of proof lies, it is certainly clear that Pippin II's grandson, the younger Pippin, sought the title of *rex Francorum* no later than 749 and perhaps even as early as 747. It is also evident that once he got the royal title in 751, he devoted the greater part of his military efforts to the conquest of the Aquitanian duchy and the elimination of its ducal house. Aquitaine was the only major region of the *regnum Francorum* that was not directly under Carolingian control during the latter part of Pippin's reign. In short, it would be very difficult even for a doctrinaire skeptic to argue that the younger Pippin was not committed to a strategy of reconstituting the *regnum Francorum* under the rule of his dynasty during approximately two decades prior to his death in 768.

I have suggested throughout this chapter that King Pippin's predecessors were no less dedicated and single-minded in the pursuit of the long-term strategy under discussion here. Pippin II clearly acted in a step-by-step fashion from the beginning of his career. First, he gave his full attention to Neustria and gained control there. While operating in Neustria, he never diverted his attention to another theater of operations. After Neustria had been secured, he turned his attention to *Fresia citerior* and followed a similar pattern of behavior. Finally, during the last years of his life, when he was already over sixty years of age, he turned his attention to Alamannia and followed a strategy similar to that which he had followed previously in both Neustria and Frisia.

Several characteristics of Pippin II's strategic thinking can be identified. First, as noted above, he operated on the offensive in one region and only in one region at a time. He did not divide his strength between raids for booty in distant lands and efforts to conquer territory in other places. Second, Pippin confined his military operations to the environs of Austrasia. Thus, he remained close to his base and kept his supply lines short. Neustria, Frisia *citerior*, and Alamannia all bordered Austrasia. Despite the great wealth of Aquitaine, Burgundy, and Provence, Pippin paid no attention to these regions of the *regnum Francorum*. Bavaria would appear to have interested him in a military sense very little. Pippin never ventured beyond the frontiers of the *regnum Francorum*; he was not at all attracted by the wealth of Spain or Italy. Finally, any notion that his army was driven by a regular need to obtain vast amounts of booty cannot be sustained from a study of his campaigns.

Charles Martel, like his father, worked in a systematic manner to secure control of the various regions of the *regnum Francorum*. After reasserting Carolingian control in Neustria, Frisia *citerior*, and Alamannia, Charles systematically worked to reintegrate Bavaria, Frisia *ulterior*, Burgundy, Provence, and

Aquitaine into the *regnum Francorum* under his leadership. He too endeavored to concentrate his forces in one area at a time, but his adversaries, especially the Muslims, first in northern Aquitaine and then in Provence, who allied with Christian magnates, made this very difficult. Nevertheless, Charles secured Frisia *ulterior*, Burgundy, and Provence and was, on the whole, overwhelmingly effective in Bavaria. His effectiveness in Aquitaine may be questioned, but only in light of events that developed almost two decades after his death.

Charles, like his father, eschewed involvements beyond the frontiers of the *regnum Francorum*. His military actions against the Saxons all were aimed at putting down rebel groups in Hesse, which traditionally was part of the *regnum*. Indeed, Charles had several opportunities to lead his armies into Spain in 732, 737, and 739 but ignored all of these in order to concentrate his military resources on conquering the remainder of the Frankish kingdom. In addition, Charles was vigorously petitioned by the pope for an alliance which, in effect, recognized him as the single most powerful ruler in the West. His role in such an alliance was to bring his armies into Italy in order to secure papal interests. However, as we have seen, he rejected all of these offers.

Charles Martel's son Pippin, first with his brother Carloman and then alone, sustained a pattern of military behavior that was consistent with that of his father and his grandfather. Of course, with the vast extension over the previous half-century of the territory that the Carolingians controlled, from Austrasia and its surrounding regions to the greater part of the *regnum Francorum*, it was more difficult to focus attention than had been the case for Pippin II. Nevertheless, Pippin and his brother systematically crushed opposition in Alamannia and Bavaria, dealt with the Saxons of Hesse and those of Eastphalia who threatened the Thuringian frontier. The Thuringians, apparently, had remained loyal to the Carolingians throughout the period under discussion. In any case, once old business had been cleaned up and Pippin had the royal title, he ruthlessly focused his attention on Aquitaine for the last nine years of his reign. Unlike his father and grandfather, Pippin was drawn briefly and unwillingly into Italy, but he refused to become bogged down there while there was still work to be done in gaining full control of the *regnum Francorum*.

The single-minded efforts of the early Carolingians for the better part of a century to pursue the reconstruction of the *regnum Francorum* provide sufficient reason to believe that they had conceived a long-term strategy to accomplish this goal. The first principle of this strategy was to move cautiously outward from the Carolingian base in Austrasia. Its second principle was to engage in a single region at a time until the conquest had been accomplished. The third principle was to avoid becoming involved beyond the frontiers of the *regnum Francorum* or to do so only when absolutely necessary and then not for the purpose of conquest. The early Carolingians did not lead their armies on raids for booty into areas that they had no intention of conquering. Clearly, they saw no purpose in making enemies simply for economic reasons or to pursue glory. I make no claims here that the early Carolingians believed that they would in their future inevitably succeed. It is clear, however, that once they had succeeded they liked to believe that their success had been inevitable. Indeed, they believed that it was God's plan.

CHAPTER TWO
Military Organization

The success of the early Carolingians both in long-term strategy and particular campaign strategies was made possible, in part, by a well-established military organization.[1] This system, which was continually developing, ultimately rested on reforms of the Roman military, especially in the West, during the later empire. Early Carolingian military organization was not a product of German forest culture so seductively described by Tacitus more than a half-millennium earlier. Indeed, from the efforts of Diocletian and his successors during the fourth and fifth centuries until the development of gunpowder toward the end of the Middle Ages, the essentials of military organization, relative effective troop strengths, strategy, and tactics demonstrate startling continuity in Rome's successor states — Byzantium and the kingdoms of the medieval West.[2]

Those men responsible for military decision-making in early medieval Europe generally possessed neither the inclination nor the resources to eliminate the vast physical infrastructure of fortified cities, fortresses, ports, and roads created by the Romans. In taking account of Roman military topography, special emphasis must be given to the process by which the *urbes* of the later Roman empire were turned into fortress cities.[3] Following the gradual dissolution of imperial power in the western half of the empire during the fifth century and the success of the Muslim invasions during the seventh and early eighth centuries, the rulers of the Romano-German kingdoms organized and augmented their forces and resources in order to control erstwhile imperial military assets. By and large these governments' military policies were not radically different from those employed by the later Roman emperors.[4]

This basic continuity stems from the fact that Western government leaders, who generally were the military decision-makers, and their advisers enjoyed considerable direct contact with the East Roman world as well as with Byzantine military forces still established in the West, as in northern Italy.[5] In addition, the corpus of ancient military science, available in books such as Vegetius' *De re Militari* (which was known in the West from the edition made at Constantinople in 450),[6] and Frontinus' *Stragemata*, mutually reinforced continuity.[7] In a reciprocal manner, access to historical information and to military handbooks provided stimuli for military commanders to take advantage of the physical and institutional legacy bequeathed by the empire. This continuity, however, should be understood not as stasis but rather as gradual and incremental change over centuries within the framework of both a physical infrastructure and an institutional system that were rooted firmly in the later Roman empire.[8]

Local Levies

The creation of great fortress cities largely during the fourth century vastly altered the empire's military topography and accelerated the militarization of the civilian population throughout the Roman world.[9] This creation of urban militias was driven, at least in part, by the need to have large numbers of armed, able-bodied citizen-soldiers available to defend the newly fortified centers of population. Thus, for example, the legislation establishing urban militia forces was well in train by 440 when Emperor Valentinian III clarified the existing but now lost regulations regarding the situation in the city of Rome itself: "We decree . . . that all are to know . . . that no Roman citizen [living in Rome] or member of a guild [in the same city] is to be compelled to do [expeditionary] military service" (*Nov. Val.* V.2).

Valentinian went on to assure each able-bodied urban dweller that "he is required to do armed service *only* on the walls and at the gates [for the defense of the city] whenever the necessity arises" (*Nov. Val.* V.2; my emphasis). Clearly, there was some anxiety among the members of the urban militia as to whether they had to leave the protection of the city walls and go into the field in order to oppose the enemy. They were required to defend the walls of the city if it should come under attack.

Finally, Valentinian called attention to the "the regulations," mentioned above, that "had been made by the Illustrious Prefect of the City," emphasizing that these regulations "are to be obeyed by all" (*Nov. Val.* V.2). Thus, Valentinian leaves the distinct impression that at least some of those who were regarded by the government as eligible to serve in the militia either were avoiding or attempting to avoid service. Indeed, efforts by civilians, not to mention regular soldiers, to avoid combat were not peculiar to the later Roman empire and are found throughout the course of Roman history and during the Middle Ages.[10]

However, despite reluctance in some quarters to bear arms, the militarization of the civilian population moved on apace in the countryside as well.[11] Also in 440, for example, Emperor Valentinian III, upon receiving intelligence regarding a projected Vandal invasion of Italy by sea, took steps for his regular soldiers and his federate allies to guard the cities and shore, and for a mobile force to be put in the field. He then observed: "Because the opportunities that are available for navigation during the summer make it uncertain where the enemy ships are going to land, we issue a warning that each and every landholder is to defend his property with his own men against the enemy should the circumstances require it" (*Nov. Val.* 9.1).

After noting that these rural militia forces served for the local defense under the command of the great landowners upon whose lands they lived, Valentinian makes clear that these rural civilians already were armed adequately: "They are to use those weapons that they have available." Apparently and perhaps with only a bit of rhetorical flourish, he indicates that he regarded such part-time troops also as being of considerable military value. Thus, with these weapons the militia forces were "to guard our province and their own fortunes" (*Nov. Val.* 9.1).

The emperor's concluding statement regards the disposition of the spoils of war: "Whatever a victor takes away from an enemy shall belong to him without any doubt." This legislation reemphasizes the emperor's expectation that the militia forces will acquit themselves well against the invaders. In addition, he allays any fears that these militia men may have harbored that the booty would be claimed by the government according to normal procedure. Thus the emperor provides an important incentive to these men to fight hard and to seek a victory that will leave the spoils of war in their hands.[12] In seeing the need to grant an exemption, the emperor recognized that these militia men would have sufficient success that the matter of booty needed to be clearly defined beforehand.

Throughout the empire, all able-bodied male adults who lived in the great fortified urban centers, which for the most part had been given new walls during the fourth century at a great expenditure of human and material resources, were organized into a militia for the purpose of defending the city. Also, men who lived in or near the many other fortifications that dotted the countryside of the West were trained to defend the walls of these *castra*, *castella*, or lesser strongholds. In the countryside, free farmers, dependent cultivators, and even slaves were given arms, trained, and mobilized for the local defense. By and large these defense obligations were limited to military operations undertaken within the *civitas*, the local administrative district in which the militia men lived. However, urban dwellers, such as those noted above at Rome, often did not wish to undertake military service in the field.[13]

The militarization of the civilian population for local defense within the institutional structures of the later Roman empire continued throughout the early Middle Ages in the Romano-German successor states of the empire, including the *regnum Francorum* of the Merovingians and the Carolingians.[14] Since participation in the local defense was a universal obligation, the largest component in these militia forces consisted of those poor free and even the unfree and slaves who lived in the area.[15] The Carolingians referred to this militia as the *lantwer* and the men who served in it as the *lantweri*.[16] Those from whom service was required was not limited in the *regnum Francorum* to men of Frankish descent. Not only did *Romani* participate but so did people who were identified as Visigoths, Basques, and even *Judei*.[17]

During the reigns of Pippin II and his early Carolingian successors, those elements in the local levies — civilians who were committed solely to serve in the defense forces of the *civitas* or the *pagus*, whether behind the walls of their fortress cities or in the countryside, and who had no other active personal military obligations — were little used. Charlemagne's ancestors were almost constantly on the offensive and thus there was little or no need to mobilize local levies for defensive purposes. When King Pippin I campaigned in Aquitaine during much of the 760s, however, the local levies of that part of the *regnum Francorum* were called up by their *dux* to defend their cities and the countryside against the Carolingian invaders from the north (see Chapter 6).

Men who were responsible for service solely for the local defense during Charlemagne's reign rarely are mentioned in the sources, because he, like Charles Martel and Pippin I, was almost constantly on the offensive. Some exceptions, noted below, occurred for forces established on the frontiers of the Carolingian world. However, after Charlemagne's death, during much of the ninth century when civil wars and especially foreign invasions frequently placed the Carolingians on the defensive, local forces once again played a prominent role in the defense of their home territories.[18] Indeed, local levies, comprised in large part of civilians, were a constant on the medieval military scene.[19] War in the *regnum Francorum* during the tenth century, following the dissolution of effective royal power in *Francia occidentalis*, for example, resembles the type of military action during the civil wars of the Merovingian era. This is well illustrated by a comparison of military operations detailed in Gregory's *Histories* and Flodoard's *Annales*.[20]

Select Levies

In Rome's Merovingian successor states some militarized "civilians," however, also were required to perform military service considerably beyond the local defense.[21] This institution, which for convenience we shall call the "select levy," is the mainland analogue of the "select *fyrd*" that flourished in Anglo-Saxon England, just as the general levy, noted above, is the mainland analogue of the "great *fyrd*."[22] The select levy, which provided the rank and file for the large expeditionary forces mustered by the early Carolingians,[23] required men to undertake offensive operations that might last several months and thus take them away from home for long periods of time.[24]

The obligation to participate in *expeditiones* (offensive military operations beyond the frontiers of one's own *civitas* or *pagus*) depended ostensibly on the wealth of the person who was to do the service.[25] Each man who possessed a *mansus*, a landed estate of between ten and eighteen hectares,[26] or someone who had an annual income equal to that produced by a *mansus*, was obligated in principle to serve in the select levy.[27] These men who served in *expeditio* very likely were provided with supplies during their entire period of service.[28] Among the expeditionary levies, however, were men specifically identified as *Franci*, and according to a very old custom (*antiqua consuetudo*), these men were required to defray the costs of food for three months of campaigning and the costs for clothing for six months of campaigning.[29] It seems likely that this *consuetudo* dated back to the later Roman empire when Salian Franks were given military lands (*terra Salica*) that could not be inherited by women, in order to sustain themselves and their families so that they could undertake operations in the field far from their homes.[30]

The armament normally carried by the poorest of the select levies appears rather simple: the short sword and the shield. Some specialized troops were armed with the bow and arrow and others with slings of the type used by David and highlighted in Latin translations of the Hebrew Bible.[31] These were minima for lightly armed men who lacked horses for combat purposes. However, any man presumably could improve upon his own equipment by obtaining a helmet, or perhaps even a mail coat, through a formal division of booty taken from the enemy or in the course of looting enemy territory or by purchase or inheritance.[32]

The richer a man was, the greater was his military obligation for service in the select levy. For example, a man who held twelve *mansi*, an estate of from 120 to 216 hectares, which was at the upper limit for personal service, was required to serve *in expeditio* fully armed and to go to war on horseback.[33] He would have had for defensive purposes a coat of mail (Lat. *lorica*, Ger. *brunia*, and, on occasion, the general Latin term *arma*),[34] a helment (Lat. *galea*, *cassis* and Ger. *helmus*),[35] a shield (*clipeus*, *scutum*)[36] with a boss or *umbo*,[37] and perhaps mail leggings (Ger. *bauga*) or greaves (Lat. *ocreae*),[38] along with all of the necessary weapons: spear (*lancea*, *hasta*),[39] sword (*spatha*),[40] and a short sword (Lat. *semispata* or *gladius* and Ger. *sax* or *scramasax*).[41]

Some percentage of fighting men in Gaul (now unrecoverable) well prior to Charlemagne's accession were traditionally armed with bow and arrow.[42] Indeed, Roman citizens, who were mandated to serve in the local militia at least from the first half of the fifth century, were required to train in the use of the bow until the age of forty.[43] Charlemagne, moreover, was interested in increasing the proportion of archers both among the elite mounted troops and especially among the far more numerous rank-and-file foot soldiers.[44] Thus, Charlemagne took men who were accustomed to wielding a sword and defending themselves with a shield in a phalanx formation and retrained them, at least in some instances, as archers.[45]

It requires neither great talent nor excessive practice for foot soldiers to become competent archers.[46] It is no more difficult to train mounted troops, who are also accustomed to fighting on foot, to use the bow and arrow when they are dismounted than it is to train regular foot soldiers to use this weapon. It is exceptionally difficult to train mounted troops to function effectively as archers from the backs of their horses.[47] Moreover, the addition of a new weapon or the substitution of a new weapon for an old one in the armamentarium of the soldier, whether mounted or not, is never a simple matter. Adopting a new weapon can raise the soldier's level of anxiety when he is unsure of his ability to use this equipment. In this context, some select levies were coming to the muster, which included regular arms inspection, with a staff (*baculum*) that they tried to pass off as a bow stave.[48]

The gap in wealth, landed and/or movable, between the individual holder of a single manse or its equivalent in income and the man who personally possessed twelve manses or their equivalent obviously was quite substantial. Thus, individuals whose wealth fell between the upper limit of twelve manses and the lower limit for personal expeditionary service, postulated here as a single manse, had a variety of military obligations. Some men, the exact extent of whose wealth cannot be ascertained, were required to come to the muster on horseback with bows but with no body armor. Other men, presumably of lesser wealth, were required to go to war on foot but with special equipment.[49] Indeed, the extent of one's wealth determined the minimum type of military equipment that was required.

A man who possessed more than twelve manses not only was required, in principle, to serve personally as a heavily armed mounted soldier but also had to support an additional expeditionary fighting man for each manse in excess of twelve that he held. Great landholders, both lay and ecclesiastical (the monastery of St. Wandrille controlled in the neighborhood of 5,000 manses),[50] were obligated to produce men for *expeditio* on the principle of one man per manse or some formula taking this base unit into consideration. Thus, in theory, a man who possessed 120 manses might be required to send a contingent of ten heavily armed mounted troops, or at the other extreme, 120 lightly armed men without mounts. Within this framework such a landholder could also be required to send some combination of men spanning the spectrum. As will be seen below, these quotas very probably were established by negotiation with royal officials on a regular basis prior to each campaign but after plans for the specific military operations had been made.

Troop Mobilization

The Carolingian government determined how many of which kinds of troops such wealthy men or women or institutions, such as monasteries and convents, were required to mobilize for any particular offensive military operation. It would have been foolish for the government to leave each landholder to his or her own devices. For example, if large numbers of lightly armed foot soldiers were needed in order to lay siege to a great fortress city such as Bourges during the forthcoming campaigning season, it would not have been very useful for those who owed troops to mobilize comparatively small numbers of heavily armed horsemen. The great military success enjoyed by the early Carolingians for the better part of a century surely may be considered prima facie evidence that, by and large, soldiers appropriate to the requirements of particular campaigns were mobilized when needed.

In this context, Charlemagne required that Abbot Fulrad of Saint Quentin bring with him on campaign machines for hurling stones (*fundibulae*) and the men who were skilled in their use.[51] Such a requirement indicates not only that such machines likely already were in existence in the abbot's arsenal but also that they were maintained in good working order. Were this assumption inaccurate, the man responsible to the king for such equipment, an abbot in this situation, had to have had specialists available who could build such machines to meet rapidly approaching deadlines. (The training of crews to operate such equipment will be discussed in Chapter 3, below.)

In addition to requiring the local authorities to provide the types of troops that were summoned for *expeditio*, the government exercised considerable control over the order of magnitude of the forces mobilized for each campaign. Indeed, it was necessary to mobilize a sufficient number of troops to meet the projected needs of the campaign strategy outlined during the planning sessions at the royal court earlier in the year. The total population of the Carolingian *regnum* north of the Alps, very conservatively put, is now estimated by scholars to have been seven to eight million.[52] In terms of age cohorts, there were likely more than two million men between fifteen and fifty-five years of age available for military service.[53]

From an administrative perspective these able-bodied men were distributed within the Carolingian *regna* throughout some six hundred to seven hundred counties.[54] Let us assume, for the sake of arithmetical convenience, that each county had a population of an approximately similar order of magnitude, 12,000 people, and 3,600 able-bodied men between the ages of fifteen and fifty-five. Let us further assume that on average only 150 men were mobilized for service in the select levy from each county. This pattern would result in utilizing approximately 4 percent of the able-bodied male population in the appropriate age cohort, as identified above, and result in a total mobilization of armies for expeditionary operations on all fronts in the 100,000 range.[55]

In documents of various kinds from throughout the Carolingian era, one finds phrases such as "all men are to go to the host" or "each and every man should be ready and fully armed."[56] On a different note there are mentions of the punishment to be meted out to "any man who did not serve."[57] However, the upper limits in land transport technology, even through the greater part of the early modern period, make it highly unlikely that armies of many more than a hundred thousand effectives with their support system could be supplied in the field in a single theater of operations.[58] By contrast, the use of water transport for supplies and/or men permitted armies of a considerably greater order of magnitude from a technical perspective.[59]

Thus, scholars have long recognized that the use of words and phrases such as "omnes" and "unumqueque hominem" in the Carolingian capitularies with regard to mobilization cannot be taken literally.[60] Indeed, the idea of calling up two million men each year for offensive military campaigning is absurd on its face if for the only reason that no men would be left at home to cultivate the land and carry out other necessary agricultural work.[61] Not incidentally, as we have seen already, not all men had the wealth qualifications to serve in the select levy. It is clear that words such as "all" and "any" in these documents must be modified by the rules and regulations concerning mobilization. Thus, the count in each *pagus* was required to keep lists of all men who were eligible for mobilization in an expeditionary force. Such lists were maintained and continued to be updated into the later ninth century, long after the major period of Carolingian military expansion had been completed.[62]

The count obviously did not customarily call up for expeditionary service all men on these lists, who were regarded as eligible for campaigning beyond the borders of the *pagus*. The count or his surrogate was permitted to summon only some of the eligible men for engagement in offensive warfare when the king issued the *ban* or mobilization order. Indeed, this selection process was fundamental to and likely a long-standing aspect of the mustering of expeditionary levies. Thus, we catch only glimpses of the mechanisms employed in the documents detailing what appear to be comital infractions or violations of the guidelines, which were intended to keep the count or the officials who served under him from abusing their power in these matters.[63] For example, from these documents, we may infer that a man who was eligible for service was not required to serve every year or perhaps was not normally required to serve in two consecutive campaigns. When his tour of duty was completed, he could not legitimately be mobilized again out of turn.[64] In addition, a free man was not to be called for service so often that his military duty would turn him into a *pauper*. Finally, no man was to be summoned for mobilization if as a result of his service he would incur debts that would force him to sell or to surrender his land.[65]

The normal turn in performing expeditionary service seems to have been mitigated by, among other things, each man's financial condition. Undoubtedly evidence had to be produced in some formal or legal context for each man to demonstrate the nature of his economic situation. Thus, the "all" terminology applies only to those men registered on the lists kept by the counts and who had been ordered to the mobilization *legitimately* for a particular campaign.[66] The "any" terminology regarding punishment, by logical extension, applies only to those men who had been summoned for service *legitimately*, but who had failed to obey the legal summons and thus were to be punished according to their offense.[67]

Professional Soldiers

Obviously, people who were sufficiently wealthy in terms of the land that they held to serve in *expeditio* personally could not be expected to perform military service every time it was required of them. For example, the holder of twelve manses might be too young or too old or too infirm to serve. The holder of twelve manses might not have the ability to fight on horseback as a heavily armed soldier or he might not have the personal inclination to serve. In most such cases, satisfactory substitutes would have been found by those men so that the required expeditionary service was performed. The alternative for unresponsive landowners was to pay fines that far exceeded the costs of supporting substitutes even at the twelve-manse level.[68]

The holder of record of one, twelve, or several hundred manses could be a woman,[69] but women were not permitted to serve in the army, even if they deemed themselves physically capable of going into battle. Thus, such women had to find a substitute or pay a fine.[70] The government had regulations to govern situations involving old men, sickly men, cowardly men, or women of whatever disposition who owned or possessed sufficient quantities of land or movable wealth to owe expeditionary service. Consequently, noteworthy numbers of able-bodied men who personally lacked sufficient wealth to owe expeditionary service but who had sufficient training to perform such service, presumably for pay, substituted for those who were summoned for expeditionary service but who were not able or willing to serve.[71]

In a similar vein, great lay and ecclesiastical landholders who possessed thousands of manses[72] were not required each year to mobilize all of the men for *expeditio* for each manse they possessed or some combination from all manses.[73] Many substantial landholders, especially among the clergy, possessed royal immunities for all or some of their lands.[74] Thus, these immunists dealt directly either with the king or with agents of the central government such as *missi dominici* rather than with the local count.[75] These immunists each year consulted with the royal court on the number of troops that they were required to mobilize and for the type or types of troops under their direct control that they were to lead to the muster.[76] These arrangements could easily be accomplished during the required visits that such very important men made to the royal court each year or in the course of other interviews with the king.[77]

It is likely, for example, that a great landholder such as the monastery of St. Wandrille, which possessed some 5,000 manses, was not required to produce approximately 5,000 lightly armed troops or a smaller number of better armed equivalents for *expeditio* each year. Nevertheless, such institutions had substantial obligations which over time were recognized to have become exceptionally burdensome.[78] However, these great landholders directly exploited approximately half their manses by keeping them in demesne. The other half of what scholars call bipartite estates were held by tenants who, in general, were of servile status and held less than a manse. More to the point, the half of the monastery's manses that was held in demesne, by and large, was very sparsely populated because they were worked by those tenants who held the other half of the monastery's lands as part of the rent for their tenements.[79] Magnates, lay or ecclesiastical, who held these great bipartite estates had to provide select levies on the basis of one man per manse for land held in demesne, creating considerable shortages of available military manpower in regard to these lands.

For a very long time the rulers of the Romano-German kingdoms in Gaul relied heavily on ecclesiastical institutions, which on the whole were wealthy,[80] in order to raise and support contingents of well-trained expeditionary troops on a regular basis for the royal army.[81] King Dagobert I (d. 639) decreed that a *descriptio* was to be made of ecclesiastical resources throughout the *regnum Francorum*, and that on the basis of this inventory a *divisio* was to be executed in which half of the church's wealth was to be listed in the records of the royal fisc (*tabulae fiscorum regalium*) as assets for the purpose of supporting soldiers (*milites*).[82]

The Carolingians carried on the tradition of using the resources of the church for military purposes. Indeed, much verbal abuse was heaped upon Charles Martel by church writers for what is depicted as his ruthless exploitation of ecclesiastical wealth.[83] This attack seems somewhat unfair since his policies were much the same as his predecessors and successors.[84] In 743, only two years after Charles Martel's death, Carloman, Charlemagne's uncle, made it clear to ecclesiastics, who were complaining to the Mayors of the Palace about the use of church lands for military purposes, that the continued exploitation of these resources by the government was necessary due to "imminentia bella." [85]

In order to ensure that the religious institutions of the *regnum Francorum* did their part for the defense of the *res publica*, the king needed a very good assessment of ecclesiastical resources, including the number and value of manses under church control. Thus, Pippin, Charlemagne's father, had the wealth (*res*) of the churches inventoried and allocations made for secular use ("descriptas atque divisas") upon becoming king in 751. He needed accurate information concerning the nature of the resources, and he had to decide what portion was to be set aside for the support of the military.[86] The survey of the resources of the monastery of St. Wandrille in 787 is but one of the surviving examples of what clearly was a regular administrative process carried out by the government directly or at government command in order to assure that the necessary resources were available to provide for the military needs of the realm.[87]

Careful estimates reveal that by the early ninth century in excess of 50 percent of the "rents" collected by the Parisian monastery of St. Germain-des-Prés were taxes to sustain the Carolingian army. These taxes were not depicted at that time as innovations imposed at the end of Charlemagne's reign. Indeed, these payments probably went back well into the eighth century as they were fundamental to the logistic support for large offensive military operations.[88]

The long-term role of the Church in helping to support the royal army is evidenced, as well, by Hincmar of Rheims' effort to protect God's resources. Looking back from the latter part of the ninth century on a history of at least a hundred and fifty years of the systematic exploitation of ecclesiastical resources for military purposes by the governments of various Carolingian Mayors of the Palace and kings, the archbishop tried to stabilize the situation to the benefit of the Church. In his effort to stem and perhaps turn back this tide of exploitation, he argued that it was customary that as much as two-fifths of Church income legitimately go to the service of the *res publica* in order to support the army. From the tone of his writing on this matter, Hincmar would likely have been very pleased if he could have established a two-fifths maximum.[89]

How these military obligations were met (in sum or in part) by the great ecclesiastical magnates and by lay aristocrats requires that we examine, at least in small part, the vast complex of resources, both material and human, that such men or institutions controlled. One such large and rich religious house, which grew to be a community of some three hundred monks, was the monastery of St. Riquier.[90] Built toward the end of the seventh century, it was awarded by King Pippin to Widmar, one of his closest and most trusted palace officials. The latter served as abbot of St. Riquier while also carrying out important missions, especially in Italy, for the king.[91] Charlemagne continued Pippin's policy of giving royal support to St. Riquier and of recognizing its great importance. He gave the monastery into the care of his close friend and "son-in-law" Angilbert.[92] St. Riquier's great library and active intellectual life are important indices of a well-rounded institution that enjoyed both immense wealth and great influence.[93]

The long-term development of the monastery of St. Riquier over more than a half-century under the leadership of Pippin's and Charlemagne's handpicked abbots should not be underestimated. However, from a military perspective, attention is more usefully focused on the economic and demographic development of the town of Centula, which surrounded the monastery. This location would seem to have been merely a *villa* when the future saint, Richarius, who was credited as "founder," was born. However, consistent with the pattern of rural economic growth beginning during the later seventh century, Centula developed into a populous town.[94]

Whether the economic growth of Centula took off in the seventh century or the early eighth century is not of importance here. What is clear is that the immense economic establishment that we see ruled by Angilbert in the latter part of the eighth century surely required several generations to develop.[95] By the early ninth century, at the latest, the population of Centula had grown to some 10,000 men, women, and children.[96] The town itself seems to have been carefully regulated and organized into artisanal districts as particular sectors (*vici*) were dedicated, for example, to smiths, furniture makers, bakers, shoemakers, butchers, fullers, furriers, winemakers, and brewers. They all paid rents to the monastery.[97]

However, the development of the town of Centula in the environs of the monastery of St. Riquier is of greatest importance in military terms and with special attention to the economic resources available to sustain the Carolingian army. One of the *vici* at Centula housed a group of shield makers (*scutarii*). The workshops used by these shield makers were located in the same *vicus* as their homes.[98] In the Plan of Saint Gall (drawn up only two or three years after Charlemagne's death), outside the sacred precincts of the cloister was not only a workshop for shield makers but also a workshop where sword blades would be ground and polished.[99] Shield makers normally were housed, as well, on royal estates.[100]

At Centula yet another *vicus* in the present context is the most important, the one dedicated solely to housing soldiers (*milites*). The inventory indicates residences in this *vicus* for 110 soldiers.[101] These men, however, were not common soldiers but elite mounted troops. Indeed, in addition to his stallion (*equus*), each *miles* was required to have in his possession, on a regular basis and ready for spot inspections, his shield (*scutum*), sword (*gladius*), and spear (*lancea*), as well as his body armor (*arma*).[102]

This armor probably was the traditional mail coat or *brunia*, commonly used by heavily armed troops during the Carolingian era, and the helmet (*helmus*), which were valued at twelve *solidi* and six *solidi*, respectively. Indeed, the entire equipment for each soldier, including the stallion at ten *solidi*, was valued at approximately forty *solidi*. By way of comparison, a cow was valued at but two *solidi*.[103] Full equipment for 110 *milites* amounted to an investment of 4,440 *solidi*. While the arms and armor would not, in general, have to be replaced except under rare circumstances, and both shields and probably swords could be repaired at Centula, itself, the stallions had an active life as war horses, following the completion of their training, for only about seven or eight years.[104]

These troops, as indicated above, were to be ready for inspection and presumably for rapid deployment. There is no indication that their term of military service was in any way limited, and it is clear that they owed nothing except military service to St. Riquier.[105] Whether these soldiers should be considered mercenaries might be a matter of a modern preference for one term rather than another, but it seems difficult to find another way to identify them.[106] More important, 110 mounted troops armed as described were prepared to fulfill a military obligation to the government on a regular basis that was owed by the monastery of St. Riquier and that accrued from the possession of 1,440 manses. However, given what is known of the wealth of St. Riquier, these 110 heavily armed and mounted soldiers were probably only part of the contingent owed by the monastery.[107]

From the perspective of the abbot of St. Riquier, or more precisely from the perspective of his potential adversaries, these mercenaries may be considered a private army sustained by the monastery. These military households or *obsequia* of the ecclesiastical magnates and surely also of lay aristocrats, however, also formed an important part of the armed forces of the royal government of the *regnum Francorum*. The composition of these *obsequia* reflected obligations to provide soldiers to the king by the magnates according to the resources that they controlled.

In this context, a well-developed practice utilized by the magnates was to train *servi* as elite fighting men and to "honor" them by making them *vassalli* ("servi . . . in bassallatico honorati sunt").[108] These *servi*, who were "in bassallatico," generally were regarded by the king as having been provided with horses, armor, shield and spear, sword and short sword.[109] At least some of the *milites*, who were billeted at Centula, likely were originally of very low social status and subsequently had been trained to serve as heavily armed and mounted fighting men. These men may be seen as an analogue of the *pueri* in the military households of Merovingian magnates.[110] As Rhabanus Maurus, who was a student of Alcuin, put it, *pueri* and *adolescentes* were supported in the households of the magnates (*principes*). There they were assigned to the tutelage of old soldiers (*antiqui milites*) to be trained to endure the harshness of warfare.[111]

Armed retinues or military households, which were supported at the expense of these great magnates, were of considerable importance to early Carolingian military organization and warfare. Even during the later Roman empire, despite the existence of a much larger standing army than that sustained by the early Carolingian kings, the imperial government relied heavily on the military forces supported by the magnates. Indeed, some such *obsequia*, like that of the Byzantine general Belisarius, for example, reached 7,000 effectives and had a complex unit system and officer corps.[112]

In general, Charles Martel and Pippin seem to have been satisfied with the performance of military retinues sustained by lay and ecclesiastical magnates. However, in 779, Charlemagne issued an edict in which he ordered that "no man is to dare to create a *trustis*," a military household.[113] This laconic command has caused considerable consternation among scholars.[114] Indeed, this royal edict of 779 obviously was contrary to long-term Carolingian policy. [115] Charlemagne's edict, however, requires some explanation. Charlemagne intended not to prohibit the establishment of *trustes* among the magnates but to prohibit the establishment of a *trustis* by any magnate *without explicit royal permission*. Thus, these four words or some such similar formulation may have appeared in the original but were lost during the process of manuscript transcription. Or, as is more likely, royal sentiment concerning this issue was so obvious that it was understood without being written into the original text.[116]

Only a few years after the edict of 779, Charlemagne not only continued to take an interest in the smooth workings of these *trustes* or *obsequia* of the magnates but also required that even the *servi* enrolled in such a military retinue were to swear an oath of loyalty to him.[117] Going back to Roman rule, the Roman imperial government had at times been ambivalent regarding the military households of the great men. From time to time, various emperors tried to outlaw units they had difficulty controlling.[118] In 779, Charlemagne was in the process of recovering from a series of setbacks — defeat in Spain and a revolt in

Saxony—that had threatened his position. His legislation regarding the control of military households is a reaction to these contemporary problems.[119]

The Royal Military Household

The most important of the military households in the *regnum Francorum*, during the period under consideration here, was that supported first by the Carolingian Mayors of the Palace and then later by the Carolingian kings. The forces established at the palace are the core of the standing army of the kingdom.[120] Moreover, a key document, which describes in some detail the very well developed early Carolingian military household, was written by King Pippin's nephew, Adalhard, who was abbot of Corbie. Substantial *fragmenta* of this tract, called *De ordine palatii*, have been preserved since the later ninth century.[121]

Adalhard, though slightly younger than Charlemagne, was raised and educated at the court of King Pippin I alongside his elder royal cousin. Indeed, a close confidant of Adalhard reported that the future abbot of Corbie shared the same *magister* with Charlemagne.[122] Adalhard was put through the training that was normally required for future secular military officers. He went on to do his initial military service, *tirocinium*, at the royal court (*palatium*). There, in addition to military training, he was educated in academic matters to the point of being *eruditus* in all aspects of worldly prudence ("omni mundi prudentia").[123]

The parts of Adalhard's *De ordine palatii* discussed here likely represent, by and large, information concerning the practices of the royal court during the later years of Pippin's reign and the early years of Charlemagne's reign, when Adalhard was in the immediate service of each of these kings.[124] Adalhard emphasized that he had eschewed any effort to provide a complete description of what we would call the central government in his *De ordine palatii*. He made clear that he could say a great deal more about both court practices and royal officials but he was setting out only those items of major importance.[125] This is the pragmatism of the Carolingian court *mentalité* masquerading in a rhetoric of brevity, also seen in the case of Rhabanus Maurus, a younger contemporary of Adalhard.[126] Adalhard's laconic approach provides a warning to his readers, then and now, that they are seeing but the higher contours of a very substantial but largely unexposed structure.

Adalhard specifically calls attention to three *ordines* or groups of fighting men who were resident at the royal court. The most important *ordo* (presumably because it was the most numerous of the *multitudo*), who were attached to the royal court and who were given consideration by Adalhard, are described as soldiers, *milites*. Adalhard portrays these troops rather pointedly as prepared to undertake military operations at a moment's notice, *expediti*.[127] It is worthwhile to link the *expediti milites* at the royal court to the *milites*, discussed above, who were billeted in the town of Centula, insofar as both forces were prepared for rapid deployment.[128]

These *expediti milites* at the court were the lowest level of the king's fighting men attached directly to the royal household and based at the palace. Adalhard makes a point of indicating that these soldiers had no servants.[129] These royal household troops, however, were supported only in part by the king and not directly. The major cost for sustaining these soldiers was undertaken by men who were attached to the royal court and whom Adalhard identifies as *domini*. These men, as will be seen below, according to Adalhard were the officers who had been assigned to command the various units of the *ordo* of *expediti milites*.[130]

Adalhard makes clear that it was through kindness (*benignitas*) and duty (*sollicitudo*) that these *domini* normally provided the *expediti milites* with food and clothing at regular intervals and with horses, as well. Also at appropriate times, the *domini* paid the *milites* in gold and silver and gave them decorations (*ornamenta*) or awards of some type. These rewards were "regulated" in some sense by the budget (*ratio*) of the commander for the support of those men who were of the rank (*ordo*) of *miles*. As a result of this fine treatment, Adalhard characterizes these *milites*, perhaps rather optimistically, as having high morale ("inflammatum animum ardentius") for their service in the royal military retinue ("regale obsequium").[131]

These *milites* assigned to the royal military household, however, also periodically received royal *donativa*, which Adalhard calls the *donum militum*.[132] Of special interest with regard to this "gift to the soldiers," however, is that it was awarded traditionally by the queen. In Adalhard's personal experience, as a youth raised at the royal court during the 750s, Queen Bertha, the wife of King Pippin I and mother of Charlemagne, was in charge of these important distributions.[133]

The honored and honorary role of the royal consort in military affairs in the West, like most early medieval military government and court practices, may be traced to imperial traditions. For example, when the Roman general Germanicus campaigned east of the Rhine in A.D. 15, he was accompanied by his wife, Agrippina. She is reported by Tacitus (*Ann.* 1.69) to have greeted the returning soldiers and to have helped to treat the wounded.[134] By the reign of Marcus Aurelius a role for the imperial consort or general's wife among the troops seems to have become firmly institutionalized. Indeed, Marcus Aurelius saw to it that his wife, Faustina, was proclaimed (posthumously, as the chronology makes clear) "mater castrorum" because of her work among the soldiers.[135] This was a frequently used title for Roman empresses thereafter and was popularized on inscriptions throughout the empire and on coins that circulated within the empire and beyond its frontiers.[136]

Whether King Pippin or members of his staff such as Fulrad and Widmar, who frequently served the Carolingian government in Italy, had seen such inscriptions or even some of the coins, is anybody's guess. The Carolingians did have access to the *Scriptores Historiae Augusta*, which contained some of this information concerning the *mater castrorum*.[137] In any case, the importance of the queen and other high-ranking ladies in relation to the soldiers at the court did not go unnoticed by the "Germans," who, as frequently observed, were drawn to *imitatio imperii*.[138] Thus, the lady of the great lord, for example, in the *Beowulf* poem, ministers to her husband's military household in peacetime much in the same way as the wife of a Roman general or emperor serves the troops. Just as German religious culture came to be suffused with Christianity so too its secular military culture came to be dominated by *romanitas*.[139]

Adalhard also emphasizes that not only were the officers (*domini*) who commanded these *expediti milites* royal officials, *ministeriales*, they are of a particular type; "they are called *capitanei*." This suggests that the *expediti milites* were organized at least into several units, each unit having as its commander a man in royal service, *ministerialis*, who was styled *capitaneus*. The use of the term *capitaneus* to modify *ministerialis*, a common term for an official at the royal court, emphasized a specific division of labor.[140] Yet the term *ministerialis*, even in the context of the royal court and connected with military service, may not always refer to a free man.[141] As discussed above, *servi* who were made *vassalli* served as elite heavily armed mounted troops, and such men might well have risen to hold unit commands. The term *capitaneus* was used later by Charlemagne in his official documents to denote the commander of a military unit.[142]

A tradition aimed at maintaining the high morale of the *milites* developed at the royal court. Adalhard refers to this tradition in a rather flowery manner as *familiaritas* and *amor dilectionis* while making clear that it concerned the relation of the *milites* to the *capitanei* or *domini* under whose command they served. Accordingly, Adalhard takes note of a custom something akin to the modern officers' mess. Thus, the *capitaneus* invited one or another or perhaps small groups of his *milites* at various times, apparently on a weekly basis, to dinner at the officers' quarters, their *mansiones*.[143]

This notion of developing a closeness between the men and their officers was already a very old tradition in the West by the second half of the eighth century. On the whole, we are witnessing a Roman tradition of the officer as the leader who is also so closely bonded with his men that he often referred to himself and wished to be considered by his men as a fellow soldier, *conmilitio*. Trajan, for example, gloried in being thought of as a fellow soldier and as a soldier's emperor. The tradition carried on through the later empire, into the Romano-German kingdoms of the early Middle Ages, and even to the present day.[144]

Charlemagne, as one might expect, was not immune from the inherent attractiveness of such a tradition that not only was redolent with the antique flavor of *imitatio imperii* but flaunted its manliness (*virtus*). Charlemagne is said to have invited his personal bodyguards, *custodes corporis*, to bathe with him in the palace pool at Aachen. On occasion, the king even invited large numbers of his palace troops, referred to by Einhard as royal *satellites*, to go swimming with him. In fact, Einhard, with a bit of exaggeration, affirms that at any one time there might be more than a hundred such men in the pool with Charlemagne. Einhard affirms that not only did Charlemagne foster this spirit of soldierly camaraderie, but the emperor seems to have enjoyed engaging in swimming races with his household troops on these occasions, even if they always let him win.[145]

Antrustiones

Among the *expediti milites* were special units seconded for service as the king's personal guard, the *custodes corporis*, and for the rest of the royal family, as well.[146] This system was a very old Western tradition that was highly developed during the later Roman empire and among the Byzantine contemporaries of the early Carolingians.[147] The institution of the royal bodyguard was firmly integrated into the institutions of the Romano-German successor states that succeeded the empire in the West. During the Merovingian era, the men who protected the king were called *antrustiones* and thus were the rank and file of the royal *trustis*, the royal bodyguard.[148]

A formulary entitled "Concerning a King's *Antrustio*," which records the process involved in "hiring" a royal bodyguard, has survived.[149] In its present form the document was drawn up toward the mid-seventh century, at the earliest. This formula was probably still in use during the early eighth century when the Carolingian Mayor of the Palace already controlled the royal household and was doing the hiring of the royal bodyguards, who protected him rather than the king.[150] Thus, the *antrustiones* served the man who had the real power, to echo what may seem to be Carolingian propaganda, rather than the man who merely possessed the royal title.[151]

At the start of this formula for the induction of an *antrustio* into royal service, "the king" asserts a basic principle: "It is appropriate that those who have promised [to us] continuing faith (*fidem*) should be given our support (*auxilium*)." This principle, obviously a very general one, extended well beyond the hiring of a bodyguard. Nevertheless, the operative word in this introductory part of the formula, which denotes the binding of the subject to the king, describes the inferior making a promise, "pollicentur," regarding his continuing faithfulness. At this point the text does not refer to his swearing an oath.[152]

The more specific elements in the formula with regard to the hiring of a royal bodyguard make clear that the would-be *antrustio* volunteered for service by going to the royal court in order to enlist as a member of the king's guards. The text of the formulary, with the name for the new *antrustio* left blank, reads on this point: "Thus, since our faithful man (*fidelis*) ————, by the will of God (*Deo propitio*), having come to our *palatio* . . . we decree and order . . ." The formula further indicates that the recruit came "with his arms [and armor] (cum arma sua)." Presumably, the would-be *antrustio* was an experienced and fully armed fighting man, a potential mercenary, who sought to "hire himself out" to the most important "captain" in the *regnum*.[153]

Following this description of the enlistment and the readiness of the future *antrustio* for military service, one finds in the formulary the long-expected mention of the oath. In short, the *antrustio* does more than simply promise his *fides*, as may be assumed from the introduction. But, "he [the *antrustio*] has there [at the *palatio*] sworn in our hand [the hand of the king] his trust (*trustis*) and his faithfulness (*fidelitas*)."[154] By having the *antrustio* swear an oath of faithfulness, the Merovingians and later their Carolingian Mayors of the Palace continued a tradition that was firmly entrenched in the West. Roman soldiers swore their faithfulness both to their commanders and to the emperor.[155]

After taking notice of the oath, the formulary concludes that as a result of the above series of actions: "We [the king] decree and order through this command (*preceptum*) that in the future the aforementioned ———— is considered to be numbered among those men [in our service] who are called *antrustiones*," and who as a result of having been admitted to this unit are to be protected by a triple wergild.[156] The thoroughgoing administrative nature of this process indicates a bureaucratic governmental culture based upon written documents. This is the case not only in terms of the use of the written formulary that outlined the process of enlistment in the corps of *antrustiones* but even more important in regard to the court's issuance of a *praeceptum*, in this case a royal document, to each *antrustio* outlining his status and guaranteeing his wergild.

Whether every *antrustio* could read his own *praeceptum* must remain a matter for speculation; I am skeptical that they could. However, the *antrustio* or members of his family might have need of this document with regard to litigation in court regarding the payment of the wergild. Thus, the documents under discussion suggest that a constellation of officials understood the value of these *praecepta* in a legal proceeding.[157]

The detailed enlistment process for the hiring of royal bodyguards for the

Merovingian *roi fainéants* and their Carolingian Mayors of the Palace hardly stopped with the establishment of Pippin as king in 751. The absence of the term *antrustio* to denote royal bodyguards at the Carolingian court does not mean that the institution of royal bodyguards came to an end. Men who in the past were called *antrustiones* guarded Charlemagne's sleeping quarters both while he was dwelling within the *regnum Francorum* and while he was on campaign beyond the frontiers.[158]

By the eighth century, *antrustiones* were recruited not only from the *Franci* but also from the *Romani* and other "ethnic" groups, as well. In addition, men who were less than fully free, *lidi* and perhaps even *servi*, also were admitted into this unit.[159] Thus, at least some of the guard units of the royal *obsequium* mirrored in the recruitment of non-Franks other units of the royal household, for example, the *schola*, in which officers, such as the Goth Witiza and his brother, were trained. Further, the *antrustiones* mirrored in a sense, as well, the retinues of the magnates in permitting men who were not wholly free to serve. The *lidi* inducted into the royal *trustis*, however, had a social status above the *servi* who were honored with *vassaticum* by various important men in the *regnum Francorum*.

The narrative sources of the early Middle Ages are not particularly forthcoming concerning the lives of the lower-class men of a secular bent who served in the military retinues of the king and his magnates. Thus, historians have made perhaps too much of the case of a young man named Isanhard, likely of Alamannic descent, who became a professional soldier. It seems that he owned some land and also a slave who helped to work the land. In regard to military matters, Isanhard was one of many small landowners who were required to serve in the select levy. Isanhard appears to have had some talent in military matters and decided that he preferred the life of a professional soldier to that of a small farmer. Thus, he sold the lands that he had inherited from his family and he sold his slave. (Both went to the monastery of Saint Gall.) He used at least part of the proceeds from these sales to purchase a horse and a sword.[160]

Traditional scenes of the enthroned emperor, frequently depicted during the later Roman empire, provide illustrations of the emperor's bodyguards.[161] These scenes were intentionally "copied" in many of their aspects by artists in the *regnum Francorum* from later Roman manuscripts.[162] During the early Middle Ages significant efforts were made in Rome's successor states and even in various polities that lay beyond the erstwhile frontiers of the empire to imitate the types of armor used during the later empire and the early Byzantine periods. The three most important items of imperial design that have a significant presence in the archaeological record are items of body armor,[163] highly decorated shields,[164] and elaborate helmets.[165]

In light of surviving artifacts of early medieval manufacture as well as late Roman pieces, Carolingian bodyguards dressed, in large part, in imitation of later Roman armor, and were not merely depicted by contemporary artists as being dressed in such armor. A policy of *imitatio imperii* was diligently pursued in the Romano-German *regna* throughout the courts in the West. Indeed, the Carolingian court imitated the later Roman court, Carolingian artists imitated later Roman artwork, and Carolingian armor makers imitated later Roman armor.[166]

Moreover, the Carolingian units of royal bodyguards were identified in the later imperial sense as a segment of the royal *schola*, and some of these bodyguards were referred to on occasion as *scholares*.[167] Even the queen had her personal unit of guards, called *scholares reginae*, who were supported through her own income.[168] The military organization of the imperial court during the later Roman empire and the early Byzantine era was rather complex.[169] Thus, in trying to understand the structure of military organization of the early Carolingian court, which vigorously pursued *imitatio imperii*, it is important to make precise distinctions when possible. Therefore, it is crucial not to confound the regular palace troops, the *expediti milites*, which constituted a highly mobile field force, with the royal bodyguards, the successors of the *antrustiones*, discussed above.

Youths in Officer Training

The second group or *ordo* of fighting men whom Adalhard mentions as being attached to the Carolingian court were the young men, apparently of rather high status, who were being trained as the future officers of the royal army. These youths are sometimes described as or compared with *discipuli*, and each of them was assigned for his training to a particular *magister*.[170] Indeed, this type of youth, mentioned in a wide variety of sources from the later Roman empire through the Merovingian era and later, was enrolled in the *schola* of the imperial or royal court.[171] It is important not to confound these future military officers and likely future counts and dukes with the rank and file of the regular military forces, *expediti milites*, based at the court or with the royal guard regiments, the erstwhile *antrustiones*.

The aristocratic young men who were being trained to be officers at the early Carolingian court very likely did a turn of service in various units of palace guards and in the units of the regular troops based at the court in order to have a wide variety of experience. Indeed, Ammianus Marcellinus (27.6.8,9) records a speech in which the Emperor Valentinian I made a point of emphasizing that as part of training, officers were to learn to bear the heat, snow, frost, thirst, and sleepless nights on campaign. The officer must not hesitate to risk his life to save his comrades in danger. This type of officer training was commonplace at the

Merovingian royal courts and, as will be seen below, in the early Carolingian *palatium*, as well.[172]

Charlemagne, in arranging for the education of his own sons, which likely mirrored his own formation at the royal court, saw to it that they were trained in horsemanship "more Francorum" (discussed in Chapter 3), as well as in the use of arms and in the hunt.[173] In the royal *schola*, however, the sons of the king and others were not limited to a military education. In addition, efforts were made to enhance their intellectual development. Indeed, Einhard makes the point that Charlemagne's sons were educated in "liberalibus studiis." Perhaps with a little exaggeration stimulated by the appreciation that one learned important lessons from books in a systematic manner that could not be easily duplicated through the vagaries of experience, Einhard asserts that these studies came "first" in importance and that the military training came afterward.[174]

It was widely recognized that learning from books was crucial to the formation of an officer. For example, Frontinus, a classical author well known to the Carolingians, put the matter of study for military purposes in the prologue to his *Strategemata*. He observed that "Commanders will be equipped with examples of good planning and foresight." He then emphasized that this knowledge "will [help them] to develop their own ability to think out and carry out operations successfully that are similar in nature [to those that they have studied]" (*Strag.* 1.1). Frontinus goes on to note that the commander who is so educated will have an added benefit insofar as he will not worry about the success of his plans because he has learned that similar plans have worked in the past (*Strag.* 1.1).

Rhabanus Maurus, mentioned above in regard to his close connection to the Carolingian court as a result of being a student of Alcuin, commented on the *De re Militari* of Vegetius. Rhabanus reiterated in his own military handbook Vegetius' notion, similar to the view expressed by Frontinus and cited above, that it is important to instruct new recruits (*tyrones*) in all manner of things ("omnimodis instituebantur") that are relevant to the military art. With such instruction, Rhabanus follows Vegetius in averring that then these *tyrones* would be prepared to carry out what they have learned rather than being afraid to act because they are uninformed.[175]

Adalhard, King Pippin's nephew, emphasizes, in a bit of long-winded hyperbole, that it is important for these young men trained at the court to bring honor to their instructor (*magister*) through their accomplishments. If they are successful, he continues, they are honored by their *magister* in return.[176] In this context, it is worth recalling Charlemagne's putative outburst, "preserved" in the *Gesta Karoli* by Notker of Saint Gall, regarding those young men who were being trained at the royal *schola* but who were reported by their officers as bringing honor neither to themselves nor to their instructors. Charlemagne is alleged to have thundered: "You young nobles, [who] have neglected the pursuit of learning and have wasted your time . . . I have no regard for your nobility . . . and know for certain that unless you immediately make up for your earlier time-wasting by serious study, you will never get anything worthwhile from Charlemagne."[177]

Whether Charlemagne ever made this speech or one like it is problematic. What is more important is the perceived tradition. It was Notker's view that in the good old days, when Charlemagne ruled, the training of an officer corps drawn from the nobility required not only the mastery of military athletics but also a highly valued and well-cultivated academic side, the *litterae studia* mentioned by Einhard.[178] Indeed, Notker distinguishes between the aristocratic youths, the sons of the *primores*, who were being trained for military command and governmental office, and boys from lower-class families (*infimi*) and those from middle-class families (*mediocres*) who were being educated at the court, as well. These nonaristocratic youths apparently were being trained for positions in the Church.[179]

The tradition that Notker perceived and popularized for his readers, however, was not a figment of his imagination. Some high-ranking military officers who served in the armies of the early Carolingians were well-educated men. For example, Wido, who as a mature man replaced Roland as commander of the Breton March sometime after 778, had received his education a good deal earlier.[180] This Wido sought a handbook from Alcuin to guide his everyday life in spiritual terms while he, himself, was thoroughly involved in "bellicis rebus." In response to Wido's need and request Alcuin composed his *De Virtutibus et Vitiis*, which was introduced by a rather complicated dedicatory letter and followed by a concluding peroration.[181] Whatever one may think of Alcuin's depth of thought or originality in this little tract, the intended reader for this handbook was no illiterate Germanic warrior concerned only with the acquisition of booty and military glory.

We have more information regarding the early career of Wido's older contemporary Witiza, a Visigoth and the son of the count of Maguelonne. Indeed, his early career serves as a model for an aristocratic officer in training. Witiza, who may have been named for the last Visigothic king, was not an ethnic Frank, as is clear even from his name. Nevertheless, he was sent to the court of King Pippin I while still a boy so that he could be educated to assume high military command.[182] He is described as being a natural leader and is reported by his biographer Ardo, who knew him, to have gained the affection of his fellow military cadets. He was, in the military jargon of the Roman empire used by Ardo, *conmilitio*.[183] Moreover, like Adalhard of Corbie, he also learned his letters very well; later in life Witiza wrote and compiled numerous Latin works.[184]

For a time Witiza was assigned for his training and education to the guard regiment responsible for the safety of the queen. He is characterized by Ardo as among the *scholares reginae*.[185] However, his posting to this unit ended before the death of King Pippin I, who transferred him to regular military service at court. When Pippin died, Witiza, who was already in his early twenties, was posted to the court of Charlemagne where he continued in military service.[186] Witiza was apparently joined at the royal court by his younger brother (his name has been lost), who was in 773 considered sufficiently well trained to go on a major campaign. Thus, both men served in the Italian campaign of 773–774, where the younger brother, who lacked Witiza's prudence, appears to have drowned while trying to ford a flooded river.[187]

By 773–774, Witiza commanded a unit of mounted troops that likely had served under him in Italy and then accompanied him on leave to Maguelonne following the victory over the Lombards.[188] This suggests that the unit was comprised of locals from the south who were going on leave at the same time as their commander. However, while returning to the north after this military leave, Witiza decided to give up the secular life and entered the monastery of Saint Seine near Dijon. At that point, he ordered his men to return to their homeland (*patria*). Thus, a very promising military career was cut short quite dramatically, but an even more influential ecclesiastical career, of the future Benedict of Aniane, was begun.[189]

The entire training program at the royal court for youths such as Witiza, as described by Adalhard, was overseen by a commander referred to as *dominus*.[190] Just as there were units of *expediti milites* stationed at the royal court under the command of *domini*, who, as already noted, were royal officials, *ministeriales*, but with the special title of *capitaneus*, there was also an overall commander, probably of similar rank, for the unit of officer candidates and the *magistri* who trained them.[191] Adalhard himself was educated at the royal court, trained by the same *magister* who trained Charlemagne, and did his initial military service, *tirocinium*, while based at the royal court.

Even Latin Carolingian court poetry contains information about training men of the upper classes as military officers. For example, much of interest concerning the training of the officer corps at the royal court can be teased from *Waltharius*, an epic poem in Latin that was written perhaps at the end of the eighth century and certainly before the end of Charlemagne's reign in 814.[192] While the poet's excellent classical education provided him with access to a plethora of Latin poetic and literary sources, which he adroitly weaves into his narrative, his studies, presumably in rhetoric, also taught him that his story had to be convincing.[193] The poet wrote for an ostensibly secular audience,[194] probably at one of the Carolingian royal courts which flourished during the period.[195]

At least some clerics who served in the royal entourage at the court where *Waltharius* was read would also be able to understand the military aspects of this poem quite well. In this context, men such as Witiza and Adalhard of Corbie, who were trained in secular *militia* at the court of King Pippin, and Rhabanus Maurus, who wrote knowledgeably on contemporary military training and tactics, come to mind.

In *Waltharius*, Walter of Aquitaine, the hero of the poem, is made a high-ranking officer, one of the *primi militiae* in the king's army, because of his ability as a military man.[196] While on campaign, he is called *ductor* when leading a unit and, in the sense of a military title or perhaps even as an indication of rank, when he is not on active military duty.[197] The king watched very carefully as Walter grew up at the royal court and as the youth developed his skills "in artibus" and especially in war games ("praesertimque iocis belli").[198] The development of physical strength (*robor*) was only part of the process of becoming a military officer, however; future *primi militiae* also had to develop their intelligence ("ingenio mentis"). As the poet put it with a modicum of exaggeration and an obvious nod to Lucan (2.52), the young men trained at court to be the best military officers were to "surpass ordinary well trained soldiers (*fortes*) in strength (*robor*) and the wise men (*sophistae*) in intellect (*animus*)."[199]

The organization of the "royal *obsequium*," as Adalhard terms the king's military household, and the *schola* for training officers, would seem to be something of an *imitatio* of the imperial household as it developed during the later Roman empire.[200] At Constantinople, for example, the imperial military household was still called the *Opsikian*, a Greek rendering of the Latin *obsequium*, meaning retinue. In 662, Constans II led the Opsikian army into Italy. By the middle of the eighth century, however, those units of the Opsikian that had been posted well outside the capital of Constantinople were reorganized and renamed. These household units were reduced to a mere 4,000 effectives who appear essentially to have been directly attendant upon the emperor as *presentales*.[201] Adalhard validates his views on the similarity of the early Carolingian court to its imperial predecessors by indicating that he had special knowledge of Constantine the Great's court.[202]

Pueri and Vassalli

Adalhard takes note of yet a third group (*ordo*) of military men attached to the Carolingian court: *pueri* and *vassalli*. They were not properly royal troops in the same way as the *expediti milites*; rather, these men were members of the military households of both the greater and the lesser officials who ostensibly had been seconded to the royal court for the purpose of serving the king. It was the duty of these royal officials to see to the provisioning of their own men.[203]

The word *puer* was traditionally the term of choice in the Merovingian era to denote an unfree military retainer who served either in the household of the king or of a magnate.[204] The terminology used to discuss this third *ordo* therefore surely brings to mind the *servi*, discussed above, who are described as being honored with *vassaticum* and equipped as elite, heavily armed mounted troops by their *domini*. The joining of the terms *pueri* and *vassalli* by Adalhard in describing the members of the military households of officials stationed at the royal court confirms their institutional similarity concerning personal status with the *servi* who were honored by their *domini*. Moreover, these *pueri* are similar in status to those men, as seen above, recruited to serve in the royal *trustis* as *antrustiones*.

Most of the professional fighting men in the *regnum Francorum* were recruited from the lower classes. Free men of sufficient wealth, as discussed earlier, already owed expeditionary service. Therefore, a substantial percentage of the military retinues very likely were *servi*.[205] In addition, the king also had *vassalli* serving in his personal military forces at the palace.[206] The *expediti milites*, discussed above, may have been considered royal *vassalli* by contemporaries, and the *milites* billeted in the town of Centula may also have been considered to have been *vassalli*. However, the term is not used explicitly to describe the men in either group, so we cannot conclude firmly that these men were considered *vassalli* by their contemporaries.

Military Lands

Not all elite or professional fighting men were in the households of the king and of the lay and ecclesiastical magnates. Like the government of the later Roman empire and later of Byzantium, the Frankish kings utilized what, for want of a proper technical term, may be called "military lands." For example, when Clovis conquered Aquitaine from the Visigoths, he established military colonies of *Franci* throughout the region. His Merovingian successors continued this practice of using military lands as they were needed, especially in territories recently brought under Frankish control.[207] In a similar vein, when King Pippin I conquered Aquitaine, he too established *Franci* in the region for military purposes.[208]

A model to consider when examining the use of military lands by governments on the erstwhile territory of the later Roman empire is provided by an edict attributed to Alexander Severus, Roman emperor from 222 to 235, that anachronistically credits him with giving lands "to the *duces* and to the *milites* of the *limitanei*." These *dona* were a later fourth-century phenomenon, made under condition that each parcel of land would belong to the *miles* who received it as long as he performed military service, and would remain in his family only if his heir entered imperial military service. In addition: "Under no circumstances were these lands to belong to civilians." The emperor also "added to these lands . . . both draft animals and slaves. . . . so that they would be able to cultivate the lands that they (the *milites*) had received."[209] Slaves were to do the agricultural work on this land so that each *miles* would have sufficient income and be available for full-time military service.

A substantial corpus of information concerning *limitanei*, like so much about the later Roman empire, was available to the Carolingians, not only from the above-mentioned *Life of Alexander Severus*, which is found in the *Historia Augusta*, but also in the *Codex Theodosianus*, which was widely used in the *regnum Francorum*.[210] One cannot even imagine how many copies of relevant parts of the *Codex* were available to men who were in a position to give advice on technical matters regarding "military lands" to the governments of the Carolingian Mayors of the Palace and later to the kings.[211]

The Carolingian Mayors and kings not only used military lands to pay some of their troops, but they also required other important men, both lay and ecclesiastical, to make such awards.[212] Much controversy, however, surrounds the institutional structures associated by scholars with the Carolingians' use of military lands.[213] Nevertheless, several points are clear. First, the Carolingians ultimately adopted the word *beneficium* to describe these military lands.[214] Indeed, no other term seems to have been used with any frequency, despite the fact that most *beneficia*, as is clear from context, were not military lands.[215] Second, the words *vassus*, its diminutive variation *vassallus*, as well as the words *homo* (man) and *miles* (soldier), were used to denote the fighting men who held such military land.[216] It is clear, however, again from context, that most *vassi*, *vassalli*, *homines*, and *milites*, did not hold military land during the early Carolingian era.[217] In addition, the word *vassus*, derived from the Celtic word *gwas* for boy, was often a synonym for the Latin *puer* in a military context, as seen above. Both words, *gwas* and *puer*, indicate a man of humble status and often a man who was a *servus*.[218] Throughout the *regnum Francorum*, men who possessed sufficient lands of their own already had well-defined military obligations to the government for *expeditio*.

A further attraction of tenure as a *beneficium* to the grantor was that, in principle, it was both limited and revocable.[219] Government officials throughout the history of the later Roman empire as well as in the Byzantine East had great difficulty in maintaining the system of military lands for the mobilization of well-trained soldiers over long periods of time. This was due to the vagaries of human demography.[220] Thus, the use of beneficial tenure might perhaps be thought to have been intended to work as a means of keeping control of the land, much of which was Church property, that had been allocated at royal command, "pro verbo regis," for grants as military land as well as for other purposes.[221]

The Carolingians were aware of such demographic vagaries as litigation frequently arose concerning *terra Salica*. This land had been entailed in the male line to assure the government of the military service of the landholder.[222] The Carolingian kings, who were constantly having surveys taken and inventories made, also struggled to keep track of the men who held military lands and the service that they owed.[223] Consequently, both Louis the Pious and Charles the Bald endeavored to keep these lists current, despite the obvious weakening of royal power at the center of government as compared to the period of Charlemagne's rule and even that of his father, King Pippin.[224]

From a military perspective, an important distinction is to be made between *vassi dominici casati*—men who had received military lands, and who, in general, no longer resided at the court—and *vassi dominici non casati*, those who remained in the royal household.[225] Some of these royal *vassi* who were *casati* received a very small amount of land, indeed, perhaps only a few *mansi*.[226] Such *vassi* were rather few in number during the reign of Pippin I and in the early reign of Charlemagne.[227] The small *beneficia* that these *vassi* received seem to have been in the nature of a reward for a long and faithful career of service in the royal military household.[228] An obvious analogue to these *casati* are retired Roman soldiers. The latter received lands and like the *vassi casati* were required to continue to play an active role, though as civilians, in military life during the later Roman empire.[229]

Other *vassi dominici*, however, were given extensive landed resources. These ranged from thirty to two hundred manses. Indeed, some men who held land at the high end of the scale were granted entire estates.[230] In all such cases this was far more land than the twelve *mansi* that were required to support a single, heavily armed, mounted fighting man of the highest quality. Finally, *vassi dominici* were distributed throughout the regions under Carolingian rule. Often these men were settled on lands that had been taken in the course of conquest or during the reintegration of territory, such as Aquitaine, into the *regnum Francorum* by King Pippin.[231] In short, each of these well-endowed royal vassals should be regarded as a sort of local commander, who was based largely in the provinces and was responsible for recruiting and leading the troops owed from his military lands in the king's army.[232] Indeed, in Aquitaine, where Pippin I had established various kinds of military settlements, even the clergy were given considerable military training (*bellicae exercitatio*). The writer who discusses this situation, a contemporary of Louis the Pious, makes special note of both equestrian skills and the hurling of missile weapons in his discussion of military drills.[233]

The highly trained fighting men and more particularly their high-ranking military officers, who were attached to the *obsequium* at the royal palace, were professional soldiers. However, when such men were given lands and left the court, their personal interests altered substantially and their role in the military markedly changed. An exceptional insight into this process is offered by the court poet who wrote *Waltharius*. He constructs a scene in which the king offers Walter, the hero of the epic and an outstanding military commander, both a wife of very high social status and extensive landed resources. As the poet explains the situation, this arrangement, if accepted by Walter, means, in effect, that he will leave the court and settle down on his estates to lead a life that was very different from his life as a professional military officer attached to the royal court.

First, the king is depicted as preparing to recognize, in direct discourse with Walter, that the latter has accomplished a great many difficult tasks (*magni labores*) while in royal *servitium*. Indeed, the poet, borrowing from Virgil (*Aen.* 9.430), has the king recognize that he esteems (*delixit*) Walter more than all of his other high-ranking military commanders (*amici*). Then, Walter is offered the opportunity to choose a wife from among the daughters of the greatest magnates of the realm. Finally, the king promises Walter that he will be given such extensive lands in the countryside and movable wealth for his home that the great magnate whose daughter he chooses to marry will not be ashamed by the poverty of his son-in-law.[234]

Walter, however, is not inclined to accept the king's offer. The poet has the hero put forth the soldier's reasons very politely but cogently. Thus, Walter emphasizes: "If I take a bride . . . first and foremost, I will be constrained in my actions by my concern for her wellbeing and by my love for her." In this vein, he continues, "because of my love for the girl, I will be diverted frequently from the king's service (*servitio regis*)." The poet has Walter point out: "I will find it necessary to build houses and to devote my attention to agriculture." And furthermore, "this, will keep me from coming to court (lit., appearing in the sight of my lord) and from devoting my usual attention [as a *primus militiae*] to the welfare of the . . . *regnum*."[235]

After emphasizing the differences between the life of an unmarried but high-ranking military officer who is attached to the court with that of a wealthy landed aristocrat, Walter explains how the latter existence limits the capacity of the professional soldier to do his duty. He generalizes in a not implausible manner "whoever has tasted pleasure thereafter is inclined to endure hardships less willingly." However, he continues, "now nothing is so sweet to me as to serve as a *fidelis* in the military household of my *dominus*." Thus, Walter goes on with his defense of the soldier who is unencumbered by wife, children, and estates: "If in the late evening or even in the middle of the night, you give me a mission, I will go wherever you order me . . . in a prepared manner and without other cares." Walter avers: "In battle there will be no anxieties that will induce me to retreat . . . neither children nor a wife will hold me back [in the course of battle] nor cause me to flee [from combat]."[236]

The *Scara*

The early Carolingians organized various types of units to carry out specific kinds of military operations. The preferred term in the narrative sources of this era for some such units was the rather unprepossessing word *scara*, although the term itself appeared much earlier.[237] This possibly quasi-technical term is the Latinized form of a word of Germanic origin that means "group."[238] The modern German word *Schar*, also meaning group, is its ultimate linguistic descendant. The use of such apparently vague terminology to denote elite military units during the early Carolingian era should hardly surprise us. Even in modern military usage, where the precision of bureaucratese is a primary *desideratum*, the equally unprepossessing word "group" and even more frequently encountered "battle group" continues to be used by the American military. Those men noted as serving in the *scara* during the period under discussion here are characterized in contemporary and near contemporary sources by terms such as *scariti*, *escariti*, and *scarii*—members of the group.[239]

Until now, scholars have exhibited uncertainty as to whether these *scarae* were regularly constituted units or *ad hoc* forces formed from a larger force for particular operations.[240] The word *scara* itself, in an etymological sense, tilts our understanding toward the notion that a *scara* initially was a part of a larger force. It is etymologically related to the spectrum of words for cutting or cutting off— scissors, shear, and shire. Similarly, a *scaritus* is a man of the group or from the group, just as a shireman is the inhabitant of the shire, that is, the region cut from a larger unit, the county. However, even if a *scara* is a part of a larger unit, an *exercitus*, as is likely at least on some occasions, this tells us nothing as to whether it was a group constituted on an *ad hoc* basis for a particular assignment or a regularly established unit of the larger force detached for one or another operation.

When we read of the *scarae* in the contemporary and near contemporary early Carolingian sources, these units do not seem to have had an identity as defined primarily by mission or combat assignment, such as infantry, cavalry, or artillery. For example, some *scarae* appear to have been composed of mounted troops, or were deployed in operations in which it would make sense to use men who were equipped with horses. Clearly, these *scarii* were deployed in operations that required rapid movement and therefore should be assumed to have been equipped with horses for such efforts. In addition, the *scarae*, on some occasions at least, seem also to have been very closely tied to the movements of the royal household, which is of importance in terms of the itinerant nature of the latter with the king and most of his *obsequium* traveling on horseback or in wagons.[241]

However, sometimes *scarae* were deployed in fortifications on garrison duty to defend the walls of strongholds should the position come under enemy attack or by their very presence to deter a hostile action. For example, in 766, Pippin deployed a *scara* in the newly captured *urbs* of Bourges and apparently in the rebuilt *castrum* at Argenton-sur-Creuse.[242] Charlemagne, early in his career, also is reported to have placed *scarae* as garrison troops for the purpose of guarding (*custodientes*) two newly rebuilt but less formidable strongholds or *castella*.[243] Such troops obviously were not required to maintain very valuable and thus expensive war horses in these rather small fortifications on a primarily defensive assignment. A garrison, or at least some of its personnel, however, used horses if only for patrolling and gathering intelligence.

Some *scarae* were units detached for various duties from the royal military household. Adalhard, for example, calls attention to the fact that men from each of the three military *ordines* based at the court and discussed above were frequently coming and going on various missions. However, he does not use the word *scara* to describe any of these units or missions. Nevertheless, Adalhard does make clear that the *expediti milites* of the royal military *obsequium* were always prepared to take military action should a critical situation arise.[244] In short, they had the same rapid deployment capacity attributed in some cases to *scarii*. It would be incautious to assert that all *scarae* in the sources are mounted units attached to the royal *obsequium*.[245] In addition to service as *custodes* in strongholds, which would separate those *scarii* from the royal court for an extended period of time, there are too many mentions of *scarii* in other contexts, especially from the early ninth century onward, to sustain a narrow meaning for *scara*.[246]

Within certain limits, for example to function as a garrison, a *scara* reported as detached from the royal court denotes a regular standing unit or more likely a formal subdivision of such a unit. As will be discussed below in detail, effective military operations require unit cohesion. Thus, the selection of men from various units for a *scara* on an *ad hoc* basis would result ostensibly in the creation of a new unit for a specific task. Such a process was likely to produce groups with less rather than more unit cohesion and would hinder rather than assist effective operations.

The author of the *Annales regni Francorum* speaks of the *scarae* established by Pippin and Charlemagne as garrisons in 766 and 776, respectively. The reviser of these accounts, who wrote early in the ninth century, refers to these same troops with the more widely known and much more precise technical military term for a garrison, *praesidio*.[247] In light of operational cohesion, the *scarae* under consideration here were already existing units that had been trained for special duty as a garrison force. This would include use of the weapons required to defend a fortification such as *ballistae* and various other types of artillery discussed below in Chapter 3.

With regard to field operations, the author of the *Annales regni Francorum*, *an.* 774, mentions that Charlemagne sent four *scarae* into Saxony. By contrast, the *Annales q.d. Einhardi*, *an.* 774, while discussing this same operation, refers to the army — the *exercitus* that is under Charlemagne's command — as having three units. The Metz annalist refers to these same units as *legiones*.[248] The use of a well-established Roman military term, which traditionally indicated a unit of regular army troops, by the well-informed and well-educated author of these *Annales mettenses*, suggests that he did not want his readers to infer that the men deployed in this situation were either expeditionary levies (men who served on a part-time basis), or some sort of *ad hoc* formation. Rather, as with a Roman legion, he wanted these men seen as professional soldiers who were formed into regular standing units.[249]

Even Latin poetry may be of some aid in helping us to grasp the operations of a court-based *scara*. As we have noted above, the training of Walter of Aquitaine to be an officer, *primus militiae* and *ductor* in the royal *obsequium*, is depicted in a manner that is remarkably consistent with nonfictional narrative sources and various types of documents. Thus, *Waltharius* also provides information regarding the rapid response capacity of mounted military units based at the royal court. For example, in one episode of this poem, the king receives exceptionally reliable intelligence (*certissima fama*) that a recently suppressed tribe (*gens*) had rejected its dependent status and that its attack on the kingdom was imminent. Walter, residing at the court, was ordered to mobilize immediately and was given command of the entire force of soldiery (*tota militia*) assigned to the task of dealing with the rebels. Very soon after he received command of this force, it was ready for action. Thus, without delay (*nec mora*), he led this army (*exercitus*) on campaign.[250] All of this leads toward the conclusion that a well-organized unit was being deployed.

Conclusion

Several important themes regarding early Carolingian military policy have been adumbrated in this chapter. With regard to military organization it is clear that Pippin II and his successors built solidly on a system devised during the later Roman empire ostensibly to fight defensive war. While they did not ignore the general levy of all able-bodied men that was required for the local defense, the early Carolingians nevertheless turned their attention to molding a system that could support extended periods of offensive warfare. Indeed, this military organization for the better part of a century sustained continuous offensive warfare and was the base upon which Charlemagne asserted his rule over the greater part of the Roman empire in the West.

In order to mobilize the large numbers of effectives that were required to sustain sieges against the great fortress cities that had been built during the later Roman empire, the early Carolingians took full advantage of the select levies, who served on the basis of their landed wealth. In addition, the early Carolingians worked diligently to create a substantial core of professional soldiers. Since all men who owned sufficient land already were required to serve on expeditions, these new professionals were recruited from among those who were too poor to owe regular offensive military service. Indeed, many and likely most men who were honored with *vassaticam* not only were landless but more often than not they probably were *servi* or *pueri*. It was not pure happenstance that the Latin term *vassus* developed from the Celtic word *gwas*, which was a synonym for *puer*. Scholars have given great attention to the royal military *obsequium*, both the *presentales*, who served at the court, and those based outside the *palatio*, as well as the retinues of the lay and ecclesiastical magnates. This has been the case especially in regard to the development of a professional army by the early Carolingians. However, this interest is highlighted in our sources, in large part, as a result of the closeness of these *vassi* to the magnates and even more particularly to the king, who are the focus of many of the various chronicles and annals. Thus, as will be detailed in Chapter 6, the militarized civilian population serving in the select levy provided the overwhelming majority of the manpower for the rank and file of the early Carolingian armies that carried out the major offensive operations. Many of these operations, which were aimed at permanent conquest, required that the great Roman fortress cities of Gaul, Italy, and, later, Spain be placed under siege. Such warfare required very large armies.

CHAPTER THREE

Training and Equipment

Throughout the history of the West, training and discipline of the armed forces have been regarded as fundamental to military success and are consistently emphasized in the military handbooks and histories that are traditionally part of the education of officers.[1] For example, in works such as Frontinus' *Stragemata* and Vegetius' *De re Militari*, which were readily available to the Carolingians (they made copies, some of which are extant), maxims are set out to emphasize the importance of both training and discipline.[2] Even Gregory of Tours in his *Histories*, though hardly classical in either form or content, makes clear through the depiction of disastrous episodes in which the basic military principles were not followed that training and discipline could not be ignored with impunity.[3]

Military training and to a lesser extent discipline cannot be divorced from how particular types of weaponry are used. Training and discipline are intended to make the best use of particular types of equipment on the battlefield as the wisdom of the time conceives such deployment.[4] The Roman government frequently encouraged auxiliaries and federates, first as allies and then as mercenaries, to continue using the armament and combat techniques that they had used beyond the frontiers of the empire. Thus, some groups, even after they had been recruited into imperial service, for a time used their traditional weapons and tactics.[5] In consequence of maintaining particular types of arms, their training techniques were little altered, as well.[6] Therefore, the many different peoples, for example, Romans, Franks, Alans, Suevi, Goths, Saxons, and Burgundians, who were drawn into the military forces of the *regnum Francorum* during the reigns of Clovis (481–511) and his sons prior to the death of King Chlotar I in 561, differed in their armament, combat techniques, and battle tactics in noteworthy ways.[7]

The military, however, saw very rapid acculturation during the latter part of the sixth century, if not earlier. As seen above in Chapter 2, virtually all of the various peoples dwelling in the *regnum Francorum* ostensibly were integrated into a system that was thoroughly conditioned by the military heritage of the Roman world.[8] A stark indicator of such change is the *francisca*, regarded in some quarters as the weapon that defined the Franks or *Franci* as an ethnic group in military terms.[9] This throwing ax, which very likely took its name from the *Franci* themselves, disappeared as a combat weapon during the later sixth century.[10] Gregory of Tours in his *Histories*, which were written at the end of the sixth century, depicts the ax not as a combat weapon widely used in warfare but rather as a sidearm that was used primarily in personal altercations. Indeed, despite his extensive discussion of violence at all levels of society from feud to war, Gregory rarely mentions the ax.[11] By the early eighth century, moreover, the author of the *Liber Historiae Francorum* believed that his readers would not even know that a *francisca* was an ax much less that it was originally a missile weapon.[12] The *francisca*, which was so closely associated with the military ethnicity of the Franks, surely symbolizes the process of acculturation.[13]

Although the military was integrated into a unified organization with similar armament, many of the various peoples dwelling in the Merovingian kingdoms and then in the realms of their early Carolingian successors continued to maintain a certain ethnic identity. This apparent continuity in identity was the result of the law; thus, Franks lived under Frankish law, Saxons under Saxon law, and so forth, including Jews who lived under *lex Judaeorum*. In this situation, legislation was needed so that, for example, people who lived under Roman law could go to court with someone who lived under Thuringian law.[14]

A curious situation evolved in which people maintained an ethnic-legal identity but were militarily integrated with regard to both organization and weaponry. These processes of military integration within the *regnum Francorum* likely played some role in the development of a tradition, especially among outsiders, as will be seen below, to refer to the fighting forces of both the Merovingian kings and the Carolingians as "Franks."[15] This labeling is an earlier analogue of that employed by Byzantine and Muslim writers who, apparently having observed the similarity of armaments and tactics used by the westerners during the first Crusade, considered these fighting men to be "Franks."[16] Under the early Carolingians, peoples from all legal-ethnic groups were required to perform military service, as we have seen above, according to their economic means. Indeed, the early career of Witiza (discussed above), who was of unambiguous Gothic descent, demonstrates ethnic integration within the army and obviously within the officer corps.

Some chroniclers of the eighth and ninth centuries speak of the "Franks" at war, but such markers may be limited not to Franks as an ethnic group, insofar as this had any military meaning in the world of the early Carolingians, nor solely to those who enjoyed Frankish juridical identity. To put a finer point on the matter, Frankish ethnicity was not meaningful in military reality but was preserved ostensibly in the context of personality of the law as, for example, in regard to *terra Salica*, discussed above. This legal tradition of ethnicity existed in a context in which both so-called Frankish *leges*—those of the Salians and those of the Ripuarians—had been thoroughly infiltrated by Roman law and massively altered by imperial influence. The processes of alteration began at least from the time of settlement within the frontiers of the empire under imperial aegis. With regard to the Salian Franks, heavy Roman influence was firmly institutionalized and can easily be traced even in the earliest redaction of *lex Salica* when Clovis commanded that a selection of these *leges* be redacted and published in Latin.[17] In short, even Frankish legal identity was highly romanized.

Our best sources of information on the training of the early Carolingians are military handbooks. For example, Vegetius' *De re Militari*, mentioned above, is only one of the many works containing valuable military information that the Carolingians copied from older, pre-Carolingian manuscripts available in the *regnum Francorum*.[18] However, Vegetius' work was copied many times, and more important, the *De re Militari* itself was the subject of a Carolingian handbook. Rhabanus Maurus, the noted scholar and ecclesiastical administrator, who was educated under the personal direction of Alcuin, one of Charlemagne's favorites, constructed a handbook that contained selections from the *De re Militari*. He provided these selections, of which only a few chapters have survived, with a commentary for use by one of Charlemagne's successors. Rhabanus declared his intention in this new handbook to eliminate from Vegetius' *De re Militari* all items not of use "tempore moderno" and thus to retain and to comment upon only those matters that were currently useful.[19]

The Vegetian materials combined with Rhabanus' commentary, despite the apparently incomplete nature of the latter's surviving handbook, provide important insights into the *desiderata* of early Carolingian military training. These texts, nevertheless, must be used carefully. Legitimate questions always may be asked regarding how closely the handbooks that set out the proper methods for training, tactics, and strategy were followed. (This question will be addressed in Chapter 5 where tactics are discussed in order to ascertain whether the training that is examined here was manifested in combat situations.)[20]

Efforts by contemporary scholars to deprecate the written culture and administrative sophistication of the early medieval era are rife. These are based, in general, upon the resuscitation of one or another invidious formulation of the long discredited "Dark Age" concept. Now, such putative insights are purveyed under the aegis of so-called anthropological "theory" which, for example, requires that we replace Western notions of trade for profit with gift exchange models created on the basis of early modern accounts of North American Indians. Western notions of real war are to be replaced with a primitive feud mentality.[21] It is claimed or implied that great leaders such as Charlemagne and the empires that they ruled are better understood if they are compared with illiterate Zulu chiefs and the sub-Saharan tribes they lead. The early medieval pursuit of *imitatio imperii* is, of course, ignored, or cast aside as mere anachronism.[22]

Narrative accounts give some sense of how the early Carolingians were using Vegetian teaching, which survives from a revision of the original work made at Constantinople in 450. For example, Vegetius advocates the training of mounted troops to dismount when necessary and to fight on foot and discusses the training required for the mastery of this combat technique.[23] Rhabanus not only includes this chapter in his handbook but provides illuminating commentary on it, which indicates that he altered some important things, sometimes radically and sometimes only slightly, for use in "modern times."[24]

The *Strategikon* of the Emperor Maurice, written circa 600, is of considerable importance in any attempt to grasp how the teaching of these two handbooks by Vegetius and Rhabanus was put into practice. The *Strategikon* is also a handbook but some of its aims are rather different from the works of both Vegetius and Rhabanus. Maurice wanted his soldiers to learn not only what they are supposed to do, but also about the techniques of the enemy. In this context, the emperor explains, in consonance with Vegetius, that his mounted troops are trained to jump off their horses so that they can fight on foot.[25] He later points out that the Franks are also well trained in the art of dismounting from their horses in order to fight on foot,[26] perhaps indicating that the Franks used the training suggested or presented by Vegetius and found in the revision of his handbook from about 450. This was recognized by Maurice in about 600, and Rhabanus made clear, as noted above, that it was still of primary importance "tempore moderno."

Training for Infantry Phalanx

In Charles Martel's famous victory at Poitiers in 732, the early Carolingian infantry phalanx is described as "standing like a wall of ice." This phalanx was the core formation of the early Carolingian army for defensive battle in the field.[27] The effective deployment of such a phalanx, as is well known from study of this formation in a variety of classical incarnations, required extensive training with the short thrusting sword and a deeply ingrained sense of discipline.[28] Rhabanus Maurus' handbook based on Vegetius' *De re Militari* gives detailed attention to training in the use of the *gladius* by foot soldiers in the phalanx formation. Indeed, Rhabanus saw this short thrusting sword as the fundamental weapon for hand-to-hand combat when he wrote during the ninth century.

Rhabanus carefully edited Vegetius' descriptions concerning "How the ancients trained recruits (*tirones*) with wicker shields and at the posts (*ad palos*)."[29] Rhabanus even changed the title of this chapter in his handbook better to describe its revised content: "How they are exercised with wicker shields and clubs."[30] Vegetius mentions in his title the posts (*pali*) or what later in the

Middle Ages would be called the "quintain."[31] By contrast, Rhabanus makes clear at the start of his treatment by way of commentary that "Individual soldiers (*milites*) were accustomed to plant individual posts (*pali*) in the ground" for the purpose of practice. According to Rhabanus (Vegetius does not discuss this), these posts are to be "rigid and about six feet or the height of an average man." The notion that an average man was six feet tall is an obvious early medieval addition as Roman soldiers on average were much shorter.

Both Vegetius and Rhabanus use the word *miles* from time to time in this chapter, which indicates that both during the later Roman empire and under the Carolingians it was normal for experienced foot soldiers (*milites*) and not merely *tirones* or recruits to practice against the rigid post.[32] Thus, the initial military training for the recruit may have been augmented by drill for the older and obviously more experienced soldier.

Rhabanus goes on to explain that "the recruit (*tyro*) came against the post as if against the enemy." In order to practice striking the enemy, the recruit carried a club (*clavus*) rather than a sword. However, this wooden substitute for the sword was intentionally much heavier than the normal *gladius* or short sword so that in combat it would be easier to wield the real weapon.[33] In his *Recapitulatio*, Rhabanus emphasizes the importance of developing the strength of a soldier's shoulders so as to enhance his strength in thrusting his sword.[34]

The short sword was traditionally used by men fighting on foot in very close order, in the manner made famous by the Spartan phalanx.[35] These troops were well known not only for the rigorous training that made their formation so formidable but also for their ferocity in battle. Therefore, when one reads the Emperor Maurice's observation regarding the Franks, "They calmly despise death as they fight ferociously in hand-to-hand combat,"[36] it is difficult not to be reminded of Plutarch's observation concerning the Spartans who "with no confusion in their hearts . . . calmly and cheerfully advanced into danger" (*Lyc.* 22.2–3).[37]

All of this hyperbole has a certain ring of romanticism and/or propaganda about it. However, the point of reference is the appearance of the soldiers as perceived by their adversaries. Nothing can be gleaned here regarding the "terrors" experienced and/or suppressed by men who are in combat or about to enter into a life-and-death struggle. If they appear to be calm or even cheerful in the face of death, however, they may well raise anxieties and lower morale in those adversaries who observe this behavior.

Each Carolingian soldier, whether *tyro* or *miles*, in the course of his training or drill placed a wooden post in front of him against which to practice. These posts, in effect, constituted a line of life-sized obstacles opposite to the line of men in training. At a signal during practice, each man pressed forward ("consurgebat") along with his fellows against the *palum* as if against his enemy ("quasi contra inimicum"). Rhabanus indicates that first the soldier practiced by jabbing at the head of the enemy and then by thrusting at the face. He followed this up with thrusts at the stomach and the sides. Finally, strokes were aimed at the knees and the lower legs. In carrying out these carefully choreographed training movements, the soldier was taught to jump in, to jump backward, and to duck to the side, while he was to cover himself with his shield so that he could not be struck by his opponent. Rhabanus concludes this chapter by emphasizing again that the shields and the swords used during training were heavier than those used during combat because as a result soldiers would find their movements much easier when they worked with the real equipment.[38]

In the next chapter, entitled "They were taught to attack with the sword by jabbing and not by slashing," Rhabanus echoes Vegetius' warning about the importance of using the sword as a thrusting weapon rather than as a slashing weapon. Like Vegetius, Rhabanus emphasizes that a jab with the sword has penetrating power, whereas the slash, which often is difficult to aim and control, may strike a bone or the enemy's shield and thus will do comparatively little damage. Rhabanus further states that the thrust or jab is delivered with the strength of the entire body (the "jumping in" exercise), while the slash is executed solely by the elevation of the right arm and carries the weight of the weapon. However, Rhabanus cautions the inexperienced that lifting the right arm high in order to strike the enemy with the greatest possible force exposes the soldier's right side, which cannot be covered by his shield, to the thrust of his adversary's weapon.[39]

The importance of the sword for thrusting rather than slashing further highlights training and discipline as well as the fact that the Franks were fighting in a phalanx formation. Although slashing is easily done and perhaps even a reflex for a man with a sword in a dangerous situation, it is inappropriate for the close order of an infantry phalanx where one could by accident easily strike one's fellow soldiers.[40] A rather effective, if exaggerated, idea of the Franks and their allies fighting in the press of an infantry phalanx formation is found in an account of the battle on the plains outside the fortress city of Toul in 612. The chronicler reports: "Where they fought against each other in the press of the battle lines (*falange in congresso certamenis contra se priliabant*) the slaughter was so great on both sides that there was no room for the dead to fall to the ground. Indeed, they remained standing as though they were still living." [41]

Although Rhabanus changed many terms in copying various chapters of the *De re Militari* and used terminology in his commentary that on occasion was different from that used in the text by Vegetius, he retained Vegetius' term *gladius* for the sword used by the Carolingian soldiers being trained to fight on foot in the phalanx formation.[42] He knew that the *gladius* was a short sword used for thrusting purposes and not a long sword used for slashing. One basis for Rhabanus' understanding of the various terms used in *De re Militari* for swords was his familiarity with Isidore's *Etymologiae*, upon which he based much of his own encyclopedia.[43]

Rhabanus may have known a great deal about different types of swords used in his own day, from the later eighth century through the mid-ninth century. The short sword of the later seventh through earlier eighth centuries likely had been developed from the short thrusting sword of the late antique era.[44] In this process of development, the early Carolingians used the longer or "long sax," which was the successor to the broad *sax*, the so-called *Breitsax* frequently found in the archaeological evidence of the seventh century.[45] These longer "short swords" ranged in length from sixty-five centimeters to eighty centimeters, including the hilt.[46] In this context, the functional similarity of the "Frankish" short sword, *sax* or *scramasax* in the Germanic languages and *gladius* or *semispatum* in Latin, to the short sword of the Spartans is worthy of emphasis in terms of its use as a thrusting weapon in the close order of highly disciplined phalanx combat.[47]

Rhabanus did not substitute the word for long sword, *spatha*, which was well known to the Carolingians, for *gladius* when describing the swords used by Frankish foot soldiers. It is important that Vegetius, when discussing one particular type of Roman infantry phalanx, indicates that the men in the first rank, whom he calls *ordinarii*, used the long sword (*spatha*).[48] Rhabanus Maurus clearly rejected this loosely structured formation, which permitted the use of a slashing weapon, as irrelevant to Carolingian infantry warfare *tempore moderno*. Rather, he accepted as his model the version of the phalanx discussed by Vegetius where the men in the front ranks of the formation not only throw spears at the outset of combat but also use the short sword, *gladius*. It is important, as well, that according to Vegetius, when deployed defensively these troops are to remain fixed in place "like a wall of iron" in order to receive the enemy attack.[49]

Exemplars of the *spatha* available to modern scholars through the archaeological record seem generally to be found in rather rich graves. *Spatha* also is found in the written sources from which it clearly can be identified as a long sword by comparison with the short sword, *semispatum* or *gladius*. The short sword of the eighth century had a sharp point and single edge while the long sword had no real point but was double-edged. The *spatha* was for slashing and the double edge enabled the soldier to cause damage both with a backhand and a forehand cut. The lack of a sharp point diminished if not totally eliminated the value of the *spatha* for thrusting at one's adversary. Obviously, the *spatha* was far better suited for combat in which the soldier had a considerable amount of space in which to maneuver, whether he was fighting on foot or on horseback.[50] That Rhabanus retained the term for a short sword (*gladius*) shows his understanding of the combat techniques used by the rank-and-file foot soldier in the Carolingian infantry phalanx. This phalanx formation was of primary importance for the Carolingians from the early eighth century when Charles Martel was victorious at Poitiers through the mid-ninth century when Rhabanus Maurus averred that he was interested in matters of value *tempore moderno*.

In the close order of the phalanx, which is made possible, in part, by the use of the short sword, each man in the unit must know what kinds of strokes he can deliver and how he is permitted to move within his formation.[51] This requires considerable training.[52] Such combat in a dense formation has been likened to a highly stylized dance.[53] Fighting men who lack sufficient training and drill may wound their own comrades because men crowded in on the sides and rear as well as on the front for all ranks except the first.[54]

The recruit trained to use the short sword also was equipped with a shield to protect himself.[55] These shields used by foot soldiers apparently were approximately eighty centimeters in diameter and had a so-called onion-shaped boss.[56] According to Rhabanus, the man fighting on foot carried a round shield, *scutum rotundum*, on his left arm.[57] However, in his description of the shield, Rhabanus departs significantly from his model. Vegetius uses the term *scutum* without any adjectival modification; he was referring to the rectangular-oblong or long-oval shield of the Roman legionary. These shields averaged approximately 1–1.2 by 0.8 meters in the fifth century, when *De re Militari* was revised at Constantinople, and perhaps as tall as 1.6 meters in the sixth century.[58]

How Rhabanus came to understand that there was a significant difference between the Roman shields being described by Vegetius and the shields used by Carolingian foot soldiers is not self-evident.[59] Nowhere in his work does Vegetius indicate the shape of the shield when he discusses the *scutum*.[60] However, Rhabanus may have seen depictions of the shields traditionally used by Roman foot soldiers on one of the many surviving monuments in territories that were under Carolingian control or to which the Carolingians had easy access.[61] In particular, attention should be given to the Vespasianic era reliefs carved into column bases located in the *praetorium* of the fortress city of Mainz, where Rhabanus served as bishop more than seven centuries after the original sculpture was executed. The Mainz reliefs depict both the long oblong and the long rectangular shields traditionally used by Roman foot soldiers into the later imperial era.[62]

Rhabanus may have based his knowledge of Roman infantry shields on late

Roman manuscript illustrations. For example, long oblong or long oval shields, associated with the infantry formations of the later Roman empire, are depicted in the manuscript of the Vatican Virgil which survives even today.[63] Later Roman public monuments, such as the mosaics in the basilica of Santa Maria Maggiore, show these kinds of infantry shields, as well.[64] It is also possible that Rhabanus had read in one of the many Roman histories, discussed above, that the Roman infantry *scutum* was not a round shield but rather a long one.[65] What is clear, however, is that Rhabanus wanted it understood that Carolingian foot soldiers in the phalanx used round shields and in this he was correct.[66]

Although Rhabanus departs from Vegetius' discussion with regard to his emphasis on the shape of the shield, he follows his model in making clear that during practice sessions the shield's weight was doubled by the addition of a wicker-work outer structure, for the same reasons extra weight was added to the training sword.[67] Moreover, Rhabanus follows Vegetius where the latter describes the normal shield, prior to its augmentation by the extra weight, as a "scutum publicum."[68] We should understand this to mean a "government issue shield," presumably a shield of some general standard size and weight that was provided to military recruits by the government, the public authority. The rough standardization of the size of the foot soldier's shield (one exact size was unlikely to fit all) would facilitate training and provide a certain uniformity to the battle line of foot soldiers.

In addition, a "government-issue shield" may have been produced by the Carolingian government and/or at the command of the government by private manufacturers for the army's use. Such organization and control of the arms industry, in general, and of shield making, in particular, might have been efforts at the *imitatio* of imperial practices.[69] Indeed, the Carolingians were well informed about the role played by the imperial government in the manufacture of arms and armor from documents such as the *Codex Theodosianus*, discussed above, and the *Notitia Dignitatum*, which were both available to the Franks.[70] Finally, the Carolingian government, like the Roman government, made well-documented efforts to maintain control of the distribution of arms within the *regnum Francorum* and its dependencies and even made efforts to prohibit the export of such items beyond the frontiers.[71]

The few surviving pieces of Charlemagne's legislation lend some support to the hypothesis that the Carolingians tried to control arms production as well as arms distribution. For example, less than two decades after his father's death, Charlemagne systematized regulations concerning the availability of shield makers under royal control. He emphasized that every *judex* was to have a shield maker (*scutarius*) in the district (*ministerium*) under his jurisdiction. He also required in this legislation that each of his royal villas have a shield maker in residence.[72] In addition to this legislation, it would seem that both important people and well-established institutions (monasteries that had been granted an immunity) needed shield makers and workshops on site.[73] In addition to staffing workshops, at least some monastic houses, such as Saint-Germain-des-Prés, required smiths who lived on lands belonging to the monastery to pay their dues in weapons they produced,[74] perhaps in an effort to ensure that armament was available locally for use by the troops whom the immunists were required to produce for *expeditio*. Finally, all magnates, both secular and ecclesiastical, were required to provide *annua dona* or *dona annualia*, a tax paid to the king on a yearly basis and usually in public at the general assembly. These "gifts" often included "weapon sets" suitable for arming soldiers in the royal *obsequium*.[75]

Some Carolingian foot soldiers also were trained in the use of the throwing spear or javelin, the bow and arrow, and the sling, as will be seen below. Slingers normally were deployed as skirmishers, a point that Rhabanus recognizes. Archers too had special tasks to perform outside the formal structure of an infantry phalanx whose men apparently used short swords as their primary weapons and shields for their protection. Archers generally do not have shields. It is likely that soldiers who were trained to throw the spear or javelin, as contrasted to archers and slingers, also were trained for combat with the short sword in the close order of an infantry phalanx. This would enable them to strike at a distance, as in the case of the Frankish phalanx that fought against the Byzantines at Rimini (see Chapter 5). However, the typical phalanx soldier probably was not trained as an archer or as a slinger.

From the archaeological evidence (both chance finds and systematically excavated graves), it appears that the spear was the most widely used weapon in the *regnum Francorum* during the early Carolingian era.[76] The pictorial evidence of the ninth century supports this judgment.[77] The wooden shafts, in general, do not survive, although sufficient very fragmentary material has been found on occasion to identify the use of ash, oak, and other hardwoods.[78] This likely can be confirmed from some written texts, as well.[79] Written evidence demonstrates that Frankish foot soldiers in a Frankish phalanx threw spears and javelins at their adversaries.[80] In many archaeological finds there are iron points that had been fitted to spears, which were missile weapons; this can be affirmed from their weight and their ballistic characteristics.[81]

What is missing from Rhabanus' handbook, however, is any discussion of the spear as a weapon used in a phalanx to present a "hedgehog" to the attackers or thrust at the enemy in hand-to-hand combat. Many spearheads found in various archaeological contexts that date from the later seventh and eighth centuries are inappropriate for use as points for missile weapons,[82] an observation sustained by the pictorial evidence from the ninth century.[83] Rhabanus may have provided sections in his handbook on these combat techniques with the spear that were subsequently lost, but this is unlikely because the Carolingian narrative sources do not describe such uses for the spear in accounts of Frankish foot soldiers deployed in massed infantry formations.

Moreover, our understanding of the early Carolingian phalanx provided by the description of Charles Martel's troops at Poitiers and Rhabanus' training regime is very similar to that found in Vegetius' handbook: "The heavy-armed soldiers [in the first two ranks] . . . stood . . . like an iron wall (*murus . . . ferreus*). They fought not only with missiles but also with swords (*gladiis*) in hand-to-hand combat. If the enemy forces fled (*hostes fugabant*), these heavily armed troops [of the phalanx] did not pursue lest the phalanx break up its own battle line (*aciem suam*) and order (*ordinationem*)."[84]

Spearheads that were unsuitable for use on missile weapons because of their great size could have been the killing points for lances such as the *conti premagni* described by Rhabanus Maurus and used largely if not exclusively by mounted troops.[85] Among these larger types were pieces thirty-five to fifty centimeters in length that had heavy cross pieces.[86] Some foot soldiers who were not normally in a phalanx may have used these nonmissile type spears in a more individualized form of combat such as in defending the walls of a fortification or while on guard duty.[87] Finally, nonmissile type spearheads cannot be presumed to have been part of a regular army weapon. A heavy spear of almost pike-like dimensions with a cross piece traditionally was required, for example, for hunting large, strong animals such as the wild boar.[88]

The foot soldiers of the early Carolingian period likely did not deploy in phalanx formation with the intention of presenting a hedgehog of nonmissile type spears to the enemy. This tactic was best used against the attack of heavily armed mounted troops deployed with the intention of breaking up the phalanx by the momentum of their charge. Thus, the hedgehog formation was intended to frighten the charging horses and perhaps even their riders sufficiently so that they refused contact. If this failed and the horse charged home, the aim was to impale either the rider or his mount. Even well-trained horses are notoriously skittish about smashing into a wall, and experienced horsemen would consider a surface that bristles with glittering points of steel even more frightening to their mounts if not to themselves.[89]

Among the adversaries the armies of the *regnum Francorum* faced over the centuries, the rulers of the Visigothic, Ostrogothic, and Lombard kingdoms often placed large numbers of heavily armed mounted troops in the field.[90] However, by the time the early Carolingian armies began their long process of military conquest only the Lombard kingdom survived, and their heavily mounted troops had not demonstrated a capacity to break an infantry phalanx by means of the shock of their charge. In addition, it is possible that Frankish foot soldiers, such as those who fought at Poitiers under Charles Martel, did not use the spear as a thrusting weapon in a phalanx context because spear shafts were easily broken in such combat. Thus, in the normal course of battle, a line of spearmen rapidly became an unpredictable admixture of some men fighting with spears, some with broken spear shafts, and others with swords.[91] Such a melange of armaments seems less effective than ranks of men armed uniformly with short swords that ostensibly are unbreakable. Finally, in support of the view that the Franks used the short sword as the primary weapon in their phalanx, the Anonymous Chronicler describes Charles Martel's troops in combat at Poitiers as using only the sword and makes no mention of spears in the hand-to-hand combat phase of the action.[92]

In actual combat, each man in the phalanx naturally tends to crowd a bit to his right in order to gain some protection from the shield his neighbor carries on his left arm.[93] Left-handers necessarily are trained out of their "abnormality" in a phalanx. In a popular poem written in the later eighth or early ninth century, the protagonist has lost his right hand in combat and his friend banters with him: "What do you say about violating the normal way of doing things (ritum . . . gentis) and girding your sword on your right thigh."[94]

However, the tendency to drift to the right, unless compensated for by extensive training, shifts the entire phalanx to the right and thus may allow the enemy to deliver a decisive attack on the left flank. In addition, the terrain of the battlefield, unless it is absolutely flat, exacerbates the problems caused by the sideways movement of each man in the phalanx. Even a small hillock or a depression in the field will, at least temporarily, separate any one man from his neighbors on the left and/or on the right, permitting experienced enemy soldiers to exploit the seam that has been established, rush into the gap, and cut into the formation. This initiative, if successful, permits an attack against the "flank" of the inner ranks of the phalanx.[95]

Attacking on Foot

Carolingian foot soldiers, of the type that Charles Martel commanded in battle at Poitiers, were trained to execute deployments considerably more complicated than simply holding their positions under the bludgeoning of an enemy attack.[96] At the heart of effective mobility for foot soldiers is the ability to march in an ordered manner. Thus, Rhabanus Maurus, while commenting upon matters that he considered to be of importance "tempore moderno," indicates that Carolingian recruits (*tyrones*) were trained in the necessary discipline of undertaking an orderly march.[97] Here, Rhabanus departs in emphasis somewhat from the model provided for him by Vegetius, who makes clear only that recruits "should be trained in marching."[98] By the later eighth or early ninth century—some fifty years before Rhabanus published his handbook—the formality of the march was thoroughly integrated into Carolingian military thought and practice. Thus, the *Waltharius*-poet, with a certain stylistic debt to Virgil, treats the movement of troops in units of rather equal size ("aequati numero") advancing in a lengthy column ("agmine longo") as a commonplace for his well-informed court audience.[99]

Hans Delbrück accepted Rhabanus' observations unhesitatingly in regard to the successful training of Frankish troops for the march,[100] despite his inclination, as observed above, to see Carolingian military efforts at all levels as primitive in comparison with both Roman and early modern practices. Delbrück brought a vast font of general knowledge to bear on this conclusion and accepted Rhabanus' evidence on the basis of *Sachkritik*, objective reality. He understood that repeatedly successful infantry forces needed to maintain effectively dressed ranks and files on the march.[101] Delbrück knew that such discipline was required even for corps of five thousand to ten thousand men; as part of his view of the early Middle Ages, he believed the Carolingians' forces were limited to that order of magnitude.[102]

Soldiers during the early Middle Ages followed the tradition of singing songs and engaging in other forms of "recitation" while on the march.[103] Some hymns written during the early Middle Ages, such as Venantius Fortunatus' *Pange lingua gloriosi proelium* and the anonymous eighth-century effort *Ab ore prolatum*, employ the "trochaic *septenarius*," which modern scholars consider the metrical form traditionally used for Roman military marching songs.[104] In addition, modern scholars have recognized the fundamental connection between the Roman military cadence and at least some of the hymns sung in early medieval religious processions.[105] Parenthetically, the need to train troops of the various household military *obsequia* as well as civilians (part-time soldiers who served in various types of militias) to participate with a certain style and discipline in the many civil and ecclesiastical ceremonies as well as in *triumphi*, in which processions were an integral element, overlapped somewhat with aspects of military training. Poems such as *Pange lingua gloriosi proelium* and Fortunatus' *Vexilla regis prodeunt* were probably used extensively both in the quasireligious milieu of the military triumph, discussed below in Chapter 4, as well as by soldiers marching into battle.

A few bits of information support Rhabanus' observations regarding the training of early Carolingian soldiers to march in an orderly and effective manner as well as Delbrück's acceptance of this as fact. From a practical perspective, the hard surface of the Roman roads permitted the soldiers to use a "cadenced pace," which made practicing the march rather simple.[106] Furthermore learning to march requires no outstanding muscular coordination, nor is it an intellectual feat.

In addition to discussing training for the march, Rhabanus emphasized the importance of maintaining cohesive formations (*ordines*) as essential for going over to the attack.[107] Medieval armies in general and Carolingian armies in particular were trained to advance in formation at a slow walk not only over the old but relatively smooth Roman roads but also over rough terrain. In the once highly controversial account of the battle of the Dyle, the *Franci* effectively advanced in formation step by step (*pedetemptim*) over very difficult ground against an emplaced enemy while under heavy enemy missile fire.[108] Medieval armies advancing under such conditions were even known to halt periodically to "check their dressing" so as not to lose the cohesion of their formations.[109]

In units where, for example, adequate spacing among the ranks and files is not maintained, unnecessary injuries may be inflicted rather easily. For example, a soldier who comes too close to the pole weapon of a man in his proper position may be injured. In a similar vein, a man who is out of position might accidentally wound a man who is in proper position. The physical essence of the march, such as the spacing of the troops, has its own inherent logic, which cannot be deconstructed or explained away as beyond the ken of "primitives."

Rhabanus Maurus further emphasizes the importance of maintaining the cohesion of the infantry formation when it moves either from a static position or the march to the offensive, whether the pace is slow because of rough terrain discussed above, or rapid. According to Rhabanus, however, rapid deployment in the attack is preferred when possible because the troops then can develop momentum.[110] The disadvantages endured by the force on the receiving end of an enemy charge will be discussed below. This same basic tactical doctrine of group cohesion was maintained for the deployment of mounted troops in combat. It was the primary *desideratum* both in striking the enemy and for military operations in general.

Rhabanus, while discussing marching drill, that is, learning *militaris gradus*, highlights this training because it made it possible for foot soldiers to attack at the run. Thus, the recruits (*tyrones*) are trained not only to charge rapidly ("irruant") against the enemy but to do so "while at the same time maintaining formation," that is, "aequaliter . . . uno parique."[111] In moving against the enemy in this manner, Rhabanus indicates that the various units must remain in their formations by each individual soldier maintaining his prescribed position in relation to the standards or banners (*vexillae*) of his particular unit.[112] In addition to maintaining formation, this rapid run (*rapidus cursus*), according to Rhabanus, permits the foot soldiers very quickly, *citius*, to take possession of key enemy positions, *oportuna loca*.[113]

The likelihood that early Carolingian foot soldiers learned through the training described by Rhabanus Maurus to march and, no less important, to attack in a cohesive manner should not be doubted. These exercises, as will be seen below, were far simpler than the highly complicated unit maneuvers on horseback that the early Carolingians practiced and effectively executed. The latter obviously were much more difficult to learn for both man and animal than marching at some sort of cadence in dressed ranks, holding their unit organization, and charging the enemy rapidly in formation.

Training in the Use of Missile Weapons

Siege warfare dominated military operations during the Middle Ages, particularly in the course of Merovingian and early Carolingian campaigns in regions that had been well-established parts of the Roman empire in the West. These regions, as we have seen above, were well defended by great fortress cities and lesser fortifications of imperial origin which dominated the military landscape. Those men who were deployed on the defensive to hold such massive urban fortifications and even lesser strongholds, *castra* and *castella*, against an enemy attack have, under normal circumstances, a very limited range of options to engage the enemy at a distance. This is true, as well, for soldiers on the offensive and deployed at a considerable distance from that fortress that they have placed under siege. Foot soldiers in the field, whether on the offensive or on the defensive, also had limited options for engaging the enemy that were different from those men engaged in siege operations.

Nevertheless, while fighting at a distance, properly trained and equipped soldiers, whether on the offensive or the defensive, deployed a variety of missile weapons to discomfort adversaries within range. The types of missile weapons under consideration here fall into two classes: (1) small or personalized weapons that were used by individual soldiers or militia men such as the throwing spear, the bow or the sling and perhaps the crossbow, and (2) large weapons, such as stone-hurling machines, that required several soldiers with the considerable skills of "artillerymen" to operate.

A second, less clear distinction may also be made regarding these two classes of weapons. The small weapons were antipersonnel in nature; they are intended to kill or to wound other soldiers or perhaps civilians and could be used against horses, mules, and camels. By contrast, stone-hurling machines were used predominantly against the enemy's material assets: walls, gates, or even smaller targets such as wagons and enemy artillery. In addition, these catapults could be used to hurl incendiaries against enemy positions. However, under appropriate conditions and in special cases various of these machines also were used with considerable effectiveness, especially when enemy troops provided a large and preferably stationary target such as the type of infantry phalanx discussed above. In special cases, it also must be noted that antipersonnel weapons such as the bow could be fitted with arrows that had been prepared in advance to deliver combustibles against material assets.

Throwing the Spear

In the surviving sections of Rhabanus Maurus' handbook, substantial elements of the four key chapters of Vegetius' *De re Militari* on the training of foot soldiers to use antipersonnel missile weapons must have been of value "tempore moderno" and were retained.[114] Rhabanus emphasizes that *tyrones* are to use the post or quintain as a target in order to practice hurling spears at the enemy. Like the shield and the sword, the practice spear is considerably heavier than the normal throwing spear or javelin (*jaculum*). However, the recruit does not use a real spear but merely a heavy spearshaft, *hastile*. Here, Rhabanus departs from Vegetius and apparently identifies the heavier spear (of which the *hastile* is the shaft) as the *hasta*. The Carolingians thus may not have normally used the *hasta* as a missile weapon during this period. This weight differential between the practice spear, which lacked a point, and the combat spear was established for the same reason that the practice shield and sword were heavier than those used in combat.[115]

Rhabanus states that the training instructor (*campidoctor*—Vegetius' technical term for specialized personnel is retained here) is to teach the recruits to throw the spear with great strength and to aim to hit the post or very close to the post.[116] Thus, the elite or well-trained spear thrower was to neutralize a particular target. Of course, not all spear throwers were expert marksmen, and a hail of spears against a mass of enemy troops was often used; this tactic is found in the Latin poetic literature.[117] As will be seen below, this dichotomy between individual targeting and a "hail of fire" has its analogue in the training and deployment of archers. Rhabanus, moreover, also emphasizes that constant practice with the throwing spear not only improves the soldier's aim but also greatly strengthens his throwing arm.[118] One rarely sees such commonplace and presumably obvious information in written form surviving from the early Middle Ages, leading some researchers, often those with a primitivist agenda, to doubt that men during this period possessed such basic information.

Training Archers

After discussing the training of recruits to throw the spear, Rhabanus follows Vegetius and moves on to the training of soldiers with the bow (*arcus*) and arrow (*sagitta*). First, Rhabanus makes clear that only the more talented and harder working (*aptiores et industriores*) among the *tyrones* were to be trained as archers.[119] This recognition of differences in ability among the rank and file of the army, whether part-time militia men or regular soldiers, by a cleric, who received his formal education during the later eighth century, is noteworthy. Rhabanus may have relied on information or advice from professional soldiers or specialized training personnel such as the *campidoctores*, or perhaps some of the *magistri*, who trained future officers at the royal court. However, Rhabanus may have inferred this information from Vegetius' specific observations that archers developed technical skills innately. Indeed, Vegetius had opined that between one-quarter and one-third of recruits for service in the infantry had sufficient aptitude to be archers. Yet even though a man had aptitude, "he should be required to practice constantly."[120]

A tradition of archery in the West among the civilian population undergirded both recruitment and training for expeditionary forces. During the later empire, as part of the policy of militarizing the civilian population, all able-bodied Roman men had to learn how to shoot a bow. They were required, in addition, to practice regularly with the weapon until they were at least forty years of age. Finally, such men were obligated by law to own both a bow and a quiver,[121] presumably filled with arrows. Regular troops were expected to have quivers with some thirty to forty arrows in them,[122] suggesting that the citizen-soldier who served as a militia man needed a similar quantity of arrows.

Three closely interrelated questions may legitimately be raised in this context, yet the answers can only be speculation. First, who produced these arrows for the militia, as contrasted, for example, to the government-run factories dedicated to the production of arms for the regular army? The making of arrows is a time-consuming process, and the men who do such work as turning properly balanced shafts, smithing satisfactory points, and cutting fragile feathers must be highly skilled. Second, through what institutional mechanisms were the arrows provided to the militia men? Finally, how were the costs of producing these missiles defrayed? The government workshops that produced bows and arrows for the regular army also probably produced this equipment for the militia, and at government expense. This interpretation rests solely upon the absence of any evidence for private enterprise in the production of this type of equipment.[123] However, men could purchase bows, arrows, and quivers for hunting purposes from private entrepreneurs who were artisans, who manufactured bows and arrows themselves, or who acted as middlemen.

Civilian possession of a bow, a quiver, and arrows, as well as bouts of regular practice legally required by the government, are well known to specialists in medieval English history as a continuing mainstay of the royal military establishment, both for offensive and defensive purposes, during the Middle Ages.[124] As among the English, so too during the later empire and early Middle Ages, it mattered little whether a man was a first-rate shot or merely average. Indeed, during the earlier period, the Roman imperial government permitted unskilled or untalented civilians to use a lighter bow that presumably was easier to handle.[125]

Experienced military men during the later Roman empire believed that given enough time, even the untrained citizen-soldier could learn to shoot adequately. The emperor Maurice, for example, wrote that civilians had to be capable of using the bow.[126] In this context, most such men would neither be recruited into the army as regular soldiers nor be required to engage the enemy in the field as the member of a local militia. The civilian archer with little or no natural talent was suited to defend the walls of the great fortress cities built during the later Roman empire. Behind these massive defenses, such archers, as will be discussed below, enjoyed a great advantage over tightly packed masses of enemy troops storming the fortifications.

Archery training for the bowman, like training with the sword and shield and with the throwing spear or javelin, discussed above, also focused on the wooden post as an individual target.[127] In Rhabanus' description of the aiming of the spear, the recruit was to select a particular target. Such training did not rule out that these archers could provide a volley of arrows against a massed enemy force. Moreover, as in previous exercises, the types of arrow used in combat and in practice varied,[128] because of the high cost of expertly feathered and properly balanced arrows with properly forged points.[129] However, by practicing with inferior arrows, the trained archer shooting with first-class missiles would find his targets on the battlefield much more effectively. Confidence built up through practice was enhanced and morale raised by having access to superior equipment in combat.

As with the other aspects of military training, discussed above, the training of archers was carefully guided by a specialist. This *magister* instructed his men to hold the bow in the left hand and to have the left arm held straight and fully extended. The right hand was used to draw back the bowstring in a controlled manner "so that the eye and the mind were to work together." Both Rhabanus and Vegetius indicate this concentration as essential to proper shooting.[130] However, where Vegetius is interested in the training of men to fight as archers both on foot and on horseback, Rhabanus pointedly omits any mention of the training of mounted archers.[131] Despite the efforts of Charlemagne, discussed above, the Carolingians had little success in training mounted archers. Rhabanus concludes his discussion of the training of *sagitarii* with an observation (not found in this chapter of Vegetius' text) concerning the great usefulness (*utilitas*) of archers in battle throughout history.[132]

The Training of Slingers

Rhabanus' discussion of slingers varies considerably from that of Vegetius.[133] Here, unlike Vegetius, Rhabanus finds the *locus classicus* for the slinger (*fundibularius*) in the biblical account of David and Goliath (1 Sam. 17:31–54). The slinger was adept in military operations on especially rocky terrain where stones for the sling were easily available.[134] By combining the account of David from the Hebrew Bible with Vegetius' *De re Militari*, Rhabanus emphasizes that experienced slingers can slaughter great numbers of their adversaries, who died when the missile hit an exposed vital spot. Rhabanus is so confident of the capability of the slinger to be exceptionally accurate that he emphasizes the lethality of the weapon even if the target was wearing armor, as was the case with Goliath, described as protected by a bronze helmet as well as by full body armor.[135]

Rhabanus adds to his discussion of slingers some of Vegetius' material concerning the *mattiobarbularii*—soldiers who were trained to hurl the *mattiobarbulus*, some sort of relatively short clublike baton that was fitted with a lead weighted head and a sharpened point.[136] Rhabanus, by contrast, depicts the implement as a lead ball used by the slinger as an alternative and presumably superior type of ammunition for his sling. He does accept, however, the notion that these lead balls may be attached to the slinger's shield for easy access.[137] Uniformly cast lead balls had more predictable trajectories and better accuracy than stones selected at random from the ground or from a streambed.

At no point in the discussion of *fundibularii* or of *mattiobarbuli* does either Rhabanus or Vegetius discuss the training of slingers.[138] Rhabanus, however, was confident that the biblical account of David's early career as a shepherd not only was well known but provided a guide to what was required for the use of the sling. In general, the techniques for using a shepherd's sling were well known to the *populus*. Rhabanus seems to believe that in the hands of the right man a sling is an exceptionally effective weapon, that spun once around the head can deliver a deadly missile on target at a maximum range of six hundred Roman feet, a distance that seems exaggerated and may well be the result of a copying error.[139] (The Roman foot was a fraction more than an inch shorter than our modern foot measure.) The slinger of the early Carolingian period was easily recruited from the rural populace, especially men who in their youth tended cattle and sheep in the meadows and mountain slopes where their charges had to be protected from predators, both two- and four-legged.

Training for Siege Warfare

Sieges dominated medieval warfare. Both the capture of fortifications and their defense were of primary importance in early Carolingian military operations. Despite the substantial evidence for various siege machines, discussed below, the most elementary and likely frequently used method for attacking an enemy stronghold, however, was by a direct assault — up and over the walls — by large numbers of men using a device as primitive as a ladder. The great fortress cities of the later Roman empire, which were preserved, by and large, throughout the Middle Ages, had walls that were generally at least ten meters high and three meters thick at the base, reinforced with projecting towers that provided the defenders with overlapping fields of fire. Many of these fortress cities had substantial moats. Lesser fortifications, such as *castra* and *castella*, also built of stone, though generally much smaller than the *urbes*, were no less formidable against the tactics of storming the walls as long as these strongholds were properly manned by highly motivated and largely local militia troops.[140]

The attacking forces could not, of course, merely forage in the countryside for ladders that were ten to twelve meters in length. This equipment had to be built either by men who were serving in the army or attached as support personnel. The men who built the ladders were trained in this skill, whether they worked while the troops were in the siege encampment during an investment or whether the ladders were transported, probably disassembled, in the baggage train as part of the *impedimenta*.

As Vegetius makes clear, some rather sophisticated techniques were used to measure the proper length for a scaling ladder. The least difficult method was to affix a string, marked off like a measuring tape, to an arrow, which was shot to the top of the wall. The man who calculates the length of the ladder ran to where the ladder was to be placed and read the marking on the string that hung down to the ground from the arrow lodged at the top of the wall.[141]

Vegetius also describes a second and far more complicated way to calculate the height of the walls. Thus, he avers, the man who does the measurements for the ladders waits for the towers and the walls to cast shadows, which are measured (presumably while the enemy is otherwise occupied). After this measurement is taken, a marked rod ten feet in length is put into the ground and its shadow is similarly measured. Thus, Vegetius affirms that the height of the city walls are ascertained from the shadow cast by the pole.[142] Although this latter method is more sophisticated than counting the marks on a measuring tape, it was hardly too difficult for the early Carolingian specialists who had been trained to prepare ladders of the correct height for scaling walls. Indeed, the far more difficult calculation of latitude by Bede was done along similar lines and was well known.[143]

In addition to measuring the distance so that the ladders could be built to the correct height, these ladders had to support the weight of at least a half dozen or so men — more than a half ton of scrambling soldiers. Building these ladders was a skill that had to be learned. Our focus here, however, will be the training and discipline required for what might perhaps appear at first glance to be one of the simplest of tactics, storming the fortress and scaling the walls.[144]

The storming tactic required a considerable amount of training for the lowliest of fighting men in the armies of the early Carolingians, as in any army. At the most elementary level, some individuals have a problem functioning at substantial heights above the ground. In addition, most men need serious physical conditioning as well as training even to climb a very tall ladder with a shield, sword, and spear while wearing some kind of armor, as well.[145] For a man to engage in deadly combat effectively with sword or spear while standing on or near the top rung of a ladder ten or twelve meters above the ground requires a certain mental toughness acquired only through frequent drill.

Very few men, in the course of their normal civilian lives, throughout the history of medieval Europe, had very much occasion to climb very tall ladders. It is less likely that many able-bodied men were accustomed to working regularly at such heights, much less to engaging in mortal combat at the top of ladders in the course of their civilian lives.[146] This lack of familiarity with operating in precarious situations at great heights may be contrasted, for example, with the likelihood that at least some and probably a great many men among the rank and file of the army's expeditionary forces in early medieval Europe regularly used a bow and arrow or spear to hunt small game.[147] However, as the discussion, below, regarding such tools demonstrates, the capacity to use various implements that have a martial potential in civilian life is considerably different from using them in combat. Although prior familiarity with these implements is traditionally well regarded in the military handbooks, the training required for military use differs markedly from the training to use similar tools in civilian life.[148]

Once a man has been mentally and physically conditioned to climb a ten-meter ladder in difficult circumstances, he had to be trained to carry on combat from this position against determined and potentially desperate men. These defenders likely saw themselves as fighting for their own lives and perhaps the lives of their wives and children, as well. The defenders, once they spied a ladder placed against the wall, were trained first to push it away from the wall so that the ladder and the men on it would fall to the ground and be killed or seriously injured. When this technique failed, but before the men on the ladder could reach the top, the defenders generally shot arrows, threw spears and stones, and perhaps dumped burning pitch on the attackers. Once the attackers reached the top of their not-too-stable "fighting platforms," the defenders (who by contrast were standing on a firm base and at least partially protected by the wall) thrust at their enemies with spears or swords.

The primitive nature of the technology under discussion here gives a universal sense—at least in the premodern West—to the description by the Greek playwright Euripides of the terrible situation endured by the soldier who was storming the walls. Thus, we learn that Kapaneus "climbed up . . . grasping the rungs of the long ladder" and "he boasted . . . that nothing would keep him . . . from seizing the city and its high towers." He bellowed his boasts while being stoned from above, probably a means of controlling his fear. Euripides continues: "He crept up having drawn his body under his shield . . . but just as he reached the cornice of the wall . . . he was hurled from the ladder by a bolt from Zeus." Thus, with "his limbs spreading apart, hair towards heaven . . . his arms and legs spun like a . . . wheel [and] the fiery corpse fell to earth" (*Phoinissai*, 1172–1186).[149]

This story about Kapaneus, who in mythology is one of the "seven against Thebes," was well known in the West. Thus, Vegetius in his *De re Militari*, which was revised in A.D. 450, chose the story of Capaneus (now Latinized with a "C") to illustrate the importance of driving the defenders from the battlements. Capaneus is credited by Vegetius, echoing the classical tradition, with inventing the method of attacking the walls with ladders. In the final analysis, however, Vegetius notes that because the defenders were not driven from the walls, Capaneus "was struck with so much force by the Thebans that it was said that he was killed by a bolt of lightning." The Christian Vegetius diplomatically omits the pagan tradition that the bolt was sent by Zeus.[150]

However hellish and precarious life on the ladder may have been for attacking troops, this experience was preceded by a no less daunting ordeal. To storm the walls of a great fortress city such as Bourges in northern Aquitaine, many hundreds of men, trained to carry, maneuver, and set up these very long and heavy ladders, were organized into carrying teams of four to six men. Although ladders of the type described above, even if constructed of live oak, did not weigh much more than a hundred or so kilograms, the carrying teams required considerable training because such long ladders are not easy to maneuver and were even more difficult to advance at the run under a hail of enemy missiles. If there were fewer than four ladder carriers not enough might remain alive and uninjured to advance the ladder to the wall.[151]

Of course, not only wooden ladders were used to scale the walls. For example, in the attack on some of the installations at Avignon in 737, Charles Martel's troops are reported by the court chronicler to have carried rope ladders.[152] By comparison with wooden ladders, these were easy to transport on campaign in baggage wagons. However, rope ladders could not be used effectively directly against the main walls of an enemy stronghold in many combat situations. Even a well-trained man could not throw the top of such a ladder, equipped with grappling hooks, ten meters or so into the air. In addition, even when the hook could be projected to the top of the wall, the hooks might not catch on in a satisfactory manner. A variety of devices, such as a throwing machine (a very heavy mounted bow-type device or a small catapult) could elevate the rope ladder appropriately. Such devices, however, would have to be placed close to the walls with all of the dangers inherent in such a maneuver. A man could throw a single rope with a grappling hook over the top of the wall and have the hook catch; then he could climb up to the top. When he reached the top, members of his unit at some prearranged signal could then attach the ladder to this rope and the man at the top of the wall would draw the ladder up to the top of the wall and put it into place. The difficulties of carrying out this dangerous and rather slow procedure in the face of enemy defenders on the wall needs little imagination. Thus, rope ladders were most effective in a sneak attack or against installations where the walls were rather diminutive by comparison with the main defenses at Avignon.

The problems involved in deploying rope ladders, especially in the face of an enemy defense on the wall, were great. However, these difficulties are further exacerbated by climbing a ten- to twelve-meter rope ladder and fighting against an enemy defender at the top. In general, few men, whether civilians of the expeditionary militia or highly trained *milites* stationed in the royal household, had reason in their daily lives to learn much about rope ladders. Thus, special training had to prepare men to use ladders of this kind, beginning with establishing the ladder securely on the wall, climbing the ladder, and finally fighting against a determined if not desperate enemy from the top of the ladder. Early medieval soldiers had to be extensively trained to use both wooden and rope ladders.

The first concern of the carrying team was to get the ladder, whether of wood or rope, to the wall in position so that it could be scaled. However, the ladder team first had to cross a killing ground under a hail of enemy arrows and other long-distance missile weapons for more than two hundred meters. Even a rather weak fifty-pound pull bow, stretched at maximum, with a thirty-inch arrow shot at a forty-five-degree elevation from the top of a ten-meter high wall, can reach in excess of two hundred meters.[153] These calculations are consistent with the observations of Rhabanus Maurus that in "tempore moderno" (the Carolingian era) a bow and arrow of the above-mentioned characteristics could be expected to have an effective range of six hundred Roman feet when shot from ground level.[154]

As the attackers drew nearer the walls, they were subjected to missiles from additional weapons. Likely, the advancing troops would come into the range of slingers at about one hundred meters at best.[155] Spear throwers would probably begin to take a toll at about thirty meters.[156] Thus, during the last thirty-meter "dash" to the wall, the attacking force would be subjected to a constant rain of missiles, arrows, stones, and spears. In the context of the phalanx, the impact of some of the lighter missiles, such as arrows, might be mitigated by the use of the *testudo* formed through the overlapping of shields. This combat technique had been made famous by the Romans, and apparently even the Vikings used it during the ninth century against their Carolingian adversaries.[157]

The situation was particularly difficult for the teams of soldiers carrying the ladders. These men needed to have their hands free in order to maneuver their burdens while running across the killing ground to the base of the fortress walls and thus could not protect themselves very easily with their shields. Most men could expect to have, at a minimum, about a 25 percent chance of being either wounded or killed by an arrow.[158] This is a best-case scenario for the soldiers in the attacking force because it assumes less than a two-hundred-meter killing ground and does not take into consideration casualties caused by slingers, spear throwers, *ballistae* of various types and stone-throwing catapults. The estimated 25 percent figure for casualties concerns only those likely to be caused by archers defending the walls.[159]

Siege Equipment

Although large numbers of men had to be trained to storm the walls and scale them with ladders, this was the most elementary way to attain the objective.[160] It generally was very costly in casualties even for successful offensive forces. Thus, throughout the early Middle Ages, as during the later Roman empire, various types of machines were deployed to diminish these risks and to increase the likelihood of success. These weapons included heavy stone-throwing machines, what is referred to here as heavy artillery, and/or battering rams. Machines of various types for throwing large and small stones and for shooting spears and arrows as well as battering rams for knocking down wooden gates and even putting substantial holes in stone fortifications had been very well developed in the West during classical antiquity.[161]

Much of this technology was passed on to the military forces of the Romano-German states in the West established on imperial territory, in part, as a result of direct continuity between the armies of the later Roman empire and those of its successor states. In addition, frequent contact with early Byzantine forces that operated in Spain, Italy, and the Balkans also served as conduits for the transfer of military technology. By the eighth century, the early Carolingians had the opportunity to obtain new technology through their campaigns against the Muslims in Aquitaine, Provence, and Septimania.[162]

The early Carolingian military had developed an effective siege train by the mid-730s at the latest. In 737, when Charles Martel sent his half-brother Duke Childebrand to besiege the fortress city of Avignon, the latter moved south into Burgundy with offensive equipment ("cum apparatu hostile"). This *apparatus*, which was worthy of special note by the court chronicler, included *machinae* for attacking the walls.[163] At the great fortress city of Bourges in 762, Pippin's most thorough and best documented siege was established, and the Carolingian ruler brought in his train *machinae* and "omni genere armorum." With these devices, according to the court chronicler, Pippin breached the walls of the *urbs*. As will be seen below in Chapter 6, the breaches in the wall were of sufficient significance that Pippin's orders to have them repaired, after the capture of the city, were worthy of mention.[164]

Light Artillery

The *scorpio*, which by the later fourth century was commonly called the *onager* or "wild ass," derived its power from a torsion system created through the use of tightly twisted sinews. (All stone-throwing machines of classical antiquity in the West were of the torsion variety.) Originally, the *onager* had been a very sophisticated two-armed stone-throwing machine that was difficult to construct and to keep in good working order. However, during the fourth century, it was modified into a much simplified and rather easily maintained artillery piece with a single arm.[165] This new *onager* was the basic stone-throwing machine for light artillery used by the Roman army during the fifth century[166] and the early Middle Ages, as well.[167]

The relatively lightly built *onager*, weighing 500–600 kilograms, could be transported fully assembled on flatbed carts or wagons, which seem to have been popular during the later Roman empire. Thus, for example, Vegetius, whose account of this weapon is independent of that provided by Ammianus Marcellinus, notes that a fully assembled *onager* can be transported on a two-wheeled cart (*carpentum*).[168] He makes clear, as well, that it was primarily an antipersonnel weapon but also could kill horses and disable enemy machines. Clearly, it was not a wall crusher.[169]

Gregory of Tours, writing in the later sixth century, discusses a heavily encumbered military baggage train that served the army of the Romano-Frankish general Calomniosus and was greatly burdened with *diversa impedimenta*, including various types of rather light siege *machinae* loaded on very slow moving wagons (*plaustra*). By contrast, heavier artillery pieces were built on the site of the siege when it became clear to Calomniosus, the commander of the campaign, that they were needed.[170]

Paul the Deacon, who served in the academic cadre at the Carolingian court during the early part of Charlemagne's reign, takes note of light artillery used to throw a severed human head over the walls of a fortress.[171] In addition, also during the eighth century, the Carolingians had machines designed to hurl small stones. According to a surviving technology manual, these missiles were first coated with an incendiary paste, then set on fire before they were launched.[172] This light artillery was based upon torsion technology, knowledge of which endured in the West throughout the Middle Ages.[173]

In addition to the *onager*, knowledge of the late Roman *fustiballus*, a sling rigged for rock throwing, was preserved. This machine, according to Vegetius, was the weapon that the *fundibulatores* were trained to operate. The *fustiballus* was mounted on a pole four feet in length. The skilled operator used two hands to lever the implement into action; apparently it was both very powerful and accurate, as Vegetius compares its hitting power with that of the *onager*.[174] This comparison by Vegetius at once affirms the fact that the *onager* should be considered light artillery, primarily antipersonnel in character, while permitting the inference that the *fustiballus*, when properly used, was a weapon of some weighty significance.

The early Carolingians also had fully assembled stone-throwing slings available for their troops. However, the term *fustiballus* dropped out of use between the revision of Vegetius' *De re Militari* during the mid-fifth century and the eighth century. Thus, the early Carolingian machine came to be called a *fundibula* after the term that had been used initially for its operator, *fundibulator*. Under the Carolingians, the latter, who must not be confused with slingers of the "Davidic" type, also were specially trained to use their weapons.[175]

Under Charlemagne, *fundibulae* were transported by wagons in the baggage train of the army, which suggests that the Carolingians deployed these relatively small "machines" in large numbers and very probably as antipersonnel weapons. They could have been used against other "soft" targets such as horses, however.[176] The round stones used as ammunition for these devices were, according to a surviving Carolingian government order, carried by pack horses and not in the wagon with the *fundibulae*. In addition, a normal wagon load of *fundibulae* was to be supplied by twenty pack horses[177] and thus the ammunition could be supplied easily to the *fundabulatores*, who as a result were given considerable mobility for deployment in terrain that was not accessible to vehicles.

Spear and Arrow Launchers

During the later Roman empire, the imperial army used a plethora of machines, which may be considered light artillery, in order to launch various types of shaft-missiles. These projectiles varied in size from lengthy "spears" to rather short bolts or arrows. The most powerful of these machines were often styled *ballistae* from which were shot short and heavy ordinance, as well as rather long spear-sized shafts, at high velocity and with great penetrating power. This weapon was fundamentally a large tension bow device mounted on a stationary platform.[178] These *ballistae* were primarily antipersonnel weapons, but some versions could drop a war elephant with a single shot. Despite its power, the *ballista* was light artillery, and Vegetius treats it in the same way as he deals with the mobile *onager*, discussed above.[179]

Vegetius comments in considerable detail on the mobile *ballista*, which is called the *carroballista*. This "field piece" was designated for deployment in various ways. It could be thoroughly integrated into troop formations or several could be organized into a separate unit as an artillery battery. The latter, deployed to the rear of the troop formations, also seem to have been constructed in various sizes. The larger *carroballistae*, those deployed in batteries, were mounted on two-wheeled carts (*carrus*, hence the name) that were drawn by two mules or two horses. The smaller *carroballistae*, deployed among the troops, were hauled on carts only by mules. Mules are far less excitable than horses and thus could be more easily integrated among the troops. A crew of eleven men, referred to by Vegetius as a *contubernia*, operated each machine.[180]

Ballistae-type machines designed to deliver shafted missiles continued to be an important weapon in the armamentarium of East Roman armies which, as noted above, were in frequent contact with the Franks, largely in Italy. Moreover, as will be seen below, these continuing contacts on the Italic peninsula also likely resulted in the transmission of a new type of heavy artillery from the Byzantines to the Carolingians or perhaps even earlier to the Merovingians. During the later sixth century, Emperor Maurice speaks of large wagons that were fitted with "revolving" *ballistae*, where one machine was mounted at each end of this horse-drawn mobile firing platform.[181] At least some of the *machinae* transported to the siege of *Convenae* on wagons in the train of the Romano-Frankish general Calomniosus, mentioned above, may have been *carroballistae*.

Late in the seventh century, the Franks' Visigothic neighbors, with whom there had been frequent military conflict, deployed a *ballista* of some type.[182] This may have been some version of the equipment the Visigoths had learned to build and operate when they acquired their knowledge of siegecraft from the Romans, almost three hundred years earlier. The Visigoths had maintained close military contact with the Byzantines on the Iberian peninsula from the mid-sixth century through the first half of the seventh century, when the latter finally were driven out of Spain after approximately three-quarters of a century of intermittent warfare. Indeed, the Visigoths continued in hostile military contact with the Byzantines, who maintained an important presence in North Africa just across the Straits of Gibraltar, until the fall of the Visigothic kingdom in Spain to the Muslims in 711.[183]

The *ballista* survived quite well in the West. The early Carolingians had formulae for the production of incendiaries delivered by a specially structured "arrow" to be fired by a *ballista*.[184] The *ballista* was used, for example, in combat operations against the Vikings that were undertaken by military forces raised in the *regnum Francorum* during the ninth century.[185] In an epic poem with noteworthy satiric passages, Abbo of Saint Germain claims that his hero could skewer seven men with a single missile shot from such a weapon.[186] Some scholars even believe that the Vikings, who began military sorties against the Carolingians during the reign of Charlemagne, had acquired this technology.[187]

Where the Franks' Anglo-Saxon neighbors to the north obtained *ballistae* remains a mystery. Nevertheless, evidence for this technology is found in tenth-century Anglo-Saxon riddles. It is obvious that *ballistae* had long been established on the island and were well known in the popular culture before they could have been incorporated into the riddle-literature.[188] Use of *ballistae* by the Visigoths, Anglo-Saxons, and Franks, like the use of this type of machine by the early Byzantines, may be one more illustration of continuity between the early Middle Ages, both West and East, with the military technology and usages of the later Roman empire.

The Crossbow

The early medieval crossbow, a rather simple hand-held weapon, was a tension bow. It gained its power in the same manner as a self bow or a recurve bow—the cord is drawn back, which flexes the bow. Then the cord is released in order to "shoot" the missile. The bow of the crossbow is fixed to a staff forming a "T," hence its name in English. Some scholars refer to this staff as a "fixed arrow guide," but this locution limits our understanding of the crossbow. Indeed, the staff of the "T" also plays an integral role in providing the place for a slot or peg or other mechanism needed to hold the cord when the span of the bow has been accomplished but before the bolt is loosed.[189]

The *ballista* technology, based on the tension bow, endured in the West for large-scale weapons. However, it also survived in much smaller versions, which provide the basis for what is known in English as the crossbow.[190] Vegetius refers to these smaller hand-held weapons as the *manuballista*[191] and the *arcuballista*.[192] While the former term disappears, the latter metamorphosed through the spoken language into the medieval French term for crossbow, *arbaleste* (modern French, *arbalète*).[193] *Arbaleste* developed from *arcuballista* through the spoken language and not as the result of the pirating of a "scientific" or "technical" term from an ancient codex by one or another medieval scholar.[194]

This "living" linguistic process does not prove conclusively that the term *arcuballista*, as used in the early Middle Ages, denotes primarily a hand-held crossbow and thus was the Latin synonym for its mutated vernacular language form, *arbaleste*. However, Paul Chevedden has quite accurately observed: "Archaeological finds in Western Europe . . . dating from late antiquity and the early Middle Ages . . . suggest that the crossbow enjoyed continuous use in the Latin West from Roman times."[195] Indeed, crossbows have been confidently identified from archaeological evidence even in the British Isles as dating from the early medieval period.[196]

The written evidence also sustains the argument for continuity. A variety of sources indicates that various Roman army units and probably auxiliary formations were equipped with crossbows throughout the imperial era.[197] This technology was so widely diffused even during the early centuries of the Roman empire that it came to be used by civilians in such diverse places as Gaul[198] and Palestine for hunting wild animals.[199] The use of the crossbow by civilian hunters even spread beyond the frontiers of the empire.[200] During the seventh century, the Byzantine army, which, as already mentioned, were in frequent contact with the Franks, also used crossbows.[201] In the West, according to the literary sources for *Francia Occidentalis*, the result is as conclusive as in the East.[202]

Heavy Artillery

New stone-throwing technology, different from and much simpler to construct than the torsion variety, which had been used in classical antiquity throughout the West, was developed by the Chinese no later than the end of the third century B.C.[203] The Muslims adopted the technology that undergirded the Chinese lever-trebuchet stone-throwing machine and made it an integral part of their siege armamentarium no later than the mid-seventh century. It was used during the investment of Mecca in 683.[204]

The Byzantines, however, may have had the new stone-throwing technology even earlier than the Muslims, if the Greek and Latin terms *manganon* and *manganum* in later seventh-century Byzantine texts describe artillery in general (both torsion and lever-trebuchet type), rather than the torsion variety alone.[205] Indeed, the Byzantine historian Theophylact Simocatta indicates that as early as the second half of the sixth century, the Byzantines had long-range catapults that could break up the walls of a stone fortress.[206] This technology was in the hands of the Avars and their Slavic allies before the end of the sixth century.[207] Emperor Maurice, during this same period, refers to such heavy artillery available to the Byzantines by the term *petrobollos*, the same term used to describe the above-mentioned Avar weapons.[208]

The early Carolingians, in addition to torsion artillery (some version of the *onager* that was small enough to be transported by cart or wagon when fully assembled), possessed some sort of heavy artillery.[209] However, whether the heavy artillery was the comparatively simple lever-trebuchet type developed by the Chinese and adopted by the Muslims and the Byzantines or merely some late imperial type of torsion device is not certain. Owing to the relative simplicity of the lever-trebuchet technology as compared to the big torsion machines, the early Carolingians probably had the new type. Carroll Gillmore has shown that the lever-trebuchet stone thrower was firmly in place in the Frankish kingdom by the mid-ninth century at the latest.[210] Her evidence, however, can be pressed back to the early ninth century and perhaps even earlier.[211] Moreover, if the author of the Carolingian court *Annals* meant the term *petraria*, cognate of the Byzantine *petrabolos*, to indicate this new type of heavy artillery, which could be used for knocking breaches in the walls of fortifications, it was already widely available in the West under the early Carolingians. The technical information required for its construction had been diffused beyond the frontiers of the Carolingian *regna* to the Saxons in the east by the early 770s.[212]

Late antique and early medieval military technology, Greek Fire being the obvious exception, could be rapidly diffused over great distances even under conditions in which communication and travel were comparatively primitive.[213] The Visigoths' acquisition during the later Roman empire of the techniques needed to sustain siege warfare has already been discussed. This pattern continued during the early Middle Ages. For example, the central Asiatic "nomadic" Avar horsemen, who first occupied a noteworthy expanse of erstwhile imperial territory during the second half of the sixth century, significantly altered their military organization in light of available technology. The Avars were already deploying sophisticated siege equipment for the investment of Byzantine fortress cities during the later sixth century, and they shared this technology with their putatively more primitive Slav allies.[214] The Saxons, who had even less direct contact with later Roman and early Byzantine military forces than the Avars and Slavs, used the "new" stone-throwing catapults, *petrariae*, by the early 770s at the latest.[215]

An *onager* of a type transported fully assembled on a flatbed cart or wagon could not hurl stones large enough to smash great breaches in the masonry defenses that had protected the fortress *urbes* of the West since the fourth century.[216] Thus, as will be discussed below in Chapter 6, the *machinae* used by Pippin that breached the walls of Bourges should be considered heavy artillery.[217] Indeed, Duke Waiofar of Aquitaine, who had based his entire defensive strategy on holding the great fortress cities of the region, recognized that Pippin's technology was too effective to resist. As the Carolingian court chronicler put it: "When Waiofar saw . . . how the king . . . had taken the exceptionally well-fortified city of Bourges with *machinae* . . . he struck to the ground the walls [*sic*] of all of the Aquitanian cities that were under his control, i.e., Poitiers, Limoges, Saintes, Périgueux, Angoulême, as well as many other cities and strongholds."[218]

If the Carolingian *petrariae* is related to the early Byzantine *petroboloi*, then the late sixth-century description of the latter by Archbishop John of Thessaloniki, who purportedly witnessed their use by the Avars during the siege of his city, is of the utmost importance.[219] Archbishop John describes a siege that seems to have taken place early in the autumn of 597.[220] On the second day of the siege, the Avars prepared their rock-throwing machines (*petroboloi*), characterized by the archbishop as being of great size.[221] The prelate's rather detailed description of these machines is fundamentally in accord with what is known of the Chinese machines and indicates a lever-trebuchet type of catapult.[222] These machines, John explains, "had quadrangular bases that tapered toward the front" and "at the base" (literally, at the ends), presumably near the corners for balance, "were affixed thick [but hollow] cylinders that were thoroughly covered in iron." Then, John indicates that "timbers of the size [used in the construction] of a large house were [inserted into these cylinders and] nailed into place." The arm of each catapult was a beam of a size similar to that used for the frame of the machine. "Slings were hung from the back side of the timbers" that were used as the arms and "from the front [of these timbers] strong ropes hung down."[223]

In this description, John neglects some facts; for example, he does not explain to his readers that in order to prepare a missile for launching, the man in charge of controlling its release held down the sling at the rear of the timber, in which the ammunition was loaded. John emphasizes, however, that "it was by pulling down [the ropes at the front end] and then releasing the sling [at the rear end], that they [the *petroboloi*] propel the stone up high [into the air] with a loud noise." John emphasizes that "when the ropes [at the front and the sling] were released, they [the machines] sent up many very large stones so that . . . no construction built by men could survive under their impact." [224]

In order to protect the crews, who operated these *petroboloi* from "enemy arrows that were shot by the defenders who manned the walls of the city," John notes that "wooden planks were attached on three sides" of the frame of the machine and thus "the men inside" were vulnerable only to missiles from above. Missile attacks from the rear were not thought to be a problem by the Avars. In addition, John explains that the Avars took measures to protect the machines from destruction by incendiary missiles, such as "fire arrows," which presented a particular danger. Thus, the Avars saw to it that the planks that were nailed to the frames of their rock throwers were covered with "freshly skinned hides." Indeed, the "bloody hides of freshly slaughtered oxen and camels were nailed onto [the planks that covered the frame of the] machines." [225]

The effectiveness of early Carolingian siege warfare was very likely based, at least in part, on the command of the lever-trebuchet stone-throwing technology described above. These machines appear to have been sufficiently simple to construct and easy to maintain that the erstwhile nomad Avars and their illiterate Slav allies mastered their use and effective deployment. This was done, according to contemporary report, with the help of information obtained from the Byzantines. Not only was the lever-trebuchet technology far simpler to service and operate than the torsion variety, but it could be built relatively easily on the site of the siege.

This pattern of technology transfer apparently went from China through various intermediaries to Byzantium. Then certain peoples, such as the Avars and those subject to them, as well as various Slav groups, who had contact with the Byzantines, were able to obtain the lever-trebuchet technology during the later sixth century. Subsequently, the technology was diffused further west to the Franks. Thus, by the time of the reign of King Pippin I, who had heavy artillery available to him during the siege of Bourges, this technology was available to the early Carolingians. They may have obtained this technology from the Muslims, however, or Charles Martel and Pippin may have learned from both the Byzantines in Italy and the Arabs who operated in Aquitaine.[226] With the very simple torsion-based single-armed *onager* for deployment as light artillery and the lever-trebuchet for heavy artillery, Pippin's engineers did not have to master the art of building, servicing, and operating the very complicated torsion-based double-armed heavy artillery used during the earlier centuries of the Roman empire.

Battering Rams

One of the oldest and more important types of military technology required for siege warfare, particularly against wooden gates, was the battering ram.[227] Early medieval commanders learned much of this technology from the Romans, as Merobaudes' account of the Visigoths' general mastery of siege warfare, discussed above, reminds us. Gregory of Tours, writing toward the end of the sixth century, discusses Merovingian armies using battering rams (*arietes*) built on wagons (*plaustra*). He notes that the men operating the machine were protected by a wicker-work frame (*cletellum*) placed over the apparatus. The frame in turn was covered with planks (*axes*).[228]

Instructions for building a battering ram, among other useful matters of military technology, were included in *Mappae Clavicula*, a handbook available to the early Carolingians, who made at least one copy of this work during the early ninth century.[229] The basic design for various important components of a battering ram is set out under the rubric "The construction of a battering ram for taking walls by assault." The wheels were to be rather small, about thirteen to fourteen inches in diameter, but they were to be four inches thick and solid rather than constructed with spokes. In addition, the instructions indicate how the wheels were to be fixed in place with dowels and wedges once the machine had been maneuvered into proper proximity to the walls for the operation of the ram.[230]

The handbook also provides considerable detail concerning how to protect the ram and the men who operate it from enemy countermeasures. The instructions for constructing the defenses for the ram indicate that the builder is to "shield [the sides of the frame] with leather." In addition, special attention was given to the roof of the ram: "Cover the top with pieces of felt, and over the felt, put pieces of leather; and over the leather four inches of sand, and over the sand, wool, so that the sand cannot move, and on top [more] pieces of leather." [231] The author of the *Mappae Clavicula* did not favor the springlike wicker-work covered with planks, described by Gregory, and seems far more interested in protecting the machine and its crew from incendiary devices by the use of "fire-blankets," which had been discussed earlier by Vegetius, than with other forms of enemy ordinance.[232] All of these measures suggest the perceived capacity of the men defending the walls to use incendiaries against the technology deployed by the attacking force.

Tortoises

"Tortoise" (*testudo*) is the name given to a roofed frame structure, which in some ways resembled a small hut, that could be maneuvered to the base of a fortress wall. The term *testudo* also was used to describe the technique employed by foot soldiers in linking their shields above their heads in order to protect themselves from various missiles, as will be discussed below.[233] Context is the obvious arbiter of what form of technology was in play. In the tortoise, a team of men equipped with digging tools tries to "sap" the wall of the enemy fortress and if necessary to construct a "mine" under the wall. The tortoise was well known to the armies of the later Roman empire[234] and to the early Byzantines.[235] In addition, various "barbarian" peoples mastered its technology soon after coming into the empire. For example, the Avars deployed tortoises in substantial numbers against the walls of early Byzantine fortress cities,[236] and the Vikings learned how to use the tortoise against Carolingian fortifications during the ninth century.[237]

As we have seen above, the Franks also built framed structures for military operations against fortress walls. These little houses with springlike roofs could withstand heavy weights dropped on them. They could also withstand incendiaries shot at or dumped on them. The "house" used to protect the battering ram, described above, was well suited for use as a tortoise, not only because it protected the sappers inside but also because these machines were equipped with wheels and thus could easily be maneuvered into place at the base of the walls of the fortress. Both the late Roman military handbooks and the early Byzantine manuals call attention to the similarity between the houses used to protect the battering ram and those constructed as tortoises.[238] The tortoise was probably one of many *machinae* used by the Franks, and the Vikings learned how to construct and deploy this technology from the Carolingians.

Defenses Against Siege Weapons

In general, many of the aforementioned machines available in the early medieval West for attacking fortifications and during sieges were also available to the defenders for protecting their strongholds. Although the defenders of urban fortresses did not need battering rams or tortoises, both light and heavy artillery for hurling stones—*onagri* and *petrariae*, respectively—as well as bow-like *ballistae* for shooting shafted missiles were important both as antipersonnel weapons and for use against enemy equipment. The incendiary technology used by attackers was also used by defenders to destroy enemy machines of various types.

In addition to the multipurpose missile-launching machines, defenders of the walls had equipment especially developed for their use. In the imperial tradition, for example, as Gregory of Tours, writing at the end of the sixth century, indicates: "The defenders threw down on the enemy [the contents of] immense vats (*cupae*)." Some of these *cupae*, Gregory notes, "were filled with stones," while others the defenders "filled with burning pitch and grease." [239] The Franks set fire to the incendiary mixture in the vats, in a manner consistent with contemporary Byzantine technology. Then the men who operated these rather primitive machines on some sort of swivel device tipped the burning "pitch and grease" onto the enemy below the walls so that the attackers and their equipment would be engulfed in flames. [240]

The *cupae* that were filled with stones did not have to be the bronze or cast-iron caldrons needed to hold the burning pitch. For example, Vegetius discusses wicker baskets filled with "stones," called "stuff" (*metallae*) in fifth-century military slang. These baskets, which were very heavy, were placed on high battlements of the fortifications (*propugnacula*), from which their contents were dropped on the men and machines near the wall. [241] The heavy weights of stone put in these baskets, moreover, marks these weapons as intended to destroy battering rams and tortoises that had to be close to the wall. [242] Half a cubic meter of stone weighs approximately 500 kilograms, and from a height of ten meters, this was capable of crushing any battering ram or tortoise on which it fell.

Skilled Personnel

The men who built the various types of equipment, discussed above, needed a broad range of technical skills. Some skills overlapped with those needed for artisanal professions including carpentry and blacksmithing, such as forging the "shoes" or cylinders from iron to hold the beams of the lever-trebuchet. The woodworkers who built the frames for the battering rams and the lever-trebuchets required little beyond their competence as builders of houses or of plows and harrows. Further, any man who could read or memorize the instructions for constructing the "fire-blanket" needed only to follow these directions in order to do his job. These tasks required very little out of the ordinary for the skilled artisan. An army on the offensive or forces on the defensive, however, needed critical numbers of these skilled artisans in order to maintain military operations.

In addition to the above-mentioned artisans who were skilled merely in normal peacetime tasks, the military required men with highly specialized knowledge to do the jobs that were peculiar to war. For example, the design and construction of a battering ram that works efficiently are complicated. Without knowledge of the physics and mathematics required to construct a battering ram, the information needed could be acquired only by long years of experience and practice under the direction of men who had learned their craft in the same way. In addition, even machines that seem simple to use, such as a mounted battering ram (as contrasted to a huge log carried by a dozen or so big soldiers), required training recruits on a regular basis by specialists, who had to learn how to build these machines and how to operate them effectively.[243]

The realities of everyday life in early medieval Europe enabled some men to gain a modicum of proficiency in the use of the bow and arrow or the throwing spear for the purpose of hunting small game; however, there was no civilian profession, on the farm or in the town, that provided basic experience in ballistics. In addition, the operation of a catapult or of the battering ram required crews of soldiers in substantial numbers to synchronize their movements under exceptionally difficult conditions, with imminent danger to life and limb.

Training Mounted Troops

During the later Roman empire, strategists advised the government to increase both the absolute number of mounted troops in the imperial army and the proportion of mounted troops to men not provided with horses. This military policy continued in force into the reign of Justinian I (d. 565) and beyond.[244] These "reforms" had been enacted despite the fact that the imperial government had instituted a long-term military strategy, as seen above, that would be characterized in modern usage as "defense-in-depth." Over time, the implementation of this new strategy increased the importance of siege warfare, resulting in a concomitant reduction in the importance of mounted troops, who have at best a small role in the investment of a fortress city.[245]

From an economic perspective, it was widely recognized in the later Roman empire, as well as in its eastern successor state in Byzantium, that the per capita resources required to support mounted troops were far greater than what was needed to sustain foot soldiers.[246] As observed above, the Carolingians also understood these cost differentials and accounted for them by requiring that men serve in the expeditionary militia according to the wealth they possessed. Nevertheless, the military decision makers in the empire's Romano-German successor states continued the imperial policy they inherited. They invested not only in the breeding and raising of expensive war-horses but also in pack horses, which increased the mobility of both mounted troops and infantry when on campaign because even horse-drawn wagons and carts, not to mention ox-drawn vehicles, moved more slowly than pack horses and needed better roads.[247]

The variety of uses to which horses were put led to the development of breeding strategies in the Romano-German kingdoms and to the implementation of policies intended to make clear the value of different types of horses.[248] These distinctions found their way into law because compositions for crimes often were reckoned in both kind and money. For example, a war-horse was usually worth three times as much as a pack horse or a draft horse and twice as much as a regular riding horse.[249] The early Carolingians followed this trend and organized the breeding of horses with the same diligence they applied to other important aspects of estate management. Consequently, Charlemagne systematized the supply of horses that was to be made available to the royal army. Among other things, he codified previous practice, which went back well beyond the days of his grandfather, Charles Martel, to ensure that large numbers of horses were raised on royal estates for governmental use.[250] In addition, Charlemagne followed his father and his grandfather in ensuring, according to a well-established *antiqua consuetudo*, the collection of the "dona annualia aut tributa publica." This "gift" to the royal court (or more accurately public tax) was paid annually and in part, at least, in war-horses by both wealthy ecclesiastics and lay magnates.[251]

An observation by Rhabanus Maurus highlights the long-term influence of Roman imperial policy with regard to the training of mounted troops and of raising good horses bred and trained for war upon the early Carolingians. Rhabanus, as noted earlier, educated under the personal direction of Alcuin, one of Charlemagne's closest advisers, during the 770s and early 780s, in a Latin work called attention to a vernacular, probably Frankish, proverb ("vulgaricum proverbium") that concerned the training of men to fight on horseback.[252] According to Rhabanus, it was common knowledge that "a boy can be trained to be a mounted fighting man (*equitem*)." However, Rhabanus emphasizes that mounted military training, like other forms of education, must begin when the boy is young. Thus, he quotes the common wisdom that the training of a mounted fighting man "can hardly ever and perhaps never be accomplished once full manhood has been reached."[253]

This folk knowledge was common among the early Carolingians — whether in German or Latin-Romance, and probably even earlier since it was already a proverb when Rhabanus was a boy.[254] The difficult business of training effective mounted troops was regarded seriously in the West over the long term. As noted above, later Roman military policy increased in the number of mounted troops in the army. Indeed, troops identifiable as *Franci* were recruited and trained to serve in imperial cavalry units during the fourth and early fifth centuries.[255]

Writers such as Vegetius indicate the importance of training mounted troops for deployment in specific tactical contexts.[256] As will be seen below, one such training regime discussed in detail in *De re Militari* had considerable influence on Carolingian training and probably on earlier Frankish practice, as well.

Training for Tactical Flexibility

The effort to maintain mounted forces was ongoing, despite their diminished value for military operations, in general, owing to the growing importance of siege warfare during the later Roman empire. This paradox was recognized by military thinkers such as Vegetius, who wrote not long after the decision had been taken to increase both the absolute number of horsemen in the imperial army as well as the percentage of mounted troops relative to foot soldiers. Thus, Vegetius discussed the training used in the armies of the later Roman empire to ensure that mounted troops were prepared to fight not only on horseback but also on foot when the tactical situation required.[257] By about 600, the Byzantine Emperor Maurice, in his military handbook, observed that the Franks, like the other northern or fair-skinned "barbarians," were consummate practitioners in the combat technique of "dismounting in order to fight on foot."[258] This development of horsemanship among so-called western "Germans," who were settled in the empire, and which is highlighted by the above-quoted proverb, was hardly anomalous. By the early fifth century there were, as noted above, several cavalry units in the imperial army composed of men who were considered "Franks" by the Roman officials who maintained the relevant military documents.

Rhabanus Maurus in his handbook averred that "tempore moderno" the training of mounted troops was important and changed little of the initial part of Vegetius' text on the matter of training those *tyrones* who had been posted from the general pool of newly recruited fighting men to special assignment for equestrian training. Like Vegetius, Rhabanus first calls attention to the need for year-round training of horsemen. For purposes of training and drill, Rhabanus emphasizes specifically that "during the winter, wooden horses are placed under a roof and in summer they are placed in a field,"[259] implying that however meager and easily constructed these facilities may have been, the Carolingian government made them available for the training of troops. The same conclusion can be drawn concerning the wooden practice horses. In addition, these enclosures constructed for winter training accommodated dozens or even hundreds of very simply built wooden horses with a great many *tyrones* practicing at the same time. As will be seen below, mounted drills were carried out by rather large units of horsemen and not by single riders.

The numbers of mounted troops involved in various complicated equestrian exercises suggest that great barnlike structures were built for these practices in winter, as had been the case during the Roman empire. For summer training, the Campus Martius, used during the empire for training soldiers, was preserved in the environs of most *urbes*. By analogy, this may also have been the case in the less developed centers of population.[260] Whether Carolingian fortifications and military encampments were equipped with special training grounds, as had been the case during the empire, is a question that specialists in medieval archaeology may perhaps find it useful to place on their research agendas. At present no specific information is available on this topic for the early medieval period.[261]

The year-round training of recruits for service as mounted troops is thoroughly consistent with the difficulties inherent in preparing youthful soldiers to fight on horseback. Frequent drill even by older and more experienced soldiers (*milites*) was required. As will be demonstrated below, the continued drill of mounted troops in a variety of combat techniques was a necessity that was widely recognized and implemented on a regular basis during the Carolingian era.

The proper training of horses for military service was not a simple matter, and a continuous history in Western civilization deals with such training in technical handbooks, and well-informed writers, especially from the upper classes, frequently referred to various technical aspects of horse training. Such observations often appear in the works of authors who were not experts in the training of horses, and the rather offhand manner and even poetic nature of their remarks suggest that they were dealing with information that was commonplace. What emerges from this literature is the obvious fact that these large and powerful animals are not born with the instinct to perform complicated military maneuvers or even to carry men into battle. Horses innately resist being ridden, and many instincts must be conditioned out of the horse's normal behavior pattern. In place of these the horse is trained to perform very complicated exercises that are largely foreign to its nature.[262]

The training of horses, in general, and for military purposes, in particular, began with three-year-olds using a *gyrus* or training circle. The training of a cavalry horse would take the better part of a year and for the course of his military service the animal required constant reinforcement under the guidance of a capable rider.[263] In early medieval Europe, written confirmation was found in no less popular a source than Virgil.[264]

After identifying the need for year-round training of troops, Rhabanus closely follows Vegetius in highlighting what both writers regard as the most important aspect of the training of mounted troops. Rhabanus gives first priority to the training of the horseman to dismount and to fight on foot at a moment's notice and to mount and go into action on horseback just as quickly.[265] However, this apparent emphasis may be the result of our not having the complete text of his handbook. Thus, it is safer to conclude that the training techniques regarding mounting and dismounting in combat situations were among the most important items in Rhabanus' handbook for use by soldiers "tempore moderno."

Whatever we may conclude regarding the complex and unresolved matter of Rhabanus' full text, in excerpting the observations that he found in Vegetius' work he gave considerable attention to the training of horsemen to mount and dismount in battle. Rhabanus explains to his readers: "First they [the recruits] try to mount without armor (*inermes*). Then they mount carrying shields (*scutati*) and wearing helmets (*galeati*), and finally, [they learn to mount] with very large pole weapons (*contos premagnos*) in their hands."[266] Rhabanus follows Vegetius in permitting the reader to infer that at the start of this training, practice in mounting was undertaken with the recruit wearing only his sheathed short sword, *gladius* (see below). These *tirones* initially wore no armor, or were *inermes*. Whereas Vegetius indicates that after the recruits had mastered the initial stages of training, they dressed in armor (were *armati*) during practice, Rhabanus provides some additional specifics and notes that these *tirones* carried a shield and wore a helmet after they had learned to mount without armor. In addition, where Vegetius uses the term *contus* to describe the pole weapon used by the Roman recruits, Rhabanus departs from the original and emphasizes the large size of this *contus*, labeling it *premagnus*. By using the phrase "contos premagnos" Rhabanus describes a weapon more like a lengthy pike, designed to be used with two hands, than a spear fit for throwing or a lance designed primarily for thrusting.[267]

Rhabanus follows Vegetius closely in describing the finesse developed by these troops through their prescribed year-round training: "This practice [of jumping on and off their horses] was so thorough that they [the recruits] were required to learn how to jump on and off their horses not only from the right side but from the left side and from the rear. In addition, they learned to jump on and off their horses even with an unsheathed sword."[268]

Rhabanus' point concerning the unsheathed sword ("cum gladiis evaginatis") is noteworthy as a putative index of the expertise developed by these soldiers. Even to nick a horse with a naked sword point or edge while mounting would cause havoc in the lines. Not only would the individual rider be hurled to the ground but men in the ranks around him would be seriously discomforted as the horse, not under control of the bit, would kick and buck in pain and panic. (To mount or dismount a horse with an unsheathed sword in hand precludes the soldier in question from carrying a large pole weapon at the same time unless it is carried on his back with some sort of strap.)[269]

This situation in which the spear and perhaps even the shield (see below) were stowed on the rider's back suggest that some early Carolingian mounted troops were armed with both a large pole weapon and a sword. Should the former be lost or broken in combat, the soldier would have to rely on his sword. However, Rhabanus follows Vegetius in noting that these horsemen carried the *gladius* or short sword, and thus were to be prepared to be integrated into a close order phalanx formation of a type described by Maurice and used by Charles Martel at the battle of Poitiers. Rhabanus mentions neither the bow nor a quiver of arrows, though either one or both might in some way inhibit the "gymnastics" described above. Finally, Rhabanus says nothing in this chapter of training horsemen with javelins or throwing spears.[270]

Rhabanus follows up his edited version of Vegetius' account in this chapter with a commentary that was not in *De re Militari*. Rhabanus writes: "Indeed, the practice of jumping [on and off their horses] flourished greatly among the Frankish people."[271] Rhabanus' brief but pregnant addition to this particular chapter of Vegetius' *De re Militari* reaffirms the observation, mentioned above, made by the emperor Maurice, several centuries earlier. The author of the *Strategikon* commented regarding the ability and predilection of "Frankish" horsemen to dismount and to fight on foot. What appears to have been true at the end of the sixth century remained true around 850, as well.

The emphasis on tactical flexibility, while reasonable, was hardly universal. For example, very heavily armed mounted troops, such as the Sarmatians of the classical era and later, were regarded by well-informed observers as not being able to fight on foot. This putative tactical inflexibility was attributed tendentiously to the great weight and rigid nature of the armor that they wore.[272] In a not dissimilar vein, the Huns, who were renowned as horsemen and were rather lightly armed not only as compared to the Sarmatians but in an absolute sense, apparently would not dismount to fight on foot. Indeed, Ammianus Marcellinus tried unsuccessfully to explain this curious situation by suggesting that the Huns' shoes were so poor that they could barely walk much less fight on foot.[273] Conversely, the Anglo-Saxons, while recognized to have instituted a military policy aimed at having good horses for the purpose of riding to battle, used their mounts only for transportation. The Anglo-Saxons rejected a training regime that would enable them to fight on horseback.[274]

Training for Mounted Combat

Descriptions of the type of training that made possible effective mounted combat — analogues of the type of training for tactical flexibility described by Rhabanus Maurus and discussed above — are not at all common. This dearth of surviving descriptions, however, is surprising since public drill was a part of the military training of elite mounted troops in the empire's Romano-German successor states.[275] The Franks were reported to have held such drills for the purpose of practicing various mounted combat techniques "often" (saepe).[276] Nithard, Charlemagne's grandson, made a detailed description (still extant) of long-standing and well-developed drill techniques used by the Carolingians for the tactical training of mounted troops.[277]

Nithard was born before 800 (before Charlemagne obtained the imperial office), although it cannot be ascertained how much earlier. It is likely that he was raised at the royal palace, where his mother, Bertha, very probably continued to dwell until Charlemagne's death in 814, although he may have been raised at the monastery of St. Riquier where her father was lay abbot. Nevertheless, it is more than likely that Nithard was educated in the imperial schola, the best educational institution in the regnum for the combined military and literary training that we know he received.[278] Very satisfactory military training was also available at St. Riquier among the milites who, as we have seen above, served at the monastery and lived in a special military compound.

Nithard was one of a noteworthy group of laymen during the early Carolingian era who obtained a rigorous literary education as well as being fully immersed in military matters. Nithard, himself, ultimately was killed in combat, but it is clear from his History that he had not squandered the opportunity to master the liberal arts.[279] Indeed, men such as Nithard and his contemporary Wido, count of the Breton March, followed in the antique tradition of military officers such as Xenophon and Caesar, who also may be regarded as intellectuals. This tradition is best illustrated for the later imperial era by the military and literary careers of Ammianus Marcellinus and Merobaudes the Younger.[280]

Nithard indicates that military drills or exercises of the type that he intends to describe for his readers and listeners were "often arranged for purposes of training" (causa exercitii) mounted troops in certain tactics. These exercises, although on occasion performed in public, were not games intended primarily to entertain an audience. In one exemplum, Nithard indicates that "two units [of mounted troops], that were approximately equal in size" were selected from among larger units and stationed at either end of a large practice field. Then, presumably at a prearranged signal, both forces "charged forward from opposite sides [of the field] toward each other," according to Nithard, "at great speed." He calls attention to the fact that the riders spurred their horses forward and indicates that the men on both sides gave the firm impression that "they were determined to engage in hand-to-hand combat." The spears were wielded in an overhand position and vibrated or shaken at the enemy.[281]

In short, this practice session began with the positioning of two approximately evenly matched forces of horsemen, probably at no less than a hundred meters distant from each other since even very good horses cannot attain "great speed" in less than about fifty meters (Nithard does not provide information regarding these units).[282] Initially they would seem to have been engaged in a cavalry charge. Presumably, the shock of the two forces slamming into each other at a combined speed of perhaps forty miles per hour (the horses on each side moving at approximately twenty miles per hour) would be instrumental in determining the winning side. The horses as well as the men had been trained to face such a potentially bone-shattering encounter.

The pole weapons carried by these horsemen consisted only of heavy spear shafts (*hastilia*) from which the iron heads had been removed to avoid any unnecessary injuries. Even when such precautions were taken, Nithard recognizes that often injuries were inflicted, but he seems rather ambiguous on whether injuries during practice were intentional or unintentional. In the course of such exercises the men involved insulted each other or, at least, bragged about their own abilities (not unlike contemporary American "trash talk" that "psychs up" the participants).[283] Indeed, such traditions are very old in the West, as seen above, in the boasting attributed to Kapaneus.

As Nithard makes clear further along, however, the military exercise he is describing was not intended to smash up either highly trained soldiers or expensive and well-trained warhorses merely for practice purposes. Nithard emphasizes: "Before contact was made [between the two onrushing forces] one side turned its back and under the protection of their shields (*umbones*) pretended to be trying to escape (*evadere . . . simulabant*)."[284] Thus, not only were the men and their mounts trained to race at each other as though prepared for hand-to-hand combat, but they also were trained to execute the feigned retreat under very closely controlled conditions, just before contact with a mounted and charging adversary. The wheeling of the horses and the repositioning of the shields required split-second timing under the conditions described by Nithard. The timing of the turns could have been less crisp if the horsemen were charging against foot soldiers deployed in a phalanx. The soldiers deployed in the latter formation would be much slower in their pursuit than an already forward-moving unit of horsemen even if the foot soldiers acted spontaneously (without a direct command) in order to execute a hot pursuit.

Nithard continues his description of the drill by noting that on signal "the force that was engaged in the feigned retreat counterattacked," that is, the men wheeled their horses, "and the [erstwhile] pursuing force [also wheeled its mounts and] then simulated flight." This process of attacking and retreating, according to Nithard, was practiced time and time again in the course of a single day of military drills. Thus, as Nithard notes "now one group feigned retreat and then the other." [285] The ability to execute a feigned retreat was well developed and a frequently practiced exercise in the armamentarium of the Carolingians.

In his *Tactica* the Greek historian Arrian identifies the particular mounted maneuver that Nithard describes in detail above. Arrian calls this maneuver the *toloutegon* (40.2) and indicates that it is of Celtic origin. In fact, he avers that the Romans learned it from the Celts. [286] According to Arrian's description, the men in each of the two training groups, carrying lance shafts, initially charged against each other, "[first] as if to provide a defense and then as if chasing after an enemy who was in flight." Then, Arrian continues, "as the horse turns, they [the men of the retreating unit] raise their shields above their heads and move them over to cover their backs." Those who are charging "vibrate their spear shafts" (40.2).

The vibration of the spear shaft, common in Latin usage and perhaps best translated into English as brandishing, is how the mounted soldier, or a foot soldier advancing at the run, maintains control of his weapon so that he can thrust it or throw it home on a target at the appropriate time. Through this vibrating motion, the rider, for example, counteracts the motion of his horse, which otherwise would dictate the movement of the spear if the man tried to hold his arm and spear in a rigid position. In addition, by shaking or brandishing the spear, the rider keeps his muscles relaxed. If he tried to hold the spear rigidly on target his muscles would be tensed, his arm would tire more easily. During the Middle Ages, men who were good at this technique of vibrating or brandishing the spear often were given the sobriquet "brisa hasta" or in English "shakespear."

In the tradition of the use of this combat technique and concomitant feigned retreat tactic, of which Nithard's account is a part, Onasander, a Greek military commentator like Arrian, emphasizes the importance of using either staffs or spear shafts, the killing points having been removed for practice purposes. Onasander notes, as well, that the cavalry should take its practice in simulated battles, which were to include "pursuits, hand-to-hand struggles, and skirmishes" (*Strategikos*, 10.6). Vegetius, whose work was available to the Carolingians, discussed very briefly some aspects of this mounted training, as well. For example, he notes that mounted troops (*equites*) were to be divided up into troop units that were armed in a similar manner ("turmas armatique similiter"). Once this had been done, two *turmae* were drilled by such a method that "sometimes they charged [at each other], then [one] retreated for a time, and then after a partial retreat they took up the attack again." [287]

Nithard's description, which is far more complete than any previous surviving Greek or Latin effort to describe this highly refined mounted exercise, permits us to understand a great deal about the training of Carolingian horsemen as well as about their precision in deployment. First, each of the two troop units mentioned above, despite charging at great speed ("veloci cursu ruebat"), was required to maintain a fully dressed front—the ranks had to be shoulder to shoulder and knee to knee. If either of the opposing lines of horsemen approached with less than a dressed rank there would have been havoc when the very sharp turns in direction were executed. Indeed, any elements from either of the opposing forces that had outrun their lines would inevitably become entangled with each other and ultimately with the slower moving troops on both sides. As with most such exercises, practice was carried out with even greater precision than in most actual battles.

The horses also had to be exceptionally well trained for these maneuvers. They were required to turn to the right or left a full 180 degrees within an exceptionally small radius while moving at high speed. In addition, during the exercise a line of equally fast moving men and horses, with whom they were on a direct collision course, approached. This technique of coming to a full stop and reversing direction in a U-turn, called a "roll back" in modern equestrian training, is well known and not simple to learn as it required considerable training both for the horse and the rider. In training, as contrasted to the drill by already well-schooled men and horses described above by Nithard, the *magister* may ride "hard at a wall or a fence, not permitting the horse to duck off to one side, until the appropriate moment giving him the signal to come neatly off the fence in a U-turn." In contemporary equestrian activities the roll back is usually carried out by a single horse and rider. In a mounted charge, however, as described by Nithard, this maneuver was carried out by serried ranks of well-trained mounted troops.[288]

In addition, these maneuvers in military exercises and in battle occurred in an atmosphere of considerable noise and uproar, which was potentially distracting to the horses if not to their riders.[289] The participants themselves generated a great deal of noise by shouting battle cries of one type or another ("ingenti clamor"), in addition to the deafening clatter of hooves, the clang of armor, and the great clouds of dust raised by numerous horses.[290] The Carolingians recognized very well that even the simple conditions of the march resulted in considerable din from the clomping of hooves and the clang of shields.[291] Under normal conditions, horses that have not been rigorously trained are easily frightened by loud noises and by just about anything else that they find to be unusual.[292]

During a charge, the horsemen, in order to keep their front dressed and both the secondary and tertiary ranks in proper order, required the advance to be carried out in close order, with perhaps two meters for maneuver within the rank and four or five meters between each of the ranks.[293] These spacing criteria likely were satisfactory for horses of no more than about fifteen hands in height. Horses of this height would appear to have been common for heavily armed mounted troops during the early Middle Ages.[294] No less important, if the turns were to be executed in a synchronized manner (essential to the task at hand), was the requirement that each horse be on the same lead.[295] Thus, each unit would turn at the same time, which could be accomplished only in response to a signal. Since verbal signals in such a situation might not be heard, flags (*signa* or *vexilla*), battle horns (*bucina*), or a combination of both were used.[296]

This practice session described by Nithard also illustrates the precise training required for the feigned retreat. This tactic had been well known in the Roman empire and, as will be seen below in Chapter 5, had been encountered by the Franks in Italy no later than the mid-sixth century. The Franks also had encountered it in subsequent campaigns, for example, against the Visigoths in the late 580s.[297] In most cases in which we have records of the use of the feigned retreat, it did not have to be performed with the great precision indicated above. However, carrying out a particular maneuver time and time again on the practice field, at the highest level of competence, was and still is generally believed to result in high quality performance on the actual field of battle. In his commentary on Vegetius' *De re Militari*, Rhabanus Maurus never tires of extolling the virtues of practice. For example, he writes, "by intelligence and practice . . . victory is provided with God's help," and "practice and continuous exercise by skilled soldiers in daily training results in victory."[298]

One final point from Nithard's account is that these equestrian accomplishments were not limited to the *Franci*. In addition to the Austrasians (likely, in general, Ripuarian Franks by legal identity), Bretons, Gascons, and even Saxons were trained as horsemen and were organized into "ethnic" units that carried out these complicated maneuvers on horseback. In short, these tactics were widely diffused among the various "peoples" who dwelled throughout the *regnum Francorum* during Nithard's adulthood in the first half of the ninth century.[299]

Whether the Bretons, Gascons, and Saxons, as contrasted to Franks, played a significant role in the armies of the early Carolingians as they did later in the history of the *regnum Francorum* is problematic. Both Charles Martel and Pippin, more often than not, found themselves in serious military conflict with these groups (see Chapter 1). Nevertheless, there is evidence for Saxon military settlement in the western part of Gaul and for Saxon mercenaries operating in both Gaul and the northerly parts of the Visigothic kingdom through the later seventh century.[300] Gascons were absorbed into the armies of King Pippin I during the 760s at the latest.[301] Finally, some Bretons served in the armies of early Carolingians commanders after about 753, when Pippin likely imposed his *ditio* on the eastern reaches of Brittany.[302]

The practice by mounted troops of keeping their line dressed during a charge, as illustrated by the requirements for the maneuvers described in Nithard's account, was not the norm solely for the feigned retreat. For a mounted charge to be successful, it had to be driven home en masse, whether against mounted troops or foot soldiers, in a unified manner. As the cliché has it, the charge was to be delivered shoulder to shoulder and knee to knee.[303] Indeed, the author of the revised court *Annals*, who was exceptionally well informed concerning what was important to Charlemagne's inner circle, describes an incident when this fundamental military precept was violated, and he rails against horsemen who fail to hold their formations.[304]

The charge of a mounted force, in a somewhat idealized version, was provided in Latin for his court audience by the *Waltharius*-poet. Thus, Walter's mounted troops with swords in their right hands and their shields on their left forearms charged the enemy: "The chests of some horses are smashed by the chests of other horses and some of the men went down [with their horses while] others were unseated by the hard shield bosses of their adversaries."[305] This was the appropriate way to drive a mounted charge home. In this context, the matter of stirrups, which scholars have claimed were essential, in fact, make little difference and are not mentioned in *Waltharius*.[306]

Conclusion

The effectiveness of early Carolingian battlefield tactics, like that of all armies in the history of Western civilization, depended upon the troops being well trained. Pippin II and his successors had well-developed training regimes for men to fight in the field both on foot and on horseback, as well as to participate in siege warfare. Many of these training techniques and drills along with their rationale are set out in the handbook *De procinctu romanae miliciae* by Rhabanus Maurus, who was schooled under Alcuin during the reign of Charlemagne. Rhabanus used Vegetius' classic text, *De re Militari*, as the base upon which he built his handbook. A detailed comparison of the surviving parts of Rhabanus' handbook with those sections of Vegetius' *De re Militari* that he used indicate many similarities with later Roman interests but also some important differences between early Carolingian needs and those of the later imperial army. With regard to the latter, for example, the Romans had a strong interest in training mounted archers while the Carolingians did not. In addition to altering Vegetius' text in many significant ways, Rhabanus added important commentary on training for the march and for the deployment of foot soldiers to attack the enemy on foot while remaining in a cohesive formation.

By contrast with Rhabanus' handbook and the descriptions of various mounted drills by Nithard, early Carolingian training for siege warfare has to be reconstructed on the basis of *Sachkritik*, objective reality. For example, the physics involved in shooting arrows and the matter of probability in ascertaining the likelihood of casualties required examination of more or less particular patterns for shooting from specific distances against a variety of enemy formations. All of these technical details, along with such other variables as the length and weight of scaling ladders, helps us to understand the training required for the troops who hauled scaling ladders across a killing field. The early Carolingian armies that carried out major siege operations against the old Roman fortress cities of Provence, Septimania, Aquitaine, and northern Italy were provided with various types of equipment, including heavy artillery, as well as with the training and discipline to scale the walls under daunting conditions.

Foot soldiers were trained to operate in the close order of the phalanx with short swords and not only stand like a wall of ice in order to turn back an enemy attack, but also to charge the enemy at a rapid pace while maintaining unit cohesion. On the march, these troops could deploy and redeploy from column to line and vice versa. The horsemen were trained in even more complicated maneuvers that enabled them to charge at high speed in formation while maintaining unit cohesion. Mounted troops mastered the techniques of the feigned retreat, a crucial ruse for undermining an enemy phalanx. It was of vital importance, as well, that horsemen were well trained to dismount in combat situations and to fight on foot using the *gladius* in the close order of the infantry phalanx. On the whole, the early Carolingians trained their soldiers to be tactically flexible, and it would be misleading to emphasize any one element as dominant outside the confines of particular situations.

CHAPTER FOUR

Morale

Military commanders throughout the history of Western civilization have recognized that a high level of morale for their troops is a *sine qua non* for effectiveness in combat.[1] As Xenophon put it for the ages: "The army that goes into battle stronger in spirit, generally will overcome its enemies" (*Anab.* III.i.42). Developing and maintaining high morale in a milieu where the soldier's survival is at issue requires a great deal of effort. Nevertheless, armies, in general, that are habitually victorious are more likely to have high morale than armies that have been defeated frequently. If, however, it were that simple, commanders would hardly have considered the matter of morale building a subject worthy of their attention.

Before an army takes the field against the enemy, the results of the forthcoming battle are unknown. In addition to which army will win, each soldier asks himself, will he survive, will he be wounded, will he be a coward or a hero, will he do his job?[2] As the *Waltharius*-poet makes clear, even the military hero has anxieties about going into battle. In addition, if he is married with a family he worries as well about his wife and children.[3] In this context, I shall examine what kinds of policies the early Carolingians developed to enable their soldiers to face these unknowns with a sense of confidence or high morale. Second, following the battle, even the soldiers of the victorious army who emerge unscathed must believe that their sacrifices in the cause of earning the victory were worthwhile. They also must believe that the sacrifices of their comrades in arms, friends, and perhaps relatives, who may not have survived or who were seriously wounded, were justified.

Angelbert, a Carolingian soldier and poet, catches much of what is eternal for the Western fighting man in his "Verses on the Battle That was Fought at Fontenoy."[4] He tells his listeners that before battle, "the first light of dawn" provided no reprieve from the "terrors of the night" that had just passed. He assigns this pessimism to the belief that "the impious demon" — the Devil — rejoices ("gaudet") in the broken peace ("rupta pace"). However, the *Waltharius*-poet, likely an older contemporary of Angelbert, tells his listeners that even the bravest fighting men experience fear as the battle begins (which undoubtedly they already knew). Indeed, "the soldiers' limbs tremble beneath their shields."[5]

All too soon, however, Angelbert remembers, the war trumpets sound ("bella clamat") and fierce fighting breaks out ("pugna gravis oritur").[6] Angelbert was deployed on a hill overlooking a stream and fought in the front line of the battle formation ("prima frontis acie"), which was heavily involved in the fighting. He laments that he was the only man to survive ("solus de multis remani") from the entire unit that had been stationed in the first line of the formation.[7]

Angelbert says nothing of the hacking and killing by which he preserved his life in combat and served loyally in the battle line. Perhaps here in this empty space, the listener to Angelbert's poem has been given at once both a sense of the "fog of battle" and the soldier's unwillingness to relive the great but very painful emotions aroused in combat. However, once again the *Waltharius*-poet provides some insight into the immense physical and emotional stress of combat. Thus, Gunther is described "as having his knees shake" as he faced a spear being thrust at his unprotected chest. In the next instant, however, he is saved from certain death at the point of his adversary's weapon by the timely interposition of his comrade's shield. When Gunther realizes that the spear thrust has been blocked, the poet observes, "he stood trembling and fearful (*tremens trepidusque stetit*), having barely escaped from death (*vix morte reversus*)."[8] Although the poet's description of these emotions and reactions fills several lines, the action takes place in a split second. The poet generalizes, however, that in battle the soldier's morale is under stress from the fear of death ("leti terror") and the hard work of combat ("labor bellandi").[9]

But with the fighting done, we return once again to Angelbert, who proclaims, "never on the field of Mars (*campo . . . Marcio*) was there a greater slaughter" — "blood flowed in waves."[10] He continues the lament in the idiom of the soldier who has lost his comrades in arms: "the brave (*fortes*) and the most battle-wise (*proelio doctissimi*) fell." He agonizes for the survivors: fathers, mothers, sisters, brothers and friends, shedding tears.[11] The "naked dead . . . who lie in unburied horror" have had a devastating effect on the brave soldier-poet, survivor of the battle line: "there they lie . . . unmoving corpses that once were men . . . waiting to be devoured by wolves and crows."[12] The night after battle was "especially horrible" as the "wounded groaned in pain," some "men died" and "the living lamented." The next day was not much better, and Angelbert finds that he can no longer bear the tears and emotional pain. He calls on the survivors to "hold their tears back as best they can."[13]

Like Angelbert, who speaks of his emotions and those of the other survivors, the *Waltharius*-poet also tries to convey the pain of loss felt by friends and relatives of those who die in battle. Thus, for example, the poem's listeners know that the youthful Pataurid will die in combat. His mother, the poet tells us, will be devastated. His bride is left without her husband to care for her. Indeed, she will not have a son and thus will be deprived of hope for the future.

Pataurid's uncle, Hagan, who views the field of combat, tries unsuccessfully to divert the youth from certain death and laments with tears and sobs the inevitable loss.[14]

However, while Angelbert focuses upon the emotional elements of pain and loss following the battle, the *Waltharius*-poet also manages to convey the physical exhaustion of combat and the campaign in general. In the latter context, when Walter returns to the palace after a vigorous campaign and bloody battle, he says, "I am worn out," literally blown out—*anhelo*, "with exhaustion" and asks for wine. In response to his request and in recognition of his condition, he is brought undiluted wine, which in military contexts is usually given to the wounded.[15] The poet's audience was aware that hand-to-hand combat was anaerobic and usually resulted in loss of breath, with the accompanying weariness in the arms and legs.[16] By battle's end, the soldier's entire body is exhausted ("omni corpore lassi").[17] Indeed, the heroic figure is the soldier who in such exhausting combat goes on and on, to the amazement of those around, who begin to "wonder why . . . the hero, who has no rest, does not begin to become tired."[18]

Unlike the *Waltharius*-poet, who wants Walter of Aquitaine's battles to be remembered in the epic tradition, Angelbert, speaking in regard to his personal feelings, demands that this cursed battle in which he has fought be forgotten. He argues that it is not to be praised in heroic song (*canatur melode*); "no glory is to come from this *pugnum*."[19] Angelbert was on the losing side, although he believed himself to have been on the side of right. Indeed, he asserts that "the law of Christians (*lex Christianorum*) was broken" by the enemy and that there was treason on his side, as well. Some of the unit commanders (*duces*) turned traitor "like Judas."[20] For the soldier, war needs meaning and purpose, some sort of justification. His mind must be steeled for the ordeal of combat so that he can overcome the immense burden of facing death, surviving the terror of the night before battle, the horrors of the struggle, and the aftermath of death and mutilation. Too many Angelberts, especially if they are unable to express their feelings in poetry or otherwise and free their consciousness from fear and doubt through such catharsis, can result the next time round in the mobilization of an army that lacks the stronger spirit.

Of great importance to high army morale is a sense of confidence in the minds and spirits of the soldiers as indicated by Xenophon, above. This means not only the sense that they *can* win, but the sense that they *will* win. A great many variables impinge upon the confidence-building process. First, in developing an expectation of victory for more than a half-century prior to the accession of Charlemagne, the armies of the early Carolingians had created a tradition of military success. The establishment of such a tradition is not, however, a matter of military policy. Clearly, commanders such as Pippin II and his successors did not set out to lose either their troops or their battles. It would be difficult, despite much stupidity among a generous selection of commanders in the course of the history of Western civilization, to identify any general, with the exception of outright traitors, who intended to have his armies defeated.

Large Armies

The early Carolingians' exceptionally successful military machine depended on the implementation of a wide variety of policies. In relation to confidence building, their policies of recruitment and organization (discussed above) resulted in the capacity to mobilize large armies regularly when necessary.[21] It is probable that the early Carolingians, like Charles Martel and his son Pippin, understood the principle that today we call "the doctrine of overwhelming force." Everything else potentially being equal, this doctrine entails the commitment and capacity to put such a numerically superior force into the field that the enemy army avoids combat and comes to terms rather than face likely defeat. In the early medieval context, this commitment also must be made for mustering troops in order to lay siege to a fortress.[22]

Having large armies that were overwhelmingly successful in their campaigns over a half-century accounts for the early Carolingians' lengthy streak of victories. Knowledge of this tradition of victory, in its turn, raised and sustained the morale of even the newest recruit from the time of mobilization to the eve of combat. This sense of confidence helped many soldiers get through that "night of fear" so poignantly emphasized by Angelbert.

However high the general morale of the soldiers, desertion was a fact of life in Carolingian armies, as in all armies in Western history.[23] The early Carolingians' pattern of success makes it clear that whatever desertion may have occurred in their armies, and these rates are not recoverable by modern scholarship, they did not have a negative impact on military operations. In short, the early Carolingians consistently had sufficiently large armies, desertion notwithstanding.

Perhaps even more important than desertion with regard to the "night of fear" was the matter of drunkenness, which did not go unnoticed as a problem or a potential problem in the West.[24] Alcohol in the form of uncut wine, as mentioned above, was recognized by the early Carolingians to have had an analgesic effect and was used to treat the wounded and raise the spirits of the exhausted. By contrast, the abuse of alcohol, which impairs the soldier in combat, undoubtedly took place in Carolingian armies. This problem fell under the official scrutiny of the central government and was dealt with in army regulations. Particular attention was given to those men who "organized" drinking bouts in which one or more of their fellow soldiers got drunk. These were prohibited. By contrast, drinking alone would seem to have been tolerated as long as the imbiber did not become drunk. However, anyone who did become drunk was to be separated from his unit. Thereafter, he was allowed to drink only water until he admitted that he had acted wrongfully, suggesting that any soldier who got drunk was placed under some form of surveillance.[25]

In specific regard to the use of overwhelming force, the soldier who fights hand-to-hand on the field of battle or storms the walls of an enemy fortress is comforted to know that he and his fellow fighting men outnumber the enemy. The "morale speeches" that are found in many medieval sources that deal with battles reaffirm the notion that soldiers who know or who believe that they are outnumbered before going into combat require a great deal of convincing that they can be victorious. Convincing "a few good men" that they are militarily superior to a much larger number of putatively less good men was a difficult task for the reason that it was contrary to the experience of battle-hardened veterans.[26]

Feeding the Troops

The larger the force the greater its logistic requirements, however. An army, according to the cliché, travels on its stomach, and feeding the army properly and on a regular basis has been recognized universally to be crucial to the maintenance of morale. As Vegetius put it: "Armies are more frequently destroyed by lack of provisions than by combat." He continues, "hunger is more cruel than the sword." Vegetius, who is basing his views on a lengthy Western tradition, further observed: "On campaign, the single most effective weapon is food. It must be sufficient for your forces while its lack will break your adversary."[27] While not all soldiers who are well fed are happy, those who suffer from a lack of supplies rarely display high morale.

The early Carolingians expended great effort to ensure logistic support to their troops. Extensive institutional arrangements were made with monasteries and other infrastructure components throughout the *regnum*, whether the army was on the march or was deployed in fixed and highly fortified siege emplacements.[28] For example, as noted above, more than half of the so-called rents collected by a wealthy monastery such as Saint-Germain-des-Prés were resources allocated to sustain the Carolingian army on campaign.[29]

In addition, the Carolingians pursued policies that were intended to sustain elements of the physical infrastructure, such as roads, bridges, and canals, that were fundamental to moving the supplies needed by the army. The road system of the Roman empire was still intact throughout the greater part of the lands of the *regnum Francorum*.[30] Even the *mansiones*, the stopping-off places along the Roman roads, were maintained along these routes.[31] The early Carolingians also maintained the "ancient custom" (*antiqua consuetudo*) that the local authorities keep roads in good repair.[32] In addition, some modest road building had been undertaken during the post-Roman period east of the Rhine, and these assets were subject as well to the *antiqua consuetudo*.[33]

The quality of early Carolingian land transport on the old Roman road system and beyond the empire's frontiers was materially aided by a noteworthy command of the science of bridge building.[34] Throughout the *regnum Francorum*, as had been the case during the Roman empire, local officials enforced the "ancient custom" of seeing to the building of new bridges and repairing old ones.[35] Charlemagne was a beneficiary of this technology and tradition. He placed a "permanent" bridge made of wood across the Rhine at Mainz, bridged the Weser, and built two bridges across the Elbe.[36] (The Carolingians were not alone in maintaining this Roman tradition of requiring local authorities to keep the road and bridges in good condition. These duties were fundamental to the so-called *trinoda necessitas* in Anglo-Saxon England.)[37]

In the context of land transport, it was Carolingian policy to maintain and develop the military technology required to move supplies. For example, prefabricated boats that could be assembled when needed were carried in the baggage train of Carolingian armies when it was known that there was a need to make river crossings that required such sophisticated equipment.[38] Supply wagons, like those of the later empire, carried inflatable animal skins while on the march; these were used for building smaller pontoon bridges and as flotation devices.[39] The Carolingians also could make the wagons watertight.[40]

Throughout the pre-modern West, the movement of men and supplies by water was far easier and a great deal less expensive than land transport.[41] The early Carolingians did not neglect this option, and as will be seen below in some detail, Charles Martel and Pippin maintained control of inland water travel for the transport of men and especially of matériel. Throughout the early Middle Ages, as in the later Roman empire, where the functioning of large armies is hardly at issue, inland water travel was well developed.[42] For example, the early Carolingians kept the Vecht canal (the successor of the *fossa Drusiana* that connected the Rhine with what is now called the Ijselmer) in operating condition.[43] Charlemagne's attempt to build a canal to connect the Rhine to the Danube and thus link the North Sea with the Black Sea reveals continuity in thinking about military and economic advantages within the framework of Roman imperial tradition. Such a project was hardly the result of some institutional memory cultivated in the primeval Germanic forests beyond Rome's frontiers.[44]

The early Carolingians maintained a highly sophisticated infrastructure capable of feeding large numbers of soldiers on campaign and during sieges. This infrastructure made such extended and elaborate military operations possible and gave the soldiers confidence over time that they would receive required supplies on a regular basis. This confidence in having proper food and equipment, in turn, contributed to the army having high morale and thus elicited from the soldiers, in general, a consistently superior overall performance, with a minimal number of desertions.

Remuneration

There has been a long-standing debate in the West regarding the proper levels of pay that soldiers should receive. For example, Tacitus had the emperor Galba aver, "I pick my soldiers, I do not buy them" (*Hist.* 1.4). The other extreme is well demonstrated by the often quoted advice to his sons by Septimius Severus: "Be agreeable, enrich the soldiers, and despise all the rest" (Dio, 76.15.2).[45] Whatever the realities of payment, soldiers who believe that their commanders or their society do not value them sufficiently rarely fight well. Under such circumstances they often demonstrate a proclivity toward disloyalty as well as low morale.[46]

As we have seen above, the *milites* who served in the royal *obsequium* of the early Carolingians are reported to have enjoyed a remarkably and consistently high level of morale. It might be cynical to suggest that this high morale was associated only with the liberal economic support that they regularly received from their *capitanei*. As noted earlier, however, the camaraderie fostered through the officers' mess may well have played a role. However, economic support provided by the *capitanei* and the *donum militum*, which the queen distributed to soldiers stationed at the royal court, looms large in the contemporary analysis of the situation provided by Charlemagne's cousin Adalhard of Corbie.[47] In short, soldiers who are well rewarded for their service have one less reason to complain.

Also among the professional soldiers, who served in the armies of the early Carolingians, were the military retinues of the lay and ecclesiastical magnates. Among the men enrolled in these *obsequia* were *servi* and *pueri*, denizens of the lower classes and in many cases unfree. Such recruits, who were honored with the status of a *vassallus* while receiving arms, armor, and horses from their *domini*, could rise in status through loyal and effective military service, while bettering the opportunities for the social and economic advancement of their children. In this context, landless men such as the lower class *vassalli* mentioned above, who were granted *beneficia* in the form of military lands, had even greater possibilities for advancement.[48] These immediate advantages and the prospect of future advantages, especially the acquisition of military land, played an important role in developing high morale in the soldiers who served in these military retinues, as well as among the troops in the royal *obsequium*.

The greater part of the rank and file of those early Carolingian armies, which were mobilized for major campaigns of conquest, was not composed of these professional soldiers. Rather, part-time militia men who possessed at least a single manse, as well as their more affluent fellow landholders, constituted the greater part of the armies mobilized for large-scale expeditions (such as the siege of great fortress cities as was the case during the conquest of Aquitaine by King Pippin I).[49] Future research may show that this type of civilian military service substituted in part for a direct tax on the land, which gradually ceased to be collected during the sixth century.[50]

Important to our understanding of how the early Carolingians maintained the morale of these part-time militia forces are the efforts, discussed above, of the central government to protect them from overzealous and/or corrupt local officials. The economic health of each militia man was given serious consideration, and for most men, who owned only small amounts of land, service was not required annually.[51] The central government considered it vital that these militia men were not to be so burdened with service that their required military duty would impoverish them. In this vein, the early Carolingians tried to ensure that the poorer men, who were required to serve in the expeditionary levies, would not be so encumbered with financial difficulties as a result of their service that they would be required to sell their land.[52]

In addition, the early Carolingians' success in their military operations over the course of a century resulted in the acquisition through conquest of considerable amounts of movable wealth and land — especially estates — as booty. While victory is a *desideratum*, the legitimate acquisition of booty in the wake of conquest is the result of a command decision to plunder the enemy's resources or annex its territory.[53] The importance to the development and maintenance of high morale, however, is the commander's subsequent decision, if taken, to provide a share of the spoils of war to the victorious soldiers. The early Carolingians did this in such a manner that chroniclers called attention to the great quantities of booty taken as an index of victory.[54] Even in entertainment literature, soldiers, after winning what is characterized as a complete victory, almost as a matter of course were permitted to plunder the bodies of the dead littering the field.[55] In the course of gaining their military success, however, early

Carolingians not only made movable wealth available to the soldiers as booty. Lands taken from various defeated enemies were, on occasion, given to the soldiers. These estates, as seen above, were to be held by their recipients in various tenures.[56]

Command Quality

Soldiers who have confidence in the ability of their commanders usually also have high morale. Thus, contemporary and near contemporary sources portray the early Carolingians as very able generals, Charles Martel, especially. The court chronicler employed by Charles' half-brother, Duke Childebrand, indicated that the famed Mayor of the Palace was known to act "daringly" (*audacter*),[57] but also "in a consistently prudent manner" (*constanter*).[58] Charles was clearly regarded as a "vigorous man in military matters" (*strenuus vir*).[59] In addition, he was reputed to have been personally "brave" (*intrepidus*)[60] and acted "wisely" (*sagace*). Indeed, Charles is seen to have been "exceptionally wise" (*sagicissimus*) in military affairs.[61] He was considered not only a "man of military talent" (*bellator*), but "a man of outstanding military talent" (*bellator insignis*) and a "man famous for his military talent" (*bellator egregius*).[62] Charles is rarely credited with actually going into combat with his men; however, when he did, he was singled out for his fighting ability and styled *belligerator*.[63] Above all, Charles Martel was regarded as a "victorious commander," a *triumphator*.[64] It is important that the early Carolingians trumpeted the view that this tradition of victory was established with the help of God, "Christo auxiliante" and "Deo auxiliante."[65]

These characterizations of Charles Martel's military ability fit rather nicely with Roman notions of what makes a good general. As Cicero put it, a good general had to be well informed on military matters, demonstrate great courage, and be regarded by his troops as having *auctoritas* (*De Imp. Pomp.* 10.28). Cicero, a pagan, also considered good luck, or as others might put it, the favor of the gods, to be of exceptional importance in the mix of virtues that brought the effective commander great and consistent victories. For Charles Martel the pagan *fortuna*, as we have seen above, became the hand of God that brought victory.

No less noteworthy is the tradition that the Roman emperor, although permitted to expose himself to danger, was required to oversee the battle in order to maintain command and control. Consequently, under normal circumstances, he was not to fight personally in the battle line.[66] Therefore, Charles Martel was praised as a *bellator*, but rarely described by the court chronicler as a *belligerator*, one actually taking part personally in hand-to-hand combat.[67]

Particularly illuminating in this context is an observation by Fredegar's Continuator, who takes note of a very bloody battle between Charles' army (*exercitus*) and that of the Frisian duke Radbod in 715. During this battle, according to the Continuator, Charles saw that his army was suffering unacceptably high losses and is reported to have ordered a retreat.[68] Charles was observing the combat from a position in which he could have a clear view of the field of battle, as a good Roman general was taught, rather than participating in the melee where one can see only one's immediate vicinity. Thus, Charles maintained command and control at a distance, and when he concluded that his battle plan had not succeeded, he could order a timely retreat and save the bulk of his army. In addition, the successful retreat permitted Charles to keep the remnants of his force intact, and as a result he attacked the enemy with greater success later in the year.[69]

The epithets cited above as illustrative of Charles Martel's military abilities likely were biased because such praise was the product of a court history that was intended to please the Mayor of the Palace and stimulate the support of his followers.[70] Yet, it is unlikely that the lengthy streak of victories by early Carolingian armies prior to the accession of Charlemagne owed nothing to the military abilities of Pippin II and his successors. Even if these men ultimately are not judged to have been among history's great military commanders, their armed forces, like the chroniclers who portrayed their deeds, had greater and greater faith in its commanders over time simply because of their continuing string of victories. For morale purposes, an enduring and plausible myth explaining exceptionally positive military performance is as useful as fact.

Court accounts of the military campaigns won by Pippin II and his successors had a limited contemporary audience. Even a program of monumental art, such as the now lost frescos that adorned the imperial *palatium* at Ingelheim and glorified the military victories of the early Carolingians, such as Charles Martel's conquest of the Frisians in 734, also likely had rather a small selection of viewers.[71] By contrast, the powerful force of the oral dissemination of great deeds popularized a tradition of Carolingian military success. Moreover, Charles Martel, Pippin, and Carloman reenforced such views. Therefore, it is important that the early Carolingians, following imperial precedent, pursued a tradition of public ceremonial (the triumph) to celebrate a careful selection of their military victories.

Fredegar's Continuator, who, as noted above, wrote his account of the early Carolingians under the patronage first of Charles Martel's half-brother and then under the auspices of the latter's son, provides compelling indications of these victory ceremonies.[72] Not every military success won by Charles, however, is recorded in language that permits the inference that there was a ceremony celebrating a triumph at the end of the campaign. For example, between 723 and

738, Charles Martel campaigned annually and never is indicated to have been unsuccessful in the prosecution of these military operations.[73] Nevertheless, on only eight occasions does the account of his success suggest that he celebrated a triumph.[74] For example, in 724 when Charles returned home, he is described as *victor*, but in 732, although he is described as *victor* again, it is explicitly indicated that he triumphed ("triumphavit"), celebrated a triumph. After his military successes in 737, Charles once more is described as *victor* but he is also described as *triumphator*, the man who celebrated a triumph.[75]

In describing Pippin's great victory over the Bavarians in 749, the Continuator emphasizes that the king returned home "with a great triumph" ("cum magno triumpho").[76] The author of the court *Annales* described Charlemagne's well-documented triumph in 774 following the conquest of the Lombard kingdom with the same formula, "cum magno triumpho," as the Continuator used to describe Pippin's ceremony a quarter-century earlier.[77] In light of additional information, which will be discussed below, the phrase "cum magno triumpho" came to be a rather traditional way to indicate that a formal victory ceremony had been celebrated by one or another early Carolingian ruler.

Our understanding of the Continuator's usage and what may seem to be the tradition sustained by the early Carolingians is clarified by an examination of his treatment of Pippin's lengthy series of campaigns, perhaps more accurately described as a war, from 760 and 768 that resulted in the conquest of Aquitaine.[78] Each year for nine consecutive years, Pippin's army fought in Aquitaine with great success. Among the highlights of these operations, which were carried out under his personal command, were the capture of the well-defended old Roman fortifications at Bourbon, Clermont-Ferrand, Bourges, and Thouars. Indeed, the siege of the great *urbs* at Bourges, which is discussed below in Chapter 6, lasted at least three months and probably longer. In addition, numerous lesser strongholds also were captured and the successful outcome of many rather small clashes in the field are noted, as well. However, none of these successes are recorded in a manner that might be construed to indicate that a triumph was orchestrated to celebrate them. The Continuator not only avoids the use of the language of triumph, he does not even describe Pippin as *victor* following any of these successes.[79]

Only in 764, the fourth year of the war, after Pippin won a significant battle in the field, does the Continuator identify the *rex Francorum* as *victor*. In addition, he indicates that Pippin celebrated a lengthy triumphal procession from the town of Digoin on the Loire eastward through Autun and on into Austrasia.[80] Pippin is reported to have campaigned in Aquitaine again in 766 with great success, that is, he is said to have obtained a great deal of booty and loot (*multa praeda* and *spolia*). The language of triumph is not used to describe his return home, however. In 767, Pippin once more led his armies into Aquitaine with considerable success, but the Continuator does not even hint that he celebrated a triumph.[81] It was only in 768, with the death of the enemy leader, Duke Waiofar of Aquitaine, and the submission of the entire region and all of its magnates that Pippin again is reported to have celebrated a triumph. At this time, the Continuator reports that Pippin went to the old Roman fortress city of Saintes "cum magno triumpho."[82]

However much the high quality of early Carolingian military leadership and their record of well-publicized victories might have stimulated the development and sustenance of high morale, they were reenforced by other closely connected patterns of behavior. For example, the early Carolingians were loath to fight unnecessarily, and on more than a few occasions, Charles Martel and Pippin accepted terms from their adversaries rather than battering them into total submission during a bloody but unnecessary battle. The prospect of the winning side suffering even the minimal losses that generally accompany a greatly one-sided encounter were avoided. Even when actually facing an enemy in the field, if an acceptable result could be gained through negotiation, such a course of action would seem to have been preferred.[83] The early Carolingians therefore very likely did not leave the impression among their troops, either among the rank and file (expeditionary levies or lower class *servi* in some magnate's *obsequium*) or among higher status professional fighting men, that the soldiery was expendable. Indeed, Pippin II and his successors did not leave the impression that the pursuit of glory and high military reputation, as ends in themselves, were *desiderata*. The virtue of caring for the well-being of one's troops was of long standing in Western tradition and helped to earn for more than one Roman emperor the highly coveted characterization of *conmilitio* or fellow soldier.[84]

In addition, like all good commanders, the early Carolingians understood the fundamental importance of having their men soundly trained and supplied with good equipment in the necessary quantities. We have already had a glimpse of the organization of the *schola* and the purpose of one of its branches in training an officer corps. As seen above, there is good reason to believe that substantial efforts were made, as well, to train the rank and file of the expeditionary forces. Furthermore, early Carolingian troops were appropriately equipped, allowing Charles Martel's armies and those of his son, Pippin, to undertake siege warfare against the great fortress cities, which, although built during the later Roman empire, were still capable of vigorous defense by adversaries of the early Carolingians. In those technical matters that lay the foundation for military victory and the development of confidence in the soldier, Charlemagne's father, grandfather, and even his great-grandfather did very well.

In this context, some scholars regard the early Carolingian heavily armed mounted forces, because of their *brunia* or mail coats, as having a significant technological advantage over their less well armed adversaries.[85] This superior defensive armament gave those who had such equipment a sense of being less vulnerable to the enemy than those who lacked such equipment. Men with *brunia*, which were expensive pieces of equipment, were only a relatively small part of the early Carolingian armies, however. In addition, this advantage was probably greatest against the Saxons, whose armament was technologically less well developed than that of the Carolingians. In wars against the Aquitanians in southwestern Gaul, the Lombards in Italy, and the Muslims on the frontiers of Spain, where the Roman imperial heritage remained strong, the Carolingians, as will be shown below, enjoyed no technological advantages worthy of note.

Motivation

When early Carolingian commanders, who were highly regarded by their soldiers, were about to order their armies to move against the enemy or to take the field in battle, they followed the long-standing Western tradition of haranguing the troops for the purpose of raising their morale.[86] We are fortunate to have preserved an account of the speech that Pippin II is depicted as delivering to his forces in 687, just prior to the march that was to take Pippin's army into enemy territory. This was during the campaign that culminated in the battle at Tertry, regarded as a great if not even a decisive victory by early Carolingians.[87]

The account of this speech is highly stylized and very probably inauthentic with regard to the specific words used. The value to historians of such battle harangues, like the speeches so much more subtly crafted by Thucydides, does not lie in whether or not they are a verbatim copy of the orations that were actually delivered by a particular individual at a particular time in a particular context. Rather, for the historian, the importance of these speeches lies in how closely contemporary values and ideas, in the present case those of the early Carolingians, are portrayed. This focus on the mentality of the speaker as conceived or perhaps understood by the chronicler and the interests of the latter's putative audience is what is known technically, in a rhetorical context, as the "criterion of plausibility."[88]

According to the Metz annalist, Pippin II began his speech by addressing the entire army (*cunctus exercitus*) as "fortissimi viri" — "the bravest men." The latter are then portrayed as "the *fideles* of Our God" — this is a divine army about which more is said below. Pippin is seen to have had a twofold purpose in this speech: to provide the soldiers with a rationale for going to war and to assure them that they are on the right side. Thus, he emphasizes that a triple necessity has required that he mobilize for war ("triplici necessitate coactus vos ad tale certamen provocare"). He continues, "listen to my speech" (me loquentem attendite) and as befits a wise commander, who understands both his men and the situation very well, he promises to speak only briefly, *breviter*.[89]

In the course of a mere 160 words, Pippin explains the need to go to war and the fact that they are fighting a "just war." He is reported to have maintained that we go to war "for the love of God" (*amor Dei*), to restore the property of the church that has been stolen ("sublatis iniuste patrimoniis ecclesiarum") by the Neustrians. He then contends that noble Franks, who are refugees from the tyranny of their Neustrian enemies, cry out for help because they believe that Pippin's forces can obtain divine help ("divinum . . . sufragium") for this just cause. Further along, Pippin emphasizes that this campaign constitutes a preemptive strike against an enemy who is planning aggression: "the *superbissimus rex* [of the Neustrians] . . . unjustly (*iniuste*) threatens the devastation of our homeland" ("vastationem patria nostrae"). Finally, their cause will be subjected to *iudicium Dei*, the judgment of God, and Pippin concludes: "We endure such battles (*certamina*) because of our love for God and his saints."[90]

Pippin provides both a legal and a practical justification for this war against the Neustrians and their king, not to mention the horrors that will attend it. He wants his soldiers to believe that their adversaries have broken the *lex Christianorum*. He does not want his men to suffer the "terror of the night" before battle and the pain of regret after the battle, as these were so eloquently expressed by Angelbert in his poem discussed above. Pippin wants no soldier, poet or otherwise, to believe that "the impious demon" rejoices in the "broken peace."[91] Rather, Pippin affirms that God is on the Carolingian side and that the *iudicium Dei* will be in their favor. No less important, however, both for encouraging the troops, who are told that they are defending their homes from a threatened invasion, and in sustaining the principle of just war is Pippin's exposure of the enemy plan to invade and devastate the Austrasian *regnum*.[92]

The so-called battle harangue seems to have been a commonplace among the early Carolingians. Indeed, toward the end of the eighth century or perhaps shortly thereafter, it infiltrated the epic genre of Latin court poetry; for example, the hero of *Waltharius*, Walter of Aquitaine, addresses a unit of palace troops, just before the unit, probably a *scara* in the Latin vernacular of royal household, was to set out on campaign from the court in a rapid deployment that could be expected to result in contact with the enemy rather quickly if not unexpectedly.[93] Walter's speech, like that of Pippin, is set in a context where combat could possibly be initiated before deployment into a formal battle formation might take place. These two speeches may be considered preemptive exhortations, as contrasted to morale-building efforts in the face of an imminent combat that was to take place in a clearly defined and well-understood tactical situation.

Walter's speech is not presented as direct discourse but rather the poet-narrator "summarizes" four important points that traditionally were common to such oratorical efforts.[94] Walter is described as encouraging his soldiery, *militia*, for the purpose of strengthening the hearts of his fighting men ("bellatorum confortat corda suorum")—raising morale.[95] In addition, he recalls their record of previous military success and thus strongly urges his troops always to remember their past victories. Having a strong record of success is very important to the development of the soldier's confidence while preparing for battle. The poet uses the term *triumphi* rather than *victoriae*, both in the plural, not only to indicate the winning of earlier battles but also to foreshadow the triumphal celebration that will take place after the victory has been won.[96]

Walter then turns from his effort to raise the morale of his men to a moral justification of their military operations. He alludes pointedly to the enemy as rebels, using the term *tyranni* in the sense of illegal holders of power. The putting down of rebels who have risen against the holder of legitimate power creates the basis for a just war. As will be seen below, the salvation of those who fight in battle for their king or his legitimately delegated commanders (especially for those who die in such a battle) requires that the cause for which they kill the enemy in combat be regarded as just.[97]

Finally, Walter addresses the broader reason for fighting wars and this one in particular. He emphasizes to the soldiers in his unit that if they fight with their accustomed superior ability ("solita virtute") not only will they be successful on the battlefield, but their victory "will instill *terror* in distant lands."[98] Here the deterrent value of military victory as the basis upon which peace is built is brutally emphasized. This thoroughly classical view was much strengthened for an early medieval Christian audience because of its acceptance by St. Augustine and subsequent development by Isidore of Seville.[99] Both these points, as we have seen above, have analogues in Pippin's speech.

In concluding his treatment of the first phase of this military operation, the poet calls very specific attention to the "fact" that after the speech, Walter rode off and "was followed by the whole army" ("sequiturque exercitus omnis") in order to advance against the enemy.[100] The implication that the poet seeks to convey to his listeners is that Walter's harangue, which emphasized the high quality of his troops, their record of great success, the justice of their cause, and the ultimate deterrent value of their forthcoming victory as a means of maintaining peace in the future, was so successful in stimulating high morale that no one deserted. Of course, Walter did not mention his own great prowess as a commander, but from the antecedent action, it is clear that his troops knew his reputation for great military success.

Spiritual Help

Although an army travels on its stomach, the soldiers do not live by bread alone. Clichés such as "there are no atheists in foxholes" are merely the modern expression of a lengthy tradition in Western civilization that illuminates the spiritual dimension of the soldier's morale.[101] The evidence is everywhere. The exceptionally important part played by religion in the Roman army has been well documented for the pagan period.[102] Constantine the Great, in the wake of his victory at the Milvian bridge and the issue of the Edict of Toleration, established a chaplain corps for his Christian soldiers.[103] The military chaplain continued to play an important role into the Byzantine period.[104]

The so-called barbarian peoples, both pagans and one or another type of Christian, such as Roman and Arian, also well understood the importance of the spiritual side of morale building for those engaged in warfare. For example, the Visigoths, after they became Christians, maintained an important role for military chaplains. Indeed, one recent interpretation of the evidence suggests that service as an army chaplain was a primary role for bishops in the Visigothic system.[105] By the seventh century, if not earlier, the Visigoths already had a well-developed mass for the king and his army when they were going out to battle. This entailed among other things prayers that the kings should have strong armies ("exercitus fortes") and loyal generals ("ducos fidos"), and that they should fight bravely while always following the Lord's teaching. Thus, the king will be the victor over his enemies. Additional prayers were said likening the Christian army to that of the Israelites: "Blessed be Israel . . . the shield of Your aid and the sword of Your Glory." A very large "marching" cross, especially blessed at the altar of the church and believed to contain a piece of the true cross, always was carried in front of the army by either a priest or a deacon. The army's standards (*banda*) also were blessed at the altar. Of particular interest from the perspective of morale is the prayer "Domine Deus, virtus salutis mee, obumbra caput meum in die belli" — "Lord God, strength of my salvation, cover my head on the day of battle."[106]

With regard to the role of religion in the development of military morale under the early Carolingians, in the *regnum Francorum*, Charlemagne's father and even his grandfather ostensibly dominated the Church and more particularly its material resources. The frequently expressed scholarly view of Charlemagne, "he stands before us as the sole master of his Church," would be little exaggerated if applied to Charles Martel and Pippin I, especially in a military context.[107] The Church role in developing the soldiers' morale owed much to government policies. No less important, the manner in which military operations were treated in contemporary historiography was also subject to policy considerations.

In contemporary and near contemporary documents, usually written by clerics, the early Carolingian *princeps* as well as the soldiers who served under his command were unambiguously represented as benefiting from the hand of God in military matters. Analogues were found in appropriate passages concerning the history of the Jews at war, which were widely available from teachings based on Latin translations of the Hebrew Bible, such as Moses' victory over Amalek and Joshua at Jericho.[108] In this context, the history of King David, a hero of the Franks in general and of the Carolingian house in particular, provides an important model throughout the Middle Ages.[109] For Christians, however, the Hebrew tradition of God's role in military victory was confirmed in Constantine's legend "Hoc signo victor eris."[110]

As we have seen above, the early Carolingian court sources cultivated the image that Pippin II and his successors won their victories with God's help, "Christo auxiliante" and "Deo auxiliante."[111] In addition, the victory ceremonies or triumphs, also discussed above, had a significant religious component. For example, Charlemagne's entry into the Lombard capital of Pavia "cum magno triumpho"[112] on the day following King Desiderius' surrender was carried out "cum hymnis et laudibus."[113] Pippin's entry into Saintes following the conquest of Aquitaine in 768, also "cum magno triumpho," probably included the hymns and *laudes* that his son was to employ in his first recorded triumph only six years later.[114]

Indeed, this image of the early Carolingians as very successful military commanders aided by God was attached, as well, to Pippin II (d. 714), Charles Martel's father. Pippin II is styled or described as *victor* in contemporary and later sources.[115] By the reign of Charlemagne and probably a good deal earlier, Pippin II's "magnos . . . triumphos" are seen to be "given to him by God" and he, too, is compared to King David. He is praised for the "unconquerable nature (*soliditas*) of his bravery" and even his ancestors (*prosapia*) are considered *invictissima*.[116] He is described as *defensor* against all the enemies of his people,[117] and frequently as *invictus princeps*, or one who wielded unconquered arms "auxiliante Domino."[118] Resting in part on Matthew (9:26), the Metz annalist observes that "the *fama* of his [Pippin's] *victoriae* and *triumphi* went out among the peoples (*gentes*)."[119] Pippin II, as Mayor of the Palace, may have had his court orchestrate a ceremonial triumph of the type attributed above to his descendants as suggested by the phrase "magnifice . . . triumphavit."[120]

A firm belief that God helped early Carolingian armies to attain victory elevated the morale of the men who went into battle. However, God's help was no random act; rather, the Franks regarded themselves as God's chosen people and the true successors of the Israelites in this regard.[121] In addition, they actively sought *auxilium Dei*. One of the main vehicles for attaining God's support was through prayer for the military success of the ruler and his army. By the early eighth century, for example, Frankish priests addressed special prayers to "Lord God, Creator of All, Terrible and Strong" so He would "grant victory to the Frankish kings." [122]

Victory by the *reges Francorum* was the subject of this prayer, despite the fact that the Mayors of the Palace held the real power. However, a mass from a somewhat later date uses the more ambiguous term *princeps* rather than *rex*,[123] suggesting that Church practice had caught up with the political reality of Charles Martel's ascendancy.[124] In this mass, the faithful pray to God to protect their *princeps*,[125] who is depicted as God's faithful servant (*fidelis famulus*), "always" and "against all adversaries" to be the *victor* in the future "cum triumphis." They also pray for his entire army (*exercitus*). Indeed, God is entreated to do all of these things through "the right hand (*per dextram*)" of His power.[126]

Throughout these prayers, reference to the Hebrew Bible—Moses, Joshua, and David, for example—are the basis for a very positive comparison with their Frankish "successors." [127] All of this late Merovingian or early Carolingian praying for military success, however, is done within the framework of the Roman imperial tradition of seeking God's help for victory. The late imperial usage in some contexts is so obvious that it appears that the *Romani* merely have been substituted for in the surviving texts by the *Franci*: for example, the enemies of the Romans, through the change of a word here and there, become the enemies of the Franks.[128]

In addition to the overall importance to good morale of instilling in the troops the firm belief that God provided victory to the *principes* and later to the *reges* of the early Carolingians, the personal feelings of each soldier regarding his own military success and spiritual salvation mattered greatly. A strong belief that God took an interest in the rank and file of the army was essential to the development and maintenance of troop morale. For example, the well-known Sacramentary of Gellone contains a mass principally "for those who are going into battle," said just as the troops were about to move out against the enemy ("in profectium hostium").[129] The mass is said for the "victory and safety" of "God's *exercitus*," making clear the special role enjoyed by these fighting men as *milites Dei*.[130] Most masses are less focused on the army; nevertheless, prayers in the Sacramentary of Angoulême, for example, were intended to save the army from suffering excessive casualties.[131] As observed above, in the Western tradition a good commander was one who did not waste his troops, and these prayers would appear to lend religious support to such doctrine.

The early Carolingians, however, also believed that the soldiers should play a regular role in Christian religious activities.[132] Thus, in the tradition of Constantine the Great [133] and his early Byzantine successors,[134] Charles Martel's son,

Carloman, ordered in 742 that selected members of the clergy were to be given specific permission to go to war ("in exercitum et in hostem pergere"). These men were ordered to accompany the army "for the purpose of divine ministry," "so that they may perform the solemn rites of the masses" to the troops. In order to say mass in the military camp and perhaps on the battlefield as well, Carolingian priests used portable altars.[135]

Carloman also decreed that the commander, that is, the *princeps*, of each army was to have on his staff one or two bishops, along with a requisite number of "chaplain priests" to carry out these rites as required. In addition, every unit commander (*praefectus*) was to have at least one priest with him on his staff.[136] This legislation was not concerned with the clerics who served in the palace "chapel," however. These men or at least some of them traveled regularly with the Mayor of the Palace and later with the king both in peace and in war.[137] Numerous Carolingian sources of a legal and epistolary nature demonstrate the effectiveness of this legislation.[138] Indeed, this legislation was so effective that an effort was made during the ninth century to forge royal *acta* that lightened these religio-military burdens on bishops.[139]

A second and very important role for at least some priests involved doing their "religious" service on the field of battle. These men were to carry holy relics ("patrocinia sanctorum") into battle for the purpose of winning supernatural support for the army.[140] In this context, the cloak of St. Martin of Tours, the famous *cappa* for which the royal chapel (*capella*) was named and where it was housed, was of primary importance.[141] This cloak was believed to have belonged to the great soldier-saint of the fourth century and was well known to have been a conspicuous part of Martin's Roman imperial army uniform.[142] The importance of the aristocratic-military holy man in Carolingian society reinforced the view of Martin as a soldier as well as a saint.[143]

Exactly which other holy relics were deployed in military operations remains obscure. The kind of general order promulgated by Carloman hardly would have been required only if the *cappa* and perhaps a small selection of other relics found in the mayoral or royal courts were to be carried into combat to support the troops spiritually.[144] Indeed, there is a lengthy history in the *regnum Francorum* of using local relics in the prosecution of locally based military operations. This tradition suggests that units mustered in various localities were accompanied in *expeditio* by at least some of their local saints.[145]

It seems that the cross in some form was also carried into battle by the early Carolingians. It is unlikely, however, that this was a large marching cross of the type used by early Byzantine armies and adopted by the Visigoths, as discussed above.[146] The early Carolingians instead used some form of banner — *vexillum* or *bandum* — on which a picture of the cross was imprinted. The Visigoths, following in the imperial tradition,[147] also had military banners blessed by the priests, and there is no reason to believe that these lacked religious significance.[148] Even some pagan Roman banners used in military operations had a sacral character.[149] As early as the sixth century banners also were used in the *regnum Francorum* in the context of a military march or procession that may perhaps have had religious overtones.[150] In addition, the *Labarum* employed by Constantine was well known in the early Middle Ages.[151]

Vigorous Carolingian dedication to *imitatio imperii* might lead one to intuit that Charlemagne's father and grandfather used some religious symbol in battle that was comparable to that employed by Constantine.[152] An early Carolingian sermon, most likely associated with Charles Martel's wars against the Muslims, calls attention on two occasions to the banner (*vexillum*) bearing the cross (*crux*) in battle.[153] In the first instance, the banner (*vexillum*) is carried into battle in front of the troops.[154] It seems possible, and this is speculation, that the banners carried into battle by Walter's *signiferi* in the *Waltharius*-epic bore one or more Christian symbols and did double duty as signals to the troops and as religious symbols to raise the soldiers' morale.[155]

In addition, soldiers during the early Middle Ages followed the tradition of singing songs or engaging in other forms of recitation while on the march.[156] These were likely the analogue of the vocal expression, *hymni* and *laudes*, mentioned above as being used in royal triumphal processions that followed military victories. In this context of procession and march, Venantius Fortunatus' *Pange lingua gloriosi proelium* and the eighth century anonymous *Ab ore verbum prolatum* are the types of hymns that likely were widely used[157] because they were written in "trochaic *septenarius*," the traditional Roman marching cadence.[158] Fortunatus' *Vexilla regis prodeunt* was probably of considerable importance in terms of both processions and religious banners discussed above.[159]

Yet, in terms of the broad spectrum of a chaplain's religious duties, neither the saying of masses for the troops nor carrying relics or banners into combat were likely their most consuming concern. Rather, these chaplains had to be available at all times to hear the confessions of the soldiers. In addition, Carloman's legislation emphasizes that these priests were to be prepared to make judgments ("iudicare") regarding the wide variety of penances to be done ("indicare poenitentiam") by the men who had confessed their sins ("qui hominibus peccata confitentibus").[160]

The hearing of confession in the spiritual regime described above was private between the priest and the person seeking absolution, as were the assignment of penance and the fulfillment of the obligations imposed on the penitent. Indeed, for Christians, in general, within the borders of the *regnum Francorum* from the later sixth century at least until early in the ninth century, the making of confession clearly was a far more frequent occurrence in a secular person's normal religious life than it had been earlier in the history of the West.[161]

Armies, as we have seen above, were of a considerable order of magnitude during the early Carolingian era, and the armed forces and their support personnel required a great many chaplains if comparatively frequent confession and penance were practiced. Just how many soldiers' confessions each priest could be expected to hear, especially in a period of great anxiety just prior to battle, cannot be assessed. Few soldiers who sought absolution on the eve of entering combat where life and limb were in the offing could be turned away if the morale of any particular individual or the unit as a whole was to be maintained. These confessions surely had to be very rapid affairs.

The academic preparation of these priests who were seconded to military duty for particular *expeditiones* was not extensive. Charlemagne's educational reforms were focused, in part, on educating large numbers of clerics for the purpose of looking after the spiritual health of the great masses of society within the empire.[162] However, since the military chaplains were clerics, who seem to have been selected for army service (so the phrase "ad hoc electi sunt" in Carloman's general order suggests), they may have been better educated than their confreres who were not summoned to war.[163] All matters concerning the army had an exceptionally high priority among the early Carolingians and thus the morale of the soldiers as well as their spiritual well being may have resulted in the selection of better-trained priests as military chaplains.

The ability of the chaplains to assign penances for sins should be seen in context of the *libelli poenitentiali*. These little pamphlets or handbooks, a copy of which each parish priest was required to have, were cobbled together in large numbers for penitential use throughout the Frankish *regna* during the eighth century on the basis of exemplars brought to the mainland from Ireland and England beginning in the seventh century at the latest. The schedules of penance provided in these little books dominated the process by which sinners were reconciled to the Lord during the early Carolingian period.[164]

The great success of these *libelli* likely was due in large part to their simple structure: an extensive list of sins to which were juxtaposed an equally straightforward list of penances. For very good reason they have come to be called "tariff books."[165] When the sinner, a soldier in the context under consideration here, completed his confession to the chaplain, he was assigned his penance according to the schedule.[166] The process was so uncomplicated (undoubtedly the intention of those who had seen to the large-scale creation of these little books) that even soldiers who were deeply ignorant or not very intelligent had little trouble understanding the principle at issue. By paying the debt that they had incurred for the sins that they had committed they were reconciled with God. As one contemporary military sermon put it: "Do not carry your sins with you into battle for Christ; but before going into battle confess to the priest."[167]

The simplification of the penitential system to meet the needs of a society that on the whole was not very deeply Christianized from a theological perspective may have had a corollary in regard to the condition of the clergy. Many of the priests mobilized to attend to the spiritual needs of the armies of the early Carolingians, not to mention those who tended their flocks throughout the *regnum Francorum* but who were not called upon for service in the military, were rather poorly educated and some may have been illiterate. Charlemagne's educational program, as noted above, was focused in part upon developing a clergy that was educated. Boniface's letter to Pope Zacharias, in which he grumbled about a poorly educated priest who had garbled a baptism rite,[168] is often cited, perhaps somewhat unfairly, by scholars who see the unpreparedness of the early Carolingian clergy as a widespread phenomenon.[169]

The simple lists of sins and schedules for penance were probably memorized by some priests who thus would be prepared to do their duty despite being unable to read well or even to read at all. Hincmar of Rheims, writing during the second half of the ninth century, was still concerned that priests memorize considerable bodies of material so that they could carry out their obligations in a satisfactory manner. Whether this may be taken as evidence that these priests could not read is problematic; a shortage of texts may also account for some priests committing various important items to memory.[170] In any case, the rather mechanical nature of the penitential process — identify the sin and locate the appropriate penance in the schedule — made it unnecessary for the priest to know much theology or to think deeply or seriously about the matter of absolution.[171]

An entry from a typical penitential regarding a particular sin and its penance for a layman reads: "If anyone is the violator of a tomb, he is to do penance for five years, three on bread and water."[172] However, for purposes of memorization by the uneducated or poorly educated priest all that was necessary was an abbreviation of the schedule, such as "homicide, adultery, perjury, fornication, three years," as found in the so-called *Poenitentiale Parisiense II*, drawn up around 750.[173]

Killing in war, unlike mundane crimes in civilian life such as homicide and adultery, was only nominally punished, and the soldiers in early Carolingian armies were made very well aware of this.[174] Perhaps most important for those soldiers who were about to enter combat was the knowledge that by killing a man (enemy soldier?) in a *bellum publicum* or in battle (*proelium*) while under the command of his king (*rex*), he was liable for a penance, in the worst case, of only forty days on bread and water.[175] In practice and in the view of some important Church figures, even these very slight penances were being ignored.[176]

Thus, Rhabanus Maurus, the great conservative among Carolingian ecclesiastical intellectuals, understood that soldiers, while under the command of the king or presumably his legitimately delegated surrogate ("in proelio commissio iussu principum"), were not required by contemporaries to do any penance after they had killed enemy troops in battle. Rhabanus also recognized that this "new tradition" was being defended on the intellectual plane despite the fact that it was in contravention of ancient practice.[177] Indeed, decades earlier, Charlemagne had dealt very severely with clerics who failed to participate in his program, and the pope traditionally gave his support to royal policy in these matters.[178] The old penitential tradition, which required that a person who had killed an enemy soldier in war and who had completed his penance should never again take up arms, had long been unenforced and was, in fact, unenforceable.[179]

With regard to the spiritual component of army morale, early Carolingian soldiers, who confessed and did penance, thus were rather easily absolved and therefore encouraged to see themselves as going off to war with souls unblemished by sin.[180] From the perspective of such soldiers, who were preparing to enter combat in "God's army" under the command of a *princeps*, who was a *famulus Dei*, the clear conscience afforded by frequent and secret confession to a priest created in many men a sense of equanimity if not spiritual elation. Despite apparent efforts by church reformers to alter the situation, secret confession was still available to soldiers as late as the battle of Fontenoy in 842.[181]

In addition to the traditional battle harangue, discussed above, which was used, at least in part, for raising soldiers' morale, prayers also seem to have been said, at least on some occasions, just before going into combat. For example, in the spring of 754, when the armies of Pippin were about to engage the forces of the Lombard king, Aistulf, in the Alpine passes leading into Italy, the Carolingian court chronicler says: "The Franks realized that neither with their allies nor with their native troops would they be able to win the battle. Thus, they called upon God and prayed for the help of the Blessed apostle Peter." Then, after the prayers had been said, "they committed themselves to the battle bravely" and "with God helping (Deo adiuuante), King Pippin won the victory."[182]

The complex of spiritual aid for the soldier, officers as well as the rank and file, can be seen in the genre that came to be known later in the history of the West as the military sermon.[183] These documents in very simple language — "Viri, fratres et patres, qui christianum nomen habetis et vexillum crucis in fronte portatis, attendite et audite!"[184] — were of great solace for the vast majority of the troops of the early Carolingian armies who understood what may still be called Latin.[185] Thus, in consonance with the liturgy for the masses, discussed above, in such sermons various themes are reiterated in a particularly repetitive style:

1. When you go to war in the name of Christ you go "deo adiuvante."[186]
2. In your prayers always invoke "deum . . . auxilium."[187]
3. Know that when you invoke God's *auxilium*, the Lord will go against your enemies.[188]

No less important was that the soldier was to confess before going into combat.[189] In one contemporary sermon confession appears five times in the first two hundred words:

1. Confess before going "viriliter in acie Christi."
2. The confession of sins is necessary ("Confessionem igitur peccatorum . . . necesse").
3. To all "est confessio necessaria."
4. Confess in order to cure the "vulnera peccatorum."
5. No one can be saved without confession ("nemo enim se sine confessione salvari posse").[190]

War, however, must be just war, as noted above, in the speech attributed to Pippin II. Thus, the soldiers are told that they are not to go to war ("bellum gerere") for worldly purposes ("pro pompa saeculare") but "pro defensione Christiani nominis et ecclesiarum dei."[191] In the matter of military conduct, it is necessary not to act "contra legem Christianam."[192] This notion of legality is further developed in the context of obtaining God's help. Thus, when the soldier is on campaign (*itinere*) to fight for God, he must follow the *lex Dei* so that Christ's angel may defend him and protect his camp (*kastra*). The sermon avers that "the shield of piety (*scutum pietatis*)" defends the soldier against his enemies.[193] Most important here, however, is that in the just war, the enemy you are fighting does not fight against you but against God.[194]

In the sermon under discussion here, the repetitive theme of God giving victory to the just cause gradually gives way to concern for the spiritual health of the soldier. The soldier who will have handed himself over ("tradiderit") to the military service of God — note the analogue with the *miles* who has handed himself over into the retinue (*obsequium*) of his secular *dominus* — will be saved. Thus, "the *remuneratio* for the soldier's *labor* will be to receive *aeternam vitam* with the Lord (*Dominus*) and he will rest in peace in paradise with the rest of his heirs."[195] For the soldier to receive these benefits when he suffers death in battle, however, he must, before going into battle, confess his sins to the priest ("antea [praelium Christi] configeatur sacerdoti").[196] Finally, the soldier is reminded, "fight for God and God fights for you."[197]

The repetitive nature, simple prose, and brevity of the sermon all fit very well with the aim of succinctly elevating the soldier's morale and cause him no psychological or spiritual confusion. Indeed, the soldier is even told that foraging (*rapina*) is justified if he needed to obtain food ("necessitas ad victualia pertinet") during the course of a just war.[198] It is important to underline the brevity of the sermon, 526 words. It survives in a copy done in a shorthand of thirty-three lines,[199] and a clerk may have copied this sermon when it was delivered by the bishop so that it could be sent as an *epistola* (thus the title in the surviving shorthand version) to other prelates as a model for a military sermon.

The religious commitment of the soldier is expressed with great effect by the *Waltharius*-poet, who depicts his hero at prayer in what he knows will be only an "intermission" between two phases of a deadly combat. First, in preparation for his prayer, Walter of Aquitaine faces the East ("contra orientalem . . . partem"). He then prostrates himself on the ground ("prostratus corpore") rather than appealing to God in the traditional standing *orans* position. Perhaps because he is cautious, as every good soldier is taught, Walter keeps his naked sword in his hand ("ensem nudum retinens") as he prays. The poet is not indulging here in satire, and he gives his listeners no reason to believe that Walter's actions constitute some sort of sacrilegious behavior.[200]

Walter prays:

> Oh Maker of things and Arranger of all
> that is made, indeed, He without whose permission
> and whose command nothing exists, I give thanks.
> I give thanks to Him who defends me from the
> hostile spears of the enemy battle formation
> (*turma*) and [He who defends me], also no less from
> disgrace. I pray to the benign Lord, contrite in
> mind (*in mente*), that He, who wishes to destroy
> sins but not the sinners, may grant to me the
> favor that these sinners may be seen by me in the
> heavenly seat [of power].[201]

Something of the ideal envisioned by early Carolingian policy makers may be identified in developing and maintaining the morale of the army on the eve of battle and in combat through spiritual means. Masses were said so that God would give victory to the early Carolingian *princeps* or *rex* and to the army. The ruler was seen as God's servant (*famulus*) and the *exercitus* as God's army. Prayers were said in order to minimize the number of casualties suffered by the soldiers. Prayers for God's aid were made not only in the soldiers' masses, but with masses and fasts being carried out in churches throughout the kingdom toward the end of the eighth century, at the latest.[202]

For the individual soldier, chaplains served with the army so that they might hear confession and impose penance. Indeed, soldiers who worried whether they had been properly baptized could be initiated on the battlefield by priests—bishops, it was decreed, were not needed in such emergencies.[203] Following confession, the troops were to go to mass and then into battle with unblemished souls—death would bring them salvation. Even in the midst of battle, however, as the *Waltharius*-poet makes clear, the soldier, with his naked sword still in hand and likely stained by the blood of his adversaries, could declare to God that he was "contrite in mind." Thus, the soldier could confess directly to God and be absolved before the battle continued. Holy Mary, Mother of God, was also sought through prayer to aid the soldier in battle.[204]

The soldiers who had confessed to priests prior to battle had great confidence that many of these same priests would be available to administer last rites should they suffer a mortal wound and in the final act oversee Christian burial in the field.[205] The salvation of soldiers who had particularly bad reputations or who somehow were thought not to have been appropriately prepared for death in religious terms also was a matter of concern. Even the man who because of his *crimines*, and soldiers surely were not immune from such behavior, was thought not to merit salvation ("non meretur gloria") had prayers said for him in order to limit the *tormenta* that his soul would suffer.[206] After some battles a fast was proclaimed for the survivors in the army so that by their sacrifice they could win remission of the sins of their *conmilitiones* who had fallen in combat.[207]

Bishops assigned to serve with the army for one or another campaign preached straightforward but repetitive sermons in simple and easily understandable Latin that emphasized the above-mentioned themes. While the army was going into battle, some of the clergy assigned to military service carried holy relics, such as the military cloak of St. Martin and the banner of the cross (*vexillum crucis*), before the troops as they all marched into battle. Hymns were recited or sung. Fortunatus' *Vexilla regis*, with sentiments indicating that as the banners of the king go forward and the mystery of the cross gleams with a depiction of the flesh that redeemed souls were favorites. Indeed, as sung in *Vexilla regis*, the tale told by the prophet David is fulfilled.[208]

After the battle was over and the military objectives were accomplished, in ceremonies God was given extensive if not total credit for the victory. These triumphs, as seen above, were quasi-religious ceremonies in which hymns and *laudes* were sung. Various other types of thanksgiving efforts of a religious nature were also undertaken. The suggestion of the sometime theologian Cath-

wulf to Charlemagne, following the capture of Pavia in 774, to offer thanksgiving "with all your armies" ("cum omnibus exercitibus tuis") and "with your
entire kingdom" ("cum omni regno tuo") was probably not an innovation.[209]
Indeed, kingdom-wide efforts of a religious nature were put into operation a
quarter-century or so earlier by Pippin when he was Mayor of the Palace.[210] By
765, broadly based liturgies for thanksgiving to God for his propitious intervention were commonplace.[211] Regular liturgical celebrations of military victories,
with what would undoubtedly have been attendant thanksgiving to the Lord of
Hosts, may have entered the calendar of the Church under the early Carolingians.[212]

On the whole, the early Carolingians were very thorough in ensuring the
spiritual comfort of their troops. This, in turn, helped to develop high morale
among the soldiers. By the reign of Charlemagne, governmental policies in this
regard resulted in the widespread belief that the gates of heaven were open to
worthy soldiers (*milites*).[213] Indeed, Pope Stephen II, when writing to Frankish
magnates in 753 (while trying to encourage King Pippin to provide military aid
to the papacy), made it clear that the soldiers who fought well in this struggle on
behalf of Rome would be assured of eternal salvation.[214] Before the middle of the
ninth century, the papacy regularized this position, and Pope Leo IV proclaimed
that any fighting man who was killed in battle and who died in the Christian
faith was not to be deprived of entry into heaven.[215]

Conclusion

High troop morale has been and continues to be a central element in military
success both in the short term and in the long term throughout Western civilization. Pippin II and his successors understood the importance of high troop
morale and undertook numerous initiatives to assure that their soldiers had the
necessary material and psychological resources. In a material sense, the early
Carolingians developed the logistic infrastructure required to keep their armies
well supplied and well equipped even when undertaking lengthy sieges far from
home. In addition, professional troops, especially those who served in the royal
obsequium, were well paid. Lower-class elements of society (poor men and even
servi) who served in the military households of the magnates were given opportunities for considerable social and economic advancement as *vassalli*. The
service of part-time militia soldiers, who participated in expeditionary service
likely in lieu of paying land taxes, was overseen by the central government to
keep their military efforts from becoming an excessive economic burden. In
addition, both professional soldiers and militia levies could obtain rewards in

the wake of successful military actions in terms of booty taken from the enemy in both movable wealth and landed resources.

In addition, the early Carolingians maintained a strategic inclination, today identified as the doctrine of overwhelming force, which generally permitted the armies of Pippin II and his successors to outnumber their adversaries. This advantage was undergirded by training and strengthened by a very able command structure. Victories were very well publicized through the use of the triumph as part of a Carolingian commitment to *imitatio imperii*. One important result of these ceremonies was that the society, in general, and those who served in the army, in particular, were well aware of a lengthy tradition of military success. Early Carolingian commanders, moreover, were not regarded as pursuing glory for its own sake and at the expense of the well-being of the rank and file of the army.

The mobilization of large armies that were supplied by an effective logistic system and imbued with a tradition of success had a psychological impact as well as practical importance. The early Carolingians also undertook key policies to sustain the spiritual well-being of the army. Sermons were delivered to the troops as the religious counterpart of the battle harangues. Both genres emphasized the just cause of the wars being fought, the army's tradition of victory, and God's role. No less important in a spiritual context was the provision of a corps of chaplains for the army who were mandated to hear confession and provide absolution so that when the soldiers went into battle they were assured of salvation in the event of death. The use of relics and religious banners on the battlefield, itself, helped to enhance the soldiers' sense of fighting a just war for God and in His name.

CHAPTER FIVE

Battlefield Tactics

The focus of military tactics is the deployment of troops in preparation for battle, the sequence of the combat, and the deployment following military engagement. The tactics a military commander uses are dictated most obviously by what knowledge he has absorbed during the course of his training and career. For example, a commander cannot order his men to execute a feigned retreat unless he knows of the existence of such a tactic. Second, even if the commander has specific knowledge of a particular tactic, he cannot expect it to succeed unless his troops have been trained previously in its execution. One cannot even imagine the execution of the *toloutegon* without the extensive training and drill discussed above in Chapter 3. In addition to the training and size of his own forces, the commander must take into consideration the size and training of the enemy force as well as its deployment in the context of the terrain, among other variables. Finally, the tactics must reflect the larger campaign strategy. Thus, a defensive deployment in a static infantry emplacement through the use of a phalanx formation might thwart an enemy advance. Conversely, a surprise mounted charge against the unprotected flank of such an infantry formation might dislodge the enemy from its position.

The purpose of the military training, discussed above, was to allow commanders to deploy their soldiers in various types of combat situations. The quality of the training of early Carolingian soldiers may be assessed, at least in part, from how well these men executed the tactics ordered by their commanders. It must be recognized at the outset, however, that soldiers such as those mobilized in the armies of the early Carolingians, who consistently succeeded over a lengthy period of time in numerous types of tactical deployments, are likely not only to have been well trained but also to have executed their tactical assignments effectively. The consistent Carolingian success over time suggests that this success was not the result of mere chance or accident.

Insights into early Carolingian military tactics can be obtained, in large part, from accounts of soldiers' "proper behavior" in battle. Conversely, when the army's execution of its mission had not been satisfactory, we can still learn something of the tactics employed from contemporary accounts of such failures. It is important, however, not to accept descriptions of errors or of other lapses by commanders or by the rank and file of the army as evidence for military norms. Indeed, monkish chroniclers and their ecclesiastical brethren often highlighted all kinds of errors as well as the failures of military discipline, using the perspective not of tactics but of clerical or religious values.[1] Some clerical writers even embellished their accounts, and these distortions have prevented some too trusting modern researchers from obtaining a balanced view of what occurred on the field of battle or during the course of a siege.[2]

It was common, if not the norm, throughout the Middle Ages for many ecclesiastical writers to depict the secular world as evil and to characterize violence, especially in war, as at or near the apex of such evil. Since military conflict was rather common, properly dedicated monks and other churchmen when writing history often manipulated the facts in order to teach their audiences the putatively appropriate religious lesson.[3] While embracing this view, these same clerics identified the life led by holy men, dedicated to peace in the model of Jesus, as the only course worth following.[4] The inclination of some modern scholars, particularly those of a primitivist bent, to accept such distortions as indicative of the norms of military behavior has been discussed above in Chapter 3.

The military handbooks available to the Carolingians, discussed above, may provide insight into a particular chronicle account of a military action. In addition, narrative accounts may confirm whether tactics discussed in the handbooks were, in fact, put into use. This type of cross-checking, however, also has its own methodological problems. For example, the handbooks, including Vegetius' *De re Militari*, taught that a general should deploy his forces preparatory for battle with the sun at his back and thus in the eyes of his adversary. When a chronicler describes such a situation, however, especially with his principal using the prescribed tactic successfully, the author may depict the use of the "proper" tactical deployment as a subtle means of praising the "book learning" of the general in question. This is especially likely if the chronicler says something to the effect that the commander who deployed his troops in a particular manner was following the teaching of Vegetius.[5] For such a chronicler the use of books in military affairs was considered to be a habit worthy of praise among the subject's contemporary readers and listeners.

When an author praises his principal, one must be very sensitive to context. Was the tactic under discussion appropriate or even possible in the situation that is being considered? For example, if the chronicler's principal deployed his forces to the east of his adversary at dusk in a Western European theater of operations, he could not position himself so that the sun was in the eyes of the enemy. This approach to the sources, originally labeled *Sachkritik* by German scholars, can be rendered into English as testing against "objective reality": does objective reality permit the described behavior?[6] Accounts that fail the test of *Sachkritik* must be disqualified as evidence for the military tactics that they purport to describe. Of course, such "errors" by a chronicler or the author of some other type of text may still tell us a great deal about his *parti pris* and/or his methods, as well as his appreciation of the interests and abilities of his intended audience.

Less dramatic, but no less important than the matter of "objective reality" is the relationship between the author of the text under consideration and his principal or patron. When, for example, the chronicler and his patron can be shown to be well acquainted and the former also demonstrates knowledge of a handbook such as Vegetius' *De re Militari*, the military commander probably also knew something of the text in question. In light of the early Carolingian court structure, discussed earlier, and the patronage dispensed by major figures such as Charles Martel's half-brother Childebrand, there seems to have been close integration between intellectuals and men of action (the members of the *magistratus*, who drew up the government's military plans).[7] Men such as Pippin's nephew Adalhard of Corbie and Witiza-Benedict, who have been discussed above in some detail, were both intellectuals and men of action who were well trained in military matters.

The fact that Einhard states that Charlemagne regularly listened to the reading of ancient histories and *gesta*[8] suggests that the king and his advisers were aware of Roman military tactics and strategy as adumbrated in these works. Indeed, the works by Ammianus Marcellinus, Velleius Paterculus, and Florus are only some of the many histories to which the early Carolingians had access and copied so that multiple exemplars were available.[9] The importance of the study of history for early medieval intellectuals, their patrons, and principals was made clear by Isidore of Seville, who said, following his classical sources, that those who would be statesmen were to read history so that they would benefit from the experience of the past.[10] Isidore's encyclopaedia was a key reference work for any educated person at the Carolingian court.[11]

Future kings' training included exposure to "book learning." Charles Martel sent his son, Pippin, Charlemagne's father, to the monastery of St. Denis for some sort of education, and also later to the comparatively highly cultured Lombard royal court at Pavia.[12] Childebrand and his son, Nibelung (Pippin's uncle and cousin, respectively), who sponsored the court chronicle of Fredegar's Continuator, were among those court figures who had more than a passing interest in history. They had the *historia* and the *gesta* of the Franks written down, and putatively they oversaw the project *diligentissime*.[13] Perhaps not incidentally, Childebrand was one of Charles Martel's most important generals and seems to have been Pippin's closest military adviser during the latter's early career.[14] That the early Carolingians were in a position to learn from books concerning training and tactics is not an issue. Indeed, classical commanders did so, and the Frankish near obsession with *imitatio imperii*, if nothing else, gave the early Carolingians sufficient impetus to do the same.

In this chapter, the focus for the study of Carolingian battlefield tactics is on two engagements: Poitiers in 732, where Charles Martel defeated the Muslims, and the Süntal in 782, where a force of Saxons under the command of Widukind defeated a Carolingian army. The battle of Rimini in 533 between the Franks and Byzantines is used here to cast light on the background of Carolingian tactics. The discussion of battlefield tactics is prefaced by a discussion of unit cohesion, a prerequisite for tactical success. Siege tactics are treated in detail in Chapter 6.

Unit Cohesion

Experienced soldiers and historians agree that unit cohesion is a *sine qua non* for success at all levels of military operation. Continuing and consistent military success over a lengthy period of time, whether on the open battlefield or in siege operations, of the type enjoyed by the armies of the early Carolingian era requires unit cohesion. Cohesion of small units or units working together within larger forces makes it possible for the latter to succeed, and large armies that are not subdivided into effective and thus cohesive smaller groups generally have little chance of success.

The question at issue, therefore, is not whether early Carolingian armies enjoyed a high level of unit cohesion but rather how this was created. Among the basic elements, discussed above, that help to bring about unit cohesion at all levels are extensive military training and high morale.[15] Under the early Carolingians, as we have seen, the elite troops, *milites*, of the royal military household were formed into relatively small units, each under its own commanding officer or *capitaneus*. Adalhard of Corbie in his *De ordine palatii* reports these units to have had high morale due in large part to regular, generous material support. However, Adalhard also draws attention to the important role of the close relations between the officers and their men. He emphasizes that the former frequently invited their men to dinner at the officer's mess and found other ways to reward them, including valuable military decorations.

This close relation between officers and the men who serve under them is of importance in the development of unit cohesion as officers at all levels of command strive to be considered *conmilitio*. The emperor Valentinian put it very well, as reported by Ammianus Marcellinus, when he emphasized that the officers were to learn to bear heat, snow, frost, thirst, and sleepless nights with their troops. Indeed, the emperor said that the commander "will not hesitate to risk his life in order to save his men who are in danger" (*Hist.*, 27.6.8,9).[16] During the Middle Ages, not only was the emperor Trajan regarded as a hero, despite being a pagan; his behavior was also thought worthy of emulation by Carolingian intellectuals, in large part owing to his great reputation as *conmilitio*.[17]

In his Latin epic, intended for an educated court audience, the *Waltharius*-poet emphasized that early Carolingian officers were to be able to endure and even surpass the hardships suffered by the men. Rhabanus Maurus, in his commentary on Vegetius' *De re Militari*, departed substantially from Vegetius in commenting on the appropriate age for the beginning of military training. He emphasizes that future officers — in particular young men trained by veteran soldiers (*milites*) in the households of important men (*principes*) — are taught to tolerate very harsh and adverse conditions. These "discomforts," according to Rhabanus, include hunger, extreme cold, and excessive heat.[18]

In living together and training together, men in such groups develop a family-like spirit that today we call bonding. This is often manifested in friendly competition between units and most important in the ethic that a soldier feels himself remiss, even shamed, if he does not fully support his comrades in battle. This closeness in such battle groups likely accounts, at least in part, for the personal despair Angelbert expresses in his poem for the loss of his friends at the battle of Fontenoy. His unit had composed the first line of the infantry phalanx and, as we have seen, he was the only man from that group to survive the battle. Angelbert knew that he had done his best in the battle line. His very close bond with his fellow soldiers was a force in the development of unit cohesion on the battlefield.

Living together, eating together, and fighting together also marked the lives of the *vassalli* and *pueri* who served in the military households of the important men seconded to the royal *palatium* in order to serve the king. These soldiers also received support from their *domini*. Indeed, there was more than a little competition for recognition as first-class soldiers among these non-royal groups, those groups of *milites* that are identified as serving in the king's *obsequium*, and probably with those of the queen's *schola*, as well. The king provided the model for the way the proper commander related to his troops, and the favor Charlemagne showed to the bodyguards and units of his *satellites*, whom he invited into the swimming pool at Aachen, may well have been copied in one way or another by the magnates.

Non-royal military units also likely partook of this same military group culture that helped to develop small unit cohesion. For example, the troop of 110 heavily armed *milites*, who served at St. Riquier, discussed earlier, was housed in its own particular neighborhood (*vicus*) near the monastery, separate from that of the other *vici* of the town. The *milites*, by sharing this common living space, enjoyed a local identity as well as a professional one and this also enhanced group identity. Troops in the retinues of secular magnates, where young boys were taken into the household for training under the guidance of old soldiers, in a manner similar to that found at the royal court, also developed a family-like relationship.

The objective conditions for small-group cohesion and high morale that obtained in regard to these professional soldiers, discussed above, fit in the tradition of Western civilization. By contrast, the situation is somewhat less obvious with regard to the civilian-soldiers or militia men mobilized for the expeditionary forces of the early Carolingians from the countryside and from towns. The local count of the *pagus* or his surrogate (the viscount) typically mobilized and led the forces from his administrative district. Therefore, the expeditionary levies of part-time militia men from early on in the history of the *regnum Francorum* enjoyed an obvious regional identity such as *Cenomanses*, men of Maine, or *Andegavenses*, men of Anjou.[19]

This narrow regional identity, based upon the *pagus*, was, as seen above in Chapter 2, further refined at the local level where men were recruited from administrative units such as the hundred or, lacking this, the village or even some smaller entity such as a villa. Where the comital authority had been bypassed by secular and ecclesiastical magnates, who had been granted immunities by the royal government, the expeditionary forces mobilized from the lands within the jurisdiction of a particular monastery, such as Fulda or St. Denis, saw themselves as the men of St. Peter and of St. Denis, respectively. If such men did not execute their assigned military duties in a proper manner, they not only would have failed to give satisfactory support to their comrades in the unit in which they served. In addition, these men failed to give the proper allegiance to the saint or saints with whom they were identified.

Social and geographical mobility tended to be rather limited during the early Middle Ages. Thus, men living within a rather small administrative circumscription, mentioned above, were often related to each other through blood and/or marriage. Therefore, geographical and familial closeness reinforced one another in giving a sense of cohesion and obligation to militia forces, similar to that among the professional soldiers in the fictive family of the *obsequia* that served the king and the magnates.

Also at the local level, various associations were based upon common secular and religious interests. Sometimes such groups were held together by oaths, *coniurationes*. The relation of these local groups to guilds of various types of craftsmen, as seen above with regard to the *vici* at St. Riquier, remains problematic, as are the origins of confraternities or prayer associations for creating social cohesion at the local level.[20] It can be ventured, however, that whatever local institutions contributed to social cohesion in civilian matters had the same effect in the military. The militia men who served in early Carolingian expeditionary forces were only part-time soldiers, primarily civilians, and thus they shared nonmilitary associations with their local acquaintances.

Yet another category of general association that developed a sense of group cohesion that carried over into military organization was that of ethnic identity. During the early Middle Ages, in general, and no less in the Carolingian era, ethnic identity enjoyed a basis in law. Thus, as will be seen below, King Pippin understood the importance of recognizing the principle of personality of the law in Aquitaine after he had reintegrated the region into the *regnum Francorum* following his final victory over Duke Waiofar in 768. In regard to ethnic identity there were, in addition to the Franks, many other groups such as Romans, Saxons, Gascons, Bavarians, Burgundians, and Alamanni living within the lands dominated by the early Carolingians. As late as 842, as we have seen above, various units were still identifiable as being composed of Saxons, Gascons, and Bretons. Indeed, such ethnic units practiced military drills against each other in highly structured training exercises.

At the very general level, the ethnic costume, broadly defined, identified military units. For example, well after the foundation of the Romano-German kingdoms on erstwhile imperial territory in the West, various ethnic groups continued to maintain peculiar ways for self-identification. Saxons, for example, were settled in military colonies in what came to be considered Merovingian Gaul. Moreover, during the later sixth century, the descendants of these men continued to cut their hair and beards in a special way that made it obvious that they still considered themselves to be Saxons. Similarly, the Bretons followed tonsorial practices that permitted them to be differentiated from both Saxons and Franks.[21]

The Gascons from south of the Garonne, by contrast, or at least mounted troops mobilized from this region, wore a distinctive ethnic costume that included a shirt with long and flowing sleeves that billowed out at the cuffs, full trousers, which were very different from those traditionally worn by Franks, as will be seen below. The Gascon horsemen tucked these trousers into rather low-cut leather boots. These Gascons also habitually wore spurs. This costume was topped, at least not in the coldest weather, with a short "rounded" cloak of some type. Setting themselves apart extended to weapons. The Gascon mounted troops apparently were best known for being armed with a throwing spear rather than with long spears or one or another particular type of sword, such as the *gladius* or *spatha*.[22]

Yet another way in which distinctions are traditionally made to give units a group identity, the *sine qua non* for unit cohesion, is through uniforms and/or other insignia, including banners. Groups of Franks, for example, early on in their history, as we have seen above, had been recruited into Roman imperial forces, and in due course, like all other soldiers, they were provided with identifying insignia and uniforms. The insignia were recorded and depicted in the *Notitia Dignitatum* as already noted. Procopius, in commenting on military matters north of the Alps, makes clear that in his time, the descendants of men who had served in Roman imperial units during the mid-fifth century in the West of Gaul were still, a century later, wearing the types of uniforms and carrying copies of the banners that their forefathers had used.[23]

The professional element of armies that had flourished during the later Roman empire were gradually disbanded in the West, and the *obsequia* of the kings and their magnates became the professional soldiers of the early Middle Ages. Indeed, in imitation of their recent past, Gallo-Roman magnates were expected to supply their household troops with uniforms or, at the least, with funds to purchase their military cloaks (*paludes*), as well as with appropriate armaments and *stipendia*.[24] Such retinues, clad in uniforms or cloaks, whether we consider them to be professional soldiers or mercenaries or some less formal type of unit, clearly had the opportunity to develop the kind of group cohesion that is under discussion here.

Frankish magnates, like their Gallo-Roman counterparts, also provided uniforms for the professional soldiers who served in their military *obsequia*. Toward the end of the fifth century, Sidonius Apollinaris describes the men who served in the household of the youthful Frankish royal prince named Sigismir. In writing to his friend Dominicius, who is characterized as greatly appreciating displays of arms and armed men, Sidonius observes that Sigismir's troops wear uniform foot gear to ankle height but with the "hairy" side of the leather on the outside. He notes as well that these men do not wear trousers but rather a "shirt" that extends to the mid-thigh and has short sleeves. These shirts exhibit an explosion of color but all apparently were of the same pattern. Over this array, the soldiers wore long military cloaks (*sagum*), all green with crimson borders. Over their right shoulder the troops wore studded sword belts and carried a short sword, *gladius*, on their left side. The shield, also carried on the left side, was white with a gilded *umbo* and a silvered rim.[25]

Providing uniforms for household troops was not limited to secular magnates. Bishop Praejectus, toward the latter part of the seventh century, provided uniforms or cloaks to the troops who served in his military retinue (*comitatus*). The soldiers who wore these costumes could be identified as the bishop's men as a result of their dress. When these mercenary soldiers deserted their episcopal employer to avoid or even to ensure his bloody fate, the first thing that they did was to throw away their uniforms ("vestibus nudati").[26] These troops had also been supplied with a rather uniform set of arms, by which they also might have been identified, and which they jettisoned ("armis expoliati") along with their uniforms when they deserted.[27] Their shields (see below) or their sword scabbards likely were marked in some uniform manner which also identified them as the bishop's men.

At the early Carolingian royal court, the members of the units of professional soldiers wore various uniforms. Notker describes with considerable hyperbole the parade of Charlemagne's army in which the officers (*duces*) appear like Joshua did in the *castra* of Gilgal (Josh. 10:6–7) and his guard units (*exercitus*) appear like that which drove the Syrians and Assyrians out of Samaria (II Kings 6:14).[28] According to Notker, ambassadors from the palace of Haroun al Rashid in Baghdad marveled at the novelty of the uniforms and arms ("novitatem . . . vestimentorum sive armorum") worn by the members of Charlemagne's *exercitus* and their officers (*proceres*) who were attached to the court.[29]

Even units of the nonmilitary household staff that served the Carolingian emperor were uniformed. For example, the uniform of the men who served the king's meals and perhaps prepared his food impressed foreign ambassadors and guests. The officer (*magister mensae*) who commanded this particular staff, a part of which went on military campaign with the king, was a high-ranking court official.[30] Charlemagne seems to have been wedded to the notion of a court society dressed in uniforms by rank and order in the context of *imitatio imperii*. He even ordered uniforms for the *janitores* who opened and closed the doors of the palace church.[31]

The military uniforms worn by the Frankish soldiers attached to the early Carolingian court seem to have been highly standardized.[32] In addition, they resemble the uniforms worn some four centuries earlier by Sigismir's *obsequium* described above. According to Notker, the palace troops had a "shiny white" uniform shirt, *camisia*, probably made either of a very finely finished bleached woolen cloth or of bleached linen.[33] The uniform "britches," designed in a segmented manner of some sort, were made of linen, dyed scarlet, and decorated with fancy embroidery. Around the lower leg, presumably from below the knee to the ankle, the soldiers wound scarlet linen wraps or what today we would call puttees. Each soldier was outfitted with leather boots that were gilded on the outside and had laces that were four feet in length. These laces or thongs were tied in a uniform and highly stylized criss-cross pattern over the puttees. The uniform cloak, *pallum*, was very long, and extended in the front and the back to the shoe tops, and very probably was made of wool since Notker emphasizes the matter of its warmth in cold weather. These cloaks were either dyed blue or bleached white and thus may have indicated further divisions within the royal guard units. Below the cloak, each soldier wore a sheathed long sword, *spatha*, probably in an over-the-shoulder harness. The sword sheath, likely constructed of thin wooden slats, had a leather covering over which a second cover of highly waxed white linen had been placed.[34]

Although we do not know whether one unit of the *obsequium regalis* was formally or informally called the "blues" and another the "whites" on the basis of the cloaks that they wore, such types of identifying sobriquets are common in military life. Some Frankish units wore striped cloaks, but whether this was in place of the blue and white cloaks (as Notker seems to think) or simply the uniform of yet other troops is problematic.[35] Cloak production for the military in the Carolingian world, if not for society in general, was monopolized by the Frisians, and cloaks were likely made of wool.[36] The Frisians also produced cloaks in gray and crimson in addition to white and sapphire blue.[37] Thus, the early Carolingians could have provided uniform cloaks to their troops in a wide variety of colors so that various military units could easily be distinguished from each other.[38]

Thus far, we have discussed briefly the uniforms of the particular military units attached to the early Carolingian court and those men who served in the military households of important lay and ecclesiastical magnates. In addition, according to court practices, the early Carolingians saw to it that virtually every group connected to the court wore uniforms or identifying *ornamenta*, such as badges of some kind. The court made a widespread effort to develop small group cohesion and group identification even beyond the military sphere proper. As noted above, Charlemagne was thoroughly wedded to the notion of a society that was dressed in uniforms by rank and order in the context of *imitatio imperii*.

From the military perspective, having uniforms could also be a liability. For example, being identified by one's uniform when on the losing side, as seen in the discussion of the mercenaries who deserted Praejectus, could be a problem. Early in the wars against the Saxons, the Franks also suffered because they were uniformed. A foraging party (*pabulatores*) of Franks returning to its camp (*castra*) in full daylight, about 3:00 P.M. (the ninth hour), was infiltrated by a substantial force of Saxons who then entered the fortification and did considerable damage. The Saxons infiltrated the foraging party and then entered the *castra*, because their trickery (*fraude*) made them indistinguishable from the Franks.[39] The Saxons' *ruse de guerre* was effective because they had either stolen Frankish uniforms or made reasonably accurate imitations.

For the development of group cohesion, in addition to uniforms, officers of various units could be identified by their helmet decorations.[40] For example, some men wore a horse tail (*equina cauda*) on their helmets, while others wore different colored crests. Walter of Aquitaine is described by the poet as wearing a "red-crested helmet."[41] Numerous manuscript illustrations from the Carolingian period depict helmets of various designs and types of crests, which still require sorting out.[42] In addition, shields were painted (*picta*) with recognizable designs; these may have been carried by soldiers or only officers.[43] As with helmets, illustrations on shields often depict various types of designs.[44]

The Battle of Poitiers

On a very bloody Saturday afternoon, 25 October 732, not far from the fortress city of Poitiers, Charles Martel's army met in open battle and soundly defeated a large Muslim force under the direct command of Abd ar Rachman al-Ghafiqi, the governor of Spain.[45] Contemporary and near contemporary descriptions of that encounter allow us to examine tactics and combat techniques used by early Carolingian fighting forces and *a fortiori* the training and the unit cohesion that made such efforts both possible and successful.[46]

The most important description of the first day of this battle is provided by a later contemporary of Charles Martel, who likely was a Christian ecclesiastic living in that part of Spain that was under Muslim domination. This author may have served at the caliphal court, where he had access to either eyewitness information from Muslim participants in the battle or official reports.[47] The anonymous chronicler writes concerning Charles Martel's army, "the northerners (*septentrionales*)," having fixed their battle line (*acies*), "were standing immobile like a wall" to await the enemy attack.[48] The chronicler then reaffirms his southern or Mediterranean perspective by observing that "they [the northerners] remained in their ranks (*manent adstricti*) like a glacier from the frozen north (*zona rigoris glacialiter*)."[49]

The observations of the Byzantine emperor Maurice, writing more than a century earlier but well acquainted with the Franks of his day, illuminate the anonymous chronicler's laconic descriptions of Charles Martel's tactics at Poitiers. In the *Strategikon*, Maurice emphasizes that the Franks normally draw up in a "dense phalanx" with an "even front."[50] Thus the dense infantry phalanx, an established tactical formation used by armies mobilized in the *regnum Francorum* in Merovingian times, continued to be a basic method of deployment by the early Carolingians and was still in use when Angelbert fought at Fontenoy during the civil wars of Charlemagne's grandsons.[51] The Frankish chronicler Fredegar reports that in a massive military encounter in 612, two large phalanxes (*falanges*) of Franks and their allies engaged in such close order combat that "there was no room for the dead to fall." He notes that "they stood in their battle lines, corpse supporting corpse, just as though they were still living."[52] Despite some likely exaggeration by Fredegar, this close order combat was sound tactical doctrine for fighting in the traditional Western infantry phalanx. Vegetius, for example, emphasizes that the first two lines of infantry in a phalanx formation are to stand immobile ("prima ac secunda acies stabat immota").[53]

At the battle of Poitiers, Charles' army stood in place while the enemy launched its attack. The anonymous southern chronicler, cited above, seems so preoccupied with the steadfastness of the Carolingian phalanx in the face of the Muslim onslaught that he neglected to indicate whether Charles Martel's troops responded to the enemy when they came into missile range by throwing spears or javelins at them and by loosing flights of arrows. As will be seen below, it is likely that the Franks possessed some sort of missile capacity. Nevertheless, after contact was made with the enemy, the Carolingian army not only did not break ranks but did not give any ground to the attackers. The Muslims, by contrast, were so badly mauled in the hand-to-hand combat that characterized the battle that the chronicler says (with considerable exaggeration), "they were slaughtered in the blink of an eye."[54] As subsequent information indicates, the Muslim army was not wiped out but retreated in considerable disorder. The northerners, however, after having killed large numbers of the attacking Muslims — including Abd ar Rachman, their commander — did not break ranks in an undisciplined hot pursuit of the fleeing enemy. Rather, the entire phalanx held its position on the field of battle until the defeated enemy completely melted away in flight. Then the Frankish army retired to its own fortified encampment as night was coming on.[55] There, as will be seen, Charles made preparations so that his army could advance against the enemy's fortified camp (*castra*) the next morning for a second day of combat.

The anonymous chronicler emphasizes that the Carolingian victory was won just as night was beginning to fall. In late October this was close to 7:00 P.M. Under normal circumstances a prudent commander such as Charles Martel, the anonymous chronicler calls him a *vir* who in "rei militaris" was *expertus*, is loath to order his men, who have just fought a hard battle, to break ranks and take off in the pursuit of a defeated enemy, especially if the pursuit is over unfamiliar ground just as night is falling.[56] Indeed, Vegetius discusses, at some length, the difficulties in maintaining a safe and effective pursuit under good conditions and points out how nighttime operations substantially favor the retreating force.[57]

As will be discussed below, Roman and medieval evidence suggest that it is difficult for a unit to retain its static position in the wake of a disorderly or even an apparently disorderly retreat by a putatively defeated enemy force. Contemporaries were aware of this problem. For any corps of troops in the pre-gunpowder age to sustain a major military action in an ostensibly immobile phalanx on foot, as the army under the command of Charles Martel did at Poitiers, they needed long periods of exceptionally effective training and drill.[58]

The larger the force the easier it is for its officers to lose command and control during both battle and an enemy retreat. The internal cohesion of small units, which is discussed above, is of primary importance in these situations.[59] Thus, it is noteworthy in this context that Charles Martel's army likely was larger than the very large force commanded by Abd ar-Rachman and thus presented greater command and control problems.[60]

Soldiers deployed to fight on foot in a phalanx must have vigorous training to hold their position in the face of an enemy attack—Charles Martel's troops stood "like a glacier from the frozen north." This defensive wall-like stance was the proper tactic in light of Charles' strategic goals in this campaign and while facing the combined force of horsemen and infantry under Abd ar-Rachman at Poitiers.[61] The anonymous chronicler mentions the Muslim "phalanxes," presumably composed of foot soldiers, whom, as will be seen below, Charles expected to meet in combat on the second day of the battle.[62] These Muslim foot soldiers were armed primarily with bows and arrows in order to strike at a distance and with swords for hand-to-hand combat.[63]

An infantry force ordered to stand firmly in place and receive the enemy attack obviously cannot take the initiative.[64] This is especially the case for a large force, such as Charles Martel's at Poitiers, because the more troops involved in any military action, the more opportunities there are for mistakes. Thus, all momentum, both physical, which is important for its shock value at the commencement of hand-to-hand combat,[65] and psychological, where anxiety is heightened by waiting in position, rests with the force on the offensive.[66]

When the attacking force includes archers, the training and discipline of the defensive force that maintains its position may perhaps be considered to have been that much more thorough and effective than in cases where the enemy lacked archers or some other significant missile-launching capacity. Abd ar-Rachman's army at Poitiers, like all other Muslim armies fighting during the later seventh and early eighth centuries in the West, had archers. Although the majority of Muslim archers were on foot, some were on horses and even on camels.[67] All these archers, with their composite recurve bows, could hammer Charles Martel's forces at a distance in excess of two hundred meters.[68] Moreover, an eyewitness to the battle of Qadisiyya in 637 reports that Muslim archers penetrated the armor of the Persian soldiers, whom they defeated.[69] We have no reason to believe that the armor used by Charles' soldiers was superior to that used by the Persians.

Even among professional soldiers, merely the sound of hundreds if not several thousand arrows rushing through the air could induce sheer terror. When missiles strike flesh, the screams of pain can unnerve even the bravest and most experienced soldier.[70] Indeed, Angelbert was tormented by the screams and groans of the wounded even after the battle was over and he was safe. Thus, the discipline of the rank and file in an immobile infantry formation, who begin to take casualties at a distance, must be very great.[71] Soldiers who have no meaningful capacity to respond can nevertheless endure even hours of enemy archery through the use of a *testudo* of shields without taking serious casualties and while maintaining their position.[72] (This requires good training, such as that enjoyed by the Spartans who fought at Platea.) At Poitiers, the Muslim archers outranged the Franks' capacity to hurl their javelins. Whatever self-bows Charles' men had, with a maximum range of perhaps six hundred Roman feet, also were less effective than the Muslims' composite recurve bows.[73]

Despite the obvious liabilities incurred by an immovable massed infantry corps, Charles Martel's decision to await an enemy attack was consistent with his overall strategy to keep the Muslim army from advancing north along the Roman road from Poitiers to Tours. If the chroniclers have presented Abd ar-Rachman's plans correctly, he intended to advance north toward the old Roman fortress city of Tours and perhaps beyond despite the fact that the onset of winter would have halted his progress sooner rather than later.

To remain militarily viable in the environs of Poitiers, however, the Muslims had to not only attack the Carolingian army but also destroy it as a functioning military force. In this context, the well-known Muslim success over the Byzantines at the Yarmouk River in 636, which resulted in the Byzantine army simply melting away, likely provided a model for the type of victory envisioned by Abd ar-Rachman.[74] In any case, Abd ar-Rachman needed a decisive victory because if significant elements of the Carolingian force survived the battle and maintained unit cohesion, these forces could be deployed to harass the Muslim line of march. Perhaps more important, the baggage train containing the booty acquired during the army's several months of successful operations was vulnerable to attack.

Like any commander who had a lengthy record of military success, Abd ar Rachman, after seeing the Carolingian deployment, probably examined the option of not engaging the Frankish army, and of making a strategic withdrawal, that is, a phased retreat in good order, that would enable him to save much of what he had gained previously during the campaign. Abd ar-Rachman undoubtedly understood that Charles enjoyed two obvious and very positive options should the Muslims retreat. If the Frankish commander withdrew his own forces safely, without taking any casualties, Charles would earn credit for having "driven" the Muslims out of the *regnum Francorum* and for having saved Tours from certain enemy attack and potential devastation. This would have been a massive propaganda victory given the importance of the shrine of St. Martin, who as Gaul's own holy soldier would have been credited with supporting the

Carolingian effort. Charles' second option, as viewed from Abd ar-Rachman's perspective, should he not commit the Muslim army to battle, was to launch forays against the retreating baggage train at the risk of taking some casualties but with the hope of seizing substantial amounts of booty. Under this option, Charles would still earn credit for having saved St. Martin's city and would possibly have greatly enriched his soldiers as well. This second option as Abd ar-Rachman understood had some chance of success since the protection of assets, even in the course of an orderly retreat, is fraught with difficulty.

Although Abd ar-Rachman was an experienced military commander and probably understood both the strategic and the tactical situation very well, there is no hint in the sources that either he or Charles Martel sought to negotiate an agreement despite the fact that they had maneuvered and counter maneuvered their armies for almost seven days before actually meeting in open battle.[75] In these circumstances, the best option for the Muslims, as Abd ar-Rachman concluded, was to fight and win a decisive battle at Poitiers. As will be seen below, Charles' aim was to entice Abd ar-Rachman to engage, so he did nothing to encourage the Muslim commander to retreat. The scene was set for a decisive battle that both generals would appear to have desired.

After Charles' forces survived enemy fire from a distance, the second phase of the battle, the hand-to-hand combat itself, also highlights the need for rigorous training and weapons drill for the members of the static infantry formation. At Poitiers, Charles Martel's soldiers relied primarily if not completely on the use of the short sword, the *gladius*.[76] These short swords, as contrasted to the long sword or *spatha*, generally varied in length from about sixty-five to eighty centimeters.[77] For equipment of this kind, one size does not fit all, and allowance has to be made for the size, strength and personal preference of each man who used such a short sword in combat. For defense, as will be seen below, Charles' men relied primarily on their shields, as is the norm in premodern phalanx warfare. The round wooden shield was the least expensive and most ubiquitous piece of defensive equipment available to the early Carolingians.[78]

In the close order of the phalanx, made possible in part by the use of the short sword, each man in the unit must know what kinds of strokes he can deliver and how he is permitted to move within his formation.[79] This requires considerable training,[80] and such combat in a dense formation has been likened to a highly stylized dance.[81] Fighting men who lack sufficient training and drill may wound their own comrades because of the men crowded in on the sides and rear as well as on the front for all ranks except the first.[82]

In actual combat, each man in the phalanx naturally tends to crowd a bit to his right in order to gain some protection from the shield that his neighbor carries on his left arm.[83] There can be no lefthanders in a phalanx despite the regular distribution in the general population of approximately one in ten; left-handers necessarily are trained to use their right hands in combat. The general view is made clear as seen above in the *Waltharius*: "What do you say about violating the normal way of doing things (*ritum . . . gentis*) and girding your sword on your right thigh?"[84]

The tendency to drift to the right, however, unless compensated for by extensive training, shifts the entire phalanx to the right and thus may allow the enemy to deliver a decisive attack on the left flank. In addition, the terrain of the field of battle, unless it is absolutely flat, exacerbates the problems caused by the sideways movement of each man in the phalanx. Even a small hillock or a depression in the field will, at least temporarily, separate any one particular man from his neighbors. With the opening of such a seam, the attackers can cut into the formation and attack the inner ranks of the phalanx on the internal flank of the exposed file.[85]

In the process of evaluating the training and tactics or combat techniques of Charles' troops at Poitiers, it is more than likely that if one of the two forces were better equipped than the other or possessed superior military technology, it was the Muslims who enjoyed the advantage over their Christian adversaries.[86] The Arabs had acquired by conquest the arms manufacturing infrastructure of what had been a large part of the eastern half of the Roman empire.[87] The production resources of the East, in addition, were far better developed than those found during the early eighth century throughout the empire's Romano-German successor states in the West.[88]

Not only did the Muslims enjoy superior manufacturing resources, but the East was much more prosperous than the West, in general. In addition to conquering many of the more wealthy regions of the Byzantine empire, the Muslims also had seized the resources of the Persian empire.[89] Thus, Muslim soldiers were vastly more wealthy than their northern opponents as they had enjoyed for a century the great masses of booty that were the rewards for conquest.[90] The Muslim soldiers also received very substantial annual salaries even as compared to the armies of the Byzantine or East Roman empire.[91] In light of the disparity in wealth and in manufacturing infrastructure, by the early eighth century the Muslims could afford better equipment than their Christian adversaries from the north. The Muslims could provide a larger proportion of their forces with body armor and helmets and also with high quality edged weapons.[92]

High quality sword blades also were produced in the *regnum Francorum*,[93] but these long swords were limited in number as compared to other types of weapons, including the short sword. In the seventh century, for example, the short sword was the dominant weapon for use in hand-to-hand combat, if the evidence provided by weapons' graves is to be regarded as decisive.[94] Generally, the long sword, *spatha*, was made of high quality pattern-welded steel. By contrast, the short sword, the *scramasax* or *gladius*, was more likely to be made of iron or rather poor quality steel.[95] From the contexts in which long swords—not to be confused with long *saxes*—are found and in which fine blades have been excavated, *spathae* belonged to wealthy men and were both costly and rare.[96]

Booty-rich Muslim soldiers wielded edged weapons that were superior in quality to the cheap and comparatively poorly made *scramasaxes* or *gladii* used by the rank-and-file foot soldiers of the Frankish phalanx. Early Carolingian infantry units were composed largely of militia men—farmer-soldiers—who as seen above, were required to do expeditionary service because they possessed a manse or two. The economic advantages enjoyed by the Muslims surely provided them with equipment that was better than that available to the vast majority of men who served Charles' army.[97]

Finally, the Muslims had the technology to construct the composite recurve bow, which was made from various layers of bone, horn, and wood. These weapons by all accounts were far superior to the wooden self-bows available to the northerners. In addition, the shorter and more powerful recurve bow could be used effectively by mounted troops. In light of the Muslims' superiority in technology and wealth, one of the few ways in which Charles Martel could hope to redress the balance at Poitiers in 732, in addition to fielding a superior number of battle-ready troops, was through better training and discipline of his soldiers.

The Muslim armies of the early eighth century, however, were already heirs to the Western military system of the later Roman empire and no longer the ragtag nomad remnants of *Arabia Deserta* who appear in the sources of the early years of the conquest. Indeed, by the period under consideration here, approximately a hundred years after the death of Mohammed, Muslim soldiers were drawn in large part from the regions that gradually had been conquered in the century prior to the confrontation at Poitiers in 732. The conquered peoples were drawn into the military service of the Muslim-run governments, and in their increasing maturity, these armies were multiethnic forces of great size and sophistication.[98] The acquisition of high quality siege equipment, discussed above, and of considerable naval assets underscores how different the armies of the later Umayyad caliphs were from the desert Arabs who had initiated the earlier conquests.[99]

From what is known of these later Muslim forces, it seems that the armies of Mohammed's successors had adopted from the peoples whom they conquered the key military values of Mediterranean civilization—training and discipline— that the early Carolingians also had adopted.[100] Thus, the main differences between the forces of Charles Martel and Abd ar-Rachman were not in their respective attention to training and discipline. Rather, Charles used the training and discipline of his forces to maintain a tactically defensive position, which was consonant with his strategic goal of blocking the Muslim advance. Thus, he enjoyed a considerable advantage over his adversaries who had to win a decisive victory in the field — a very difficult feat against a numerically superior, psychologically determined, and well-drilled infantry force — in order to continue their advance northward. In short, with almost everything else being equal in the comparatively primitive technological milieu of early eighth-century warfare, the well-drilled defensive force in open battle generally enjoyed the advantage.[101]

As noted above, Charles Martel managed to maintain command and control of his infantry phalanx in the wake of the Muslim rout, a discipline not easily accomplished despite the imminent onset of night. Normally, the victors wanted to acquire booty from the defeated enemy, the dead, the wounded, and potentially from those who were in flight.[102]

In addition, some soldiers, who while in battle feel themselves to have been in serious peril of losing their lives, experience what is often labeled in modern psychological terminology as "blood lust" or "killing frenzy." Thus, the apparent freedom stimulated by the enemy's flight, combined with a desire for revenge, psychologically releases the defenders to undertake the offensive regardless of what orders they may have been given to hold position. This condition, which modern scholars have come to call the "berserk syndrome," often requires the soldiers who are so affected to exhaust themselves physically and/or psychologically before they are able to stop killing and again come under the effective discipline of their officers.[103] In contexts such as these, but not necessarily as extreme as the so-called berserk syndrome, commentators on warfare throughout the history of Western civilization traditionally observe that a military unit is, beneath the veneer of its training, a mob awaiting its opportunity to escape from the discipline that created it.[104] Therefore, the description of Charles' wall of soldiers standing as if frozen in place has the ring of a grudging compliment.

The commanders of troops on the attack who engaged in offensive action against a phalanx such as that deployed by Charles Martel at Poitiers developed what has come to be called the feigned retreat. This tactic (see above regarding the training for the *toloutegon*) could be executed by mounted troops, whether heavily or lightly armed, or even by men fighting on foot or combinations of both horsemen and foot soldiers.[105] In effect, the force on the offensive charges the enemy phalanx but after engaging the front ranks finds that it is unable sufficiently to penetrate the defensive position and thus to break up its solid formation. Therefore, at a prearranged signal or signals, which could be visual (flags) or auditory (trumpets) or a combination of the two, the attacking force feigns a disorderly retreat in the hope and often in the expectation that the troops in the phalanx will break ranks and charge after the now presumably defeated enemy. However, at a second prearranged signal (again the repertoire of signaling devices is considerable and the various techniques are not mutually exclusive) the retreating force moves to the second stage of this *ruse de guerre* and halts its retreat. In a third phase, the men, having stopped their disorderly feigned retreat, reform their lines. Finally, in the fourth phase, the reformed units counterattack against their now thoroughly disorganized pursuers, whose formations have been decisively undermined during the pursuit and whose officers ostensibly have lost command and control.[106]

The Battle of Rimini, 553

For specialists in Western medieval history and especially in military history, this feigned retreat tactic is best known from its use on at least two occasions and with moderate success by William the Conqueror during the battle of Hastings on 14 October 1066.[107] However, the battlefield feigned retreat, as contrasted to the strategic feigned retreat (which might go on for miles and well beyond the battlefield proper), entered the tactical repertoire of armies in the West a great many centuries earlier than William's deployment at Hastings.[108] The Byzantine commander Narses used a feigned retreat effectively against a well-emplaced formation of Merovingian troops in Italy on a plain outside the fortress city of Rimini, south of Ravenna, in 553.[109]

Perhaps a decade or so after this battle, the Byzantine historian Agathias began collecting information for his *History*, which ultimately dealt with the East Romans and their neighbors for the period A.D. 552–559. Agathias accumulated a considerable body of very detailed information on this campaign, both from contemporaries and from documents.[110] Even strong critics of the *History* recognize that Agathias gave a very high priority to research, and he ranked research second only to the study of "the classics." These ancient works, according to Agathias, were to be imitated in terms of their style but not in terms of their content. He also gave a high priority to ascertaining the "truth" and claims that he was intent upon avoiding what he characterizes as the contemporary tendency of writers to flatter famous people. On the whole, Agathias is judged to have been exceptionally curious in searching out obscure details and it is recognized that he worked very hard.[111]

Concerning the battle at Rimini, Agathias undoubtedly had the benefit of participant and/or nonparticipant eyewitness accounts, which would seem to have been of an authoritative character. By medieval standards, and by early medieval standards in particular, Agathias' treatment of the military operations of both the Franks and the Byzantines is rather full if not complete. Perhaps more important, the account does not suffer from the antiviolence bias of religious authors that so frequently infects the accounts of military operations provided by clerics in medieval Western Europe. Agathias was a lawyer, which does not seem to have impinged upon his presentation of the relevant military facts.[112]

Agathias' account is worthy of discussion at some length for several reasons. First, he illuminates early medieval command thinking with regard to the use of the feigned retreat. Second, the "victimization" of this particular army, which had been recruited in the *regnum Francorum*, provided very obvious practical knowledge to the numerous survivors who returned home north of the Alps and to those of their posterity who learned the details of the battle. This knowledge could be used, in turn, by creative Frankish officers to devise proper tactical responses to an enemy's use of the feigned retreat in the future. Third, by seeing how the feigned retreat was used, the more intelligent and creative among the survivors could develop this tactic so that it might be added to the Frankish armamentarium. Finally, and of great importance here, Agathias provides an opportunity to gain considerable insight into the training and discipline of an expeditionary force, which was mobilized in the *regnum Francorum* and was operating in the field more than one thousand kilometers from home a century and a half or so before Charles Martel succeeded to the office of Mayor of the Palace.

The Merovingian corps, whose personnel Agathias refers to as "Franks" and which Narses engaged in the plain outside Rimini in 553, was detached from the main invasion force that had entered the peninsula earlier in the year. The corps had been seconded to undertake foraging operations when it was brought to battle by Narses. This group of Franks, Agathias notes, numbered some two thousand effectives—approximately one-third of a Roman legion of the later Republic or early empire in order of magnitude—and was composed of approximately equal numbers of foot soldiers and mounted troops. In addition, the foraging unit had packhorses and wagons in order to bring supplies back to the main army.[113]

When Narses, from his office in one of the towers high atop the fortress walls of Rimini, saw these foragers at work, he ordered his personal guard regiment to prepare to attack them. Agathias puts this force at *bandon*-strength, a cavalry unit of three hundred effectives. Some men in the unit were armed with bows and arrows while others had only javelins as missile weapons. When his troops had been prepared for combat, Narses rode out into the countryside at the head of his unit with the aim of scattering the enemy foragers and depriving them of the supplies that they had gathered.[114]

However, the Frankish foragers, either upon seeing the approaching Byzantine force or at least signs of an approaching force, perhaps from a dust cloud, did not flee nor did they rush to attack Narses' *bandon*. Rather, the Franks joined together from their widely scattered and presumably assigned locations and rapidly drew up in a defensive formation.[115] This tactical response by two thousand troops to what would appear to have been a much smaller enemy force suggests that Agathias was overcounting the Frankish corps or undercounting Narses' own troop strength. Such a manipulation of numbers is not uncommon in medieval sources, especially for boosters with regard to the size of the forces against which their home side was engaged.[116]

Before we draw any firm conclusions concerning the possible exaggeration of numbers, however, the entire situation needs to be surveyed. In deciding to deploy in a defensive position, the Merovingian commander undoubtedly considered the corps of enemy troops bivouacked outside the walls of Rimini. This force, not to be confused with Narses' *bandon*, was under the command of Theudebald, the son and successor of Vaccarus as king of the Warni and an important Byzantine ally. The Warni, as a "tribal" unit under the direct command of its king, was considerably larger than a mere detachment of Frankish foragers.[117] The Byzantine regular forces under Narses' personal command was perceived by the Frankish commander to be the vanguard of a much larger force. The latter was assumed to include Theudebald's Warni, as well as however many of the local militiamen who were available at Rimini for the defense of their city and its environs.

The Merovingian commander, in this early stage of a rapidly developing and possibly very dangerous situation, may not yet have obtained solid intelligence regarding the full strength of the enemy force before he deployed. Narses' total force may have been only at *bandon*-strength or well in excess of the three hundred effectives reported by Agathias. Nor can we know whether the Franks' commander at the time of the decision to form up in a defensive position had conclusive information concerning the size of the Byzantine army or merely reacted to a cloud of dust emanating from the direction of the fortress at Rimini. The commander of this Frankish foraging unit, by deploying on the defensive in the manner described above, acted according to sound military doctrine of the later Roman empire (and earlier).[118]

Agathias reports that the foragers, who "had been sent by their commanders to pillage and plunder the countryside," were seen by Narses to be "scattered" and "dispersed" throughout the countryside while "stripping the fields" and "dragging off draft animals."[119] From a tower only thirty feet in height, Narses or perhaps his younger and more sharp-eyed officers of the watch could see some seven miles in any direction over relatively flat terrain.[120] As soon as the approach of the Byzantine force was detected, and, as will be seen below, Merovingian commanders used scouts, the Franks immediately broke off their plundering and came together very quickly into a defensive formation.[121] Such a rapid response by these soldiers undoubtedly was the result of previous planning and drill, including some sort of a prearranged signal system.[122]

Agathias reports concerning the Franks: "They closed ranks, both the infantry and cavalry, and deployed themselves into a compact formation which, though it was not of great depth, (that would not have been possible in light of their numbers) nevertheless constituted a solid formation of shields that was flanked in the appropriate manner by the cavalry which was covering the wings."[123] The training and discipline of this unit seem remarkable in light of the rapidly developing situation at hand.

Agathias' observation that the Frankish foraging unit could not deploy in deep formation, as apparently was expected practice, due to an insufficiency in the number of troops, initially might seem puzzling. Indeed, two thousand effectives in virtually any medieval context and especially during the early Middle Ages, when some scholars (even military historians) believe armies to have been very small, hardly could be considered a paltry force incapable of forming a deep phalanx.[124] With a front extended over a distance of some four hundred meters, a force of two thousand effectives fighting on foot and spaced at approximately one-meter intervals along the front could deploy at a depth of five ranks equal in size.

Agathias' curious parenthesis, however, is made clear by the fact that the Franks' commander extended his front so that the flanks were covered by thick forest on either side.[125] Agathias did not choose to make an explicit connection between the shallow formation and the extension of the front to the forested land on the flanks, evidently assuming that his readers did not need any commentary on this basic tactical point. His silence here may be taken as *prima facie* evidence of the relative sophistication that he expected of his readers in regard to military matters.[126]

The Franks, as modern military commentators would say, acted "by the book." The commanders of the foraging unit had established signals for rapidly reforming their force at a prearranged site should they learn that some danger had arisen from the direction of the fortress city of Rimini or another quarter.[127] It is clear, in addition, that the Franks acted with great caution and practice as they deployed into a well-defined defensive formation consistent with the nature of the terrain as the enemy drew closer but well before any contact could be initiated.

The decision by the Frankish commander to extend his front so that his flanks rested on densely wooded terrain indicates his military experience. He was aware of the possibility that the Byzantine mounted troops likely would attempt to execute a flanking movement if the opportunity arose. The Frankish commander's well-placed confidence that his soldiers could carry out this difficult deployment from the deep or dense column, which Narses apparently had expected to see facing him, to an extended front — virtually a deployment from column to line — in the face of an oncoming enemy mounted force further attests to substantial training, drill, and discipline.

The Frankish commander, by basing his right and left flanks on wooded terrain, seems to have been favoring a completely defensive deployment. However, as a result of ordering his mounted troops to remain on horseback and by deploying them on the wings of his formation, he also retained the capacity, should the opportunity arise, to take the offensive. Thus, if the Byzantine commander were to err by making the sole focus of his attack the men fighting on foot at the center of the Frankish formation and if these troops held firmly, as their "descendants" were to stand at Poitiers, the Frankish horsemen could strike the attacking force on either or both flanks in a partial envelopment and perhaps even carry out a complete envelopment that would enable them to attack from the rear as well. Mounted attacks on the flanks and rear of an enemy force, as contrasted to a head-on charge against a well-dressed front, were the most effective way to deploy horsemen in combat against either foot soldiers or mounted troops throughout the history of the West.

It is possible, as defenders of a "primitivist" perspective might have it, that any one of the above-mentioned actions that Agathias reports the Frankish commander to have taken might have been the result of happenstance or dumb luck or perhaps even "barbarian cunning." However, all of the actions taken by the Frankish commander, when evaluated in their ensemble, are the hallmark of rigorous training, frequent drill, and rigorously enforced discipline. Agathias, who surely was no friend of the Franks when this account was written, has not a single negative word to say about their preliminary military deployment at Rimini; in fact, he credits the Frankish commander of this force of two thousand men with having deployed in a "perfect formation" given the tactical situation with which he was faced.[128]

By contrast, Charles Martel deployed his army at Poitiers in a considerably different manner, but his forces were not necessarily less disciplined. For example, Charles did not deploy the mounted troops, traditionally an important part of all large Frankish armies, to the flanks.[129] Tactically, he seems to have committed himself completely to a defensive battle, which as we have seen was aimed primarily at thwarting the enemy advance northward in the direction of Tours and thus was fully consistent with Carolingian strategic goals. Since none of the sources mention Charles' mounted forces, he must have ordered all or most of the men on horseback to dismount and join the battle line on foot. This was a drill to which they were well accustomed, as seen above.

One may speculate that Charles, who, as we have seen, was a very prudent commander of considerable experience, deployed at least a small force of mounted troops to the rear of his infantry formation. Such a precaution was called for in the eventuality that the Muslims, whose armies often were composed in significant part of mounted troops, carried out a flanking movement. The use of such a tactic by Abd ar-Rachman was unlikely at Poitiers because Charles' army, as noted above, outnumbered the Muslim force. Nevertheless, a mounted reserve, even a rather small force, could easily delay such a flanking effort until a sufficient number of foot soldiers in the phalanx could be redeployed to face enemy forces attacking from a new direction. Every good commander strives to deploy for battle so that he will not be surprised by an enemy counter-deployment.

Unlike Agathias, my primary interest in the battle at Rimini between the Franks and the Byzantines is not to call attention to the details of Narses' superb execution of the feigned retreat tactic. Nor is it my intention to reaffirm the well-established fact, noted above, that Merovingian armies — like those of their Carolingian successors — were composed, often in substantial part, of troops prepared to fight on horseback. (Nevertheless, the more detail we can gather on all such tactics and fighting techniques from reliable sources, the better.) In the present context, however, the object is to understand, using Agathias' account, how difficult it was for even a well-disciplined force of the type engaged outside of Rimini to resist the temptation to pursue a defeated or apparently defeated enemy in the face of a real or feigned retreat.

Agathias reports that when Narses saw the strength of the Frankish position, he halted his troops within missile range of the enemy phalanx and ordered both his archers and his javelin throwers to aim at the men in the front ranks. This "direction of fire" is revealing. An effort that is intended to pick off foot soldiers in the front ranks, who are well protected by shields, in order to thin the lines is far less effective than sending a hail of arrows down on their potential targets from as high above as possible.[130] As noted previously, even the sound of a rain of arrows can hurt the morale of well-trained soldiers.

A hail of arrows, however, is easily blunted by an emplaced force through the use of the *testudo*, or shields placed overhead in an overlapping "turtle-shell," which the enemy arrows, even falling close to the maximum speed of thirty-two feet per second squared, cannot penetrate. Indeed, as a Continuator of the *Annals of Fulda* put it in describing the use of the *testudo*, the Carolingian soldiers placed their "shields over themselves in the manner of a roof (*scuta super se in modum tecti).*"[131] Obviously, Narses avoided deploying his missiles en masse because he knew that the Franks could use the defensive *testudo* technique to nullify the overall effects of such an archery tactic.[132] Even the Vikings learned how to use the *testudo* in the ninth century, likely as a result of their frequent conflicts with the Franks.[133]

In any case, Agathias indicates that the missile attacks by the Byzantine archers and javelin throwers had no noteworthy effect on the front line of the enemy phalanx. He reports that the Franks "stood firm and immoveable behind a wall of shields."[134] Agathias, a man from the Mediterranean world like the anonymous chronicler who reported on the battle of Poitiers, however, makes no subsequent reference to this Frankish phalanx standing like a "glacier from the frozen north." Nevertheless, the basic Frankish infantry formation used at Rimini was similar to that deployed at Poitiers almost 180 years later. What was significantly different was that at Poitiers, the Arabs eventually closed with Charles' men and were cut down in hand-to-hand combat, while at Rimini, the Franks answered the enemy barrage of arrows and javelins with a counter-barrage of missiles. Again, training undergirded the continued discipline of the Frankish phalanx under fire in this battle.[135]

Another important difference between the Frankish forces at Rimini and those at Poitiers was that in maneuvering prior to the earlier battle, the Franks were not seeking to engage the enemy. Charles Martel, by contrast, encouraged an enemy attack and did nothing overt to frighten off the Muslims whom he outnumbered. For example, he did not deploy horsemen on the flanks, which would warn the Muslim commander that his forces faced the possibility of partial or total envelopment by a rapidly moving mounted force. Perhaps more important, Charles did not have pits or ditches dug in the killing ground that fronted his formation. This old and well-tested tactic was intended to break the momentum of a mounted charge and discomfort any force, mounted or on foot, that approached the phalanx at some pace but with more élan than care. Indeed, the Thuringians had used it effectively against the Franks' mounted troops on the banks of the Unstrut in 531.[136]

At Rimini, Narses quickly understood that he could not sufficiently "soften up" the Frankish shield wall with missile fire so that he might subsequently launch a mounted charge and break up the phalanx, even though the Franks, as Agathias noted, were deployed in a shallow line formation rather than in their normal and much deeper broadly fronted column formation. Thus, Narses employed what Agathias considers a "barbarian tactic"—the feigned retreat—which he claims was commonly used by the Huns. Having decided on this new deployment, Narses ordered his forces "to turn their horses" and "to retreat at a mad gallop as though they were fleeing in terror." This was done, according to Agathias, to lure the Franks from their emplacements onto the open plain.[137]

The execution of the feigned retreat went so well, Agathias reports, that the Franks "immediately" left their secure position in order to take off after the Byzantines "in hot pursuit." This Frankish redeployment, Agathias reports, was led by the mounted troops, who had been stationed on the flanks of the infantry formation. The horsemen apparently were followed in short order by the "bravest and the swiftest" of the foot soldiers. Agathias fails to make clear whether the Frankish commanders ordered the hot pursuit.[138] Indeed, unless enemy prisoners had been taken by the Byzantines and successfully interrogated, and some account of these interrogations had been provided to Agathias, he had no way of knowing whether the Frankish commander ordered the pursuit or whether he had lost command and control of his forces at a crucial stage of the battle.

The response of his mounted troops to the enemy feigned retreat cannot be considered *prima facie* evidence for a complete breakdown of discipline. The proper tactical response to the feigned retreat was long known in the Roman West not only from repeated practice in training and in battle but from texts such as Arrian's *Contra Alanos* and the Latin writers who used this and similar accounts of proper deployment in these rather complicated circumstances.[139] It was crucial for the defending force to switch to the offensive very quickly and carefully. If the transition were not rapid then it would be difficult to gain the full advantage should the retreat prove to have been real rather than feigned. The redeployment, Arrian emphasizes, had to be done very carefully if the retreat turned out to be feigned so that the effectiveness of the enemy force in the launching of a counterattack could be thwarted.[140]

In response to a retreat, whether feigned or real, the commander of the force that was redeploying from the defensive to the offensive, dispatched units of mounted troops, previously stationed either on the flanks or in reserve behind the infantry phalanx, in rapid but not hot pursuit of the retreating enemy. The key difference between a rapid pursuit and a hot pursuit was that the pursuing force in the former deployment maintained formation, but in the latter case, horsemen broke formation and moved at their own very fast pace in search of targets of opportunity. The rapid pursuit was intended as a type of harassment, analogous in some ways to skirmishing prior to a battle, and was intended to keep the enemy soldiers engaged in a feigned retreat from stopping their flight, reforming their units, and finally counterattacking. In a proper response by the force moving from the defensive to the offensive, the rapid pursuit by the horsemen was to be followed up by a much slower advance by a substantial part of the infantry force. The latter were to come forward in close formation in order to provide support and protection should the enemy be able to reform and launch an effective counterattack against the pursuing mounted troops.[141]

If Agathias is correct in noting that the Frankish horsemen immediately undertook a hot pursuit (and thus broke formation), then from the start they had violated proper procedure if not perhaps discipline. In fact, the Frankish commander may have ordered a hot pursuit, presuming that he had been fooled by the effectiveness of the enemy ruse, and thus the horsemen would have been following orders by undertaking their redeployment from their static defensive position. Such a situation would reveal command error based upon an inaccurate evaluation of intelligence rather than a loss of command and control due to a lack of discipline among the troops.

Agathias, however, was not an eyewitness, and even those men who were the closest eyewitnesses to the very rapidly developing events on the battlefield at Rimini — the Byzantine mounted troops who were in the process of executing a feigned retreat — had their backs turned to the pursuing Frankish horsemen. As a result, even the Byzantine combatants might not have known whether the enemy had broken formation from the outset of their redeployment and advance or whether this hot pursuit began only at some later point in the action when the Byzantines appeared "certainly," but quite erroneously, to the Franks to have been engaged in a real rather than in a feigned retreat. Indeed, as Agathias put it in a congratulatory manner, "the Romans . . . played their roles so convincingly . . . that they raced away looking to everyone as though they were panic-stricken fugitives."[142] Surely, legitimate caveats may be adduced regarding loss of command and control of the Frankish horse. By contrast, it is clear that the hot pursuit if not the actual redeployment undertaken by the Frankish foot soldiers, who broke ranks at one time or another during the second stage of the engagement, violated proper tactical procedure and probably their standing orders, as well.

Narses successfully executed the final phases of the feigned retreat and slaughtered perhaps as many as some nine hundred Franks. Most of these casualties, Agathias indicates, were enemy foot soldiers, who, once out of formation and widely scattered on the field of battle, were easy prey to Narses' army. Because the Frankish mounted contingent putatively outnumbered the Byzantine horse under Narses' direct command by a more than a three-to-one margin, the Byzantines were probably strongly supported by the Warni under the command of King Theudebald in this phase of the battle. The Frankish mounted troops, however, escaped with a comparatively small number of casualties. In these circumstances, the forage that the Franks had collected in the countryside, and likely their wagons and pack horses as well, were captured either by the troops in Narses' *bandon* or by his Warni auxiliaries.[143]

Narses' great success with the use of the feigned retreat at Rimini against the Franks was much heralded, and, as we have seen, some twenty years or so after the battle, Agathias wrote a detailed report of it in his *History*. Emperor Maurice, who was writing his *Strategikon* at the end of the sixth century, either knew at first-hand Agathias' account or had considerable information from one or more other sources concerning this battle. In any case, Maurice generalized in his *Strategikon* regarding the Franks' great susceptibility to this "barbarian" *ruse de guerre*, the feigned retreat.[144]

Maurice observed concerning the Franks: "They are easily broken by a feigned retreat which is followed by a sudden turning back [and counterattack] against them."[145] Maurice may have surmised from Agathias' account or perhaps from other sources that the Frankish defeat at Rimini was the result of a loss of command and control. Thus, he asserts, relevant to the present context, that the Franks "are disobedient to their leaders" and "they despise good order, especially on horseback."[146] It is clear, however, by contrast with the situation at Rimini and Maurice's possible generalization from it, that Charles Martel's phalanx at Poitiers did not break ranks and engage in an undisciplined hot pursuit of a beaten or only a presumably defeated enemy. In addition, as already noted, whatever mounted troops that may have been attached to Charles Martel's force at Poitiers either had dismounted and fought on foot within the phalanx or were deployed to the rear as a reserve and thus deliberately were kept out of the action.[147]

Carolingian foot soldiers of the type that Charles Martel commanded in battle at Poitiers were, in addition, capable of considerably more complicated deployments than simply holding their positions under the bludgeoning of an enemy attack. The capacity to restrain these troops from undertaking a very risky counterattack at dusk following an enemy retreat, as discussed above, is further evidence for their discipline. These Frankish troops were also capable of advancing to the attack in a disciplined and orderly manner. Thus, at dawn on the day following the above described victory, Charles, who had already formed up his troops inside the *castra* that his army had constructed prior to the first day of battle, began his march against the enemy's fortified encampment.[148]

The Frankish troops most likely were deployed in a broadly fronted but very deep marching column in order to take advantage of the first-class Roman road near which both forces had been encamped and which ran north-south from Tours to Poitiers. Indeed, the formality of the march by a large army was thoroughly integrated into Carolingian military thought and practice. Rhabanus Maurus went into considerable detail so as to remind his readers in the summary or *Recapitulatio* of his handbook regarding the importance of maintaining troop formations (*ordines*) while on the march.[149] And as seen above,

Hans Delbrück on the basis of *Sachkritik* accepted Rhabanus' observations un-hesitatingly regarding the successful training of Frankish troops with regard to their ability to maintain formations in regard to units ranging as high as ten thousand men.[150]

At Poitiers on Sunday, 26 October 732, Charles Martel, upon reaching the environs of the enemy's fortified camp (*castra*), within which numerous tents and pavilions had been erected in neatly standing rows, halted his forces. The court chronicler reports that from this position Charles sent out scouts in order to reconnoiter the enemy position in preparation for an all-out assault on the Muslims' fortified position.[151] Charles' precaution is diametrically opposed to the Emperor Maurice's assertion regarding the standard operating procedure of the Franks. The emperor, though recognizing the importance of scouts for suc-cessful military operations, indicates rather ambiguously that the Franks either are neglectful in their deployment of scouts or do not use them at all. Maurice leaves the reader to infer that the failure to take full advantage of scouts hurt the Franks (and anyone else who fails to employ this basic intelligence-gathering technique).[152]

In contrast to Maurice's observation and in consonance with the contem-porary report of Charles Martel's action, Rhabanus Maurus emphasizes the gen-eral principle that scouts are to be used "as, indeed, necessity requires it" and that such necessity "occurs frequently in the course of warfare (*bellum*)." Rha-banus gives particular attention to the situation in which "the enemy *castra* is to be scouted (*explorare*)" and notes that this is to be done "very quickly" and that "even more quickly, the scouts are to return to report [to the commander]." In short, not only was obtaining intelligence a high priority for Frankish military operations, but the intelligence also must be fresh. Stale information, as military commanders know, is likely inaccurate information.[153]

Rhabanus, however, did not find this information regarding the impor-tance of scouting the enemy and particularly of scouting the enemy *castra* in Vegetius' *De re Militari*, book I, chapter 9, where he had found the discussion, treated above, regarding the training of foot soldiers to use the *militaris gradus* (to march in military step according to a particular cadence), and upon which he was commenting. Rhabanus, by adding the scouting information to the sec-tion on marching, emphasizes a sequence of events similar to that in the court chronicler's account of Charles Martel's deployment on the second day of the battle of Poitiers. First, Charles Martel, as we have seen, marched his soldiers out of camp in the direction of the enemy's fortified position. Then he sent out scouts to reconnoiter the Muslim *castra*.

Charles Martel's scouts subsequently reported their findings to him. The Frankish commander then redeployed his troops from the long and deep column that had been necessary for the march south toward Poitiers along the Roman road. This redeployment was to a lengthy formation in line ("aciem instruit"), which was required to launch an attack against the defenses of the enemy's fortified encampment (*castra*). Following the redeployment, if Fredegar's Continuator is to be believed, Charles (characterized here, in a departure from the norm, as *belligerator*) personally commanded the charge against the enemy camp. His army attacked the enemy camp rapidly ("inruit") and breached the defenses, literally "overthrew their tents" ("tentoria eorum subvertit") pitched within the circuit of the fortification.[154]

Rhabanus, while discussing marching drill (*militaris gradus*), emphasized the importance of this training, as we have seen above, because foot soldiers could attack at the run. Thus, soldiers are trained not only to charge rapidly ("irruant") against the enemy but also to do so "while maintaining formation" ("aequaliter . . . uno parique").[155] Rhabanus indicates that in moving against the enemy in this manner the various units needed to sustain the cohesion of their formations by maintaining the prescribed position in relation to their standards or banners (*vexillae*).[156] One purpose of the implementation of this rapid run ("rapido cursu") while maintaining formation is, according to Rhabanus, to permit the foot soldiers to take possession of key enemy positions, *oportuna loca*, very quickly, *citius*.[157]

The rapid occupation of *oportuna loca* resonates acutely with the events on the second day of battle at Poitiers. Charles, as we have seen, sent out his scouts to reconnoiter the enemy position, and they may have reported to him that some sections of the perimeter fortification of the enemy *castra* were ill-defended. Muslim losses on the previous day would have left Charles' enemies somewhat shorthanded for the defense of a perimeter constructed when they were at full strength. These putatively ill-defended positions could be characterized as *oportuna loca*, to use Rhabanus' phrase, that had to be taken very quickly, before the Muslims could reinforce them. Thus, after obtaining intelligence from his scouts, Charles redeployed the Frankish army into line and rapidly charged ("inruit") the enemy's fortified encampment.

Rhabanus' discussion emphasizes the significance of using scouts for the purpose of reconnoitering an enemy *castra*, the need for fresh intelligence, and the importance of a rapid attack on foot in formation in order to capture *oportuna loca* — desiderata consistent with Charles Martel's tactics on the second day of the battle at Poitiers. Indeed, Rhabanus was of an age and socially positioned not only to have known men who had fought at Poitiers but also to have met them in court circles.[158] Nevertheless, whatever he knew about the battle of Poitiers in 732 was not necessarily the reason he chose this chapter on training for the march to diverge from Vegetius' discussion and provide his own commentary. Still, that the pattern of operations Rhabanus identified as being by the book "tempore moderno" was consistent with what Charles Martel had done more than a century earlier at Poitiers.

The Continuator, recording the court version of the situation, who indicates that the battle resulted in the breaching of the walls of the Muslim fortifications and the capture of the *castra*, also recognizes that Charles' army very quickly inflicted a threefold slaughter on the enemy ("ad proelium stragem conterendam").[159] This magnitude of the casualties inflicted by Charles' troops, however rhetorically disguised, should not mask the likelihood that for every three Muslims who were either killed or wounded, at least one Carolingian suffered a similar fate. The anonymous chronicler who conflates the two phases of the battle reports that the Muslims suffered very serious casualties and even annihilation; he does not dwell on Carolingian losses.[160]

After inflicting this second and likely even more massive defeat on the Muslims in the course of two days, however, Charles remained cautious and made no concerted effort to follow up this victory. According to the anonymous chronicler, Charles feared an enemy ambush in this territory with which he and his men, by and large, were unfamiliar. Indeed, the week-long maneuvering between the two forces prior to the battle had not permitted Charles to obtain much information concerning the situation south of Poitiers because this would have put his scouts behind the enemy position. Because the area to the south was not well known to the Carolingian army, Charles ordered his troops to be exceptionally careful while hunting down those enemy troops who had escaped but who apparently were believed to have remained in the region. He is said to have had no intention of pursuing the Muslims in an extended effort—an accurate appraisal of his post-battle campaign strategy.[161]

A sufficient body of fresh intelligence was not all that was needed for a successful pursuit in force of the remnants of the retreating Muslim army. Charles likely had some of the resources available to undertake an effective pursuit, but not everything. For example, a well-rested corps of mounted troops with fresh horses would be required. He likely had the fresh horses, but his mounted troops may have dismounted in order to fight on foot and thus were battle weary from two successive days of brutal and costly combat. In addition to fresh men and fresh horses, a well-stocked supply train of considerable mobility (likely with pack horses rather than wagons or carts) that was already prepared for such a potentially lengthy pursuit had to be available. In short, like all military operations, the tactic of pursuing the enemy in an effective manner rests in large part on objective realities such as the availability of reliable intelligence, well-rested troops, fresh horses, and sufficient supplies.

Battle in the Süntal

The author of the revised court *Annals*, who was exceptionally well informed concerning what was of importance to Charlemagne's inner circle, describes a battle in the Süntal mountains against the Saxons in 782 that is particularly revealing of proper tactics.[162] The annalist recounts a selection of details regarding a military operation in which a large Carolingian army under divided command (a procedure about which he seems also to have had serious reservations, as will be seen below) was deployed to suppress a sudden and unexpected Saxon revolt.[163] This Carolingian army likely was principally composed of the levy of expeditionary troops that had been mustered from throughout the "Ribuarian province" with its capital at Cologne. Most of this rapidly mobilized levy was foot soldiers who possessed a manse or two. This entire "Ribuarian" force served under the direct command of Theodoric, Charlemagne's cousin, who was responsible for its mobilization.[164]

A second unit, described in the court *Annals* as a *scara*, was composed solely of East Frankish mounted troops.[165] This *scara* was under the direct command of three of Charlemagne's most senior government officials (*ministri*): Adalgisus the Chamberlain (*camararius*), Geilo the Count of the Stables (*comes stabuli*), and Woradus the Count of the Palace (*comes palatii*).[166] The rank and file of this force were a select element of the expeditionary levy drawn from at least four counties or *pagi* in that part of the *regnum Francorum* considered *Francia orientalis*.[167]

Since this latter force was composed only of mounted troops, these men were a select element of the select levy. As discussed in Chapter 2, most members of the select levy were rather undistinguished men who possessed a manse or two and did not have horses, while a small minority who possessed twelve manses were required to serve as heavily mounted troops. The composition of this group of horsemen, however, was not limited to men who possessed at least twelve manses (heavily armed mounted troops). Lightly armed mounted troops, who possessed less than twelve manses, also served as expeditionary levies, and nothing in the account suggests that all of the horsemen of this East Frankish select levy were heavily armed.

In addition to the above-mentioned mounted troops and foot soldiers, mobilized from the expeditionary levies in the East Frankish *scara* and the Ribuarian unit, respectively, there was a third group of fighting men attached to the forces under the command of Adalgisus, Geilo, and Woradus. These troops were the real professionals of the Carolingian army, sustained in the military households of the palace officials, the counts, and the other important men who served in East Frankish *scara*.[168] For example, the annalist's report that twenty aristocrats (*clari*) and nobles (*nobiles*) were killed in the battle[169] permits the inference that there were more than twenty such important men in the *scara*; it would have been odd if all the magnates mustered for these operations had been killed.

The Saxon forces were under the direct command of a talented military leader, Widukind, who in previous encounters with Frankish armies had frequently outwitted and outmaneuvered Charlemagne's generals.[170] Widukind's army numbered well in excess of five thousand effectives.[171] By contrast, the Carolingians, as noted above, had been mobilized in great haste in order to keep the rebels from moving on the offensive and did not enjoy its accustomed numerical advantage over the Saxons, which has been characterized, above, as "overwhelming force."[172] The Saxons, who had been preparing their revolt for some time, outnumbered the Franks in terms of absolute numbers of effective troops prepared for combat at that time in the campaign.[173] Some elements of the Carolingian force, that is, the *scara*, were likely of superior quality.

When the Ribuarian unit commanded by Theodoric made contact with the East Frankish levy, a planning council was held in which Adalgisus, Geilo, Woradus, and Theodoric are reported to have been the principals. It is not clear whether all, some, or even any of the *comites*, *clari*, or *nobiles* took part in these deliberations. In any event, the annalist reports that Theodoric suggested that scouts (*exploratores*) should be sent out to locate the Saxon encampment and to estimate both the strength of the enemy force and evaluate its tactical deployment. Then, according to the annalist, Theodoric urged that "if the terrain were appropriate," the two forces—the mounted East Frankish *scara* and the Ribuarian levies—together should attack the Saxons. Adalgisus, Geilo, and Woradus agreed to both elements in Theodoric's plan. The annalist characterized both the "suggestions" and the fact that they were accepted by the other commanders as "admirable."[174]

Theodoric's insistence that both Carolingian armies attack the Saxons at the same time may be taken as *prima facie* evidence for the enemy's substantial numbers if not numerical superiority. The *desideratum*, articulated by Theodoric, that battle should be given only if the nature of the terrain were appropriate seems to be an obvious reference to the importance that Charlemagne's cousin gave to the mounted troops of the East Frankish *scara*. They could be deployed to their best advantage against superior numbers of enemy foot soldiers if they could engage on horseback against either the enemy's flank or to attack from the rear. It was known that the Saxon force was somewhere in the Süntal mountains, and under normal conditions in such terrain the horsemen would be required to dismount in order to fight on foot. This concern for keeping the mounted arm of the force viable supports the inference that the Saxons likely outnumbered the Franks and that a battle simply between foot soldiers would favor the former.

In due course, the Carolingian scouts found where in the Süntal mountains the Saxon army was encamped and reported to their commanders the fact that it was ensconced in a fortified position (*castra*). With this information in hand, the four leaders decided to divide the army. Theodoric, whose forces, as already suggested, were largely lacking in horsemen, initially was to remain in place in order to block any imminent Saxon movement westward toward Frankish territory. Thus, Theodoric established a *castra* of his own on the left bank of the Weser along the route that the Saxons would have to follow if they were to move west from their present position. The mounted forces under the command of Charlemagne's three *ministri*, Adalgisus, Geilo, and Woradus, who obviously could move much more quickly than Theodoric's foot soldiers, then crossed the river and circled the Süntal in order to place the Saxons between themselves and Theodoric's position.[175]

The two Carolingian forces now began closing the pincer in order to trap the Saxons between them. The Saxons could not advance west toward the Weser without exposing themselves to an attack against their rear from the east nor could they retreat to the east without exposing themselves to an attack on their rear from the west. In the former case, Theodoric's troops would act as the anvil while the troops led by Adalgisus, Geilo, and Woradus would play the role of the hammer. In the latter case, the roles of the two Carolingian armies would be reversed. This classic pincer movement was a traditional Carolingian tactic employed well into the ninth century.[176]

However, at this crucial point in the campaign, the *ministri* in command of the mounted forces of the East Frankish *exercitus* decided not to follow the plan, discussed above, upon which they had agreed. Adalgisus and his co-commanders did not wait for the arrival of Theodoric's army from the west so that the two forces could trap the Saxon between them and, if the situation were propitious, initiate a joint attack. Indeed, having taken up their position to the east of the Saxon encampment, the *ministri* decided to engage the enemy in the open field. The annalist emphasizes the folly of this decision to attack prematurely, indicating particular annoyance that Adalgisus and his fellow commanders (according to the commonly held view) did not wait for the arrival of Theodoric's forces because they did not want to share the "glory of victory" with him and his men. This very forceful condemnation, correct or not, makes clear that proper Carolingian military doctrine eschewed the pursuit of glory as a valid military goal.[177]

In fact, the situation was not as simple as the annalist wanted his readers

to believe. The Saxon commander, who in this case was Widukind, himself, obtained intelligence that led him to appreciate the difficulties inherent in his strategic position. He understood that the Saxons had to engage and defeat the
East Frankish *scara*, which already was not too far distant from their camp, before Theodoric's Ribuarian force arrived and the two armies converged on their
position and encircled it. Once the two Carolingian armies had linked up in the
environs of the Saxon camp, the Franks could wait for increasing numbers of
reinforcements until overwhelming force was at hand. As more time passed and
additional enemy forces arrived, the Saxon position would become increasingly
untenable until executing a successful breakout became impossible.

The Saxon commander thus drew the conclusion that he had to lure the
East Frankish *scara* into engaging prematurely, before Theodoric's army arrived on the scene. Widukind was aware that Adalgisus and his co-commanders
would not lead a mounted charge against a fortified position and that Charlemagne's *ministri* would not order their horsemen, inferior in number to the Saxons', to dismount and storm the *castra* on foot. Indeed, as will be seen below in
Chapter 6, a minimum numerical advantage of four effectives to one was necessary for an attacking force storming a fortification. Thus, Widukind ordered
his troops to march out of the protection of the *castra* in order to challenge the
Carolingians, whom the Saxons probably outnumbered, to attack them.[178]

The Saxons—well-trained foot soldiers—deployed into line formation
with their backs to the wall of the camp. The court annalist, who reported the
battle on the basis of information provided by eyewitness informants, observes:
"The Saxons stood in their battle line (*in acie*) in front of their fortified encampment (*castris*)."[179] Some of the Saxons likely also were ordered by Widukind
to remain hidden within the camp, so that when the Frankish horsemen began
their advance against the Saxon battle line, those men could pop up from hiding
and pepper the attacking force with various types of missile weapons before the
mounted troops reached the Saxon phalanx.

The annalist's concern, as noted above, was not only with the stupid decision of the *ministri* to fight for glory rather than to follow the plan upon which
they had agreed. In addition, he was enraged by the terribly poor performance
of the Frankish horsemen in the battle. Once the decision to attack was made,
the annalist emphasizes that "each and every one [of the Franks] charged at the
Saxons with as much speed as he could generate," "as fast as his horse could
carry him." Such a charge, in which each horse was pushed all out, resulted in
the ranks of horsemen not being dressed. Thus, according to the annalist, "since
the charge had been so poorly executed, the battle (*pugnam*) [that followed]
also was a disaster." He continues, "once the fighting began, the attacking force
was enveloped by the Saxons and almost all [of the Franks] were killed."[180]

The annalist emphasizes both important facts about mounted tactics as well as key tactical errors. As the annalist and his audience knew, not all horses are capable of the same maximum speed at any time. When each man rides as fast as his horse can travel against the enemy there will be no unified battle line of mounted troops to crash simultaneously into the enemy formation. In addition, since there is no proper attacking formation of the type discussed above by Nithard, and thus no unified front, if the attack fails to break the enemy formation, the force cannot execute a feigned retreat in order to lure the enemy from its position. This type of pell-mell mounted charge, the annalist affirms, is not the proper way to attack a prepared battle line.[181]

The annalist presents the traditional wisdom that a mounted charge, like a charge on foot, was to be executed *en masse*. This was firm doctrine among the Franks' Byzantine neighbors in Italy, as illustrated, for example, by Maurice's instructions to his mounted troops. He emphasizes that in launching an attack, troops are not to fall behind their rank nor are they to get ahead of the standard that guides their line or rank. He also emphasizes that each soldier knows that he is to "move forward even with the front rank," meaning that the spacing between the ranks is to be kept. Finally, Maurice makes it clear that troopers "do not . . . charge out [of formation] in an impetuous manner and thus cause their ranks to be broken up."[182] Given the demands of the *toloutegon*, as described in considerable detail by Nithard and discussed above, the breaking of ranks by horsemen during a charge would lead to serious problems. Throughout the early Middle Ages and beyond, the imperative that mounted troops be kept together in formation in order to charge home as a group was well understood and constitutes what is now called fundamental "cavalry doctrine."[183]

The court annalist makes clear that the charge executed by the East Frankish *scara* in the Süntal was unsuitable for attacking an enemy battle line; however, he points out that such a deployment at top speed and ignoring proper formation was appropriate for "chasing down fugitives from behind and gathering up booty."[184] Here, the annalist is discussing the final phase of what previously had been a controlled pursuit. This phase in the deployment of a mounted force is initiated only after the enemy formation has been broken and the pursuing unit is sure that it has not been duped by an attempted feigned flight. This form of "hot pursuit," as we have seen above in discussing both the feigned retreat tactic and the countermeasures that were to be taken in order to thwart it, was, like the feigned retreat, itself, well integrated into the Carolingian tactical armamentarium.

The criticisms and asides of the court annalist in dealing with the debacle in the Süntal mountains provide insights into what was well known to the highly trained military officers who commanded early Carolingian armies. Indeed, the proper tactics of a mounted charge, whether against foot soldiers or against mounted troops, were so well known that a detailed although perhaps idealized version could be provided in Latin in the form of court poetry. The *Waltharius*-poet wants his listeners or readers to visualize two opposing forces in which the horsemen, to whom he gives his full attention, are to be seen as the primary tactical element in the battle.[185] Thus, in the first phase of the account, the reader learns that the topography of the area where the battle presumably is to be fought is composed of a broad expanse of flat lands and fields,[186] an ideal milieu for combat between mounted forces. Walter, the hero, personally scouted the area he has chosen for the battlefield ("locum pugnum conspexerat"), a decision he attempts to actualize through the adroit maneuver of his forces.[187] In the process of scouting the battlefield, he made a count of the enemy force, as well.[188] Then Walter deployed his army throughout the above-mentioned flat lands and fields in battle order ("aciem . . . digessit").[189]

After this initial deployment in line of his entire army, some part of Walter's force (see below) was deployed on foot to shoot arrows at the enemy. Walter ordered his remaining mounted troops, his main striking force, to advance to within the spear-throwing range of the enemy.[190] As we have seen above, this was a distance of about thirty or forty meters at most. Walter's mounted troops were not archers, as the poet refers to these mounted troops throwing only spears and exhausting their supply of this weapon.[191] Charlemagne, as noted earlier in Chapter 2, had tried and failed to develop a corps of mounted archers.[192] For the poet's audience, Walter's men who engaged as archers had dismounted and deployed on foot somewhere behind the line of horsemen or perhaps on their flanks.[193]

Once the two mounted forces to whom the poet gives his attention have come to a halt, they begin the first phase of the battle. He indicates that trumpets (*classica*) were sounded by both sides, by the relevant personnel who had been trained in the necessary signals and at the orders of their respective commanders. The soldiers in both armies then send up very loud battle cries from all parts of their formations.[194] The sounding of the trumpets, although a signal of sorts, was not the signal for a mounted charge. Rather, following the sounding of the trumpets, the horsemen begin to throw their spears, and those men who were equipped with bows loosed their arrows at the enemy. The poet depicts both the spear throwers and the archers, despite their obvious close range, sending their missiles in a high arc, as contrasted to directed "fire" at individual targets in the facing battle line.[195]

When the troops on both sides exhausted their missiles, the first phase of the battle ended.[196] At this point, the mounted troops under Walter's command were ordered to redeploy from the line formation (*acies*), in which they were

spread in a broad front and from which position they had launched their javelins, into a deep column to prepare for a charge. The term used is *cuneus*, by
which the poet indicates a pointed column of sorts.[197] The troops undoubtedly
were given some sort of signal to indicate when they were to halt their forward
movement, but the poet fails to mention this signal. (A poem, however "realistic" it may be in some of its military descriptions, cannot include every detail
and especially those that lack dramatic purpose. The fact that the poet mentions
signals sufficiently recognizes this technology without overburdening the poem
with indications of each time that these were used.)

The poet informs his listeners of the beginning of the second of phase of
the battle by suggesting that Walter's mounted troops were being commanded
by the numbers in a three-step drill. First: "each of the soldiers reaches for his
sword." The implied synchronicity here would lead those listening to believe
that a command or signal had been given. The second in a series of commands is
"they draw their flashing swords."[198] At the third step in the command sequence,
the soldiers "revolve their shields," that is, move them from their backs, where
they were kept out of the way during the first phase of the battle in which the
horsemen were throwing their spears, and place them on the left forearms.[199]

The troops were put through a three-step drill to begin what we have identified here as the second phase of the battle, but none of the mounted troops
prepares to engage the enemy in hand-to-hand combat with lances. Neither the
conti praemagni nor the thrusting spears, discussed above, which were treated by
Rhabanus Maurus and Nithard, respectively, are mentioned by the *Waltharius*-
poet. The mounted troops in this particular literary account attack only with
their swords.

The poet, however, does emphasize that the horsemen "revolve their
shields." This latter movement of the shield is important as it helps to illuminate much of the preceding handling of various weapons, discussed above. Prior
to loosing his missile weapons each horseman had removed his shield from his
left forearm and placed it on his back where it hung from a cord, the same maneuver used by the "retreating" troops in the *toloutegon*, previously discussed
and described in detail by Nithard. The horseman who was loosing his missiles
at the enemy placed his shield on his back in order to obtain greater physical
flexibility in the saddle and thus hurl his spear farther and more accurately. A
trade-off was involved: the man who stowed his shield away was as a result more
vulnerable to enemy missiles.[200]

Once Walter's mounted troops had their swords in their right hands and
their shields on their left forearms, the first segment of the second phase of
the battle—preparation to charge—was complete. The charge itself was the second segment of the second phase and the two opposing forces are depicted as

riding pell-mell at each other. Despite the silence of the poet on this point, one can safely assume that here too there was some signal, perhaps another blast of trumpets and an answering howl of war cries similar to that which inaugurated phase one. In any case, the charge brought the mounted troops together in a crash of considerable concussive impact. The poet describes the collision: "The chests of some horses are smashed by the chests of other horses and some of the men went down [with their horses while] others were unseated by the hard shield bosses of their adversaries." [201] The wording of the reciprocal smashing of the horses' chests was borrowed from Virgil and may be suspect in terms of the damage done in such a clash.[202] The horses on each side had traveled at most fifteen or twenty meters before crashing into each other and likely could not have reached the lethal speed required to smash a horse's chest.[203]

What is important from a tactical perspective, however, is that the distance covered between the two lines of horsemen was very short. Thus, breaks in the ranks of horsemen could not be created by the excessive speed of one or another horse or the efforts of an undisciplined rider to race ahead of his fellow soldiers.[204] In addition, Walter's forces were charging in column while the enemy force remained in line. This meant not only that Walter's troops remained in a compact mass but that they easily broke the enemy line. The statement that in the press of the first contact between the two forces, one or another horseman was able to unseat an adversary by smashing him with his shield boss is not fanciful. In this situation, a rider would be able to use his individual upper body strength in coordination with the speed of his horse to bring down an adversary.

The melée that followed the initial charge forms the third phase of the battle. Here, the poet quite naturally focuses his attention on the hero, Walter, depicted as cutting a wide swath through the enemy formation. Wherever Walter strikes, to the left or the right, men die and fear is instilled in the survivors who catch a glimpse of his epic effectiveness. Concomitantly, Walter's bravery, leadership, and invincibility on the battlefield undoubtedly raise the morale of his men and lower the morale of their adversaries. The epic exaggeration of the hero's exploits should not mask the fact that his men were fighting very effectively, as well. Finally, after the enemy suffered substantial casualties ("strages") and had its resolve to continue the battle broken, the poet reports, "having slung their shields on their backs, they fled giving [their horses] free rein." [205]

As the fourth phase of the battle begins — retreat and pursuit — we again see the fleeing mounted troops revolve the shield to protect the horseman's back. The poet describes the retreat as "at once, they all turned their backs." [206] Here the commander of the force that executed the retreat probably gave some sort of signal to his troops in order to execute a uniform retreat. The poet's audience expected even a defeated force to reflect vigorous training and drill.

The *Waltharius*-poet is not describing a simulated or feigned retreat; how-ever, the depiction of this "real" retreat technique is very similar to that de-scribed above by Nithard when he discusses the "roll back" or *toloutegon*. In a classic manner of the effective cavalry commander, Walter then led his men in a pursuit that is even "more cruel and more daring" than the initial charge. In what would seem to have been a hot pursuit, Walter and his men "continued the slaughter," "struck down more of their adversaries," and "killed even more fugitives." [207] The pursuit was carried on until Walter's force had won complete victory ("plenum . . . triumphum").[208]

Walter judged that the enemy forces were executing a real retreat rather than a feigned retreat. Then, Walter had yet one more signal given by his trum-peter (perhaps he even gave the signal himself; see below), not to move after the enemy in the tight formation, in which an enemy turnabout was expected, but in hot pursuit. This legitimate example of moving at top speed and ignoring proper formation was, as the court chronicler put it, appropriate for "chasing down fugitives from behind and gathering up booty." [209]

With the enemy driven from the field and fully defeated, Walter's victori-ous forces began plundering the bodies of their defeated adversaries. The army "rushes upon the dead and despoils all [that comes to hand]." [210] Since Walter's force represents a model of discipline and effectiveness, there is no doubt in the listener's mind that Walter has given his permission for the enemy to be de-spoiled and that this was conveyed to the troops through some sort of signal. When Walter concludes that sufficient looting had taken place, he recalls his troops and orders them into a line formation (*agmin*) by blowing a signal on his own horn (*cornus*).[211]

The "fictional" account of Walter's victory provides a model for the way in which certain types of mounted troops were to operate in a complex of specific combat situations. The troops were required to remain under the very tight con-trol of their *ductor* throughout the operation. Everything was done by signals, even if the poet did not mention all of the signals at the appropriate time. All operations were to be executed in a controlled sequence in which each trooper went through a type of drill in which first he prepared to draw his sword, then he drew his sword, then he fixed his shield in place, and finally he executed the charge. Any reader or listener at the court who was well acquainted with military discipline and training saw that Walter's men were operating "by the numbers." Even the defeated enemy is expected to be well disciplined; indeed, Walter's ad-versaries seem, in general, to be the mirror image of his own force. Thus, for example, the defeated forces execute a *toloutegon* under difficult conditions in a real retreat situation and manage to get their shields placed on their backs in the required manner.

Two points emerge from the treatment of this battle in addition to the importance of training, discipline, and obedience. First, good leadership is essential. The only real difference between the two armies in the poem would seem to be the presence of Walter as commander. The second point, which emerges from the first, is never underestimate the enemy. Those early Carolingians, who knew something of the Byzantine military manuals or had seen East Roman armies in drill or in combat, could not ask for a more disciplined force than that represented in the *Waltharius*, even if it was a poetic ideal.

Conclusion

The examination of early Carolingian tactics at the battle of Poitiers indicates that the phalanx was the basic formation for the deployment of a large mass of soldiers fighting on foot in a defensive posture. These soldiers were exceptionally well trained and could withstand the attack of both high-quality foot soldiers and mounted troops who had superior weapons and were better protected with armor. Indeed, Muslim armies had demonstrated their excellence against the armies of the East Roman empire and the Persians for more than a century prior to their defeat at Poitiers. Early Carolingian soldiers fighting on foot could deploy from column to line and carry out effective attacks on foot, as well. In short, the training of early Carolingian foot soldiers, discussed above in Chapter 3, was effective.

From the foregoing discussion of early Carolingian mounted troops, three distinct types of units would appear to have been armed and trained. Rhabanus Maurus focuses upon men who were trained to be equally adroit in fighting on foot and on horseback. These men carried swords, shields, and very long lances. Rhabanus indicates that these mounted troops carried the *gladius*, which suggests that when on foot they could fight effectively in a closely formed phalanx. Nithard, by contrast, gives his full attention to mounted troops who were adroit in mounted maneuvers. Great emphasis is given to carrying out a close order charge and to execute the feigned retreat tactic in the most difficult circumstances—against an oncoming mounted force. Nithard describes these troops as being equipped with thrusting spears, not extra-long lances, and shields. Although they probably carried swords, Nithard does not mention these weapons in regard to this particular training exercise. The *Waltharius*-poet emphasizes mounted troops who carried throwing spears, swords, and shields. These men were trained to deploy from riding column to line so that they could hurl their spears and then to redeploy in column in order to charge the enemy.

It is anachronistic to think of the mounted troops to whom Rhabanus Maurus gave his attention as dragoons—men trained to fight both on foot and on horseback. Less problematic is characterizing the men described in *Waltharius* as heavy cavalry who were trained to bring their charge home with such force that a horse's chest putatively could be smashed by the impact. Finally, the drill that Nithard describes seems more likely to have been executed by more lightly armed cavalry. Given the momentum built up in the charges described by Nithard, a heavy cavalryman who rode pell-mell at an oncoming enemy mounted force and then turned very abruptly in formation would endanger the horses. The feigned retreats carried out both by William's heavy cavalry at Hastings and Narses' *bandon* at Rimini were focused on tricking men who were fighting on foot and in a static position, and thus the change in direction for the horses would not have to have been so abrupt as in situations where the adversaries were enemy horsemen.

The early Carolingians' repertoire of tactics was quite ordinary and not innovative in terms of the late Roman past of which they were heirs. The armies of Pippin II and his successors, however, seem to have executed well on the basis of extensive training and drill, unit cohesion, high morale, and sound leadership. Although the debacle in the Süntal mountains shows that these armies were not immune from the stupidity of poor generalship or from failure to carry out their assignments, over the greater part of a century, early Carolingian armies in the field significantly and consistently outperformed their adversaries.

CHAPTER SIX
Campaign Strategy and Military Operations

A key element in any successful military organization is the ability to prepare detailed plans for campaigns such as that executed by Pippin against the fortress city of Bourges in 762, which is discussed below. These efforts rest, in part, on the capacity to acquire and evaluate sufficient intelligence to assure soundly conceived operations. How early in their rise to power the early Carolingians began to develop the formalized procedures that are intrinsic to such a system is unclear.[1] Adalhard of Corbie, in his *De ordine palatii*, demonstrates the functioning of a well-developed intelligence establishment by the latter part of King Pippin's reign.

Although Adalhard made it clear to his readers that he provided only the highlights of the administration of the royal palace, he discussed military planning and intelligence matters in considerable detail. Once each year, according to Adalhard, the *rex Francorum* held a special court (*placitum*), attended only by his most important court advisers (*praecipuii consiliarii*) and by a small selection of very important *seniores* drawn to the court from outside the regular palace staff. Adalhard had attended some of these meetings during the course of his early career and probably some later on as well. Thus, on the basis of personal experience, he reports that those who attended the *placitum* discussed problems identified by the palace staff and made specific plans for future military operations.[2]

In consonance with Adalhard's description, court writers note the important role that military planning played in the procedures of the royal court. Thus, for example, the Metz annalist, who wrote ca. 805, emphasizes how Pippin II, Charles Martel's father, relied on the expertise of a specialized group of military planners for the preparation of his major campaigns. The annalist calls this group, which was based at the royal court, "the *magistratus*."[3] Less than two decades later, Einhard indicates somewhat cryptically that Pippin, Charlemagne's father, had taken over the planning responsibilities for military operations even before he became king. According to Einhard, Charlemagne was constantly occupied by his military planning.[4] In short, by the later eighth century, detailed military planning was seen as a virtue in successful rulers.

By the reign of Charlemagne, the military planners were considered *magistri* in the quasi-technical language of the court's Latin vernacular—or so it seems from the account of the Metz annalist. In addition, these planners, again following the Metz annalist, constituted a rather formal group of specialists characterized by the then novel term *magistratus*. Thus, as suggested above, the author of the *Annales mettenses priores* projected the formal military planning function backward into the later seventh century. He writes: "When Pippin [II] had received the plan [or advice], i.e., *consilium*, from the *magistratus*, which it had been considering in its meeting (*quod apud se versabat*), he was exceptionally pleased [and] he mobilized the army *exercitus*."[5] This minimalist interpretation may or may not be fair to Pippin II or to the truthfulness of the Metz annalist.

The king viewed matters of "war and peace," as Adalhard puts it, as being of paramount importance to this group called the *magistratus* by the Metz annalist. Indeed, Adalhard indicates that he concurred with the king's views in this matter of establishing military priorities.[6] Also, the king sought to obtain information from all parts of his *regnum* through a wide intelligence-gathering network.[7] This mentality so thoroughly infiltrated court circles that it was a commonplace in the Latin entertainment literature meant for the royal entourage. In *Waltharius*, gathering intelligence is such a matter-of-fact process that when the king receives "certissima fama" of a pending enemy attack he sends a rapid response unit of mounted troops from the court to crush the invaders.[8]

Concerning the workings of the court planning and intelligence staff, Adalhard reports that data collected from throughout the realm was brought to the court. Government functionaries then separated what was useful and factual from gossip and unsubstantiated rumor and provided written summaries to the council members to aid them in their planning. These intelligence reports were structured into titled units ("denominata") and then further organized into chapters ("ordinata capitula").[9]

It is unfortunate that none of these planning documents have survived. However, as will be seen below, these texts were regarded as highly sensitive by the royal court and their circulation inhibited greatly by the perceived need for security and secrecy. Most of these documents were also ostensibly time conditioned in their value. Thus, the most likely reason for their failure to survive was the general inclination to have the expensive parchment upon which they were written scraped and reused for subsequent reports or other purposes.

Adalhard indicates that on the basis of the information provided to the planning group, decisions had to be made as to whether one or another Carolingian army would be deployed on the offensive and which other armed forces were to be mobilized so as to remain on the defensive. In this context, strategy was considered in terms of what we would call theaters of operation. Adalhard seems to imply, however, in consonance with established Western strategic thinking, that offensive military operations on more than one front at the same time were avoided.[10]

When the council obtained the necessary information, in the above-mentioned reports, "it determined, after lengthy deliberations, what action (*actio*) or troop deployments (*ordo agendi*) were to be carried out in the future," during the forthcoming campaigning season.[11] This account closely parallels the Metz annalist's description, quoted above, of Pippin II's response to receiving the campaign plan developed by his *magistratus*. From a semantic perspective, however, the experts' determination of the best campaign strategy for any particular year is not the same as giving the orders regarding what the ruler was to do upon receipt of the report.

This gathering of military officers and intelligence experts described by Adalhard may be characterized as a "war council."[12] Its role was not limited to undertaking lengthy deliberations in order to establish a broadly conceived military strategy on an annual basis for all of the potential theaters of operation in which the early Carolingians were involved. The council also paid close attention to matters of security. The senior military advisers who were invited to attend the palace meeting, as well as the staff permanently attached to the palace, who arranged and summarized the available intelligence data for the *magistratus*, recognized that the plans made by this group and subsequently approved by the king were to be kept carefully guarded secrets.[13]

Numerous observations made by Adalhard concerning the importance of maintaining secrecy indicate that Pippin and Charlemagne operated on the premise that today we call a need-to-know basis.[14] Secrecy, according to Adalhard, thwarted those "persons, who, because of the information [that they could obtain], might wish to stop or to undermine [the plans of the government]"; when secrecy was maintained, such people "were not able to do this."[15] The early Carolingian rulers and their advisers regarded their overtly committed enemies as well as their potential adversaries as having an avid interest in acquiring valuable intelligence concerning Carolingian military strategy and planning. Thus, the early Carolingians obviously perceived their adversaries as capable of potentially damaging spying efforts in order to secure information.

Keeping secrets from the enemy was but one half of intelligence operations at the early Carolingian court, as it is today. The other half of such operations was the gathering of explicit military information concerning the enemy, potential adversaries, and friends and allies.[16] Adalhard depicts the Frankish kings under whom he served as so eager to obtain information that they sought to question personally, or as we would say, "debrief," everyone who came to court.[17]

This type of royal interest extended to the mentality of contemporary Latin poetic literature that circulated in the early Carolingian royal courts. For example, in *Waltharius* the *rex Francorum* notices that a fish served to him for dinner was not a local variety and became suspicious. (The poet implies such suspiciousness was a very positive value.) The king summoned the head of the court kitchens in order to learn where he had obtained this "foreign" fish, saying: "This kind of fish to my knowledge is not found in *Francia*; they come from foreign territory beyond the frontiers." The chief cook explained to the king that he had obtained it from the man who operated the ferry that transported people across the Rhine where it passes the old Roman fortress city of Worms. The king then ordered the ferryman to be brought to him and personally interrogated the man. The ferryman had obtained the fish from a well-armed stranger who had recently crossed the river in his boat. The poet gives the ferryman's report to the king in great detail through direct discourse, suggesting not only that the monarch required very complete answers to his questions but that the court would consider this to be a normal debriefing. After receiving this intelligence and discussing it with his advisers, the king assembled a group of well-armed men from his entourage under his personal command to ride out and overtake the intruder.[18]

Reality and fiction likely were not very far apart here. Thus, Adalhard reports that all men who visited the royal court on official business, and especially those who had been summoned to attend one or another of the "general assemblies," were required to carry out intelligence-gathering efforts prior to their arrival. These men of all ranks were expected to provide information regarding domestic matters and what was happening beyond the frontiers if they had information of this kind. They were instructed in advance of their visit to acquire intelligence from their own people, from strangers, from friends, and from enemies. Indeed, what we call "raw information" from any source apparently was valued by the Carolingian court, even from slaves.[19]

According to Adalhard's account, the early Carolingian government sought the usual types of intelligence information, for example, concerning local disturbances and rumblings of local discontent within the *regnum*. Regarding foreign matters, Adalhard indicates that information concerning the potential for revolt by subject peoples and intelligence concerning people from beyond the frontiers who were planning attacks on the *regnum* were highly prized.[20] Even in discussing intelligence gathering, Adalhard phrases the *desiderata* in terms of just military actions, averring that the king wants to suppress revolts and defend the frontiers. Nothing is said of gathering information for wars of aggression or unprovoked invasion of foreign territories so that they might be conquered or plundered.

In addition to the planning of military strategy and the gathering of domestic and foreign intelligence, Adalhard pays considerable attention to logistical matters. Detailed planning was necessary in order to sustain the large numbers of people associated with the court. These logistical demands included the care and feeding of the household troops, the rank and file of the military house-hold.[21] The military units that composed the royal *obsequium*, as we have seen earlier, were an important element both at the court and in the early Carolingian army, itself.

With regard to logistics, Varro's *Libri Logistorici*, a handbook that provided methods for the calculation of logistic needs for late Roman and perhaps even for early medieval commanders, may not have survived into the early Carolingian period.[22] Nevertheless, amassing and organizing large quantities of food in order to supply both the court and the army required no more than the basic arithmetic that rustics commanded in order to count the hundreds of eggs, chickens, pigs, and *modii* of grain that they regularly raised and/or collected. However, it was hardly necessary for the skills that were required for logistic planning to be grasped by every peasant.

Arithmetical skills of an elementary nature were well developed through-out society through the very widespread use of the so-called finger calculus, also called the "*Calculus* of Victorius." This ancient system of calculation uses the finger joints similar in several ways to the counters of an abacus. Knowledge of the finger calculus was widely defused throughout early medieval society and, in one or another variation, is even used today in some parts of Europe. The finger calculus allowed people to add, subtract, multiply, and divide into the tens of thousands without worrying about the putative difficulties that many modern observers believe were inherent in the use of Roman numerals.[23]

At a higher level of society, young men who attended school at the Caro-lingian court learned more complicated arithmetical skills. The often discussed "Propositions for Sharpening Youth," associated with Alcuin but going back to Bede and probably earlier, illustrate a level of numeracy and a capacity to handle interesting number problems that few contemporary college students in the United States can be expected to solve. Many practice problems in "Propo-sitions" evidence a definite application to military matters,[24] especially "pack-ing problems," which taught formulae regarding how to calculate the number of houses or barracks that could be fit within the walls of a fortification.[25] Of course, a universally numerate society with a high level of mathematical train-ing and knowledge was as unnecessary for the working out of early Carolingian logistic problems as it was for the compilation of Domesday Book by William the Conqueror's bureaucrats.

*   *   *

As discussed above in Chapter 1, the topic of strategy can be separated into long-term strategy and campaign strategy. The former has been examined in detail with regard to the deployment of military assets, if and when necessary, for the purpose of securing a significant political goal — in the present context, the reconstruction of the *regnum Francorum* under direct Carolingian rule. Each campaign undertaken by the early Carolingians in pursuit of their long-term strategy required specific planning within the framework of a particular goal, for example, Charles Martel's effort to capture the fortress city of Narbonne from the Muslims in 737. For each campaign, the Carolingian *magistratus* decided the order of magnitude of the forces considered necessary and what types of fighting men (mounted troops, foot soldiers, artillery) they would need. In addition, they had to decide what kinds of equipment were required, how much food had to be made available, and a myriad of other details.

The information available for the strategy of the many early Carolingian campaigns differs greatly. Some campaign strategies, such as Pippin II's prior to the battle of Tertry in 687, are well documented. Others, such as Charles Martel's early punitive campaigns against the Saxons in Hesse, are poorly documented. In addition, evidence for military operations, to carry out the campaign strategy, differs markedly in both quantity and quality. There is usually a direct relation concerning the surviving information for a particular campaign strategy, the operations that were undertaken to execute the strategy, and the role of both the campaign strategy and military operations in the long-term strategy.

King Pippin's Conquest of Aquitaine

Of all early Carolingian campaign strategies developed for the offensive purpose of gaining control of territory and holding it, King Pippin's efforts, which focused on the capture of the great fortress city of Bourges, are the best documented. Not surprisingly, the military operations undertaken to execute this strategy are also among the best documented of those undertaken by Pippin I and his predecessors.[26] Thus, the campaign strategy and military operations that focused upon the capture of Bourges illustrate early Carolingian capabilities in these two important areas of early medieval warfare. However, the matter of documentation is not the only reason for this emphasis. This campaign strategy and the military operations through which it was realized were arguably the most difficult and complex of all early Carolingian efforts. Thus, we may evaluate the capabilities of Pippin's military establishment under the most challenging circumstances that it faced.

The Early Carolingians' Aquitanian Adversaries
By the mid-seventh century, the dukes of Aquitaine had managed to usurp royal power and ruled independently of the Merovingian *rois fainéants* and their

Mayors of the Palace in the north.[27] These dukes, moreover, maintained the structures of Merovingian military organization wherever possible through the implementation of policies similar to those that Clovis and his successors had pursued. Throughout Aquitaine, the fortified *urbes* remained the capitals of the *civitates*, which continued to be the units of local political organization. For the Aquitanian dukes, these fortress cities remained fundamental to the defense of the region and thus continued to be of great importance for military purposes.[28] The major cities, most of which had been walled and fortified since the later Roman empire, were provided with garrisons and defended as well by the locally recruited levies of civilian militiamen.[29]

At Bourges in 760, for example, there were at least two separate garrison units serving simultaneously within the *urbs* in addition to the local militia. One of these units was stationed there temporarily, and its members were referred to by contemporaries simply as *homines*.[30] These men did not live permanently at Bourges because their families were not settled in the city or in the general area. The other garrison force was composed of Gascons, and, in contrast to the former, they were established permanently at Bourges and had their families with them. Fredegar's Continuator, who as noted above may be considered an early Carolingian court chronicler, indicates that Pippin, after capturing these Gascon garrison troops, required them to swear an oath of faithfulness to him so that subsequently they could serve in his military forces.[31]

In addition to the major cities, such as Clermont-Ferrand, Bourges, and Toulouse, strongholds of lesser prominence built by the Romans throughout the region also were garrisoned.[32] For example, a troop of Gascons was stationed at Thouars in northern Aquitaine. The fort (*castrum*) at Bourbon was garrisoned by a unit called *homines Waiofarii*, or the men of (Duke) Waiofar. These troops may have been organized on the same basis as the garrison unit at Bourges referred to simply as *homines*. At Loches, some thirty miles southeast of Tours, the garrison was designated simply as *custodes*.[33] During the Merovingian era this term *custodes* was used frequently to denote garrison troops; such was the case at the nearby city of Tours.[34]

In addition to the garrisons stationed in the many cities and strongholds of Aquitaine, the dukes utilized various kinds of levies. The *Romani* of Orléans, who opposed Pippin's advance into Aquitaine in 742, were descendants of the locally raised levies from that *civitas* which had flourished during the Merovingian era. The use of the term *Romani* by a later eighth-century Frankish chronicler may well suggest his perception of this continuity, but more likely reflects his perception of the legal ethnic identity of the men in question.[35] The force led by Count Chilping of the Auvergne in 764 is described in terms similar to those used to denote levies in the Merovingian sources. Count Chilping also reinforced his levy with a Gascon unit, temporarily on detached duty from the garrison in the city of Clermont-Ferrand, which appears to have been its normal billet.[36]

The expeditionary elements of the local levies were sometimes grouped together into larger forces under the command of the duke of Aquitaine or his representative. In 761, Duke Waiofar called upon Count Chunibert of Bourges and Count Bladinus of the Auvergne to mobilize the expeditionary forces under their respective commands for an attack on Chalon-sur-Saône. Both the Auvergne and the Berry had institutionalized and well-established select levies operating late in the sixth century. Indeed, the former levy can be traced back into the early sixth century when it served in *expeditio* as part of the Visigothic military establishment.[37] Waiofar reinforced these *civitas*-based expeditionary levies with other troops and led this army against Chalon-sur-Saône. This force probably did not include Gascons, since Fredegar's Continuator appears to mention these southerners when they took part in military action.[38]

The Continuator's description of Waiofar's force, which engaged the Carolingians in 765, reveals that a Gascon levy did not normally form a regular part of the army of the Aquitanian duke but was constituted rather as a special and identifiably separate force.[39] In 765, the duke led "a large army," probably a group of reinforced locally recruited select levies drawn from the *civitates* for expeditionary service, and "a large levy of Gascons." The Continuator further notes that these Gascons were the same people who were once called Basques.[40] Such a clearly identifiable Basque levy had served under the duke of Aquitaine almost a half-century earlier, when in 719, Duke Eudo led a *hostis Vasconorum* against Charles Martel across the Loire and as far north as the region of Paris.[41] The Gascon levy, mobilized by the duke for expeditionary purposes, should be distinguished from the numerous garrisons composed of Gascons who were based in various fortress cities and other fortified places throughout Aquitaine.

Also important in the military organization of independent Aquitaine were the units of armed retainers employed by the magnates and established in their *obsequia* or military households. The outstanding example of such a magnate was Remistanius, who was Duke Waiofar's uncle but held no official position in his nephew's government. Nevertheless, he was so rich and powerful and his *obsequium* so formidable in armament and numbers that he used these household troops to attack strongly fortified positions that were defended not merely by locally raised general levies but by regular Carolingian garrisons, as well.[42]

The military usefulness of such household units is also well illustrated by an episode involving a battle in the field between Count Ammanugus of Poitiers and Abbot Wulfard of St. Martin at Tours. The count led the forces from his *obsequium* on a raid north-northeast into the Touraine and is reported by a hostile source to have initiated a plundering operation. The abbot, however, also personally led a force of household troops on campaign against Ammanugus' force. Abbot Wulfard deployed his *homines* so as to intercept Count Ammanugus' column, and in the battle that followed the count and a great many of his men were killed. The abbot successfully defended the region around Tours with his military household in a manner similar to that of a local levy or a garrison.[43]

Whether we label these troops, who were supported in the households of lay and ecclesiastical magnates such as Remistanius and Abbot Wulfard, "mercenaries" or as members of an *obsequium* is a matter of definition. Any duke or king who wanted to rule over a large area had to command the support of the leaders of these groups. Through the Merovingian era, important men employed *obsequia* of armed retainers. Rulers and would-be rulers purchased the support of these magnates and their followers with all kinds of wealth, moveable and landed, their own and that taken from others. For example, Eudo, while Duke of Aquitaine, was successful for a time in giving lands from the church in the Bourges area to various magnates to ensure their loyal military support.[44]

Both the usefulness of these household units and the complexity of the Aquitanian military organization that the early Carolingians faced are well illustrated by Duke Waiofar's efforts to weaken Pippin's control in the Narbonnaise in 762. Along with other magnates and their *obsequia*, Waiofar's cousin Count Mantio, in this instance reinforced by a levy of Gascons, set out to ambush a Carolingian force stationed at Narbonne while it was outside the city on patrol. Though Mantio apparently succeeded in gaining an initial tactical advantage, presumably through the element of surprise, the Carolingian force was able to recover its formation and counterattack. Count Mantio was killed, along with all of his household troops, the other magnates with their men, and a great many Gascons. Those Gascons who survived the battle fled the battlefield on foot, and the Franks took their horses as booty.[45] The Frankish unit, which succeeded despite its weakened tactical position and the apparent size of the Aquitanian force, which was composed of several groups of fighting men, was well trained and well led. It may have been quite large, as well, in light of the diversity of its opposition and the initial tactical advantage that the latter enjoyed.

Despite this defeat, the Gascons continued to play an important role in the Aquitanian military organization. These men from south of the Garonne had been under Merovingian suzerainty intermittently since the sixth century. Early in the seventh century, King Dagobert I (d. 639) placed the Basque territory under the administrative and military command of a Saxon duke and established the region as something of a frontier march with the Visigoths in Spain. By the early eighth century, a Gascon regional levy was a significant part of the

military organization of the Aquitanian duke. This regional levy served far beyond the frontier of Gascony and even beyond the borders of Aquitaine. In fact,
as seen above, this force was engaged in military operations under the command
of the Aquitanian duke north of the Loire River.[46] In terms of its regional organization and its capacity to engage in lengthy campaigns, it may perhaps be compared to the regional levy of Champagne, which the Merovingian kings organized during the sixth century and which served as far from its home base as
northern Italy.[47]

The Gascon regional levy was not, however, as has already been noted, the
only type of forces mobilized from south of the Garonne. Gascon garrison forces
were established with their families and very far from home in various fortress
cities in the north of Aquitaine. Units of Gascons also served in field forces such
as the one led by Count Mantio. These men may have been stationed in Aquitanian *centenae*, military colonies located north of the Garonne. Gascon fighting men settled with their families far from home, however, should probably be
considered mercenaries, an analogue of the *foederati* of the later fourth and fifth
centuries who were used by the government of the later Roman empire.[48]

In addition to using Basques or Gascons, men of Frankish origin served in
the Aquitaine dukes' military forces. In his victory over the Muslims at Toulouse
in 715, Duke Eudo led a force composed jointly of Aquitanians and Franks.[49] A
generation earlier, a noteworthy group of Frankish troops had settled in Aquitaine, and Eudo may have drawn his Frankish supporters from among these men
and their descendants.[50] The Franks who served Eudo may also have been descendants of garrison troops settled in Aquitaine by early Merovingian monarchs. Clovis began this process of military colonization. Following his victory
over the Visigothic king Alaric II in 507 and the integration of most of Aquitaine into the *regnum Francorum*, Clovis established Frankish military units in
Toulouse, Rodez, Saintes, and Bordeaux. Frankish military colonists probably
also were settled in many other fortified cities and *castra*.[51]

The continuity in military organization in Aquitaine from the Merovingian
era to the period of ducal independence is worth emphasizing. The three basic
organizational categories, which persist and would appear to have flourished,
are the general levies used ostensibly only for local defense; the select levies used
both for local defense and for *expeditio*; and the armed *obsequia* of the magnates
(including the duke), which were deployed either in attendance upon the *dominus* as a military household of *presentales* or in some sort of garrison situation.
The ability of the Aquitanian duke and/or his officers to use fighting men from
two or three organizational units at the same time, as seen above, suggests considerable strategic flexibility. The use of free men, as well as dependent followers
and perhaps even those who were less than free, illustrates the diversity of classes

from which these fighting men were drawn. The heterogeneous nature of the Aquitanian military from the "ethnic" standpoint is illustrated by the incorporation of *Romani*, *Wascones* (*Vaceti*), *Aquitani*, and *Franci* into various units.

Preparations for the Carolingian Conquest of Aquitaine

For almost a decade (760–768), King Pippin fought against Duke Waiofar in an ultimately successful long-term effort to bring Aquitaine under direct royal control. Thus, for all intents and purposes, the reconstruction of the *regnum Francorum* as it had existed at the death of King Chlotar I in 561 was completed under Pippin's rule, fulfilling the major *desideratum* of early Carolingian long-term strategy. Because this effort led by Pippin is unusually well documented in comparison with other early Carolingian military initiatives, it is possible to ascertain the structure of Pippin's military organization, strategy, and tactics he developed to gain his victory within the framework of the military policies that the early Carolingians had adopted in order to attain their long-term strategic goals.

In 761, Pippin's armies captured the important fortified places of Bourbon, Chantelle, and Clermont-Ferrand. In the Auvergne, he also obtained control of many other strongholds by making agreements with the local commanders. Pippin continued his campaigning the following year and after an elaborate siege took the city of Bourges; his forces also captured the fortress at Thouars in 762. By 766–767, most if not all of the fortified places in Aquitaine were in Pippin's hands. In 768, following the death of Duke Waiofar, the Frankish conquest was completed and Pippin issued a capitulary to provide the legal outline of the reintegration of the region into the *regnum Francorum*.[52]

As in the days of the later Roman empire and the Merovingian era, warfare in Aquitaine focused upon the fortified cities and other strongholds in the region.[53] Pippin's military objectives therefore were similar in many ways, not only to those pursued by the Visigothic kings who seized Aquitaine from Rome and garrisoned its strong places, but also to those of the Merovingians who drove out the Goths and later fought over the region in their civil wars.[54] To sustain this type of warfare in a consistent manner, effective siege operations had to be maintained over a lengthy period of time. For example, Pippin's army, when attacking Bourges, erected around the city a breastwork that included ramparts for the placement of siege engines as well as other weapons of various kinds. The Carolingians, therefore, deployed a considerable corps of engineers and artillerymen to help them capture their objective in this instance.[55]

By 766, recognizing Pippin's command of siege warfare, Duke Waiofar withdrew his garrisons from the fortified cities and strongholds that still remained under his control. Waiofar apparently also understood that Pippin was intent upon maintaining a military organization in Aquitaine similar to that which had flourished there since the later Roman empire, based in large part upon a highly militarized civilian population, the use of local levies, and the defense of both fortified cities and lesser strongholds. Therefore, in an effort to thwart Pippin's objectives, at least in the short term, Waiofar ordered that the walls were to be razed in the fortified places from which he withdrew his garrisons.[56]

However, the ability to do much more than breach, much less to raze, the types of fortifications under consideration here, which in many cases had ten-meter-high walls that were often three to four meters thick, on rather short notice and without substantial manpower, was a hopeless task. Waiofar's men may have achieved occasional breaches in the walls and perhaps the burning of wooden gates, as compared to the hyperbolic descriptions in the contemporary sources. Nevertheless, Pippin ordered the "rebuilding" of these fortifications, and though all work of this type was both costly and time-consuming, he is reported to have spared no expense and gave this task high priority. At Bourges, for example, as soon as the city (*urbs*) had fallen to the Carolingian army, Pippin commanded that the walls be repaired; he also placed the entire district (*civitas*) under the jurisdiction of his counts (*comites*). Pippin had the walls of the fort (*castrum*) at Argenton-sur-Creuse (Indre) repaired and placed this stronghold under his *comites*, as well. Before his death in 768, Pippin restored most of the fortified places that had been sabotaged and then abandoned by Waiofar's forces.[57] Indeed, the fortress cities of Aquitaine remained great defensive bastions throughout the Middle Ages.[58]

Like those counts who were given command at Bourges, the counts who were detailed to secure at least some of the newly repaired fortifications have been called "comtes-gouverneurs." It has been claimed that their office was a new one created by Charles Martel.[59] These *comites* commanded garrisons at forts and fortified cities; for example, the *comites* Australdus and Galemanius served with their men as a garrison for Narbonne. We also know that these garrisons were not permanently settled in new homes with their families. The troops served for a time as a garrison and then were moved on to another task. Thus, Count Australdus, after garrisoning Narbonne with his men, was assigned to defend the Chalon area, where he was detailed to cooperate with count Adalard of Chalon. Other *comites* also served under Adalard in this area.[60]

It is clear that Adalard of Chalon was the regular count of the *civitas*, but that the other *comites*, like Australdus, were not the usual type of count who served as the administrative and military head of a *civitas*. The title *comes* as applied to men like Galemanius and Australdus seems to have been an honor given to a worthy fighting man, probably one with a military household of his own, who could be used in a great variety of military and paramilitary operations. Another possibility is that these men commanded units of the royal household troops. In either case, far from being an innovation introduced by Charles Martel, such *comites* had their institutional origins in later Roman and Merovingian practices.

Throughout the later Roman empire, the term *comes* denoted elite military personnel who were accorded high status in the imperial army and who generally had some honored relation with the emperor. In Gaul during the later fifth century, for example, a Gallo-Roman magnate named Titus commanded and supported, at his own expense, a unit of household troops that performed with considerable effectiveness. Emperor Leo was so impressed by the armed exploits of Titus and his men (who may have been mercenaries) that he invited him to come to the eastern part of the empire and gave him the title *comes*.[61] In the Merovingian era, important men who performed military functions received the title *comes*. Such men, however, did not hold the office of count of the *civitas*. Some were associated with the court and were sent on military missions by the king.[62]

Even the independent dukes of Aquitaine accorded the title of *comes* as an honor to various men who used their household troops in a manner approved by the government. For example, Waiofar's garrison commander at Thouars, which was only a *castrum* and not a *civitas*, was called *comes*. In addition, a contemporary notes that Waiofar's cousin Mantio also held the title of *comes*, as did several of the magnates who served with him. None of these men, however, was the administrative and military head of a *civitas* during the period immediately under consideration here.[63]

Pippin also used *comites* of this type for tasks other than as commanders of garrison units. He employed them, for example, to guard the queen, to undertake special missions such as to hunt down his enemies, and also to support the forces led by a count of the *civitas*.[64] Thus, the use of *comites* for military and paramilitary operations in Aquitaine was not an innovation developed by Charles Martel that his son Pippin then imposed upon a conquered region. Instead, *comites* who were not assigned to serve as the military and civil head of a *civitas* were a relatively old institution used in the later Roman empire, adopted by the Merovingians, and continued to be employed both by the independent dukes of Aquitaine as well as by the early Carolingians under Charles Martel and Pippin. The honorable nature of the *comes* intitulation, in this context, likely results from the idea of being close to the king, a royal "companion."

When used for garrison duty, these *comites* with their armed forces served only on temporary assignment. For example, Count Australdus was transferred from garrison duty at Narbonne to more active duty in the area of Chalon-sur-

Saône. The *comites* established at Bourges in 762 were soon replaced by Chunibert, who was appointed count of the *civitas* as part of Pippin's regular administration.[65] For garrison purposes, Pippin gave command of the *castrum* within the city of Bourges to Remistanius, an Aquitanian magnate; he was to defend the *castrum* against Waiofar.[66] In the *civitas* of Berry, Pippin also encamped a special military unit of Franks (*scara Francorum*). This group may have been similar to the forces raised from a *centena* or, given the substantial size of some *scarae* deployed, both by the Merovingians and the early Carolingians, as seen above, such large units may have been mobilized from several *centenae*. Any of the *scarae* mentioned in these sources may also have been an element of the *obsequium regalis*. The *centena* was "a Frankish settlement, part military and part colonizing in function, living under a royal official (of imperial origin) called the *centenarius*" and which persisted in Aquitaine under Merovingians, independent dukes, and the early Carolingians.[67]

Pippin established garrisons and special units throughout Aquitaine. Various terms used in the sources to denote these units are *homines suis*, that is *homines Pippini*, and *custodes*. These two terms may cover similar groups by providing information from different perspectives. That the *homines* of Pippin are described in regard to their relation to the king may be evidence for their being members of the royal military household, who were on detached duty. But it may also mean only that these *homines* had taken a personal oath of faithfulness to the king. The term *custodes*, by contrast, refers to the military role that these men played as garrison troops. Thus, a *homo Pippini* could also be a *custos*, but not all *custodes* were members of the royal household on detached duty. It is likely, nevertheless, that every *homo* whom Pippin assigned to be a *custos*, even if a member of some magnate's *obsequium*, had taken an oath of faithfulness to the king much as every Roman soldier took an oath both to his commander and to the emperor.

The Carolingian garrisons at Angoulême and at Argenton were composed at least in part of Franks, and in the Bourges area another Frankish unit was established. Fredegar's Continuator took pains to distinguish between the *Franci*, who were used as garrison troops, and those *custodes* whom he did not consider *Franci*.[68] The latter units may have been composed of indigenous troops, perhaps even the same men who had served as garrisons during Waiofar's regime. As noted earlier, Pippin was not averse to using Remistanius and his Aquitanian household troops at Bourges, and most of these men were probably *Romani* in legal terms.

In this context, when Pippin obtained an oath of faithfulness from the Gascons, whom he had captured at Bourges in 762, he did so because he intended to use these men for military purposes. We cannot ascertain, however, whether these or other Basques were among the *custodes* whom Pippin deployed in strongholds throughout Aquitaine. The term *custodes* was used in a very general manner to denote garrison troops both during the Merovingian period and in Aquitaine under the independent dukes.[69]

As noted earlier, anyone who hoped to rule a large area needed to secure the loyalty of the magnates of the region and to obtain through them the support of their military households or *obsequia*.[70] Thus in 765, Pippin "purchased" the support of Remistanius, Waiofar's uncle. Pippin gave Remistanius gold, silver, costly cloths, horses, and arms. Whether one chooses to characterize Remistanius as a mercenary captain is more a matter of style than substance. In any case, Pippin also made Remistanius the administrator of half of the Bourges district as far west as the Cher River and gave him command of the fort, *castrum*, within the city. Remistanius' orders were to hold Bourges against Waiofar, his nephew and erstwhile *dominus*.[71] Other Aquitanian magnates also joined Pippin. For example, Count Chunibert of Bourges, after losing his city to the Carolingians in 762, swore an oath of faithfulness to Pippin, who reinstalled him as count. By 766, many of the Aquitanian magnates realized that Waiofar's cause was lost and offered their support to Pippin.[72]

Shortly before his death in 768, Pippin issued a capitulary for the purpose of regularizing Carolingian control in Aquitaine. In this edict, he directed that the principle of the personality of the law would obtain in the region just as it had under the independent dukes, the Merovingian kings, the Visigothic kings, and the later imperial government. Thus, Pippin gave support to the customs and traditional institutions of the various peoples dwelling in Aquitaine.[73] Obviously, not far from Pippin's mind when he issued this capitulary was the military value of the *Romani*, who constituted the vast majority of the population in the region and had shown at Orléans, for example, that they were still arms worthy. In addition, this attention to ethnic interests likely pleased Pippin's Basque subjects, who had been ubiquitous in military operations throughout Aquitaine during the 760s. This order suggests that Pippin either already had or was about to reconstitute, now under royal control, the general levies of the *civitates* for local defense and the select levies that were required to perform *expeditio*. In short, it was a *desideratum* of early Carolingian military policy to maintain a thoroughly militarized civilian population.

Furthermore, Pippin reaffirmed an old Merovingian and imperial military regulation regarding foraging. For example, when Clovis invaded Aquitaine in 507 during his campaign against the Visigoths, he issued a series of orders that placed church property off-limits to foragers, in principle, and promised the ecclesiastical authorities that they would be compensated for any losses suffered at the hands of his army. He permitted his mounted troops to take only grass and water for their horses from the countryside without compensation.[74] Similarly, Pippin issued a capitulary making clear that his troops must not loot and pillage the region; he limited them to taking only wood, water, and grass.[75]

No less important, however, were Pippin's efforts to maintain the basic tax in kind, the *annona militaris*, through which fodder was provided for the horses and for the pack animals of those soldiers, *viri militares*, who needed this support to help them sustain the costs of campaign (*expeditio*).[76] These taxes, which commonly came to be called *fodrum* (fodder), before the end of the eighth century, were a continuation of one aspect of an impost that had been collected during the later Roman empire.[77] As a result of Pippin's efforts, the military *annona* continued to be collected in Aquitaine as it was throughout the rest of the *regnum Francorum*.[78] While this tax burden fell upon all those who possessed land, poor men, who lacked the resources to participate in expeditionary operations, may well have felt the impact more acutely.[79]

Pippin's military organization in Aquitaine preserved the basic structures that he found there. For example, the magnates with their military *obsequia* were encouraged. In addition, he used men on detached service from the royal *obsequium* and troops recruited from the indigenous populations to garrison both the fortress cities and lesser strongholds, these latter units being mercenaries of a sort. In addition, Pippin legislated continued use of local levies for the local defense and of wealthier people for service in expeditionary levies.

Though his military organization indicates continuity, Pippin removed Gascon garrisons from some places and established personnel from the north in some locations. He did, however, continue to use non-Frankish garrisons of *custodes*. His capitulary, which explicitly recognized the personality of the law, gave particular emphasis to the rights of the Romans and of the Salian Franks. Thus, the majority of those Franks whom he placed in Aquitaine were drawn from those Romanized or Latinized Salians who earlier had settled in Neustria, and not from the Ripuarians, who, in general, were settled further to the east and likely had a higher proportion of German speakers in their midst. The reaffirmation of the Salian law would be appreciated by the descendants of those Franks who had been settled in Aquitaine since the early sixth century. Pippin's recognition of the legal identity of the *Romani* also strongly suggests that the local levies of Aquitaine, composed largely of *Romani* (like the unit he had encountered further to the north at Orléans), would continue to be used.

Offensive Campaign Strategy
The sources for Pippin's extended and successful effort to conquer Aquitaine during 760–768 provide a substantial body of information regarding his campaign strategy.[80] Of all Pippin's campaigns carried out in this context, however,

the effort executed in 762 that resulted in the capture of the formidable old Roman fortress city of Bourges in northeastern Aquitaine and the *castrum* of Thouars in the west of the duchy is the best documented. Therefore, this part of the chapter, dealing with campaign strategy, will focus on the efforts that culminated in the siege of Bourges. The siege itself and the capture of the city will be treated in the context of Pippin's military operations.

Pippin's diplomatic preparations for his projected annexation of Aquitaine, which he planned to initiate in 760, began following his Saxon campaign of 757.[81] Either before the end of the sailing season in 757 or when the Mediterranean route to Constantinople again became open in 758, the Carolingian king sent an embassy (*legatio*) to the Byzantine emperor, Constantine V Copronymus. The latter rapidly responded by dispatching imperial *legati* with many gifts to Pippin. Through these agents, the king and emperor swore "amicitias et fidem" to each other.[82] Pippin and Constantine had maintained good relations for several years prior to this exchange of embassies, and although they had not concluded a formal alliance previously, such a prospect was not far from the mind of the emperor and must have appealed to the Carolingian ruler.[83] In any case, given these close and friendly relations between Constantinople and the Carolingian court, it would have been exceptionally impolitic for Pippin not to have informed Constantine regarding his plans to bring Aquitaine under direct royal control by whatever means necessary and thereby to extend the *regnum Francorum* to the frontiers of Muslim-controlled Spain.[84]

The swearing of *amicitia* and *fidis* was a traditional diplomatic usage of a quasi-technical nature during the later Roman empire and among the Byzantines, indicating that an alliance of some sort had been arranged.[85] The exchange of oaths between proxies for their principals, the Frankish king and the Byzantine emperor, suggests that Fredegar's Continuator was copying the above-mentioned official usage. The possibility of an alliance of some kind between the Carolingians and Constantinople should not be ruled out in summary fashion.[86] Indeed, the negotiations between Pippin and Constantine concerning the possibility that the former's daughter, Gisla, might be married to one of the latter's sons, likely were still in progress.[87] At the very least, in these exchanges with Pippin, Constantine was not expressing any formal opposition to Carolingian policy with regard to Aquitaine.

Fredegar's Continuator, whose account ostensibly represents a contemporary view from the Carolingian court, indicates that during 758 and 759 Pippin did not undertake any offensive military campaigns. This period of peace undergirded an effort by Pippin to husband the human and material resources of the Carolingian realm for the planned invasion of Aquitaine. During this two-year period, Pippin had at least as good reason to take the field against the Lombards as he had had, for example, in 754 and 755. The Italian settlement, which he had made in 755, simply broke down. Beginning in 758 and continuing through 759 and beyond, Pope Paul continuously sought help from Pippin against what the Roman pontiff characterized as a Lombard-Byzantine axis. Nevertheless, Pippin was not deterred from his plans regarding Aquitaine and kept his armies at home. The *amicitia* or agreement between Pippin and Constantine, however, may have required that the former stay out of Italian affairs for some stipulated period of time.[88]

In 760, after working to secure his relations with Constantinople and resting his armies for two campaigning seasons, Pippin sent an ultimatum to Waiofar, the Aquitanian duke. The Carolingian monarch demanded through his *legati* that the duke restore all church properties that he had confiscated. In addition, Pippin commanded that Waiofar preserve the immunities that previous Frankish kings had granted to these ecclesiastical institutions. Waiofar therefore was to keep ducal officials (*judices*) and tax collectors (*exactores*) out of lands belonging to churches that had received relevant immunities. Indeed, these immunists were to have a direct relation with the king which was not to be mediated by the duke or his officials.[89] Further, Pippin demanded that Waiofar pay the wergild of those Goths who had given their support to the Frankish king and whom the duke subsequently had executed. Finally, Waiofar was to return to Pippin as prisoners all of the latter's *homines* who had fled from the Frankish kingdom to Aquitaine and joined the duke's service.[90]

With the benefit of hindsight, by the winter of 757–758, at the latest, Pippin and his advisers had begun to plan for the conquest of Aquitaine. Despite considerable pressure to the contrary from the pope, Pippin had managed to stay out of Italy and to conserve the military resources of the *regnum Francorum* for two years. He also very likely secured the neutrality of the Byzantines, if not their encouragement. When everything was as ready for war as Pippin could make it, he began his diplomatic initiative with an ultimatum to the Aquitanian duke that could be expected to result in military conflict. As the Carolingian monarch saw the situation, Waiofar would have difficulty accepting royal demands. Such acquiescence would seriously undermine Aquitanian independence or autonomy and reduce the duke's position to that of a high official in the service of the Carolingian monarch.

As the situation evolved under Pippin's guidance, through the Continuator's account, the early Carolingians understood two important and basic maxims about war and peace that were passed on in the West from antiquity through writers of the later Roman empire. First, Vegetius' often quoted maxim, "Igitur qui desiderat pacem, praeparet bellum," seems to have been almost second nature in Carolingian tradition.[91] Second, Augustine's complex view that justified war as the price of peace is no less relevant. Augustine recognized that the just ruler cannot avoid war because he will be compelled to it by the actions of his adversaries.[92] As presented by the court chronicler, Pippin's position with regard to the rebels in Aquitaine who were abusing the church established the justice of this war.

Therefore, the *casus belli*—Waiofar's rejection of Pippin's ultimatum—would be seen as the Carolingian king's defense of God's church against one of its many despoilers, if an account of the situation consistent with that provided by the Continuator were effectively bruited about. The Continuator wrote, "Waiofar defied all these things that King Pippin had mandated through his legates,"[93] and the language used here is exceptionally important. The verb *mando, mandare*, encourages the reader to believe that Pippin had sent a *mandatum* to Waiofar. Whether this is what Pippin did, or was what the Continuator wanted his readers to believe the king had done, puts a rather subtle point of constitutional-legal history at issue. Under Roman law, which was much appreciated in the empire's successor states, a *mandatum* given by the issuing power to a subordinate provides the latter with the legitimate right to act for the former. Thus, Pippin, by issuing a *mandatum* to Waiofar, was treating the Aquitanian duke as a royal official who was empowered to act for the king in carrying out the latter's orders.[94]

The court chronicler continued his narrative by emphasizing that the king "was compelled unwillingly" by Waiofar's failure to carry out the *mandatum* and therefore "mobilized an army (*exercitus*)" with which "he marched toward Aquitaine."[95] In any case, the court chronicler was establishing Pippin in the position, under Roman law, of a legitimate ruler who was in the process of undertaking a "just" military operation against a rebellious government official who had refused to carry out his duties under a *mandatum* issued by his rightful superior. From a military perspective, Pippin was pursuing his diplomatic initiative of trying to bring a wayward province back under central governmental control by other than diplomatic means.

As will be seen, this invasion launched in the campaigning season of 760 was merely a raid in force intended to probe the weaknesses of Waiofar's defenses and, if possible, accomplish the Aquitanian duke's capitulation without a full-scale war. After celebrating Easter during the first week of April at Jupille near Liège, Pippin moved his court south, probably to the frequently used royal residence at Attigny where the army was ordered to muster.[96] Not long after 1 May, the traditional date for the mobilization of Carolingian armies for the spring campaigning season, Pippin was ready to move his forces south into Aquitaine.[97]

From Attigny, or a nearby *Campus Martius*, the army marched south for about a week's travel time, or about 160 kilometers, through the Champagne to the district of Troyes. There the force stopped in order to rest the horses, re-supply where necessary, and repair the equipment after this initial "shakedown" phase of the operation.[98] It cannot be ascertained whether additional units from the Burgundian parts of the kingdom joined Pippin's army at this time, but after only a short rest of two or three days, the march was resumed along the Roman road south. Sens to the north was bypassed, and after at least three days on the march, the column again stopped, this time at the great fortress city of Auxerre.[99]

From Auxerre, Pippin's army continued southwest to the region of Nevers, a march of approximately 170 kilometers that under good conditions would have brought Pippin's army to the right bank of the Loire River by the late afternoon of the fifth day out of Auxerre. The main part of Pippin's army stopped at Mêves, some thirty-five kilometers north of Nevers on the Loire, however, in order to cross the river.[100] Pippin chose to cross at Mêves because if the Aquitanians were aware of his movements, they would expect him to cross the river at Nevers, which was on the direct Roman road to Bourges, Waiofar's northern capital in Aquitaine.[101] Waiofar's troops could have deployed to hinder Pippin's forces or, at the very least, have spies in the area to report that an army had crossed into Aquitaine, including intelligence regarding the size of the Carolingian invasion force and an estimate of its capabilities.

No permanent bridge at Mêves is mentioned. In addition, during the spring, the waters of the Loire in this region traditionally are high. Thus, it likely took Pippin's forces well into the second day after reaching Mêves if not longer to prepare a pontoon bridge and perhaps also to fit the usual flotation devices needed to bring the necessary supply wagons across the river.[102] This estimated timing is based upon the fact that the sources report no difficulties. Thus, within three to four days, the Carolingian army likely was across the Loire and on the road that led west to Bourges.

River crossings within enemy territory or from friendly territory into enemy territory were recognized by late Roman and early medieval commanders as one of the more dangerous maneuvers an army could undertake.[103] Therefore, Pippin, whose entire military career is a model of prudence and sound military practice, probably not only put reconnaissance parties across the river to ascertain if an enemy ambush were being prepared but also established a beachhead on the left bank of the Loire before committing the main body of his forces and supplies to the crossing. Such was standard operating procedure as found in the military handbooks.[104]

Once across the Loire, Pippin's forces departed from the road to Bourges and slashed southward, burning their way through the eastern reaches of the

Berry and the Bourbonais. The army finally halted at Doyat on the frontier of the Auvergne, about 150 kilometers almost due south of the Mêves river crossing and established a fortified base camp (*castra*). From this stronghold Pippin's forces were safely positioned so that they could project raids into the countryside.[105] Pippin's army was moving fast, but not more than about thirty kilometers per day, for if they went much faster their mounts might not be battle ready if they needed to deploy and engage the enemy on horseback.[106] In enemy territory, Pippin's army could not expect to replace their worn-down animals, and thus the greatest care had to be taken of the limited number of valuable horses any army could bring with it on campaign.[107]

From its base camp at Doyat, the Carolingian army raided along the frontier long and hard enough to get the attention of Duke Waiofar; this was Pippin's intention.[108] Finally, after considerable damage had been done, Waiofar, who had received intelligence concerning the Carolingian raid in force, sent Otbertus and Dadinus, two *missi*, to Pippin to arrange for the termination of hostilities. After negotiations between Pippin and the envoys, which the Continuator depicts as little more than an exercise in "begging for peace" by the latter, it became clear that Waiofar had no stomach for a war with the Carolingian king at that time. Thus, the two sides agreed that Pippin would stop the *bellum* at once and that Waiofar would hold a court (*placitum*) at which all of the properties in dispute would be returned to their rightful owners. In addition, Pippin received Adalgarius and Itherius (two prominent supporters of Waiofar) as hostages, and oaths by the duke's representatives strengthened his pledge to restore church property and ecclesiastical privileges.[109]

With an apparent minimum of effort, notwithstanding the Continuator's somewhat exaggerated account of the Carolingian army's accomplishments — "they burned the greatest part of Aquitaine with fire" and "returned home without casualties" — Pippin succeeded. Matters still were less than settled, as Aquitaine was not yet under direct royal rule. Moreover, after Pippin had withdrawn his forces from Aquitaine and the campaigning season had ended, Waiofar, who was no longer directly threatened by an army in the field on his own territory, sent another delegation to the Carolingian court. Count Chunibert of Bourges, Count Bladinus of the Auvergne, and Bishop Bertelannus of Bourges were instructed to "renegotiate" the agreement made at Doyat earlier in the year. Pippin is reported to have displayed "great anger" toward this embassy, and Waiofar's distinguished envoys did not accomplish their mission.[110]

In the spring of 761, Waiofar ignored the promises that he had made through his legates at Doyat and launched a well-planned raid into the *regnum Francorum*. The duke played directly into Pippin's hands, since the latter's aim was the domination of Aquitaine, by conquest if necessary. Pippin was still in need of a *casus belli*, and could not have ignored the *supplicatio* of Waiofar's representatives at Doyat during the campaigning season of 760.[111] Nor could he have refused the oaths, apparently given in good faith in the Aquitanian duke's name, promising that he would restore the church lands that had been confiscated.

Pippin, nevertheless, knew his man and lured Waiofar into breaking the peace by making it easy for the Aquitanian duke to launch a retaliatory attack into Frankish-held territory the following year. Pippin's *ultimata* imposed very harsh, even debilitating terms on the duke.[112] Pippin's show of anger toward the high-level embassy sent to the Carolingian royal court later in the year—an obvious diplomatic posture—was calculated to insult the aristocratic envoys and may have been intended to preclude a peaceful resolution of the differences between the two men short of Waiofar's complete capitulation.[113]

To lure Waiofar into a compromising hostile initiative, Pippin's defense of the Burgundian frontier east of the Berry did not deter an invasion; indeed, the Carolingian ruler made it easy for Waiofar to launch a successful attack in the region of Autun and Chalon-sur-Saône. Provoked by Pippin's actions and offered an easy opportunity for retaliation, Waiofar broke the oaths given in his name, initiated a *bellum* against the lord king, and inflicted serious damage on the *regnum Francorum*.[114] Who could then deny in the wake of Waiofar's perjury and aggression that Pippin had a just *casus belli*?[115]

A brief examination of Waiofar's success in this campaign provides considerable insight into the military situation that Pippin faced as he prepared his campaign strategy for the conquest of Aquitaine. In April 761, Waiofar led a large army comprised of the select levies from the Berry and the Auvergne, as well as several other *civitates*, in an attack on the *regnum Francorum*.[116] Since the Aquitanian duke's plan was to ravage the region in the neighborhood of Autun and Chalon-sur-Saône, the army was mustered in the region of Bourges north of the confluence of the Loire and the Allier.[117] Waiofar's forces would have to cross only the Loire and after passing safely to the north of the frontier fortress city of Nevers would be exceptionally well positioned to move south and then due east along the Roman road that ran to Autun and then on to Chalon. From the banks of the Loire, Autun was less than a four-day march, even with horse-drawn carts to carry supplies when going in and to haul booty out while leaving enemy territory. Chalon was merely two days further east on the same route, 160 kilometers in all, from the crossing of the Loire.[118]

In the course of ten days or two weeks, Waiofar's forces ravaged the Autunais region and also the territory of the Chalonais, including the *suburbana* of Chalon itself. In addition, Waiofar went out of his way to insult Pippin personally by burning down the royal villa (*villa publica*) of Mailly.[119] The contemporary report, though hostile to Waiofar, recognizes that the Aquitanian duke and his men then returned home with a large quantity of spoils and considerable booty ("multa spolia et praeda").[120] This major raid in force was aimed at both acquiring considerable quantities of loot and causing damage. No effort was made to take or even to attack Carolingian cities or for that matter any type of fortifications that were under Pippin's control.[121] The Carolingian local levies apparently were not called out either at Autun or at Chalon to engage the invaders in the field. Indeed, if these defense forces had been mobilized, Waiofar's army, which clearly relied on rapidity of movement, likely would have avoided contact if possible.[122]

Pippin was at Düren, a villa located between Cologne and Aachen, holding an assembly of his magnates to discuss affairs of state when he learned of Waiofar's invasion. Messengers could travel the five hundred or so kilometers, as the crow flies, between Autun and Düren, with exchanges of horses and riding during daylight hours, in less than five days if the *tractoria* (state messenger system) were working at full efficiency.[123] Pippin knew, once he received intelligence regarding the nature of Waiofar's army, whose mission was clear from its lack of siege equipment, that the enemy would be long gone before any forces at Düren could reach the area under attack.[124]

Rather than try to chase down Waiofar's army, Pippin decided to launch a major counterinvasion of eastern Aquitaine, with the immediate goal of capturing and/or reducing regional strongholds and seizing the fortifications at Clermont-Ferrand. That Pippin had such a campaign in mind prior to Waiofar's aggression is likely in light of the Carolingian ruler's previous record of prudent political and military planning, but cannot be proved. In any case, Pippin sent out orders that "all Franks" who were eligible for service in this campaign were to muster on the right bank of the Loire at the fortified city of Nevers.[125] Pippin, himself, moved south from Düren and issued a summons to mobilize an *exercitus*, which was not the same army as the general force, but likely units of the royal military household based in cantonments outside the presence of the king.[126] He then continued in a general southerly direction along the Roman roads that he had used the previous year, marching through the region of Troyes to Auxerre and then on to Nevers.[127]

After having crossed the Loire in the shadow of Nevers' massive urban fortifications, Pippin moved his large force about four days' march to the *castrum* of Bourbon. After closely surrounding the stronghold, he ordered the walls to be stormed from all directions. Pippin had bypassed Bourbon in 760 but obviously had had it scouted thoroughly. Thus, he knew that with sufficient manpower he could take the walls by storm and that a lengthy siege would not be required. Bourbon was duly captured and reportedly then burned. Waiofar's men who were serving in the garrison were taken prisoner. However, Pippin spared the local population that lived within the town and had served in the local levy to defend the walls. In addition, there is no mention that he had the town looted. This relatively benign treatment may have been part of an overall plan intended to pacify the inhabitants of the region and avoid embittering them unnecessarily during the process of annexation.[128]

Upon rendering Bourbon indefensible, at least temporarily, Pippin put his entire army on the road to Auvergne, 120 kilometers or about four days' march at best to the south. During this march, he apparently treated the countryside much more roughly than he had the previous year. This is marked by a change in emphasis in the court chronicler's account.[129] Along the road south to Auvergne, Pippin captured Chantelle, one of the several strongholds of the region alluded to above. Chantelle also apparently fell by storm but the commanders of many other fortifications (*castella*) in the region handed them over to the Carolingian ruler rather than face assault.[130] What terms Pippin imposed cannot be ascertained but it was customary for the king to be lenient with regard to those who surrendered without opposition.

When the army reached its destination of Auvergne, Pippin's forces constructed fortified encampments. Not long after his defensive positions were established, Pippin attacked the *castrum* of Clermont, which served as a citadel of sorts for the *urbs* of Auvergne.[131] Clermont was taken by storm and set on fire. Fredegar's Continuator reports that a great many people were killed, "as many women and children as men." Bladinus, the count of the Auvergne, apparently sallied from the urban fortifications with a large force of Gascon mercenaries who had been stationed there as garrison troops. This counterattack failed, the *urbs* was captured, and among the prisoners were a great many Gascons. Pippin had these men executed and Count Bladinus was held in chains as a prisoner of war.[132]

The entire region of the Auvergne was devastated and its local strongholds surrendered. Pippin rendered temporarily indefensible all the fortifications he captured during this campaign. After this campaign had been completed, Pippin considered the Auvergne to be integrated into the *regnum Francorum*, and thus under his royal control (*dominium*). In addition, units of the Carolingian army, apparently not under Pippin's direct command, were sent in a raid in force from Auvergne as far as Limoges, some two hundred kilometers to the west, in order to harry the land and terrorize its population. The Carolingian army is reported by the court chronicler to have returned home "unscathed" but with a great deal of plunder and spoil. God's help, "Deo auxiliante," was given overall credit for the victory, and this triumphalist characterization of the situation indicated that the war was regarded as just.[133]

Seen in the very short term, Pippin's campaign strategy in 761 was very different from his campaign strategy during the previous year. The earlier effort was a raid in force, intended either to secure Waiofar's submission or to provoke the duke into taking the kind of major hostile action that would provide Pippin with an obvious just cause to undertake a full-scale war of conquest aimed at bringing Aquitaine under direct Carolingian rule. At the same time, the campaign of 760 also served as an intelligence-gathering operation preparatory to either a future peaceful Carolingian occupation or a major invasion aimed at the reconquest of the region. Although Waiofar's attention was gained by the devastation that Pippin's forces wrought in 760, the chroniclers do not report, as is their wont, that the army returned home with noteworthy quantities of spoils. The lack of any mention of spoils may perhaps confirm the view that Pippin was interested in a peaceful solution if possible.

By contrast, the campaign strategy executed in 761 heralded the beginning of the reconquest of Aquitaine. Waiofar could still submit, and Pippin may even have permitted him to retain the office of *dux*.[134] However, Waiofar had provided Pippin with a just *casus belli* on three counts. The Aquitanian refused to execute the king's *mandatum*, he violated the pact made at Doyat (in effect, an act of perjury), and he attacked Carolingian assets in Burgundy. Thus, Pippin set out to nullify Waiofar's major bases in the east at Bourbon and in the Auvergne. This limited strike could be seen in the short term as proportional retaliation for Waiofar's raid into Burgundy. However, the basic issues were that Waiofar recognize Pippin as his superior, and that in his capacity as a royal official, *dux*, he ensure that the *tributa* and *munera* (traditional taxes that previous dukes had directed to the *reges Francorum* from their subjects in the Aquitanian province) were paid on an annual schedule.[135]

Pippin's successful campaign in 761, in addition, made it exceptionally difficult for the Aquitanian duke to make a major thrust against the Carolingians' western frontier in the future, as he had done with some success earlier in the year. However, in the longer term, Pippin's campaign strategy in 761, which deprived Waiofar of his bases in the eastern part of Aquitaine, undermined the capacity of the duke's army to cut Carolingian supply lines that would originate in Burgundy. For example, a fortress city such as Nevers, on the right bank of the Loire, was ideally positioned and, as will be seen below, seems to have been the main Carolingian base from which campaign forces were projected into northeastern Aquitaine for an attack on Bourges.

In addition, Pippin's campaign strategy in both 760 and 761 left the impression among his Aquitanian adversaries that his regular invasion route into their territory would originate in Austrasia and that he would use Nevers as his base for crossing the Loire. According to this reading of Pippin's behavior, Nevers could be seen as the likely location for the muster of the Carolingian army in future invasions of Aquitaine. However, in preparing his strategy for the campaign in 762, Pippin spent the winter and early spring in the heart of Neustria at Quirzy, about one hundred kilometers northeast of Paris. As late as 18 April, Easter Sunday, Pippin was at Quirzy. Thus, if Waiofar had spies reporting on the Carolingian ruler's movements, as is likely, Pippin and his military advisers, the *magistratus*, seemed to be exploring new offensive options for the invasion of Aquitaine.[136]

Pippin, however, had decided no later than mid-March that he would launch a two-pronged attack into Aquitaine. Troops drawn primarily from Austrasia would, as in the previous year, muster at Nevers. This army would cross the Loire and lay siege to Bourges, the Carolingian monarch's primary target and the strategic key to the military control of northeastern Aquitaine. Waiofar regarded it as his capital, or at least as the capital of Aquitaine, *caput Aquitaniae*.[137] Here Pippin tried to duplicate what he had done so effectively in 755 and 756 when he forced the surrender of Pavia, the Lombard capital, and won a short and comparatively bloodless victory.

Pippin was not eager to have his Austrasian army, heavily laden with machines and supplies for the siege, encounter an Aquitanian field force, however. Thus, he mobilized a second column, raised in Neustria, likely to muster in the region around Tours on the Loire or at Angers about a hundred kilometers further to the west on the banks of the same river. After crossing the Loire, this likely smaller column was to attack the important border stronghold of Thouars on Aquitaine's northwest frontier, more than four hundred kilometers westnorthwest of Bourges.[138]

Pippin intended to attract Waiofar's attention and lure the Aquitanian duke into that western region with his field army. Pippin set up this ruse by spending the early spring in Neustria, signaling his intention to command an invasion force that was to attack in the west. If this ruse were to be successful, the Carolingian forces, which were coming from Austrasia in the east and mustered at Nevers, could establish a siege at Bourges without dealing with an enemy army nearby in the field. If Pippin's strategic thinking as it developed during the winter of 761–762 can be plausibly reconstructed, the planners at Quirzy seem to have assumed that Waiofar would focus his attention on the forces raised in Neustria because these troops seemed to be under the Carolingian king's direct command. Thus, from Waiofar's perspective, wherever Pippin was to be found, the Carolingians' major effort would be launched. Pippin, like his father, Charles Martel, had a long history of personal and effective military leadership, and this could not have been unknown to the Aquitanian duke.[139]

Military Operations

It is not clear exactly when Pippin assumed personal command of the siege operations at Bourges. This great fortified city, which since Merovingian times had been a major military base and key to the control of northeastern Aquitaine, would not be easy to capture should force be required.[140] The Roman fourth-century walls of Bourges enclosed approximately 26 hectares within a roughly oval-shaped perimeter that had a circuit of 2,600 meters. Forty-six semicircular hollow towers projected from the walls at roughly fifty-meter intervals, and four gates have been identified, each with two U-shaped towers to provide additional protection. These towers and the gate fortifications created overlapping fields of fire for men deployed either with regular bows or crossbows in the towers or on the walls. The areas between the towers and in front of the gates therefore were extremely effective killing grounds. The walls, averaging approximately two and a half to three meters in thickness, were of the exceptionally strong ashlar construction commonly used throughout the late Roman world for building urban defenses.[141]

Pippin and his advisers understood that taking Bourges by force would require not only an army of a substantial order of magnitude with the skills requisite to attack a great fortress city but also an exceptionally sophisticated siege train. In addition, Waiofar's field army, which had been so successful in Burgundy the previous year, could not be ignored. If Pippin were successful temporarily in luring his enemy far to the west, tricking the Aquitanian duke into believing that he was protecting Thouars, Waiofar could eventually work his way back to the east. The potential threat posed to Pippin's operations by this Aquitanian army as well as by the considerable force of local levies and mercenary troops stationed at Bourges required noteworthy precautions for the investment of the city.[142]

As Fredegar's Continuator indicates, the Carolingians first established fortified encampments (*castra*) in strategic positions around Bourges.[143] These encampments provided immediate protection for the invading army against a force that might sally out from the city and/or from an enemy force already in the field. Thus, Pippin's operations met the standard that had been used in the West for centuries.[144] These procedures were well documented in the military handbooks and histories, which along with the practical experience that was provided by operations in the field, had served as the basis for the education of military commanders in the West for more than a millennium.[145] The building of fortified camps for a siege as well as for other purposes was also standard operating procedure for the Byzantines with whom the Franks already had substantial direct contact during the previous three centuries.[146]

In addition, the Frankish *castra* in the environs of Bourges likely were sited so that Pippin's army could interdict entry into and exit from the city. The early Carolingians had considerable experience in laying siege to and capturing major fortress cities, such as Bourges, which had been built during the later Roman empire. For example, Charles Martel had, among many other such *urbes*, on two separate occasions besieged and taken the fortress city of Avignon, which during the early Middle Ages had proven consistently to have been a particularly difficult target.[147]

Closer in time and of greater importance to our understanding of what the Carolingians were doing in 762 at Bourges, and as a possible guide to estimating the complexity of Pippin's military operations, were his successful invasions of the Lombard kingdom in 754 and 755. In both cases, after the Carolingian armies broke through the alpine defenses that King Aistulf had established, Pippin struck directly at the well-fortified city of Pavia, the Lombard capital.[148] In 754, after Pippin established a fortified camp (*castra*) in the environs of Pavia, he dispatched raiding parties to forage throughout the countryside and to ravage and burn what could not be carried away. This policy included the destruction of the small Lombard military encampments (*castra*) that dotted the region in the neighborhood of Pavia and the capture of their inhabitants.[149] The latter apparently were held as prisoners but they do not seem to have been considered hostages.[150]

In contrast with his military operations around Pavia in 754, Pippin employed rather different tactics in the second phase of his campaign strategy in 755. First, as in 754, he saw to it that the entire region around Pavia was entirely devastated; all movables and especially foodstuffs were commandeered following normal military practice in the West. However, in the second phase of his operation, he deployed his army all around the city and did not merely base these forces in a single fortified encampment (*castra*). The court chronicler, who was now working under the patronage of Pippin's cousin, observed that the Carolingian army encamped around the walls of Pavia ("circa muros Tincini") so that no one could escape ("ita ut nullus exinde evadere potuisset") from the city. This observation by the Continuator permits the inference that Pippin vallated the entire circuit, that is, he built a continuous encircling siege wall.[151] In doing this, he was following a procedure that Charles Martel had employed during the siege of Narbonne in 737.[152] Whether Pippin established a contravallation in 755 to protect his emplacements from attack by enemy forces already in the field cannot be ascertained. Such a decision would have depended upon his view of the threat posed by the supporters of the Lombard king, Desiderius, who were then deployed in other parts of the *regnum* but could in principle be mobilized to relieve the siege of Pavia.

Pippin's operations at Bourges in 762 incorporated several methods he employed when he laid siege to the Lombard capital at Pavia in 754 and 755. For example, the main fortified encampment established by the Carolingians in the environs of Bourges was constructed on a site about three hundred meters southeast of the walls of the *urbs*. This position, opposite the gate that is now called the Port de Lyon and along the old Roman road between Bourges and Nevers, apparently had an earlier incarnation as a Roman *castrum*.[153] From an offensive perspective, this fortification in Pippin's hands and fully defended provided a strong base for interdicting all substantial movement to the east by the forces of Count Chunibert, who was in command of the Aquitanian defense effort at Bourges.[154]

This fortification in the direction of Port de Lyon was not large: 200 meters by 160 meters, enclosing 32,000 square meters. Nevertheless, the area within the walls of the *castrum*, and perhaps in their environs, as well, was inhabited. A church dedicated to Saint Austregisel, which had been built during the previous century, was located within the walls.[155] A stone church was superior to chapel tents and portable altars for the performance of religious services which, as noted in Chapter 4, were an important *desideratum* for maintaining the morale of the troops on campaign. In addition, housing for men and/or animals, facilities for drawing water, and civilian labor that could be commandeered within this stronghold were regarded by Pippin as assets to the military operation that was under way.

Nevers had been the main base for Pippin's operations against enemy assets in eastern Aquitaine during the previous two years. It was the closest fortified city, under direct Carolingian control and in secure contact with his Austrasian and Burgundian centers of power, to Bourges. Thus, the old Roman *castrum* that impeded access to Port de Lyon gave Pippin complete control of part of an important link in his supply route (see below) along the old Roman road between Nevers and Bourges. Indeed, in light of the various advantages outlined above, this stronghold was an ideal site for Pippin's army headquarters.

The *castrum* was insufficiently large to protect the entire Carolingian army (see below). If Pippin had based his entire force, even initially, in and around this stronghold, he would have left three of Bourges' four gates without Carolingian troop emplacements. The Carolingians' other *castra*, which had to be constructed in the environs of Bourges, therefore must be assumed to have been opposite the remaining three gates of the city. Port Saint-André in the north wall opened onto the Roman road that led to Orléans, Port d'Auron in the west wall opened on the Roman road to Tours, and Port Gordaine in the east wall opened on the Roman road that led to Saint-Satur (*Cortunum Castrum*).[156]

No compelling archaeological evidence has been uncovered to sustain this speculation regarding the possible location of Pippin's fortified camps in the environs of Bourges. As Fredegar's Continuator makes clear, however, Pippin intended to besiege the *urbs* and this required that access to each of the main gates be interdicted.[157] His fortifications, even initially, had to block the roads that radiated from each of these gates to keep a relief force of any considerable size or even small troop units from entering the city. In addition, messengers could enter or leave the fortress at will, were the gates not blocked by the besieging force. Finally, a properly protected supply train could get through to Bourges if Pippin failed to control the roads into the city.

From a defensive perspective, even with appropriately positioned fortified encampments, Pippin's army could not interdict forces from sallying out of the gates of Bourges and deploying in the field, but they could ensure that this tactic could be executed only at some considerable cost. For a unit of five hundred men to exit through a five-meter-wide gate and to deploy in formation outside the wall required ten to fifteen minutes from the time the head of the column had passed through the gate. However, troops in fortified positions with various missile weapons, discussed earlier, could inflict substantial casualties on a force that tried to deploy outside the walls.

Once the Carolingian army was in its defended emplacements at Bourges, a thoroughgoing foraging operation was undertaken throughout the surrounding area, again following standard operating procedure for the initiation of a siege.[158] Fredegar's Continuator, with some hyperbole, depicts the region as being devastated as a result of these foraging efforts.[159] Unfortunately, most early medieval writers fail to make a distinction between regular foraging operations, which were intended to augment an invading army's supplies, and an intentional effort to undermine the productivity of a region for a lengthy period of time by destroying its capital infrastructure. The latter, which, for example, necessitated the cutting down or burning of grape vines and olive trees, had to be the result of a predetermined policy to which the perpetrator would have to dedicate considerable planning, resources, and time.[160] Since it was Pippin's clear intention not only to conquer the Berry but to integrate it directly into that part of the *regnum Francorum* which he ruled, it is highly unlikely that he departed from traditional wisdom and destroyed the capital infrastructure of the region.[161]

Pippin and his advisers knew early in the campaign that a protracted siege would be necessary. Thus, Pippin ordered additional steps to be taken in order to perfect the interdiction of relief to the city and to protect the besieging army. In a second and far more costly and time-consuming initiative, some of the *castra* discussed above were linked by lines of vallation, which established a circuit of siege walls completely around Bourges.[162]

Lines of contravallation likely were also put in place to protect the besieging army from any attack from the rear by an enemy relief force. The possibility that Waiofar could put an army into the field similar to the one that had operated so effectively the previous year in Burgundy could not be ignored by King Pippin, who was known for his prudence. Count Chunibert, in fact, had refused to surrender his city on favorable terms prior to the initiation of hostilities and in the face of a very formidable Carolingian force. This behavior signaled to Pippin that the count of Bourges believed that the duke of Aquitaine could and likely would send an army capable of raising the siege.[163]

The task of preparing the siege of Bourges, as briefly described above, provides important insights into the Carolingians' military infrastructure. Fredegar's Continuator makes clear that Pippin's army fully encircled Bourges with a wall, constructed of earth but probably reinforced with wooden supports (see below) and topped by a rampart. This wall, according to the Continuator, had two main purposes: to stop all traffic in and out of Bourges, and to serve as a protected firing platform for the catapults (*machinae*) and all kinds of other siege engines ("omni genere armorum") that were to be used by Pippin's men, whose aim was to batter and breach the walls of the city as well as to kill enemy personnel.[164]

In order to encircle the *urbs* of Bourges, the Carolingian vallation had to have a circumference between 3,200 and 4,400 meters. The former figure puts the siege wall less than 100 meters from the outer defenses of the city of Bourges, placing both the defenders and the besiegers within the range of archers on both sides and well within range of the heavy artillery. The latter suggestion puts the vallation 300 meters from the city and permits the siege fortifications to be linked directly to the *castrum* on the road to Nevers. In such a case, however, the city and the Carolingian vallated siege positions would not be within archery range of each other. If Pippin's forces also constructed a contravallation, at least twenty meters between the two siege walls was required for maneuvering artillery into place, for easy access and turning room for wagons, and perhaps even for the protection of horses.

Vallation and contravallation of the type traditionally used in the West from ancient times through the Middle Ages did not require a sophisticated engineering knowledge or advanced surveying skills. For example, much more complex earthen walls, which were of considerably greater extent than those likely constructed by Pippin's forces at Bourges, were built by the Danes as early as 737.[165] Indeed, Pippin's younger contemporary King Offa of Mercia, whose resources were inferior to those of his Carolingian neighbors, built the famous dike that bears his name which ran for more than two hundred kilometers across England's western frontier with Wales.[166] The kind of sophisticated technical knowledge demonstrated by Charlemagne's engineers, who, a little later in the eighth century, designed and undertook the effort to build a Rhine-Main-Danube canal, was far superior to what was needed for the type of wall building under consideration here.[167] In any case, the early Carolingians had available a substantial corpus of Roman surveying works with illustrations and maps.[168]

Nevertheless, the construction of four major siege *castra*, as well as at least a single siege wall of at least 3,000 meters, and possibly a contravallation of greater size, required considerable manpower and large numbers of basic tools. As with the armies of the later Roman empire and the early Carolingians' Byzantine contemporaries, the equipment for building fortifications while on campaign was a standard part of the *impedimenta*, along with a great many other items, carried on Carolingian war carts. A partial list of standard implements useful for building *castra* and siege walls is in one of the very few surviving Carolingian military *capitula*: "In your carts (*carris*) there are to be various kinds of equipment, i.e., hatchets (*cuniada*), saws for stone cutting (*dolaturia*), augers (*tarratros*), carpenter's axes (*assias*), spades for ditch digging (*fosorios*), iron shovels (*palas ferreas*), and all the rest of the tools (*utensilia*) that are necessary for an army on campaign (*hostem*)." [169] With equipment of the type that traditionally was part of a Carolingian baggage train, sufficient manpower, and engineers, Pippin's army was capable of building the siege works alluded to by Fredegar's Continuator.

Vegetius discusses briefly the various types of earthen walls with ramparts and ditches that were commonly constructed since the later Roman empire in *De re Militari*. He describes defenses that are to be used "when there is no pressing danger," the kind of fortified encampment "for one night or for brief occupation in the course of a march." For this temporary type of ditch and wall fortification, two methods are described. In one, "sods are cut from the earth and from these a type of wall is built, three feet high above the ground." [170] Then on the top of this "rampart . . . stakes or wooden posts are set up." [171] Or, "when the earth is too loose for it to be possible to cut the turf like a brick, the ditch is dug in 'temporary style,' five feet wide, three feet deep, and with the rampart rising on the inner side." [172]

The handbooks also provide information for more permanent fortified encampments to be constructed "when enemy forces present a more serious danger." Such encampments may have ditches from nine to seventeen feet in width. Apparently, it was most common:

to fortify the perimeter of the camp with an appropriate ditch, i.e., one that is twelve feet wide and nine feet below ground level. Above the ditch, embankments are built [of wood] and . . . filled with the earth that has been dug out from the ditch; these walls rise to a height of four feet. Thus, the ditch is thirteen feet deep [from the bottom to the top of the wall] and twelve feet wide. On top of the wall stakes of very strong wood are fixed.[173]

In more elaborate fortified camps, "battlements and turrets" constructed of wood were placed on top of the embankment itself.[174]

These data provided by Vegetius in his *De re Militari* are confirmed by other handbooks, as well as by traditional Byzantine usage.[175] Pippin's close advisers, such as Fulrad, who ultimately was made abbot of St. Denis and went on to serve Charlemagne, likely learned a great deal about Byzantine methods and ideas while working in Italy.[176] However, it would be rash to suggest that Pippin's men followed one or another handbook in a slavish manner. Rather, these data provide merely a glimpse of the order of magnitude of the task that lay before Pippin as the Carolingians planned the siege emplacements needed to pursue the effective investment of Bourges.

We are not informed whether Pippin ordered nine-foot ditches or twelve-foot ditches to be dug or whether the earthen embankments that his men constructed were three feet or four feet above ground level. We do know, according to a court source, that there were ditches and earthen walls and that the latter were topped by wooden ramparts. Not only were the earthen walls sufficiently solid to support the weight of the artillery which Pippin had placed on them, but also these embankments withstood the recoil of the catapults. Finally, Pippin's wall, excluding the *castra* and contravallation, was at least 3,000 meters in circumference.

A ditch-and-wall complex that was far below imperial Roman standards of the later empire and below contemporary Byzantine standards still required a substantial amount of highly organized labor and large quantities of the best iron tools available to do a first-rate job in minimum time. While a low standard is used here to avoid exaggerating Carolingian accomplishments, there is no reason to believe that Pippin skimped with regard to military matters. A worst-case situation — a 3,000-meter wall with a ditch three meters in breadth and perhaps two meters deep — required that 18,000 cubic meters of earth be excavated. This task alone, under optimal conditions based on experiments done with nineteenth-century hand tools, which were far superior to the type of equipment used during the mid-eighth century, is estimated to have required 72,000 man-hours of labor, or 7,200 man-days of digging.[177]

This estimate does not include the labor needed for cutting and preparing the wood to build the revetments that held the earthen walls, nor does it include cutting and shaping the wood for building the palisade or rampart that crowned the earthen wall. If a contravallation was also built, these minimum labor figures would have to be doubled. Still unaccounted for are the labor, equipment, and resources used to build the *castra* or shelters for the men, for the horses, and for the safe storage of supplies.[178] In short, the Carolingian siege complex at Bourges built by Pippin's forces during the campaigning season of 762 may have required more than 30,000 man-days of labor.

The same logistic problems inherent in conducting a highly sophisticated siege of a major fortified city surfaced throughout the fourth to eleventh centuries in the West. This is due, in large part, to the static nature of the available technology.[179] This technology, as discussed earlier, dictated the minima in terms of number of troops required to defend the walls of a fortification and thus determined the order of magnitude of any army which sought to capture a city such as Bourges by military force. A reasonably well-trained fighting man, equipped with a bow, was required by early medieval defense doctrine to defend approximately each one and one-third meters of wall.[180] In light of this ratio, the 2,600-meter circuit wall of the fortress city at Bourges required more than 2,000 militia men for its defense.

As Fredegar's Continuator makes clear, however, Bourges was defended not only by its own local levy but also by a unit of garrison troops stationed there by Duke Waiofar. In addition to this garrison, there was a force of Gascons, who most likely should be considered mercenaries, deployed for the defense of the city.[181] The exceptionally elaborate precautions taken by Pippin for the defense of his besieging army, which have been discussed above, permit some important inferences regarding the order of magnitude of the contingent of men deployed to defend Bourges. Indeed, Pippin regarded the enemy forces ensconced at Bourges as a formidable lot, with a predictable capacity to sally forth against a besieging force should its defensive positions not be tactically sound.

The details of Pippin's operational deployment, described here, seem well planned and based on substantial intelligence data rather than guesswork. If we can "rethink" Pippin's information, the Aquitanian forces gathered to defend Bourges were of a considerable order of magnitude. As mentioned above, a militia force of levies of approximately 2,000 able-bodied men, committed only to the local defense, was required simply to defend the walls of the city. Such a force, in principle, excluded the select levies, who could be called out for expeditionary service, as had been the case the previous year for Waiofar's invasion of Burgundy. Thus, these select levies could not be counted on in all possible circumstances to defend the walls when the *urbs* was attacked. In light of what is known of the population of the Berry in the early Middle Ages, it is unlikely that in the mid-eighth century, the expeditionary levies of the region numbered less than 500 men.[182] The minimal local levies combined with the select levies, who were eligible for expeditionary service but who were probably at Bourges in the spring of 762, numbered about 2,500 at a minimum.

The defenders of Bourges, however, were only partly composed of these

2,500 local and select levies. Another 2,000 to 2,500 fighting men came from the special troops that Waiofar specifically dispatched to defend Bourges and from the Gascon mercenaries given special attention by Fredegar's Continuator, bringing the total number of defenders to about 5,000 able-bodied men. Not included in this estimate are the ubiquitous household troops, both free and unfree, who served in the military *obsequia* of the secular and ecclesiastical magnates of Bourges and the nearby countryside.[183]

By contrast, Pippin's army at Bourges had to be several orders of magnitude larger than the force that defended the city. The Carolingians' besieging army had to be of sufficient size both to build the extensive siege works alluded to by Fredegar's Continuator and to defend those men who undertook the construction work. Once a minimum 3,000-meter siege wall had been completed, some 3,000 fighting men were required simply to defend it from enemy attack. The ratio of defenders to length of wall required to defend a fortress is considerably smaller than the ratio of men to length of wall for the defense of a siege vallation. Those defending the former have interior lines of communication and movement which make it possible to deploy easily from one part of the city wall to another in case of a sharply focused enemy attack. In order to go from one part of a siege vallation to another, however, troops move around its circumference rather than across its diameter. Thus, the defenders of a siege work found it necessary to deploy greater manpower than those holding an interior wall of the same perimeter.

In addition, the besieging army needed to be a certain size in relation to the defending force to capture a large and well-garrisoned fortress city such as Bourges. An attacking force had to be at least four times larger than the forces mobilized for the defense.[184] Indeed, Pippin understood these basic offensive-defensive force ratios when he besieged the fortress city of Pavia in 754 and in 755. As a result, the Lombard king, Aistulf, surrendered without resisting the overwhelming force of the Carolingian army.[185] Pippin also demonstrated his understanding of these ratios in 761, when he took several very strong fortifications by storm.

When invading Italy and capturing Pavia in succession, Pippin placed in the field more than 1,000 kilometers from home forces of an order of magnitude that defeated the Lombards in the alpine passes and cowed King Aistulf into surrender at Pavia. By contrast, in 571 when the Lombards first captured Pavia, one of the strongest fortress cities in the West, it was only after a three-year siege.[186] Pippin may have been able to mobilize expeditionary forces in the 60,000 range that his son Charlemagne mustered later in the eighth century.[187] For his siege of Bourges, however, Pippin did not need even 40,000 men, and his force likely was in the 20,000–25,000 range. This force would have been in the same range as three to four strengthened legions of the earlier Roman empire.[188]

The Carolingian army deployed to take Bourges likely was mobilized in the environs of Nevers about the first of May, the beginning of the campaigning season. If this force struck its camp on the banks of the Loire within a week, it could have begun its siege operations (building the *castra* discussed above) around the middle of the month.[189] It is unlikely that the army moved out before the traditional date, since grass for the horses and/or oxen needed to haul the supply carts, as well as for the soldiers' mounts, could not be assured before the middle of April.[190] Some units that were mustered in the more northerly and easterly parts of the *regnum Francorum* needed one to two weeks to reach Nevers for a 1 May mobilization. In addition, the spring flood of the Loire had to be sufficiently calmed for pontoon bridges to be placed across the river.[191]

Despite the foraging carried out by the Carolingians in the eastern Berry, as reported by Fredegar's Continuator, which was probably completed by the end of May, Pippin's forces could not live off the land in the region of Bourges for a significant length of time.[192] In addition, Pippin's baggage train, which departed from Nevers with the army, could not have carried the foodstuffs necessary to feed only the personnel, much less the animals required for a protracted siege. Twenty days' supply of victuals for an army of 20,000 men, for example, which in the worst case required a kilogram of milled wheat per man per day, amounted to more than 400 tons.[193] In order to transport such a load, approximately 800 wagonloads pulled by 1,600 horses would be needed.[194] Livestock, including cattle, sheep, and even pigs, traditionally were herded along with the baggage train. Although these animals might move more slowly than horse-drawn carts and have to be fed, it was cheaper and easier than hauling dressed carcasses preserved in salt. In any case, fresh meat tasted better than preserved meat.[195]

Once Pippin's army was established at Bourges, a carefully planned logistic effort was necessary to provide the besieging force with supplies on an ongoing basis. The relatively short eighty or so kilometer distance between the Carolingian base at Nevers and the siege encampment at Bourges provided Pippin with immense advantages. A column of supply wagons for the Carolingian besieging force, loaded from boats that had sailed the Loire to the depot across from Nevers, could make a round trip between the left bank of the river and Bourges along the Roman road in less than a week. This timetable provided every draft horse its required day of rest during each seven-day period of work. Each day on average a wagon train composed of a minimum of forty vehicles would have to arrive at Pippin's camp with grain to feed the troops.[196]

Exactly how long the Carolingian siege of Bourges lasted is unknown. As compared to the description of Pippin's preparations, the course of the siege is only vaguely described in the sources. Fredegar's Continuator observed: "After many men had been wounded and even more had been killed and the walls had been breached, he [Pippin] took the city and restored it to his rule by right of battle (iure proelii)."[197] The emphasis on the large number of casualties, however, suggests a long and bloody operation with several efforts to storm the walls before the city was taken.[198] Thus, the failure of the Continuator, who was writing for Pippin's cousin and close ally, Count Nibelung, to gloat over the extent of enemy casualties while bragging about Carolingian good fortune, as was his custom, suggests that both sides suffered greatly.[199]

The city was taken; it did not surrender. Therefore, the Continuator makes the point that following the capture of Bourges, Pippin showed "great mercy" to the men who had been stationed to defend the city by Duke Waiofar, sending them back to their homes in Aquitaine. By contrast, Pippin forced the Gascon mercenaries, who were also part of the garrison at Bourges, to take an oath of faithfulness to him and to join his army. Pippin sent the wives and children of these Gascons back to *Francia* on foot to be held as hostages to ensure the loyal service of their menfolk. Count Chunibert of Bourges was also required to swear an oath of faithfulness to Pippin. Initially, however, the count of Bourges was kept as a prisoner under close guard in the royal household.[200]

From the Continuator's account, it is possible to sketch some aspects of the military action at Bourges. The Carolingian vallation of the city, described by the Continuator, kept the garrison and the inhabitants from receiving any noteworthy infusion of supplies or reinforcements. However, the failure of the commander, Count Chunibert, to expel noncombatants suggests that the storehouses within the city were sufficiently well stocked with grain and that hunger was not a problem.[201] In addition, the count's refusal to surrender implies that he expected that a relief force would arrive to raise the siege — Waiofar had command of a significant field army — and/or that Pippin could not take the city.

The Continuator emphasizes that Pippin's army was well equipped with siege machines, some of which were mounted on the vallation that cut off access to and egress from the city. In addition, the Continuator makes clear that the *urbs* was taken only after significant breaches were made in the walls, not the gates. The sequence of events, combined with the Continuator's emphasis on the large number of Carolingians wounded and even more killed, suggests that Pippin ultimately won the victory by storming the city, the most costly way to take a heavily fortified and well-defended objective.

In terms of understanding Pippin's operations at Bourges, however, our attention needs to be drawn to the breaches made in the massive old Roman stone walls of this magnificent fortress city. Following the capture of Bourges, Pippin had the walls repaired. Taking a well-defended city by storm after considerable bombardment results in considerable damage, probably inflicted by heavy artillery from Pippin's army. The victory, therefore, was a major accomplishment for the Carolingian engineers and catapult teams, which enabled the attacking force to go through the walls rather than over them.

Whether Pippin's forces had available to them the "new" lever-trebuchet technology, as discussed above, for their heavy artillery cannot be asserted with complete confidence. However, unless all of the breaches made in the walls of Bourges were the work of battering rams, which is highly unlikely, the Carolingians' stone-throwing machines must have hurled heavy projectiles with considerable accuracy. This heavy artillery should not be confused with the light artillery, probably *ballistae* and *onagri*, which the Continuator's account suggests were deployed on the top of the siege walls. These devices, as seen in Chapter 3, were deployed largely for antipersonnel purposes and could be transported easily on flat-bed carts or wagons. Thus, Pippin probably used the heavy lever-trebuchet artillery (Latin, *petrariae*; Greek, *petraboloi*) to damage the great stone walls of Bourges in order to breach them.[202]

Finally, after disposing of the captured enemy troops who had been stationed at Bourges and ordering the walls of the *urbs* to be repaired, Pippin likely dismantled the extensive siege works his forces had built. As the archaeological evidence suggests, however, the *castrum* on the road from Bourges to Nevers, which helped to protect the Carolingian supply route, was excepted from this order. In general, leaving the vallation and contravallation in place could be a danger to the new rulers should Waiofar attempt to recapture the city. Indeed, Pippin's attention to repairing the breaches in the walls, as indicated by the Continuator's emphasis, suggests that the Carolingian ruler believed an attack by Waiofar was possible and even likely. Finally, Pippin defended Bourges by placing his own garrison troops in the city, and he reorganized the government of the region in the short term by placing it under several of his own counts.[203]

The campaigning season of 762, however, was not over for Pippin. Before leaving Aquitaine, he led a force into the northwestern part of the region in order to capture the well-fortified and strongly garrisoned *castrum* of Thouars. Fredegar's Continuator may leave an impression that Pippin moved his entire army with its siege train to Thouars from Bourges after he captured the latter.[204] If this were the Continuator's intention, the large army that had been victorious at Bourges, despite undertaking an exhausting siege effort and suffering substantial casualties, needed an extensive effort merely to prepare to march more than 400 kilometers through enemy territory during the heat of the summer in what amounted to a wholly new campaign. For example, after at least three and perhaps even four months in their siege emplacements at Bourges, substantial equipment repairs would be required. In addition, the force would have to be re-victualed for a lengthy march, at least three weeks for a mounted column using pack horses or horse-drawn carts for their supplies. If ox carts were used to haul supplies, the march would take at least six weeks. A unit of only 5,000 effectives would require 200 horse-drawn carts merely to carry food for the soldiers; for a substantial siege train the number of carts would have had to have been vastly increased. Oats for only 5,000 stall-fed horses would require a minimum of 500 horse-drawn carts, and thus food for another 1,000 horses would also have to be transported.[205] In short, the movement of a large and undoubtedly tired force through enemy territory during the hottest part of summer with the prospect of facing an attack or at least serious harassment from hostile Aquitanian forces, which had not yet been defeated in the field, is unlikely.

Yet, Fredegar's Continuator credits Pippin's army, directly upon arriving at Thouars, with establishing a siege wall around this well-fortified stronghold. He emphasizes, as well, that the *castrum* was well defended. Specific mention is made of a special Gascon garrison, likely a mercenary force, and undoubt-edly, like all fortified centers of population in the *regnum Francorum*, there were also the militarized citizens of the local levy. Finally, the Continuator avers that Thouars was captured with "extraordinary speed."[206] His frame of reference here may well have been the comparatively prolonged siege of Bourges.

The Continuator's account of this second campaign concerning the army that took Thouars is somewhat condensed and therefore potentially opaque to the reader. The author's rather narrow focus on Pippin's activities likely re-sulted in telescoping the facts into a condensed time-frame. The Continuator was probably correct in asserting that Pippin went to Thouars after Bourges fell. Yet the Frankish king must have been accompanied by a relatively small force, perhaps 1,000 to 2,000 mounted household troops who used pack horses to carry their supplies and thus could move with some speed. However, it is doubt-ful that Pippin brought the entire army from Bourges to Thouars or that he brought a substantial siege train. It is more likely that one Carolingian army, mustered in Neustria, had already laid siege to Thouars in May while a second force, mustered at Nevers, attacked Bourges. Evidence for a simultaneous opera-tion at Thouars, which the Continuator initially ignored because Pippin was at Bourges, are the construction of the vallation that encircled Thouars and the prosecution of a siege. Indeed, it is almost incomprehensible that Pippin would initiate a second major campaign at the end of summer against Thouars *de novo* under the circumstances that the Continuator would seem to suggest.

Pippin thus had no need to initiate a fully developed investment when he arrived at Thouars. Pippin probably marched a corps of elite troops west from Bourges to Thouars, where the men who were defending the *castrum* were informed that Bourges had been taken and realized that their situation was hopeless. Either they surrendered or Pippin's army at Thouars, strengthened by the reinforcements brought from Bourges, launched a surprise attack and took the fort, explaining the Continuator's observation that Thouars "was taken with extraordinary speed."

In any case, the Continuator did not comment on Carolingian casualties at Thouars, although he noted that after taking the stronghold, Pippin ordered it to be burned out. No mention is made of the treatment of the civilian inhabitants nor of enemy casualties. Pippin took the Gascon garrison, or what was left of it, back to *Francia*. It is not clear, however, whether these Basques were prisoners or merely mercenaries who subsequently would be recruited for Pippin's army. The commander of the garrison, a "count" whose name is not mentioned, was taken back to *Francia* as a prisoner of war by Pippin.[207]

Pippin's campaign strategy and military operations in 761 and especially in 762 demonstrated the overwhelming superiority of the Carolingian military and particularly of its siege train to the Aquitanians. Indeed, Waiofar thoroughly grasped these facts. As Fredegar's Continuator put it: "Waiofar, lord of Aquitaine, saw how the king had stormed the fortress of Clermont, and had taken Bourges, the best defended city and capital of Aquitaine, with siege engines, and that he had not been able to do anything to stop it."[208]

The Carolingian chronicler then discusses Waiofar's strategic response to Pippin's tactical superiority. The Aquitanian duke, the Continuator reported, "razed [sic] the walls of all the Aquitanian cities under his control, i.e., Poitiers, Limoges, Saintes, Périgueux, Angoulême, and many other cities and other fortified places the region." Of course, these walls were merely damaged and not razed, but the extent of damage is not relevant to our understanding of Waiofar's decision. He chose to pursue a war of maneuver against Pippin, who was intent upon conquering Aquitaine. Ultimately, the superior Carolingian forces wore down Waiofar in a six-year war of attrition, which illustrates yet another pattern of campaign strategy with concomitant military operations.[209]

Conclusion

King Pippin's campaign strategy and military operations, which centered on the conquest of Aquitaine and the capture of the fortress city of Bourges, demonstrate the complexity and sophistication that is involved at both levels. The campaign strategy in this context was probably the most complex undertaken by the early Carolingians. Charles Martel's campaign strategy that led to the capture of the Muslim-held fortress cities of Provence and Septimania likely were very complex, but these strategies, which entailed arrangements for the use of Lombard troops, are not well documented. From an operational perspective, Pippin's efforts in northern Italy against the Lombards also required immense sophistication.

Every campaign requires a strategy, and the early Carolingians planned and executed several score efforts in the pursuit of long-term strategic goals. Even the most limited of campaign strategies, conceived by a successful commander, rests upon his knowledge that necessary human and material resources will be available when he needs them. Thus, the government that succeeds militarily, and particularly one that succeeds over the long term, must execute a matrix of military policies concerning the recruitment of soldiers and their organization. In addition, troops must be highly motivated and have good morale. Finally, military success requires detailed planning, and government bodies must be organized to make these plans.

Conclusion

The early Carolingians successfully pursued a long-term strategy during the better part of a century that enabled them to reconstruct the *regnum Francorum* under the control of their dynasty. In following this strategy, Pippin II and his successors were not diverted by opportunities for financial enrichment in the short term through raids and campaigns outside the *regnum Francorum*. They tended to avoid fighting merely for immediate material gain and focused their efforts on conquest. In addition, the early Carolingians preferred bloodless diplomatic success to unnecessarily destructive warfare, and they did not pursue military glory for its own sake. Early Carolingian leaders rarely entered combat themselves; rather, like Roman generals, they maintained command and control of their armies from positions where they could observe the course of action and respond to tactical situations as they developed.

In order to sustain the above-mentioned long-term strategy, the early Carolingians developed a sophisticated military organization geared primarily for offensive warfare and territorial conquest. This was based largely on the system that had flourished in the Merovingian era, which rested on much that had survived from the later Roman empire. Although the general levy of all able-bodied men was maintained for the local defense in each district, Pippin II and his successors had little need for it, as most of their operations were for offensive purposes in hostile territory. For these operations, the early Carolingians relied extensively on the highly militarized civilian population, which had to serve in the select levy for expeditionary purposes beyond the boundaries of the *pagi* or *civitates* in which they lived. This ability to recruit soldiers from among farmers and urban-dwellers enabled the early Carolingians to mobilize large armies required for besieging the old Roman fortress cities that dominated the military topography of the West. Charles Martel, if not his father, Pippin II, grasped the significance of what today we call "the doctrine of overwhelming force."

Since each person who held at least one manse was required to do military service or provide a substitute when summoned, the rank and file of large early Carolingian armies was composed, in general, of part-time militia men who were mobilized either in the cities or in the countryside. In addition, there were professional soldiers, sustained in the military households of the lay and ecclesiastical magnates. These great landholders were obligated to send the army contingents that were consistent in size and type of armament with the wealth that they possessed. A monastery with many thousands of manses, for example, had to send the army a very large contingent. The largest and most proficient of the professional forces were those of the royal *obsequium*, some of whose units were attached to the court while others were established in various types of military colonies throughout the *regnum Francorum*. The royal court, in imitation of imperial practice, also maintained a *schola* for the training of an officer corps. In magnate households, veteran soldiers trained the military retinues. Since wealthy landowners were required to serve personally or find substitutes and to find additional troops to fulfill the quotas demanded from their lands, most professional soldiers were recruited from the ranks of the poor and even the unfree because small landowners were already required to do military service when summoned. Success in military service as a professional soldier therefore provided potential upward mobility for poor men and their families.

The effectiveness of the military organization, which was undergirded by policies sustained and sometimes initiated by the early Carolingian government, depended on the troops being well trained. This training was exceptionally well developed in all areas of military specialization, including fighting on foot, fighting on horseback, and executing lengthy sieges of the great fortress cities built during the later Roman empire. All of these efforts were supported by the necessary technology. The early Carolingian armies that carried out major siege operations against the old Roman fortress cities of Provence, Septimania, Aquitaine, and northern Italy had various types of equipment, including heavy artillery, as well as the training and discipline to scale the walls under daunting conditions. Foot soldiers were trained to operate in the close order of the phalanx with short swords and were sufficiently disciplined not only to stand like a wall of ice in order to turn back an enemy attack, but also to charge the enemy at a rapid pace while maintaining unit cohesion. On the march, these troops mastered the military step which enabled them to deploy and redeploy from column to line and vice versa. Mounted troops were trained in even more complicated maneuvers than the foot soldiers, and this drill enabled them to charge at high speed in formation. Horsemen mastered the techniques of the feigned retreat, which was a crucial ruse for undermining an enemy phalanx, and were well trained to dismount under battlefield conditions and to fight in the phalanx on foot.

A dedicated and consistent long-term strategy, undergirded by efforts to sustain a military organization with large, well-trained and well-equipped armies, required additional government policies which resulted in high troop morale. The early Carolingians' sophisticated logistical system supplied their armies effectively for long periods of time at distances of one thousand kilometers or more from their home bases. These well-fed soldiers enjoyed a tradition of military success that could be attributed, in part, to the high quality of their commanders. These early Carolingian commanders are to be regarded as *conmilitiones* because they did not squander their troops in an irrational pursuit of personal glory.

The early Carolingians also gave their soldiers both material and spiritual rewards for their service. Booty was shared and professional soldiers were well paid. As a corollary to these positive undertakings, efforts were made to prevent the economic distress of the part-time militia soldiers who were frequently mobilized for lengthy campaigns far from home. On the spiritual level the early Carolingians provided a panoply of religious services to their soldiers and sustained what today we would consider propaganda efforts in order to assure the troops as well as their families who remained at home that they were fighting just wars and that God was on their side.

Early Carolingian long-term strategy, military organization, troop training, and morale building all contributed to the unit cohesion that enabled the armies of Pippin II and his successors to execute their battle tactics effectively. The early Carolingians developed three types of mounted troops which were armed and trained in various ways for executing different types of tactical maneuvers. Considerable attention was given to the training of "dragoons," which likely was the preferred Frankish mode. These men were prepared to fight on horseback with large pike-type lances and on foot with inexpensive short swords in a tightly packed phalanx formation. There were also units of more lightly armed horsemen who were particularly well trained in a wide variety of complicated mounted maneuvers, including the difficult feigned retreat. Finally, units of horsemen carried javelins to attack the enemy at a distance and used swords rather than lances in order to drive home their charge. There was no noteworthy progress in trying to develop units of mounted archers.

Early Carolingian siege tactics and equipment were at least as effective as the development of battlefield tactics and equipment and enabled the armies of Charles Martel and his successors to capture the great fortress cities with their formidable defensive walls dating from the later Roman empire. Every campaign that was a part of the early Carolingian long-term strategy to reunite the *regnum Francorum* had its own time-limited strategy which was executed through specific military operations.

Short-term strategic objectives and the operations to carry them out varied immensely. For example, Charles Martel's punitive raids against Saxon villages in Hesse during the early 720s were very different from his siege of the old Roman fortress city of Narbonne a decade and a half later. Pippin's siege of Bourges, one of the early Carolingians' most complicated campaign strategies and military operations, makes clear how through the effective implementation of government policies regarding military organization, training, equipment, supply, and tactics, his efforts succeeded and led to the reintegration of Aquitaine into the *regnum Francorum*.

An examination of early Carolingian warfare must dispel any notions of primitivism or the utility of comparison with North American Indians and nonliterate sub-Saharan tribes. King Pippin I's military organization, system of supply, training, and tactics, for example, had far more in common with that of his Byzantine and Muslim contemporaries than with that of any Zulu chief. The early Carolingians built directly on the remains of imperial institutions that their Merovingian predecessors had preserved. In addition, the early Carolingians learned from their Byzantine and Muslim neighbors, who also were heirs to aspects of the later Roman military establishment.

In the matter of warfare, at the least, the idea that there was a Western European Dark Age that ultimately was enlightened by some later Renaissance cannot be sustained. Efforts by postmodern social scientists, self-styled literary theorists, and Germanic primitivists to bring back a Dark Age of one type or another greatly undermine our understanding of early Carolingian institutions and the talented men who made them work so effectively. The early Carolingians built upon surviving imperial military topography, adopted late antique technology, and effectively utilized their classical intellectual inheritance to prepare the way militarily for Charlemagne's resuscitation of the Roman empire in the West.

The Organization of Naval Assets

The Romans had developed extensive naval resources throughout the region that was to fall under the rule of the Merovingian kings and its environs.[1] In addition to coastal fleets with well-established harbors where even mounted troops could be landed from especially constructed horse transports in battle-ready condition there were river fleets as well. All kinds of port installations were developed which facilitated not only military operations but also civilian maritime and riverine activity.[2] Thus, civilian merchant activity flourished in blue water and on the rivers, while fishermen also plied their trade.[3] In short, there was no dearth of experience in the full spectrum of naval operations. Widespread civilian activity meant that a substantial segment of the population living along the coasts and on the riverbanks was available to provide support for the imperial military operations that were concerned with the transport of troops and/or supplies.

When the Romano-German kingdoms replaced the imperial governing authority in Gaul, basic continuity may be observed. For example, during the later fifth century, the Gallo-Roman aristocrat Namantius, who was a close friend and confidant of the celebrated author Sidonius Apollinaris, commanded a major naval squadron. This force operated along Aquitaine's Atlantic coast and had attached to it a military force trained to fight on land as well as on the sea.[4] In a support context, the Gallo-Roman lady Geneviève, who later was made a saint for her numerous good works, organized fleets of merchant vessels that were capable of supplying Paris for a five-year period while the city was under loose siege by the Frankish king Clovis.[5]

Clovis' lack of the requisite naval assets to thwart the provisioning of Paris during this early period of his reign, when he relied primarily upon ethnic Franks for his military support, should not be surprising.[6] During the later Roman empire, the *Franci* as an ethnic group were not much interested in naval matters as indicated by the silence of the written sources.[7] The imperial government, which traditionally posted so-called barbarians for the kinds of duty to which they were well suited, failed to recruit *Franci* in any noticeable manner either for riverine fleets or for units that operated in open water.[8] In addition, the written sources do not describe types of ships associated with the *Franci* as an ethnic group.[9]

By contrast with their failure to identify Frankish ships, the Roman sources often describe the kinds of ships and sailing techniques that putatively were peculiar to so-called ethnic groups.[10] The often-cited effort by Caesar (*Bell. Gall.*, 3.13) to describe the ships built by the *Veneti* is a *locus classicus* in the present context. In addition, the early medieval sources are packed with information regarding Viking ships but nothing of specifically Frankish ships.[11] Memorable, as well, is the oft-discussed distinction made by Alfred the Great between his new ships, which were "higher" than "Danish" and "Frisian" ships.[12] With regard to ethnicity and ship types, it was rumored that Charlemagne could, at great distance, discern the different peculiarities of ships sailed by Jewish merchants, Moors from North Africa, traders from Britain, and Vikings.[13] Finally, there is no compelling archaeological evidence for a particular type of ship that can be associated with ethnic Franks.[14]

However, by the latter part of Clovis' reign a multi-ethnic military force was serving at the command of the Merovingian king and his successors.[15] For example, in Armorica, as noted earlier, the descendants of Roman soldiers, who were still wearing imperial uniforms and carrying their ancient banners, were part of the Merovingian army as late as the mid-sixth century. With regard to naval operations, Theudebert I defeated Danish raiders at sea off the Austrasian coast during the mid-520s at the earliest,[16] likely commanding a fleet based in the erstwhile Roman naval installation on the Sambre (the only known major naval military installation in the region).[17] The sailors who manned the ships that carried Theudebert's army to victory against the Danes probably were descendants of men who formerly had served in Roman units, rather than ethnic Franks, in light of obvious continuity with late imperial institutions in so many other areas of the Merovingian military.

Just as the walls of cities and lesser fortifications survived into the Middle Ages, so too did many of Rome's naval installations.[18] The enduring character both of the physical structure of these installations, such as ports, in the West, and of a continuing "civilian" capacity to participate effectively in naval activities throughout the early Middle Ages, is perhaps most thoroughly illustrated in regard to the Norman conquest of England. William the Conqueror, as duke of Normandy, neither maintained a permanent fleet as part of his military establishment nor did he support a corps of regular naval personnel. However, it was hardly mere good luck that enabled him to mobilize a fleet of some 700 ships with well-trained crews in order to sail in September of 1066 for England. The fact that his invasion fleet embarked for England from the erstwhile Roman port of Saint-Valery-sur-Somme and made landfall at the former Roman port of Anderita (Pevensey), where facilities were available to disembark his mounted troops in battle ready condition, was the result of careful planning.[19]

Naval Assets in the North

During the period immediately following the emergence of the Romano-German *regna*, the examples of Namantius and Geneviève illustrate the capacity to utilize all kinds of available ships and ostensibly "civilian" naval personnel for military purposes. The same pattern persists after the dissolution of Carolingian power, as indicated by William the Conqueror's operations. Under the early Carolingians, too, the government had extensive naval assets at its disposal. As discussed very briefly in Chapter 1, Charles Martel and his advisers knew by the early 730s that the Carolingians would have to impose a measure of direct control over Frisia *ulterior*, either to assert or to maintain control over the very lucrative trade into the North Sea from its bases on the lower Rhine at Durstede and Utrecht.[20] This meant an invasion of the home islands, which could be accomplished only with naval force.

In 733, Charles Martel mobilized a combined naval and land operation to undertake a punitive raid deep into Frisian territory.[21] This campaign, which was carried out with the help of naval craft, penetrated as far as the island of Westergo. A band of "rebels" based on this island, the only ones who opposed Charles, met the Carolingian army in battle, apparently on the island, and were entirely destroyed. The remaining inhabitants of Westergo recognized their subject status in regard to the Mayor of the Palace, or as the Metz annalist put it, "He subjugated them to his *ditio* and they promised him their faith (*fidem*)."[22] In connection with this operation, three points are noteworthy: Charles took hostages; he did not permit his men to plunder the island; and he made no effort to undermine the Frisian practice of paganism.[23] This strongly suggests that once the opposition, at least as Charles conceived it, had been eliminated, he was more interested in a peaceful *modus vivendi* with the people of Westergo than in maintaining hostilities.

The court chronicler reports that the next year, however, the Frisians rose in an exceptionally vicious revolt ("nimis crudeliter rebellantem").[24] These new rebels may have interpreted Charles' apparent leniency to the inhabitants of Westergo after his victory the previous year as a sign of weakness. The phrase "nimis crudeliter" may also indicate that those who had treated with Charles on Westergo, that is, promised faith and recognized his *ditio*, were viciously punished by their fellow Frisians. In any case, a second "revolt" in as many years, this one led by the apparent ruler of the *gens Frisionum*, Duke Bubo, was under way by early 734.[25] As will be seen below, this revolt, like the previous one, does not seem to have been very broadly based.

Most likely building on information that he had obtained during the operations in 733 and more current intelligence, Charles prepared a large-scale invasion of the Frisian main islands. The Mayor mobilized what his court chronicler called a large fleet ("navium copia"). Charles also prepared an army (*exercitus*) in order to undertake a naval invasion ("navale evectione") of the Frisian islands. In short, the ships were used to transport a military force.[26] From a juridical perspective, an effort was made to demonstrate the just nature of this military operation. Thus, according to the official explanation, the Frisians are depicted as being in revolt against Charles, their rightful ruler.[27]

As the Continuator describes the invasion, Charles' fleet entered upon the high seas ("alto mare").[28] Thus, it is almost certain that he mustered his army at Utrecht and moved from the Rhine through the Vecht canal (the old *fossa Drusiana* that was kept in operation) into what today is called the Ijselmer.[29] From there, the Carolingian army sailed approximately ninety nautical miles to Westergo, where they found no rebel army. Apparently, the inhabitants of the island kept their promise and respected the fact that they had given hostages to Charles. The Carolingian army then reembarked and sailed another twenty-five nautical miles to the island of Ostergo. No action is reported to have been undertaken at this landing either. Neither of these two Frisian villages or their populations appear to have been harmed by Charles' forces and no booty is indicated as having been taken.[30]

Charles was not leading a raid in force against the major Frisian home islands intended to destroy enemy material assets, severely discomfort the population, and acquire large amounts of booty. Rather, Charles' strategic goal was either to obtain the surrender of the Frisian *dux* Bubo and assure his acquiescence to Carolingian *ditio*, or to bring him to battle and, if necessary, to destroy his army in combat. In order to pursue this strategy, Charles searched out Bubo, who, despite his "nimis crudeliter" revolt, apparently was not very eager to engage the Carolingian army in the field or on the water. In the context of Charles' landings at both Westergo and Ostergo, none of the sources mention booty, captives, or the destruction of Frisian property, despite the fact that the latter were pagans and that the Carolingians were engaged in a "just war."

After penetrating more than 110 nautical miles into the Frisian home islands and reaching Ostergo, Charles turned his fleet around, presumably after receiving additional intelligence, and sailed south. Apparently, Carolingian scouts had located Duke Bubo with his army (*exercitus*) either in the estuary of the river Boorne, almost due east of Westergo or, as is more likely (see below), on the banks of the river.[31] Bubo may have been in the area of Oldeboorne, one of the three major population and commercial centers in Frisia, along with Dokkum and Durstede, the latter already being in Carolingian hands.[32] Having entered the mouth of the Boorne River, Charles, who was seeking a confrontation while Bubo was trying to avoid battle, likely blocked naval egress from the estuary by linking his boats together across the mouth of the river.

After making it impossible for Bubo to retreat, Charles landed the bulk of his army on the banks of the Boorne. There, following standard operating procedure for early Carolingian armies, he ordered a fortified encampment (*castra*) to be constructed.[33] Charles then brought Bubo to battle, and the sources make it clear that the Carolingians won a decisive victory ("exercitum Frigionum prostravit") but also that Duke Bubo was killed in combat.[34] Charles' army had no mounted troops in this battle; not only do the sources fail to mention either horses or mounted Carolingian troops, but there is no external evidence for the existence of horse transport vessels at this time in the northern parts of Europe.[35] It is possible that Duke Bubo commanded some mounted troops in the army that he had mobilized, as the Frisians had units that were able to deploy on horseback.[36] There is no evidence, however, for Frisian use of mounted troops in the campaign under consideration here.

Charles treated this area of Frisia that had supported Duke Bubo far differently than he had treated Westergo on two separate occasions in 733 and 734 and Ostergo in 734. After defeating Bubo's army on the banks of the Boorne, Charles ordered the pagan shrines (*fana*) near the battle area to be broken up into small pieces and then burned. In addition, Charles ordered this same region, which apparently was quite rich—another reason to identify it with Oldeboorne—to be stripped of its moveable wealth. Thus, the court chronicler indicates that Charles returned to the *regnum Francorum* with a great mass of spoils and booty ("magna spolia et praeda"), presumably carried away in boats that were confiscated from the Frisians. Charles is described in this account of the campaign as *victor*, and, as seen in Chapter 3, this may indicate that he celebrated a triumph of sorts on his return home.[37]

Fredegar's Continuator is surprisingly consistent in mentioning when the early Carolingians used boats in one or another particular combat. The fact that the Continuator does not make clear that the battle under consideration here was a naval battle suggests that it was fought on the land.[38] In addition, the necessary inference to be drawn from the Continuator's observation that the Carolingian forces built a fortified camp (*castra*) is that Charles considered the possibility that his men might be attacked on land by the Frisian army. This information, combined with the fact that the Continuator does not mention a sea battle, indicates that Charles' army fought on the banks of the Boorne near the camp and not on the water. Indeed, no other source that mentions this clash provides any reason to believe that this was a naval battle.[39]

Whether or not this battle was fought on the land or on the water, however, is not relevant to the fact that Charles needed to have available to him many ships for his Frisian operations in both 733 and 734. These ships had to be capable of sailing from Utrecht, and likely from farther afield, through the Vecht canal, across the Ijselmer, out to the islands of Westergo and Ostergo, and then back again into the estuary of the Boorne. It is important, therefore, that the Carolingians controlled the emporium of Durstede,[40] where many scores if not hundreds of ships of the type Charles needed likely could have been found at any time during the sailing season.[41]

In order better to understand Charles' operations on the Rhine river and on the sea, it is important to know what types of ships were available. In this context, the so-called *hulc* (or perhaps more accurately the proto-*hulc*) was of primary importance.[42] This vessel takes its name from the fact that it was built on top of a huge hollowed-out log.[43] Such proto-*hulcs* are known from the archaeological record, specifically the Utrecht boat. This particular craft was built during the early Carolingian era or may be a somewhat later model very similar to that used during the eighth and ninth centuries.[44] Pictorial evidence for this type of boat appears on the coins struck at the Carolingian port of Durstede during the reign of Charlemagne and his son Louis the Pious.[45]

These proto-*hulcs* apparently had a relatively low freeboard and were propelled by a single sail. They had no oars for propulsion but had at least one steering oar. From the design of the Utrecht ship it is clear that they had one deck.[46] How actual combat might be orchestrated from such a vessel is not easy to envision; men armed with bows or crossbows could shoot at their adversaries from the deck and over the gunwales of the ship, but men could probably not climb the mast and use it as a firing platform. In addition, with a sail and one or two steering oars, one could maneuver a proto-*hulc* into position where the men on it could board another vessel, probably using grappling hooks and/or planks, in order to engage in hand-to-hand combat.[47]

In both 733 and 734 the soldiers being transported on Charles' vessels did not engage in ship-to-ship combat. As far as these campaigns are concerned the Carolingian soldiers were passengers being transported to a theater of operations. A ship with the dimensions of the Utrecht boat, almost eighteen meters in length and about four meters at the beam, was primarily a merchant craft designed for hauling cargo. By contrast, a warship, constructed for combat, was likely to have a ratio of length to beam closer to 7:1 rather than 4:1. Warships of the north during this era are believed by scholars to have been oared vessels, although this did not preclude them from having sails as well.[48]

A proto-*hulc* with the dimensions of the Utrecht boat has been estimated to have carried twenty-three tons of cargo.[49] Its deck area was in excess of seventy meters square. Fifty to sixty soldiers could comfortably be accommodated on deck as "passengers" for a several-days voyage, and in an emergency situation double that number could be transported for a short duration. In relatively calm weather, a considerable number of additional men might be accommodated below deck. (In wartime, the mission remains paramount and the short-term physical comfort of the troops, provided they remain combat ready, is rarely a controlling priority.) Since even a hundred men at 100 kilograms per man amounts to a load of only 10,000 kilograms, a Utrecht-type proto-*hulc* could carry more than three tons of additional cargo. Large quantities of equipment, which included not only weapons but also the tools that were needed to construct a *castra*, food, and probably tents, as well, could easily be transported on these vessels.

Unlike the *hulc*, which is often described by scholars as having a banana shape, the early Carolingians also had available to them more boxy ships with flat bottoms. These ships also operated under sail and lacked oars for propulsion. Scholars tend to characterize this boxy shaped craft as a "proto-cog."[50] Examples of this type of ship are depicted on ninth-century coins minted on the island emporium of Haithbau in southern Denmark.[51] The region in which this emporium was located enjoyed exceptionally close trade relations with both Utrecht and Durstede during the early Carolingian era. Thus, Charles Martel probably was as likely to find proto-cogs in the ports under his control as proto-*hulcs*. Scholars have suggested that the cog was the basic Frisian ship, the proto-*hulc* coinage of Durstede notwithstanding.[52]

In 733 and 734, Charles Martel very likely commandeered both proto-*hulcs* and proto-cogs along with their crews, captains, and navigators or pilots for his naval operations against the Frisians.[53] Both types of ship obviously were capable of moving the Carolingian army with its equipment to and among the Frisian islands. Charles also commandeered some oared craft that could travel much more rapidly, at least for shorter distances, than ships that relied solely on their sails. These could be used for scouting operations to gather intelligence. In this context, one should think of some descendant of Vegetius' *scarfa exploratoria*, which had both oars and sails.[54] Such ships would also have been commandeered from nonmilitary business for naval service as needed with their crews and captains.[55] Some type of obligation for expeditionary service may have been imposed on men who lived along the banks of rivers or in coastal regions and who owned or sailed ships, as was the case in Anglo-Saxon England.[56]

The order of magnitude of Charles Martel's operations in these naval campaigns must be estimated. During the later seventh and early eighth centuries, the Frisians mobilized formidable military and naval forces in their frequent wars against the early Carolingians. These campaigns, as seen above, often were fought not in the Frisian islands but on the mainland and sometimes within Frankish territory. For example, Duke Radbod defeated Charles Martel's army in the field in the region of the Ardennes and then launched a successful raid as far south as Cologne. Earlier Frisian naval forces had penetrated as far up the Rhine as Cologne, where they demanded and obtained tribute (see Chapter 1).

In light of these experiences, it would have been imprudent for Charles, who grasped the importance of the doctrine of overwhelming force, to have ventured into the Frisian heartland by ship without a very formidable army. However, for Charles to have led even a rather small army of 5,000 men into Frisia *ulterior*, he would have needed approximately 100 proto-cogs and/or proto-*hulcs*, each of which on average had the carrying capacity of the Utrecht ship. Thus, the court chronicler's report that Charles mobilized a "large fleet" in 734 suggests that he also mobilized a large army.[57]

It was possible for the Romans to transport large armies by water and supply them easily from their ships on the lower Rhine. As a point of comparison, in 358, the emperor Julian built some 400 ships to transport his forces and the supplies they required into the lower Rhine region. He already had 200 ships at his disposal, and thus his entire fleet came to some 600 craft. These ships not only were capable of being used on the Rhine but also were capable of crossing the English Channel. This campaign was undertaken against an alliance of several "Germanic" groups in the region, and the number of troops led by Julian during this operation likely was in excess of 20,000 effectives.[58]

The combination of proven Frisian military strength and the early Carolingian penchant for mobilizing large forces suggests that the army Charles led into Frisia in 734 was likely in excess of 5,000 men. However, what conclusions we may draw concerning the order of magnitude of Charles' army in these naval campaigns against the Frisians rests, in large part, on what we can say concerning the order of magnitude of his fleet. This, in turn, depends on what archaeologists in the future learn concerning the upper limits of the size and carrying capacity of the early eighth-century ships available to the Carolingians in this region of the North Sea.

Naval Organization in the South

During the first part of the campaigning season of 737, Charles Martel captured the fortress city of Avignon following a close investment with various *machinae*.[59] He then advanced with a large army and his formidable siege train from Provence across the Rhône into Septimania in order to attack the Muslim-held fortress city of Narbonne. It is not clear how he managed this river crossing but either boats or a pontoon bridge were necessary.[60] His men probably commandeered boats customarily used by civilians on the Rhône for fishing and trading purposes, as previous military commanders had done.[61] Whether he had to have a special type of ship constructed in order to ferry the above-mentioned *machinae* across the river seems likely.[62]

Following the pattern employed at Avignon earlier in the campaign, Charles established a close siege at Narbonne. However, after several weeks of investing this massive fortification, he received intelligence that an enemy relief force was on its way to the Narbonne region by sea from Spain for the purpose of raising the siege. The Muslim commander planned to sail his ocean-going fleet into the Étang de Sigean, about fifteen kilometers south of Narbonne. Once anchored outside the bay, he was to disembark his troops and send them ashore in rather small, oar-propelled landing craft carried by his ships. After landing on the shore, the army planned to advance north toward Narbonne in order to drive the Carolingian army from the environs of the city and break the investment.[63]

Charles mobilized a substantial part of his army and marched out of his siege emplacements, probably along that part of the Via Domitia that led from Narbonne to Elne. He then established a base camp on the banks of the Berre River in the valley of Corbières, where much earlier a Visigothic *palatio* had served as an occasional royal residence.[64] Charles' march from Narbonne to the banks of the Berre was approximately fifteen kilometers and likely took the better part of a day. It is unclear, however, whether the Carolingian army awaited the Muslim landing at the mouth of the Berre or whether the Muslims had already landed when he arrived.

Leaving aside Charles' intelligence-gathering capability, it is clear that the Muslim relief army had sailed its fleet into what is today called the Étang de Sigean. Of necessity, these seagoing ships anchored off l'Isle de l'Aute, which now is less than one thousand meters from the mouth of the Berre but probably was a lot closer, within normal swimming distance, in Charles' day.[65] Using small, shallow-draft landing craft, the Muslim army disembarked on the north bank of the Berre.[66]

There, Charles' army fought what the court chronicler characterizes as a tough battle against the enemy relief force. The Muslims, however, were soundly defeated. After the death of the emir, Omar-ibn-Chaled, who was in command of the army, "the survivors, who wished to escape, tried swimming out to the invasion fleet that was anchored in the bay and struggled to board the ships." [67] Indeed, the pursuit by Charles' force was so vigorous that the Muslims were unable to refloat their landing craft. Once they saw that the Muslims were trying to swim out to the larger ships anchored on the seaward side of the bay, Charles' men quickly floated the small boats that the Muslims had used to land on the river bank, caught up to many of the swimmers, and are reported to have speared some of them and drowned others.[68] Some of the Carolingian soldiers had sufficient knowledge of how to row the small landing craft, but this can hardly be considered naval training. Indeed, there is no reason to believe that the early Carolingians controlled naval assets in the south.[69]

Pippin's Naval Efforts

Yet one more example of early Carolingian naval operations suggests the rather ad hoc nature of such matters. In 749, Pippin, Charles Martel's son, mustered an army (*exercitus*) for an invasion of Bavaria in order to put down Duke Odilo, who had led his people in revolt. The Carolingian force on the march is described as being exceptionally well equipped—"cum magno . . . apparatu." Pippin's force crossed the Bavarian frontier and stopped on the banks of the Inn, where the army, following standard early Carolingian procedure, built a fortified encampment (*castra*) before making preparations for assaulting the enemy on the far side of the river. The Bavarians were equipped with boats and apparently were ready to engage Pippin's force on the river itself. In any case, when Odilo came to understand, probably after a parlay, that Pippin was prepared to annihilate the Bavarians in a naval battle ("navale proelium"), the duke surrendered.[70]

From where did the Carolingian fleet materialize that would make possible a naval battle? The sources do not mention Pippin ordering his troops to engage in a crash program of ship building. In any case such an effort would have taken a long time for which our understanding of the chronology makes no allowance.[71] By contrast, Pippin and his advisers understood that in seeking to deal with the Bavarians, the army would have to cross several rivers. Thus, the Continuator's observation that Pippin's army was exceptionally well equipped, "cum magno . . . apparatu," might be taken to indicate that they carried with them the means to operate effectively as a military force on the water.

Exactly what equipment to which the Continuator referred cannot be ascertained, but Carolingian technology and practice allows limited speculation. For example, the Carolingians had the technology to build and deploy prefabricated boats. These vessels were capable of being broken down into pieces of such manageable size that they could be carried in the baggage train on wagons or in some cases on pack horses.[72] The early Carolingians also likely carried with them inflatable boats made from animal skins.[73] This technology may well have been analogous to that used by the Carolingians to make their supply wagons "watertight" and this in turn allowed the army to float their supply wagons on a river or stream.[74]

Conclusion

From these accounts of early Carolingian naval operations, and in the absence of other evidence, there is no reason to believe that Pippin II or his successors sustained a fleet of warships or that they kept a fleet of troop transports ready for military deployment. In addition, we have no basis to conclude that the early Carolingians supported a corps of professional naval personnel trained to sail either warships or transports. Rather, operations in both 733 and 734, as well as the episodes in the environs of Narbonne and on the banks of the Inn, strongly suggest a pattern of ad hoc behavior. This is especially the case with regard to matters in 737, where enemy craft were commandeered on the banks of the Berre. The episode in 749 against the Bavarians seems to have been the result of careful logistical planning for a lengthy march that required the crossing of rivers. The fact that prefabricated boats could be used in actual military operations should not be surprising, but it was unlikely to have been the primary purpose for their development.

These two episodes make clear that certain elements in the multiethnic expeditionary forces available to Charles Martel and Pippin were fully capable of handling oared boats in armed hostilities. Thus, some troops were capable of actually "fighting" — if spearing fugitives in the water may be considered combat — while on board a craft on a river or in a bay. The skills required to handle oared craft and to fight while on board were available in the course of the everyday life of a fisherman or a sailor on a merchant craft. This training was far less demanding than teaching men to maneuver ten- to twelve-meter ladders, scale them under combat conditions, and then fight while teetering far above the ground on a platform fifty or so centimeters in width, as was the case for siege warfare training.

Finally, Rhabanus Maurus, in his commentary on Vegetius' *De re Militari*, made clear that "tempore moderno" it was important for the soldiers of the Carolingian army, like their Roman predecessors, to know how to swim and to swim well.[75] It is noteworthy in this context that the ethnic Franks, traditionally, do not seem to have been very good at swimming during their early history.[76]

However, the early Carolingians were not totally uninterested in military matters that concerned the water. The prefabricated boats and floatable wagons are of considerable importance. In addition, the use of this equipment required training, time, organization, and resources.

Notes

Preface

1. The observations by Walter E. Kaegi, Jr., "The Crisis in Military Historiography," *Armed Forces and Society*, 7 (1980), 299–316, are of great importance here. Note also the acute observations by Gordon Craig, "Delbrück: The Military Historian," in *Makers of Modern Strategy from Machiavelli to the Nuclear Age*, ed. Peter Paret et al. (Princeton, 1986), 352–353.

2. Charles Oman, *On the Writing of History* (New York, 1939), 159–160.

3. Walter Goffart, "Two Notes on Germanic Antiquity Today," *Traditio*, 50 (1995), 9–30; and Bernard S. Bachrach, "Anthropology and Early Medieval History: Some Problems," *Cithara*, 34 (1994), 3–10, provide some observations on these problems.

4. See, for example, the articles by Bernard S. Bachrach, "Animals and Warfare in Early Medieval Europe," *Settimane di Studio del Centro Italiano di Studi sull'alto Medioevo*, 31 (Spoleto, 1985), 1, 707–764, and "A Picture of Avar-Frankish Warfare from a Carolingian Psalter of the Early Ninth Century in Light of the *Strategicon*," *Archivum Eurasiae Medii Aevi*, 4 (1984), 5–27. Both are reprinted in *Armies and Politics in the Early Medieval West* (London, 1993), with the same pagination. See also Bernard S. Bachrach, "Some Observations on the Bayeux Tapestry," *Cithara*, 27 (1987), 5–28. I hope in the future to publish a monograph on early medieval arms and armor that will address some of the difficult problems raised by the use of manuscript illustrations and other artifacts.

Chapter 1. Long-Term Strategy

1. Paul Kennedy, "Grand Strategy in War and Peace: Toward a Broader Definition," in *Grand Strategies in War and Peace*, ed. Paul Kennedy (New Haven, 1991), 1.

2. Compare here the observations by Edward Mead Earle, "Introduction," in *Makers of Modern Strategy*, ed. Edward Mead Earle (Princeton, N.J., 1943), viii; and those by Basil Henry Liddell Hart, *Strategy*, 2nd revised ed. (New York, 1974). In this context, Brian Bond, *Liddell Hart: A Study of His Military Thought* (London, 1973), is also useful. The dearth of philosophical rigor in this tradition is made evident in the treatment by Kennedy, "Grand Strategy in War and Peace: Toward a Broader Definition," 1–7, and 185–186, for additional literature. Kennedy and the tradition that he represents in this regard seem to have little interest in either the methodological or epistemological problems involved in the development of definitions.

3. It is perhaps ironic that the most important historical discussion of grand strategy in recent times for ancient and medieval historians, Edward N. Luttwak, *The Grand Strategy of the Roman Empire: From the First Century A.D. to the Third* (Baltimore,

1976), avoids definitions. Perhaps even more ironic is that his critics, while arguing vigorously that the Roman empire had no grand strategy, also fail to offer definitions. This point is made by Everett Wheeler, "Methodological Limits and the Mirage of Roman Strategy," *Journal of Military History*, 57 (1993), 7–41, 215–240.

4. For example, Benjamin Isaac, *The Limits of Empire* (Oxford, 1990), vigorously attacks Luttwak, without taking him to task for failing to provide a methodologically valid definition of grand strategy. Wheeler also does an excellent job of exposing the rhetorical devices used by the critics of Luttwak ("Methodological Limits," 7–41, 215–240). See also the examples provided by Arther Ferrill, "The Grand Strategy of the Roman Empire," in *Grand Strategies in War and Peace*, ed. Paul Kennedy (New Haven, 1991), 71–85 and 196–199; and Isaac, *The Limits of Empire*, which are both excellent in their efforts to manipulate the reader. Both scholars excel in the techniques of persuasion and know the sources well.

Contrary to the norm, Wheeler, "Methodological Limits," 10, makes a brave effort to develop something like a definition by summarizing some of the insights put forward by Kennedy, "Grand Strategy in War and Peace," 4–5. However, Wheeler is aware that the characteristics he emphasizes do not meet the criteria of necessity and sufficiency.

5. The immense response to the work of Luttwak, cited above, is a good example of the heuristic value of discussions regarding grand strategy. For an excellent examination of many of the arguments see Wheeler, "Methodological Limits," 7–41, 215–240.

6. Ferrill, "The Grand Strategy of the Roman Empire," 78.

7. Kennedy, "Grand Strategy in War and Peace," 4.

8. Kennedy, "Grand Strategy in War and Peace," 1–2.

9. Allan R. Millett, Williamson Murray, and Kenneth H. Watman, "The Effectiveness of Military Organizations," in *Military Effectiveness*, ed. Allan R. Millett and Williamson Murray, 3 vols. (London and Boston, 1988), I, 12. This pseudo-definition, in a epistemological sense, is cited with apparent approval by Kennedy, "Grand Strategy in War and Peace," 185, n. 3.

10. Kennedy, "Grand Strategy in War and Peace," 2–3, with the cited literature.

11. Cf. the summary by Kennedy, "Grand Strategy in War and Peace," 4–6.

12. It is anachronistic to consider Pippin II a Carolingian because the term derives from the name of his son Charles Martel. It is customary to consider Pippin II either a Pippinid, for his maternal grandfather Pippin, or on occasion an Arnulfing, for his relationship to the distinguished bishop of Metz, who was a paternal ancestor and perhaps a great-uncle.

13. *Annales mettenses priores*, pp. 12–13.

14. The basic modern work on this text has been done by Hartmut Hoffmann, *Untersuchung zur karolingian Annalistik* (Bonn, 1958), 9–68; and Irene Haselbach, "Aufstieg und Herrschaft der Karolinger in der Darstellung der sogenannten *Annalen Mettenses priores*," *Historische Studien*, 412 (1970), 1–208. Numerous other studies, moreover, have been written to explain the Metz annalist's controlling assumptions, and there is no consensus. For example, Walthar Schlesinger, "Kaisertum und Reichsteilung. Zur *divisio regnorum* von 806," in *Forschung zu Staat und Verfassung, Festgabe für Fritz Hartung*, ed. R. Dietrich and G. Oestreich (Berlin, 1958), 9–51, and reprinted in Walthar Schlesinger, *Beiträge zur deutschen Verfassungsgeschichte des Mittelalters*, 2 vols. (Göttingen, 1963), I, 193–232, with an afterword on 345.

15. Haselbach, "Aufstieg und Herrschaft," 34, makes a compelling argument that the Metz annalist had available to him some sort of narrative source that dealt with Pippin's reign but which is no longer extant. She believes this lost source was a "chronicle" but also sees the influence on the text (38) of Seutonius' biographical writings, so well known from the annalist's contemporary, Einhard. Louis Halphen, *Études critique sur l'histoire de Charlemagne* (Paris, 1921), 50, called attention to the similarity of the annalist's treatment of Pippin II's career to certain aspects of *vitae* which are prominent in early medieval hagiographical writing.

16. For the sake of brevity I will only note three areas in which long-term or programmatic capitularies were markedly successful. With regard to Charlemagne's orders to establish schools, to produce tens of thousands of book-length manuscripts, and to control the coinage, see, respectively: (1) Pierre Riché, *Écoles et enseignement dans le haut moyen âge* (Paris, 1979), 11–118; and cf. M. M. Hildebrandt, *The External School in Carolingian Society* (Leiden, 1992); and the review of Hildebrandt by Bernard S. Bachrach, *History of Education Quarterly*, 33 (1993), 99–101; (2) Rosamond McKitterick, *The Carolingians and the Written Word* (Cambridge, 1989), 163; and John Contreni, "The Carolingian Renaissance: Education and Literary Culture," in *The New Cambridge Medieval History*, ed. Rosamond McKitterick (Cambridge, 1995), II, 711; and (3) Mark Blackburn, "Money and Coinage," in *The New Cambridge Medieval History*, II, 538–559, and esp. 548–552, with the bibliographies, 984–987.

17. See, for example, Simon Adams, "Tactics or Politics? 'The Military Revolution' and the Hapsburg Hegemony, 1525–1648," in *Tools of War: Instruments, Idea, and Institutions of Warfare, 1445–1871*, ed. John A. Lynn (Urbana, Ill., 1990), 28–52; and David Parrott, "Strategy and Tactics in the Thirty Years' War: The 'Military Revolution,'" *Militärgeschichtliche Mitteilungen*, 18 (1985), 8–21.

18. For the general background see Bernard S. Bachrach, "Logistics in Pre-Crusade Europe," in *Feeding Mars: Logistics in Western Warfare from the Middle Ages to the Present*, ed. John A. Lynn (Boulder, 1993), 57–78; idem., "Animals and Warfare," 707–764; and idem., "Medieval Siege Warfare: A Reconnaissance," *Journal of Military History*, 58 (1994), 119–133. For some case studies, see two articles by Bernard S. Bachrach, "On the Origins of William the Conqueror's Horse Transports," *Technology and Culture*, 26 (1985), 505–531; and "Some Observations on the Military Administration of the Norman Conquest," in *Anglo-Norman Studies VIII*, ed. R. Allen Brown (Woodbridge, 1986), 1–25.

19. It is clear that during the 650s, Grimoald, the son of Pippin I, orchestrated a Carolingian usurpation of the royal title in Austrasia. This failed after several years and led to disastrous short-term consequences for the Carolingians including Grimoald's execution. However, the usurpation was well known to Grimoald's descendants through the *Liber Historiae Francorum*, ch. 43; and obviously was regarded as somewhat of an embarrassment by the early ninth century. The Metz annalist, for example, ignored the episode. Richard Gerberding, *The Rise of the Carolingians and the Liber Historiae Francorum* (Oxford, 1987), 47–66, provides a satisfactory account of Grimoald's failed efforts. More recently, Matthias Becher, "Der sogenannte Staatsstreich Grimoalds," in *Karl Martell in Seiner Zeit*, ed. Jörg Jarnut, Ulrich Nonn, and Michael Richter (Sigmaringen, 1994), 119–147, unconvincingly has argued that there was no usurpation.

The observations by Theodor Schieffer, *Winfrid-Bonifatius und die Grundlegung von Europas* (Freiburg, 1954), 25, that Grimoald's lack of success influenced the manner in which the Carolingians subsequently pursued the kingship, certainly helps to account for the caution exercised by Pippin prior to his elevation in 751.

20. Regarding Pippin and Charles Martel's interest in securing the Frankish royal title for his family see Jörg Jarnut, "Die Adoption Pippins durch König Liutprand und die Italienpolitik Karl Martells," in *Karl Martell in Seiner Zeit*, ed. Jörg Jarnut, Ulrich Nonn, and Michael Richter (Sigmaringen, 1994), 217–226, with the literature cited there.

21. Theodor Breysig, *Jahrbücher der fränkischen Reiches, 714–741* (Leipzig, 1869); and Ludwig Oelsner, *Jahrbücher des fränkischen Reiches unter König Pippin* (Leipzig, 1871); and Heinrich Hahn, *Jahrbücher des fränkischen Reiches, 741–752* (Berlin, 1863), still provide the most comprehensive references to the sources.

22. For an excellent discussion of the manuscripts see Walter Goffart, "From *Historiae* to *Historia Francorum* and Back Again: Aspects of the Textual History of Gregory of Tours," in *Religion, Culture, and Society in the Early Middle Ages: Studies in Honor of Richard E. Sullivan*, ed. Thomas F. X. Noble and John J. Contreni (Kalamazoo, 1987), 55–76; and reprinted in Walter Goffart, *Rome's Fall and After* (London, 1989), 255–274.

23. The most thorough study of the geography of the *regnum Francorum* during the Merovingian era remains Auguste Longnon, *Géographie de la Gaule au VIe siècle* (Paris, 1878).

24. Gregory, *Hist.*, bk. III, ch. 3.

25. *Carm.*, IX, 1, lines 75–76.

26. Boniface, *Epist.* no. 109.

27. Gregory, *Hist.*, bk. II, ch. 27.

28. See the discussion by Bernard S. Bachrach, "Procopius and the Chronology of Clovis's Reign," *Viator*, 1 (1970), 21–31, and reprinted with the same pagination in *Armies and Politics in the Early Medieval West* (London, 1993).

29. For the date see Bachrach, "Procopius and the Chronology of Clovis's Reign," 21–31; and Mark Spencer, "Dating the Baptism of Clovis, 1886–1993," *Early Medieval Europe* 3 (1994), 97–116.

30. Gregory, *Hist.*, bk. III, ch. 7.

31. Gregory, *Hist.*, bk. IV, ch. 9.

32. Fredegar, *Chron.*, bk. IV, ch. 72.

33. This is clear from the basic introduction to Philip Grierson and M. Blackburn, *Medieval European Coinage* I, *The Early Middle Ages (5th-10th Centuries)* (Cambridge, 1986), 81–154, which is the best general account.

34. For general reference to the levying of trans-Rhenish troops, see Gregory, *Hist.*, bk. IV, ch. 49. Examples of Alamanni are found in Gregory, *Hist.*, bk. III, ch. 32; and Fredegar, *Chron.*, bk. IV, ch. 68. Concerning Thuringian levies see Fredegar, *Chron.*, bk. IV, ch. 38. It is somewhat more difficult to identify troops who were recruited from Hesse but it is likely that many of the Saxons who served in Merovingian armies and military colonies were recruited from settlements in this region rather than from Saxony proper east of the river Weser. For Saxons serving in the armies of the Merovingian kings, see, for example, Fredegar, *Chron.*, bk. IV, ch. 38.

35. See, for example, *Lex Allamannorum*, Cod. B, *incipit*; and *Lex Baiuvariorum*, *prol.*

36. The exaggerated views of Ian Wood, "Frankish Hegemony in England," in *The Age of Sutton Hoo: The Seventh Century in North-Western Europe*, ed. M. O. H. Carver

(Woodbridge, 1992), 235–241, go well beyond the evidence. Wood's point is a rhetorical use of the fact that Berchar was killed after the battle, not in the battle, to assert that he continued to rule after the battle. This is pure tendentiousness on Wood's part for the purpose of diminishing the role of warfare in politics.

37. See below regarding the comparison of Merovingian and Carolingian operations with regard to northern Spain.

38. For this controversial topic, see Georg Löhlein, *Die Alpen- und Italienpolitik der Merowinger im VI. Jahrhundert* in *Erlanger Abhandlungen zu mittleren und neuen Geschichte*, ed. B. Schniedler and O. Brandt (Erlangen, 1932), 1–81; Robert Holtzmann, "Die Italienpolitik der Merowinger und des Königs Pippin," in *Das Reich: Idee und Gestalt. Festschrift für Johannes Haller*, ed. H. Dannenbauer and F. Ernst (Stuttgart, 1940), 95–132; and Reinhard Schneider, "Fränkische Alpenpolitik," in *Die Transalpinen Verbindungen der Bayern, Alemannen und Franken bis zum 10. Jahrhundert*, ed. Helmut Beumann and Werner Schröder (Sigmaringen, 1987), 23–49.

39. Julia M. H. Smith, *Province and Empire: Brittany and the Carolingians* (Cambridge, 1992), 33–47.

40. See, for example, Martin Lintzel, "Die Sachsenkrieg Chlothars I," *Sachsen und Anhalt*, 4 (1928), 1–13; and Martin Lintzel, "Die Tributzahlungen der Sachsen an die Franken zur Zeit der Merowinger und König Pippins," *Sachsen und Anhalt*, 4 (1928), 13–28. These are reprinted in Martin Lintzel, *Ausgewählte Schriften*, 2 vols. (Berlin, 1961), I, 64–73, 74–86, respectively.

41. Here I follow the reconstruction of the chronology for Grimoald's efforts established by Gerberding, *The Rise of the Carolingians*, 47–66.

42. *Annales mettenses priores*, p. 2; and Gerberding, *The Rise of the Carolingians*, 123.

43. Here I follow the identification of the kings, mentioned above, as found in *Liber Historiae Francorum*, ch. 46. For the argument that Pippin and Martin brought Dagobert II back to Austrasia, see Gerberding, *The Rise of the Carolingians*, 78–80.

44. For the titles see *Liber Historiae Francorum*, ch. 46; but cf. Fredegar Cont., ch. 3. It is possible that Martin held the title of *dux* in a territorial sense, as duke of Champagne. In general, see Archibald R. Lewis, "The Dukes in the *Regnum Francorum*, A.D. 550–751," *Speculum*, 51 (1976), 381–410, for a useful introduction concerning the varied use of the title.

45. Concerning the order of magnitude of the armies of the early Carolingians, see below. Gerberding, *The Rise of the Carolingians*, 83, perceptively observed in support of the notion that Pippin and Martin established Dagobert II as king: "It seems highly unlikely that . . . Pippin's position was such that he could have raised a following sufficiently large . . . without himself having the attracting power of a king." Cf. Bernard S. Bachrach, *Merovingian Military Organization: 481–751* (Minneapolis, 1972), 107, where I speculate that Pippin II's grandson, Pippin, and the latter's brother, Carloman, put a puppet king, Childeric III, on the throne of the *regnum Francorum*, after a lengthy interregnum, in order to legitimize their efforts to mobilize expeditionary levies.

46. *Liber Historiae Francorum*, ch. 46; and Fredegar Cont., ch. 3. Wood, *The Merovingian Kingdoms, 450–751* (London, 1994), 257, sees the account in *Liber Historiae Francorum* as the preferred narrative source for the career of Pippin II because it has a clear Neustrian "political stance." However, Wood (233) uses the highly conjectural case of

Rupert of Salzburg to undermine the above-cited observation of the *Liber Historiae Francorum* regarding Pippin's domination of Austrasia from ca. 675. Indeed, Wood concludes that "an anti-Pippinid party *still* (my italics) existed in Austrasia in the 690s." It is doubtful that Wood's conjectures regarding Rupert amount to proof for the existence of an "anti-Pippinid party" in Austrasia in the 690s. The most that can perhaps be said regarding Rupert is that he had a personal falling out with Pippin and chose to accept a Bavarian "offer" to work in Salzburg. However, even if one were to accept Wood's hyperbole regarding Rupert's "anti-Pippinid party" as existing ca. 696, when he went to Bavaria, there is absolutely no warrant to project such a hypothetical party back to 675.

Not all scholars see Rupert as succumbing to ignominious flight from the Rhineland ca. 696 because as a leader of a putative anti-Pippinid party he could no longer tolerate the hostility generated by the Austrasian leader. For example, J. M. Wallace-Hadrill, *The Frankish Church* (Oxford, 1983), 73–74, 147–148, sees Rupert as a missionary "episcopus et abbas" educated in the Irish tradition, who was imposed upon a "more or less willing" Bavarian duke. Indeed, the latter apparently had reservations in seeing a "Frankish" enclave established in Bavarian territory at Salzburg. Thus, as Wallace-Hadrill emphasizes, Rupert kept his distance from the Bavarian capital at Regensburg.

Pippin's extensive diplomatic efforts to manipulate the Austrasian aristocracy and especially his *Klosterpolitik*, so well developed by Gerberding, *The Rise of the Carolingians*, 96–105, should not be seen as a sign that Carolingian control was weak but rather as a description of the means by which these rulers maintained control in an aristocratic society. Cf. for example, Ronald Syme, *The Roman Revolution*, 2nd ed. (Oxford, 1951), for a classic discussion of diplomacy in an aristocratic society.

47. Karl Ferdinand Werner, "Les principautés périphériques dans le monde franc du VIIIe siècle," *Settimane di studio del Centro Italiano di studi sull'alto medioevo*, 20 (Spoleto, 1972), 483–532.

48. The use of the phrase "infinita turba populi Austrasii" by the author of *Liber Historiae Francorum*, ch. 46, implies a force that was not composed of predominantly highly professional soldiers drawn from the military households of the magnates, which would be comparatively few in number. Fredegar Cont., ch. 3, also uses the term *populus* in a manner that does not suggest specialized troops. See below regarding early Carolingian military organization.

49. *Liber Historiae Francorum*, ch. 46; and Fredegar Cont., ch. 3. However, it is not without interest that *Annales mettenses priores*, whose author sought to outline a process of Carolingian success according to God's plan, omitted mention of the defeat at Lucofao.

50. *Liber Historiae Francorum*, ch. 47; Fredegar Cont., ch. 4; and *Annales mettenses priores*, p. 6.

51. *Annales mettenses priores*, p. 2. Paul, *Hist.*, bk. VI, ch. 37, provides a romanticized version of Pippin's effort.

52. Both Fredegar Cont., ch. 3; and *Liber Historiae Francorum*, ch. 46, make clear that Duke Martin and a substantial number of his troops were killed after he had agreed to terms of surrender that Ebroin's negotiators had sworn to uphold.

53. Fredegar Cont., ch. 4; *Liber Historiae Francorum*, ch. 47; and *Annales mettenses priores*, p. 6.

54. Fredegar Cont., ch. 4; and *Liber Historiae Francorum*, ch. 47, who adds that

Ermenfrid brought gifts to Pippin. Wood, *The Merovingian Kingdoms*, 234, concludes that these "gifts" absolve the Austrasian *dux* of guilt. This would seem to be based upon the assumption that the giving of "gifts" in this society "derationalizes" subornation of a criminal act.

55. *Annales mettenses priores*, p. 6.

56. Fredegar Cont., ch. 4; *Liber Historiae Francorum*, ch. 47; *Annales mettenses priores*, p. 6.

57. Fredegar Cont., ch. 4; and *Annales mettenses priores*, p. 6, which refers to a substantial number of important Neustrian magnates who were forced into exile by Ebroin and found support at Pippin's court. With the death of Ebroin these men returned to their homes.

58. This marriage only took place toward the end of the decade and after much tribulation. The suggestion that Ansfledis was Waratto's second wife is based, in part, upon the fact that her daughter Anstrudis was a potential bride for Drogo who could not have been more than ten years of age ca. 681. Waratto, however, had a son named Ghislemar, who during the early 680s was a grown man and thus presumably could not have been Ansfledis' son. Cf. Gerberding, *The Rise of the Carolingians*, 124, who dates Drogo's birth to ca. 675.

59. *Liber Historiae Francorum*, ch. 47; Fredegar Cont., ch. 4; and *Annales mettenses priores*, p. 6, all credit Ghislemar with considerable ability and experience, but none seems to like him.

60. Gerberding, *The Rise of the Carolingians*, 90–91, suggests that Ghislemar's rift with his father was likely due to one or a combination of the following factors: personal ambition, a reaction of the local elements in the Rouen area, and disapproval of his father's "dangerous alliance with Pippin" ("a clearer prevision than his father of the dangers to come"). I would not argue against Ghislemar being strongly motivated by personal ambition. However, if Ansfledis was Ghislemar's stepmother, then the opposition to his father's alliance with Pippin was a rational reaction against a plan that would have placed Drogo in competition for the office of Mayor of the Palace with the full backing of his stepmother and Pippin. As will be seen below, Berchar's marriage to Ghislemar's half-sister played a role in his obtaining that office.

61. Fredegar Cont., ch. 4.

62. *Liber Historiae Francorum*, ch. 47; Fredegar Cont., ch. 4; and *Annales mettenses priores*, p. 6, all tell much the same story.

63. *Liber Historiae Francorum*, ch. 47; Fredegar Cont., ch. 4; and *Annales mettenses priores*, p. 6, all provide some detail for the reconstruction of the situation. For a full discussion see Gerberding, *The Rise of the Carolingians*, 92–93.

64. On the Neustrian side, Ansfledis was the driving force behind the plan to have her daughter, Anstrudis, married to Drogo. See *Liber Historiae Francorum*, ch. 48, and for the marriage, *Annales mettenses priores*, p. 16. This conclusion is arrived at by reading back from her hostility to Berchar and her interest in the marriage of Anstrudis and Drogo ca. 687. Paul J. Fouracre, "Observations on the Outgrowth of Pippinid Influence in the 'Regnum Francorum' After the Battle of Tertry," *Medieval Prosopography*, 5.2 (1984), 4, sees this marriage as being of crucial importance.

65. Cf. Gerberding, *The Rise of the Carolingians*, 92.

66. While the Mayor should not be confounded with the abbot of the same name,

the latter was a major figure in the Champagne and an adversary of Pippin. He was assassinated shortly after 692. Cf. the coverage by Gerberding, *The Rise of the Carolingians*, 101–103.

67. *Annales mettenses priores*, pp. 7–8.

68. Fredegar Cont., ch. 5.

69. Fredegar Cont., ch. 3, emphasizes that the prelate played a key role in the negotiations that led to the death of Duke Martin.

70. Cf. Gerberding, *The Rise of the Carolingians*, 102–103.

71. *Annales mettenses priores*, p. 8.

72. Recent scholarship has tended to devaluate the impact of Carolingian military operations and to place greater emphasis on Pippin's use of diplomacy in gaining the support of various aristocratic factions. With regard to the putative impact of the victory at Tertry see, for example, Gerberding, *The Rise of the Carolingians*, 92–94; and Fouracre, "Pippinid Influence," 1–31. Paul J. Fouracre, "Frankish Gaul to 814," in *The New Cambridge Medieval History: c. 700–c. 900*, II, ed. Rosamond McKitterick (Cambridge, 1995), 85–86, reiterates his earlier views.

While it is important to emphasize the key role played by diplomacy in the expansion of Pippinid power—winning the war is not the same as winning the peace—it is crucial not to diminish the importance of military victory. Thus, for example, a comparison of Pippin's position in Neustria following the defeat at Lucofao with his position in the region following his victory at Tertry, as will be seen below and contrary to Fouracre's thesis, makes clear that military victory has its positive side and military defeat some very strong negatives.

73. *Liber Historiae Francorum*, ch. 48. See the discussion and the literature mustered by Gerberding, *The Rise of the Carolingians*, 93–94, who rightly points out that Pippin's involvement is a scholarly conjecture. Wood, *The Merovingian Kingdoms*, 260, asserts "Despite his defeat at Tertry, it was not the battle which ended Berchar's rule, but his mother-in-law." There is no evidence that Berchar's "rule" survived his defeat at Tertry and successful flight from the battlefield.

74. For the marriage see *Annales mettenses priores*, p. 16. Fouracre, "Pippinid Influence," 4.

75. *Annales mettenses priores*, p. 12.

76. Fouracre, "Pippinid Influence," 5.

77. *V. Ansberti*, ch. 21; *Gesta Abbatum Font.*, II, 1. See the discussions by Eugen Ewig, "Die fränkischen Teilreiche im 7. Jahrhundert (613–714)," *Trierer Zeitschrift*, 22 (1954), 141, and reprinted in Eugen Ewig, *Spätantikes und fränkisches Gallien: Gesammelte Schriften (1952–1973)*, 2 vols., ed. Hartmut Atsma (Munich, 1976, 1979), I, 172–230; and A. Halbedel, "Fränkische Studien: Kleine Beiträge zur Geschichte und Sage des deutschen Altertums," *Historische Studien*, 132 (Berlin, 1915). Cf. Gerberding, *The Rise of the Carolingians*, 97, who appears to be unwilling to concede that Gripho, despite his "Carolingian" name, was more than a "loyal follower" of Pippin.

78. Cf. the discussion by Fouracre, "Pippinid Influence," 5, who also emphasizes the small number of surviving documents.

79. *CLA*, no. 576.

80. See the discussion by Fouracre, "Pippinid Influence," 7, regarding this family and the chronology.

81. These percentages rest upon the data developed by Fouracre, "Pippinid In-

fluence," 6–7, and are subject to the methodological caveats that he correctly identifies. Fouracre notes that the homeland of a considerable number of the men in the sample cannot be identified and that the number of Austrasians likely is an undercount.

82. Cf. the treatment of this matter by Fouracre, "Pippinid Influence," 9–10.

83. For example, Fouracre, "Pippinid Influence," 5, argues on the basis of the Tironian notes in *CLA*, no. 577, that Pippin did not assume the title of Mayor of the Palace before 695, eight years after the victory at Tertry. Fouracre interprets this possible lapse of time between the victory at Tertry and the assumption of the mayoral office as an index of Pippin's weakness in Neustria. In contrast, *Liber Historiae Francorum*, ch. 48, leaves the impression that the period of time between the battle of Tertry and Pippin's assumption of the title of Mayor was not very long at all. Cf. Gerberding, *The Rise of the Carolingians*, 93, who does not mention the interpretation of the Tironian notes cited above, follows the *Liber* which, as he has shown generally is not biased in favor of the Carolingians but is essentially a Neustrian account.

84. *Liber Historiae Francorum*, ch. 48; and Gerberding, *The Rise of the Early Carolingians*, 93, for the chronology.

85. In one of his many special pleadings, Wood, *The Merovingian Kingdoms*, 264, tendentiously accepts the information provided by Bishop Ansebert's hagiographer (*V. Ansberti*, chs. 22, 24–26) for the saint's putative popularity post mortem in the area of Rouen as evidence for Pippin's supposed weakness in Neustria. See also Ian Wood, "Saint Wandrille and Its Hagiography," in *Church and Chronicle in the Middle Ages: Essays Presented to John Taylor*, ed. Ian Wood and Graham Laud (London, 1991), 11–12.

86. Cf. Fouracre, "Pippinid Influence," 9–11 and Gerberding, *The Rise of the Early Carolingians*, 115, who both rather curiously seem to judge the extent of Pippin's control of Neustrian affairs during his own lifetime on the basis of events that occurred after his death. Not unexpectedly, Wood, *The Merovingian Kingdoms*, 267–272, follows suit.

87. Cf. Fouracre, "Pippinid Influence," 11, who recognizes Pippin's use of diplomacy in governing Neustria but takes this as a sign of the weakness of his position. Even the mayoral office, Fouracre observes, may not have "guaranteed unchallengeable power and influence" to Pippin. Since even the greatest of the Roman emperors never had "guaranteed unchallengeable power and influence," Fouracre has set the standard a bit too high.

88. See the discussion by J. M. Wallace-Hadrill, "War and Peace in the Early Middle Ages," *Transactions of the Royal Historical Society*, 5th series, 25 (1975); and reprinted in J. M. Wallace-Hadrill, *Early Medieval History* (Oxford, 1975), 23; and in greater detail, Lawrence Markus, "Saint Augustine's Views on the 'Just War'," *Studies in Church History*, 20 (1983), 1–13.

89. Bede, *Hist.*, bk. V, 10. See the comment by J. M. Wallace-Hadrill, *Bede's Ecclesiastical History of the English People: A Historical Commentary* (Oxford, 1988), 182; and Wolfgang Fritze, "Zur Enstehungsgeschichte des Bistums Utrecht: Franken und Friesen 690–734," *Rheinische Vierteljahrsblätter*, 35 (1971), 107–115. For the general picture, H. Halbertsma, "The Frisian Kingdom," *Berichten van de Rijksdienst voor het Oudheidkundig Bodemonderzoek*, 15–16 (1965–1966), 70.

90. Even Gregory of Tours, who was no supporter of war, illuminated this strategic error for his more attentive readers. Gregory, *Hist.*, bk. III, ch. 6; and see the discussion by Bernard S. Bachrach, "Gregory of Tours as a Military Historian," in *Gregory of Tours*, ed. K. Mitchell and I. Wood (Leiden, 2000), forthcoming. With regard to Pip-

pin II's successors see Breysig, *Jahrbücher der fränkischen Reiches, 714–741*; and Oelsner, *Jahrbücher des fränkischen Reiches unter König Pippin*, for the activities of Charles Martel and his son Pippin, respectively.

91. *V. Wilfridi*, chs. 26–27; and Bede, *Hist.*, bk. V, ch. 19. See the discussion by H. Halbertsma, "The Frisian Kingdom," 69–70.

92. It is not clear whether the coinage during this period of Frisian independence was intended as a mark of that independence or as merely an economic advantage that helped to sustain the profitability of the emporium. In any case, there seems to be general agreement that the Durstede coinage between ca. 670 and ca. 695 was not controlled from the *regnum Francorum*, whereas earlier it was controlled by the Merovingians. For the basic information see Grierson and Blackburn, *Medieval European Coinage*, I, 150–154.

93. Halbertsma, "The Frisian Kingdom," 69–71.

94. With regard to the wealth generated by the emporium see Stéphane Lebecq, *Marchands et navigateurs frisons du haut moyen âge*, 2 vols. (Lille, 1983), 1, 156–163.

95. Note the omission of Burgundy from the list provided in *Annales mettenses priores*, pp. 12–13; and cf. the discussion by Werner, "Les principautés périphériques," 493.

96. *Annales mettenses priores*, p. 13.

97. *Annales mettenses priores*, p. 2. Cf. Matthias Werner, *Der Lütticher Raum in frühfränkischer Zeit* (Göttingen, 1980), esp. 335, 347–348, 469, who endeavors to prove that Pippin I held extensive lands in the Liège-Maastricht area. Cf. Gerberding, *The Rise of the Carolingians*, 121, who disputes this claim and is likely correct. However, this debate does not affect the conclusions that Pippin I was in charge of the government of this region or the description of its geographical extent.

98. Regarding the disappearance of Aldgisl and the rise to power of Radbod, see the discussion by Halbertsma, "The Frisian Kingdom," 70–71.

99. Cf. Bede, *Hist.*, bk. V, ch. 10, who also refers to Radbod as *rex*. This may have been an Anglo-Saxon tradition, e.g., Willibaldus, *V. S. Bonifatii*, ch. 5; and Boniface, *Epist*, no. 15.

100. Cf. Halbertsma, "The Frisian Kingdom," 70–71.

101. See *Liber Historiae Francorum*, chs. 49, 50; Fredegar Cont., chs. 6, 7; *Annales mettenses priores*, pp. 13, 17, 18; and Bede, *Hist.*, bk. V, ch. 10.

102. Fritze, "Zur Enstehungsgeschichte des Bistums Utrecht," 107–115; and Halbertsma, "The Frisian Kingdom," 70–71.

103. Halbertsma, "The Frisian Kingdom," 70–71.

104. For the *castrum* at Durstede see Fredegar Cont., ch. 6; who is followed by *Annales mettenses priores*, p. 17. However, archaeologists have yet to find remains of the *castrum*.

105. Bede, *Hist.*, bk. V, ch. 10.

106. The basic argument was made by Alexander Bergengruen, *Adal und Grundherrschaft im Merowingerreich* (Wiesbaden, 1958), 113–120; and recently rehearsed by Gerberding, *The Rise of the Carolingians*, 126–128.

107. Marios Costambeys, "An Aristocratic Community on the Northern Frankish Frontier, 690–726," *Early Medieval Europe*, 3 (1994), 55–61, quotation on 61.

108. For the "many wars," see *Liber Historiae Francorum*, ch. 49.

109. Bede, *Hist.*, bk. V, ch. 10. Costambeys, "An Aristocratic Community," 61.

110. The argument put forth by Costambeys, "An Aristocratic Community," 39–62, is based upon three key points: charters issued by the Toxandrian magnates differ significantly in some key terminology from traditional charters of the period outside the region; these charters indicate a lengthy period of landholding but no recent revolutionary change; and the charters indicate no evidence for these Toxandrian magnates holding familial lands in the Mosel-Eifel region.

111. *Annales mettenses priores, an.* 692 (p. 13). Efforts to redate this battle on the basis of presumed relative chronology in other sources are not compelling. Indeed, as seen above, the legal process dealing with the expropriation of the Amalberti in Neustria was only completed in 692.

112. *Annales mettenses priores, an.* 692 (p. 13).

113. Bede, *Hist.*, bk. V, ch. 10.

114. Gerberding, *The Rise of the Carolingians*, 117–126.

115. Halbertsma, "The Frisian Kingdom," 70–71.

116. Fredegar Cont., ch. 6; and *Annales mettenses priores*, p. 17.

117. *Annales mettenses priores*, p. 17.

118. Fredegar Cont., ch. 6; and *Annales mettenses priores*, p. 17.

119. Concerning the geography of the region, see William H. TeBrake, *Medieval Frontier: Culture and Ecology in Rijnland* (College Station, Tex., 1985), 53–103; A. M. Lambert, *The Making of the Dutch Landscape*, 2nd ed. (London, 1985); and Lebecq, *Marchands et navigateurs*, 1, 119–124.

120. Bede, *Hist.*, bk. V, ch. 11, provides the basis for this chronology. After Pippin's capture of Utrecht, he established the missionary headquarters for Willibrord in the old Roman fortress. See the discussion by Halbertsma, "The Frisian Kingdom," 70–71.

121. *Liber Historiae Francorum*, ch. 50; and *Annales mettenses priores*, p. 18.

122. The basic work remains Wilhelm Levison, *England and the Continent in the Eighth Century* (Oxford, 1946), 45–69, and his essay "St. Willibrord and His Place in History," in Wilhelm Levison, *Aus rheinischer und fränkischer Frühzeit* (Düsseldorf, 1948), 314–329. See also Wallace-Hadrill, *The Frankish Church*, 142–147; Rosamond McKitterick, "England and the Continent," in *The New Cambridge Medieval History: c. 700–c. 900*, II, ed. Rosamond McKitterick (Cambridge, 1995), 64–84; and Costambeys, "An Aristocratic Community," 39–62, for extensive references to more recent scholarly literature.

123. See, particularly, Wallace-Hadrill, *The Frankish Church*, 144–145; and the earlier study by Levison, "St. Willibrord," 314–329.

124. Costambeys, "An Aristocratic Community," 39–62, correctly argues that Willibrord's policies may have differed from Pippin's in specific matters. However, whatever differences the two men might have had, Pippin always gave Willibrord full support.

125. The Alamannic dukes established their independence of the *regnum Francorum* during the second third of the seventh century. See, for example, Reiner Butzen, *Die merowinger östlich des mittleren Rheins* (Würzburg, 1987), 132. However, cf. Werner, "Les principautés périphériques," 504, who leans on *Erchanberti Breviarium*, ch. 1, a later ninth-century text.

126. *Annales mettenses priores, ann.* 709, 710, 712. *Annales S. Amandi, ann.* 709, 710, 711, 712; *Annales Tiliani, ann.* 709, 710, 711, 712; *Annales Mosellani, an.* 710; and *Annales Laureshamenses, an.* 710. N.b. *Annales Alamannici*, ed. Lendi, *an.* 711; and *Annales Nazariani*, ed. Lendi, *an.* 710.

127. *Annales mettenses priores, ann.* 709, 710, 712. Rolf Sprandel, *Der merovingische Adel und die Gebiete östlich des Rheins*, in *Forschung zur oberrheinischen Landesgeschichte*, V (Freiburg im Breisgau, 1957), 117, would seem to accept Pippin's war aims as set out by the annalist. In contrast, J. M. Wallace-Hadrill, "A Background to St. Boniface's Mission," in *England Before the Conquest: Studies in Primary Sources Presented to Dorothy Whitelock*, ed. P. Clemoes and K. Hughes (Cambridge, 1971), and reprinted in J. M. Wallace-Hadrill, *Early Medieval History* (Oxford, 1975), 141–142, sees Pippin as having "shown the way" for Charles Martel's ultimate conquest. Bruno Behr, *Das alemannische Herzogtum bis 750* (Frankfurt am Main, 1975), 178–179, represents a consensus when he concludes that Pippin's success was rather localized.

128. These dates are provided by *Annales mettenses priores, ann.* 708, 711.

129. *Annales Mosellani, an.* 709; and *Annales Laureshamenses, an.* 709.

130. For a basic survey see Behr, *Das alemannische Herzogtum bis 750*, 175–179.

131. *Annales S. Amandi, an.* 709; *Annales Tiliani, ann.* 709; and *Annales mettenses priores, ann.* 709.

132. *Annales mettenses priores, an.* 709. Concerning the language of victory ceremonies, see below.

133. *Annales S. Amandi, an.* 709; *Annales Tiliani, an.* 709. Both detail the bad weather and a lack of crops to harvest in the spring.

134. *Annales S. Amandi, an.* 710; *Annales Tiliani, an.* 710; and *Annales mettenses priores, an.* 710 for the details.

135. *Liber Historiae Francorum*, ch. 50; Fredegar Cont., ch. 7; and *Annales mettenses priores, an.* 711.

136. *Annales S. Amandi, an.* 711; and *Annales Tiliani, an.* 711. Horst Ebling, *Prosopographie der Amsträger des Merowingerreiches von Chlothar II. (613) bis Karl Martell (741)* (Munich, 1974), is unable to identify Walericus.

137. *Annales S. Amandi, an.* 712; and *Annales Tiliani, an.* 712.

138. *Annales mettenses priores, an.* 712.

139. *Annales mettenses priores, an.* 713.

140. Breysig, *Jahrbücher des fränkischen Reiches*, 1–48, is still useful as a guide.

141. Fredegar Cont., ch. 10.

142. Fredegar Cont., ch. 10; *Liber Historiae Francorum*, ch. 53; and cf. the detailed discussion in *Annales mettenses priores*, pp. 23–25. Regarding the date, note Wilhelm Levison, "A Propos du Calendrier de S. Willibrord," *Revue Bénédictine*, 50 (1938), 37–41 and reprinted in Levison, *Aus rheinischer und fränkischer Frühzeit*, 344. Gerberding, *The Rise of the Carolingians*, 139–140, n. 39, sees Charles' area for military recruitment limited to Austrasia at this time.

143. Fredegar Cont., ch. 10, asserts that Ragamfred and King Chilperic offered to Eudo the rule (*regnum*) of Neustria and many gifts for his *auxilium* against Charles. Eudo was an exceptionally important man who had decisively defeated the Muslims in 721 and had been in close contact with Pope Gregory II prior to this victory. See the discussion by Michel Rouche, *L'Aquitaine des Wisigoths aux Arabes: 418–781: Naissance d'une région* (Paris, 1979), 108–113.

It is possible that Eudo had envisioned advancing his interests beyond the Loire ca. 700, when Pippin is said to have led an army to Bourges. See the discussion by Rouche, *L'Aquitaine*, 131, which rests on *Miracula S. Austregisilii*, ch. 5. However, the *Miracula* survives in an eleventh-century reworking and this episode likely refers to the siege operations carried out by Pippin II's grandson, King Pippin I, which are discussed below.

144. The group at issue here is that led by Bishop Savaric of Auxerre and his descendants in the next generation. In 697, Savaric, himself, as Gerberding, *The Rise of the Carolingians*, 103–104, has shown, supported Pippinid policy in Neustria. After Savaric's death, Charles appointed the dead prelate's relatives, Eucherius and Ainmar, bishops of Orléans and Auxerre, respectively. These men served Charles loyally in many wars against the Muslims until the late 730s. Toward the end of the decade, Charles removed them from power for reasons that apologists for the bishops depict as unjust. Cf. Wood, *The Merovingian Kingdoms*, 263, 266, 276–277, who attacks Gerberding's discussion of Savaric's support for the Pippinids in 697 on the basis of Charles' rough treatment of Eucharius and Ainmar some forty years later. Wood puts forth the curious argument that Eucherius and Ainmar supported Charles' military operations for two decades because he was too weak to get rid of them. N.b. the behavior of Antenor, a dominant magnate in Provence, who like Savaric supported Pippinid aims in 697, is rather different, as will be seen below.

145. See, for example, *Annales S. Amandi, an.* 715; *Annales Tiliani, an.* 715; and *Annales Petaviani, an.* 715. Cf. the three studies below by Lintzel, "Die Sachsenkrieg Chlothars I"; "Die Tributzahlungen der Sachsen an die Franken"; and "Karl Martells Sachsenkrieg im Jahre 738 und die Missionstätigkeit des Bonifatius," *Sachsen und Anhalt*, 13 (1937), 59–65. These are reprinted in Martin Lintzel, *Ausgewählte Schriften*, I, 64–73; 74–86; 87–92, respectively.

146. *Liber Historiae Francorum*, ch. 51; Fredegar Cont., ch. 8; and *Annales mettenses priores, an.* 714.

147. Willibaldus, *V. S. Bonifatii*, ch. 4, indicates that both Utrecht and Durstede were already in Radbod's hands when Boniface arrived there in 716.

148. The naval attack is discussed in *Gesta Abbatum Font.*, ch. 3; and the operations of this year are mentioned in *Annales S. Amandi, an.* 716. Cf. Fredegar Cont., ch. 9, who would seem to have condensed two Frisian attacks on Cologne, the first "navali ordine" and the second without a naval component, mentioned below, into a single episode.

149. *Liber Historiae Francorum*, ch. 52; and Fredegar Cont., ch. 8, for the alliance.

150. Gerberding, *The Rise of the Carolingians*, 130–132, provides a useful discussion of Charles' early support and expands upon these views in "716: A Crucial Year for Charles Martel," in *Karl Martell in Seiner Zeit*, ed. Jörg Jarnut, Ulrich Nonn, and Michael Richter (Sigmaringen, 1994), 205–216.

151. See the discussion by Gerberding, *Rise of the Carolingians*, 134–135.

152. *Liber Historiae Francorum*, ch. 52; Fredegar Cont., ch. 10.

153. *Liber Historiae Francorum*, ch. 51; and Fredegar Cont., ch. 10.

154. *Liber Historiae Francorum*, ch. 52; and Fredegar Cont., ch. 9. N.b. *Annales mettenses priores*, p. 23, reverses the temporal relationship between the encounter at Amblève, see below, and the attack on Cologne.

155. *Liber Historiae Francorum*, ch. 52; and Fredegar Cont., ch. 9. *Annales mettenses priores*, p. 22, accounts, in part, for the undisciplined encampment of the Neustrians and the Frisians by the "summer weather," which was unseasonably warm for April in this region.

156. *Liber Historiae Francorum*, ch. 53, indicates that Charles tried to arrange peace. *Annales mettenses priores*, pp. 23–25, notes that Charles sent his *legati* to Ragam-

fred to inform him that he was willing to make peace on the basis of the status quo ante, i.e., prior to the death of Pippin II. If the Metz annalist, who describes the battle in great detail, were an elderly man when he wrote in 805, he could have had access not only to men who had fought in the Carolingian army or even in the Neustrian army at Vinchy but also to men who had been party to the negotiations prior to the battle. See also Fredegar Cont., ch. 10.

157. Fredegar Cont., ch. 10, mentions the pursuit to Paris; as do *Annales mettenses priores*, p. 25. Cf. Gerberding, *The Rise of the Carolingians*, 140, who follows Wallace-Hadrill's mistranslation of this passage and concludes that the Continuator says that Charles "took Paris." Gerberding then extends this misreading to the treatment of Charles' pursuit by the Metz annalist. Gerberding provides no basis for rejecting the texts that indicate Charles "usque Parisius civitate properavit" except for the fact that *Liber Historiae Francorum*, ch. 53, fails to mention this additional humiliating detail suffered by his Neustrian countrymen. Indeed, the use of the term *civitas* strongly suggests that the Continuator was talking about the region of Paris and not about the *urbs*. In any case *properavit* means that Charles advanced rapidly, not that he captured the city.

158. *Liber Historiae Francorum*, ch. 53; and Fredegar Cont., 10, both stress the importance of the ravishing of enemy territory, the taking of captives, and the acquisition of large amounts of booty. *Annales mettenses priores*, p. 25, especially emphasizes that the entire region was thoroughly worked over (*subacta*) in the course of looting. Nb. the Metz annalist makes a point by using *subacta* to mean thoroughly ravaged rather than the traditional language for conquest, as noted above, in his discussion of Pippin II's wars against the Alamanni, which resulted in the Mayor's *ditio* being imposed on the conquered. The most obvious and the most rapid line of march for Charles' army from the Paris region to Cologne was through the valley of the Oise and the valley of the Sambre. N.b. *Liber Historiae Francorum*, ch. 53, indicates that Charles' army plundered several *regiones*.

159. *Liber Historiae Francorum*, ch. 53; and Fredegar Cont., ch. 10.

160. For the background on these Thuringian dukes see Hubert Mordek, "Die Hedenen als politische Kraft im austrasischen Frankenreich," in *Karl Martell in Seiner Zeit*, ed. Jörg Jarnut, Ulrich Nonn, and Michael Richter (Sigmaringen, 1994), 345–366. See *Echternach*, II, ed. Wampach, no. 97, for Heden's act of 717.

161. *Echternach*, II, ed. Wampach, no. 39, for Heden's act of 704.

162. Alcuin, *V. S. Willibrordi*, ch. 13.

163. For 719 see *Annales Alamannici*; *Annales Laureschamenses*; *Annales Tiliani*; *Annales S. Amandi*; *Annales Petaviani*; and *Annales Nazariani*. None of the above provide a cause of death and thus he may have died naturally.

164. N.b. *Annales Laureschamenses*, an. 722; *Annales Petaviani*, an. 722; and *Annales Nazariani*, an. 722, all indicate that military operations were carried out in the "northern region" (*bella contra aquiloniam*). However, none of these accounts specifically mentions Frisia or the Frisians. From the chronology, as will be seen below, it is likely that these efforts were carried out against Saxons or the group called "Dani-Saxones." Cf. Costambeys, "An Aristocratic Community," 59.

165. This region also included the Frisian port at Domburg on the island of Walcheren. Alcuin, *V. S. Willibrordi*, ch. 13; and see Lebecq, *Marchands et navigateurs*, I, 142–145.

166. Costambeys, "An Aristocratic Community," 57–59, briefly indicates the order

of magnitude of the aid going to Willibrord through Charles Martel and his dependents in Toxandria. Gerberding, "716: A Crucial Year," 205–216, rightly emphasizes the great importance of Willibrord to Charles' success. However, he seems greatly to underestimate the importance of key military victories won by Charles (215). N.b. Ebling, *Prosopographie der Amtsträger*, identifies no secular officials for Frisia under either Pippin or Charles Martel who might be seen as governing the entire territory. I am prepared to believe that Willibrord functioned as Charles' "governor" for the region. Indeed, Willibrord's immense responsibilities may help account for his need of Boniface as an assistant between 719 and 721, as well as his efforts to keep the latter as his assistant even after 721. See Levison, *England and the Continent*, 65.

167. See, for example, *Annales S. Amandi, an.* 715; *Annales Tiliani, an.* 715; and *Annales Petaviani, an.* 715.

168. See, for example, *Annales Alamannici, an.* 718, ed. Lendi; *Annales Nazariani, an.* 718; *Annales S. Amandi, an.* 718 *Annales Tiliani, an.* 718; and *Annales Petaviani, an.* 718.

169. Under 718 see *Annales Alamannici*, ed. Lendi; *Annales Nazariani*; *Annales S. Amandi*; *Annales Tiliani*; and *Annales Petaviani*.

170. Rouche, *L'Aquitaine*, 111–113, deals with Eudo's policies.

171. Fredegar Cont., ch. 10; and *Liber Historiae Francorum*, ch. 53.

172. *Liber Historiae Francorum*, ch. 53; and Fredegar Cont., ch. 10. Cf. *Annales mettenses priores*, p. 25, which condenses the flight of Eudo and the negotiations into a single episode with the apparent purpose of trumpeting the Aquitanian duke's fear of Charles.

Although Eudo refused battle with Charles in 719 and had retreated ignominiously, the Aquitanian duke was capable of fielding a formidable army on his own. In 721, he defeated a major Muslim army in the southern part of Aquitaine. The Aquitanian duke may have wanted to avoid fighting the Muslims in the south and the Austrasians in the north at the same time. The Muslim governor in Spain, As-Samh, invaded Aquitaine in 719 and captured the city of Narbonne. Eudo also may have believed that alliance with Charles might be of value in the future, correctly, as the events of October 732 at Poitiers were to demonstrate. Conversely, Eudo's earlier alliance with Ragamfred may have been motivated by a desire to obtain Neustrian support for his wars with the Muslims in the south. With *regnum* in Neustria, Eudo would have the legal right to mobilize soldiers from the region.

173. For the year 720 see: *Annales Guelferbytani*, ed. Lendi; *Annales Nazariani*, ed. Lendi; *Annales Alamannici*, ed. Lendi; *Annales Laureshamenses*; *Annales S. Amandi*; *Annales Tiliani*; *Annales Laubacenses*; and *Annales Petaviani*.

174. Willibaldus, *V. S. Bonifatii*, ch. 6.

175. Boniface, *Epist.*, no. 63.

176. This interpretation is contrary to most contemporary writing on the subject, which tends to emphasize Boniface's independence. See, for example, McKitterick, "England and the Continent," 73, where Boniface's personal submission to Charles in 722 is treated in rather muted terms.

177. Cf. Lintzel, "Karl Martells Sachsenkrieg," 87–92.

178. For various aspects of the process by which the Carolingians gained control of Hesse, see Walter Schlesinger, "Early Medieval Fortification in Hesse: A General Historical Report," *World Archaeology*, 7 (1976), 243–260, with the immense body of scholarly works cited there; and David Parsons, "Sites and Monuments of the Anglo-Saxon

Mission in Central Germany," *The Archaeological Journal*, 140 (1983), 280–321. With regard to some provocative ideas concerning the relations between settlement and religious houses see Hans-Jürgen Nitz, "The Church as Colonist: The Benedictine Abbey of Lorsch and Planned Waldhufen Colonization in the Odenwald," *Journal of Historical Geography*, 9 (1983), 105–126; and from an even more general perspective Walter Janssen, "Some Major Aspects of Frankish and Medieval Settlement in the Rhineland," in *Medieval Settlement: Continuity and Change*, ed. Peter Sawyer (London, 1976), 41–60.

179. Fredegar Cont., ch. 11, indicates that Charles, after forcing Ragamfred to take refuge at Angers, then laid siege to the city but did not take it. Instead, he ravaged the region and returned home with a great amount of booty, *plurima spolia*. The date of this operation is usually put in 724, the year after Charles' illness, but that chronology is hardly certain. This military operation may have taken place as early as 721. Cf. Wood, *The Merovingian Kingdoms*, 273, who suggests that Ragamfred established himself at Nantes and then "invents" a siege of this old Roman fortress city by Charles in 724.

180. *Annales mettenses priores*, p. 26, where it is also noted that Charles took Ragamfred's son as a hostage in order to ensure the father's continuing loyalty. The sources seem to conflate two Carolingian operations against Ragamfred at Angers. After the first (Fredegar Cont., ch. 11), Charles returned home with great amounts of booty. In the second, discussed here, Ragamfred led a force against Charles' assets but was again chased back to Angers.

181. Regarding Ragamfred's survival until 731 see the slightly different accounts for this year in *Annales Guelferbytani*, ed. Lendi; *Annales Nazariani*, ed. Lendi; *Annales Alamannici*, ed. Lendi; *Annales Laureshamenses*; *Annales S. Amandi*; *Annales Tiliani*; *Annales Laubacenses*; and *Annales Petaviani*. There is no basis in the sources to support the claim by Werner, "Les principautés périphériques," 510, that "Raginfred . . . conservait, jusqu'à sa mort en 731, une principauté," or the conclusion by Fouracre, "Pippinid Influence," 2, that "Ragamfred . . . continued to resist Charles Martel from his base at Angers until his death in 731." Ebling, *Prosopographie der Amtsträger*, 207, whom Fouracre cites to support this argument, merely indicates, following *Annales Petaviani, an.* 731, that Ragamfred died in that year. No evidence is produced of Ragamfred's "continued" resistance to Charles. It is unlikely that Charles, who defeated the Muslims at Poitiers in 732, would tolerate "resistance" at Angers as late as 731.

182. Breysig, *Jahrbücher des fränkischen Reiches*, 46.

183. The dates of Charles' retaliatory raids against the Saxons in 718 and 720 are firm. However, this third operation is very difficult to date. See, for example, Lintzel, "Karl Martells Sachsenkrieg," 87.

184. Fredegar Cont., ch. 12, reports that a year passed between the Saxon "rebellion" and Charles' campaign in the south. However, as diplomatic evidence, discussed below, suggests, Charles may have mobilized an army and invaded Alamannia in 724.

185. *Annales mettenses priores*, p. 4.

186. Fredegar Cont., ch. 12. Late sources, e.g., Sigibert of Gembloux in the eleventh century, suggest that there was a battle between Charles and Landfrid, but there is no contemporary confirmation. See Behr, *Das alemannische Herzogtum*, 182.

187. *Lex Alamannorum, prologus*; and Fredegar Cont., ch. 25, which makes clear that the laws (*jura*) to which the Alamanni were subject had been imposed by the Carolingians. See the discussion by Werner, "Les principautés périphériques," 506, n. 51; and Behr, *Das alemannische Herzogtum*, 186–187, for the date 724/725. Cf. Wood, *The Mero-*

vingian Kingdoms, 285, who, to diminish the importance of the early Carolingians, concludes that Landfrid asserted his "independence" and issued the *Lex Alamannorum* in his own name.

188. For discussions of the documentation see Behr, *Das alemannische Herzogtum*, 101–102, who follows J. F. Böhmer and Engelbert Mühlbacher, *Resgesta Imperii: Die Regesten des Kaiserreichs unter den Karoligern, 751–918* (Innsbruck, 1908), 15.

189. See *V. Arnulfi*, ch. 13; along with the perceptive observations of Werner, "Les principautés périphériques," 497, n. 28, who also provides a discussion of the relevant scholarly literature.

190. See the observations by Werner, "Les principautés périphériques," 498, n. 29, with the literature cited there concerning Dagobert's military colonies in Alamannia.

191. Fredegar Cont., ch. 12; and *Annales mettenses priores*, p. 26.

192. See, for example, Cicero, *Att.* 5.20.2; and Virgil, *Aen.*, 6.681.

193. For the year 725, see *Annales S. Amandi*; *Annales Tiliani*; and *Annales Laubacenses*, which indicate only that this was Charles' first expedition into Bavaria. Fredegar Cont., ch. 12, makes no specific mention of combat, and only *Annales Petaviani* indicate that Charles did any fighting there.

194. Fredegar Cont., ch. 12; and *Annales mettenses priores*, p. 26.

195. Cf. Herwig Wolfram, *Die Geburt Mitteleuropas: Geschichte Österreichs vor seiner Entstehung, 378–907* (Berlin and Vienna, 1987), 96–97.

196. Paul, *Hist.*, bk. VI, ch. 58; with the discussion and literature cited by Thomas F. X. Noble, *The Republic of St. Peter: The Birth of the Papal State, 680–825* (Philadelphia, 1984), 31–32 and the quotation.

197. *Monumenta Noval.*, ed. Cipolla, no. 1 (p. 9). Cf. Ian Wood, in his review of Geary (*Aristocracy in Provence* in *French History*, 1 [Stuttgart, 1987], 118–119), who prefers to see Abbo in 726 as being hostile to Charles Martel.

198. Fredegar Cont., ch. 12; and *Annales mettenses priores*, p. 26.

199. Fredegar Cont., ch. 12; and *Annales mettenses priores*, p. 26. Regarding the various family relationships see Jörg Jarnut, "Untersuchungen zur Herkunft Swanahilds, der Gattin Karl Martells," *Zeitschrift für bayerische Landesgeschichte*, 40 (1977), 345–349.

200. Timothy Reuter, "Plunder and Tribute in the Carolingian Empire," *Transactions of the Royal Historical Society*, 5th ser., 35 (1985), 75–94, clearly sets out this popular "primitivist" view of military organization, which takes as its starting point notions of a German warrior aristocracy based upon literary fantasies such as the *Beowulf* epic and which seriously undervalues the vast institutional infrastructure that the West inherited from the later Roman empire.

201. For the year 728, see the curious observation in *Annales Alamannici*, ed. Lendi, that the *Franci* did not do anything. *Annales S. Amandi* indicate that Charles went to Bavaria, but *Annales Tiliani* indicate that there was no fighting. Neither Fredegar Cont. nor *Annales mettenses priores* mention Charles' effort in this context.

202. See under the year 731: *Annales Nazariani*, ed. Lendi; *Annales Alamannici*, ed. Lendi; *Annales Laureshamenses*; *Annales S. Amandi*; *Annales Laubacenses*; and *Annales Petaviani*. Only *Annales Tiliani* report any fighting and this annalist reports fighting as a matter of course, e.g., *ann.* 725, 728, 730, when none of the other annalists report military action. However, *Annales mettenses priores*, pp. 26–27, follows the account in *Annales Tiliani*, *an.* 731, and embellishes it with material from Fredegar Cont., ch. 13, who endeavors to characterize Eudo and the Aquitanians as traitors who sought help from the Mus-

lims. Michel Rouche, "Les Aquitans ont-ils trahi avant la bataille de Poitiers?" *Le Moyen Age*, 74 (1968), 5–26, effectively exposes the problems with the Continuator's effort.

203. In 730, Duke Landfrid of Alamannia died: *Annales Nazariani*, ed. Lendi; *Annales Alamannici*, ed. Lendi; *Annales Laureshamenses*. By contrast, *Annales S. Amandi*; *Annales Laubacenses*; and *Annales Petaviani* all indicate that Charles went into Alamannia "against Landfrid" and *Annales Tiliani* actually indicate that there was fighting. Both Fredegar Cont. and *Annales mettenses priores* ignore Charles' efforts in regard to Alamannia. No sources indicate that spoils were taken. Whether Charles invaded Alamannia in order to punish Landfrid for having expelled Pirmin from Richenau two or three years earlier or whether Charles came to Alamannia following Landfrid's death to arrange the succession of the new duke or perhaps both is beyond the scope of the present discussion. See Behr, *Das alemannische Herzogtum*, 190.

204. This campaign is discussed in considerable detail in subsequent chapters.

205. Gregory, *Hist.*, bk. III, ch. 29, provides an account of this successful campaign after which Childebert I built the church of St. Vincent in Paris. In addition, Dagobert I was regarded by contemporaries as capable of executing formidable military operations in Spain; see Fredegar, *Chron.*, bk. IV, ch. 73.

206. See, for example, Karl Leyser, "Early Medieval Warfare," in *The Battle of Maldon*, ed. Janet Cooper (London, 1993), 87–108, and reprinted in Karl Leyser, *Communications and Power in Medieval Europe: The Carolingian and Ottonian Centuries*, ed. Timothy Reuter (London and Rio Grande, 1994), 29–50.

207. *V. Eucherii*, chs. 7–9. Cf. Gerberding, *The Rise of the Carolingians*, 139, n. 39, who argues that Charles acted against Eucharius not in 732 but in 737. He bases this dating on the conclusion that Charles appointed Eucherius as bishop of Orléans in 722 rather than in 717 as most scholars correctly maintain. The argument against 717 put forth by Gerberding is twofold. First, he assumes that Charles did not "control" Orléans in 717. This depends upon Gerberding's assumption that the decisive victory by the Carolingians over Ragamfred on 21 March 717 did not leave Orléans in Charles' power. Gerberding also fails to note that Charles was at the old roman fortress of Orleans in 719 with a major army, as seen above. This permits the inference that he was in a position to control matters at Orléans no later than 719. Finally, Gerberding argues that since *V. Eucherius*, ch. 8, indicates that the bishop of Orléans was deposed and exiled after Charles defeated the Muslims in Aquitaine with the help of the Burgundians, the text must be referring to Charles' victory in 737 because he could not have had Burgundians in his army as early as 732. In this context, Gerberding dismisses as of no consequence the fact that the conflict in 737 was not fought in Aquitaine but in Septimania. Moreover, Gerberding fails to note that Bishop Ainmar of Auxerre served at the head of a "Burgundian" contingent with Charles at Poitiers in 732 (*Gesta episcoporum Autissiod.*, ch. 27). For a critical reading of this passage of the *Gesta*, on this point cf. Annalena Staudte-Lauber, "Carlus Princeps Regionem Burgundie Sagiciter Penetravit. Zur Schlacht von Tours und Poitiers und dem Eingreifen Karl Martells in Burgund," in *Karl Martell in Seiner Zeit*, ed. Jörg Jarnut, Ulrich Nonn, and Michael Richter (Sigmaringen, 1994), 80–81. Staudte-Lauber, 93, n. 81, dismisses Gerberding's efforts to overturn the traditional date of 732, for the deposition of Eucherius as bishop of Orléans by Charles, and asserts that it is incorrect (*unrecht*).

208. *V. Eucherii*, ch. 4, attempts to portray Eucherius' elevation to the episcopal seat as having taken place in a canonical manner but admits, nevertheless, that his appointment depended upon Charles' approval.

209. *V. Eucherii*, chs. 4, 7 (*inimicus humani generis*), and 8. See, for example, Wood, *The Merovingian Kingdoms*, 275–276, who ignores the obvious bias of *V. Eucherii*.

210. See Staudte-Lauber, "Carlus Princeps," 92–99.

211. Fredegar Cont., chs. 14, 18.

212. *Gesta episcoporum Autissiod.*, ch. 27, and the discussion by Fouracre, "Pippinid Influence," 8.

213. Regarding Maurontus, see Fredegar Cont., chs. 20, 21. Staudte-Lauber, "Carlus Princeps," 92–99, argues a version of the cliché "my enemy's enemies are my friends." However, there is no inherent reason to believe that because Charles punished both groups they were in league against him.

214. *V. Eucherii*, ch. 8.

215. *V. Rigoberti*, chs. 9, 12.

216. Fredegar Cont., ch. 14.

217. F. L. Ganshof, "Charlemagne et le serment," *Mélanges d'histoire du Moyen Age dédiés à la mémoire de Louis Halphen* (Paris, 1951), 259–290; translated as "Charlemagne's Use of the Oath," in F. L. Ganshof, *The Carolingians and the Frankish Monarchy: Studies in Carolingian History*, trans. Janet Sondheimer (London, 1971), 111–124, which provides a good introduction to this subject with the focus on the reign of Charlemagne. However, Charlemagne was acting within the framework of a tradition that went all the way back to the later Roman empire and its army. See the observations in Chapter 2.

N.b. Fredegar Cont., ch. 14, uses the term *infideles* here as the contrapositive of *fideles* and not as a synonym for Muslim or pagan. See, for example, ch. 13, where the Continuator uses Saracens; ch. 19, when he means pagans; and ch. 20, where he interchanges Saracens with Ishmaelites. In this section of the account the court chronicler does not use "infidel" to mean either a non-Christian or Muslim.

218. Fredegar Cont., ch. 14; and n.b. *Annales mettenses priores*, p. 27, which glosses *leudes* as *duces*.

219. Fredegar Cont., ch. 14.

220. Regarding the importance, in general, of seeing the behavior of the principals during this era in late antique terms see Werner, "Les principautés périphériques," 483–532.

221. Fredegar Cont., ch. 18, and the discussion below.

222. *V. Eucherii*, ch. 7. Cf. Staudte-Lauber, "Carlus Princeps," 85, n. 38.

223. This campaign is discussed in detail in the Appendix: "The Organization of Naval Assets."

224. Fredegar Cont., ch. 15. In light of the high quality and general effectiveness of the armies of the Aquitanian duchy (summarized by Rouche, *L'Aquitaine*, 115), it is inconceivable that Charles would have risked an invasion with anything but a large army. In addition, the fact that Charles chose to call a council of his magnates prior to launching the invasion indicates that he required their support. In addition, he also likely sought counsel because he was, as will be seen below, aiming to alter Carolingian policy toward Aquitaine.

225. Regarding travel time and logistics see Bachrach, "Animals and Warfare," 707–764.

226. Although Fredegar Cont., ch. 15, might perhaps be considered biased in reporting this peaceful progress, he is sustained by the various early Carolingian annals. For example, under the year 735, see *Annales S. Amandi*; *Annales Mosellani*; *Annales Laureshamenses*; *Annales Laubacenses*, *Annales Alamannici*, ed. Lendi, and *Annales Na-*

zariani, ed. Lendi. Indeed, only *Annales Tiliani*, *an*. 735, report any fighting and, as observed above, it was this annalist's habit to record fighting whenever an army was led into the field.

227. See Werner, "Les principautés périphériques," 483–532, for the phenomenon, in general, and 499–502, in regard to Aquitaine, Rouche, *L'Aquitaine*, 87–109, who treats the period 614–718 as "la marche vers l'indépendance," and 111–132, treats the period 718–781 as "la fin de l'indépendance."

228. Fredegar Cont., ch. 15; and with slight variation *Annales mettenses priores*, p. 28.

229. This information is discussed from a somewhat different perspective by Rouche, *L'Aquitaine*, 114–115.

230. Fredegar Cont., ch. 15.

231. Charles Higounet, *Bordeaux pendant le haut moyen âge* (Bordeaux, 1963), 22–23.

232. Robert Latouche, *The Birth of Western Economy: Economic Aspects of the Dark Ages*, trans. E. M. Wilkinson (London, 1961), 134.

233. Gregory, *Liber gloria confessorum*, ch. XLV.

234. See, for example, the discussion by Bachrach, *Merovingian Military Organization*, 9, 12, 17, 20–21, 29, 37–38, 53, 55, 101, 105, 111, 127.

235. With regard to Italy, see Dick Harrison, *The Early State and the Towns: Forms of Integration in Lombard Italy, AD 568–774* (Lund, 1993).

236. *Annales mettenses priores*, p. 28. Cf. Rouche, *L'Aquitaine*, 115–116, who believes that Hunoald and his brother Hatto revolted against Charles and held the ducal title by force. This putative revolt, however, is not recorded in earlier sources. Rouche recognizes that Charles turned back the previous efforts of the Aquitanian *duces* to have themselves considered *reges*.

237. Fredegar Cont., ch. 15.

238. Bernard S. Bachrach, "Quelques observations sur la composition et les caractéristiques des armées de Clovis," in *Clovis, histoire & mémoire*, 2 vols., ed. Michel Rouche (Paris, 1997), 1:700–701.

239. Under the year 736, see, for example, *Annales S. Amandi*; *Annales Tiliani*; and *Annales Petaviani*. Rouche, *L'Aquitaine*, 116, believes that Charles' armies were defeated by the Aquitanians because the court chronicler does not discuss the invasion. However, as will be seen below, Charles' military operations in Septimania could hardly have been undertaken if potentially hostile Aquitanian and Gascon forces were positioned along his routes of march and supply lines.

240. *Annales Laureshamenses*; *Annales Alamannici*, ed. Lendi, and *Annales Nazariani*, ed. Lendi. Cf. Rouche, *L'Aquitaine*, 519, n. 36.

241. Fredegar Cont., chs. 41, 42, 49, calls attention to Auxerre as a crucial road center for military operations on the route between the Austrasian Rhineland and Aquitaine. See also Fredegar, *Chron.*, bk. IV, chs. 58, 90, for the route south from Sens through Auxerre and Autun to Lyons.

242. *Gesta episcoporum Autissiod.*, ch. 27, is the only source for the fate of Ainmar. However, it was written ca. 875, more than a hundred and forty years after the events under consideration, and confuses matters on a number of points. For example, Eudo is depicted as the prisoner rather than his ostensibly obscure son Hatto. See, for example, Staudte-Lauber, "Carlus Princeps," 80, n. 13. Cf. Wood, *The Merovingian Kingdoms*, 276,

who does not recognize the confusion of Eudo, who was never taken prisoner by Charles, for Hatto and fails to take account of the anti-Carolingian bias of the *Gesta*.

243. For the disablement of Hatto at the hands of Hunoald, see *Annales mettenses priores*, p. 36, which dates this event to 744. There is, however, no corroborating source for the date and no reason to believe that Hatto survived the reign of Charles Martel. Rouche, *L'Aquitaine*, 519, n. 36, rightly expresses his perplexity in regard to the date provided by the above-cited annals and indicates his "impression" that 736 is the likely date for Hatto's blinding and imprisonment. In recognition of the pro-Carolingian bias of the Metz annalist, events that cast a poor light on the Carolingians' adversaries might be thought to be suspect. However, if the rough treatment of Hatto is regarded as historical fact, the Metz annalist may have placed the event chronologically in a context that would best advance his argument. Thus, I would suggest 737 as the likely date for Hunoald's imprisonment of his brother.

244. *V. Pardulfi*, ch. 21.

245. Fredegar Cont., ch. 18. Unfortunately, the Continuator confounds this very limited operation at the city of Lyons with Charles' reorganization of the political structure of Provence in the south (the region between the city of Marseilles and the Arlate). Neither the city of Lyons nor the Lyonnaise were part of the southern district. These were fundamentally different operations and the Continuator's account has resulted in much unnecessary confusion.

246. Ganshof, "Charlemagne's Use of the Oath," 111–124, treats this problem as noted above for the reign of Charlemagne.

247. Fredegar Cont., chs. 20, 21, surely permit this inference.

248. Abbo and his family are best known from the former's *testamentum*, which now has been authenticated firmly by Ulrich Nonn, "Merowingische Testamente. Studien zum Fortleben einer römische Urkundenform im Frankenreich," *Archiv für Diplomatik*, 18 (1972), 1–129. An easily accessible text of this document with a somewhat problematic translation is in Patrick Geary, *Aristocracy in Provence: The Rhône Basin at the Dawn of the Carolingian Age* (Stuttgart, 1985), 38–79 and 125–131, where Abbo's family is discussed.

249. Geary, *Aristocracy in Provence*, 132–143.

250. Whether Abbo was a supporter of Charles as early as 722 or perhaps in 726, or only joined the Carolingians sometime between 733 and 737, remains a matter of controversy as highlighted by Wood, in his review of Geary (*Aristocracy in Provence*), 118–119.

251. Fredegar Cont., ch. 18.

252. Fredegar Cont., ch. 20; *Chronicon Moissacense*, 292. For the year 737 see *Annales S. Amandi*; *Annales Tiliani*; *Annales Petaviani*; *Annales Laureshamenses*; *Annales Alamannici*, ed. Lendi, and *Annales Nazariani*, ed. Lendi. Cf. Rouche, *L'Aquitaine*, 520, n. 38.

253. Fredegar Cont., chs. 20, 21. Modern scholars have made much of Maurontus' role in these events but, in fact, the Continuator is the only independent source to mention his activities. Even *Annales mettenses priores*, pp. 28–30, treats him as an unimportant element in the events of the period. Rouche, "Les Aquitains," 5–26, argued successfully that Eudo had not allied with the Muslim governor of Spain but that the Continuator was spreading Carolingian propaganda. However, the Continuator's charge that Maurontus allied with the Muslims is supported by Abbo, *Testamentum*, ch. 56. Wood, *The Merovingian Kingdoms*, 284, gets this right.

254. *Chronicon Moissacense*, 292, for the Franks, Burgundians, and surrounding *nationes* that were subject to his *ditio*. More briefly see for the year 737: *Annales S. Amandi*; *Annales Tiliani*; and *Annales Petaviani*. *Annales Laureshamenses*; *Annales Alamannici*, ed. Lendi, and *Annales Nazariani*, ed. Lendi.

255. Rouche, *L'Aquitaine*, 111–112, regarding the previous Muslim offensives.

256. Regarding the death of Duke Hucbert see Wolfram, *Die Geburt Mitteleuropas*, 97; and Jörg Jarnut, *Agilolfingerstudien. Untersuchungen zur Geschichte einer adligen Familie im 6. und 7. Jahrhundert* (Stuttgart, 1986), 118.

257. Wolfram, *Die Geburt Mitteleuropas*, 97–98.

258. Boniface *Epist.*, nos. 44, 45. Cf. Wallace-Hadrill, *The Frankish Church*, 154, who accepts that Odilo gave his permission for Boniface to work in Bavaria and Pope Gregory's claim to have ordered the effort. In short, Wallace-Hadrill does not discount the protocol of diplomatic language here. As discussed above, Boniface clearly recognized that he could accomplish nothing without Carolingian military support or the threat of its use. In addition, Boniface's mission in Bavaria took place, as will be seen below, in a context of papal efforts to gain Carolingian military support against the Lombards. The notion that Odilo or Pope Gregory, much less both of them, acted as Boniface's principals in Bavaria without first obtaining the support of Charles Martel is not credible.

259. Cf. Fredegar Cont., ch. 19 and ch. 11, but especially *Annales mettenses priores*, p. 26, where it is clear that the Saxons, who were attacked by Charles in 724, lived on the west bank of the Weser. Indeed, the *Annales Petaviani*, *an.* 718, makes clear that in 718, Charles also attacked Saxons on the west bank of the Weser.

260. *Annales regni Francorum*, *an.* 808, provides a description. For the date based upon archaeological evidence see James Graham-Campbell, *The Viking World* (New Haven and New York, 1980), 208–209.

261. Even John Haywood, *Dark Age Naval Power: A Reassessment of Frankish and Anglo-Saxon Seafaring Activity* (London, 1991), who (*passim*) grossly exaggerates putative early references to Saxon naval prowess, is unable to find any information for the period under discussion here. Indeed, no permanent naval force was likely kept by the Saxons, who nevertheless could find sufficient boats available when needed to cross the Rhine (Fredegar Cont., ch. 19). Operations to circumnavigate the Danevirke obviously required naval assets of an order of magnitude far different from that required to cross the Rhine. N.b. when Haywood discusses the Daneverke (124–125), which he recognizes was built in 737, it seems not to have occurred to him that a "naval power" would hardly have been deterred by it.

262. See for the year 737: *Annales Petaviani*; *Annales Laureshamenses*; *Annales Alamannici*, ed. Lendi; and *Annales Nazariani*, ed. Lendi. For the details: Fredegar Cont., ch. 19; and *Annales mettenses priores*, p. 28.

263. Fredegar Cont., ch. 19, as understood by Wallace-Hadrill, *Fredegar*, 93.

264. Fredegar Cont., ch. 19, "quam plures hospitibus ab eis accepit."

265. *Annales mettenses priores*, p. 30. Wallace-Hadrill, *Fredegar*, 93, finds this reading acceptable, as well.

266. Paul, *Hist.*, bk. II, 32; bk. III, ch. 16, with regard to their peculiar use in Lombard Italy. In general, see Walter Goffart, *Barbarians and Romans, A.D. 418–584: The Techniques of Accommodation* (Princeton, 1980). A great deal more work needs to be done concerning the various means by which soldiers were supported.

267. Fredegar Cont., ch. 21; *Annales mettenses priores*, p. 30; Paul, *Hist.*, bk. VI, ch. 54. For the dating of the last mentioned account see the literature cited by Noble, *The Republic of St. Peter*, 41–42, n. 131.

268. Fredegar Cont., ch. 21; *Annales mettenses priores*, p. 30, Paul, *Hist.*, bk. VI, ch. 54. See for the year 739: *Annales Petaviani*; *Annales Laureshamenses*; *Annales Alamannici*, ed. Lendi; and *Annales Nazariani*, ed. Lendi.

269. Fredegar Cont., ch. 21.

270. *Annales mettenses priores*, p. 30. The operation undertaken by Charles' son Pippin and Duke Childebrand in 740 was, as Fredegar Cont., ch. 24, makes clear, to firm up the defenses of the frontiers (*fines*) of the Burgundian region.

271. Fredegar Cont., ch. 23. Neither Frisia nor Hesse were indicated in the list of regions that formed Charles' *principatus* but these likely formed part of a much extended Austrasian *regnum*.

272. *Cod. Carol.*, nos. 1 and 2.

273. Fredegar Cont., ch. 22. *Annales mettenses priores*, pp. 30–31, for papal abandonment of the *dominatio* of the emperor (*imperator*) and for Charles providing *defensio*. See also *Chron. Moissacense*, 292, which covers the same ground. Gregory III believed that he needed Charles' military support against the Lombards. However, the pope also knew that Charles was a close ally of King Liutprand. In this context, therefore, Gregory made his highly extravagant offer to Charles Martel. Noble, *The Republic of St. Peter*, 40–48, provides a good guide to the abundant controversies on this episode.

274. Fredegar Cont., ch. 22; *Annales mettenses priores*, pp. 30–31; and *Chron. Moissacense*, 292.

275. Fredegar Cont., ch. 22; and *Cod. Carol.*, nos. 1 and 2.

276. It is generally agreed that the title of *Patricius Romanorum*, which was conferred upon Pippin and his sons by the pope in 754, signaled their responsibility to use Carolingian military forces to protect Rome. Noble, *The Republic of St. Peter*, 278–80, discusses the nuances of the literature in useful detail. See the important study by F. L. Ganshof, "Notes sur les origines byzantines du titre 'Patricius Romanorum,'" *Annuaire de l'institut de philologie et d'histoire orientales et slaves*, 10 (1950), 261–282.

277. Fredegar Cont., ch. 23, a strong supporter of Pippin's "rights," omits Gripho from his account of the *divisio*. By contrast, the Metz annalist, who commanded the details of this *divisio*, reports the tripartite nature of Charles' disposition of the *regna* that he ruled (*Annales mettenses priores*, p. 32). See also *Annales q.d. Einhardi, an.* 741, which recognizes that Gripho was one of Charles' legitimate heirs, i.e., one of his "filios heredes."

278. Fredegar Cont., ch. 23; and is followed on this point by *Annales mettenses priores*, p. 31. Cf. Rudolf Schieffer, "Karl Martell und seine Familie," in *Karl Martell in Seiner Zeit*, ed. Jörg Jarnut, Ulrich Nonn, and Michael Richter (Sigmaringen, 1994), 305–315, whose criticisms of Charles Martel's actions regarding the succession of his sons seem a bit unrealistic in light of the complexity of the political situation during the last years of the mayor's life. The role of the magnates is also to be identified when Charles' son, Pippin, divided the *regnum Francorum* between his two sons, Charlemagne and Carloman, in 768. Fredegar Cont., ch. 53; *Annales regni Francorum, an.* 768; and the possible ambiguity of the *Annales q.d. Einhardi, an.* 769.

279. *Annales mettenses priores*, p. 31, indicates that Charles "principatum suum inter filios suos aequa lance divisit."

280. *Annales mettenses priores*, p. 32.

281. Fredegar Cont., ch. 23.

282. The principles by which later divisions, primarily the *divisio* of 843, were executed have been illuminated brilliantly by F. L. Ganshof, "Zur Entstehungsgeschichte
und Bedeutung des Vertrages von Verdun (843)," *Deutsches Archiv für Erforschung des
Mittelalters*, 12 (1956), 313–330, and translated as "The Genesis and Significance of the
Treaty of Verdun (843)," by Janet Sondheimer in F. L. Ganshof, *The Carolingians and the
Frankish Monarchy: Studies in Carolingian History* (London, 1971), 289–302. Concerning
the *divisio* of 768, see A. Kroeber, "Partage du royaume des Francs entre Charlemagne
et Carlomann Ier," *Bibliothèque des Chartes*, 20 (1856), 341–350; Siguard Abel and Bern-
hard Simson, *Jährbucher des fränkischen Reiches unter Karl dem Grossen*, 2 vols., 2nd ed.
(Leipzig, 1883–1888), I, 23–40; Arthur Kleinclausz, *Charlemagne* (Paris, 1934), 4–6 and
map 1; Louis Halphen, *Charlemagne et l'empire carolingien* (Paris, 1949), 41–42; Peter
Classen, "Karl der Grosse und die Thronfolge im Frankenreich," *Festschrift für Hermann
Heimpel* (Göttingen, 1972), III, 24; and Rosamond McKitterick, *The Frankish Kingdoms
Under the Carolingians: 751–987* (London, 1983), 371, map 2.

283. Even the Bible (Num. 23:1–2; Josh. 18:4–6) makes it clear that a *descriptio*
was a necessary prerequisite for a *divisio*. Ganshof, "The Genesis and Significance of
the Treaty of Verdun," 293, 301, n.30. Charlemagne's biographer, Einhard, who served at
the Carolingian court and knew many men who had been trained and had served at the
court of King Pippin I, insists that the *divisio* of the *regnum Francorum* that was made by
the latter in 768 had as its model Charles Martel's *divisio* of 741. Einhard, *V. Karoli*, bk. I,
ch. 3. Einhard's view that Charles received in 768 the part of the *regnum Francorum* that
his father Pippin had received in the *divisio* of 741, and that Carloman received the part
in 768 that his uncle Carloman had received in 741, has led scholars to be skeptical about
the truth of the account. It is clear that the basis for the *divisio* of 768 was not exactly the
same as that of 741. However, Einhard's error on this point does not permit us to assume
that he also erred when he indicated that a formal *divisio*, which Carolingian administrators understood to require a *descriptio*, had been made between Pippin and Carloman
following the death of Charles Martel.

During the seventh and early eighth centuries, especially when Charles Martel was
Mayor of the Palace, great magnates systematically took control of vast amounts of ecclesiastical property. Scholars have not fully appreciated the record keeping intrinsic to
these efforts. For background see Bernard S. Bachrach, "Charles Martel, Mounted Shock
Combat, the Stirrup and Feudalism," *Studies in Medieval and Renaissance History*, 7
(1970), 49–75 and reprinted in *Armies and Politics in the Early Medieval West* (London,
1993), with the same pagination, here 66–72, with the literature cited there; Bernard S.
Bachrach, "Fulk Nerra's Exploitation of the *facultates monachorum*, ca. 1000," in *Law,
Custom, and The Social Fabric in Medieval Europe: Essays in Honor of Bryce Lyon*, edited
by Bernard S. Bachrach and David M. Nicholas (Kalamazoo, 1990), 29–49; and Bachrach,
"Logistics in Pre-Crusade Europe," 63, 68. A useful handlist of Carolingian *descriptiones*
is provided by R. H. C. Davis, "Domesday Book: Continental Parallels," in *Domesday
Studies: Papers read at the Novocentenary Conference of the Royal Historical Society and
the Institute of British Geographers: Winchester, 1989*, ed. J. C. Holt (Woodbridge, Suffolk,
1987), and the review by Bernard S. Bachrach in *Albion*, 20 (1988), 450–455.

With regard to specific accusations concerning the expropriation of ecclesiastical
landed assets by Charles Martel see esp. Hincmar, *Epist.* no. 7. Concerning Charles' repu-

tation see Ulrich Nonn, "Das Bild Karl Martells in mittelalterlichen Quellen," in *Karl Martell in Seiner Zeit*, ed. Jörg Jarnut, Ulrich Nonn and Michael Richter (Sigmaringen, 1994), 9–21.

284. See, for example, the various documents mentioned in three articles by Walter Goffart, "From Roman Taxation to Medieval Seigneurie: Three Notes: 1. The *Iugum* in Ostrogothic Italy; 2. The Ambulatory Hide; 3. Flodoard and the Frankish Polyptych," *Speculum*, 47 (1972), 165–187, 373–394; "Old and New Merovingian Taxation," *Past and Present*, 96 (1982), 3–21; and "Merovingian Polyptychs: Reflections on Two Recent Publications," *Francia*, 9 (1982), 55–77. These are reprinted in Walter Goffart, *Rome's Fall and After* (London, 1989), 167–211; 213–231, 233–253, respectively.

285. See, for example, Geary, *Aristocracy in Provence*, 12–31, regarding the highly unlikely circumstance in which Abbo's *testamentum* survived, and 80, n. 1, for the failure of the various *descriptiones* upon which this document is based to survive.

286. Bachrach, "Charles Martel," 66–72; and Bachrach, "Fulk Nerra's Exploitation of the *facultates monachorum*," 29–49; Davis, "Domesday Book," 35–39.

287. For the year 751: *Annales Guelferbytani*; *Annales Nazariani*; and *Annales Alamannici*, all edited by Lendi. See the discussion by Ganshof, "The Genesis and Significance of the Treaty of Verdun," 294, with the literature cited there; and also Davis, "Domesday Book," 30.

288. *Annales mettenses priores, an.* 741 (pp. 32–33).

289. See, for example, *Gesta Consulum*, 47, "Semper enim contra novum principem nova confestim bella emergunt."

290. Most recently see Wood, *The Merovingian Kingdoms*, 288. However, Noble, *The Republic of St. Peter*, 66, is not immune to exaggeration, either.

291. Wood, *The Merovingian Kingdoms*, 288, refers to "the Saxons" as though there were some sort of unified political force. He would appear to make no distinction between those living within the *regnum Francorum*, e.g., the Saxons of Hesse, and those who did not live within the Frankish kingdom.

292. Fredegar Cont., ch. 23.

293. *Annales mettenses priores*, pp. 28, 33.

294. *Annales mettenses priores, an.* 743 (p. 33). Cf. Herwig Wolfram, "Baiern und das Frankenreich," in *Die Bajuwaren*, ed. Hermann Dannheimer and Heinz Dopsch (Salzberg, 1988), 134–135.

295. Fredegar Cont., chs. 25, 26, presents the facts and *Annales mettenses priores*, p. 35, presents the information that indicates an alliance had been made. However, he includes only Odilo and Hunoald in the alliance. Cf. *Annales Guelferbytani*, ed. Lendi, *an.* 741, regarding the Alamannic count Theudebald.

296. *Annales mettenses priores*, p. 33.

297. Fredegar Cont., chs. 25; *Annales mettenses priores*, p. 33; *Annales regni Francorum, an.* 742; and *Annales q.d. Einhardi, an.* 742.

298. *Annales mettenses priores*, p. 33; *Annales regni Francorum, an.* 742; and *Annales q.d. Einhardi, an.* 742.

299. Fredegar Cont., ch. 25; *Annales mettenses priores*, p. 33; *Annales regni Francorum, an.* 742; and *Annales q.d. Einhardi, an.* 742.

300. Fredegar Cont., ch. 25. See the brief discussion by Behr, *Das alemannische Herzogtum*, 194–196.

301. Fredegar Cont., ch. 25; *Annales mettenses priores*, pp. 33–35; *Annales regni*

Francorum, an. 742; and *Annales q.d. Einhardi, an.* 742. See Wolfram, "Baiern und das Frankenreich," 135; and Behr, *Das alemannische Herzogtum,* 194–196. A papal legate named Sergius was in the Bavarian camp during this period and there has been much scholarly speculation on this matter. See, for example, the perceptive observations by Noble, *The Republic of St. Peter,* 65.

302. *Annales mettenses priores,* p. 33; *Annales regni Francorum, an.* 742; and *Annales q.d. Einhardi, an.* 742. Cf. Fredegar Cont., ch. 26, who misplaces this effort in 744.

303. *Annales mettenses priores,* p. 33; *Annales regni Francorum, an.* 742; and *Annales q.d. Einhardi, an.* 742. Cf. Fredegar Cont., ch. 26, places this effort in 744. For a general account with good background, see Rouche, *L'Aquitaine,* 116–118.

304. Fredegar Cont., ch. 26, regarding Carolingian casualties.

305. See the observations by Bachrach, *Merovingian Military Organization,* 107. Werner Affeldt, "Untersuchungen zur Königserhebung Pippins," *Frühmittelalterliche Studien,* 14 (1980), 112, 125–126, takes the more general position that the lack of a king could provide Carloman's and Pippin's enemies with a legal excuse to disobey their orders.

306. *Annales mettenses priores,* p. 33; *Annales regni Francorum, an.* 742; and *Annales q.d. Einhardi, an.* 742. Cf. Fredegar Cont., ch. 26. Cf. Behr, *Das alemannische Herzogtum,* 197–199.

307. Fredegar Cont., ch. 29; *Annales mettenses priores,* p. 37. *Annalium Petavianorum cont. an.* 746, suggest that Carloman felt remorse for having killed many thousands of men (*multa hominum milia*). Cf. Behr, *Das alemannische Herzogtum,* 193–194.

308. See the discussion by Hans Jänichen, "Warin, Rudhard und Scrot," *Zeitschrift für Würtemburgische Landesgeschichte,* 14 (1955), 372–384.

309. Fredegar Cont., ch. 28, had reported neither Hunoald's very successful raid into the region of Chartres nor the Aquitanian duke's alliance with Odilo of Bavaria. The Continuator may have been less well informed regarding this situation than the Metz annalist. It is more probable that the Continuator chose not to dwell in detail on Hunoald's capitulation in 745 because the Continuator's readers would want to know what had happened between the successful invasion of Aquitaine in 742 by Pippin and Carloman and their invasion in 745. When discussing matters in 745, the Continuator thoroughly dissimulates by referring to the Carolingians' adversaries as "Gascons." See, therefore, the more complete account in *Annales mettenses priores,* p. 36. Rouche, *L'Aquitaine,* 117–119, covers this well.

310. *Annales mettenses priores,* p. 36, with the discussion by Rouche, *L'Aquitaine,* 119.

311. See, for example, Fredegar Cont., ch. 30; *Annales regni Francorum, an.* [*sic*] 746; *Annales q.d. Einhardi, an.* [*sic*] 746; and *Annales mettenses priores,* pp. 37–38. See for 747: *Annales Laureshamenses; Annales Alamannici, Annales Guelferbytani,* ed. Lendi; *Annales Nazariani; Annales S. Amandi cont.; Annales Laubacensium cont.; Annalium Petavianorum cont.* N.b. the Metz annalist uses the phrase "Dei omnipotentis se servitio mancipare" when describing Carloman's subjection of himself to the service of God. This should be seen in the context of the papal self-identification as "servus servorum Dei." However, the discussion above of Hunoald's subjection of himself to the service of Pippin and Carloman with similar language is a very different matter.

Many scholars have tried without success to see Carloman as having been driven from office by Pippin. See, for example, Dieter Riesenberger, "Zur Geschichte des Hausmeiers Karlmann," *Westfalische Zeitschrift,* 120 (1970), 271–286, with a review of the earlier literature. It is quite probable that Carloman was motivated by religious enthusi-asm as argued by Karl Heinrich Krüger, "Königskonversionen im 8. Jahrhundert," *Früh-mittelalterliche Studien*, 7 (1973), 169–222.

312. *Annales mettenses priores*, pp. 39–40. The information provided by *Annales regni Francorum, an.* [*sic*] 746; and especially by *Annales q.d. Einhardi, an.* [*sic*] 746, per-mit the inference that Gripho was freed by his brother Pippin.

313. *Annales mettenses priores*, p. 40.

314. All of the sources date the establishment of Gripho in the West with his head-quarters at Le Mans as following his capture after his failed uprising in Bavaria in 749. *Annales regni Francorum, an.* 748; *Annales q.d. Einhardi, an.* 748; and *Annales mettenses priores*, pp. 41–42. This chronology, however, is highly unlikely, as Pippin would have been rewarding Gripho for causing great trouble in both Eastphalia and Bavaria. In addi-tion, Gripho, after getting free following the disaster in Bavaria, fled to Aquitaine and sought refuge there with Duke Waiofar. Cf. Wood, *The Merovingian Kingdoms*, 289, who has Hunoald rather than Waiofar acting as Aquitanian duke at this time. Fredegar Cont., ch. 35, followed by *Annales mettenses priores, an.* 750 (p. 42), clearly indicates that the duke in question was Waiofar.

315. The key study regarding this march is J.-P. Brunterc'h, "Le duché du Maine et la marche de Bretagne," in *La Neustrie: Les Pays au Nord de la Loire, 650 à 850*, 2 vols., ed. Hartmut Atsma (Sigmaringen, 1989), I, 29–127. A useful summary is provided by Smith, *Province and Empire*, 44–47. *Annales regni Francorum, an.* 748; and *Annales q.d. Einhardi, an.* 748, both call this territory a *ducatus*.

316. *Form. Andecav.*, no. 37, provides a basis for understanding how levies were to be mobilized from the region. See, Smith, *Province and Empire*, 45, n. 53.

317. *Annales regni Francorum, an.* 747; *Annales q.d. Einhardi, an.* 747; and *Annales mettenses priores*, pp. 40–41.

318. *Annales regni Francorum, ann.* 743, 744; *Annales q.d. Einhardi, ann.* 743, 744; *Annalium Petavianorum cont., an.* 744; and *Annales mettenses priores*, pp. 33–34.

319. *Annales regni Francorum, an.* 747; *Annales q.d. Einhardi, an.* 747; and *Annales mettenses priores*, pp. 40–41.

320. Fredegar Cont., ch. 31; *Annales regni Francorum, an.* 747; *Annales q.d. Ein-hardi, an.* 747; and *Annales mettenses priores*, pp. 40–41.

321. Fredegar Cont., ch. 31.

322. N.b. Fredegar Cont., ch. 31, speaks of the Wends having *reges*—more than one king.

323. Fredegar Cont., ch. 31.

324. *Annales mettenses priores*, p. 41, for the loss of Seeburg; and Fredegar Cont., ch. 31, concerning the general surrender.

325. *Annales regni Francorum, an.* 748; *Annales q.d. Einhardi, an.* 748; and *Annales mettenses priores*, p. 41.

326. Fredegar Cont., ch. 31; Gregory, *Hist.*, bk. IV, ch. 14; and Fredegar, *Chron.*, bk. IV, ch. 74.

327. *Annales regni Francorum, an.* 748; *Annales q.d. Einhardi, an.* 748; and *Annales mettenses priores*, p. 42. See the discussion by Wolfram, *Die Geburt Mitteleuropas*, 100.

328. Fredegar Cont., ch. 25, regarding Childrudis' marriage and the role of Sun-nichildis. N.b. the Continuator employs the ancient cliche "with the advice of her wicked stepmother (*consilio nefario nouerce*)."

329. A useful recounting of Gripho's position is made by Walter Mohr, *Studien zur*

Charakteristik des karolingische Königtums im 8. Jahrhundert (Saarlouis, 1955), 13–47. We need not, however, accept his notion that Charles Martel had intended to make Gripho his sole heir in order to appreciate the young man's potential importance.

330. For Franks settled in Western Bavaria under Charles Martel see Freidrich Prinz, "Herzog und Adel im agilulfingischen Bayern. Herzogsgut und Konsensschenkungen vor 788," *Zeitschrift für bayerische Landesgeschichte*, 25 (1962), 283–311.

331. *Annales regni Francorum, an.* 748; and *Annales q.d. Einhardi, an.* 748, maintain that Gripho "subjugated the *ducatus* to himself and held both his sister and her son as prisoners." *Annales mettenses priores*, pp. 41–42, tells the same story. N.b. Fredegar Cont., ch. 32, does not mention either Odilo's death or Gripho's efforts. See the discussion by Herwig Wolfram, "Tassilo III. und Karl der Grosse—Das Ende der Agilolfinger," in *Die Bajuwaren*, ed. Hermann Dannheimer and Heinz Dopsch (Salzburg, 1988), 160.

332. *Annales regni Francorum, an.* 748; and *Annales q.d. Einhardi, an.* 748; and *Annales mettenses priores*, pp. 41–42. Cf. Behr, *Das alemannische Herzogtum*, 198–199.

333. *Annales regni Francorum, an.* 748; and *Annales q.d. Einhardi, an.* 748. Wolfram, *Die Geburt Mitteleuropas*, 100.

334. Curiously, Fredegar Cont., ch. 32, writes about the Bavarians accepting the advice (*consilium*) that had been given by evil people (*nefandi*) but does not mention Gripho.

335. *Annales regni Francorum, an.* 748; and *Annales q.d. Einhardi, an.* 748; and *Annales mettenses priores*, pp. 41–42. See, above, where it is noted that these sources place Pippin's award of the twelve counties to Gripho in the wrong chronological framework.

336. Fredegar Cont., ch. 32.

337. Fredegar Cont., ch. 32. The military aspects of this campaign are discussed below.

338. *Annales regni Francorum, an.* 748; and *Annales q.d. Einhardi, an.* 748; and *Annales mettenses priores*, pp. 41–42. It is well beyond the reach of this study to engage in the enduring controversy regarding Tassilo's juridical position vis-à-vis the Carolingians. Much of the early literature is dealt with by Hermann Krawinkel, *Untersuchungen zum fränkischen Benefizialrecht* (Weimar, 1937), 48–65, and Krawinkel's own views are critically evaluated by Charles E. Odegaard, *Vassi and Fideles in the Carolingian Empire* (Cambridge, Mass., 1945), 90–96. The vast body of literature on the use of *beneficium* here to describe the nature of Pippin's act is surveyed in great detail by Charles E. Odegaard, "Carolingian Oaths of Fidelity," *Speculum*, 14 (1941), 284–296.

339. *Cod. Carol.*, no. 3 (p. 480), indicates the pope's *desideratum* that there be a close working relationship between Rome and *Francia*.

340. For the negotiations themselves see Fredegar Cont., ch. 33.

341. These matters have received a vast amount of attention to which Noble, *The Republic of St. Peter*, 65–70, is a useful guide.

342. These are briefly summarized by Fredegar Cont., ch. 33.

343. He may also have made an effort to reassimilate eastern Brittany into the *regnum Francorum* in 753. This is problematic, but if the campaign was undertaken, it was offensive, as well. The only source for this is *Annales mettenses priores*, p. 44. For a full and convincing treatment of this episode see Julia M. H. Smith, "The Sack of Vannes by Peppin III," *Cambridge Medieval Celtic Studies*, 11 (1986), 17–27.

344. In 753, operations were undertaken in the region between the Weser and the Rhine north of the Teutoburger forest. The Saxons apparently had attacked the strong-

hold of Iburg near Osnabrück and Bishop Hildegar, who likely led the Cologne levies to protect the region, was killed there. Pippin then apparently engaged the Saxons somewhere in the valley of the Else before it reached its confluence with the Weser in the area of Rehme and won a decisive victory (*Annales regni Francorum, an.* 753; *Annales q.d. Einhardi, an.* 753; Fredegar Cont., ch. 35). The campaign of 758 also was carried out within the *regnum Francorum*. Indeed, the focus of fighting was the stronghold at Sythen on the Lippe only fifty kilometers east of the Rhine. The Saxons apparently were using this fortification as a base from which to raid the surrounding area. *Annales regni Francorum, an.* 758; and *Annales regni Francorum, an.* 758.

345. *V. Stephani II*, ch. 8. Cf. Noble, *The Republic of St. Peter*, 72–73, who argues that the pope did not ask Pippin for help in 752 because no alliance existed between them. If they had no alliance in 752 this was also true in 753 when the pope did ask Pippin for help. With Frankish envoys easily available to the pope in Rome in 752, it is more than likely that Stephen was aware of Pippin's negative attitude toward military involvement in Italy.

346. Fredegar Cont., ch. 37.

347. *V. Stephani II*, chs. 31, 32, where the idea for a diplomatic settlement is credited to the pope. Indeed, Pippin may well have taken Stephen's advice on this matter when the campaign was already well under way because he trusted the pope's judgment and did not want to fight.

348. *Annales mettenses priores*, p. 47. I cannot follow Noble, *The Republic of St. Peter*, 75–77, who argues that "Pepin . . . did want to intervene in Italy."

349. This is a controversial topic. See the discussion by Noble, *The Republic of St. Peter*, 70–71, with the literature cited there.

350. Fredegar Cont., chs. 35, 36, 37, 38; *Annales regni Francorum, ann.* 755, 756; and *Annales q.d. Einhardi, ann.* 755, 756.

351. Einhard, *V. Karoli*, ch. 6.

352. Einhard, *V. Karoli*, ch. 6. Indeed, it is a sign of Pippin's great authority that he prevailed in the face of serious opposition to the invasion among some exceptionally important men. Cf. the discussion by Holzmann, "Die Italienpolitik der Merowinger," 5–7, 39–42, who stresses traditional links of friendship with the Lombards. These links, however, were hardly as strong or consistent as Holzmann would have his readers believe.

353. Fouracre, "Pippinid Influence," 12, and 20–21, n. 12, for a useful review of the literature, which shows that these pre-World War II views carried over into the early 1980s. Gerberding, *The Rise of the Carolingians*, 93, n. 8, expands the list.

354. Three rather recent works in English: Fouracre, "Pippinid Influence," 1–31; Gerberding, *The Rise of the Carolingians*, 92–145; and Costambeys, "An Aristocratic Community," 39–61, provide a helpful introduction to the bibliography on this topic, which is mostly in German and dedicated to local history.

Chapter 2. Military Organization

1. In general, the scholarly focus has been on the military exploits of Charlemagne and his successors while rather little attention has been given to the early Carolingians. A useful selection of the older literature is cited in Bachrach, "Military Organization in Aquitaine," 1–2, notes 1–5; and Bernard S. Bachrach, "Charlemagne's Cavalry: Myth and Reality," *Military Affairs*, 47 (1983), 181–187 and also reprinted in *Armies and*

Politics, 11–12, notes 1–2. Among the more important recent works are Reuter, "Plunder and Tribute," 81–100; Timothy Reuter, "The End of Carolingian Military Expansion," in *Charlemagne's Heir: New Perspectives on the Reign of Louis the Pious (814–840)*, ed. Peter Godman and Roger Collins (Oxford, 1990), 391–405; Leyser, "Early Medieval Warfare," 29–50; and Philippe Contamine, *La Guerre au Moyen Age*, 4th ed. (Paris, 1994), 98, 100, 102–104, 128, 145, 318–319.

2. The long-term view of this pattern is sketched in Bernard S. Bachrach, "On Roman Ramparts," in *Cambridge Illustrated History of Warfare*, ed. Geoffrey Parker (Cambridge, 1995), 64–91; and in considerably more detail in Bernard S. Bachrach, "Early Medieval Europe," *Warfare and Society in the Ancient and Medieval Worlds: Asia, the Mediterranean, Europe, and Mesoamerica*, ed. Kurt Rauflaub and Nathan Rosenstein (Cambridge, Mass., 1999), 271–307.

3. Regarding the monumental physical infrastructure see, for example, R. M. Butler, "Late Roman Town Walls in Gaul," *Archaeological Journal*, 116 (1959), 25–50; H. von Petrikovits, "Fortifications in the North-Western Roman Empire from the Third to the Fifth Centuries A.D.," *Journal of Roman Studies*, 61 (1971), 178–218; Stephen Johnson, *Late Roman Fortifications* (Totowa, N.J., 1983); Albert Grenier, *Manuel d'archéologie gallo-romaine* (Paris, 1934), vol. 6:1; Dietrich Claude, *Topographie und Verfassung der Städte Bourges und Poitiers bis in das 11. Jahrhundert* (*Historische Studien*, 380, Lübeck-Hamburg, 1960); Carl-Richard Brühl, *Palatium und Civitas*, I, *Gallien* (Cologne, 1975); and Adrien Blanchet, *Les enceintes romaines de la Gaule* (Paris, 1907).

There, of course, remains the vestige of a school of thought that saw the late antique *urbes* as "empty shells." However, even the bizarre arguments by Guy Halsall, *Settlement and Social Organization: The Merovingian Region of Metz* (Cambridge, 1995), a recent devotee of this nonsense, who asserts that Metz became a ghost town during the fifth century, do not go so far as to suggest that the walls disappeared, as well. The building of a massive cathedral within the walls of Metz during the first half of the fifth century, however much Halsall would wish it not to be there, is prima facie evidence for a substantial and wealthy interest concerning what was going on within the walls.

4. Jim Bradbury, *The Medieval Siege* (Woodbridge, 1992); Bernard S. Bachrach, "Grand Strategy in the Germanic Kingdoms: Recruitment of the Rank and File," in *La noblesse romaine et les chefs barbares du IIIe au VIIe siècle*, ed. Françoise Vallet and Michel Kazanski (Paris, 1995), 55–63; and Bachrach, "Medieval Siege Warfare," 119–133.

5. For example, Bachrach, *Anatomy of a Little War: A Diplomatic and Military History of the Gundovald Affair: 568–586* (Boulder, 1994), who provides considerable information regarding the later sixth century; and T. S. Brown, *Gentlemen and Officers: Imperial Administration and Aristocratic Power in Byzantine Italy A.D. 554–800* (Rome, 1984).

6. See, for example, *De re Militari*, bk. I, *praef.*, ch. 8; bk. III, *praef.*

7. L. D. Reynolds, "Frontinus," in *Texts and Transmission: A Survey of the Latin Classics*, ed. L. D. Reynolds and P. K. Marshall (Oxford, 1983), 167–172. See the discussion by J. Brian Campbell, *The Emperor and the Roman Army, 31 B.C.-A.D. 235* (Oxford, 1984), 326–327, and regarding the early Middle Ages see Bachrach, "Some Observations Concerning the Education of the 'Officer Corps' in the Fifth and Sixth Centuries," in *La noblesse romaine et les chefs barbares du IIIe au VIII siècle*, ed. Françoise Vallet and Michel Kazanski (Paris, 1995), 7–13.

8. Jean Durliat, *Les finances publiques de Dioclétien aux Carolingiens (284–889)* (Sigmaringen, 1990), with regard to a useful though perhaps somewhat rigid model for

continuity in fiscal organization, in general, and particularly concerning the fiscal organization of the military. See Bernard S. Bachrach, "Military Lands in Historical Perspective," *Haskins Society Journal*, 9 (2001), forthcoming. A useful view of a particular process of development is outlined by Herwig Wolfram, "Karl Martell und das fränkische Lehenswesen. Aufnahme eines Nichtbestandes,"in *Karl Martell in Seiner Zeit*, ed. Jörg Jarnut, Ulrich Nonn, and Michael Richter (Sigmaringen, 1994), 61–78.

9. Bachrach, "Grand Strategy," 55–63; and cf. Hugh Elton, *Warfare in Roman Europe, A.D. 350–425* (Oxford, 1996), 102–103.

10. See, for example, Campbell, *The Emperor and the Roman Army*, 11–13, 307–310, with the literature that he cites.

11. Bachrach, "Grand Strategy," 55–63; and Luttwak, *Grand Strategy*, 132–133.

12. *Nov. Val.* 9.1; and Adolf Berger, *Encyclopedic Dictionary of Roman Law* (Philadelphia, 1953), 600–607, 641, 768.

13. Bachrach, "Grand Strategy," 58–59.

14. Regarding local defense forces in the Merovingian period see Bachrach, *Merovingian Military Organization*, 66; Margarete Weidemann, *Kulturgeschichte der Merowingerzeit nach den Werken Gregors von Tours*, 2 vols. (Mainz, 1982), 2, 240–242; and Reuter, "Plunder and Tribute," 90.

15. It would be odd, indeed, if this were not the case in light of what we know about Carolingian social structure. For the service of dependents and the unfree, see Bachrach, "Grand Strategy," 57, in the Merovingian era; and for the Carolingians see Reuter, "Plunder and Tribute," 90.

16. Helen Maud Cam, *Local Government in "Francia" and England* (London, 1912), 37; and F. L. Ganshof, "Charlemagne's Army," in *Frankish Institutions Under Charlemagne*, trans. B. and M. Lyon (Providence, R.I., 1968), 59–61.

17. Concerning Basques and Visigoths, see below, and regarding Jews see Bernard S. Bachrach, *Early Medieval Jewish Policy in Western Europe* (Minneapolis, 1977); and Karl Ferdinand Werner, "*Hludovicus Augustus*: Gouverner l'empire chrétien—Idées et réalités," in *Charlemagne's Heir: New Perspectives on the Reign of Louis the Pious (814–840)*, ed. Peter Godman and Roger Collins (Oxford, 1990), 78.

18. This would seem to be the thrust of Reuter, "The End of Carolingian Military Expansion," 391–401, but I am not sure I understand fully the organizational structures he would appear to have identified. For a clearer discussion of the continued participation of the poor and even of the unfree in the local defense, see Cam, *Local Government*, 130–131.

19. Bachrach, "On Roman Ramparts," 64–91, provides a general treatment of this subject, which nevertheless is in need of considerable further research.

20. For good examples from Gregory's *Histories* see the discussion in Bachrach, *Anatomy of a Little War*; and compare Flodoard, *Annales, ann.* 919–967, passim.

21. There is general agreement on this point as narrowly defined here. See, for example, Bachrach, *Merovingian Military Organization*, 69; Weidemann, *Kulturgeschichte der Merowingerzeit*, I, 250; and Reuter, "The End of Carolingian Military Expansion," 395–396. However, as the scholars noted above indicate, there is comparatively little agreement on the basis for such service and the mechanisms used by the government to decide who would serve and who would be exempt from such expeditionary service.

22. C. Warren Hollister, *Anglo-Saxon Military Institutions on the Eve of the Norman Conquest* (Oxford, 1962), 38–102.

23. See Ganshof, "Charlemagne's Army," 60, who reviews the capitulary and

other evidence briefly. Reuter, "The End of Carolingian Military Expansion," 395, would appear to accept the assumption that Carolingian armies "depended to a significant extent on the kind of military service referred to in these capitularies, namely a *Volksauf-gebot* of free men." However, Reuter believes that this situation lasted until shortly after 800 A.D., at which time, he argues, the composition of the army was changed substantially. These putative changes he sees as being caused by a fundamental shift in Carolingian military strategy during the ninth century from offensive warfare to defensive warfare. I hope to discuss Reuter's suggestions concerning what has been characterized as Carolingian "grand strategy" during the latter part of Charlemagne's reign in a subsequent study.

24. Ganshof, "Charlemagne's Army," 66–67; and Bachrach, "Logistics in Pre-Crusade Europe," 70. Cf. Eckhard Müller-Mertens, *Karl der Grosse, Ludwig der Fromme und die Freien* (Berlin, 1963), 129–130, and 140–141, who argues that this constant campaigning over a lengthy period of time at high costs economically to these relatively poor levies exhausted their resources in the long term. Reuter, "The End of Carolingian Military Expansion," 395–396, rejects Müller-Mertens' model in a highly nuanced and complicated argument that takes us well beyond the chronological scope of the present study.

25. There is a long-standing argument regarding the criteria that were used by the Carolingian government for the mobilization of men for *expeditio*, i.e., offensive warfare beyond the confines of the local administrative region in which the fighting man lived. The early Carolingian sources do not speak directly to this matter. However, by early in the ninth century Charlemagne issued *capitula* that make clear that a specific quantity of wealth, landed and/or movable, was the prerequisite for military service. See, for example, *Cap. reg.* no. 48, ch. 2; no. 49, ch. 2; and 50, ch. 1. In addition, see no. 165, ch. 6, where brothers left their inheritances undivided so that only one was required to serve while the others who were impecunious avoided service. These texts provide no reason to believe, however, that the use of wealth as a criterion for military service was an innovation introduced by Charlemagne following his acquisition of the imperial title. Rather it would seem that Charlemagne and his successors merely were fine tuning existing wealth-based obligations.

Nevertheless, Reuter, "The End of Carolingian Military Expansion," 398, is surely correct when he observes: "It will not do simply to take the capitulary provisions of the period 800–830 and project them indefinitely into the Frankish past." The same may be said for provisions enacted only during the period 800–814, i.e., the latter part of Charlemagne's reign. Particular requirements in the provisions cited above certainly were prescriptive and constituted orders for the alteration of the status quo ante. Nevertheless, the institutional base that Charlemagne was attempting to alter had provided for the previous two generations of Carolingian military success. Two generations should hardly be thought of as stretching the interpretation of continuity prior to ca. 800 "indefinitely into the Frankish past."

The *Königsfreien* hypothesis deployed by some scholars, especially in the immediate post-World War II era, to explain these select levies is no longer competitive. See, for example, the fine survey by Franz Staab, "A Reconsideration of the Ancestry of Modern Political Liberty: The Problem of the So-Called 'King's Freemen' (*Königsfreie*)," *Viator*, 11 (1980), 51–69; and Reuter, "The End of Carolingian Military Expansion," 395.

26. Concerning the size of the manse "on average," see F.L. Ganshof, *Feudalism*, trans. Philip Grierson (3rd Eng. ed., New York, 1964), 37. There is immense controversy

concerning the designation *mansus* and its purposes, for example (but not limited to) the use of the term as an agricultural unit or as a unit of assessment. Regarding these matters, which are well beyond the scope of this military history, see David Herlihy, "The Carolingian Mansus," *Economic History Review*, 13 (1960), 79–89; and more recently Adriaan Verhulst, "Economic Organisation," in *The New Cambridge Medieval History*, ed. Rosamond McKitterick (Cambridge, 1995), II, 488–499, with the bibliography cited 975–976.

27. The manse was the material or economic base that undergirded the military "reforms" being made by Charlemagne. In the above-mentioned capitularies, the *mansus* or fragments of a *mansus* or multiples of *mansi* or their monetary equivalents in terms of income are used for all calculations in the determination of military service. In addition, the minimum requirement was being raised to three manses by Charlemagne from a previous floor, probably one manse (*Cap. reg. Fr.* no. 48, ch. 2). In these reforms Charlemagne established, as well, that a man who goes off to war required a minimum of six *solidi* in income (*Cap. reg. Fr.* no. 48, ch. 2) in order to sustain himself and his family while he did his military duty. It is possible that the wealth requirement prior to Charlemagne's reforms was less than three manses but more than one manse. It would be difficult to postulate a base below one manse simply on economic grounds. Thus, for example, on a comparative basis the one-manse hypothesis is not inconsistent, allowing for inflation, with the average 1.5-hide allotment to a *miles*, i.e., a well-armed foot soldier, in Domesday book. For a detailed discussion of these matters see Bachrach, "Military Lands," forthcoming.

28. Cam, *Local Government*, 128; and Ganshof, "Charlemagne's Army," 67, survey the relevant texts.

29. See, for example, *Cap. reg. Fr.*, no. 74, ch. 8; and for additional evidence with discussion see Bachrach, "Quelques observations sur la composition et les caractéristiques des armées de Clovis," 1:698–699.

30. Thomas Anderson, Jr., "Roman Military Colonies in Gaul: Salian Ethnogenesis and the Forgotten Meaning of *Pactus Legis Salicae* 59.5," *Early Medieval Europe* 4 (1995), 129–144, has recently reexamined the vast literature on the ethnogenesis of the Salian Franks in an very effective manner. For other recent examinations, but very different in nature, see David Harry Miller, "Ethnogenesis and Religious Revitalization Beyond the Roman Frontier: The Case of Frankish Origins," *Journal of World History*, 4 (1993), 277–285; and Jean-Pierre Poly, "La Corde au cou: Les Franks, la France, et la Loi Salique," in *Genèse de l'état moderne en Méditerranée. Paris, 287–320* (Paris, 1993), 287–320.

The relation of the so-called *Reihengräberzivilisation* and the Franks as an ethnic group is very controversial. For a Germanic approach, see Joachim Werner, "Zur Entstehung der *Reihengräberzivilisation*: Ein Beitrag zur Methode und frügeschichtliche Archäologie," *Archaeolgoia Geographia*, 1 (1950), 139–167; Heiko Steuer, *Frühgeschichtliche Sozialstrukturen im Mittleuropa. Eine Analyse der Auswertungsmethod des archäologischen Quellen* (Göttingen, 1982); and Heiko Steuer, "Archaeology and History: Proposals on the Social Structure of the Merovingian Kingdom," in *The Birth of Europe: Archaeology and Social Development in the First Millennium A.D.*, ed. Klaves Ransbourg (Rome, 1989), 100–122. Cf. Edward James, "Cemeteries and the Problem of Frankish Settlement in Gaul," in *Names, Words and Graves*, ed. Peter H. Sawyer (Leeds, 1979), 55–89; and Guy Halsall, "The Origins of the *Reihengräberzivilisation*: Forty Years On," in *Fifth-Century Gaul: A Crisis of Identity?* ed. J. Drinkwater and H. Elton (Cambridge, 1992), 196–207.

The last mentioned study must be used with great care as the author has very idio-syncratic views regarding the nature of evidence. For my views in detail, see Bachrach, "Quelques observations sur la composition et les caractéristiques des armées de Clovis," I, 695–698.

31. See the detailed discussion, below, in Chapter 3.

32. The background to the matter of taking booty and its distribution is dealt with by Bachrach, "Quelques observations sur la composition et les caractéristiques des ar-mées de Clovis," I, 700–701, with the literature cited in n. 55. Cf. Weidemann, *Kultur-geschichte der Merowingerzeit*, II, 279–281. Although there are numerous illustrations of lightly armed fighting men by Carolingian artists, information from the written sources is slight and likely due to the fact that what is very well known to contemporaries gen-erally requires little discussion. See Ganshof, "Charlemagne's Army," 65. N.b. *Cap. reg. Fr.*, I, 32, ch. 64, which indicates that one of the guards for each supply wagon that is sent off on campaign is to be equipped with a shield and a spear. The observations of Hans Delbrück, *History of the Art of War Within the Framework of Political History*, trans. Walter J. Renfroe, Jr. (Westport, Conn., 1982), III, 29, on this armament are important. See also Simon Coupland, "Carolingian Arms and Armor in the Ninth Century," *Via-tor*, 21 (1990), 35–38, 46–48, whose work, by and large, includes the eighth century in his discussions, as well.

33. *Cap. reg. Fr.*, I, no. 44, ch. 6. See Cam, *Local Government*, 138; and Ganshof, *Feudalism*, 37.

34. Concerning the *brunia*, see *Lex Rib.* ch. XL, ch. 11 (XXXVI, ch. 11); and *Cap. reg. Fr.*, I, no. 44, ch. 6. Cf. Ganshof, "Charlemagne's Army," 158, n. 48, who wonders whether the *lorica* mentioned in no. 77, ch. 9, is a synonym for a *brunia* or perhaps some other sort of body armor. The *lorica* is also mentioned in no. 44, ch. 5; and *V. Landiberti*, ch. 13. For *arma* see *Cap. reg. Fr.*, I, no. 25, ch. 4; and *Carmen de Conversione*, line 40, for shining armor. In general, see Martin Last, "Die Bewaffnung der Karolingerzeit," *Nach-richten aus Niedersachens*, 41 (1972), 77–93. Cf. F. L. Ganshof, "A propos de la cavalerie dans les armées de Charlemagne," *Académie des Inscriptions et Belles-Lettres: Comptes rendus des séances* (1952), 533, who takes note of Charlemagne's efforts to keep mail coats from being exported beyond the frontiers and would seem to assume that this is evidence for the widespread use of body armor. See, in general, Coupland, "Carolingian Arms and Armor," 38–40.

35. References to helmets are found in *Cap. reg. Fr.*, I, no. 77, ch. 9; *V. Landiberti*, ch. 13; *Carmen de Conversione*, line 41, for a pointed *galea* and *Lex Rib.* ch. XL, ch. 11 (XXXVI, ch. 11), respectively. See Ganshof, "A propos de la cavalerie dans les armées de Charlemagne," 533–534; Last, "Die Bewaffnung der Karolingerzeit," 77–93; and Coup-land, "Carolingian Arms and Armor," 32–35.

36. For *clipeus*, see *V. Landiberti*, ch. 13; and *Lex Rib.* ch. XL, ch. 11 (XXXVI, ch. 11); and *Cap. reg. Fr.*, I, no. 25, ch. 4, for the *scutum*. Cf. the discussion by Ganshof, "A pro-pos de la cavalerie dans les armées de Charlemagne," 534; and Coupland, "Carolingian Arms and Armor," 35–38.

37. *Carmen de Conversione*, line 44, where *umbo* is used by synecdoche for the entire shield.

38. Concerning the leg protections, see *Cap. reg. Fr.*, I, no. 40, ch. 7; *Lex Rib.* ch. XL, ch. 11 (XXXVI, ch. 11). See Notker, *Gesta Karoli*, bk. II, ch. 17, regarding the Latin usage. Cf. Ganshof, "Charlemagne's Army," 65–66, concerning leg protections; but he

does not discuss the Latin term. See also Coupland, "Carolingian Arms and Armor," 41–42.

39. Regarding spears of various types, see *Cap. reg. Fr.*, I, no. 25, ch. 4; *Lex Rib.* ch. XL, ch. 11 (XXXVI, ch. 11); and *V. Landiberti*, ch. 13. See the discussion by Coupland, "Carolingian Arms and Armor," 46–48. These likely should not be confused with throwing spears, e.g., *telae*, as in *Carmen de Conversione*, line 44; and *spicula*, line 45. As will be seen below in Chapter 3, some important distinctions must be made among spears that were used for throwing purposes, i.e., javelins in modern American usage, pole weapons used for thrusting purposes by foot soldiers, and pole weapons used by mounted troops.

40. *V. Landiberti*, ch. 13; *Cap. reg. Fr.*, I, no. 25, ch. 4; *Carmen de Conversione*, line 46, and *Lex Rib.*, ch. XL, 11 (XXXVI, ch. 11), where mention is also made of a sheath (*scoigilum*). Coupland, "Carolingian Arms and Armor," 42–46.

41. See *Cap. reg. Fr.*, I, no. 25, ch. 4, for the short sword. See the discussion in Chapter 3.

42. Holger Riesch, " 'Quod nullus in hostem habeat baculum sed arcum' Pfeil und Bogen als Beispiel für technologische Innovationen der Karolingerzeit," *Technikgeschichte*, 61 (1994), 209–226, makes clear that the bow and arrow was a consistent element in the arsenal of the Franks, as it was of a segment of those fighting men whom they already found in Gaul when they settled there. For the heterogeneous background of the fighting men integrated into the armies of Clovis and his successors, see Bachrach, *Merovingian Military Organization*, 3–17. For the use of the bow and arrow in Gregory of Tours' writings, see Weidemann, *Kulturgeschichte der Merowingerzeit*, II, 267. An important source in the context of the early Carolingian era is *V. Lamberti*, ch. 13, in which Dodo, the *domesticus* of Pippin II, supported a large military household in which his *pueri*, when fully armed, carried a bow and a quiver of arrows.

43. Maurice, *Strategikon*, bk. I, ch. 2. This text is discussed in considerable detail in Chapter 3.

44. Ganshof, "Charlemagne's Army," 65, suggests that this increased interest in the development of archery began with Charlemagne and occurred as a result of his campaigns against the Avars, who were known to have considerable expertise in this area. Ganshof also entertains the possibility that Charlemagne was stimulated to develop a greater role for his archers because of his hostile contacts with the Slavs. See Bernard S. Bachrach, "A Picture of Avar-Frankish Warfare." Karl Rübel, "Frankisches und spätrömisches Kriegswesen," *Bonner Jahrbücher*, 114 (1906), 138, suggests that Frankish arrowheads of the Carolingian era only are to be found in the context of fortifications from later in Charlemagne's reign and takes special note of the situation in Westphalia. However, Rübel seems to be relying on the capitulary evidence for his dating of the arrowheads in what becomes a rather circular argument. In any event, arrowheads are also found in Merovingian graves. See Joachim Werner, "Bewaffnung und WaffenBeigabe in der Merowingerzeit," *Settimane di Studio del Centro Italiano di Studi sull'alto Medioevo*, 15.2 (Spoleto, 1968), 105. Cf. Riesch, " 'Quod nullus,' " 209–226, who nevertheless collects a substantial body of information, as does Coupland, "Carolingian Arms and Armor," 48–50.

45. See, for example, *Cap. reg. Fr.*, I, no. 77, ch. 9, which has "lance, shield, and bow with two cords and twelve arrows"; no. 32, ch. 64, indicates that one guard on each supply wagon on campaign was to be equipped with a quiver [with arrows] and a bow.

See Delbrück, *Art of War*, III, 29, regarding this text. The illustrations of archers by Caro-lingian artists do not necessarily include the shield and spear as part of their equipment.

46. Maurice, *Strategikon*, bk. I, ch. 2.

47. While important people in the Western tradition are often lauded for their accomplishments with the bow and arrow, especially with regard to the hunt, there is a definite prejudice in the matter of nobles using the bow in combat. See, for example, the useful introductory study by A. T. Hatto, "Archery and Chivalry: A Noble Prejudice," *Modern Language Review*, 35 (1940), 40–55. This topic would repay detailed study.

48. *Cap. reg. Fr.*, I, no. 77, ch. 17: "Quod nullus in hoste baculum habeat sed ar-cum." The officials who encountered such an excuse, as postulated above, used the term *baculum* in their reports to the king. Thus, he in turn used it, as well, in order to make clear that the piece of wood in question (a *baculum*) was not to be considered a legiti-mate bow stave. The effort by H. von Mangoldt-Gaudlitz, *Die Reiterei in den german-sichen und frankischen Herren bis zum Ausgang der deuschen Karolinger* (Berlin, 1922), 61, to emend the reading of *baculum* to *jaculum* is plausible in orthographic terms but fails to take into account the lack of this usage, i.e., *jaculum*, in the military capitularies and the obvious fact that no one could attempt to pass off a javelin with a fixed metal point as a bow stave. Cf. Riesch, " 'Quod nullus,' " 209–226; and Coupland, "Carolingian Arms and Armor," 48.

49. F. L. Ganshof, "Benefice and Vassalage in the Age of Charlemagne," *Cam-bridge Historical Journal*, 6 (1939), 160, notes that a holding of four manses likely required some sort of more elaborate equipment than the holder of a single manse. *Cap. reg. Fr.*, I, no. 77, ch. 9; and no. 75, may be referring to men who hold fewer than twelve manses but who have various types of armament in excess of a spear and shield.

50. *Gesta Abbatum Font.*, 45. This information was gathered in a public survey ordered by Charlemagne in 787. There is no reason to believe that during the previous quarter-century or so the monastery of St. Wandrille had increased its landed wealth substantially; for that matter, there is no evidence that its landed wealth had suffered any noteworthy decreases.

51. *Cap. reg. Fr.*, I, no. 77, ch. 10.

52. David Herlihy, "Demography," in *Dictionary of the Middle Ages*, ed. J. R. Strayer, 12 vols. (New York, 1984), IV, 139–140. Cf. Reinhard Schneider, *Das Frankenreich* (Munich, 1982), 124; and Eduard Hlawitschka, *Vom Frankenreich zur Formierung der eu-ropäischen Staaten- und Völkergemeinschaft, 840–1046* (Darmstadt, 1986), 8, who permit the conclusion that Charlemagne's empire as a whole had a population in the neighbor-hood of twenty million.

53. See Ansley Coale and Paul Demeny, *Regional Model Life Tables and Stable Populations* (Princeton, 1966), passim, who provide the basic data regarding age cohorts. The imposition of the oath of loyalty to the king upon twelve-year-old males, who were regarded as capable of doing military service, would naturally increase the pool of able-bodied men to considerably in excess of two million. Concerning the oath see F. L. Gan-shof, "Charlemagne's Use of the Oath," 114.

54. Karl Ferdinand Werner, "*Missus-Marchio-Comes*: Entre l'administration cen-trale et l'administration locale de l'Empire carolingien," *Histoire comparée de l'adminis-tration (IVe-XVIIe siècles)*, ed. Werner Paravicini and Karl Ferdinand Werner (Munich, 1980), 191, discusses the number of counties.

55. Delbrück, *The Art of War*, III, 21, conjures up a figure with no source material

or supporting argument that 100 men were mobilized for expeditionary service for each 50,000 in the total population. This would mean that on a population base of about eight million people, approximately 16,000 able-bodied men in the appropriate age cohort would be called up for expeditionary service. This figure is well below one percent of the approximately two million males who would be eligible for military service on an age cohort basis. However, if Delbrück means that 100 men go off to war for each 50,000 men in a total population of eight million, then only some 4,000 could be mustered for offensive military operations, or 0.0002 percent of men available on the basis of their age cohort.

56. See, for example, *Cap. reg. Fr.*, I, no. 25, ch. 6; no. 34, ch. 13; and no. 77, ch. 9.

57. See, for example, *Cap. reg. Fr.* I, no. 27, ch. 1; no. 33, ch. 7; no. 44, ch. 19; and no. 50, ch. 19.

58. See regarding these matters the pathbreaking work of Donald Engels, *Alexander the Great and the Logistics of the Macedonian Army* (Berkeley, 1978); and regarding the technology of transport see Parrott, "Strategy and Tactics in the Thirty Years' War"; and Simon Adams, "Tactics or Politics?" 28–52.

59. With regard to water transport see, for example, the discussion by Engels, *Alexander the Great*, 26–27; and the case study by Bernard S. Bachrach, "The Siege of Antioch: A Study in Military Demography," *War in History*, 6 (1999), 127–146. Regarding Carolingian use of naval assets see Appendix in this volume.

60. Cam, *Local Government*, 31; and Ganshof, "Charlemagne's Army," 60. Delbrück, *The Art of War*, III, 31–32, goes so far as to argue that texts that have the word "all" do so as a result of careless copying and that the word "not" before it was accidentally omitted.

61. See the discussion by Durliat, *Les finances publiques*, 315–321. This is not to say that women cannot or did not do various types of agricultural work. The point is that extracting some 30 percent of the labor force from crucial work on a regular basis is not plausible.

62. Concerning these military and military-related lists see, for example, *Cap. reg. Fr.* I, no. 67, ch. 4; no. 18; no. 123, ch. 6; II, no. 19, 7; 321, ch. 27; and *Annales S. Bertani, an.* 869; and the commentary by Werner, "*Hludovicus Augustus*," 81–82. Carolingian society was a list-making culture: see, in general, McKitterick, *The Carolingians and the Written Word*; and with particular attention to administrative list making, see the pioneering work by James Westfall Thompson, "The Statistical Sources of Frankish History," *American Historical Review*, 40 (1935), 625–645, and more recently Davis, "Domesday Book," 15–39.

Cf. Delbrück, *The Art of War*, III, 33–36, who vehemently attacks the notion of a written culture, the existence of lists of any kind for military purposes, and any serious military administration. Concerning this extreme "primitivism" and its modern supporters, which is intended to sustain the notion of the Germanic nature of early medieval society, see the brief remarks by Bachrach, "Anthropology and Early Medieval History," 3–10; and the important observations by Goffart, "Two Notes on Germanic Antiquity Today," 9–30. Bernard S. Bachrach, "Early Medieval Military Demography: Some Observations on the Methods of Hans Delbrück," in *The Circle of War*, ed. Donald Kagay and L. J. Andrew Villalon (Woodbridge, 1999), 3–20.

63. *Cap. reg. Fr.* I, no. 44, chs. 15, 16, indicates efforts by the central government to thwart free men from being oppressed by the local officials.

64. *Cap. reg. Fr.* I, no. 50, ch. 6, provides evidence for the count's violation of these regulations.

65. *Cap. reg. Fr.* I, no. 34, ch. 12; and no. 73, ch. 3.

66. Reuter, "The End of Carolingian Military Expansion," 398, perhaps exaggerates when he observes: "Yet nowhere in the sources for the Merovingian or early Carolingian period is there anything which looks like a possible selection mechanism." The capitulary evidence regarding abuses, discussed here, dates from shortly after Charlemagne's coronation as emperor, but is merely the earliest surviving mention of the abuses that by their very nature, e.g., gradual impoverishment, must be considered a long-term process. Indeed, no internal evidence in these capitularies permits the inference either that the traditional mechanisms for selection or their abuse was something new. Rather, the abuses, themselves, that Charlemagne sought to correct were in essence deviations from a pattern that likely took a considerable amount of time, in general, to cause serious problems.

Charlemagne's later enactments regarding the Saxons and the Frisians (*Cap. reg. Fr.*, I, no. 49, chs. 2 and 3, respectively), which establish universal service for the local defense and selective service for expeditionary levies on the basis of wealth, likely should be seen, in principle, as establishing a system similar to that which existed in parts of the *regnum Francorum*. It would be a mistake, however, to assume that these enactments mirrored exactly the mechanisms in place earlier in the *regnum Francorum*. Cf. Reuter, "The End of Carolingian Military Expansion," 399–400, who seems to have glimpsed part of the picture but is misled perhaps by his unnecessary emphasis on a massive and rather sudden alteration in Carolingian "grand strategy" from offensive war to defensive war following Charlemagne's coronation.

67. These basic policies should not be confounded with special exemptions given by the king for all kinds of service. See the brief discussion by Cam, *Local Government*, 133–134. For a more detailed discussion of the working of demographic patterns see Bachrach, "Military Lands," forthcoming.

68. Ganshof, "Charlemagne's Army," 67–68, concerning fines; and Cam, *Local Government*, 134–135, regarding substitutes. Delbrück, *The Art of War*, III, 16–17, calls attention to these fines but believes that they were a ruse developed by the Carolingians in order to raise a tax. He bases this assumption on the belief that Charlemagne had no military use for these levies because the Carolingians had very small armies. Nevertheless, Delbrück does believe, apparently in this particular context alone, not only that the lists were made but also that they were kept current by the relevant government officials so that the fines could be assessed and collected. See the critique of Delbrück's argument by Bachrach, "Early Medieval Military Demography," 3–20.

69. Concerning women holding allodial land see Alexander C. Murray, *Germanic Kinship Structure: Studies in Law and Society in Antiquity and the Early Middle Ages* (Toronto, 1983), 201–215.

70. I have not found an example of a woman going off to war on expeditionary service for this period. But if such a case were to be identified, it surely would be an aberration, rather than evidence for a norm, and hardly the basis upon which to rest a quantitative argument. I have little doubt, however, that rather bizarre stories of women engaged in helping to defend a fixed position, e.g., Paul, *Hist.*, bk. I, ch. 8, may mask a kernel of truth.

71. See *Cap. reg. Fr.*, no. 50, chs. 1–9; and cf. the commentary by Durliat, *Les finances publiques*, 317–321. The discussion of *servi*, who were honored with the status of

a vassal, i.e., *vassaticum*, and provided with arms, and who are discussed below, would seem to fit the description of poor men who were armed and trained for expeditionary military service.

72. For a glimpse at the great wealth under consideration here, see Hans-Werner Goetz, *Life in the Middle Ages from the Seventh to the Thirteenth Century*, trans. Albert Wimmer and ed. Steven Rowan (Notre Dame, Ind., 1993), 112–113.

73. See, for example, the information gathered by Ganshof, "Charlemagne's Army," 63.

74. The surviving *acta* for the reigns of both Pippin and Charlemagne indicate that immunities were the focus of more *acta* than any other single subject. See *Dip. Carol. passim*.

75. For the basic outlines of the immunity, see M. Kroell, *L'immunité franque* (Paris, 1910). This is not to say that the count was not an officer of the central government. However, as an official of the central government, who was serving at the local level, he is carefully distinguished in official documents from those government officials who were attached directly to that part of the royal administration based at the palace. Cf. Barbara Rosenwein, *Negotiating Space: Power, Restraint, and Privileges of Immunity in Early Medieval Europe* (Ithaca, N.Y., 1999), who fails to grasp the military significance of immunities.

76. See, in general, Cam, *Local Government*, 100–104, for specific attention to the responsibility for military service owed by magnates who had been granted immunities.

77. Adalhard, *De ordine palatii*, ch. VI (30), with the putative additions by Hincmar. See the discussion by Cam, *Local Government*, 128.

78. N.b. the complaints of abbots such as Ardo, *V. Benedicti*, ch. 39; and Servatus Lupus, *Epist.* nos. 16, 24, 45, concerning the great economic burden imposed by the requirements that they have their forces participate in expeditionary military operations. Such whining, like most complaints concerning taxes throughout the history of Western civilization, was probably a topos of sorts. However, the existence of these great burdens surely was not a fantasy.

79. Easy access to the basics of this bipartite organization of estates is provided by Verhulst, "Economic Organisation," 489–499.

80. Concerning the wealth of the church, see Emile Lesne, *Histoire de la propriété ecclésiastique en France*, 6 vols. (Lille, 1910–1943), II.1, 224, whose estimate that one-third of the arable land in Gaul was in the hands of the church has been generally accepted.

81. Friedrich E. Prinz, "King, Clergy and War at the Time of the Carolingians," in *Saints, Scholars and Heroes: Studies in Medieval Culture in Honour of Charles W. Jones*, ed. M. King and W. Stevens (Collegeville, Minn., 1979), II, 301–329; and cf. Weidemann, *Kulturgeschichte der Merowingerzeit*, II, 238–246.

82. Letaldus, *Miracula Martini Abbatis Vertavenis*, ch. 7. For a very helpful discussion of the original Merovingian text that underlay Letaldus' reworking see Thomas Head, *Hagiography and the Cult of the Saints* (Cambridge, 1990), 221; cf. Bachrach, "Fulk Nerra's Exploitation of the *facultates monarchorum*, ca. 1000," where I did not give sufficient weight to the Merovingian texts at Letaldus' command.

83. Bachrach, "Charles Martel," 66–69; Wolfram, "Karl Martell und das fränkische Lehenswesen," 61–77; Nonn, "Das Bild Karl Martells," 9–33.

84. Bachrach, "Charles Martel," 66–69; and Wolfram, "Karl Martell und das fränkische Lehenswesen," 61–77.

85. *Cap. reg. Fr.*, I, no. 11, ch. 2.

86. *Annales Guelferbytani, an.* 751; *Annales Alamannici, an.* 751; and *Annales Na-zariani, an.* 751.

87. For other examples, see the rather incomplete but nonetheless very useful list compiled by Davis, "Domesday Book," 15–39.

88. Jean Durliat, "La polyptyque d'Irminon pour l'Armée," Bibliothèque de l'Ecole des Chartes, 141 (1983), 183–208; John Percival, "The Precursors of Domesday: Roman and Carolingian Land Registers," in *Domesday Book: A Reassessment,* ed. Peter Sawyer (London, 1985), 5-27. N.b. the use of polyptychs goes back into the Merovingian era; see Robert Fossier, *Polyptyques et Censiers* (Brepols, 1978), who provides a useful introduction to this genre of document. Also considerable attention should be given to the insightful critique by Goffart, "Merovingian Polyptychs: Reflections on Two Recent Publications," in *Rome's Fall and After* (London, 1989), 233–253.

89. Hincmar of Rheims, *Collectio de Ecclesiis et Capellis,* 119–120. Cf. the important discussion by Janet Nelson, "The Church's Military Service in the Ninth Century: A Contemporary View?" *Studies in Church History,* 20 (1983), 15–30, and reprinted in Janet Nelson, *Politics and Ritual in Early Medieval Europe* (London, 1986), 111–132. Bachrach, "Charles Martel," 66–69, who takes note of Hincmar's efforts to blame Charles Martel for what had been and continued to be a basic aspect of military financing in the *regnum Francorum.*

90. Concerning the size of the monastery, see Ursmer Berlière, "Le nombre des moines dans les anciens monastères," *Revue Bénédictine,* 41 (1929), 231–261; 42 (1930), 19–42, whose data makes clear that St. Riquier under the leadership of Angilbert was one of the largest houses in the *regnum Francorum.* This is hardly surprising in light of Angilbert's closeness to Charlemagne.

91. Concerning Widmar's career see, in general, Susan A. Rabe, *Faith, Art, and Politics at Saint-Riquier: The Symbolic Vision of Angilbert* (Philadelphia, 1995) 74, 180, n. 50.

92. Concerning Angilbert's background, in general, Rabe, *Faith, Art, and Politics,* 52–54, with the literature cited there. Regarding Angilbert's "marriage" to Charlemagne's daughter Bertha see Suzanne Wemple, *Women in Frankish Society: Marriage and the Cloister, 500–900* (Philadelphia, 1981), 79. Concerning the program of religious building at St. Riquier see most recently Rabe, *Faith, Art, and Politics,* 81–82, with her discussions of the relevant sources and literature.

93. Brief discussions of the library with relevant literature are found in Wallace-Hadrill, *The Frankish Church,* 346–348, and McKitterick, *The Carolingians and the Written Word,* 176–178.

94. Hariulf, *Chron.* (*Hariulf, Chronique de l'abbaye de Saint-Riquier Ve siècle-1104,* ed. Ferdinand Lot [Paris, 1894]), bk. I, chs. iv and vi, respectively, for reference to Centula as a *villa* and then as a *vicus.* Robert Fossier, *La Terre et les hommes en Picardie,* 2 vols. (Paris, 1968), I, 191–192, calls attention to this terminology and sees it as a contradiction. Indeed, he then assumes that the term *vicus* must be an error, presumably by a later writer who was reading conditions of the eighth century back into the seventh century, and rejects the notion of considerable economic development at Centula prior to 630.

95. Fossier, *La Terre et les hommes,* I, 193, sees Centula as already well developed when Angilbert became abbot, and in *Polyptyques et Censiers,* 28–29, Fossier calls attention to an inventory of the monastery's wealth executed at the order of Louis the Pious in 831.

96. Information concerning the town is published in Hariulf, *Chron.*, ed. Lot, appendix 7, 306–308, and is generally believed to have been a part of the inventory of 831 mentioned above. However, Theodore Evergates, "Historiography and Sociology in Early Feudal Society: The Case of Hariulf and the 'Milites' of Saint-Riquier," *Viator*, 6 (1975), 35–49, has argued that both the text of the inventory of 831 and the *descriptio* of Centula are later medieval documents. *Au fond*, it is Evergates' conviction that the term *miles*, which appears in these texts, was not used to denote secular fighting men in Carolingian times. This is clearly incorrect. For example, it is clear that Adalhard identified *milites* serving as part of the military household in the courts of both Pippin I and Charlemagne (*De ordine palatii*, V [22, 27]). In addition, Hincmar of Rheims, *Ad Carolum Calvum*, col. 1050, not only writes of *milites* in the sense of secular fighting men but identifies them as holding *beneficia*. This terminology is even found in Carolingian epic poetry. See, for example, *Waltharius*, ed. Strecker, line 409; and below for the date. Rabe, *Faith, Art, and Politics*, 192, n. 42, effectively criticizes the nonmilitary arguments made by Evergates.

Hariulf, *Chron.*, ed. Lot, appendix 7, provides the figure of 2,500 households to which I have applied a conservative multiplier of four in order to estimate the order of magnitude of the population as a whole. A multiplier of five, for which some specialists in medieval demography argue and which is not impossible, would provide a figure of 12,500. See the relevant demographic work in Herlihy, "Demography," 146. Fossier, *La Terre et les hommes en Picardie*, I, 191–194, accepts the information concerning the demographic and economic development of Centula in the early Carolingian era.

97. Hariulf, *Chron.*, ed. Lot, appendix 7, 306–308.

98. Hariulf, *Chron.*, ed. Lot, appendix 7, 307.

99. Walter Horn and Ernest Born, *The Plan of St. Gall*, 3 vols. (Berkeley, 1979), I, 347–348, II, 191. It is not clear whether these craftsmen were fully involved in the making of swords or whether they were involved in only two phases of a very complex process.

100. *Cap. reg. Fr.*, no. 32, ch. 62.

101. Hariulf, *Chron.*, ed. Lot, appendix 7, 308, lists the number of houses and in Hariulf, *Chron.* bk. III, ch. 3, the names of 100 of these *milites* are listed who were then housed in the above-mentioned houses. It seems that the contingent based at Centula was ten men short of its maximum.

102. Hariulf, *Chron.*, ed. Lot, appendix 7, 308. The use of the term *gladius* for sword here will be discussed in Chapter 3.

103. See the discussion by Ganshof, "Charlemagne's Army," 65–66, and based on the conversion values provided by *Lex Rib.*, XL (XXXVI), ch. 11.

104. Warren Treadgold, *Byzantium and Its Army; 284–1081* (Stanford, 1995), 151, n. 82, argues that twenty years is a plausible average period of employment for a war horse. However, a twenty-year-old horse is old by any calculation. This, however, is not much help in ascertaining average lifespan of an ordinary war horse, average working life of a war horse, or (more to the point) average useful years of a war horse. Horses are fragile animals, and very sick or injured horses are extremely difficult to treat. A broken leg, for example, means the end of the horse. By contrast, a soldier who breaks his leg will likely recover. Thus, when figuring averages for the useful life of a war horse we must take into consideration all those that die, either from natural causes or in combat, well before they ceased to be of use for military operations. Even more to the point is the fact that a horse needed to be three or perhaps even four years of age to carry heavy loads

under arduous conditions. In addition, it takes at least a year or two, during the period of growth to full strength, to train a war horse properly. Concerning the difficulties in training a war horse, see the exceptionally important article by Carroll Gillmore, "Practical Chivalry: The Training of Horses for Tournaments and Warfare," *Studies in Medieval and Renaissance History*, n.s. 13 (1992), 7–29. And as J. K. Anderson, *Ancient Greek Horsemanship* (Berkeley, 1961), 98, points out, a horse does not get all of its permanent teeth until four to four and a half years of age.

105. Hariulf, *Chron.*, ed. Lot, appendix 7, 308. N.b. it is in the nature of these documents to record what is owed to the institution that takes the inventory (polyptych) in question. Thus, much information that would be of great interest to historians is omitted from such documents.

106. The knotty problem of finding satisfactory modern terms to describe various types of medieval fighting men is well illustrated in this case. For example, all mercenaries are not styled *milites* and all men styled *milites* in our sources surely are not mercenaries. For some interesting observations on the problem of trying to define mercenaries, see John Schlight, *Monarchs and Mercenaries; A Reappraisal of the Importance of Knight Service in Norman and Early Angevin England* (Bridgeport, Conn., 1968).

107. Unfortunately, that part of the inventory of 831 that lists the total number of manses belonging to St. Riquier was not included in Hariulf, *Chron.*, ed. Lot, bk. III, ch. 3.

108. *Cap. reg. Fr.*, no. 25, ch. 4, from which it is clear that this was a well-established practice. N.b. *arma* in this text should be taken to mean armor. See the general discussion by Bachrach, "Military Organization in Aquitaine Under the Early Carolingians," *Speculum*, 49 (1974), 20.

109. *Cap. reg. Fr.*, no. 25, ch. 4. The use of the terms *spatha*, and *semispatha* for long and short swords, is discussed, below, in the section on "The Royal Military Household."

110. Paul Guilhiermoz, *Essai sur l'origine de la noblesse en France au moyen âge* (Paris, 1902) 52–57, 67–68, 72, n. 107.

111. Rhabanus Maurus, *De Procinctu romanae Miliciae*, ch. III.

112. See Bernard S. Bachrach, "The Imperial Roots of Merovingian Military Organization," in *Military Aspects of Scandinavian Society in a European Perspective, A.D. 1–1300*, ed. Anne Norgard Jorgensen and Birthe L. Clausen (Copenhagen, 1997), 28.

113. *Cap. reg. Fr.*, no. 20, ch. 50.

114. See, for example, Odegaard, *Vassi and Fideles in the Carolingian Empire*, 125. n. 90, with the extensive literature cited there; and Reuter, "Plunder and Tribute," 81–82, with the literature cited in n. 42.

115. There is little doubt that these retinues were of importance. Indeed, scholars have leaned toward overestimating the importance of these *obsequia* to the Carolingian military, in general, at the expense of the expeditionary levies. See, for example, Reuter, "Plunder and Tribute," 81–82, with references to Tacitus and an argument going back to the German *Urzeit*. Unfortunately, some exceptionally tenacious historiographical myths have grown up regarding the so-called *comitatus* and the institutions that putatively were brought west from the German forests. See the effective criticism of this tendency by Steven C. Fanning, "Tacitus, Beowulf and the Comitatus," *Haskins Society Journal* 9 (2001), forthcoming. In a more general sense, the study by Goffart, "Two Notes on Germanic Antiquity Today," 9–30, is indispensable.

116. Cf. the discussion by Bachrach, "Military Organization in Aquitaine," 15, which I have modified here somewhat.

117. *Cap. reg. Fr.*, I, no. 25, ch. 4. The discussions by Odegaard, "Carolingian Oaths of Fidelity," 284–296; and Ganshof, "Charlemagne's Use of the Oath," 111–124, taken together provide a good introduction to this subject.

118. Bachrach, "Grand Strategy," 59; and cf. Ramsey MacMullen, *Soldier and Civilian in the Later Empire* (Cambridge, Mass., 1967), 119–151.

119. F. L. Ganshof, "Une crise dans le règne de Charlemagne, les années 778 et 779," in *Mélanges d'histoire et de littérature offerts à Monsieur Charles Gilliard* (Lausanne, 1944), 132–144.

120. See the broad-ranging discussion of this institution by J. O. Prestwich, "The Military Household of the Norman Kings," *English Historical Review*, 96 (1981), 1–35; and for further elaboration, Stephen Morillo, *Warfare Under the Anglo-Norman Kings, 1066–1135* (Woodbridge, 1994), 60–66. The observations of Régine Le Jan-Hennebicque, "Satellites et bandes armées dans le monde franc (VIIe–Xe siècles)," in *La combattant au moyen âge* (Nantes, 1990), 97–109, are perceptive, but she tries to draw too many overarching conclusions from too small a base of evidence.

121. Hincmar, *De ordine palatii*, ed. Gross and Schieffer, ch. III (12), records the title of the original work by Adalhard. In addition, Hincmar indicates that he was personally acquainted with Adalhard, who died in 826. Gross and Schieffer, 10, make clear that Hincmar composed his version of this text sometime after 5 August 882 but before 21 December 882, and speculate (11) not implausibly regarding the possibility that Adalhard's version was written either for Charlemagne's son Pippin, who was made king in Italy in 782, or for the latter's son Bernard (811–814). Adalhard served as regent and adviser to both. However, exactly when Adalhard actually wrote or perhaps more accurately dictated his *De ordine palatii* is a subject in need of further study.

Provisionally, I would suggest that Adalhard wrote early in the reign of King Pippin of Italy, i.e., ca. 782–783, when he assumed the duties of governing the young king's *regnum*, since the text presumably was to be used as a tool to develop the organization of the new Carolingian central government to be based at Pavia. The sooner such a work was written the more value it would have had for organizing the government of the new *regnum*. By 811, when Bernard succeeded his father, King Pippin, the government of the Italian *regnum* had been in rather successful operation for more than a quarter century. There would have been no substantial reason to provide the new ruler with a tract based upon information that was already more than forty years old, i.e., dating to Adalhard's youthful experiences at the court of King Pippin I, and that dealt with institutions that had flourished in the *regnum Francorum* north of the Alps. By contrast, when Hincmar included parts of Adalhard's tract in his version of the *De ordine palatii*, he made substantial additions and some revisions. It is unclear to me why Hincmar, *De ordine palatii*, ed. and trans. Maurice Prou (Paris, 1884), does not appear in the bibliography of the Gross and Schieffer edition (cf. 18) and that his valuable notes were not fully utilized.

Louis Halphen, "*De ordine palatii* d'Hincmar," *Revue historique* 183 (1938), 1–9, and reprinted in Louis Halphen, *A travers l'histoire du moyen âge* (Paris, 1950), 83–91, calls attention to the literary and rhetorical nature of the text, in general, and assumes unnecessarily that this is evidence both of massive interpolation by Hincmar and inaccuracy. In short, Halphen believes that the text is of little historical value for understanding how either Pippin I's or Charlemagne's court was organized. Heinz Löwe, "Hinkmar von Reims und der Apocrisiar," in *Festschrift für Hermann Heimpel*, 3 vols. (Gottingen, 1972), 3, 197–225, argues that this text is of value only for the later ninth century. However, Josef Fleckenstein, "Die Struktur des Hofes Karls des Grossen im Spiegel von Hinkmars *De ordine palatii*," *Zeitschrift des Aachener Geschichtsvereins*, 83 (1976), 5–22, has concluded sensibly that the work is of substantial value for our understanding of the early Carolingian court. I would agree insofar as secular matters are at issue.

122. Paschasius Radbertus, *V. S. Adalhardi*, ch. 7.

123. Paschasius Radbertus, *V. S. Adalhardi*, ch. 7. Of course one must be careful lest the possible exaggerations often found in the *vita sancti* genre of literature provide a misleading picture. However, mention of Adalhard's *tirocinium*, i.e., initial military service, suggests a measure of honesty by a writer who personally was very well acquainted with his subject. For useful general overviews of Adalhard's career see, for example, Paul Bauters, *Adalhard van Huise (750–826) abt von Corbie en Corvey* (Oudenaarde, 1964); and Henri Peltier, *Adalhard, Abbé de Corbie* (Amiens, 1969).

124. Although we do not know exactly when Adalhard wrote *De ordine palatii*, he refers to institutional practices of Pippin's reign as well as to those of Charlemagne's reign (ch. IV [14, 15]). Adalhard left the royal court in ca. 771 after a major disagreement with Charlemagne. A rapprochement between the two men was effected, however, during the early 770s and in ca. 776, Charlemagne ostensibly established his cousin as abbot of the very important monastery of Corbie. Adalhard is known to have returned from time to time to the court of Charlemagne and also to the court of Louis the Pious for rather brief visits, but he neither played an official role at the royal court nor spent much time there after ca. 771. Thus, it is very likely that whatever detailed knowledge Adalhard had of the workings of the Carolingian court dated from the reign of Pippin I and from the early part of Charlemagne's reign. We cannot, however, rule out the possibility that Adalhard added some bits and pieces of information from later periods. In addition, it is unfortunate that the detailed work has not been done to identify how Hincmar dealt with the ostensibly secular parts of the *De ordine palatii* under consideration here. Cf. Löwe, "Hinkmar von Reims und der Apocrisiar," 197–225.

125. Adalhard, *De ordine palatii*, ch. IV (17). Fleckenstein, "Die Struktur des Hofes Karls des Grossen," 5–22, provides a useful summary of sections of the text.

126. See also Einhard, *V. Karoli, praef.*

127. Adalhard, *De ordine palatii*, ch. V (27).

128. Previous discussion of rapid deployment has ignored the *expediti milites* based at the court and the *milites* based at Centula. Thus, Ganshof, "Charlemagne's Army," 63–64, discusses rapid deployment forces on the basis of early ninth-century evidence. He sees the possibility that Charlemagne instituted rapid deployment but thinks it is more likely that Louis the Pious was responsible. Werner, "*Missus-Marchio-Comes*," 198, n. 117, however, emphasizes that rapid deployment was more likely developed by Charlemagne. Reuter, "The End of Carolingian Military Expansion," 394–395, sides with Werner and emphasizes the defensive nature of rapid deployment. This is not compelling because Reuter takes note of the "first appearance" of such forces undertaking military operations in Italy. The long-range capacity of these forces, i.e., mobilized in the Trier area in 817 and sent to Italy, is of the greatest importance and thus their potential for offensive operations beyond the frontiers cannot be ignored.

129. Adalhard, *De ordine palatii*, ch. V (27). *Absque ministeriis*, the phrase that I have translated as "without servants," is sound Latin usage. However, it is likely less common than the translation others have preferred, i.e., "without [having] a [particular] assignment." The latter meaning obviously would permit the inference that *expediti milites* had a general assignment but no particular assignment presumably as compared to the

other two *ordines* of fighting men at the court. However, while those young men who were training to be officers (see below) may perhaps be considered to have had an assignment insofar as they were at the *palatium* to learn how to be officers, the third *ordo*, composed of *vassali* and *pueri*, cannot be argued to have had any particular assignments.

This passage has caused numerous problems because of the difficulty some scholars have had in grasping the notion of *expediti milites* as a military force. See, for example, Prou, *Hincmar*, 66–68; and followed by Gross and Schieffer, *Hincmar*, 81. By contrast, see Peltier, *Adalhard, Abbé de Corbie*, 82, who seems to be a bit more on track. Ardo, *V. Benedicti*, ch. 29, also discusses the *milites* who are based at the court, i.e., "milites aulae regiae." See, as well, Notker, *Gesta Karoli*, bk. I, ch. 11. Cf. the treatment of these texts by Paul Guilhiermoz, *Essai sur l'origine de la noblesse*, (Paris, 1902), 112, n. 24.

130. Adalhard, *De ordine palatii*, ch. V (27).

131. Adalhard, *De ordine palatii*, ch. V (27).

132. Adalhard, *De ordine palatii*, ch. V (22). Georg Waitz, *Deutsche Verfassungsgeschichte*, 8 vols., 2nd ed. (Berlin, 1893–1896), III, 549, is correct in seeing these as gifts to the *milites*; and Nelson, "The Church's Military Service," 126, is likely correct in seeing these gifts in money if for no other reason than the comparative ease with which cash can be transferred in a ceremonial context. In addition, cash was the usual imperial gift to the soldiers and the role of *imitatio imperii* was never far from the minds of the Carolingian rulers.

Unfortunately, Schieffer and Gross (72, n. 165) totally confuse the *dona annua*, which was given by the great magnates to the king, with the *donum militum* given by the king through the aegis of the queen to the palace troops. Reuter, "Plunder and Tribute," 81, is on the right track with regard to the *donum militum*, but if I have understood him correctly (82) he has misinterpreted the very positive, even perhaps festive, spirit of Adalhard's account.

133. Adalhard, *De ordine palatii*, ch. V (22).

134. Cf. Campbell, *The Emperor and the Roman Army*, 40.

135. See, for example, *Vit. Marc. Ant. Phil*, 26.8.

136. The basic information for the early empire is collected by Campbell, *The Emperor and the Roman Army*, 95–97.

137. Concerning Roman empresses exercising actual authority over the imperial military household, or at least one or two units stationed there, see the examples of Agrippina issuing orders to *milites* and the episode between Justina and Ambrose discussed by Richard I. Frank, *Scholae Palatinae: The Palace Guards of the Later Roman Empire* (Rome, 1969), 22–23, 107–109, respectively. These events were also recorded in sources known to the Carolingians. Regarding the availability of the *Scriptores* to the Carolingians, see P. K. Marshall, "Scriptores Historiae Augustae," in *Texts and Transmission*, 354–356; and Bernhard Bischoff, *Manuscripts and Libraries in the Age of Charlemagne*, trans. and ed. Michael Gorman (Cambridge, 1994), 118, 120, 150.

138. Regarding *imitatio*, see the classic work of Michael McCormick, *Eternal Victory: Triumphal Rulership in Late Antiquity, Byzantium and the Early Medieval West* (Cambridge, 1986). N.b., as well, the fascinating letter that Servatus Lupus (*Epist.*, no. 37) a good friend of both Einhard and Rhabanus Maurus, wrote to his king where he notes that he was sending him a very brief summary of the deeds of the emperors, likely Aurelius Victor, *Epitome de Caesaribus* (Levillain, I, 165, n. 4). In this letter, Servatus Lupus called special attention in this context to Trajan and Theodosius "because from their

deeds (actibus) you are likely to find many things that you can imitate in a most profitable (utilissime) manner."

139. See, for example, *Beowulf*, ed. Klaeber, lines 607–641. I am unconvinced by Michael I. Enright, *Lady with a Mead Cup: Ritual, Prophecy and Lordship in the European Warband from La Tène to the Viking Age* (Portland, Ore., 1996), esp. 29, who seems to think that the involvement of the high ranking "lady" with the military forces attached to her husband's court is evidence that she was partaking in an *ur-* and *echt-* Germanic custom when the "evidence" he proffers postdates by many centuries the Roman evidence, discussed above, and which he seems to have chosen to ignore. It is exceptionally difficult to identify pre-Roman and pre-Christian Germanic customs after the German-speaking people in question had been in contact with both the Roman Empire and Christianity for centuries.

140. Adalhard, *De ordine palatii*, ch. V (27). Cf. the notes by Prou, *Hincmar*, 66–68.

141. Adalhard, *De ordine palatii*, ch. V (27). See, for example, Friedrich Keutgen, "Die Entstehung der Deutschen Ministerialität," *Vierteljahrschrift für Sozial- und Wirschaftsgeschichte*, 8 (1910), 1–16, 169–195, 481–547, for background. Cf. Benjamin Arnold, *German Knighthood, 1050–1300* (Oxford, 1985), 35–41, who provides a lucid account of contemporary scholarship which rejects the notion of continuity between the Carolingians and later German history in this area.

142. See, for example, notice of *capitanei*, who command royal units that are not based at the court, in *Cap. reg. Fr.*, no. 48, ch. 3; these will be discussed below.

143. Adalhard, *De ordine palatii*, ch. V (28).

144. Bachrach, "Education of the 'Officer Corps'," 7–9; and on the modern scene see Omar N. Bradley and Clay Blair, *A General's Life: An Autobiography* (New York, 1983).

145. Einhard, *V. Karoli*, ch. 22.

146. If, as noted above, one follows the interpretation that the *expediti milites* had no regular assignments rather than that they lacked servants, then the corps of royal bodyguards must be seen as yet another special unit, i.e., a unit especially designated to guard the king and other members of the royal family, rather than as a special unit chosen from among the *milites*. For the role of household troops in guarding the king's children, see Einhard, *V. Karoli*, ch. 19, where the rather general term *satellites* is used.

147. See, for example, Frank, *Scholae Palatinae*, for a detailed examination of these institutions.

148. Maximin Deloche, *La trustis et l'antrustion royal sous les deux premières races* (Paris, 1878), remains basic but is badly in need of revision.

149. *Marculfi Formulae*, I, 18.

150. For the dating problems of this formula see Rudolf Buchner, *Die Rechtsquellen* (Weimar, 1953), 51–52, who notes two possible dating patterns, i.e., ca. 650 and 721–735.

151. Regarding Pippin's oft discussed question to Pope Zacharias, see Pierre Riché, *The Carolingians: A Family who Forged Europe*, trans. M. I. Allen (Philadelphia, 1993), 67.

152. *Marculfi Formulae*, I, 18.

153. *Marculfi Formulae*, I, 18.

154. *Marculfi Formulae*, I, 18.

155. Campbell, *The Emperor and the Roman Army*, 22–23.

156. *Marculfi Formulae*, I, 18.

157. See, in general, McKitterick, *The Carolingians and the Written Word*.

158. Cf. Notker, *Gesta Karoli*, bk. II, ch. 3, where a special story is confabulated as

noted by Edward Dutton, *The Politics of Dreaming in the Carolingian Empire* (Lincoln, Neb., 1994), 12. N.b. Le Jan-Hennebicque, "Satellites et bandes armées," 97–105, who sees changes in terminology as having much greater significance than suggested here.

159. This is a controversial matter for which the basic text is *Recapitulatio legis salicae*, ch. 30. Cf. the extended discussion by Deloche, *La trustis et l'antrustion royal*, 66–79 and the refutation by Simeon L. Guterman, *The Principle of the Personality of Law in the Germanic Kingdoms of Western Europe from the Fifth to the Eleventh Century* (New York, 1990), 6–7.

160. *Urkundenbuch S. Gallen*, ed. Wartmann, no. 31. See, for example, the great weight placed by Marc Bloch, *Feudal Society*, trans. L. A. Manyon (London, 1962), 152; and Lynn T. White, *Medieval Technology and Social Change* (Oxford, 1962), 29, on this example. As a landowner who owed military service, Isanhard obviously already possessed both a spear and a shield.

161. F. L. Ganshof, "Die uitrusting van de lijfwachters der Karolingische koningen en keizers," *Genste bijdragen tot de kunstgeschiedenis*, 12 (1949–1950), 122–126. See also Richard Delbrück, *Spätantike Kaiserportraits* (Berlin, 1935), 79, 86, 94; and F. W. Deichmann, *Frühchristliche Bauten und Mosaike von Ravenna* (Baden-Baden, 1958), pl. 368.

162. See Ganshof, "Die uitrusting van de lijfwachters der Karolingische koningen en keizers," 122–126, which remains the basic study. However, see Bachrach, "A Picture of Avar-Frankish Warfare," 5–27, where it is shown that Carolingian artists added contemporary details of various types. The research by Coupland, "Carolingian Arms and Armor," 36–37, supports this conclusion.

163. John F. Haldon, "Some Aspects of Byzantine Military Technology from the Sixth to the Tenth Centuries," *Byzantine and Modern Greek Studies*, 1 (1975), 15–16, with the literature cited there.

164. See, for example, the materials published by Joachim Werner, "Ein langobarischen Schild von Ischl an der Als," *Bayerische Vorgeschichtsblätter*, 18–19 (1952), 45–58; S. Fuchs, "Bronzebeschläge des Langobardenzeit aus Italien," *Mitteilungen der deutschen archaeologischen Instituts, römische Abteilung*, 55 (1950), 100–113; Sune Lundquist, "Sköld och svärd ur Vendel," *Fornvännen*, 45 (1950), 1–24; and Rupert Bruce-Mitford et al., *The Sutton Hoo Ship Burial*, 3 vols. in 4 (London, 1978), 2, 99.

165. H. Klumbach, ed., "Spätrömische Gardehelme," *Münchner Beiträge zur Vor- und Frühgeschichte*, 15 (1973); and Russell H. Robinson, *Armour of Imperial Rome* (London, 1975), 62–139, for the background. Regarding various types of copies, see Sune Lundquist, "Vendelhjälmarna Uesprung," *Fornvännen*, 20 (1925), 181–207; Greta Arwindsson, "A New Scandinavian Helmet from the Vendel-Time," *Acta Archaeologica* 3 (Copenhagen, 1932), 21–46; Greta Arwindsson, "A New Form of Scandinavian Helmet from the Vendel Time," *Acta Archaeologica* 5 (Copenhagen, 1934), 31–59; and Rupert Bruce-Mitford et al. *Sutton Hoo*, 3 vols. in 4 (London, 1978), 2, 220–223. Joachim Werner, "Zur Herkunft der frühmittelaltliche Spangenhelm," *Praehistorische Zeitschrift*, 33–34 (1949–1950), 178–193, provides a valuable general review of helmets.

166. It is not my intention here to argue that there was no originality among early medieval artists, in general, and Carolingian artists, in particular. Regarding the exceptionally knotty matter of artistic originality, see the very useful essay by Lawrence Nees, "The Originality of Early Medieval Artists," in *Literacy, Politics, and Artistic Innovation in the Early Medieval West: Papers Delivered at "A Symposium on Early Medieval Culture," Bryn Mawr College, Bryn Mawr, PA*, ed. Celia M. Chazelle (New York, 1992), 77–133.

167. Notker, *Gesta Karoli*, bk. II, ch. 17.

168. Ardo, *V. Benedicti*, ch. 1. The queen's guards would seem to have been comprised both of fully trained adult soldiers and of young men of high status who were being trained in the queen's *schola*. Witiza, as will be seen below, is one of the latter.

169. A good introduction is provided by Frank, *Scholae Palatinae*.

170. Adalhard, *De ordine palatii*, ch. V (28).

171. Notker, *Gesta Karoli*, bk. I, ch. 26, speaks of Charlemagne's "scola tyronum"; and ch. 11, makes reference to "scholares alae" but this is evidently a mistranscription of "scholares aulae." Cf. Guilhiermoz, *Essai sur l'origine de la noblesse*, 66, n. 80.

172. Bachrach, "Education of the 'Officer Corps'," 7–9.

173. Einhard, *V. Karoli*, ch. 19.

174. Einhard, *V. Karoli*, ch. 19, makes clear that education in "liberalis studiis" was not military training. Charlemagne also had his daughters educated in these "liberal arts." Einhard's placement of book learning before military training may well have been the order of things since one must be of a certain physical strength to engage in serious training of this type.

175. *De Procinctu romanae Miliciae*, ch. III.

176. Adalhard, *De ordine palatii*, ch. V (28).

177. Notker, *Gesta Karoli*, bk. I, ch. 3.

178. Notker, *Gesta Karoli*, bk. I, ch. 3.

179. Notker, *Gesta Karoli*, bk. I, ch. 3.

180. Cf. Smith, *Province and Empire*, 52–53, 67–68.

181. Alcuin, *De Virtutibus et Vitiis*, cols. 613–638; and for the letters at the beginning and end of the handbook see Alcuin, *Epist.*, no. 305. Luitpold Wallach, "Alcuin on Virtues and Vices: A Manual for a Carolingian Soldier," *Harvard Theological Review*, 48 (1955), 175–195, provides a useful introduction to the text and its problems, but I do not agree with all of his interpretations.

182. N.b. this information comes from Ardo, *V. Benedicti*, ch. 1, but we know about Witiza only because he became a celebrated monk who took the name Benedict and is known to posterity as Benedict of Aniane. Much the same training noted here for Witiza was undertaken by Adalhard.

183. Ardo, *V. Benedicti*, ch. 1, where his comrades are referred to as his *conmilitiones*.

184. Ardo, *V. Benedicti*, chs. 5, 18, 38, 42.

185. Ardo, *V. Benedicti*, ch. 1.

186. Ardo, *V. Benedicti*, ch. 1. For the service and concerning his age, ch. 42, where it is indicated that he died on 11 February 821 in his seventies. Thus, Witiza may have been born any time between ca. 742 and ca. 750.

187. Ardo, *V. Benedicti*, ch. 2, describes the situation but does not say explicitly that Witiza's brother died. Ardo merely indicates that Witiza almost drowned while trying to save him and that as a result he vowed to abandon secular life. Nothing more, however, is heard of Witiza's brother.

188. Ardo, *V. Benedicti*, ch. 2, provides a time frame that justifies this interpretation.

189. Ardo, *V. Benedicti*, ch. 2.

190. Adalhard, *De ordine palatii*, ch. V (28).

191. Cf. Notker, *Gesta Karoli*, bk. I, ch. 11, who refers to a cadre of officers at the court which includes *duces*, *comites*, *praefecti*, and *proceres* of various ranks (*dignitates*). All of these will be discussed below. N.b. Notker places the military *magistri* below the above-mentioned officers. Some evidence developed in the section on military training may suggest that the *magistri* were what today we would call drill sergeants or training officers.

192. The dating of this poem is highly controversial and I have been swayed by many of the arguments presented by Karl Ferdinand Werner, "*Hludovicus Augustus*," 103–123, for an early date, with 104–105, n. 384, 121, for a review of the literature. In addition, Werner's method based upon investigation of the ideas within the poem itself must be followed. Of considerable importance as well is the material presented by Alf Önnerfors, *Die Verfasserschaft des Waltharius-Epos aus sprachlicher Sicht* (Düsseldorf, 1978), 42–46, for an early ninth-century date. However, my own inclination is to look to the later eighth century, i.e., prior to the final conquest of the Avars, in a rather complicated argument that is likely to be no less controversial than previous discussion but which I hope to publish in the future. N.b., however, *Waltharius*, ed. Strecker, lines 764–767, are an attack on Saxon pedantry. Seen in the perspective of an early date, this may be taken to be poking fun at Alcuin and his Saxon origins. Alcuin left the royal court in 796 to become abbot of St. Martin at Tours and died in 804.

193. See, for example, the information compiled by Karl Strecker and easily available in his edition of *Waltharius* (Berlin, 1947), 123–151. Cf. Herman Althof, *Waltharii Poesis. Das Walthariuslied Ekkehards I. von St. Gallen*, 2 vols. (Leipzig, 1899, 1905), II, 9–371.

194. Werner, "*Hludovicus Augustus*," 107, n. 189.

195. The part of the poem, itself, that is under consideration here is set in the court of Attila the Hun and thus the action putatively takes place more than three and a half centuries prior to the time that it actually was written. There is no reason to believe that the poet, however, had any written sources available to him in Latin, which are now lost, that would have provided the kind of detailed information found in *Waltharius* concerning Attila, his army, or his court. For example, Ammianus Marcellinus' *Histories* were available to the Carolingians to provide information concerning the Huns in the fourth century but these do not provide the kind of information found in *Waltharius* and it seems clear that the poet did not use Ammianus. Indeed, he appears to have done research neither on the Huns nor on the Avars. The latter, however, were well known to the Carolingians. See, for example, Bachrach, "A Picture of Avar-Frankish Warfare," 5–27.

Rather, the poet very obviously uses his knowledge of the Carolingian court to construct many of the substantive details of his story. Whether the court where the poet gained his experience was that of Charlemagne at Aachen, his son King Charles in Italy, from which much of the Avar war was prosecuted, or the court of Louis the Pious in Aquitaine, from which operations against the Muslims in Spain were orchestrated, is a subject that requires further investigation. Cf. Werner, "*Hludovicus Augustus*," 109, who argues that the poet had available to him information both from the Aquitanian court and from a northern milieu.

196. *Waltharius*, ed. Strecker, line 106. This is a common phrase in the classical sources for army officers. See Althof, *Waltharii Poesis*, 50, for citations to Ovid, Valerius Maximus, and Justin.

197. *Waltharius*, ed. Strecker, lines 208 and 360, respectively. It is likely that the author was interested in having the "title" seen in light of Virgil's frequent use of the term.

198. *Waltharius*, ed. Strecker, lines. 101–102. See, below, Chapters 3 and 4 with regard to the training of soldiers.

199. *Waltharius*, ed. Strecker, lines. 103–104. See for the classical context the comments in the edition by Strecker, *Waltharius*, 125.

200. A still very valuable examination of the military structure of the imperial court during the later empire is Frank, *Scholae Palatinae*.

201. Treadgold, *Byzantium and Its Army*, 23–31, 70–72.

202. Adalhard, *De ordine palatii*, ch. III (13).

203. Adalhard, *De ordine palatii*, ch. V (28). N.b. in discussing the support of these *pueri* and *vasalli*, Adalhard makes clear that the magnates who were responsible for them are not to permit them to engage in rapine and theft. This admonition at once provides evidence for the putative ability of these men to carry out paramilitary operations such as foraging but also strikes a note that illegal activities are taking place. It is my sense, however, that this admonition is an interpolation into Adalhard's text by Hincmar because it is rather more consistent with the frequently reported lack of discipline associated with the later ninth century as contrasted to the reign of Pippin I and the early period of Charlemagne's reign. See Reuter, "Plunder and Tribute," 82–83, who gathers examples of abuses carried out by the military households of various magnates during the period after Charlemagne and also attributes the comments, noted above, about abuses to Hincmar. However, Reuter makes no effort to distinguish between Adalhard's original text and Hincmar's putative additions.

204. See Guilhiermoz, *Essai sur l'origine la noblesse*, 52–57, 67–68, 72, n. 107; who is followed by Reuter, "Plunder and Tribute," 82–83.

205. The best discussion of "vassals" in the present context remains Odegaard, *Vassi and Fideles*, 3–50. However, because Odegaard concentrates on the capitularies and on military service he omits much about "vassals" who are merely "commended men" of low status but who are not in the military household of a magnate or the king. Concerning such men see Susan Reynolds, *Fiefs and Vassals: The Medieval Evidence Reinterpreted* (Oxford, 1994), 84–85.

206. Odegaard, *Vassi and Fideles*, 14–50.

207. See J. M. Wallace-Hadrill, *The Long-Haired Kings and Other Studies in Frankish History* (London, 1962), 31; Bachrach, *Merovingian Military Organization*, 12, with the sources cited there; and Rouche, *L'Aquitaine*, 355–356.

208. Rouche, *L'Aquitaine*, 357–358.

209. *V. Sev. Alex.*, 58, 4–5. See the discussion by Bachrach, "Grand Strategy," 56; and cf. MacMullen, *Soldier and Civilian*, 13.

210. A helpful introduction is provided with very useful bibliography by Dafydd Walters, "From Benedict to Gratian: The Code in Medieval Ecclesiastical Authors," in *The Theodosian Code*, ed. Jill Harries and Ian Wood (Ithaca, N.Y., 1993), 200–216; and of course F. L. Ganshof, *Recherches sur les capitulaires* (Paris, 1958).

211. For the Merovingian background, see the introductory observations by Ian Wood, "The Code in Merovingian Gaul," in *The Theodosian Code*, ed. Jill Harries and Ian Wood (Ithaca, N.Y., 1993), 159–177; and McKitterick, *The Carolingians and the Written Word*, 48–55, for a list of Carolingian legal manuscripts.

212. Reynolds, *Fiefs and Vassals*, 92–100, who nevertheless adds the important caution that not all and likely not even most *beneficia* were given for military purposes. See, in particular reference to Charles Martel and the early Carolingians, the recent study by Wolfram, "Karl Martell und das fränkische Lehenswesen," 61–78.

213. An excellent treatment of the early history of these debates is provided in Carl Stephenson, "The Origin and Significance of Feudalism," *American Historical Review*, 46 (1941), 788–812 and reprinted in Carl Stephenson, *Medieval Institutions: Selected Essays*, ed. Bryce D. Lyon (Ithaca, N.Y., 1954), 205–233. Reynolds, *Fiefs and Vassals*, 1–114, explains the problems at issue very clearly.

214. Regarding the background on *beneficium*, see two works by Paul Roth, *Geschichte des Beneficialwesens von den ältesten Zeiten bis ins zehnte Jahrhundert* (Erlangen, 1850); and *Feudalität und Unterthanverband* (Weimar, 1863); Krawinkel, *Untersuchungen zum fränkischen Benefizialrecht*; Emile Lesne, "Les diverses acceptions du terme 'beneficium' du VIIIe au IXe siècle," *Revue historique de droit français et étranger*, ser. 4, 3 (1924), 5–56; and Reynolds, *Fiefs and Vassals*, 78–79, 84–105.

215. Lesne, "Les diverses acceptions," 5–56, who is followed by both Ganshof, *Feudalism*, 9–12; and Reynolds, *Fiefs and Vassals*, 93–104, although with very different emphases.

216. Odegaard, *Vassi and Fideles*, 14–50; and Reynolds, *Fiefs and Vassals*, 22, 84–88, 94–97, 99–105. In the Carolingian context it seems clear that all free men, in principle, were the king's *fideles*, i.e., his loyal subjects, but not all royal subjects held *beneficia* from the king or from some other person at the monarch's direction. Cf. Ganshof, *Feudalism*, 21–26, who envisions the vast spread of vassalage more or less at royal direction during the latter part of the reign of Charlemagne.

217. Reynolds, *Fiefs and Vassals*, 33, for the general point and the discussion of the men at court above. See Bachrach, "Charles Martel," 70–72; and followed by both Nelson, "The Church's Military Service," passim; and Reuter, "Plunder and Tribute," 82–83. See also Wolfram, "Karl Martell und das fränkische Lehenswesen," 61–78.

Ganshof, *Feudalism*, 24, would seem to emphasize that a considerable number of *vassi* who served the king at the court did not possess military lands. His observation, "By the end of Charlemagne's reign it seems likely that a vassal who had carried out his services satisfactorily might normally hope sooner or later to receive a benefice in some part by the empire," is an appropriately cautious statement but remains undocumented.

N.b. *Cap. reg. Fr.*, no. 20, ch. 9, deals with royal *vassi* who did not possess *beneficii*, but among other services, were required to carry out paramilitary operations for peacekeeping purposes. The "superiores vassos" established "infra palatio," who are discussed by the author of the *Annales Laureshamenses*, *an.* 802, could well have been royal *vassi* without benefices as suggested by Ganshof, *Feudalism*, 36. However, these *Annales* are concerned in this entry not with the absolute poverty of these *vassi* but their poverty relative to the wealth of the great lay and ecclesiastical officials who served the royal court.

218. Bloch, *Feudal Society*, 155–157; and Odegaard, *Vassi and Fideles*, 16. In this context, it is noteworthy that in the Western tradition regular soldiers, in general, and especially in the Roman empire, were never very highly regarded in social terms. By and large, soldiers came from the lower strata of society. Campbell, *The Emperor and the Roman Army*, 9–10, 176–181, 207–208.

219. By the mid-ninth century a strong hereditary component tended to become infused into the process of holding military lands. For example, even those ecclesiastics

such as Hincmar of Rheims (*Ad Carolum Calvum*, col. 1050), who worked diligently to protect Church resources, recognized that a bishop who had given a *beneficium* to a soldier (*miles*) was bound to give it in turn to that soldier's sons if they were fit for military service. One can note here a similarity to the edict of Alexander Severus discussed above. Note the various interpretations by Lesne, "Les diverses acceptions," 5–56; Ganshof, *Feudalism*, 9–12; and Reynolds, *Fiefs and Vassals*, 93–104.

220. See Bachrach, "Military Lands," forthcoming

221. Ganshof, *Feudalism*, 40–49; and Reynolds, *Fiefs and Vassals*, 78–79, 89–91.

222. Bachrach, "Quelques observations sur la composition et les caractéristiques des armées de Clovis," 1659–697. Cf. Murray, *Germanic Kinship*, 177–215, with regard to the background.

223. The Carolingian rulers and, indeed, their subjects would seem almost to have been obsessed with taking inventories and making lists. Of course, this was a Roman imperial tradition that the Merovingians did not ignore. Of fundamental importance to this view is the work of McKitterick, *The Carolingians and the Written Word*. See, as well, Davis, "Domesday Book: Continental Parallels," 15–39; and Percival, "The Precursors of Domesday," 5–27, whose late eleventh-century English focus does not permit the reader fully to appreciate Carolingian administrative practice. Durliat, *Les finances publiques*, passim, develops the evidence in its proper context. Cf. F. L. Ganshof, "Charlemagne et l'usage de l'écrit en matière administrative," *Le Moyen Age*, 57 (1951), 1–25; and translated as "The Use of the Written Word in Charlemagne's Administration," in F. L. Ganshof, *The Carolingians and the Frankish Monarchy*, trans. Janet Sondheimer (London, 1971), 125–142, who is far too pessimistic, consistent with his immediate postwar discouragement regarding the fate of Europe.

224. Regarding Charles the Bald, see the data amassed regarding the administrative structures required to collect the Danegeld by Einar Joranson, *The Danegeld in France* (Rock Island, Ill., 1923); concerning the drawing up of lists, see Simon Coupland, "Charles the Bald and the Defence of the West Frankish Kingdom Against the Viking Invasions: 840–877" (Ph.D. diss., Cambridge, 1987), 96, with the relevant literature.

225. See Ganshof, "Benefice and Vassalage," 151–153.

226. Ganshof, *Feudalism*, 37.

227. This is the inference to be drawn from the observations by Ganshof, *Feudalism*, 24, who as the strongest proponent of the notion that beneficed vassals became common does not see it having a rapid development under the early Carolingians.

228. Ganshof, *Feudalism*, 24, observes: "By the end of Charlemagne's reign it seems likely that a vassal who had carried out his services satisfactorily might normally hope sooner or later to receive a benefice in some part of the empire."

229. MacMullen, *Soldier and Civilian*, 103–113, for the Romans and for the continued military role played by the *vassi casati*, see Ganshof, "Charlemagne's Army," 60. The analogy is mine.

230. Ganshof, "Benefice and Vassalage," 151–152, regarding wealthy *vassi casati*; and also Ganshof, *Feudalism*, 37, concerning the order of magnitude of military lands. He is followed by J. F. Verbruggen, "L'armée et la stratégie de Charlemagne," in *Karl der Grosse*, I, ed. W. Braunfels (Düsseldorf, 1965), 422.

231. Ganshof, "Benefice and Vassalage," 154–155, concerning the implantation of vassals in newly acquired territories.

232. Ganshof, *Feudalism*, 63–64; cf. Reuter, "The End of Carolingian Military Ex-

pansion," 394, who does not seem to appreciate the full breadth of Carolingian military thinking in this matter because of his focus on "defensive" strategy.

233. Astronomer, *V. Hludowici*, ch. 19. N.b. the author writes in order to condemn such practice.

234. *Waltharius*, ed. Strecker, lines 132–139. Actually, this is recorded as direct discourse between the queen and her husband as she advises him regarding the words to speak in the above-quoted manner to Walter. As will be seen below, the king acts as his wife suggests. Cf. line 138: "Amplificabo quidem donis te rure domique," with Hermoldus Nigellus, *In honorem Hludovici*, I. 179: "Si sibi rura, domus seu praedia multa darentur."

235. *Waltharius*, ed. Strecker, lines 149–155.

236. *Waltharius*, ed. Strecker, lines 158–164.

237. The first notice of *escariti*, i.e., members of the *scara*, would seem to be datable to the early seventh century, i.e., 610. See Fredegar, *Chron.*, bk. IV, ch. 37; and the discussion by Bachrach, *Merovingian Military Organization*, 81, 87–88, 109. The assertion by Verbruggen, "L'armée et la stratégie," 421, that the *scara* appeared toward the middle of the eighth century, is incorrect. He seems to have recognized this error but without grasping the manner in which it undermines the specifics of his argument for rapid cavalry development toward the mid-eighth century. See J. F. Verbruggen, "L'art militaire dans l'empire carolingien (714–1000)," *Revue belge d'histoire militaire*, 25 (1980), 292–295; and J. F. Verbruggen, *The Art of Warfare in Western Europe During the Middle Ages: From the Eighth Century to 1340*, 2nd ed. revised and enlarged (Woodbridge, 1997), 14, where he calls attention to Fredegar, *Chron.*, bk. IV, ch. 74, concerning the use of the term *scara* in 631. For references to the earlier literature and its many controversies see Delbrück, *The Art of War*, III, 51–54.

238. Verbruggen, *The Art of Warfare*, 20–21, would seem to believe that *scara* is a technical term, but as will be seen below this has not been established.

239. Verbruggen, "L'art militaire," 292–294; and for additional terms or at least variant orthography, see Ganshof, "Charlemagne's Army," 64.

240. For the general picture, see Ganshof, "Charlemagne's Army," 64; and Verbruggen, "L'armée et la stratégie," 421, where it is argued that *scara* is a technical term that is used as a replacement for *trustis*. He argues that the *scara* was, in fact, another name for the royal military household composed of cavalry troops. Here he follows Delbrück, *The Art of War*, III, 25, but see 52–54, for a variety of other interpretations.

241. Fredegar Cont., ch. 52; and perhaps *Annales regni Francorum*, *an.* 773, and likely *an.* 774; see Delbrück, *The Art of War*, III, 52–54.

242. *Annales regni Francorum*, *an.* 766. See the discussion by Verbruggen, "L'armée et la stratégie," 421; and Delbrück, *The Art of War*, III, 52.

243. *Annales regni Francorum*, *an.* 776. See the discussion by Verbruggen, "L'armée et la stratégie," 421; and Delbrück, *The Art of War*, III, 52.

244. Adalhard, *De ordine palatii*, ch. V (28).

245. Delbrück, *The Art of War*, III, 25, seems to lean in the direction of characterizing the *scara* as either the royal military household or more likely parts of it at a given time. Verbruggen, *The Art of Warfare*, 20–21, seems to be less nuanced.

246. See the material collected by Delbrück, *The Art of War*, III, 52–53.

247. *Annales q.d. Einhardi*, ann. 766, 776.

248. *Annales mettenses priores*, *an.* 774.

249. In principle, the assertion by Verbruggen, *The Art of Warfare*, 13–14, that ver-

nacular and/or vernacular-based, i.e., Latinized vernacular words, have greater precision than traditional Latin terminology must be treated with great caution, at least for the period under consideration here.

250. *Waltharius*, ed. Strecker, lines 170–180, and line 194, for evidence that this was a mounted force.

Chapter 3. Training and Equipment

1. J. Brian Campbell, "Teach Yourself How to Be a General," *Journal of Roman Studies*, 77 (1987), 13–29; and Bachrach, "Gregory of Tours as a Military Historian," forthcoming.

2. Regarding maxims concerning discipline and training see, for example, Frontinus, *Stragemata*, bk. IV, chs. 1 and 2; and for Vegetius, *De re Militari*, bk. I, ch. 1; bk. III, ch. 10, and passim. The basic introduction to Carolingian collections of books is Bischoff, *Manuscripts and Libraries*, 56–75. Also of importance in this context is Donald Bullough, "Roman Books and Carolingian *renovatio*," *Church History*, 14 (1977), and republished with corrections in Donald Bullough, *Carolingian Renewal: Sources and Heritage* (Manchester, 1991), 1–38. Concerning the availability of the *Stragemata* of Frontinus to the Carolingians see L. D. Reynolds, "Frontinus," *Texts and Transmission: A Survey of the Latin Classics*, ed. L. D. Reynolds and P. K. Marshall (Oxford, 1983), 171–172, and particularly for the use of this text by Paul the Deacon when he was at Charlemagne's court; and for the availability of the *De re Militari* of Vegetius, see Bischoff, *Manuscripts and Libraries*, 144.

3. Bachrach, "Gregory as a Military Historian," forthcoming.

4. The most obvious, if perhaps a rather extreme example, is the relationship between the type of armor used, particularly the hoplite shield, the phalanx formation, and the peculiar tactics developed for its deployment. For a good general view see Victor Hanson, *The Western Way of War: Infantry Battle in Classical Greece* (New York, 1989), 56–88; and in more specific detail J. K. Anderson, "Hoplite Weapons and Offensive Arms," in *Hoplites: The Classical Greek Battle Experience*, ed. Victor Hanson (London and New York, 1919), 15–37.

5. Cf. Elton, *Warfare in Roman Europe*, 128–154.

6. Elton, *Warfare in Roman Europe*, 94.

7. For the background, see Bachrach, *Merovingian Military Organization*, 3–17; and with a sharper focus Bachrach, "The Imperial Roots of Merovingian Military Organization," 25–31.

8. See Bachrach, *Merovingian Military Organization*, 36–128; and it is clear that *fragmenta* of ethnic identity were preserved in some military colonies during the second half of the sixth century; see Gregory, *Hist.*, bk. IV, ch. 18. However, it is arguable that Gregory, consistent with his *parti pris*, calls attention to these "ethnic" military colonies because they were oddities. Cf. Elton, *Warfare in Roman Europe*, 132–133, who appears to be unaware of previous scholarly work on these colonies.

9. Procopius, *BG*, xxv, 1 ff.; with the discussion by Bernard S. Bachrach, "Procopius, Agathias and the Frankish Military," *Speculum*, 45 (1970), 435–441, regarding Procopius' exaggerations. Isidore, *Etymol.*, XVIII, 6, 9, discusses the *francisca* and affirms that it takes its name from the Franks.

10. Regarding the ax, see, for example, the great attention given to it by Procopius, *BG*, xxv, 2–3. However it is not given attention by either Agathias, *Hist.*, bk. II, 5. 3–4; or Maurice, *Strategikon*, II. 3. 2. The basic work on the value of Procopius' and Agathias' descriptions in this context remains Bachrach, "Procopius, Agathias and the Frankish Military," 21–31. Cf. Elton, *Warfare in Roman Europe*, 60, who does not appear to grasp the fact that these accounts have fundamental differences in matters of significant detail.

11. Gregory, *Hist.*, bk. II, ch. 27; bk. VII, ch. 14, bk. VIII, ch. 19. See Bachrach, *Merovingian Military Organization*, 134, for discussion of these accounts.

12. Anon., *Liber Historiae Francorum*, ch. 10, where he is expanding upon Gregory, *Hist.*, bk. II, ch. 27, when he writes, "bipenne, quod est francisca," and later in the same chapter: "franciscam eius, quod est bipennis." Gerberding, *The Rise of the Carolingians*, 36–37, does not seem to grasp that the author of the *Liber Historiae Francorum*, cited above, was glossing the term because his readers did not know that the *francisca* was an ax.

13. Procopius, *BG*, xxv, 1ff.; with the discussion by Bachrach, "Procopius, Agathias and the Frankish Military," 435–441, concerning Procopius' exaggerations.

14. For background, see Simeon L. Guterman, *From Personal to Territorial Law: Aspects of the History and Structure of the Western Legal-Constitutional Tradition* (Metuchen, N.J., 1972); and Guterman, *The Principle of the Personality of Law*.

15. Regarding the generalized term "Frank" to describe the multi-ethnic armies of the *regnum Francorum*, see the discussion of the work of Procopius and Agathias by Bachrach, "Procopius, Agathias and the Frankish Military," 435–441, with the scholarly literature cited there.

16. R. C. Smail, *Crusading Warfare, 1097–1193*, 2nd ed. (Cambridge, 1995), simply adopts the Byzantine-Muslim convention of referring to the crusaders as "Franks." John France, *Victory in the East: A Military History of the First Crusade* (Cambridge, 1994), 18, discusses some of the problems visualized by contemporaries as a result of this rather undifferentiated classification.

17. Murray, *Early Germanic Kinship*, passim; Anderson, "Roman Military Colonies in Gaul," 125–144; and Bachrach, "Quelques observations sur la composition et les caractéristiques des armées de Clovis," 696–698.

18. See, for example, L. D. Reynolds, "Ammianus Marcellinus," *Texts and Transmission*, 6–8; M. Winterbottom, "Caesar," *Texts and Transmission*, 35–36; M. Winterbottom, "Curtius Rufus," *Texts and Transmission*, 35–36; L. D. Reynolds, "Eutropius," *Texts and Transmission*, 159–162; P. K. Marshall, "Florus," in *Texts and Transmission*, 164–166; L. D. Reynolds, "Justinus," in *Texts and Transmission*, 197–199; L. D. Reynolds, "Livy," in *Texts and Transmission*, 205–214; R. J. Tarrant, "Lucan," in *Texts and Transmission*, 215–218; L. D. Reynolds, "Sallust," in *Texts and Transmission*, 341–349; P. K. Marshall, "Scriptores Historiae Augustae," in *Texts and Transmission*, 354–356; M. D. Reeve, "Suetonius," in *Texts and Transmission*, 399–406; R. J. Tarrant, "Tacitus," in *Texts and Transmission*, 406–409; P. K. Marshall, "Valerius Maximus," in *Texts and Transmission*, 428–430; and L. D. Reynolds, "Velleius Paterculus," in *Texts and Transmission*, 431–433. In this context, the fate of the Latin translations of Josephus' works, which also were available, are much in need of detailed study. See the observations of M. L. W. Laistner, *Thought and Letters in Western Europe* (rev. ed., Ithaca, N.Y., 1956), 100, 161, 266, 304.

19. Rhabanus Maurus, *De Procinctu romanae Miliciae*, 450; and Rhabanus, *Ep.*

no. 57, for the epistolary prologue. See the brief discussion by Riché, *Écoles et enseigne-ment*, 302.

20. However, one may wonder whether government regulations concerning ar-mament, for example, were promulgated merely so that these royal commands could be ignored by the men for whom they were intended. Perhaps even more puzzling is the assumption by some scholars that handbooks were written and/or copied at the order of men of importance, who were graced with more than a modicum of intelligence and educational sophistication, so that these expensively produced parchments could be left unread until "discovered" by the epigones who peopled one or another later renaissance. For example, Alexander Murray, *Reason and Society in the Middle Ages* (corr. ed. Oxford, 1985), would seem to believe that the Western tradition—recognizing that one could learn from books to control the world in which one lived—died sometime during the later Roman empire and was only reborn during the so-called renaissance of the twelfth century.

21. Norbert Ohler, *Krieg und Frieden im Mittelalter* (Munich, 1997), 8–10.

22. Bernard S. Bachrach, "Anthropology and Early Medieval History," 3–10.

23. Vegetius, *De re Militari*, bk. I, ch. 18.

24. Rhabanus Maurus, *De Procinctu romanae Miliciae*, ch. VI.

25. Maurice, *Strategikon*, bk. I, ch. 1.

26. Maurice, *Strategikon*, bk. XI, ch. 3.

27. See below, Chapter 5, dealing with tactics.

28. Hanson, *The Western Way of War*, passim.

29. Vegetius, *De re Militari*, bk. I, ch. 11.

30. Rhabanus Maurus, *De Procinctu romanae Miliciae*, ch. IV.

31. White, *Medieval Technology and Social Change*, 149, for the medieval use of the quintain.

32. Rhabanus Maurus, *De Procinctu romanae Miliciae*, ch. IV.

33. Rhabanus Maurus, *De Procinctu romanae Miliciae*, ch. VI.

34. Rhabanus Maurus, *De Procinctu romanae Miliciae*, ch. XIII.

35. Anderson, "Hoplite Weapons and Offensive Arms," 27; and Hanson, *The West-ern Way of War*, 165.

36. Maurice, *Strategikon*, bk. XI, ch. 3.

37. Cf. the discussion by Hanson, *The Western Way of War*, 99.

38. Rhabanus Maurus, *De Procinctu romanae Miliciae*, ch. VI; and paraphrased in the *Recapitulatio*, ch. XIII. Rhabanus by and large follows Vegetius, *De re Militari*, bk. I, ch. 11, but omits any discussion of this type of practice for gladiators who obviously were of no interest to the Carolingians.

39. Rhabanus Maurus, *De Procinctu romanae Miliciae*, ch. VII. In the *Recapitula-tio*, ch. XIII, Rhabanus emphasizes the importance of thrusting and of arm strength.

40. It is of considerable importance that the Spartans, who were arguably the most effective of the Greeks in the use of the massed infantry phalanx, used the short stabbing sword. See the discussion by Anderson, "Hoplite Weapons and Offensive Arms," 27–28, where it is noted, as well, that drill was important.

41. Fredegar, *Chron.*, bk. IV, ch. 38.

42. Rhabanus, *De Procinctu romanae Miliciae*, ch. VI; and Vegetius, *De re Militari*, bk. I, ch. 9.

43. Rhabanus Maurus, *De Universo*, bk. XX, ch. 6.

44. Information concerning the weapons used by fighting men in the empire's Romano-German successor states is plentiful. However, much of this information, which comes from archaeological finds and from descriptions in Greek and Latin sources, is not easily interpreted. In addition, the vast corpus of archaeological material, in general, dates from considerably earlier than the eighth century which is under consideration here. For background see, for example, Karl Raddatz, "Die Bewaffnung der Germanen vom letzten Jahrhundert vor Chr. Geb. bis zur Völkerwanderungzeit," *Aufstieg und Niedergang der Römischen Welt*, 2. 12.3, ed. Hilda Temporini (Berlin, 1985), 281–361; H. Böhme, *Germanische Grabfunde des 4 bis 5 Jahrhunderts zwischen unterer Elbe und Loire* (Munich, 1974); Wilfrid Menghin, *Das Schwert im frühen Mittelalter: chronologische-typologischen Gräbern des 5. bis 7. Jahrhunderts* (Stuttgart, 1983); but cf. Weidemann, *Kulturgeschichte*, vol. II, 258–265, who points to Gregory of Tours' inconsistent usage of various terms for long and short swords. She correctly makes the clear distinction, however, between the *spatha* as a long sword and *gladius* as a short sword.

45. The key work in the present context with regard to dating the archaeological evidence is the methodological study by Patrick Périn and R. Legoux, *La datation des tombes mérovingiennes. Historique, méthodes, applications* (Geneva, 1980). This work establishes something close to a sound working chronology to the end of the seventh century and into the early eighth century. For easy access to the general picture on the short sword from the archaeological evidence for the period, see Patrick Périn and Laure-Charlotte Feffer, *Les Francs*, 2 vols. (Paris, 1987), I, 93, 109. Of additional interest in a broader perspective, see D. A. Gale, "The Seax," *Weapons and Warfare in Anglo-Saxon England*, ed. Sonia Chadwick Hawkes (Oxford, 1989), 49–62.

46. The so-called long *sax*, which appears to be dominant during the eighth century, is in need of more detailed study. See, however, Frauke Stein, *Die Adelsgräber des achten Jahrhunderts in Deutschland*, 2 vols. (1967), Textband, 13, n. 11; and Tafelband, 105, 106, for the distribution of the long *sax*. For some useful illustrations of the long *sax*, see Menghin, *Das Schwert im frühen Mittelalter*, cat. nos. 140, 144, 147, which provide exemplars in a range from 66 cm to 76 cm. Whether the short sword, i.e., the long *sax* in the present context, became obsolete during the ninth century remains controversial and is well beyond the scope of the present discussion. Coupland, "Carolingian Arms and Armor," 42–43, seems to be on the right track.

47. Anderson, "Hoplite Weapons and Offensive Arms," 27; and Hanson, *The Western Way of War*, 165.

48. Vegetius, *De re Militari*, bk. II, ch. 15.

49. Vegetius, *De re Militari*, bk. II, ch. 17.

50. Eduard Salin, *La civilisation mérovingienne*, 4 vols. (Paris, 1957), III, 58, believes that the long sword was used by the Carolingians as a weapon for foot soldiers. However, White, *Medieval Technology and Social Change*, p. 146, sees this as rather odd since Salin (90–94, 109) seems committed to the notion that these long swords were introduced into the West through Asian nomad horsemen. However, as seen above, Vegetius (*De re Militari*, bk. I, ch. 15), makes clear that Roman *ordinarii*, who fought on foot in a loose formation, used the *spatha*.

51. See Anderson, "Hoplite Weapons and Offensive Arms," 29–30, who explores the Greek evidence.

52. W. K. Pritchett, *The Greek State at War*, 4 vols. (Berkeley and Los Angeles, 1971–85), II, 208–231.

53. Cf. Anderson, "Hoplite Weapons and Offensive Arms," 29–30, who while recognizing the connections with dance among the Greeks doubts its value. See also Pritchett, *The Greek State at War*, II, 213–219, who examines the role of gymnastics in training.

54. For the debate concerning the training required for effective operation within the phalanx see Hanson, *The Western Way of War*, 31–32; and Anderson, "Hoplite Weapons and Offensive Arms," 30–31, where the high levels of Spartan training are contrasted with putative Athenian "amateurism." The rhetorical topos, which one also finds in Victorian England, lauds the gifted amateur at the expense of so-called professionals. See also Pritchett, *The Greek State at War*, II, 210–212, who sees the topos of amateurism at work among the Athenians. The Romans, by contrast, saw training, drill, hard work, and dedication as positive values, and these values are in evidence among the Carolingians as well. This will be seen, below, in the discussions of the handbooks by Vegetius and Rhabanus.

55. Rhabanus Maurus, *De Procinctu romanae Miliciae*, ch. VI.

56. The estimates of the diameter of these round shields by Coupland, "Carolingian Arms and Armor," 36, which are based upon a careful comparison of numerous manuscript illustrations, are likely to be of the correct order of magnitude. However, his apparent anxiety regarding the archaeological evidence for smaller round shields (37) discussed by Stein, *Adelsgräber des achten Jahrhunderts*, Textband, 19, 77, is probably misplaced. These smaller shields, especially those in the 50 cm range, were very likely carried by mounted troops. See below for further discussion regarding the shields used by horsemen.

In regard to the archaeological evidence, the material survivals are not sufficient to permit statistically significant conclusions. In addition, even though it is useful to think of the general uniformity of government-issue shields, *scuta publica*, the variation in the size and strength of individual soldiers or militia men can easily account for a difference of five or ten centimeters in the diameter of any particular shield. Further, most of our archaeological information regarding shields comes from "reconstructions" based upon more or less fragmentary material. Thus, assertions regarding the diameter of any particular shield must be regarded as approximate. Finally, it may be suggested that from the perspective of *Sachkritik*, our knowledge of what role the shield is thought to have played in the combat techniques used by soldiers in various formations establishes limits for the size of the shield. When these estimates are considered in relation to the size and strength of the men involved in the above-mentioned type of combat, Coupland's hypothesis regarding the dimensions of the early Carolingian round shield become more than plausible.

57. Rhabanus Maurus, *De Procinctu romanae Miliciae*, ch. VI.

58. Vegetius, *De re Militari*, bk. I, ch. 11. Elton, *Warfare in Roman Europe*, 115, discusses long oval shields used by the Romans. See, as well, the material evidence provided by David Nicolle, *Medieval Warfare Source Book* (London, 1995), 20, 21, 40.

59. It would be far-fetched to suggest that Rhabanus was influenced here by Tacitus, *Germania*, 43.6.4, who describes the Gothones, Rugii, and Lemovii as using round shields (*rotunda scuta*) and short swords (*breves gladii*). However, *Germania* was known at Fulda in the ninth century, where Rhabanus was abbot, and perhaps earlier. See M. Winterbottom, "Tacitus," in *Texts and Transmission*, 410; and Bischoff, *Manuscripts and Libraries*, 150. However, there is no tradition during the early Middle Ages of treating any

of the three above-mentioned "Germanic" peoples as being related either to the Carolingians or to the Franks.

60. Vegetius, *De re Militari*, bk. I, chs. 4, 20; bk. II, chs. 12, 15–17; bk. III, chs. 4, 8, 14, always uses the word *scutum*, without modification.

61. H. Russell Robinson, *The Armour of Imperial Rome* (New York, 1975), for examples from the Lyons region (pl. 200); and from the Antonine Wall (pl. 201) about which Rhabanus could possibly have learned from his teacher Alcuin or one of the many other Englishmen who frequented the Carolingian royal court and provincial schools. For additional exemplars from the reliefs in the forum of Trajan and from the column of Trajan, see pls. 238, 239. See also pls. 463–466, 468, 469, 476, 477, 495.

62. Robinson, *The Armour of Imperial Rome*, pls. 196, 197, 198, 199. Of particular interest in the present context is pl. 196, where a foot soldier thrusting a short sword is shown carrying a rectangular shield.

63. Nicolle, *Medieval Warfare Source Book*, provides a good photograph (40) of these shields from the Vatican Virgil MS 3225, fol. 73v.

64. For the mosaics at Santa Maria Maggiore, see the photograph in Nicolle, *Medieval Warfare Source Book*, 19. Information from late Roman monuments of various types influenced Carolingian artists in many ways, and much work needs to be done in this area. See, for example, Bachrach, "A Picture of Avar-Frankish Warfare," 5–27; and Coupland, "Carolingian Arms and Armor," 33, 40–41, 43–44.

65. For the long shield see, for example, Livy, *Hist.*, XXXVIII.17.3, which seems to have been available at Mainz, Tours, and the royal court. See L. D. Reynolds, "Livy," *Texts and Transmission*, 208–213; and Bischoff, *Manuscripts and Libraries*, 140–141. It seems unlikely that Rhabanus had access to Apuleius, *Met.*, 10.1.8, regarding shields. See L. D. Reynolds, "Apuleius," *Texts and Transmission*, 15–16.

66. For Carolingian foot soldiers using the round shield see Coupland, "Carolingian Arms and Armor," 35–38, who provides references to a plethora of manuscript illustrations to sustain his point. However, his observation (36) "Unfortunately, written sources give no indication as to the . . . shape, or construction of Frankish shield" is incorrect. The observation by Rhabanus under discussion here confirms the information found in the manuscript illustrations.

67. Rhabanus Maurus, *De Procinctu romanae Miliciae*, ch. VI; and Vegetius, *De re Militari*, bk. I, ch. 11.

68. Rhabanus Maurus, *De Procinctu romanae Miliciae*, ch. VI; and Vegetius, *De re Militari*, bk. I, ch. 11.

69. For the diversity of imperial practice during the later empire, see S. T. James, "The *fabricae*: State Arms Factories of the Later Roman Empire," in *Military Equipment and the Identity of Roman Soldiers: Proceedings of the Fourth Roman Military Equipment Conference, 1986*, ed. J. C. Coulston (Oxford, 1988), 257–331.

70. Concerning the *Notitia Dignitatum* see M. D. Reeve, "*Notitia Dignitatum*," in *Texts and Transmission*, 253–257, with the literature cited there.

71. Coupland, "Carolingian Arms and Armor," 39, 44–45.

72. *Cap. reg. Fr.*, no. 32, ch. 45, for the counties, and ch. 62, for the *villae*.

73. The evidence here is fragmentary. Documentary evidence survives from the monasteries of Corbie and St. Riquier. However, perhaps more important in this regard is the Plan of St. Gall, which likely was a blueprint of sorts for the fitting out of all such workshops. See Walter Horn and E. Born, *The Plan of St. Gall*, 3 vols. (Berkeley, 1979), I,

347–348, II, 190–191; *Consuetudines Corbeienses*, ed. Semmler, 367; and Hariulf, *Chron.*, ed. Lot, appendix 7, 307, where an entire neighborhood, *vicus*, is devoted to the houses and workships of the *scutarii*.

74. See the discussion by Coupland, "Carolingian Arms and Armor," 47, n. 193.

75. Hincmar, *Ad Carolum Calvum*, cols. 1050D–1051A, in consideration of the history of this *donum*, classifies it as a tax for the support of the army. *Cap. reg. Fr.*, no. 217, ch. 4, uses the phrase "dona annualia aut tributa publica." For the background on this controversial issue see Lesne, *Histoire de la propriété ecclésiastique en France*, vol. 2.2, 411–419; and Waitz, *Deutsche Verfassungsgeschichte*, III, 591; IV, 107–110. This was an ancient tax that may well have had precedents in Roman imperial institutions. The earliest Carolingian example can be dated to 755, i.e., *Cap. reg. Fr.*, no. 14, ch. 6, where the term *munera* is used. The same term is also used in 766 by Fredegar Cont., ch. 48. However, while the example in *Formulae Bituricenses*, no. 18, is Carolingian it may have had earlier roots. In 755 the giving of *munera* at the assembly was already a well-established institution. Cf. Reuter, "Plunder and Tribute," 85, n. 56, who, while admitting that the Carolingian sources consider this "an ancient institution," believes that "it seems to have begun and ended with the Carolingians." Coupland, "Carolingian Arms and Armor," 36, confuses the *donum militum*, discussed above, with the *annua dona* or *dona annualia* that is under consideration here. However, it is possible and perhaps likely that the *annua dona* given to the king by the magnates was, in turn, used by the court to provide the *donum militum* to members of the military branch of royal *obsequium*.

76. See, for example, Stein, *Adalsgräber des achten Jahrhunderts*, Textband, 9–18, 78–84. For comparative data from Anglo-Saxon England, see Heinrich Härke, "Early Saxon Weapon Burials: Frequencies, Distributions and Weapon Combinations," in *Weapons and Warfare in Anglo-Saxon England*, ed. Sonia Chadwick Hawkes (Oxford, 1989), 71–83.

77. Coupland, "Carolingian Arms and Armor," 47, takes this position but is at times too trusting of the connection. On the whole, however, he seems to be correct.

78. For a selection of examples see Peter Paulsen, *Alamanische Adelsgräber von Niederstotzingen* (Stuttgart, 1967), 104–105; Ingo Stork, "Friedhof und Dorf, Herrenhof und Adelsgräb," in *Die Alamannen* (Stuttgart, 1997), 307. I owe these references to Ms. Cornelia Paulus of the Institut für vor- und Frühgeschichte in Munich. See also Bruce-Mitford, *Sutton Hoo*, vol. 2, 272.

79. *Waltharius*, ed. Strecker, line 186, alludes to spear shafts made of cherry wood and of ash; line 771, cherry wood; 1288 mentions ash and possibly apple; and line 1295, ash. See the discussion by Althof, *Waltharii Poesis*, pp. 66, 225, 333, 334. Admittedly the poet borrows from Virgil and Ovid (*Waltharius*, ed. Strecker, 127, 138), but not always, and, as seen above, the use of hardwoods are required for spear shafts.

80. Agathias, *Hist.* bk. I, ch. 21. 4.

81. See, for example, Stein, *Adalsgräber des achten Jahrhunderts*, Textband, 9–18, 78–84; and Peter Paulsen, "Flugellanzen: Zum archäologischen Horizont der Wiener Sancta lancea," *Frümittelalterliche Studien*, 3 (1969), 289–312.

82. See, for example, Stein, *Adalsgräber des achten Jahrhunderts*, Textband, 16–18, 90–92; and Paulsen, "Flugellanzen," 289–312.

83. See the general observations by Coupland, "Carolingian Arms and Armor," 47.

84. Vegetius, *De re Militari*, bk. II, ch. 17. Vegetius recognized, in this context, that

once the line and order of the phalanx had been disestablished, the enemy could counter-attack and take advantage of the situation even without having executed a feigned retreat.

85. Rhabanus Maurus, *De Procinctu romanae Miliciae*, ch. XII.

86. See, for example, Stein, *Adalsgräber des achten Jahrhunderts*, Textband, 16–18; and Paulsen, "Flugellanzen," 290–299, where these spear points are described in his catalogue. I am skeptical of the notion that the "winged" spear developed in the course of the eighth century if by this is meant a spear with a heavy cross piece. J. Aymard, *Essai sur les chasses romaines des origines à la fin du siècle des Antonins* (Paris, 1951), pls. xxii, xxiv; and J. K. Anderson, *Hunting in the Ancient World* (Berkeley, 1985), pl. 46, provide examples of much earlier spears with a heavy balk. See below for further discussion of the spear with a cross piece used by mounted troops but note the frequently discussed grave no. 1782 from Krefeld-Gellep with a coin of Anastaius (491–518) and a "winged" spear. For access to this exemplum, see Menghin, *Das Schwert im frühen Mittelalter*, cat. no. 84.

87. Coupland, "Carolingian Arms and Armor," 47, adduces evidence that suggests the Franks were unused to using light throwing spears. This information concerns the period toward the mid-ninth century. However, he undermines his own conclusion by noting that references to Franks throwing spears during the later ninth century are confined to descriptions of sieges. This surely permits the inference that through the ninth century, the Carolingians retained their light spears for throwing purposes, as the evidence discussed above suggests, and used heavy spears for thrusting in hand-to-hand combat. In addition, to make throwing the spear practical it was necessary, as will be seen below, to train with a heavier spear.

88. Aymard, *Essai sur les chasses*, pls. xxii, xxiv; Anderson, *Hunting in the Ancient World*, pl. 46; and Jörg Jarnut, "Die frümittelalterliche Jagd unter Rechts-und Sozialgeschichtlichen Aspekten," *Settimane di studio del Centro Italiano di studi sull'alto medioevo*, 31 (Spoleto, 1985), 746–798, who focuses on neither the techniques of hunting nor technology but does affirm the often made connection between hunting and military training.

89. John Keegan, *The Face of Battle* (New York, 1976), 96, sums up the general view quite accurately.

90. Regarding the mounted troops of the Ostrogothic kingdom, see Herwig Wolfram, *History of the Goths*, trans. Thomas J. Dunlap (Berkeley, 1979), 302–305; and White, *Medieval Technology and Social Change*, 9–10, who provides access to the relevant literature concerning the debate on the importance of mounted troops in the armed forces of the Visigothic kingdom. For Lombard heavily armed mounted troops (Procopius, *BG*, bk. VII, ch. xxxix, 20) which also were well trained to fight on foot (Procopius, *BG*. bk. VIII, ch. xxxi, 5); but note Bachrach, *Merovingian Military Organization*, 39–40, where, for example, the armies of the *regnum Francorum* were superior to those of their southern neighbors on the battlefield.

91. Hanson, *The Western Way of War*, p. 146, recognizes that most spears were broken at first impact. Cf. John Lazenby, "The Killing Zone," in *Hoplites: The Classical Greek Battle Experience*, ed. Victor Hanson (London and New York, 1991), 96–97, who believes that the spear lasted longer in the fight but ultimately the hoplite generally found it necessary to resort to the use of his sword. Victor Hanson, "Hoplite Technology in Phalanx Battle," in *Hoplites*, 72–74, continues to recognize that spear shafts were fragile

but now argues that the butt spike, obviously not present on Carolingian spears, made the broken shaft a formidable though seriously reduced weapon. Keegan, *The Face of Battle*, 100–101, comments intelligently on the difficulties of wielding a spear in very close quarters.

92. Anon., *Chron.*, 362, mentions only that Charles' men cut down the Arabs by the sword, i.e., "gladio enecant" and notes as well that after the battle they sheathed their swords. These are the only two mentions of Carolingian weapons, and the latter might be thought perhaps to be a synecdoche.

93. Delbrück, *The Art of War*, I, 23.

94. *Waltharius*, ed. Strecker, lines 1429–1430.

95. Concerning the danger caused by gaps in the line see, for example, A. H. Jackson, "Hoplites and the Gods: The Dedication of Captured Arms and Armour," in *Hoplites*, 240; and Hanson, *The Western Way of War*, 160–170.

96. See Fredegar Cont., ch. 13, and the discussion below in Chapter 5.

97. Rhabanus Maurus, *De Procinctu romanae Miliciae*, ch. V.

98. Vegetius, *De re Militari*, bk. I, ch. 9.

99. *Waltharius*, ed. Strecker, line 44. Cf. Vergil, *Aen.*, 7, 698; 8, 595.

100. Delbrück, *The Art of War*, II, 636.

101. See, for example, *History of the Art of War*, I, 81–87.

102. *The Art of War*, III, 22–23.

103. Albert Koeniger, *Die Militärseelsorge der Karolingerzeit: Ihr Recht und ihre Praxis* (Munich, 1918), 56–57.

104. Fortunatus, *Pange lingua gloriosi*, ed. Bulst, 20; and *Ab ore prolatum*, ed. Dreves and Blume, 51.82–83 (78). See William Beare, *Latin Verse and European Song* (London, 1957), 15–19, regarding the Roman marching cadence. He is followed by Joseph Szövérffy, "Venantius Fortunatus and the Earliest Hymns to the Holy Cross," *Classical Folia*, 20 (1966), 110–112, 121–122.

105. Szövérffy, "Venantius Fortunatus and the Earliest Hymns to the Holy Cross," 110–112.

106. Cf. Keegan, *The Face of Battle*, 90, who was apparently acquainted with Delbrück's views on this matter and perhaps more important was not thinking about the rather high quality of the Roman roads.

107. Rhabanus Maurus, *De Procinctu romanae Miliciae*, ch. XIII.

108. *Annales Fuldenses*, an. 891, regarding the very lengthy history of misunderstanding the term *pedetemptim*. In this context (Bachrach, "Charles Martel," 51–53), the *Franci* were unaccustomed to advancing slowly over very rough terrain under a barrage of enemy missiles. There is no reason to suggest on the basis of this text that the *Franci* were unaccustomed to advancing in a "step by step" fashion. See also Timothy Reuter, *The Annals of Fulda* (Manchester, 1992), 122, n. 9. Indeed, the training described by Rhabanus, under discussion here, makes it clear that such discipline was not a chronicler's fantasy.

109. See the perceptive observations by Keegan, *The Face of Battle*, 90.

110. Rhabanus Maurus, *De Procinctu romanae Miliciae*, ch. V.

111. Rhabanus Maurus, *De Procinctu romanae Miliciae*, ch. V.

112. Rhabanus Maurus, *De Procinctu romanae Miliciae*, ch. XIII.

113. Rhabanus Maurus, *De Procinctu romanae Miliciae*, ch. V.

114. Rhabanus Maurus, *De Procinctu romanae Miliciae*, chs. VIII, IX, X, XI; and

cf. Vegetius. *De re Militari*, bk. I, chs. 14, 15, 16, 17. It is important to note that the *ango*, which had been the primary spear or, at the least, one of the more important throwing spears used during the era of the Merovingians, seems to have disappeared during the eighth century as noted by Werner, "Bewaffnung und Waffenbeigabe," 107. Cf. Coupland, "Carolingian Arms and Armor," 47, who argues that during the ninth century the throwing spear, which was no longer the *ango*, was used primarily in sieges "where close combat was excluded." Rhabanus, as will be seen below, does not limit the use of the throwing spear to siege warfare.

115. Rhabanus Maurus, *De Procinctu romanae Miliciae*, ch. VIII.

116. Rhabanus Maurus, *De Procinctu romanae Miliciae*, ch. VIII.

117. See, for example, *Waltharius*, ed. Strecker, lines 181–186, with immense debt to the language of Virgil. See *Waltharius*, ed. Strecker, pp. 126–127.

118. Rhabanus Maurus, *De Procinctu romanae Miliciae*, ch. VIII.

119. Rhabanus Maurus, *De Procinctu romanae Miliciae*, ch. IX.

120. Vegetius, *De re Militari*, bk. I, ch. 15.

121. Maurice, *Strategikon*, bk. I, ch. 2, deals with the training of militia men to be archers in the midst of a chapter concerning regular cavalry troops. This seems like an authorial interpolation in which Maurice was led to discuss militia men in an inappropriate context as a result of his estimation of the importance of the bow and arrow. Cf. John F. Haldon, *Recruitment and Conscription in the Byzantine Army, c. 550–950: A Study on the Origins of the Stratiotika Ktemata* (Vienna, 1979), 24, who sees these men as "recruits" and suggests in defense of this view the unlikely prospect that men might be recruited for the regular army up to the age of forty. It seems to me that the age limit is indicative of service in a militia of citizen-soldiers.

122. For regular army archers, see Maurice, *Strategikon*, bk. I, ch. 2.

123. Regarding the workshops, see A. H. M. Jones, *The Later Roman Empire, 284–602: A Social, Economic, and Administrative Survey*, 2 vols. (Norman, Okla., 1964), 834–836.

124. See the information conveniently assembled by Jim Bradbury, *The Medieval Archer* (New York, 1985), 160–164. However, there is a great deal more to learn about this topic.

125. Maurice, *Strategikon*, bk. I, ch. 2.

126. Maurice, *Strategikon*, bk. I, ch. 2; see note 121.

127. Rhabanus Maurus, *De Procinctu romanae Miliciae*, ch. VIII, where Rhabanus follows Vegetius, *De re Militari*, bk. I, ch. 15, very closely. However, in the *Recapitulatio*, ch. XIII, Rhabanus calls attention to the use of bundles of reeds or sticks as targets.

128. Rhabanus Maurus, *De Procinctu romanae Miliciae*, ch. VIII, where Rhabanus follows Vegetius, *De re Militari*, bk. I, ch. 15, very closely.

129. Far too little research has been done regarding both the production of arrows and their cost. See the useful introductory material provided by J. C. Coulston, "Roman Archery Equipment," in *The Production and Distribution of Roman Military Equipment*, ed. M. C. Bishop (Oxford, 1985), 264–270; and Coupland, "Carolingian Arms and Armor," 49–50.

130. Rhabanus Maurus, *De Procinctu romanae Miliciae*, ch. VIII, where Rhabanus follows Vegetius, *De re Militari*, bk. I, ch. 15, very closely. Cf. Maurice, *Strategikon*, bk. I, ch. 1; and bk. XII, pt. B, ch. 3, attacks the notion of carefully aimed archery and advocates that bowmen both on horseback and on foot are to shoot as rapidly as possible.

131. Rhabanus Maurus, *De Procinctu romanae Miliciae*, ch. VIII; and cf. Vegetius, *De re Militari*, bk. I, ch. 15.

132. Rhabanus Maurus, *De Procinctu romanae Miliciae*, ch. VIII. N.b. Vegetius, *De re Militari*, bk. I, ch. 15.

133. Rhabanus Maurus, *De Procinctu romanae Miliciae*, ch. X. N.b. Vegetius, *De re Militari*, bk. I, ch. 16.

134. For a detailed study of slingers as background to the discussion here, see W. B. Griffiths, "The Sling and Its Place in the Roman Imperial Army," in *Roman Military Equipment: The Sources of Evidence. Proceedings of the Fifth Roman Military Equipment Conference, 1988*, ed. C. van Driel-Murray (Oxford, 1989), 255–279.

135. Rhabanus Maurus, *De Procinctu romanae Miliciae*, ch. X. N.b. Vegetius, *De re Militari*, bk. I, ch. 16. See also M. Korfmann, "The Sling as a Weapon," *Scientific American*, 229 (1973), 35–42.

136. Rhabanus Maurus, *De Procinctu romanae Miliciae*, ch. X. Cf. Vegetius, *De re Militari*, bk. I, ch. 16. For the clublike weapon used during the later empire, see Vegetius' younger contemporary, the anonymous author of *De Rebus Bellicis*, ch. 10. In the *Recapitulatio*, ch. XIII, Rhabanus discusses practice in throwing one-pound stones. It is not clear, however, whether this is merely a strengthening exercise or actual practice with a rather crude weapon that can be used by men defending the walls of a fortification.

137. Rhabanus Maurus, *De Procinctu romanae Miliciae*, ch. XI. The Carolingians used a *fundibula*, but this term also could be applied to a much larger sling-type device for hurling stones, the sort of light artillery that was also an antipersonnel weapon. See *Cap. reg. Fr.*, I, no. 77, ch. 10.

138. Rhabanus Maurus, *De Procinctu romanae Miliciae*, chs. X, XI; and Vegetius, *De re Militari*, bk. I, chs. 16, 17.

139. Rhabanus, *De Procinctu romanae Miliciae* (*Recapitulatio*), ch. XIII.

140. It was possible for early medieval armies to build ramps of sorts to bring them closer to the top of the wall. See the discussion of a ramp, apparently built to the gates, in Bachrach, *Anatomy of a Little War*, 142–143; and also Josiah Ober, "Hoplites and Obstacles," in *Hoplites: The Classical Greek Battle Experience*, ed. Victor Hanson (London, 1991), 195, n. 25.

141. Vegetius, *De re Militari*, bk. IV, ch. 30.

142. Vegetius, *De re Militari*, bk. IV, ch. 30.

143. See the discussion by Wesley M. Stevens, *Bede's Scientific Achievement: Jarrow Lecture, 1985* (Jarrow, Durham, 1985); and "Cycles of Time: Calendrical and Astronomical Reckonings in Early Science," *Time and Process: Interdisciplinary Issues, The Study of Time VII*, ed. J. T. Fraser and Lewis Rowell (Madison, Conn., 1993), 27–51.

144. See the comparable problems faced in the ancient world as discussed in learned detail by Paul B. Kern, *Ancient Siege Warfare* (Bloomington, Ind., 1999).

145. *Essentials of Fire Fighting*, ed. Michael A. Wieder, Carol Smith, Cinthia Brackage, 3rd ed. (Stillwater, Okla., 1992), 241–289, makes clear that even under modern conditions with considerable technological advancement, working with ladders is a complicated matter that requires considerable training, especially under dangerous conditions.

146. Workers in the building trades, instead of using high ladders, used scaffolds of various types. See, for example, Bernard S. Bachrach, "The Cost of Castle-Building: The Case of the Tower at Langeais, 992–994," in *The Medieval Castle: Romance and Reality*, ed. K. Reyerson and F. Powe (Dubuque, Iowa, 1984), 46–62 (four plates), and the literature cited there.

147. See, for example, Jarnut, "Die frümittelalterliche Jagd," 746–798.

148. See, for example, Rhabanus Maurus, *De Procinctu romanae Miliciae*, chs. IV, XIV; who follows Vegetius, *De re Militari*, bk. I, chs. 2–7 and esp. ch. 7, with some modification.

149. Cf. the translation by W. P. A. Childs, *The City Reliefs of Lycia* (Princeton, 1978), 72–73, which I have followed at several points. See the excellent discussion of this topic by Ober, "Hoplites and Obstacles," 181–183, where Childs' translation is reproduced unmodified; and note as well the important article by Yvon Garlan, "De la poliorcétique dans les 'Phéniciennes' d'Euripide," *Revue des études anciennes*, 68 (1966), 264–277.

150. Vegetius, *De re Militari*, bk. IV, ch. 21.

151. Bernard S. Bachrach, and Rutherford Aris, "Military Technology and Garrison Organization: Some Observations on Anglo-Saxon Military Thinking in Light of the Burghal Hidage," *Technology and Culture*, 31 (1990), 7–9, 14–17.

152. Fredegar Cont., ch. 20.

153. Bachrach and Aris, "Military Technology," 6. For interpretation of Byzantine texts as contrasted to modern physical assessment, see W. McCleod, "The Range of the Ancient Bow," *Phoenix* 19 (1965), 1–14; and cf. A. D. H. Bivar, "Cavalry Equipment and Tactics on the Euphrates Frontier," *Dumbarton Oaks Papers*, 26 (1972), 283, with regard to Byzantine mounted archers ca. 600.

154. Rhabanus Maurus, *De Procinctu romanae Miliciae*, ch. XIII.

155. Rhabanus Maurus, *De Procinctu romanae Miliciae*, ch. XIII, probably exaggerates when he suggests that the sling had an effective range of 600 Roman feet. However, the transmission of the text may have been confused at this point where Rhabanus is also discussing the range of the bow and arrow, which he also puts at 600 Roman feet and which, as seen above, is highly credible. See, in general, Korfmann, "The Sling as a Weapon," 35–42; and Griffiths, "The Sling and Its Place in the Roman Imperial Army," 255–279.

156. Adrian Goldsworthy, *The Roman Army at War: 100 B.C.-A.D. 200* (Oxford, 1996), 196–201, points out that the Roman *pilum* was usually hurled at about 30 meters, but that longer ranges could be attained by men throwing down upon the enemy from the height of a wall. The modern javelin, which is scientifically designed to achieve maximum distance, can be thrown approximately 100 meters by world-class athletes, who are specifically trained in special techniques, following a 20-meter "run-up."

157. Abbo, *De bello Parisiaco*, bk. I, lines 267, 302.

158. Bachrach and Aris, "Military Technology," 6–7, 14–17.

159. Bachrach and Aris, "Military Technology," 14–17.

160. The Hebrew Bible, from which the Carolingians frequently accepted tuition, often emphasizes the vast numbers of soldiers required to storm the walls of a fortress city, but perhaps nowhere as eloquently as in Joel 2:7–9, where these operations are seen as a simile for a swarm of locusts. See the discussion with many examples by Kern, *Ancient Siege Warfare*, 49–51.

161. The best work is E. W. Marsden, *Greek and Roman Artillery: Historical Development* (Oxford, 1969); and *Greek and Roman Artillery: Technical Treatises* (Oxford, 1971). However, some useful ideas and suggestions are in W. Sackur, *Vitruv und die Poliorketiker. Vitruv und die christliche Antike. Bautechnisches aus der Literatur des Alterums* (Berlin, 1925); Yvon Garlan, *Recherches de poliorcétique grecque* (Athens, 1974); and Otto Lendle, *Text und Untersuchungen zum technischen Bereich der antiken Poliorketik* (Wiesbaden, 1983). Also, Kern, *Ancient Siege Warfare*, passim.

162. The basic work on continuity is in Gustav Köhler, *Die Entwickelung des Krieg-wesens und der Kriegführung in der Ritterzeit von Mitte des 11. Jahrhunderts bis zu den Hussitenkriegen*, 3 vols. (Breslau, 1886–1909), I, 140–221, which was accepted by Charles Oman, *A History of the Art of War in the Middle Ages*, 2 vols., 2nd ed. (London, 1924), I, 136–140. The notion of continuity is given fundamental support, but only in general terms, by Kalervo Huuri, *Zur Geschichte des mittelalterlichen Geschützwesens aus orientalischen Quellen* (Helsinki, 1941), 53–62.

Rudolph Schneider's claim (*Die Artillerie des Mittelalters* [Berlin, 1910], 1–26) that the period from ca. 500 to the later ninth century in the West was ostensibly devoid of artillery cannot be sustained, nor can his belief that the Vikings reintroduced artillery into the West later in the ninth century. Schneider was overreacting to some of Köhler's more exaggerated claims while holding the notion that the so-called barbarian invasions, which he calls the *Volkerwanderung*, destroyed any continuity from the later Roman empire to the Romano-German kingdoms of the early Middle Ages. In short, Schneider embraces an exaggerated version of the "Dark Ages." In this context, I find perplexing the apparent acceptance of some of Schneider's more extreme views regarding the absence of siege artillery in early medieval western Europe by R. Rogers, *Latin Siege Warfare in the Twelfth Century* (Oxford, 1992), 255–266. I agree, however, with Rogers' observation (269) that "Schneider's thesis for the total eclipse of torsion artillery . . . was not conclusively proven."

W. T. S. Tarver, "The Traction Trebuchet: A Reconstruction of an Early Medieval Siege Engine," *Technology and Culture*, 36 (1995), 137–143, is among those who would seem to see the "barbarians" as incapable of maintaining late Roman imperial torsion technology for no other reason than they were barbarians. Yet, for some reason, he believes that in the thirteenth century men once again learned how to build these machines, which putatively had not existed for almost a millennium, and used them as toys. He asserts (141) that "the ancient means of producing them [*onagri*] had perished" and contends (142) that "A Byzantine survival of some form of torsion artillery . . . is possible but highly unlikely." There is no evidence to support this assertion and *a priori* the Byzantines cannot be dismissed as barbarians.

Evidence for the use of siege artillery in the early Middle Ages is provided by Donald H. Hill, "Siege-Craft from the Sixth to the Tenth Century," in *De Rebus Bellicis. Part I, Aspects of the De Rebus Bellicis: Papers Presented to Professor E. A. Thompson*, ed. M. W. C. Hassal (Oxford, 1979), 111–117; and particularly important are the researches by Carroll Gillmore, "The Introduction of the Traction Trebuchet into the Latin West," *Viator*, 12 (1981), 1–8. A major problem with the critics of Köhler's position, indeed, even those who recognize the use of artillery during the early Middle Ages, is the implicit assumption that two separate types of artillery technology, i.e., the torsion type and the lever-trebuchet type, could not coexist. Thus, in terms of understanding the development and diffusion of technology in historical conditions, the notion of Huuri, *Zur Geschichte*, 56–65, that there was a period of transition during which both types were used, likely is correct.

163. Fredegar Cont., ch. 20. N.b. the difference in phraseology where the Continuator, while discussing the Carolingians' siege emplacements, indicates that Charles "castra ponit" at Avignon, and concerning Narbonne he says "castraque metatus," in addition to placing a "munitionem in girum."

164. Fredegar Cont., ch. 43.

165. The basic description of the modified machine is in Ammianus Marcellinus, *Hist.*, bk. XXIII, ch. 4, lines 4–7. Most of this history of the *onager* or *scorpio* is well summarized by Marsden, *Greek and Roman Artillery: Technical Treatises*, 249–265. The *onager*, which purportedly got its name, "wild ass," because of its vicious "kick," had to be mounted on an exceptionally resilient platform. N.b. the folk explanation for the kick of the *onager* would seem to have referred to the habit of the wild ass of kicking stones with his hind legs, an interesting example of how the "arcane" knowledge of the engineer — the kick being the equal and opposite reaction of the machine to the launching of its missile — is made comprehensible by the uneducated public. The laws of motion, of course, existed before Newton "discovered" them. The new name for this equipment may have been introduced when its design was fundamentally altered.

Additional observations of importance are to be found in J. G. Lendels, *Engineering in the Ancient World* (Berkeley, 1978), 132, regarding simplification that took place in the fourth century; and more generally Paul E. Chevedden, "Artillery in Late Antiquity: Prelude to the Middle Ages," in *The Medieval City Under Siege*, ed. Ivy A. Corfis and Michael Wolfe (Woodbridge, 1995), 135–138, who also accepts the view that the *onager* was simplified from a complicated two-armed machine to a one-armed machine that was easier to build, maintain, and operate.

166. Vegetius, *De re Militari*, bk. II, chs. 10, 25; bk. III, 14; bk. IV, chs. 8, 9, 22, 29, 44. Cf. Chevedden, "Artillery in Late Antiquity," 133, who does not seem to be aware that the modern text tradition of Vegetius' handbook rests upon a revision done at Constantinople in 450 A.D.

167. Much of the argument regarding the supposed disappearance of the *onager* rests upon a misreading of the later Roman texts and a failure to examine the early medieval texts carefully. For example, Schneider (*Artillerie*, 50–60), in addition to his belief in a technologically primitive Dark Ages, concluded that torsion artillery had to be transported to the siege already constructed. Really heavy artillery could not be transported by land due to the primitive nature of wagons. Thus, parts of a machine could be prefabricated and assembled on site. He also argued, however, that evidence for baggage trains in the early medieval sources is absent and thus they did not transport artillery. Since they did not transport artillery, he concluded that they could not have used torsion artillery.

Gregory, *Hist.*, bk. VII, ch. 35, who discusses a heavily encumbered military baggage train with *diversa impedimenta* loaded in their very slow-moving wagons (*plaustra*) and carrying battering rams and other *machinae*, refutes Schneider's argument regarding baggage trains. Thus, following Schneider's logic, torsion artillery could still have been available for sieges during the early Middle Ages since there were baggage trains to transport them. For a discussion of this baggage train mentioned by Gregory in its military context and the use of its *machinae*, see Bachrach, *Anatomy of a Little War*, 133–134. Even if Schneider had been correct regarding baggage trains, there was no reason why torsion artillery could not have been preserved for defensive purposes within already existing fortifications. Here, of course, Schneider relied upon his notion of a primitive Dark Ages to dismiss such a possibility in the West.

168. Vegetius, *De re Militari*, bk. II, ch. 25. I am unsure why Marsden, *Greek and Roman Artillery: Technical Treatises*, 264, thinks this vehicle is a four-wheeled wagon. Regarding the maximum carrying capacity of carts and wagons during the later Roman empire and the early Middle Ages, which in turn have controlled our discussion, above,

of the weight of the *onagri* in use, see Albert Leighton, *Transport and Communication in Early Medieval Europe, A.D. 500–1100* (Newton Charles, England, 1972), 70–87.

169. Vegetius, *De re Militari*, bk. IV, ch. 23.

170. Gregory, *Hist.*, bk. VII, ch. 35. See the discussion by Bachrach, *Anatomy of a Little War*, 132–136.

171. Paul, *Hist.*, bk. V, ch. 8, where Paul uses the term *petraria* or rock thrower; this machine appears to have been but one of the *diverses machinae* (bk. V, ch. 7.) deployed at the siege.

172. See *Mappae Clavicula*, MS P, ch. 58v, where the term *palestra* is used, an obvious archaic rendering of the Greek *bal[l]istra*, and MS S, ch. 42, where the term *petrariae* is employed rather than *onager*. By the eighth century in the West, the term *onager* had gone out of fashion. Thus, as seen above, Paul, *Hist.*, bk. V, ch. 8, and the author of MS S of the *Mappae Clavicula* used the new term for heavy artillery, see below, for light artillery, as well. By contrast, the author of MS P used the archaic *ballista*. For the use of the term *ballista* as archaic for a stone thrower, see Chevedden, "Artillery in Late Antiquity," 138–152.

173. It is not my intention here to trace the use of torsion artillery beyond the early Carolingian era. Tarver, "The Traction Trebuchet," 141, cites conclusive evidence that this technology was known during the thirteenth century in the West. Since Tarver believes that knowledge of this technology was lost in the West in the fourth century, however, he seems to suggest that it was rediscovered at some later date.

174. Vegetius, *De re Militari*, bk. III, 14, and bk. IV, ch. 8.

175. *Cap. reg. Fr.*, I, no. 77, ch. 10. Cf. Gillmore, "Traction Trebuchet," 6; and Hill, "Siege-Craft from the Sixth to the Tenth Century," 113.

176. *Cap. reg. Fr.*, I, no. 77, ch. 10.

177. *Cap. reg. Fr.*, I, no. 77, ch. 10. Cf. Hill, "Siege-Craft from the Sixth to the Tenth Century," 113.

178. Vegetius, *De re Militari*, bk. II, ch. 10; bk. III, ch. 24; bk. IV, chs. 9, 18, 22, 29. Procopius, *BG*, I, 21. 14–18. By and large Chevedden, "Artillery in Late Antiquity," 138–142, is on the right track.

179. Vegetius, *De re Militari*, bk. II, ch. 10; bk. III, ch. 24; bk. IV, chs. 9, 18, 29.

180. Vegetius, *De re Militari*, bk. II, ch. 25; bk. III, chs. 14, 24. Chevedden, "Artillery in Late Antiquity," 142, reviews the earlier material in detail.

181. Maurice, *Strategikon*, bk. XII.B, chs. 6, 18.

182. *Lex Visigothorum*, bk. VIII, 4. 23. Much more work is required not only on Visigothic weaponry but on their military in general.

183. Concerning the end of the Visigothic kingdom see the fascinating article by Luis A. García Moreno, "Covadonga, Realidad y Leyenda," *Boletín de la Real Academia de la Historia*, 194 (1996), 353–380, with the literature cited there.

184. *Mappae Clavicula*, MS P, 58.18, uses the Greek spelling *palestra* while MS S, 41.17, uses a variation of the Latin *balesta*.

185. Abbo, *De bello Parisiaco*, bk. I, line 87; bk. II, lines 242–243; and the discussion by Gillmore, "Traction Trebuchet," 5, n. 18. The siege technology described in great detail by Abbo requires additional study.

186. Abbo, *De bello Parisiaco*, bk. I, line 109, where the term *sagitta* is used. Due to the poetic form this is likely a shorthand for "sagittis ballistariis," i.e., *ballista*-spears. See the use of this terminology by Vegetius, *De re Militari*, bk. III, ch. 24.

187. Schneider, *Die Artillerie*, 1–26, believes that the Vikings introduced heavy ar-

tillery into the West. See also the comments by Bernard Rathgen, *Das Geschütz im Mittelalter* (Berlin, 1928), p. 601, on Viking artillery.

188. *Exeter Book*, ed. Gollancz, no. 17 (II, 106). See the discussion by Bradbury, *The Medieval Archer*, 18, who believes that the Anglo-Saxon text describes a *ballista*.

189. Nicole Pétrin, "Philological Notes on the Crossbow and Related Missile Weapons," *Greek, Roman and Byzantine Studies*, 33 (1992), 276–278, asserts in a purely arbitrary manner: "A bow with a fixed arrow-guide is not a crossbow; the distinguishing feature of the crossbow is not its crosspiece but its mechanical release." Pétrin (281–282, n.37), further insists that a crossbow must have a "stirrup, lock and trigger." Her argument in defense of this pronouncement is the belief that without these elements, "the Arabs *might not* have considered it a crossbow" (my italics).

There surely were a wide variety of so-called arrow guides, used throughout Asia and the Middle East. See the extensive bibliography compiled by Chevedden, "Artillery in Late Antiquity," 144, n. 58; and for the possibility that it was used by the Byzantines see David Nishimura, "Crossbows, Arrow Guides, and the *Solenarion*," *Byzantion*, 58 (1988), 422–435. There is no evidence for the use of arrow guides of the type discussed above in the West and little for the Byzantines. See, for example, Taxiarchis G. Kolias, *Byzantinische Waffen: Ein Beitrag zur byzantinischen Waffenkunde von den Affangen bis zur lateinischen Eroberung* (Vienna, 1988), 239–253.

190. The efforts of Bert S. Hall, "Crossbows and Crosswords," *Isis*, 64 (1973), 527–533, to see these as torsion devices have been rejected. See Duncan B. Campbell, "Auxiliary Artillery Revisited," *Bonner Jahrbücher*, 186 (1986), 131; and Chevedden, "Artillery in Late Antiquity," 142–143.

191. Vegetius, *De re Militari*, bk. IV, ch. 22. Chevedden, "Artillery in Late Antiquity," 141, and 147 n. 71 for a review of the literature.

192. Vegetius, *De re Militari*, bk. II, ch. 15; bk. IV, chs. 21, 22. Chevedden, "Artillery in Late Antiquity," p. 140, and n. 43, who reviews recent discussions of ammunition for shaft-missile weapons.

193. Marsden, *Greek and Roman Artillery: Historical Development*, 2.

194. Pétrin, "Philological Notes on the Crossbow," 285–286, and the literature cited there make this point well.

195. Chevedden, "Artillery in Late Antiquity," 145, is here referring only to surviving physical evidence. Additional material of value is in two studies by Egon Harmuth, "Die Armbrustbilder des Haimo von Auxerre," and "Ein arabische Armbrust," both in *Zeitschrift der Gesellschaft für historische Waffen- und Kostümkunde*, n.s. 12 (1970), 127–130; and n.s. 25 (1983), 141–144. See also Raphael Loewe, "Jewish Evidence for the History of the Crossbow," in *Les Juifs au regard de l'histoire: Mélanges en l'honneur de Bernhard Blumenkranz*, ed. Gilbert Dahan (Paris, 1985), 87–107.

196. See, for example, J. M. Gilbert, "Crossbows on Pictish Stones," *Proceedings of the Society of Antiquaries of Scotland*, 107 (1975–1976), 316–317; and A. M. MacGregor, "Two Antler Crossbow Nuts and Some Notes on the Early Development of the Crossbow," *Proceedings of the Society of Antiquaries of Scotland*, 107 (1975–1976), 317–321. The efforts of Strickland, "Military Technology and Conquest," 358, to cast doubt on the evidence is, at best, inconclusive.

197. The early military evidence is discussed by Campbell, "Auxiliary Artillery Revised," 117–132; and cf. Chevedden, "Artillery in Late Antiquity," 142–145, who reviews the early evidence and the scholarly controversies regarding it.

198. The most thorough examination of the evidence for the hunting crossbow is

Dietwulf Baatz, "Die römische Jagdarmbrust," *Archäeologisches Korrespondenzblatt*, 21 (1991), 283–299; but see, as well, Kolias, *Byzantinische Waffen* 240–241; and Egon Harmuth, *Die Armbrust* (Graz, 1975), 18–19. More recent studies are surveyed by Chevedden, "Artillery in Late Antiquity," 142–145. Curiously, Pétrin, "Philological Notes on the Crossbow," 277, wants to consider these hunting crossbows to be fixed arrow guides despite the fact that the mechanism that is used to hold the cord in place when the bow has been spanned is clearly visible in the Polignac exemplum (Emile Espérandieu, *Recueil général des bas-reliefs de Gaule romaine*, 2 [Paris, 1908], no. 1679, p. 442).

199. Loewe, "Jewish Evidence for the History of the Crossbow," 92, regarding Palestine in the third century A.D.

200. Loewe, "Jewish Evidence for the History of the Crossbow," 91–92, where mention is even found in the Babylonian Talmud using the loan word "balistri."

201. Maurice, *Strategikon*, bk. XIIb, ch. 5. See the discussion by John Haldon, "Solenarion—The Byzantine Crossbow," *Historical Journal of the University of Birmingham*, 12 (1970), 155–157; George Dennis, "Flies, Mice and the Byzantine Crossbow," *Byzantine and Modern Greek Studies*, 7 (1981), 1–5; and Kolias, *Byzantinische Waffen*, 239–253. Cf. Nishimura, "Crossbows, Arrow Guides, and the *Solenarion*," 422–435, who has tried to show that the Solenarion was an arrow guide. However, Chevedden, "Artillery in Late Antiquity," 147, and n. 71, has shown that Nishimura has misread the scholarly research and demonstrates that "The studies he [Nishimura] cites to support this interpretation, rather than advocating his view, are clearly opposed to it." Pétrin, "Philological Notes on the Crossbow," 287–291, has a more positive view of Nishimura's work and gets the eleventh-century Byzantine information terribly confused.

202. Strickland, "Military Technology and Conquest," 358 n. 20, correctly indicates: "The evidence for the use of the crossbow in ninth- and tenth-century France is helpfully collected and discussed in *Carmen* [Catherine Morton and Hope Munz, *Carmen de Hastingae Proelio of Guy Bishop of Amiens* (Oxford, 1972), 112–115]." Loewe, "Jewish Evidence for the History of the Crossbow," 87–107, affirms continuity, as well. Cf. Pétrin, "Philological Notes on the Crossbow," 265–291, whose treatment of the evidence is far too selective.

203. Joseph Needham, "China's Trebuchets, Manned and Counterweighted," in *On Pre-Modern Technology and Science: Studies in Honor of Lynn White, Jr.*, ed. Bert S. Hall and Delno C. West (Malibu, Calif., 1976), 108–109. See also for a general picture H. Franke, "Siege and Defense of Towns in Medieval China," ed. F. Kierman, *Chinese Ways in Warfare*, (Cambridge, Mass., 1974), 167–174. For additional literature, see Tarver, "The Traction Trebuchet," 144–145.

204. Huuri, *Zur Geschichte*, 127–192, developed the Arabic evidence in great detail. However, Donald Hill, "Trebuchets," *Viator*, 4 (1973), 100, and n. 4, provides an exact date by correcting Huuri's translation, and concludes that this technology was known to the Muslims by 660. The secondary literature is reviewed by Tarver, "The Traction Trebuchet," 144, n. 141.

205. Gillmore, "The Traction Trebuchet," 5–8, and esp. 27; and Tarver, "The Traction Trebuchet," 143–144, both satisfactorily rehearse the philological evidence, upon which, in my opinion, no fundamentally sound conclusions can be drawn about the nature of the machines being described.

206. Theophylact Simocatta, *Hist.*, ed. De Boor-Wirth, bk. II, ch. 16. 9–11, where a Byzantine soldier named Busas gives away the secret of building these siege machines to

the Avars in order to save his life. For details concerning these machines, see John, *Miracula S. Demetrii*, ed. Lemerle, XIV, 152–155. The two texts are effectively connected by Speros Vryonis, Jr., "The Evolution of Slavic Society and the Slavic Invasions in Greece: The First Major Slavic Attack on Thessaloniki, A.D. 597," *Hesperia*, 50 (1981), 378–390. Concerning Busas and the transfer of siege engine technology from the Byzantines to the Avars, see the discussion by Michael Whitby, *The Emperor Maurice and His Historian: Theophylact Simocatta on Persian and Balkan Warfare* (Oxford, 1988), 118–119, who doubts the historicity of this story. He denies neither that the Byzantines had the type of heavy catapults under discussion here nor that the Avars had them. Cf. Whitby, *The Emperor Maurice*, 118, who ventures the highly unlikely hypothesis that the nomad Avars brought this heavy artillery to the West. However controversial the interaction between the Byzantines and the Avars may be in this context, both had the lever-trebuchet before the end of the sixth century.

207. John, *Miracula S. Demetrii*, ed. Lemerle, XIV, 152–154. Paul Lemerle, *Les plus anciens recueils des miracles de Saint Démétrius*, 2 vols. (Paris 1979), II, 54, n. 65, and 96–103, provides an analysis and discussion of Avar siege operations. But cf. Vryonis, "The Evolution of Slavic Society," 384 n. 23, who expresses general reservations regarding Lemerle's commentary but fails to provide specifics.

208. Maurice, *Strategikon*, bk. 10, ch. 3.

209. Leighton, *Transport and Communication*, 70–87, discusses the capacity limits of both carts and wagons during this period. Since there is no archaeological evidence for the *onager* and descriptions found in the sources are insufficiently technical for making accurate reproductions, various scholars have experimented with a variety of models. These models were far too heavy to carry on a flatbed wagon of the early medieval era and thus cannot relate to the *onagri* that are discussed by Vegetius, *De re Militari*, bk. II, ch. 10; bk. III, ch. 14; bk. IV, chs. 8, 9, 22, 29. For an example of such huge models, see R. W. F. Payne-Gallwey, *The Crossbow, Mediaeval and Modern, Military and Sporting*, 2nd ed. (London, 1958), appendix, 18. Rogers, *Latin Siege Warfare*, 256, formulates his objection for the continued use of the *onager* on the notion put forth by Payne-Gallwey that this was a huge machine that required a massive baggage train. He appears to have been unaware of the capacity limitations of later Roman and early medieval vehicles. Thus, if the *onager* was hauled on a cart, as Vegetius makes clear, or even on a wagon, it could not have been the heavy machine that Payne-Gallwey and Rogers believe that it was.

210. Gillmore, "Traction Trebuchet," 5–6; and on some details cf. Huuri, *Zur Geschichte*, 55–56, 84. *Annales regnum Francorum, an.* 776, speak of *petraria*.

211. See Bachrach, "Military Organization in Aquitaine," 28; and Gillmore, "Traction Trebuchet," 6. N.b. Astronomer, *V. Hludowici*, ch. 16, talks about the *mangones* used by the Carolingian army at the siege of Tortosa in 808–809.

212. *Annales regnum Francorum, an.* 776, speak of *petraria*. Cf. Gillmore, "Traction Trebuchet," 5–6.

213. Greek Fire, a petroleum-based compound that burned on the water, was used by Byzantine naval forces to great effect. The basic work remains J. R. Partington, *A History of Greek Fire and Gunpowder* (Cambridge, 1960).

214. Vryonis, "The Evolution of Slavic Society," 378–390, summarizes the evidence discussed above in an effective manner.

215. *Annales regnum Francorum, an.* 776, refers to the Saxons using *petraria*. The author of the *Annales* sees these stone throwers as a type of *machina*. The assertion by

Schneider, *Die Artillerie*, 23, that this reference to *petraria* is an interpolation is without merit.

216. See the discussion by Gillmore, "Traction Trebuchet," 2, 4.

217. Fredegar Cont., ch. 43, regarding the breaching of the walls of Bourges. Concerning models and simulations, heavier machines could throw heavier loads even further. See, for example, the experiments discussed by Payne-Gallwey, *The Crossbow*, app., 11; E. Schramm, *Die antiken Geschütze der Saalburg* (Berlin, 1918), 30; H. Diels, *Antike Technik*, 3rd ed. (Leipzig, 1924), 99; and Marsden, *Greek and Roman Artillery: Technical Treatises*, 254–255, for various reconstructions. The calculations made *infra* are estimations based upon these experiments. One of the virtues of the *onager* is that it could be adjusted so that greater distance, within limits, could be attained with lighter missiles, and heavier loads, within limits, could be hurled over shorter distances. See Vegetius, *De re Militari*, bk. IV, chs. 8, 22. The range of the machine could be altered easily by adjusting the length of the sling which held the load to be launched. Marsden, *Greek and Roman Artillery: Technical Treatises*, 263.

218. Fredegar Cont., ch. 46. We know that at best Waiofar only damaged the walls of these fortifications. See regarding this matter, Bernard S. Bachrach, "Early Medieval Fortifications in the 'West' of France: A Technical Vocabulary," *Technology and Culture*, 16 (1975), 531–569.

219. John, *Miracula S. Demetrii*, ed. Lemerle, XIV, 148–154. Vyronis, "The Evolution of Slavic Society," 378–390.

220. John, *Miracula S. Demetrii*, ed. Lemerle, 134. There is a lively debate regarding the date of this siege. Here, it seems, that Paul Lemerle, "La composition et le chronologie des deux premiers livres des Miracula S. Demetrii," *Byzantinische Zeitschrift*, 46 (1953), 354; but cf. Lemerle, *Les plus anciens recueils*, I, 50–56; and Vyronis, "The Evolution of Slavic Society," 378–390, have made a good case for 597, which the arguments by Whitby, *The Emperor Maurice*, 117, do not overturn.

221. John, *Miracula S. Demetrii*, ed. Lemerle, XIV, 139, 146, 151–154. I am unconvinced that Vyronis, "The Evolution of Slavic Society," 384, has done a service to those ignorant of the Greek language when he translates *petroboloi* as *balistrae*. The latter term does not occur in the original text of the *Miracula* and has its own special meaning very different from that of a *petrobolos*. See, for example, Ammianus Marcellinus, *Hist.* bk. XXIII, 4, 1–3; and Vegetius, *De re Militari*, bk. II, ch. 10; bk. III, ch. 24; bk. IV, chs. 9, 18, 29, where the *ballista* "shoots" long spears. Cf. Tarver, "Traction Trebuchet," 145.

222. Tarver, "Traction Trebuchet," 144–145, is correct here.

223. John, *Miracula S. Demetrii*, ed. Lemerle, XIV, 151.

224. John, *Miracula S. Demetrii*, ed. Lemerle, XIV, 151.

225. John, *Miracula S. Demetrii*, ed. Lemerle, XIV, 151.

226. Cf. Hill, "Siege-Craft from the Sixth to the Tenth Century," 111–117. It may be emphasized, as well, that the Lombards had stone-throwing machines that Pippin's armies captured in the Alpine forts in 755 and 756. In addition, when King Aistulf surrendered Pavia to King Pippin in both of the above-mentioned years, the early Carolingians took over whatever new technology that the Lombards may have possessed. See Fredegar Cont., chs. 37, 38. The Lombards had much closer contact with the Byzantine military than either the Merovingians or the Carolingians. Indeed, the Lombards actually took over fortress cities directly from the Byzantines, where later Roman and Byzantine military equipment was found. See Harrison, *The Early State and the Towns*.

227. For the background see Marsden, *Greek and Roman Artillery: Historical Development*, 50–54, 100, 104–105, 109, 113, 124–126, 177; and Lendle, *Text und Untersuchungen*, 188–194.

228. Gregory, *Hist.*, bk. VII, ch. 37; and see the discussion by Bachrach, *Anatomy of a Little War*, 135–136.

229. Regarding the MSS see 3–14.

230. I quote here the translation by Smith and Hawthorne, *Mappae Clavicula*, ch. 270, which I have modified. The editors, 69, n. 186, observe "this whole paragraph is more than usually obscure." See regarding some important technical matters, Rutherford Aris and Bernard S. Bachrach, "*De Motu Arietum* (On the Motion of Battering Rams)," in *Differential Equations, Dynamical Systems, and Control Science: A Festschrift in Honor of Lawrence Markus*, ed. K. D. Elworthy, W. Norrie Everitt, and E. Bruce Lee (New York and Hong Kong, 1993), 1–13.

231. *Mappae Clavicula*, chs. 162, 266–276.

232. Vegetius, *De re Militari*, bk. IV, chs. 14, 15.

233. Neither the infantry *testudo* nor that used for providing protection for sappers should be confused with the *testudo* used by Roman mounted troops. See concerning the last mentioned, Ann Hyland, *Training the Roman Cavalry from Arian's "Ars Tactica"* (Dover, N.H., 1993), 115–131.

234. See, for example, Vegetius, *De re Militari*, bk. IV, chs. 13, 14.

235. See, for example, Anon., *Strategy*, ed. Dennis, ch. 13.

236. John, *Miracula S. Demetrii*, ed. Lemerle, XIV, 139.

237. See Abbo, *De bello Parisiaco*, bk. I, line 99, where the term *muscilis* is used. Cf. Vegetius, *De re Militari*, bk. IV, chs. 13, 16.

238. Vegetius, *De re Militari*, bk. IV, chs. 13–16; and Anon., *Strategy*, ed. Dennis, ch. 13.

239. Gregory, *Hist.*, bk. VII, ch. 37.

240. For a wide variety of commonly known sixth-century methods, see Anon., *Strategy*, ed. Dennis, ch. 13, lines 61–91; 121–135.

241. Vegetius, *De re Militari*, bk. IV, ch. 6.

242. Anon., *Strategy*, ed. Dennis, ch. 13, lines 61–71, where the importance of the stones being of heavy weight is discussed.

243. Aris and Bachrach, "*De Motu Arietum*," 1–13.

244. This is the orthodox position as presented by Dennis in his edition of the *Strategikon*, viii; and also Haldon, "Some Aspects of Byzantine Military Technology," 12–13. Cf. Elton, *Warfare in Roman Europe*, 106–116, whose demurrers are not sustained.

245. Bachrach, "Early Medieval Europe," 271–307, for an explanation of imperial strategy in this context.

246. Treadgold, *Byzantium and Its Army*, 118–157.

247. Bachrach, "Animals and Warfare," 123–124.

248. Regarding background on breeding in the early Middle Ages see Bachrach, "Animals and Warfare," 711–712; R. H. C. Davis, *The Medieval Warhorse: Origin, Development and Redevelopment* (London, 1994), 49–51; Ann Hyland, *The Medieval Warhorse: From Byzantium to the Crusades* (Dover, N.H., 1994), 62–63.

249. See, for example, *Lex Alamannorum*, LXII, 1, 2, 3; *Lex Baiuvariorum*, XIV, 11, 12; *Lex Gundobada*, IV, 1; *Lex Ribuaria*, 40, 11. For further discussion of this topic, Bachrach, "Animals and Warfare," 711–712.

250. *Cap. reg. Fr.*, no. 32, Davis, *The Medieval Warhorse*, 51–53, has it basically right regarding Charlemagne. Cf. Karl Brunner, "Continuity and Discontinuity of Roman Agricultural Knowledge in the Early Middle Ages," in *Agriculture in the Middle Ages*, ed. Del Sweeney (Philadelphia, 1995), 22–23, who leaves the impression that Charlemagne's legislation was merely wishful thinking.

251. Concerning the royal military household, which has been discussed above in considerable detail, see Adalhard, *De ordine palatii*, ch. V. Cf. Reuter, "Plunder and Tribute," 81–82, whose account much simplifies Adalhard's description. See *Cap. reg. Fr.*, no. 217, ch. 4, which Hincmar, *Ad Carolum Calvum*, cols. 1050D-1051A, considered a tax for the support of the army. This is a controversial matter but the tax revenue it raised was not great. Reuter, "Plunder and Tribute," 87.

252. Rhabanus Maurus, *De Procinctu romanae Miliciae*, ch. IV. White, *Medieval Technology and Social Change*, 32, 149–150, n. 1, seems to make the curious argument that this "Frankish proverb," which must go back beyond Rhabanus' living memory and that of the oldest contemporaries of his youth, is evidence for revolutionary change.

253. Rhabanus Maurus, *De Procinctu romanae Miliciae*, ch. IV.

254. If Rhabanus had suspected that this vernacular saying was of recent vintage, he would not have described it as a "proverb," which implied then, as it implies today, that the saying was very old. In view of the highly competitive nature of intellectual life at the Carolingian court, certain kinds of factual exaggeration were difficult to sustain and errors often cost the man who made a "mistake" a considerable loss of face. See, for example, in Peter Godman, *Poets and Emperors: Frankish Politics and Carolingian Poetry* (Oxford, 1987), 68–69, a discussion of Theodulf's attacks on Alcuin. N.b. *Waltharius*, ed. Strecker, lines 755–769, where the poet takes a not so oblique swipe at Alcuin's fancy "Saxon" use of words.

255. Bachrach, *Merovingian Military Organization*, 14.

256. See, for example, Vegetius, *De re Militari*, bk. I, ch. 18; and see also Maurice, *Strategikon*, bk. II, passim.

257. Vegetius, *De re Militari*, bk. I, ch. 18.

258. Maurice, *Strategikon*, bk. XI, ch. 3.

259. Rhabanus Maurus, *De Procinctu romanae Miliciae*, ch. XII; and cf. Vegetius, *De re Militari*, bk. I, ch. 18.

260. Brühl, *Palatium und Civitas*, provides information regarding the military practice field, i.e., *Campus Martius*, in the environs of the great Roman fortress cities that were the central places of the *regnum Francorum*.

This use of the term *Campus Martius* for a permanent topographical feature of a fortress city should not be confused with the place where troops were mustered prior to going off to war during the Merovingian and Carolingian eras. The latter use of the term likely was adopted by analogy with the Romans' use of the term in a topographical sense. Concerning the early medieval "Field of Mars," where troops were inspected prior to campaign, see Bernard S. Bachrach, "Was the Marchfield Part of the Frankish Constitution?" *Medieval Studies*, 36 (1974): 78–85. Reprinted in *Armies and Politics in the Early Medieval West* (London, 1993), with the same pagination and the literature cited there.

261. Specialists in Roman imperial history have made a very good beginning on this subject. See, for example, Roy W. Davies, *Service in the Roman Army* (New York, 1989), 93–123, which is basic. Unfortunately, his views on medieval matters (e.g., 269, n. 256) cannot be given much weight.

262. For the necessary background see J. K. Anderson, *Ancient Greek Horsemanship* (Berkeley, 1966); Hyland, *Training the Roman Cavalry*; and Gillmore, "Practical Chivalry."

263. Hyland, *The Medieval Warhorse*, 115–117.

264. Hyland, *Training the Roman Cavalry*, 24–26.

265. Rhabanus Maurus, *De Procinctu romanae Miliciae*, ch. XII.

266. Rhabanus Maurus, *De Procinctu romanae Miliciae*, ch. XII.

267. Cf. White, *Medieval Technology and Social Change*, 149, n. 1.

268. Rhabanus Maurus, *De Procinctu romanae Miliciae*, ch. XII.

269. Maurice, *Strategikon*, bk. I, ch. 1.

270. It is possible that Rhabanus discussed the use of a throwing spear by Carolingian horsemen in a chapter that did not survive in transmission.

271. Rhabanus Maurus, *De Procinctu romanae Miliciae*, ch. XII.

272. See, for example, Tacitus, *Hist.*, bk. I, ch. 79. See Haldon, "Some Aspects of Byzantine Military Technology," 16–17, regarding the continued use of Sarmatian-type armor.

273. *Hist.*, XXXI.2.6. Otto Maenchen-Helfen, *The World of the Huns: Studies in Their History and Culture* (Berkeley, 1973), 206–207.

274. Strickland, "Military Technology and Conquest," 359–360, reviews the problem once again.

275. Regarding this tradition in the Ostrogothic kingdom and in the Visigothic kingdoms, see Delbrück, *History of the Art of War*, III, 241, and Verbruggen, *The Art of Warfare*, 31–32. However, the apparent effort to connect these sophisticated "war games" with a putative Germanic tradition credited to the Tencteri by Tacitus, *Germania*, ch. 32, is misleading in institutional terms.

276. Nithard, *Hist.*, bk. III, ch. 6. See the discussion by Bernard S. Bachrach, "*Caballus et Caballarius* in Medieval Warfare," in *The Study of Chivalry*, ed. Howell Chickering and Thomas H. Seiler (Kalamazoo, 1988), 206 n. 69.

277. Nithard, *Hist.*, bk. III, ch. 6, does not in any way leave the impression that any of these drills were innovations.

278. See Janet Nelson, "Public *Histories* and Private History in the Work of Nithard," *Speculum*, 60 (1985), 280–293, concerning Nithard's private life. In addition to the basic details of his very high quality education, the hypothesis that Nithard was raised at the royal court is suggested by the fact, emphasized by Astronomer, *V. Hludowici*, ch. 21, that Charlemagne liked to keep his daughters with him at Aachen but that after the emperor's death Louis the Pious sent them from the court.

279. Nelson, "Public *Histories* and Private History," 282–289, has some useful observations on this important group of educated laymen.

280. Bachrach, "The Education of the 'Officer Corps,'" 7–13.

281. Nithard, *Hist.*, bk. III, ch. 6. See the discussion by Bachrach, "*Caballus et Caballarius*," 206, n. 69.

282. A Roman imperial practice ground excavated at Tomen-y-mûr measured 122 x 97.5m. See the discussion by Davies, *Service in the Roman Army*, 98.

283. Nithard, *Hist.*, bk. III, ch. 6; and regarding insults and bragging in considerable detail, see *Waltharius*, ed. Strecker, lines 581–1061, passim.

284. Nithard, *Hist.*, bk. III, ch. 6.

285. Nithard, *Hist.*, bk. III, ch. 6.

286. However, in *Tactica*, 44.1, Arrian indicates that "the turns and feigned re-

treats" were learned from "the Sarmatian and Celtic shaft carriers" whose "cavalry took turns to charge" in practice sessions. This reference to the Sarmatians rather than any particular information regarding the Huns of Attila's time or earlier may have been the *locus classicus* for Agathias' observations.

287. Vegetius, *De re Militari*, bk. I, ch. 27. Concerning this tradition, see Davies, *Service in the Roman Army*, 102–107. In the surviving parts of Rhabanus Maurus, *De Procinctu romanae Miliciae*, no mention is made of these tactics. Yet, as we have seen, they not only were in Vegetius' tract; they were also used *tempore moderno* as made clear by Nithard, Rhabanus' younger contemporary, in the above-cited discussion. The absence of a section in the surviving text of *De Procinctu romanae Miliciae* strengthens the hypothesis, suggested above, that not all of the original ninth-century handbook has survived.

288. Hyland, *Training the Roman Cavalry*, 33, 36 n.50, 44 (for the quotation), 76, 94, 96 n. 20, 155–156.

289. Hyland, *Training the Roman Cavalry*, 24–36.

290. Nithard, *Hist.*, bk. III, ch. 6.

291. See, for example, *Waltharius*, ed. Strecker, lines 45–46.

292. Hyland, *Training the Roman Cavalry*, 75, 121. One is always astonished by how quiet the audience remains during the exercises in an equestrian contest.

293. The importance of close order charge has been so often emphasized in the course of the study of cavalry in the West that it is almost a cliché. See, for example, Verbruggen, *The Art of Warfare*, 74, who quotes the cliché "If you throw a glove on their helmets, it would not fall to ground within a mile." However, such a close packing of the men and horses makes it impossible to maneuver and especially to carry out the "roll back" described by Nithard. Cf. Hyland, *Training the Roman Cavalry*, 117. Indeed, the Byzantines (Maurice, *Strategikon*, bk. IX, ch. 9) allotted on a minimum basis and under conditions of the march a space of approximately a meter in width and two and half meters in length for each horse.

294. N.b. the calculations by Hyland, *Training the Roman Cavalry*, 117, based upon Maurice, *Strategikon*, bk. IX, ch. 9.

295. Gillmore, "Practical Chivalry," 16; and Hyland, *Training the Roman Cavalry*, 33.

296. Concerning the use of signals during the early Carolingian era, see, for example, *Passio Praejecti*, ch. 29, where there are specific mentions of war trumpets. This text was likely written within a quarter century or so of Bishop Prajectus' murder in 676. Considering the recall of the troops with the use of the *cornus* and the *signiferi* mentioned in *Waltharius*, ed. Strecker, lines 208 and 211, respectively, as being drawn on Frankish models may be problematic, but I lean in that direction.

297. Bernard S. Bachrach, "The Feigned Retreat at Hastings," *Medieval Studies*, 33 (1971), 344–347.

298. Rhabanus Maurus, *De Procinctu romaniae Miliciae*, praef., ch. I.

299. Nithard, *Hist.*, bk. III, ch. 6.

300. Gregory, *Hist.*, bk. 10, ch. 9,; Fredegar, *Chron.* bk. IV, chs. 54, 55, 58; *Passio Praejecti*, ch. 30; and Julian, *Hist. Wambae Regis*, ch. 25. These references are intended to be illustrative and not exhaustive.

301. Fredegar Cont., chs. 43, 48, concerning the Gascons.

302. Pippin made major inroads in Brittany around 749–752 when he likely cap-

tured and then sacked the fortress city of Vannes. Some time prior to 778, and perhaps as early as 753, a Carolingian march was established in eastern Brittany that likely included Nantes and Rennes if not Vannes as well. Indeed, substantial lands in the area of eastern Brittany were in the hands of Frankish religious houses and the Carolingian rulers during this period. The relevant sources and scholarly literature are discussed by Julia M. H. Smith, "The Sack of Vannes by Pippin III," *Cambridge Medieval Celtic Studies*, 11 (1986), 17–27.

303. Matthew Bennett, "*La Règle du Temple* as a Military Manual or How to Deliver a Cavalry Charge," in *Studies in Medieval History Presented to R. Allen Brown*, ed. C. Harper-Bill, C. J. Holdsworth, and J. L. Nelson (Wolfeboro, N.H., 1989), 7–19; and Verbruggen, *The Art of Warfare*, 97–102.

304. *Annales q.d. Einhardi, an.* 782. Other sources, with the exception of the *Annales regni Francorum, an.* 782, ignore this debacle while the latter works hard to sanitize the entire operation to the benefit of the Carolingians.

305. *Waltharius*, ed. Strecker, lines 194–195.

306. See the detailed examination of the state of the question of stirrups and mounted combat by Kelly DeVries, *Medieval Military Technology* (Peterborough, Ont., 1992), 95–122.

Chapter 4. Morale

1. See, for example, J. C. M. Baynes, *Morale* (London, 1967); F. M. Richardson, *Fighting Spirit: A Study of Psychological Factors in War* (London, 1978); Karl von Clausewitz, *On War*, trans. Michael Howard and Peter Paret (Princeton, 1976); J. T. MacKurdy, *The Structure of Morale* (Cambridge, 1943). For the Middle Ages, see the general observations by Verbruggen, *The Art of Warfare*, 58–61; and the lengthy series of articles by John Bliese: "Aelred of Rievaulx's Rhetoric and Morale at the Battle of the Standard, 1138," *Albion*, 20 (1988), 543–556; "The Battle Rhetoric of Aelred of Rievaulx," *Haskins Society Journal*, 1 (1989), 99–107; "Rhetoric and Morale: A Study of Battle Orations from the Central Middle Ages," *Journal of Medieval History*, 15 (1989), 201–226; "When Knightly Courage May Fail: Battle Orations in Medieval Europe," *The Historian*, 53 (1991), 489–504; "The Just War as Concept and Motive in the Central Middle Ages," *Medievalia et Humanistica*, n.s., 17 (1991), 1–26; "The Courage of the Normans—A Comparative Study of Battle Rhetoric," *Nottingham Medieval Studies*, 35 (1991), 1–16; "Deliberative Oratory in the Middle Ages: The Missing Millennium in the Study of Public Address," *Southern Communication Journal*, 59 (1994), 273–282; "Rhetoric Goes to War: The Doctrine of Ancient and Medieval Military Manuals," *Rhetoric Society Quarterly*, 24 (1994), 105–130; "Fighting Spirit and Literary Genre," *Neuphilologische Mitteilungen*, 96 (1995), 417–436.

2. For some interesting observations regarding these matters, see Contamine, *War in the Middle Ages*, 250–259; and more important, Verbruggen, *The Art of Warfare*, 36–54. Cf. the curious notion proffered by Georges Duby, *The Legend of Bouvines: War, Religion, and Culture in the Middle Ages*, trans. Catherine Tihanyi (Berkeley, 1990), 102–104, that courage was discovered in the twelfth century.

3. *Waltharius*, ed. Strecker, lines 163–164.

4. This poem is discussed at some length by Peter Godman, *Poetry of the Carolingian Renaissance* (London, 1985), 48–50, who provides a text and translation 262–265;

for additional observations Peter Godman, *Poets and Emperors*, 151–153. There is also a translation with text by Helen Waddell, *Mediaeval Latin Lyrics*, 4th ed. (New York, 1933), 102–105. Godman places Angelbert's poetry within the context of the civil war between Louis the Pious' sons. However, my interest in the poem, as will be seen below, is with the emotions of the soldier to help define the bigger picture. I have benefited from both of the above-cited translations but the renderings below are my own.

5. *Waltharius*, ed. Strecker, line 1284.

6. V. 1.

7. Vv. 8 and 9.

8. *Waltharius*, ed. Strecker, lines 1327–1328 and 1331–1332 for the shaking knees and trembling body, respectively.

9. *Waltharius*, ed. Strecker, lines 1344–1345.

10. V. 3.

11. V. 7.

12. V. 14.

13. Vv. 13, 15.

14. *Waltharius*, ed. Strecker, lines 846–851.

15. *Waltharius*, ed. Strecker, lines 223–224, for the post-campaign exhaustion followed by strong wine, and line 1410 with regard to strong wine for the wounded. Cf. Statius, *Theb.*, 11,7, "fessus anhelet."

16. *Waltharius*, ed. Strecker, lines 721–722.

17. *Waltharius*, ed. Strecker, lines 721–722; 1422.

18. *Waltharius*, ed. Strecker, lines 829–830.

19. V. 12.

20. Vv. 3, 5.

21. For the greater part of the twentieth century, scholars have believed that medieval armies and especially early medieval armies were very small. This has, in general, been the legacy of Hans Delbrück. Werner, "Heeresorganization und Kriegsführung," 792–843, challenged this consensus and his views that the Carolingians had very large armies are now the norm (see the magisterial synthesis by Philippe Contamine, *La Guerre au Moyen Age*, 101–103). For a thoroughgoing critique of Delbrück's methods, see Bernard S. Bachrach, "Early Medieval Military Demography," 3–19.

22. Verbruggen, *The Art of Warfare*, 283, admitted that Charlemagne commanded large armies but refused to commit himself regarding their order of magnitude. Verbruggen, "L'Armée et la stratégie," 433, makes the point that because of the size of the forces that Charlemagne could muster, he was able to use a strategy of convergence, i.e., pincer movements, with several armies attacking the enemy from different directions. Thus, the size of his forces and their deployment positioned him to overwhelm the enemy. However, Verbruggen asserts that Charles Martel and Pippin did not use this strategy because their armies may have been too small.

The evidence for large armies and the deployment of overwhelming force among the early Carolingians, however, suggests that Charlemagne was not an innovator in this regard. See, for example, Fredegar Cont., chs. 8, 24–26, 32, 35, 42, 47, 48, for large armies and ch. 17 "navium copia"; for the enemy coming to terms without a fight, see chs. 27, 28, 31, 32, 38, 48; for the enemy fleeing without a fight, see chs. 31, 32, 47; and for the enemy with a big army fleeing without a fight, see ch. 47. Even Pippin II, Charles Martel's father, is credited with large armies by the author of the *Liber Historiae Francorum*, chs. 46, 48.

23. Ganshof, "Charlemagne's Army," 68.

24. For background, see Hanson, *The Western Way of War*, 126–131; and Goldsworthy, *The Roman Army at War*, 261–262.

25. *Cap. reg. Fr.*, I, no. 50, ch. 6.

26. See the several articles by Bliese, "Rhetoric and Morale," 206, 208, 214–215, 220; "The Courage of the Normans," 4, 12; "Deliberative Oratory in the Middle Ages," 277; and "Fighting Spirit and Literary Genre," 421. This tradition, of course, is found in the Hebrew Bible (Leviticus 27:7) and was transmitted to the Muslims, where the image of a properly motivated small force is presented in the Koran, ch. VIII, concerning Mohammed's victory at the battle of Bedr in 624. John Bagot Glubb, *The Great Arab Conquests* (London, 1963), 196, calls attention to the report that chapter VIII of the Koran was recited before the Muslim troops prior to going into battle against the Persians at Qadisiyya in 637.

27. Vegetius, *De re Militari*, bk. III, ch. 3.

28. Concerning troop supply requirements, which are discussed below in Chapter 6 regarding operations, see *Cap. reg. Fr.*, no 74, ch. 8, where this is already described as an *antiqua consuetudo*. For the institutionalization of the logistic system see Wilhelm Störmer, "Zur Frage der Functkion des kirchlichen Fernbesitzes im Gebiet der Ostalpen vom 8. bis zum 10 Jahrhundert," in *Die Transalpinen Verbindungen der Bayern, Alemannen und Franken bis zum 10 Jahrhundert*, ed. H. Beumann (Sigmaringen, 1987), 379–403; and for the very successful detailed application of Störmer's methods, see Charles R. Bowlus, *Franks, Moravians, and Magyars: The Struggle for the Middle Danube, 788–907* (Philadelphia, 1995).

29. Jean Durliat, "La polyptyque d'Irminon pour l'Armée," *Bibliothèque de l'Ecole des Chartes* 141 (1983), 183–208.

30. Concerning the continued use of Roman roads, see Raymond Chevallier, *Roman Roads*, trans. N. H. Field (Berkeley, 1976), and with greater detail, Jean Hubert, "Les routes du moyen âge," in *Les Routes de France, depuis les origines jusqu'à nos jours* (Paris, 1979), 25–56.

31. F. L. Ganshof, "*La Tractoria*: Contribution à l'étude des origines du droit de gîte," *Tijdschrift voor Rechtsgeschiedenis*, 8 (1928), 69–91; and Carlrichard Brühl, *Fodrum, gistum, servitium regis: Studien zu den wirtschafts Grundlagen des Königtums im Frankenreich un in den fränkischen Nachfolgestaaten deutschland, Frankreich, Italien vom 6 bis zur Mitte des 14 Jahrhunderts*, 2 vols. (Cologne, 1968). I, 65–67.

32. See, for example, *Cap. reg. Fr.* I, no. 91, ch. 4; no. 93, ch. 7.

33. Werner, "*Missus-Marchio-Comes*," 232, with the literature cited there.

34. Marjorie Nice Boyer, *Medieval French Bridges: A History* (Cambridge, Mass., 1976), 13–27, provides some background on the early Middle Ages. Of considerable importance regarding the science of bridge building in this context is *Mappae Clavicula*, ch. 102; and cf. the discussion by Victor Mortet, "Un formulaire du VIIIe siècle pour les fondations des édifices et de ponts d'après des sources d'origine antique. Nouvelle édition critique," *Bulletin Monumentale*, 71 (1907), 422–465.

35. *Codex Theodosianus*, XV, 3.6; see the normal requirements as evidenced in *Dip. Karol.* no. 91; and various regulations as set out in *Cap. reg. Fr.* I, no. 91, ch. 4; no. 93, ch. 7. Work on bridges is considered an *antiqua consuetudo* in these documents.

36. Einhard, *V. Karoli*, chs. 17, 31, for the Rhine bridge; *Annales Petaviani, an.* 796, for the Weser bridge; and *Annales regnum Francorum, an.*, 789; and *Annales q.d. Einhardi, an.* 789, for the Elbe bridges.

37. W. H. Stevenson, "Trinoda Necessitas," *English Historical Review*, 29 (1914),

689–703, are emphasized by Nicholas Brooks, "The Development of Military Obligations in Eighth- and Ninth-Century England," in *England Before the Conquest: Studies in Primary Sources Presented to Dorothy Whitelock*, ed. Peter Clemoes and Kathleen Hughes (Cambridge, 1971), 69–84.

38. Astronomer, *V. Hludowici*, ch. 15.

39. Anon., *De rebus bellicis*, ch. XVI, 1,2; and Ammianus Marcellinus, *Hist.*, 24.3.1. More generally, see the discussion by J. Homell, "Floats and Buoyed Rafts in Military Operations," *Antiquity*, 19 (1945), 73–79.

40. *Cap. reg. Fr.*, no. 32, ch. 64.

41. Leighton, *Transport and Communication in Early Medieval Europe*.

42. See Haywood, *Dark Age Naval Power*, 87–104; and regarding the Romans see Chester G. Starr, *The Roman Imperial Navy*, 2nd ed. (Cambridge, 1960), 124–166; Lionel Casson, *Ships and Seamanship in the Ancient World*, 2nd ed. (Baltimore, 1995), 329–343; and Chester G. Starr, *The Influence of Sea Power on Ancient History* (New York, 1989), 79–81.

43. See the discussion in Appendix.

44. For details concerning the efforts to build the canal, see Hans Hubert Hofmann, "*Fossa Carolina*: Versuch einer Zussammenschau," in *Karl der Grosse*, I, 437–453.

45. This subject is well treated by Campbell, *The Emperor and the Roman Army*, 181–198.

46. Campbell, *The Emperor and the Roman Army*, 165–168, 176–198.

47. Adalhard, *De ordine palatii*, ch. V (27).

48. Bachrach, "Military Lands," forthcoming.

49. Verbruggen, "L'armée et la stratégie," 431–432, emphasizes the importance of seeing that the early Carolingian armies were "composed, in general, of vassals and free men who had a certain minimum of wealth." However, he is not very specific regarding the ratios. As will been seen below, the free men of necessity comprised the larger element in the great armies of conquest.

50. Walter Goffart, "Old and New Merovingian Taxation," *Past and Present*, 96 (1982), 3–21, and cited here in the reprint Goffart, *Rome's Fall and After*, 231, n. 71, observes, "active military service was the alternative to tribute." The word "tax" might reasonably be substituted for tribute in this context.

51. *Cap. reg. Fr.* I, no. 50, ch. 6, provides evidence for the count's violation of these regulations.

52. *Cap. reg. Fr.* I, no. 34, ch. 12; and no. 73, ch. 3. Verbruggen, "L'armée et la stratégie," 426–429, emphasizes the heavy burden experienced by the expeditionary levies because of their frequent service. However, he fails to make clear that the deleterious effect seems to develop only during the early ninth century. See also Müller-Mertens, *Karl der Grosse*, 129–130, and 140–141, who follows Verbruggen, and cf. Reuter, "The End of Carolingian Military Expansion," 395–396.

53. The successful commander's decision to permit his troops to plunder is not a *pro forma* result of winning the battle. See, for example, the orders given by Clovis to restrict plundering in Aquitaine (*Cap. reg. Fr.* no. 1, chs. 1, 2) in the context of the war against the Visigoths. By contrast, Theuderic I, Clovis' son, promised booty prior to victory as a means of encouraging his soldiers (Gregory, *Hist.*, bk. III, ch. 11). In a similar vein, simply because troops may be identified as engaged in plundering does not mean that they had been given permission. On occasion, officers, even men of such authority as

Clovis, are known to have lost command and control of one or another element of their forces. See Bachrach, "Quelques observations sur la composition et les caractéristiques des armées de Clovis," 1700–701; and note the material collected by Reuter, "Plunder and Tribute," 79. See also *Lex Baiuv.*, ch. II. 4, where plunder may be taken only on the order of the duke to whom the power has been delegated by the king. Cf. André Crépin, "Les dépouilles des tués sur le champ de bataille dans l'histoire, les arts et la pensée du haut moyen âge," in *La guerre, la violence et les gens au moyen âge*, ed. Philippe Contamine and Olivier Guyotjeannin, 2 vols. (Paris, 1996), I, 15–24, for a collection of anecdotes that support his point regarding the putative normalcy of despoiling those who had fallen on the field of battle. However, he fails to engage sources, such as those noted above, which illustrate the realities of military command impinging upon a soldier's desire for booty.

54. Regarding Charles Martel and Pippin, see, for example, Fredegar Cont., chs. 6, 11–13, 17, 18, 20, 25, 32, 35, 37–39, 42–44; and for the early career of Charlemagne, *Annales regni Francorum*, ann. 772, 774, 775; and *Chron. Laurissense Breve*, 34. Verbruggen, "L'armée et la stratégie," 429, emphasizes the division of the booty with the troops during the early period, i.e., Charlemagne followed the policies of his father and grandfather, but sees a diminution in these practices according to the chroniclers later in the ninth century. Reuter, "Plunder and Tribute," 78–80, follows Verbruggen's view regarding the later period but projects it into the earlier period as well. Regarding the later period, which is beyond the scope of this study, that although victories and conquests were fewer, the sources do not condemn the later Carolingians for their parsimony toward their soldiers.

55. *Waltharius*, ed. Strecker, lines 206–207. The language used here—"caperet plenum . . . triumphum" for winning a complete victory—likely is intended to attract attention to the notion of a ceremonial triumph, further evidenced in lines 209–212, discussed below.

56. Cf. Verbruggen, "L'armée et la stratégie," 422, who focuses upon large grants. However, many such estates were divided to support the retinue of the large landholder. See also *Cap. reg. Fr.* no. 16, ch. 1, for a discussion of the movement of families to take advantage of new opportunities for settlement.

57. Fredegar Cont., chs. 13, 17.

58. Fredegar Cont., ch. 10.

59. Fredegar Cont., ch. 19.

60. Fredegar Cont., chs. 10, 20.

61. Fredegar Cont., ch. 18.

62. Fredegar Cont., ch. 20.

63. Fredegar Cont., ch. 13.

64. Fredegar Cont., ch. 13.

65. See, for example, Fredegar Cont., chs. 8, 13, 15, 19, 20, 32, 37, 42, and 43.

66. Campbell, *The Emperor and the Roman Army*, 59–69, covers the material very well but hesitates to characterize the role attributed by contemporaries and near contemporaries to the commander as military doctrine despite the strong evidence he musters to support such a conclusion.

67. Fredegar Cont., chs. 8, 10, 15, 18–20.

68. Fredegar Cont., ch. 8. Verbruggen, *The Art of Warfare*, 4, compellingly argued that for the modern scholar to understand medieval warfare and especially tactics he must be alert to the significance of even the tiniest of details provided by the sources.

69. Fredegar Cont., ch. 9.

70. For example, this encounter is treated somewhat differently by the somewhat negative author of the *Liber Historiae Francorum*, ch. 52, and a great deal more favorably by the more partial author of the *Annales mettenses priores*, p. 21. However, Fredegar Cont., ch. 9, is the account relied upon above. N.b. the observations by Roger Collins, "Deception and Misrepresentation in Early Eighth Century Frankish Historiography," in *Karl Martell in seiner Zeit*, ed. Jörg Jarnut, Ulrich Nonn, and Michael Richter (Sigmaringen, 1994), 235–247, are useful in reaffirming the court-centered *parti pris* of the Continuator, which has long been recognized.

71. Hermoldus Nigellus, *Hon. Hlud.*, 4, 2156–2163.

72. In analyzing this evidence I follow the methodology developed by McCormick, *Eternal Victory*, 372–373.

73. Fredegar Cont., chs. 11–21.

74. Fredegar Cont., chs. 11, 14, 15, 17, 19, 20, 21.

75. Fredegar Cont., chs. 11, 13, 20.

76. Fredegar Cont., ch. 32.

77. *Annales regni Francorum., an.*, 774; and the discussion by McCormick, *Eternal Victory*, 372.

78. Fredegar Cont., chs. 41–52.

79. Fredegar Cont., chs. 42–44.

80. Fredegar Cont., ch. 47.

81. Fredegar Cont., chs. 48–51.

82. Fredegar Cont., chs. 48–52.

83. See, for example, Fredegar Cont., chs. 27, 28, 31, 32, 38, 48, for early Carolingian willingness to accept terms.

84. Campbell, *The Emperor and the Roman Army*, 32–59, regarding *conmilitio*.

85. Verbruggen, *The Art of Warfare*, 19–20.

86. For this tradition see a selection of studies by Bliese, "When Knightly Courage May Fail," 489–504; "Deliberative Oratory in the Middle Ages," 273–282; "Rhetoric Goes to War," 105–130; and "Fighting Spirit and Literary Genre," 417–436.

87. *Annales mettenses priores, an.* 690 [*sic*] 687 (8–9). For a discussion of the value of these annals, see above. N.b. Haselbach, "Aufstieg und Herschaft der Karolinger," 34, who plausibly argues that the author of the *Annales* used an earlier chronicle source for the reign of Pippin II. Whether the Metz annalist used an earlier chronicle or perhaps some sort of career-biographical account similar to that used by Paul the Deacon for his history of the bishops of Metz, he had material of a non-annalistic nature that he tried to squeeze into an annalistic format with only limited success. See Walter Goffart, "Paul the Deacon's 'Gesta episcoporum Mettensium' and the Early Design of Charlemagne's Succession," *Traditio*, 42 (1986), 59–93. With regard to the importance of Tertry see the somewhat revisionist views of Fouracre, "Pippinid Influence," 1–31.

88. See, for example, the discussion by Nancy Partner, "The New Cornificius: Medieval History and the Artifice of Words," 12; and Roger Ray, "Rhetorical Scepticism and Verisimilar Narrative in John of Salisbury's *Historia Pontificalis*," 66, 83–84, both in *Classical Rhetoric and Medieval Historiography*, ed. Ernst Breisach (Kalamazoo, 1985).

89. *Annales mettenses priores, an.* 690 [*sic*] 687 (p. 8). For general background on the just war see Frederick Russell, *The Just War in the Middle Ages* (Cambridge, 1975), who deals basically with canon law and theology. For the idea of the just war in the

present context see the excellent study by Bliese, "Just War as Concept and Motive," 1–26, which, although limited to the central Middle Ages, makes clear that the justifications are constant. In fact, they are rather constant through the later Roman empire; see Doyne Dawson, *The Origins of Western Warfare: Militarism and Morality in the Ancient World* (Boulder, 1996), 111–165.

90. *Annales mettenses priores, an.* 690 [*sic*] 687 (p. 8).

91. *Versus de Bella*, vv. 1, 3, 5.

92. Bliese, "Just War as Concept and Motive," 6–7, calls attention to the importance of the defense of the *patria* as a motive for just war in harangues to the troops made by commanders.

93. *Waltharius*, ed. Strecker, lines 170–178. Both Althof, *Waltharii Poesis*, II, 63; and Strecker, *Waltharius*, 126, find echoes of both classical and biblical phraseology in these lines. However, nothing in these echoes undermines the "originality" of the poet's effort to convey ideas relevant to the Carolingian court.

94. *Waltharius*, ed. Strecker, lines 175–178. With regard to these themes see, for example, two studies by Bliese, "Rhetoric Goes to War," 105–130; and "When Knightly Courage May Fail," 489–504.

95. *Waltharius*, ed. Strecker, line 175; and Strecker, *Waltharius*, 126, where he calls attention to II *Kings* 11:25; and Virgil, *Aen.* 11.415.

96. *Waltharius*, ed. Strecker, lines 175–176, for the speech; the foreshadowed events referred to as a *triumphus* are found in lines 211–212. In line 206 *triumphus* is used again in the context of this same campaign as a synonym for *victoria* and again foreshadows the ceremony noted above. McCormick, *Eternal Victory*, does not seem to treat this "fictional" triumph, but it may be classified under his rubric of a "splendid parade" (p. 292, n. 59).

97. *Waltharius*, ed. Strecker, line 177. For a discussion of the term *tyranni* in the context of illegitimate power during the early Middle Ages see Bernard S. Bachrach, "Gildas, Vortigern and Constitutionality in Sub-Roman Britain," *Nottingham Medieval Studies*, 32 (1988), 126–140; and reprinted in *Armies and Politics in the Early Medieval West* (London, 1993), with the same pagination.

98. *Waltharius*, ed. Strecker, line 178; and Strecker, *Waltharius*, 126, where the locution is shown to have been used both by Prudentius, *Psych.*, 156; and Virgil, *Aen.*, 11,415.

99. Wallace-Hadrill, "War and Peace in the Early Middle Ages," 19–20, 23–24.

100. *Waltharius*, ed. Strecker, line 180.

101. Contrary to its title, Bernard J. Verkamp, "Moral Treatment of Returning Warriors in the the Early Middle Ages," *Journal of Religious Ethics*, 16.2 (1988), 223–249, has little to say regarding the early Middle Ages. However, the work does examine many of the important issues regarding morale and spiritual matters in a general sense.

102. The basic work remains Alfred von Domaszewski, *Die religion des römischen Heeres* (Linz, 1895), but see more modern treatments by J. Helgeland, "Roman Army Religion"; and Eric Birley, "The Religion of the Roman Army, 1895–1977," both in *Aufstieg und Niedergang der Römischen Welt*, ii *Die Principat*, II 16.2, ed. Hildegard Temporini (Berlin, 1978), 1470–1505, and 1506–1541, respectively. The latter reviews Domaszewski's work.

103. Cf. A. H. M. Jones, "Military Chaplains in the Roman Army," *Harvard Theological Review*, 46 (1953), 239–240. For some useful background regarding early Christian

views see Henri F. Secrétan, "Le christianisme de premiers siècles et le service militaire," *Revue de théologie et de philosophie*, n.s. 2 (1914), 345–365.

104. Albert Michael Koeniger, *Die Militärseelsorge der Karolingerzeit: Ihr Recht und ihre Praxis* (Munich, 1918), 21–23, for the early period. A comprehensive study of Byzantine military chaplains is needed.

105. Ralph W. Mathisen, "Barbarian Bishops and the Churches 'in barbaricis gentibus' During Late Antiquity," *Speculum*, 72 (1997), 664–697, esp. 677, 679–683.

106. *Ordo quando rex cum exercitu ad prelium egreditur*, ed. Férotin, cols. 149–153, passim. This last prayer—biblical echoes aside—likely is to be understood as something more than a desire to be safe from enemy archery. However, the locution may have had a basis in the realities of military technology at some time in the past.

107. F. L. Ganshof, "L'Eglise et le pouvoir royal dans la monarchie franque sous Pépin III et Charlemagne," *Settimane di Studio del Centro Italiano di Studi sull'alto Medioevo*, 7 (Spoleto, 1960), 95–141; and translated as "The Church and the Royal Power Under Pippin III and Charlemagne," in Ganshof, *The Carolingians and the Frankish Monarchy*, trans. J. Sondheimer (London, 1971), 205–239, and 206, for the quotation. N.b. Notker, *Gesta Karoli*, I, 25, refers to Charlemagne as "head bishop of the bishops." This does not speak to institutional formalities but rather to the realities of power.

108. See the discussion by Etienne Delaruelle, "Essai sur la formation de l'idée de Croisade," *Bulletin de littérature ecclésiastique*, 42 (1941), 27–31; and the mention of these by McCormick, *Eternal Victory*, 345.

109. See, for example, by Delaruelle, "Essai sur la formation de l'idée de Croisade," 28–31; and Eugen Ewig, "Zum christlichen Königsgedanken im Frühmittelalter," in *Das Königtum. Seine geistigen und rechtlichen Grundlagen, Vorträge und Forschungen*, 3 (1956), 7–73; and for the citation here see the reprint in Ewig, *Spätantikes und fränkisches Gallien*, I, 11, 46, 52. More recently note Oswyn Murray, "The Idea of the Shepherd King from Cyrus to Charlemagne," in *Latin Poetry and the Classical Tradition: Essays in Medieval and Renaissance Literature*, ed. Peter Godman and Oswyn Murray (Oxford, 1990), 10–13.

110. In this context, note should be taken of Rufinus of Aquilea's translation of Eusebius' *Vita Constantini* and also of *Legenda Sancti Silvestri*. See regarding the former, J. E. L. Oulton, "Rufinus's Translation of the Church History of Eusebius," *Journal of Theological Studies*, 30 (1929), 164–168; and M. Villain, "Rufin d'Aquilée et l'histoire ecclésiastique," *Recherches de science religieuse*, 33 (1946), 188–199; regarding the latter, see C. B. Coleman, *Constantine the Great and Christianity* (New York, 1914), 161ff.; and Wilhelm Levison, "Konstantinische Schenkung et Silvesterlegende," in *Miscellanea Francesco Ehrle* (Rome, 1924), II, 159–247.

In addition to the conversion of Constantine there was available Gregory of Tours' account of Clovis' conversion (*Hist.*, bk. II, chs. 30–31), and probably the account in the Anon., *V. Remigii*, which played an important role in Hincmar, *V. Remigii*, written later in the ninth century. In short, the role of God in military victory as seen in the Western tradition can hardly be neglected in trying to understand Charlemagne's views. A brief but useful summary of the importance of Constantine to the early Carolingians is to be found in Delaruelle, "Essai sur la formation de l'idée de Croisade," 31–33, with additional literature.

111. See, for example, Fredegar Cont., chs. 8, 13, 15, 19, 20, 32, 37, 42, and 43.

112. *Annales regni Francorum, an.* 774.

113. *Chron. Laur. breve*, ed. Schnorr von Carolsfeld, 31; and the important discussion by McCormick, *Eternal Victory*, 374.

114. Fredegar Cont., ch. 52.

115. See, for example, *Liber Historiae Francorum*, ch. 48, who is apparently followed by Fredegar Cont., ch. 5. However, the latter seems to use the term without prompting from the *Liber* in ch. 6. *Annales mettenses priores, an.* 688 (p. 6), follows in the tradition of the above-mentioned sources, but p. 10 uses the term on his own as is the case in *an.* 710 (p. 18).

116. *Annales mettenses priores, an.* 688 (pp. 1–4).

117. *Annales mettenses priores, an.* 688 (p. 4).

118. *Annales mettenses priores, an.* 688 (p. 4); *an.* 691 (p. 12), *an.* 692 (13, 15).

119. *Annales mettenses priores, an.* 672 (p. 15).

120. *Annales mettenses priores, an.* 709 (p. 18).

121. See particularly *Lex Salica*, Prolog.

122. *Das Palimpsestsakramentar im Codex Augiensis. CXII, ein Messbuch altester structur aus dem Alpengebiet. Texte und Arbeiten*, 2, ed. Alban Dold and Anton Baumstark (Beuron, 1925), 37. Here I follow the argument and translation by McCormick, *Eternal Victory*, 344–345.

123. *Bobbio Missal*, ed. Lowe, 64–65; and McCormick, *Eternal Victory*, 345.

124. Ewig, "Zum christlichen Königsgedanken im Frühmittelalter," vol. I, 42, n. 181.

125. *Bobbio Missal*, ed. Lowe, no. 493:151.

126. *Bobbio Missal*, ed. Lowe, no. 493:151–152. I have departed from the interpretation by McCormick, *Eternal Victory*, 345, only slightly in regard to the phrase "ita eum . . . esse iubeas" which he translates as "that You . . . may bid him." The sense should be God "ordering" rather than "bidding" his faithful servant (*fidelis famulus*). The emphasis on command in modern English usage is better carried by "order" rather that "bid" in what is, in effect, a military context.

127. See McCormick, *Eternal Victory*, 345.

128. See McCormick, *Eternal Victory*, 345–347, with the sources and literature cited there.

129. *Sacramenatarium Gellonense*, ed. A. Dumas and J. Deshusses, 430:2750 (p. 431); and Bernard Moreton, *The Eighth-Century Gelasian Sacramentary: A Study in Tradition* (Oxford, 1976), 187–191. McCormick, *Eternal Victory*, 347, is correct in seeing the army rather than the commander as the focus of this mass.

130. *Sacramenatarium Gellonense*, ed. A. Dumas and J. Deshusses, 430:2755 (p. 432).

131. *Le sacramentaire gélasien d'Angoulême*, ed. P. Cagin (Angoulême, n.d. [1919]), fol. 167v., no. 2310, Moreton, *Eighth Century*, 192–193; and McCormick, *Eternal Victory*, 349.

132. The basic work on the Carolingian clergy and the army remains Koeniger, *Die Militärseelsorge*, and with much greater nuance on several important points, Michael McCormick, "The Liturgy of War in the Early Middle Ages: Crisis, Litanies, and the Carolingian Monarchy," *Viator*, 15 (1984), 1–23.

133. Jones, "Military Chaplains in the Roman Army," 239–240.

134. Koeniger, *Die Militärseelsorge*, 21–23; J.-R. Vieillefond, "Les Pratiques religieuses dans l'armée byzantine d'après les traités militaires," *Revue des Etudes Anciennes*,

37 (1935), 322–330; and Paul Goubert, "Religion et superstitions dans l'armée byzantine à la fin du VIe siècle," *Orientalia Christiana Periodica*, 13 (1947), 495–500.

135. Ludwig Arnzt, "Der Feldaltar in Vergangenheit und Gegenwart," *Zeitschrift für Christliche Kunst*, 28 (1915), 94.

136. *Cap. reg. Fr.*, no. 10, ch. 2. Cf. the discussion by Koeniger, *Die Militärseelsorge*, 14–15, who may give too much credit to Boniface in light of the government control of the church. However, he suggests (p. 20) that the edict issued in 742 merely formalized and systematized previous practice. This is not implausible, as the first written evidence for some institutions during the early Middle Ages is known to come sometime after the institution itself was well established on an "informal" basis. For additional background, see Ernest Hildesheimer, "Les clercs et l'exemption du service militaire à l'époque franque," *Revue d'histoire ecclésiastique de France*, 29 (1943), 5–18.

It is not clear why Prinz, "King, Clergy, and War," II, 305, believes that the *princeps*, whom the legislation designates as having a clerical staff, refers only to Carloman. If this were the case then Prinz would have to conclude that only those forces commanded by Carloman would have chaplains to minister to the soldiers and only units commanded by *praefecti* in Carloman's armies would have chaplains. However, Prinz sees these other requirements as general rather than specific to armies under Carloman's direct command. Wilfried Hartmann, *Die synoden der Karolingerzeit im Frankenreich und in Italian* (Paderborn, 1989), provides a useful reference guide to relevant legislation.

137. Koeniger, *Die Militärseelsorge*, 44. For the standard modern work, see Josef Fleckenstein, *Die Hofkapelle der deutschen Könige*, 2 vols. (Stuttgart, 1959); and for the itinerant court see Brühl, *Fodrum, gistum, servitium regis*, vol. 1.

138. Koeniger, *Die Militärseelsorge*, 26, regarding the epistolary sources, and 47–48, regarding the legal sources.

139. Koeniger, *Die Militärseelsorge*, 32–33.

140. *Cap. reg. Fr.*, no. 25, ch. 2. Cf. the discussion by Koeniger, *Die Militärseelsorge*, 19.

141. Walahfrid, *De exord*, ch. 32; with the discussion of this relic in war by Koeniger, *Die Militärseelsorge*, 19; and McCormick, *Eternal Victory*, 357. Regarding the background on St. Martin's relics, see Raymond Van Dam, "Images of Saint Martin in Late Roman and Early Merovingian Gaul," *Viator*, 19 (1988), 1–27; and for the royal chapel see Fleckenstein, *Die Hofkapelle*, for the basic overview.

142. Johannes van den Bosch, *Cappa, Basilica, Monasterium et le culte de saint Martin de Tours, Etude lexicologique et sémasiologique*, Latinitas Christianorum primaeva, 13 (Nijmegen, 1957), 7–37, does little to clarify the importance of St. Martin's cape for military operations.

143. Prinz, "King, Clergy, and War," 309–311, concerning the Carolingian view of such aristocratic holy men.

144. See Koeniger, *Die Militärseelsorge*, 19, 44–46; and McCormick, *Eternal Victory*, 357–358, for a variety of examples.

145. McCormick, *Eternal Victory*, 333–334, illuminates some of the instances in which holy relics were used in a local context within the *regnum Francorum* to help secure military victory and not incidentally to raise the morale of both soldiers and civilians.

146. Vieillefond, "Les pratiques religieuses," 322.

147. Goubert, "Religion et superstitions," 496, calls attention to the Byzantine use of banners emblazoned with crosses.

148. *Ordo quando rex cum exercitu ad prelium egreditur*, ed. Férotin, col. 152, where the term *banda*, as preferred by the Byzantines, is used. The inclination of Carl Erdmann, *The Origin of the Idea of Crusade*, trans. M. W. Baldwin and Walter Goffart with a foreword and additional notes by M. W. Baldwin (Princeton, 1977), 6, 22, 30 n. 72, 39, 43 n. 44, 82 n. 58, to affirm the dubious generalization that Visigothic tradition was unrelated to the tradition that was developed in the *regnum Francorum* underestimates the connection between the early Carolingians and men of Visigothic ethnicity. For example, the influential family of Witiza, discussed above, would be a primary example of such a close interaction. On a broader level see, for example, Fredegar Cont., ch. 41, for Visigothic dependents of King Pippin I in Aquitaine, and ch. 53, which makes clear that Septimania was part of the Carolingian *regnum*. For the later Merovingian background of interaction between the Visigothic kingdom and the *regnum Francorum* in regard to the very important area of ceremonial, see, in addition to the almost half-century long career of Queen Brunhild, McCormick, *Eternal Victory*, 441.

However, the most telling evidence for the untenabililty of Erdmann's position concerning early Carolingian-Visigothic connections regards the liturgy for the sick, the dead, and for burial. Edmund Bishop, *Liturgica Historica: Papers on the Liturgy and Religious Life of the Western Church* (Oxford, 1918), 168, established that Visigothic (Mozarabic) liturgy dominated in these areas. As is pointed out by Frederick S. Paxton, *Christianizing Death: The Creation of a Ritual Process in Early Medieval Europe* (Ithaca and London, 1990), 138–140, this process of integrating Visigothic liturgy into Frankish institutions is now regarded as having been the work of Benedict of Aniane (the abovementioned Witiza), rather than Alcuin, whom Bishop had credited with the effort.

149. Alfred von Domaszewski, *Das Fahnen im römischen Heere* (Vienna, 1885), 2; and Helgeland, "Roman Army Religion," 1477.

150. Gregory of Tours, *Hist.*, bk. V, ch. 4. Despite the scholarly controversy regarding the use of these banners in a putatively ecclesiastical context, the existence of the banner is not at issue. See the discussion by Erdmann, *The Idea of Crusade*, 41, n. 35.

151. See Erdmann, *The Idea of Crusade*, 36–39.

152. McCormick, *Eternal Victory*, 328–384, for the *regnum Francorum*. Efforts to see the Christian banner as in some way related to pagan Germanic origins are seriously discouraged by Erdmann, *The Idea of Crusade*, 38, n. 21.

153. Anon., *Epist. consol. ad pergantes bellum*, ed. Schmitz, tab. 10, lines 7 and 22. Hermann Schmitz, *Miscellanea Tironiana* (Leipzig, 1896), 29–30, is followed by Karl Künstle, "Zwei Dokumente für altchristlichen Militärseelsorge," *Der Katholik*, 3rd ser. 22 (1900), 122, in maintaining an early eighth-century date but suggesting Visigothic Spain for its origin. Erdmann, *The Idea of Crusade*, 28, n. 68, believes the ninth-century wars against the Northman to be more probable but provides no supporting argument. By contrast, Koeniger, *Die Militärseelsorge*, 51–52, fits this sermon effectively into the eighth-century milieu of required private confession and preoccupation with tariff penances (see below) that dominated the soldiers' religious life under the early Carolingians.

In further support of the eighth-century date, the soldiers were expected to understand the sermon. Thus, a ninth-century date in a context of the wars against the Northmen toward the middle of the ninth century would postdate by a considerable period of time Alcuin's language reforms, which are believed to have undermined the ability of the average "Latin" speaker to understand the newly formalized Latin liturgy.

Additional opposition to a context driven by the Northmen is the characterization of the enemy as "persecutores christianorum et ecclesiarum" (line 22), which fits the Muslims far better than the Northmen. The importance of confession by the troops before battle to their priests was, as will be noted below, under serious clerical attack by the early ninth century. In addition, the fact that priests are hearing confession as contrasted to bishops finds little support in a Visigothic context. Finally, the fact that the sermon survives in Tironian notes lends doubt to a Visigothic hypothesis—at least for the text in its shorthand version.

154. Anon., *Epist. consol. ad pergantes bellum*, ed. Schmitz, tab. 10, line 7: "vexillum crucis in fronte portatis" in an erudite context refers to the sign of the cross placed on the forehead of the baptized or (in an even more arcane interpretation) to the injunction in the Hebrew Bible (Exod. 13:9; Deut. 6:8) that imposed upon all adult males the requirement of placing holy scripture on one's forehead. However, as the discussion of this sermon below makes clear, this document was a simplistic and rather repetitive series of injunctions and promises intended to motivate the soldier and to give each fighting man the sense that he was a soldier of God. The second use of the phrase, "vexillum sanctae crucis" (line 22), where the "banner of the holy cross" is said to have been despised by the persecutors of Christians and of the Church, makes a connection with the baptismal sign of the cross on the forehead rather remote, although a sophisticated argument can be made. We cannot rule out the possibility that the bishop who wrote this sermon intended it for the soldier to be taken in a simple manner and for the scholar in a complex manner.

155. *Waltharius*, ed. Strecker, line 214.

156. Koeniger, *Die Militärseelsorge*, 56–57.

157. Fortunatus, *Pange lingua gloriosi*, ed. Bulst, p. 128; and Anon., *Ab ore verbum prolatum*, ed. Dreves and Blume, 51.82–83 (78).

158. See William Beare, *Latin Verse and European Song* (London, 1957), 15–19, regarding the Roman marching cadence; who is followed by Joseph Szövérffy, "Venantius Fortunatus and the Earliest Hymns to the Holy Cross," 110–112; 121–122.

159. *Vexilla regis prodeunt*, ed. Bulst, 129. Szövérffy, "Venantius Fortunatus and the Earliest Hymns to the Holy Cross," 115–118.

160. *Cap. reg. Fr.*, no 25, ch. 2. Koeniger, *Die Militärseelsorge*, 16, emphasizes that confession and penance get special attention here. Regarding the general spiritual character of the period see Jean Chelini, *L'aube du moyen âge: Naissance de la chrétienté occidentale. La vie religieuse des laïcs dans l'Europe carolingienne (750–900)* (Paris, 1991).

161. See, for example, Bernhard Poschmann, *Die abendländische Kirchenbusse im frühen Mittelalter* (Breslau, 1930), 73–91; Oscar Daniel Watkins, *A History of Penance*, 2 vols. (London, 1920), II, 632–664; R. C. Mortimer, *The Origin of Private Penance in the Western Church* (Oxford, 1939), 72–154; and H. G. J. Beck, *Pastoral Care of Souls in Southeast France in the Sixth Century*, Analecta Gregoriana, 51 (1950), 211–216, 221–222. Also of help are the summary observations by Rosamond Pierce (McKitterick), "The 'Frankish' Penitentials," *Studies in Church History*, 11, ed. Derek Baker (Oxford, 1975), 31–39, which provides a brief but excellent introduction to this complicated subject.

162. Riché, *Ecoles et enseignement*, 65–75, and 352–353.

163. *Cap. reg. Fr.*, no. 10, ch. 2. Perhaps I am making too much of the use of the

word "electi" because it is traditionally used to denote "elite troops" in the contemporary sources rather than "selecti," which indicates that the priests were chosen to serve by a higher authority. Koeniger, *Die Militärseelsorge*, 17, is correct in suggesting that the bishop in each diocese picked those priests who would serve in the army.

164. See, for example, Poschmann, *Die abendländische Kirchenbusse im frühen Mittelalter*, 73–91; Watkins, *A History of Penance*, II, 632–664; and Pierce, "The 'Frankish' Penitentials," 31–39.

165. See, for example, the following works by Cyrille Vogel, *La discipline pénitentielle en Gaule des origines à fin du VIIe siècle* (Paris, 1952); *Les "Libri paenitentiales"* (Brepols, 1978); and "Les rituels de la pénitence tarrifée," in *Liturgia opera divina e umana. Studi offerti à S. E. Mons. A. Bugnini, Biblioteca Ephemerides Liturgicae*, Subsidia 26 (Rome, 1992), 419–427.

166. By the early ninth century some clerical intellectuals were much annoyed by the rather mechanical and putatively uncanonical processes that dominated confession and penance. See the brief but useful summary by Pierce, "The 'Frankish' Penitentials," 31–34.

167. Anon., *Epist. consol. ad pergantes in bellum*, ed. Schmitz, tab. 10, lines 4–5.

168. Boniface, *Epist.*, no. 68. N.b. Boniface's letter is known only from a *fragmentum* in the pope's reply.

169. See, for example, R. Emmet McLaughlin, "The Word Eclipsed: Preaching in the Early Middle Ages," *Traditio*, 46 (1991), 111.

170. Cf. McLaughlin, "The Word Eclipsed," 110–111, who calls attention to Hincmar's views as evidence for the domination of society by orality.

171. See the texts gathered by Pierce, "The 'Frankish' Penitentials," 31–34.

172. *Poenitentiale Burgundense.*, ed. Schmitz (II, 321), XV: "Si quis sepulcri violator fuerit V an pen[e]eat III ex his in pane et aqua."

173. *Poenitentiale Parisiense II*, ed. Schmitz (II, 330), ch. 60.

174. In addition to *De remediis peccatorum*, ed. Schmitz (II, 657), ch. 6; and *Poenitentiale Parisiense II*, ed. Schmitz (I, 687), ch. 52, cited above, see, for example, *Poenitentiale Bedae*, ed. Schmitz (I, 559), ch. 6; *Poenitentiale Cummeani*, ed. Schmitz (I, 655), ch. 2, "Si quis cum rege in proelio occiderit hominem, XL dies paenit"; *Poenitentiale Valicellanum II*, ed. Schmitz (I, 356), ch. 13: "Si quis cum rege in prelio hominem occiderit, XL dies peniteat in pane et aqua; qui jussu Domini sui occiderit hominem, similiter XL dies peniteat"; and *Poenitentiale Valicellanum I*, ed. Schmitz (I, 264), ch. 11, "Si quis cum rege in proelium hominem occiderit, XL dies peniteat."

An even more lengthy list is compiled by Erdmann, *The Idea of Crusade*, 17, n. 32, with the apparent intention (16–18) of suggesting that penances were even more heavily imposed on Carolingian soldiers than is suggested by the penance books. Cf. Delaruelle, "Essai sur la formation de l'idée de Croisade," 44, n. 105, who criticizes Erdmann for casting his net too widely in seeking to demonstrate the hard nature of military penance of soldiers who killed legitimately in a just war. Raymund Kottje, *Die Tötung im Kriege: Ein moralisches und rechtliches Problem im frühen Mittelalter* (Barsbüttel, 1991), 1–2.

175. *De remediis peccatorum*, ed. Schmitz (II, 657), ch. 6; *Poenitentiale Parisiense II*, ed. Schmitz (I, 687), ch. 52. See the observations by Kottje, *Die Tötung im Kriege*, 1.

176. Kottje, *Die Tötung im Kriege*, 3–4, demonstrates the insufficiency of Erdmann's position regarding penance and calls attention to several texts, including the *leges* of the

Frisians redacted ca. 800, which assigns no penance for legitimate killing by soldiers in war.

177. Rhabanus Maurus, *Poenit.*, ch. 4, which was written in 841; and also Rhabanus Maurus, *Epist.*, 32, in which he explained the situation to Archbishop Otgarius of Mainz in 842. The length and detail of Rhabanus' argument suggests that ecclesiastical intellectuals, unnamed in either text, were arguing that no penance should be done by those men who had followed legitimate orders, i.e., acted "jussu principum." In short, Rhabanus likely would not have believed that he needed substantial authority for his position if he were merely dealing with a popular custom that had no intellectual support. See the discussion by Kottje, *Die Tötung im Kriege*, 6–7.

178. McCormick, "The Liturgy of War," 4–5.

179. See Koeniger, *Die Militärseelsorge*, 53–54. The curious insistence by Erdmann, *The Idea of the Crusade*, 17, that "a provision was in force that penitents should not bear arms and should never again participate in war after having completed their penance," has an air of unreality about it. In loc. cit., n. 34, he recognizes that "these rules could not be implemented in wartime." Since the rule was ancient (see for background Henri F. Secrétan, "Le christianisme de premiers siècles et le service militaire," *Revue de théologie et de philosophie, n.s.* 2 (1914), 345–365) and unenforced by the early Carolingians, who undertook military campaigns on a regular basis, the prohibition was not in force. Kottje, *Die Tötung im Kriege*, 2–6, ostensibly demolishes Erdmann's position noted above.

180. Koeniger, *Die Militärseelsorge*, 50–52.

181. Nithard, *Hist.*, bk. III, ch. 1.

182. Fredegar Cont., ch. 37.

183. Koeniger, *Die Militärseelsorge*, 51.

184. Anon., *Epist. consol. ad pergantes in bellum*, ed. Schmitz, tab. 10, line 7. The effort by Erdmann, *The Idea of the Crusade*, 16 n. 31, to argue that this text is not a sermon because the word *epistola* appears in the title of the manuscript is tendentious on two counts. First, the original of the text does not survive; the title exists only in a copy in shorthand. Second, the use of the word *epistola* in the title of a document does not disqualify a text from being a sermon (see below). The document in question in the form that we have it is a sermon that was intended for a large audience. McLaughlin, "The Word Eclipsed," 77–122, apparently is unaware of this text.

185. There seems to be a general consensus that until the reform efforts of Alcuin, begun late in the eighth century, at the earliest, took hold in a significant manner—here there is disagreement regarding the pace of change—Latin was the vernacular. A very useful guide is Roger Wright, "Review Article: Michael Banniard, *Viva voce: Communication écrit et communication orale du IVe au IX siècle en occident latin* (Paris, 1992)," *Journal of Medieval Latin*, 3 (1993), 78–94, with the literature cited there.

186. Anon., *Epist. consolat. ad pergantes in bellum*, ed. Schmitz, tab. 10, lines 9–10.

187. Anon., *Epist. consolat. ad pergantes in bellum*, ed. Schmitz, tab. 10, line 12.

188. Anon., *Epist. consolat. ad pergantes in bellum*, ed. Schmitz, tab. 11, line 3.

189. Anon., *Epist. consolat. ad pergantes in bellum*, ed. Schmitz, tab. 11, lines 5–6.

190. The complete text (MS CLM. 14410, fols. 81v-83v,) was published for the first time from the above-mentioned Munich MS by Koeniger, *Die Militärseelsorge*, 68–72; see 68, for the crowded treatment of confession. For further discussion, see Joseph Michael Heer, *Ein karolingische Missionskatechismus* (Freiburg, 1911), 60–62, who argues that the sermon in question was intended for Carolingian troops in the Avar wars. However, in

his review of Heer's monograph, Joseph Schmidlin (*Zeitschrift für Missionwissenschaft*, 2 [1912], 258) shows that this sermon could have been written for soldiers in the wars against the Saxons. The early Carolingians fought frequently against the Saxons and nothing in the sermon ties the text explicitly to the reign of Charlemagne. Koeniger's inclination (loc. cit. 51) toward an earlier date would seem to be influenced by the heavy emphasis on penance and on priests hearing confession.

Cf. Erdmann, *The Idea of the Crusade*, e.g., 16, n. 31, who doubts the value of early Carolingian texts and recognizes that these undermine his efforts to identify various of the matters under discussion here as primarily post-Carolingian, i.e., developments of the later ninth and tenth centuries. By contrast, Delaruelle, "Essai sur la formation de l'idée de Croisade," 24–45, sees much of interest regarding the matter of the "crusade idea" in a broad sense prior to the later ninth century. McLaughlin, "The Word Eclipsed," 77–122, appears to have been unaware of this text.

191. Anon., *Epist. consolat. ad pergantes in bellum*, ed. Schmitz, tab. 10, lines 13–14.

192. Anon., *Epist. consolat. ad pergantes in bellum*, ed. Schmitz, tab. 10, line 15.

193. Anon., *Epist. consolat. ad pergantes in bellum*, ed. Schmitz, tab. 10, lines 18–19.

194. Anon., *Epist. consolat. ad pergantes in bellum*, ed. Schmitz, tab. 10, line 21.

195. Anon., *Epist. consolat. ad pergantes in bellum*, ed. Schmitz, tab. 10, line 25, tab. 11, line 1.

196. Anon., *Epist. consolat. ad pergantes in bellum*, ed. Schmitz, tab. 11, lines 4–5.

197. Anon., *Epist. consolat. ad pergantes in bellum*, ed. Schmitz, tab. 11, line 8.

198. Anon., *Epist. consolat. ad pergantes in bellum*, ed. Schmitz, tab. 10, lines 15–16. Cf. Erdmann, *The Idea of Crusade*, 18, who emphasizes clerical hostility toward rapine but does not discuss the above-cited sermon in this context which obviously provides a different view. Concerning the matter of foraging and the inflammatory vocabulary used by ecclesiastical writers, which in turn many modern scholars misunderstand, see the important article by Elisabeth Magnou-Nortier, "The Enemies of the Peace: Reflections on a Vocabulary, 500–1100," in *The Peace of God: Social Violence and Religious Response in France Around the Year 1000*, ed. Thomas Head and Richard Landes (Ithaca and London, 1992), 58–79. She makes clear that foraging in friendly territory was permitted only with the permission of the commander. However, if survival were at issue, the soldier could take what he needed under the teaching of the church. *Rapina*, however, required that the goods taken be paid for at a later time but without penalty.

199. Anon., *Epist. consolat. ad pergantes in bellum*, ed. Schmitz, tab. 10, 1–25, tab. 11, 1–8.

200. *Waltharius*, ed. Strecker, lines 1158–1160.

201. *Waltharius*, ed. Strecker, lines 1161–1167.

202. McCormick, *Eternal Victory*, 358–359.

203. See, for example, *Cap. reg. Fr.*, no. 13, ch. 7, issued in 755.

204. Abbo, *De bello Parisiaco*, bk. I, lines 315–319, 332–352.

205. The basic outline for the early Carolingian period is provided by Paxton, *Christianizing Death*, 92–127, although he does not follow up the military aspects of the situation. Kottje, *Die Tötung im Kriege*, deals with the military context but concentrates on the later Carolingians.

206. *Sacramentary of Gellone*, no. 2923; and see the discussion by Paxton, *Christianizing Death*, 99.

207. See, for example, Nithard, *Hist.*, bk. III, ch. 1, whose report would seem to suggest custom rather than innovation.

208. Fortunatus, *Vexilla regis prodeunt*, ed. Bulst, 129.

209. Cathwulf, *Epist.* (7); and see the discussion by McCormick, *Eternal Victory*, 359.

210. Two letters by Pope Zacharius, *Epist.*, no. 60, ed. Tangl; and *Cod. Carol.*, no. 30, to Boniface and Pippin, respectively, would seem to sustain this observation as argued by McCormick, "Liturgy of War," 17.

211. McCormick, "Liturgy of War," 15–16.

212. See the imaginative suggestion by McCormick, *Eternal Victory*, 360–361, regarding the successful *pugnae* of Charles Martel that were added to St. Willibrord's Calendar at specific dates.

213. Hermoldus Nigellus, *Elegia*, line 3.

214. *Cod. Carol.*, no. 6.

215. See the discussion by Wallace-Hadrill, "War and Peace in the Early Middle Ages," 32.

Chapter 5. Battlefield Tactics

1. Verbruggen, *The Art of Warfare*, 11, for a general condemnation, and Matthew Strickland, *War and Chivalry: The Conduct and Perception of War in England and Normandy, 1066–1217* (Cambridge, 1996), 75–97, who provides a great deal of very useful information on this subject.

2. See the discussion by Bachrach, *Anatomy of a Little War*, 79–81, for a good example of this practice.

3. Few monks went as far as Ademar of Chabannes, who forged documents and made up entire narrative accounts from the whole cloth. See, for example, Richard Landes, *Relics, Apocalypse, and the Deceits of History: Ademar of Chabannes, 989–1034* (Cambridge, Mass., 1995).

4. See, for example, Goffart, *Narrators*, 219–220.

5. See, for example, the discussion of this problem by Bernard Bachrach, "The Practical Use of Vegetius' *De re Militari* During the Early Middle Ages," *The Historian*, 47 (1985), 239–255.

6. The development during the later nineteenth century of what the Germans called *Sachkritik* was particularly important to the writing of military history. See Delbrück, *The Art of War*, I, 16–17, 20. However, Delbrück failed to utilize the method with sufficient rigor in regard to his studies of the Carolingians. See Bachrach, "Early Medieval Military Demography," 3–20. Concerning the background on Delbrück see Arden Bucholz, *Hans Delbrück and the German Military Establishment* (Iowa City, 1985); and the insightful observations by Gordon A. Craig, "Delbrück: Military Historian." Keegan, *Face of Battle*, 87–88, provides a very good explanation of the method without, however, discussing its nineteenth-century intellectual roots. It may be added, as well, that military planners must use *Sachkritik* as a fundamental part of their work, as in the question: can we move 10,000 men from point A to point B in ten days with adequate supplies." Thus, in a Collingwoodian sense the historian "rethinks" the problem in a manner consistent with the way in which those in the past were likely to have thought through the decisions which they made.

7. See, for example, two articles by Donald Bullough, "*Aula Renovata*: The Caro-

lingian Court before the Aachen Palace," *Proceedings of the British Academy*, 71 (1985), 267–301; and "Roman Books and Carolingian *renovatio*," 1–38. The brief remarks by Riché, *Ecoles et enseignement*, 65–69, are also of interest.

8. Einhard, *V. Karoli*, ch. 24.

9. Reynolds, "Ammianus Marcellinus," 6–8; Marshall, "Florus," 164–166; and Reynolds, "Velleius Paterculus," 431–433.

10. Isidore, *Origines*, I, xliii. See the discussion by Jacques Fontaine, *Isidore de Séville et la culture classique dans l'Espagne wisigothique* (Paris, 1959), 180–185, regarding Isidore's view of history; and the general observations by Pierre Riché, *Education and Culture in the Barbarian West: Sixth Through Eighth Centuries*, trans. J. Contrini (Columbia, S.C., 1976), 261.

11. Laistner, *Thought and Letters*, 218–220.

12. Riché, *Ecoles et enseignement*, 51, 66. Cf. Giles Brown, "Introduction: The Carolingian Renaissance," in *Carolingian Culture: Emulation and Innovation*, ed. Rosamond McKitterick (Cambridge, 1994), 5, who argues that Pippin's close connection with St. Denis and his stay there do not prove that he had access to any formal education at the monastery. Brown does not, however, address Riché's suggestions regarding the intellectual richness of the court at Pavia and its possible influence on Pippin.

13. See the introduction by Wallace-Hadrill to Fredegar Cont., xxvi–xviii, lvi; and explicitly ch. 34.

14. See, for example, Fredegar Cont., chs. 20, 24.

15. See the general discussion by Verbruggen, *The Art of Warfare*, 27–28, 51, 58–60, 63.

16. See the discussion by Bachrach, "The Education of the 'Officer Corps,'" 8–9.

17. Regarding Trajan's reputation, see Campbell, *The Emperor and the Roman Army*, 37–38, 45–47; and regarding Carolingian views on the importance of Trajan as a model, see, for example, Lupus, *Epist.*, no. 37. A study of Trajan's medieval *Nachleben* is a *desideratum*. N.b. Verbruggen, *The Art of Warfare*, 51, who provides examples of the enduring importance of these values from the High Middle Ages.

18. Rhabanus Maurus, *De Procinctu romanae Miliciae*, ch. III, where Rhabanus' commentary departs greatly from Vegetius, *De re Militari*, bk. I, ch. 4.

19. Regarding the identification of levies in regional terms based upon the *civitas* in which they were mustered, see Bachrach, *Merovingian Military Organization*, 154.

20. Hans-Werner Goetz, "Social and Military Institutions," *The New Cambridge Medieval History*, II, ed. Rosamond McKitterick (Cambridge, 1995) 477–478, provides an introduction with some bibliography. However, this is a topic which requires considerable new research. Efforts by the government to discourage some of these groups and particularly *coniurationes* or sworn associations must be seen in particular contexts that require further investigation. Traditional arguments redolent with the whiff of "class struggle" are less than convincing.

21. Gregory of Tours, *Hist.*, bk. X, ch. 9.

22. Astronomer, *V. Hlud.*, bk I, ch. 4.

23. See the discussion by Bachrach, "Procopius and the Chronology of Clovis's Reign," 22–24.

24. Sidonius Apollonaris, *Epist.*, V, 7, 3.

25. Sidonius Apollonaris, *Epist.*, bk. IV, no. 20.

26. Anon., *Passio Praejecti*, ch. 29.

27. Anon., *Passio Praejecti*, ch. 29.

28. Notker, *Gesta Karoli*, bk. II, ch. 6.

29. Notker, *Gesta Karoli*, bk. II, ch. 8.

30. Notker, *Gesta Karoli*, bk. II, ch. 6, for the *magister* and his uniformed staff. *Waltharius*, ed. Strecker, line 438, where mention is made of the *magister* who was in charge of the cooks at the royal court.

31. Einhard, *V. Karoli*, ch. 26.

32. Notker, *Gesta Karoli*, bk. I, ch. 34, provides a very full but problematic account of these uniforms and I have treated it as such. Notker saw the household troops who had accompanied King Charles III in his visit to St. Gall in 883 and obtained information concerning the uniforms of the "ancient" Franks, i.e., the distant predecessors of these "modern" soldiers, from the men who were in the royal guard. By the "ancient" Franks, Notker means the generation prior to that of Charlemagne and then that of the great emperor, himself.

33. Notker, *Gesta Karoli*, bk. I, ch. 34, and cf. bk. II, ch. 21, where there seems to be no awareness that linen was likely more expensive than wool.

34. Notker, *Gesta Karoli*, bk. I, ch. 34.

35. Notker, *Gesta Karoli*, bk. I, ch. 34.

36. Lebecq, *Marchands Frisions*, I, 131–134.

37. Notker, *Gesta Karoli*, bk. II, ch. 9. Lebecq, *Marchands Frisions*, I, 131–134.

38. Notker, *Gesta Karoli*, bk. II, ch. 21, seems to think that the color spectrum of Frisian cloaks was vast.

39. *Annales q.d. Einhardi, an.,* 775.

40. *Waltharius*, ed. Strecker, line 556, for the general point.

41. *Waltharius*, ed. Strecker, line 698, concerning the horse tail and line 334 for the red crests.

42. Coupland, "Carolingian Arms and Armor," 32–35, provides a very satisfactory picture of the state of the question, but much more work is necessary.

43. *Waltharius*, ed. Strecker, line 798.

44. Coupland, "Carolingian Arms and Armor," 34.

45. The date is unnecessarily controversial and the conclusions by Rouche, "Les Aquitains," affirming the value of the Latin sources for 732 are sound. See also Rouche, *L'Aquitaine*. Roger Collins, *Early Medieval Spain: Unity in Diversity, 400–1000* (New York, 1983), 146–149, argues that the Arab sources are unreliable for the kind of detail at issue and reinforces this position with particular attention to the matter of the date for the battle of Poitiers, for which he accepts the 732 date (167, 254). He reiterates these arguments against the Arab sources in Roger Collins, *The Arab Conquest of Spain: 710–797* (Oxford, 1989), 23–26. However, in a curious lapse (89–90) he accepts the Arab dates. In the course of this later lapse, Collins fails to mention Fredegar's Continuator, chs. 13, 14, who was the contemporary court chronicler for Charles Martel's family, and provides a relative chronology that strongly supports 732 for the year of the battle.

46. An extensive scholarly literature dealing with this battle is marked by serious conflicts over most points. However, no modern scholar now claims that the Carolingian army fought on horseback during the first day of the battle. By contrast there is a consensus that Charles Martel deployed his forces on foot. See, for example, Marcel Mercier and André Seguin, *Charles Martel et la bataille de Poitiers* (Paris, 1944); and Jean Deviosse, *Charles Martel* (Paris, 1978).

47. From a historiographical perspective, see M. C. Diaz y Diaz, "La historiografía hispana desde la invasíon hasta el año 1000," *Settimane di Studio del Centro Italiano di Studi sull'alto Medioevo*, 16 (Spoleto, 1970), I. 313–355. and reprinted in M. C. Diaz y Diaz, *De Isidoro al siglo XI* (Barcelona, 1976), 205–234.

48. Anon., *Chron.*, 361. N.b. Vegetius, *De re Militari*, bk. I, ch. 20; and bk. III, ch. 17, who emphasizes the importance of the men in the phalanx standing like a wall.

49. Anon., *Chron.*, 361.

50. Maurice, *Strategikon*, bk. XI, ch. 3.

51. The poem by Angelbert, discussed earlier, in which the author indicates that he fought in the first battle line, gives every indication that he was fighting on foot and says nothing to suggest that he was involved in mounted combat.

52. Fredegar, *Chron.*, bk. IV, ch. 38.

53. Vegetius, *De re Militari*, bk. II, ch. 17.

54. Anon., *Chron.*, 362.

55. Anon., *Chron.*, 362.

56. Anon., *Chron.*, 362, who, nevertheless, chides the Northerners for having "despicably" failed to follow up their victory despite the fall of night. If the chronicler's judgment here is be taken seriously then it is prima facie evidence of his own ignorance of good generalship. However, it is more than likely, given his apparent though inconsistent southern sympathies, that he was trying to discredit the Northerners.

57. Vegetius, *De re Militari*, bk. III, ch. 22,

58. For the broad picture, see Klavs Randsbourg, *Hjortspring: Warfare and Sacrifice in Early Europe* (Aarhus, 1995); regarding the Greeks, see Anderson, "Hoplite Weapons," 28–29, where a year of basic training was required for all new recruits and subsequent practice was deemed necessary. Vegetius, *De re Militari*, focuses upon training in great detail. Indeed, he generalizes on the matter in several chapters, e.g., bk. II, ch. 23; bk. III, chs. 4, 10. As will be seen below, Rhabanus Maurus, *De Procinctu romanae Miliciae*, focuses on training as well.

59. A comparison of the Spartan phalanx and particularly its small unit interior organization with the infantry formations of the other Greek city-states demonstrates the general principle very well. See John Lazenby, "The Killing Zone," in *Hoplites*, 103–104.

60. Anon., *Chron.*, 361, emphasizes that while the Muslim army was very large, i.e., Abd ar Rachman saw the land filled up with "multitudine sui exercitus," Charles' army was even larger. However, since the author was perhaps sympathetic to the Muslims, he may have been exaggerating the order of magnitude of the "northern" victorious force. See above regarding the discussion of Delbrück's insights regarding the respective sizes of the enemy army and the army from one's homeland as reported by chroniclers.

61. Some detailed work is needed on the armament, combat techniques, and tactics of Muslim armies during the later seventh and early eighth centuries. A synthesis of sorts has been sketched for the first few decades of Muslim expansion by Donald R. Hill, "The Camel and the Horse in the Early Arab Conquests," in *War, Technology, and Society in the Middle East*, ed. W. J. Parry and M. E. Yapp (Oxford, 1975), 32–43; and he is followed by Fred McGraw Donner, *The Early Islamic Conquests* (Princeton, 1981). Patricia Crone, *Slaves on Horses: The Evolution of the Islamic Polity* (Cambridge, 1980), 37–41, provides a fine discussion of the "integration" of conquered peoples which leads ineluctably to the conclusion that the army, which operated in Spain ca. 732, was very different from what it had been ca. 632. Regarding changes that took place in the Muslim military

establishment, see Al-Bayan wa'l-Tabyin Al-Jahiz, writing during the early ninth century, who compares early Muslim armament and combat techniques with some of the massive developments that took place in the period following the early conquests, after about 650, under the influence of the Byzantines and Persians. For a convenient translation, see Bernard Lewis, *Islam from the Prophet Muhammad to the Capture of Constantinople*, 2 vols. (New York, 1974), I, 214–217. For earlier influences see, for example, Jones, *Later Roman Empire*, 154, 278, 294, 611, who notes that various Arab units fought as mercenaries for both the Persians and the Byzantines.

Claudio Sánchez-Albornoz, *Entorno a los orígenes del feudalismo*, 3 vols. (Mendoza, 1942) I, 136–251, treats the role of what he calls *la caballería* of the Muslims from the conquest of North Africa to the end of the eighth century largely on the basis of translated Arabic sources. His aim is to show that "Arab cavalry" was neither the numerically preponderant nor tactically dominant arm of the Muslim armies that conquered Spain and which later were projected into Gaul. In this observation, Sánchez-Albornoz is likely correct. However, he seems to have been overly influenced by the fact that some elements in the early Muslim armies were desert nomads. Thus, he sets out to demonstrate that these forces were not the same type of nomad fighting men as those who ranged over the steppes of South Russia on horseback, e.g., Huns, and rightly observes that in the early days of conquest the camel was of primary importance.

Sánchez-Albornoz does recognize, however, that the Muslim armies in Spain included "small" numbers of mounted troops. To put a percentage on these vague conclusions is hazardous, but if only 10 to 20 percent of the Muslim armies were composed of mounted troops, these forces cannot be ignored. Nevertheless, such small percentages would still make the mounted troops in Muslim armies far inferior in terms of both numbers and tactical importance to the armies of the Byzantines whom they defeated, whose lands they ruled, and whose people they recruited subsequently for military service. Ann Hyland, *Medieval Warhorse*, 47, argues that with control of Byzantine resources, "Arab cavalry soon became the main arm of the Arab forces." Here she seems to be extrapolating from some of the information provided by Hill, "The Camel and the Horse." However, Donner, *Early Islamic Conquests*, 193, alludes to a source mentioning Muslim horsemen in the 5,000 range. The figures provided by Hyland, *Medieval Warhorse*, 55–57, suggest that in Spain during the 720s, the entire Muslim field army was in the 30,000 range and this force may have included 30 percent mounted troops.

62. Anon., *Chron.*, 361., regarding the units of Muslim *falangae*. The term "phalanx" in the Western tradition is reserved, in general, for the description of units deployed on foot.

63. Donner, *The Early Islamic Conquests*, 222.

64. Hanson, *The Western Way of War*, 135–137.

65. Keegan, *Face of Battle*, 99, discusses the technique by which the force on the defense can "wrong-foot" the enemy offensive force by taking a backward step. This defensive maneuver, of course, requires considerable training, for if not prearranged it can throw the men further to the rear off-balance.

66. With regard to the fear that is felt by even the best trained troops, see the brilliant discussion by Hanson, *The Western Way of War*, 96–104.

67. For the basic philological background, see Friedrich Wilhelm Schwarzlose, *Die Waffen der alten Araber aus ihren Dichtern dargestellt* (Leipzig, 1886), 246–319; and for a general treatment see Hill, "The Camel and the Horse," 38–40. In the early years of

the conquest Muslim mounted archery was poor, but it improved considerably during the first decades of conquest. Donner, *The Early Islamic Conquests*, 222, emphasizes that mounted troops used lances. Crone, *Slaves on Horses*, 38, calls attention to archery regiments, e.g., the Qiqaniyya, named for the region in which they were raised. Glubb, *The Great Arab Conquests*, 142, discusses the Muslim's capacity to begin battle even as early as in the first decades following Mohammed, with a "cloud of arrows," and (189) calls attention to the tradition that Saad ibn abi Waqqas, who commanded the Muslim army at the Yarmouk in 636, was renowned as a young man for his ability as an archer. N.b. the well-known Oman petroglyphs depict men on horseback with lances, and mounted troops with swords and shields, foot soldiers with swords and shields, and others with bows but no mounted archers. A collection of these has been brought together in accessible form by Nicolle, *Arms and Armour*, I, 196–197 for the literature; II, nos. 508–515B, for the pictures. N.b. Nicolle includes material that dates from much earlier than the crusading era. Regarding changes that took place in the Muslim military establishment see Al-Bayan wa'l-Tabyin Al-Jahiz (trans. Lewis, *Islam from the Prophet Muhammad to the Capture of Constantinople*, I, 214–217).

68. Muslim archery was based upon the composite recurve bow, used in the Middle East and the steppes of South Russia. These bows, however, not only were difficult to make, but also required considerable skill to keep in good repair. In the climate of northern Europe, the composite bow, which was very sensitive to wet or even damp weather, was exceptionally difficult to keep in first-class working condition. Some scholars suggest that these recurve bows, when in top working condition and in the hands of professional archers, had a reliable range of some 300 meters.

The basic works are J. C. Coulston, "Roman Archery Equipment," and also J. C. Coulston, "Late Roman Armour, 3rd-6th centuries A.D.," *Journal of Roman Military Equipment Studies*, 1 (1990), 139–160. For the Persian side see Bivar, "Cavalry Equipment and Tactics on the Euphrates Frontier," and H. Russell Robinson, *Oriental Armour* (London, 1968), 23–25, with very helpful illustrations of both mounted and foot archers. In this context, it is of considerable importance that Arab mercenaries, prior to the emergence of Islam, were frequently employed by both the Romans and the Persians. See, for example, Jones, *Later Roman Empire*, 154, 278, 294, 611.

69. Hill, "The Camel and the Horse," 38, for the discussion of the superiority of Arab archery to Persian archery at Qadisiyya.

70. Keegan, *Face of Battle*, 33–34, 87–88, develops a discussion of technical matters in the context of *Sachkritik*; and 87, 94–95, examines the effect of archery from this perspective. See, as well, Hanson, *The Western Way of War*, 140, for the endemic fear of missile weapons that can infect men in a stationary position. Cf. Maurice, *Strategikon*, bk. XI, ch. 3, who notes that the Franks are not able to suffer pain calmly.

71. Whatever missile capacity Charles Martel's army maintained was of limited value in this battle, in light of not only the account by the Anon., *Chron.*, of the first day of the battle, discussed here, but also information provided by Fredegar's Continuator concerning operations on the second day of the battle, discussed below. Neither author mentions the Carolingian missile weapons in the context of battle at Poitiers in 732. It is possible that Charles did not use his archers or spear throwers so as to encourage the Muslims to charge and close with his phalanx.

72. Anderson, "Hoplite Weapons and Offensive Arms," 21–22.

73. Agathias, *Hist.*, bk. II, ch. 5.4, writing during the second half of the sixth cen-

tury, claims that the Franks did not use the bow for military purposes, and Maurice, *Strategikon*, bk. XI, ch. 3, writing at the end of the sixth century, does not discuss their ability as archers. Thus, the use of the bow for offensive operations in the field, where the Byzantines were apt to gain information regarding Merovingian military forces, is controversial. However, there is early evidence (Gregory, *Hist.*, bk. I. ch. 9, quoting Sulpicius Alexander) that the Franks used the bow and arrow in military operations as contrasted merely for hunting. Indeed, according to this account they used the tactic of a hail of arrows and that the arrow points were smeared with poison. Some possible support for knowledge of poison arrows is found in *Lex Salica*, XVII.2, where the fine of 62.5 solidi is levied on someone who uses them. More important in the present context, however, is *Lex Salica*, XXIX.6, where a composition of 35 solidi must be paid if someone illegally cuts off the second finger "with which one shoots an arrow." This composition is also found in *Lex Rib.*, V.7., but is set at 36 solidi. N.b. *Lex Baj.*, IV, 23, takes note of fighting men with bows and with other types of missile weapons and IV. 21, also takes note of the use of poisoned arrows. For the use of the bow in Merovingian Gaul, cf. Weidemann, *Kulturgeschichte*, II, 267.

The Carolingian use of the bow for military purposes is much less controversial. See, for example, Riesch, "Quod nullus," 209–226, who makes clear that the bow and arrow was a consistent element in the arsenal of Frankish armies, as it was of a segment of those fighting men whom the Franks found in Gaul when they settled there. For the heterogeneous background of the fighting men integrated into the armies of Clovis and his successors see Bachrach, *Merovingian Military Organization*, 3–17. An important source in the context of the early Carolingian era is *V. Lamberti*, ch. 13, in which Dodo, the *domesticus* of Pippin II, supported a large military household in which his *pueri*, when fully armed, carried a bow and a quiver of arrows. Coupland, "Carolingian Arms and Armor," 48–50, by and large also affirms the use of the bow by the Carolingians. Rhabanus Maurus, *De Procinctu romanae Miliciae*, ch. XIII, for the putative maximum range of Carolingian bows.

In the north, where the self bow was used but the composite bow was generally not, there is considerable information regarding the Anglo-Saxon neighbors of the early Carolingians. For some good illustrations of the self bow used in the north, see Bradbury, *The Medieval Archer*, 18, 19, 24. A plethora of misunderstanding and argument regarding the so-called long and short self bows are judiciously corrected by James Holt, *Robin Hood* (London, 1982), 79.

The composite bow was not unknown to the Franks, however. For example, archery units of the later Roman empire stationed in the north used this type of weapon as noted by Coulston, "Roman Archery Equipment," 224–225. Coupland, "Carolingian Arms and Armor," 49, also believes that there is some evidence for knowledge of the composite bow by the early Carolingians because it was used by their Byzantine neighbors and also apparently by their Lombard neighbors.

74. Glubb, *The Great Arab Conquests*, 178–179.

75. Anon. *Chron.*, 360.

76. Anon. *Chron.*, 362. The use of the term *gladius* to describe the weapon used by Charles' troops might incline the reader to believe that a rhetorical figure had been put in play by the author rather than an accurate description of the combat. However, Isidore of Seville (*Etymol.* bk. XVIII, ch. 6), comments extensively on different types of swords, including the *gladius*. The well-educated Anonymous, who was living in Spain

and writing in Latin, undoubtedly knew Isidore's work. Thus, whatever rhetorical figure might have been adduced by using the word *gladius*, he focused on the short thrusting sword that was appropriate for use in the infantry phalanx.

77. Stein, *Die Adelsgräber des achten Jahrhunderts*, Textband, 13.

78. Coupland, "Carolingian Arms and Armor," 35–38.

79. See Anderson, "Hoplite Weapons and Offensive Arms," 29–30, who explores the Greek evidence.

80. Pritchett, *The Greek State at War*, II, 208–231.

81. Cf. Anderson, "Hoplite Weapons and Offensive Arms," 29–30, who while recognizing the connections with dance among the Greeks, doubts its value. See also Pritchett, *The Greek State at War*, II, 213–219, who examines the role of gymnastics in training.

82. See Hanson, *The Western Way of War*, 31–32; and Anderson, "Hoplite Weapons and Offensive Arms," 30–31.

83. Delbrück, *The Art of War*, I, 23.

84. *Waltharius*, ed. Strecker, lines 1429–1430.

85. Concerning the danger caused by gaps in the line, see, for example, A. H. Jackson, "Hoplites and the Gods: The Dedication of Captured Arms and Armour," in *Hoplites*, 240; and Hanson, *The Western Way of War*, 160–170.

86. Donner, *The Early Islamic Conquests*, 223, speaks about the low level of Muslim military technology during the first quarter century of the conquest. However, the success of the conquest surely contributed to the rapid adoption of much more advanced equipment. See, for example, Al-Jahiz, trans. Lewis, I, 214–217.

87. The basic work on the late imperial and early Byzantine background is S. T. James, "The *fabricae*: State Arms Factories of the Later Roman Empire," in *Military Equipment and the Identity of Roman Soldiers: Proceedings of the Fourth Roman Military Equipment Conference, 1986*, ed. J. C. Coulston (Oxford, 1988), 257–331, and useful background for the Roman period is provided by M. C. Bishop, "The Military *fabrica* and the Production of Arms in the Early Principate," in *The Production and Distribution of Roman Military Equipment*, ed. M. C. Bishop (Oxford, 1986), 1–42. See also Ramsey MacMullen, "Inscriptions on Armor and the Supply of Arms in the Roman Empire," *American Journal of Archaeology*, 64 (1960), 23–40.

88. The classic but now dated study by Marc Bloch, "The Problem of Gold in the Middle Ages," in *Land and Work in Medieval Europe*, trans. J. E. Anderson (Berkeley, 1967), 186–229, still repays careful study.

89. See, for example, Michael G. Morony, *Iraq After the Muslim Conquest* (Princeton, 1984).

90. Glubb, *The Great Arab Conquests*, 218–219; and Donner, *The Early Islamic Conquests*, 231; Hyland, *The Medieval Warhorse*, 106–108.

91. Regarding Byzantine military pay, see Treadgold, *Byzantium and Its Army*, 119–157.

92. Schwarzlose, *Die Waffen der alten Araber*, 322–348 regarding armor, 349–351 concerning helmets, 351–356 for spears, and 210–245 concerning swords. See Glubb, *The Great Arab Conquests*, 142; and cf. Donner, *The Early Islamic Conquests*, 223, who is discussing the very early Muslim armies when he opines regarding their lack of body armor. However, it is important to distinguish between Muslim armies to ca. 650 and those of the later seventh and early eighth centuries, when Byzantines and Persians were inte-

grated into the military forces of Islam. See, for example, Crone, *Slaves on Horses*, 37. N.b. Al-Jahiz, trans. Lewis, 214–217, with regard to sophisticated equipment.

93. Salin, *La civilisation mérovingienne*, III, 57–115, provides what remains the basic account of the manufacture of the long sword; and Menghin, *Das Schwert im frühen Mittelalter*, 15–21, whose work focuses on the long sword, and especially see his catalogue of more than 150 such weapons. A. Zeki Validi, "Die Schwerter der Germanen nach arabishcen Berichten des 9–11. Jahrhunderts," *Zeitschrift der Deutschen Morgenländischen Gesellschaft*, 90 (1936), 19–36, points to Muslim admiration for swords produced in the West. This theme is followed by Coupland, "Carolingian Arms and Armor," 44–45, but also takes note of a variety of sources that indicate that the Carolingians coveted swords manufactured by the Muslims.

94. Werner, "Bewaffnung und Waffenbeigabe in der Merowingerzeit," 107.

95. Salin, *La civilisation mérovingienne*, III, 97, 105–107, 112, 196, identifies high quality pattern-welded *spathae*, while the short sword (45–57) was of lesser quality. Whether Salin's samples are representative in a statistical sense is another matter. For a more recent review, see Gale, "The Seax," 71–83. See also Stein, *Die Adelsgräber des achten Jahrhunderts*, Textband, 13.

96. Menghin, *Das Schwert im frühen Mittelalter*, 15–21; and Stein, *Die Adelsgräber des achten Jahrhunderts*, who deals with what she calls noble graves from the eighth century but which should be termed rich graves.

97. Anon., *Chron.*, 361, notes that Charles' men were armed in a formidable manner ("ferrea manu perardua") but pointedly does not hint that they were better armed than their Muslim adversaries. This is important because in the same sentence in which he speaks of the armament of the Franks, the anonymous chronicler does assert that the Christian army was larger than the force led by Abd ar Rachman.

98. Crone, *Slaves on Horses*, 37–41.

99. Aly Mohamed Fahmy, *Muslim Sea Power in the Eastern Mediterranean from the Seventh to the Tenth Century A.D.* (London, 1980).

100. See Al-Jahiz, trans. Lewis, I 214–217.

101. See the basic work by Kelly DeVries, *Infantry Warfare in the Early Fourteenth Century: Discipline, Tactics, and Technology* (Suffolk, 1996).

102. See the warnings in Maurice, *Strategikon*, bk. VII, ch. 14.

103. See, for example, Lazenby, "The Killing Zone," 101. However, this is an exceptionally important subject which has not received the kind of attention for any period of Western history that it deserves. A significant pioneering work is Jonathan Shay, *Achilles in Vietnam: Combat Trauma and the Undoing of Character* (New York, 1994), esp. 77–99, where, among other things, certain physiological observations on "specific brain neurotransmitter function and impulsive violence" of the modern "berserkers" are marked to be in need of further study.

This use of the "berserk" model must take into account a literary critique by Klaus von See, "Exkurs zum Haraldskvaedhi: Berserker," in *Edda, Saga, Skaldendichtung: Aufsätze zur skandinavischen Litaratur des Mittelalters* (Heidelberg, 1981), 311–317, where the phenomenon is traced to a ninth-century poet and found generalized ostensibly in thirteenth-century imitators. Whether the apparent development of a literary topos or theme is to be taken to mean that pure invention or fantasy is at issue in the Scandinavian material is quite another matter but well beyond the scope of the present study. Concerning the berserker, see also the curious observations by Hilda Ellis Davidson, "The Training of Warriors," in *Weapons and Warfare in Anglo-Saxon England*, ed. Sonia Chadwick Hawkes (Oxford, 1989), 12–17, who, in general (11–23), finds the tales of Zulu warriors and North American Indians to be more important evidence for our understanding of early medieval military training than the rigors of the *Campus Martius*, where generations of "Germans" were systematically trained and drilled in the Roman tradition. Concerning this evocation of "primitivism," see the searching critique by Goffart, "Two Notes on Germanic Antiquity Today," 9–30.

104. For some acute general observations, see Verbruggen, *The Art of Warfare*, 44–46. However, as Hanson, *The Western Way of War*, 96–104, makes clear, the rise of fear and panic that defeats discipline is greatest when the battle is about to begin.

105. See for background Bachrach, "The Feigned Retreat at Hastings," and Stephen Morillo, *The Battle of Hastings* (Woodbridge, 1996), 190–193.

106. See the analysis of this tactic by Arrian, *Acies Contra Alanos*, ed. Roos. For the only complete English translation see Bernard S. Bachrach, *A History of the Alans in the West* (Minneapolis, 1973), 128–132. Cf. A. B. Bosworth, "Arrian and the Alani," *Harvard Studies in Classical Philology*, 81 (1977), 217–255, who, despite his hypercritical assertions regarding the accuracy of this translation (217, n. 2), provides a commentary that departs neither significantly nor frequently from it. Bosworth's own idiosyncratic commentary (e.g., he refers to the Parthian king, Vologaeses II, as paying "Danegeld" ca. 135 A.D.) does not take into consideration the feigned retreat. Lamentably, Bosworth declined to offer his own translation of this difficult text.

107. Bachrach, "The Feigned Retreat at Hastings," 344–347.

108. See Bernard S. Bachrach, "The Origin of Armorican Chivalry," *Technology and Culture*, 10 (1969), 166–171; and reprinted in *Armies and Politics in the Early Medieval West* (London, 1993), with the same pagination.

109. Agathias, *Hist.*, bk. I, ch. 21. 1–7. See the all too brief discussion by Bachrach, *Merovingian Military Organization*, 27–28.

110. Hans von Schubert, *Die Unterwerfung der Alemannen unter die Franken* (Strassburg, 1884), 99–101, argues that Agathias may have had available to him military documents and perhaps even some sort of "daybook" that an erstwhile member of Narses' staff could have provided for his perusal. Cf. Avril Cameron, *Agathias* (Oxford, 1970), who, 43, acknowledges that Agathias likely had "an informant highly placed in the Roman army, or possibly actually an Italian." On 40, n. 2, however, she argues that Schubert has too high an opinion of Agathias' sources and concludes this on the basis of the fact that the latter provides useful information regarding both the Franks and the Alamanni. Cameron affirms that Agathias sought out contemporary oral testimony (40) but rejects Schubert's arguments regarding written sources, in part, because of the "vagueness of some of his [Agathias'] battle accounts." If Cameron is correct some of Agathias' battle accounts are vague, some are not. The account under discussion here is far from being vague and, in addition, is not discussed by Cameron either here or in Avril Cameron, "Agathias on the Early Merovingians," *Annali della Scuola Normale Superiore di Pisa*, ser. 2, 37 (1968), 95–140.

111. See, for example, Cameron, *Agathias*, 31–37, who examines Agathias' "approach to history." While recognizing the "virtues," noted above, she sees the work largely in a negative light and judges Agathias' *History* by modern historiographical standards. Nevertheless, she tends to defend Agathias' details regarding the Franks (Cameron, "Agathias on the Early Merovingians," 96), while being less imaginative than Schubert, *Die Unterwerfung der Alemannen unter die Franken*, 93–125.

112. Cf. Cameron, *Agathias*, 50–51, 54, 120–121, who tries to convict Agathias of

maintaining a bias in favor of the Franks so as to support a putatively contemporary diplomatic rapprochement between the Byzantines and one or another king in the *regnum Francorum*. In these efforts, Cameron omits discussion of the episode under discussion here, where, as will be seen below, the Franks err seriously. Regarding Byzantine-Frankish diplomacy in this regard, see Bachrach, *The Anatomy of a Little War*.

113. Agathias, *Hist.*, bk. I, ch. 21, 4–5. For the uses of carts, wagons, and pack horses, see Bachrach, "Animals and Warfare," 716–726.

114. Agathias, *Hist.*, bk. I, ch. 21, 4–5.

115. Agathias, *Hist.*, bk. I, ch. 21, 6.

116. See the discussion by Bachrach, "Early Medieval Military Demography," 3–20.

117. Agathias, *Hist.*, bk. I, ch. 21, 2, mentions, in a deceptively offhand manner, the encampment of Theudebald's forces outside the walls of Rimini at this time.

118. This was sound military doctrine according to late Roman practice as indicated, for example, by Vegetius, *De re Militari*, bk. III, ch. 16.

119. Agathias, *Hist.*, bk. I, ch. 21, 4, 6.

120. These data regarding the capacity of unaided human sight at various distances are developed in Bachrach, "On the Origins of William the Conqueror's Horse Transports," 505–531.

121. Agathias, *Hist.*, bk. I, ch. 21, 6.

122. Maurice, *Strategikon*, bk. XI, ch. 3, remarks on the Franks using prearranged signals.

123. Agathias, *Hist.*, bk. I, ch. 21, 6.

124. See Bachrach, "Early Medieval Military Demography," 3–20, regarding a continued doctrinaire belief in small armies.

125. Agathias, *Hist.*, bk. I, ch. 21, 8.

126. Cf. Cameron, *Agathias*, 37, who concludes somewhat dismissively that Agathias provides "a military history written by a lawyer."

127. Maurice, *Strategikon*, bk. XI, ch. 3, discusses the use of signals by the Franks. N.b. Gregory, *Hist.*, bk. IV, ch. 47, who in the paramilitary context of a pursuit makes reference to the use of horns and trumpets for signaling purposes. However, because a pursuit is at issue and he is not friendly to Chlodovech, the son of King Chilperic, who is in flight, Gregory likens the operation to the hunt for a deer.

128. Agathias, *Hist.*, bk. I, ch. 21, 8.

129. In addition to the lengthy discussion, above, of the mounted troops who fought at Rimini, it is noteworthy that Maurice, *Strategikon*, bk. XI, ch. 3, is concerned with the charge of the Frankish horsemen. For further discussion of mounted troops in the Merovingian and early Carolingian armies, see Bachrach, *Merovingian Military Organization*, 14–15, 19–20, 26–28, 58–60, 117–122, 134–137; Bachrach, "Military Organization in Aquitaine," 1–33; and Bachrach, "Charles Martel," 49–75.

130. Keegan, *Face of Battle*, 93–94, provides a very intelligent discussion of the use of archery against a mass of troops.

131. *Annales Fuldenses* [Regensburg continuation], *an.* 894.

132. The earliest mention I have found of the use of a *testudo* of this type in a Carolingian military context is in Abbo, *De bello Parisiaco*, bk. I, lines 266, 302, but with language that leads to the conclusion that it was a well-known tactic and not an innovation of the later ninth century. However, in Anglo-Saxon England during the eighth century, as indicated by Aldhelm's letter to Eahfridus (*Epist.*, no. 4), Aldhelm takes it as a com-

monplace that his correspondent will understand that archers will break up a phalanx that is protected by a *testudo*. In addition, it seems that the artist who executed the carvings on the so-called Franks' casket may have tried to depict a *testudo*. A good picture of this carving is found in Robert Hardy, *Longbow: A Social and Military History*, 3rd ed. (London, 1992), 30; and see Bradbury, *The Medieval Archer*, 19, for further comment.

133. Abbo, *De bello Parisiaco*, bk. I, lines 266, 302.

134. Agathias, *Hist.*, bk. I, ch. 21, 4.

135. Agathias, *Hist.*, bk. I, ch. 21, 4.

136. Gregory, *Hist.*, bk. III, ch. 7. See the brief discussion by Bachrach, *Merovingian Military Organization*, 135–136.

137. Agathias, *Hist.*, bk. I, ch. 22, 1, 2.

138. Agathias, *Hist.*, bk. I, ch. 22, 2, 3.

139. See, for example, regarding different types of feigned retreats, Frontinus, *Stragemata*, bk. III. ch. 9; and Maurice, *Strategikon*, bk. IV, chs. 2, 3; bk. VI, ch. 2; bk. VIII, ch. 2.91.

140. See Arrian, *Acies Contra Alanos*, 131–132; and Maurice, *Strategikon*, bk. XI, ch. 2.

141. Arrian, *Acies Contra Alanos*, 131–132.

142. Agathias, *Hist.*, bk. I, ch. 22, 4.

143. Agathias, *Hist.*, bk. I, ch. 22, 5–7.

144. Maurice, *Strategikon*, bk. XI, ch. 3. This chapter contains a melange of information that requires some sorting out. Some refers to the Franks as an ethnic group and was long out of date by the time Maurice gathered his information, while other facts are ostensibly contemporary with the period in which the author wrote.

145. Maurice, *Strategikon*, bk. XI, ch. 3.

146. Maurice, *Strategikon*, bk. XI, ch. 3.

147. Charles Martel also may have had some reservation about the discipline of his mounted troops in the forthcoming battle against the Muslims and therefore ordered them to dismount or deployed them to the rear where they could not launch a charge without specific orders and this only after considerable redeployment of the foot soldiers in front of them.

148. To this point in the narrative, Anon. *Chron.*, 362, provides the detailed account that I have followed. However, in speaking of events following the battle, he tells his readers that during the night all the Muslims silently slipped away from their camp in close marching order but left all their tents and other equipment behind. This account, as will be seen below, is diametrically opposed to the account of events provided by Fredegar's Continuator, ch. 13, regarding events that took place on the day after the battle described above. Since the Continuator, as already noted, was commissioned by Charles Martel's brother, Count Childebrand, who likely was an eyewitness if not a participant, I have followed this account regarding the second day of hostilities.

149. Rhabanus Maurus, *De Procinctu romanae Miliciae, Recapitulatio*.

150. Delbrück, *History of the Art of War*, II, 636.

151. Fredegar Cont., ch. 13.

152. Maurice, *Strategikon*, bk. II, ch, 11, for the importance of scouts, and bk. XI, ch. 3, for the Franks' putative neglect their use.

153. Rhabanus Maurus, *De Procinctu romanae Miliciae*, ch. V.

154. Fredegar Cont., ch. 13.

155. Rhabanus Maurus, *De Procinctu romanae Miliciae*, ch. V.

156. Rhabanus Maurus, *De Procinctu romanae Miliciae*, ch. XIII.

157. Rhabanus Maurus, *De Procinctu romanae Miliciae*, ch. V.

158. Rhabanus was well acquainted with the nature of early Carolingian warfare. As a privileged student during the later 770s and into the early 780s before taking up a plethora of administrative duties throughout the *regnum Francorum*, he likely had contact with elderly men who in their youth had fought at Poitiers more than forty or so years earlier or in similar battles during subsequent campaigns in which the phalanx formation had been deployed.

159. Fredegar Cont., ch. 13. N.b. this account fails to mention the week-long maneuvering prior to the battle, telescopes the two days of battle into a single day, and thereby completely ignores the victory of the Frankish phalanx on the first day of combat, discussed above. In addition, the Continuator leads his readers to believe that Abd ar Rachman was killed during Charles' attack on the Muslim encampment.

160. Anon., *Chron.*, 161.

161. Anon., *Chron.*, 162, who recounts the reluctance to pursue but avers that all significant action took place on the first day, completely contrary to Fredegar's Continuator, cited above, who sees the main action taking place as a battle for the Muslim camp.

162. *Annales q.d. Einhardi, an.* 782. Other sources, with the exception of the *Annales regni Francorum, an.* 782, ignore this debacle.

163. *Annales regni Francorum, an.* 782, emphasizes the fact that Charlemagne was caught unaware by this revolt; while *Annales q.d. Einhardi, an.* 782, does not focus upon this aspect of the situation.

164. *Annales q.d. Einhardi, an.* 782. Cf. *Annales regni Francorum, an.* 782, which ignores Theodoric and his levies completely.

165. *Annales regni Francorum, an.* 782, emphasizes that originally this unit was constituted at Charlemagne's command in order to suppress raiding operations by Slavs on the Elbe frontier. A force of Saxons was to accompany the East Frankish units, and the author characterizes this total force as an *exercitus*. However, when the Carolingian commanders learned of the Saxon revolt, they dismissed the Saxon contingent from their army and proceeded against the rebels. The author refers to this remaining East Frankish force as a *scara*. *Annales q.d. Einhardi, an.* 782, makes it very clear that this East Frankish force was composed solely of mounted troops.

166. *Annales q.d. Einhardi, an.* 782, emphasizes the official court titles of these commanders. By contrast, *Annales regni Francorum, an.* 782, simply refers to them as *missi*.

167. *Annales q.d. Einhardi, an.* 782, calls attention to the fact that four counts were killed in the battle under consideration here. It is unlikely that all the counts involved in these operations died in combat.

168. *Annales q.d. Einhardi, an.* 782, calls special attention to the members of these military retinues and avers that a great many of them chose to die at the side of their principal rather than to retreat from the field of battle, presumably without orders to withdraw, and thus to save their lives. Here, the *Annales* affirm the importance of loyalty and perhaps of obedience—no retreat without proper orders. However, he is also demonstrating skepticism, in military terms, regarding values that result in the apparent unnecessary deaths of numerous professional troops. Indeed, this author hints that since the commanders had fouled up so badly, the rank and file were not obligated to

die for these mistakes. For some important insights regarding how historians have mis-understood the values of the *comitatus*, see Steve Fanning, "Tacitus, Beowulf, and the Comitatus," *Haskins Society Journal* 9 (2001), forthcoming.

169. *Annales q.d. Einhardi, an.* 782.

170. *Annales q.d. Einhardi, an.* 782; and *Annales regni Francorum, an.* 782.

171. *Annales regni Francorum, an.* 782, indicates that when Charlemagne once again asserted his authority in the region, he forced the Saxons to surrender the rebels. The rebels, numbered at 4,500, were all executed by royal order for the crime of treason. According to *Annales q.d. Einhardi, an.* 782, 4,500 was a minimum estimate and all the prisoners were executed in a single day. Obviously, not every participant in Widukind's victory in the Süntal mountains was captured and turned over to Charlemagne for exe-cution. Widukind himself escaped, and he probably had his personal military retinue with him when he avoided capture.

A substantial effort has been made to undermine both the notion of the execution, for which deportation has been substituted, and the figure of 4,500 executed traitors. Martin Lintzel, "Die Vorgänge in Verden im Jahre 782," *Niedersachs. Jahrbuch*, 15 (1938), 1–37, and reprinted in Lintzel, *Ausgewälte Schriften* I, 147–173, reviews the older literature and tries with no success to undermine the 4,500 figure. His strongest argument, 30–36 (169–173), is based upon Delbrück's often discussed methods which as shown by Bach-rach, "Early Medieval Military Demography," 3–20, are not sound when dealing with the early Middle Ages.

When Lintzel wrote, the Saxon population during the Carolingian era was esti-mated to have been at least a half-million (Erich Keyser, *Bevölkerungsgeschichte Deutsch-lands*, 2nd ed. [Leipzig, 1941], 71, 130). Martin Lintzel, "Karl der Grosse und Widukind," reprinted in Lintzel, *Gesammalte Werke*, I, 199–224; and Lintzel, "Die Schlacht am Sün-tel," in *Ausgewälte Schriften*, I, 144–146, adds nothing new here. Cf. also Louis Halphen, "La conquête de la Saxe," *Revue historique*, 130 (1919), 252–278; reprinted in Louis Hal-phen, *Études critiques sur l'histoire de Charlemagne* (Paris, 1921), cited here at 161–167.

172. Halphen, "La conquête de la Saxe," 163–164, also concludes that the Carolin-gian army was not of great size but for reasons that I cannot wholly accept because they are based, in part, on *a priori* assumptions regarding the order of magnitude of a *scara*.

173. Cf. Lintzel, "Die Vorgänge in Verden im Jahre 782," 1–37; and Lintzel, "Karl der Grosse und Widukind," 199–224.

174. *Annales q.d. Einhardi, an.* 782.

175. *Annales q.d. Einhardi, an.* 782. Cf. the discussion by Lintzel, "Die Schlact am Süntel," 146, regarding the geography.

176. For the traditional Carolingian use of the pincer deployment, see Verbruggen, "L'armée et la stratégie de Charlemagne," 433–435; and Verbruggen, *The Art of Warfare*, 313–319.

177. *Annales q.d. Einhardi, an.* 782.

178. *Annales q.d. Einhardi, an.* 782. Evidence for the Saxons, who deployed outside the *castra*, outnumbering the East Frankish *scara* may be inferred from the fact that the former were capable of enveloping the latter, even though the latter were mounted and took up more space per capita.

179. *Annales q.d. Einhardi, an.* 782.

180. *Annales q.d. Einhardi, an.* 782.

181. *Annales q.d. Einhardi, an.* 782.

182. Maurice, *Strategikon*, bk. III, ch. 5.

183. For a plethora of medieval examples, see Verbruggen, *The Art of Warfare*, 97–102; and for a useful discussion of these developments into modern times, see Bennett, "*La Règle du Temple* as a Military Manual," 15–19.

184. *Annales q.d. Einhardi, an.* 782.

185. *Waltharius*, ed. Strecker, lines 180–214. This account is problematic because the poet is putatively describing a battle between the Huns and one of their subject peoples who are in revolt. Walter of Aquitaine is the leader of the Hunnic host in the epic portrayal. As mentioned earlier, however, the poet knew nothing of the Huns. It is possible that the poet knew something about the Avars, who dominated Pannonia during the early Carolingian era and against whom Charlemagne not only fought but was dramatically victorious. However, as will be suggested below, there is little or nothing in the poet's description of this battle that echoes the practice of the Avars.

186. *Waltharius*, ed. Strecker, line 180.

187. *Waltharius*, ed. Strecker, lines 180–181. N.b. *Annales Fuldenses, an.*, 891, where King Arnulf personally reconnoiters the enemy position, and the discussion by Bachrach, "*Caballus et Caballarius*," 185.

188. *Waltharius*, ed. Strecker, lines 180–181, "Ecce locum pugnae conspexerat et numeratam / Per latos aciem campos digessit et agros." It is argued here that the adjective "numeratam," i.e., "counted," is a synecdoche for "numeratam [hostem]," "the counted enemy force." This reading is possible because *hostis* can be either masculine or feminine. Cf. Wieland, *Waltharius*, 56, whose gloss would have "numeratam" refer to Walter's own "aciem" with some meaning such as "he arranged the battle line by the numbers." This is a creative interpretation for "numeratam," which is in the accusative singular. However, despite the problem in grammar, it is not an unattractive possibility in light of the sophisticated nature of early Carolingian military training. For another example of a synecdoche in this episode see line 195.

There were numerous ways to count the enemy force and experienced soldiers were supposed to know how to do this. See, for example, Maurice, *Strategikon*, bk. IX, ch. 5, where various problems are discussed. Accurate estimation of forces up to the 20,000–30,000 range was thought to be possible. To count troops on the march was considered exceptionally difficult, and mounted troops on the march created even greater problems as experienced commanders knew how to mask the true numbers of their forces. However, when the size of one's forces was not disguised, their estimation by the enemy was correspondingly less difficult.

189. *Waltharius*, ed. Strecker, line 181.

190. *Waltharius*, ed. Strecker, line 182.

191. *Waltharius*, ed. Strecker, line 190.

192. I am unconvinced that the poet is using the Avars rather than the Franks as his model. The Avars, of course, were noted as mounted archers and the bow was their main weapon. However, there is little reason to believe that the Avars or the Huns, for that matter, drove home a mounted charge in column with swords, as is the case in the remainder of the battle described by the *Waltharius*-poet. With regard to the Avars and their depiction by the early Carolingians, see Bachrach, "A Picture of Avar-Frankish Warfare," 5–27.

193. *Waltharius*, ed. Strecker, line 189. Of course, an argument from silence can rarely be conclusive. Nevertheless, the poet's silence on these points with regard to Walter's horsemen should not be ignored.

194. *Waltharius*, ed. Strecker, lines 183–184. Weiland, *Waltharius*, 57, interprets "hinc indeque" as "everywhere."

195. *Waltharius*, ed. Strecker, lines 185–189. Virgil has influenced the poet's vocabulary here as shown by Strecker, *Waltharius*, 126–127. However, there is no reason to believe that the poet's description of the tactics was affected by this classical influence.

Above, we have seen how Narsus ordered "direct fire" against a Frankish force and the reasons for this. The mounted troops of early Carolingian armies were trained to use the *testudo* technique as were Frankish foot soldiers: it is clear (line 192), as will be seen below, that each horseman removed his shield from his left forearm and placed it on his back where it hung from a cord, so that he could hurl his spears more efficiently.

196. *Waltharius*, ed. Strecker, line 192.

197. *Waltharius*, ed. Strecker, line 184, reverses the two terms in this context and provides the listener with an obvious contrasense insofar as he has the troops throw their spears while deployed in column, which for the most part is not effective and probably objectively not possible. It may be too much to expect that the description of a battle in Latin poetry, with all of the concomitant demands of meter, to have everything in the right place and to include all relevant military details.

198. *Waltharius*, ed. Strecker, line 193.

199. *Waltharius*, ed. Strecker, line 192.

200. Gernot Wieland, *Waltharius* (Philadelphia, 1986), 57, has the sequence of events confused here.

201. *Waltharius*, ed. Strecker, lines 195–195.

202. Strecker, *Waltharius*, 127.

203. Bennett, "*La Règle du Temple* as a Military Manual," 15–19, examines the horse's speed and keeping the ranks properly dressed.

204. See the discussion by Bennett, "*La Règle du Temple* as a Military Manual," 15–19.

205. *Waltharius*, ed. Strecker, lines 196–202.

206. *Waltharius*, ed. Strecker, line 201.

207. *Waltharius*, ed. Strecker, lines 203–205.

208. *Waltharius*, ed. Strecker, lines 203–205.

209. *Annales q.d. Einhardi, an.* 782.

210. *Waltharius*, ed. Strecker, line 207.

211. *Waltharius*, ed. Strecker, lines 208–209.

Chapter 6. Campaign Strategy and Military Operations

1. P. O. Long and Alex Roland, "Military Secrecy in Antiquity and Early Medieval Europe: A Critical Reassessment," *History and Technology*, 11 (1994), 259–290, do not treat the Carolingians. Their conclusions regarding the lack of importance of secrecy, however, are not consistent with early Carolingian behavior.

2. Adalhard, *De ordine palatii*, ch. VI (30).

3. *Annales mettenses priores, ann.* 690, 692 (pp. 8, 13, respectively).

4. Einhard, *V. Karoli*, chs. 1 and 17, respectively.

5. *Annales mettenses priores, an.* 690 (p. 8). My assumption that the author of the Metz annales is projecting contemporary conditions backward, of course, is not proof that Pippin II, Charles Martel's father, lacked a well-organized planning staff.

6. Adalhard, *De ordine palatii*, ch. VI (30).

7. Adalhard, *De ordine palatii*, ch. VII (34).

8. *Waltharius*, ed. Strecker, ll. 170–179.

9. Adalhard, *De ordine palatii*, ch. VII (34).

10. Adalhard, *De ordine palatii*, ch. VI (30).

11. Adalhard, *De ordine palatii*, ch. VI (30).

12. The early Carolingians encouraged the development of expertise in particular areas; for example, a veritable cadre of experts in Italian affairs served both Pippin and Charlemagne. See the observations by Karl Ferdinand Werner, "*Hludovicus Augustus*," 31–32 n. 102.

13. Adalhard, *De ordine palatii*, ch. VI (30).

14. Adalhard, *De ordine palatii*, chs. V (20), VI (31).

15. Adalhard, *De ordine palatii*, ch. VI (30).

16. Vegetius, *De re Militari*, bk. III, chs. 5, 6, 9.

17. Adalhard, *De ordine palatii*, ch. VII (36).

18. *Waltharius*, ed. Strecker, ll. 428–463.

19. Adalhard, *De ordine palatii*, ch. VII (36).

20. Adalhard, *De ordine palatii*, ch. VI (36).

21. Adalhard, *De ordine palatii*, chs. V (23–25, 27).

22. See Sidonius Apollinarus, *Epist.* VIII, vi, 13–18; and the discussion by Bachrach, "The Education of the 'Officer Corps' in the Fifth and Sixth Centuries," 7–13. When these valuable books, which were much in use during the later fifth century, actually disappeared has yet to be discovered.

23. See the discussion by E. Alföldi-Rosenbaum, "The Finger Calculus in Antiquity and in the Middle Ages: Studies on Roman Game Counters I," *Frühmittelalterliche Studien*, 5 (1971), 1–9; and the additional remarks by Dhuoda, *Manuel pour mon fils*, ed. and trans. Pierre Riché (Paris, 1975), 294–295 nn. 5, 6. For a sound appreciation of "scientific" accomplishment in the early Middle Ages, see Wesley M. Stevens, "Cycles of Time," 51. Cf. Alexander Murray, *Reason and Society in the Middle Ages* (corr. ed. Oxford, 1985), 156, who takes the fact that errors crept into manuscripts and were on occasion recopied as evidence for a general failure in early medieval society to do practical arithmetic. This, despite his admission that "No one knows for sure how Bede did his sums," and one could add much else as well. But cf. 451 n. 64.

24. Alcuin, *Propositiones ad acuendos juvenes*, chs. 4, 9, 13, 19, 27, 28, 29, 32, 33, 34, 52, 53, provides situations with logistic and military related value. Cf. Murray, *Reason and Society*, 153, 155, 164, who provides most of the relevant facts regarding this text, but his interpretation of the capabilities of the Carolingians to make practical use of arithmetic for military purposes and particularly with regard to logistics is far wide of the mark. This is not to say that the men and boys at Charlemagne's court were mathematicians, but that arithmetic is all that was required.

25. Alcuin, *Propositiones ad acuendos juvenes*, chs. 27, 28, 29. I want to thank my graduate student Peter Burkholder, who has worked on this text and called to my attention the order of difficulty in calculating answers to these problems. With regard to barracks see the Trelleborg fortresses, which were both "packed" and measured according to the Roman foot, see Peter H. Sawyer, *The Age of the Vikings* (London, 1962), 129–135.

26. Oelsner, *Jahrbücher des fränkischen Reiches unter König Pippin*, remains a useful guide.

27. The basic work in now Michel Rouche, *L'Aquitaine*, 111–132; also of value is Philippe Wolff, "L'Aquitaine et ses Marges," in *Karl der Grosse: Lebenswerk und Nachleben*, I, ed. W. Braunfels and Helmut Beumann (Düsseldorf, 1965), 269–306.

28. For my earlier and more general views regarding Aquitanian military organization see Bachrach, "Military Organization in Aquitaine." Cf. Rouche, *L'Aquitaine*, 350–361.

29. In general, see Butler, "Late Roman Town Walls in Gaul"; von Petrikovits, "Fortifications in the North-Western Roman Empire from the Third to the Fifth Centuries A.D."; and Steven Johnson, *Late Roman Fortifications*, 82–135. With regard to continuity of the physical artifacts and consistency of terminology see Bachrach, "Early Medieval Fortifications in the 'West' of France: A Technical Vocabulary," *Technology and Culture*, 16 (1975). On garrisons see Rouche, *L'Aquitaine*, 354–358.

30. Fredegar Cont., ch. 43.

31. The question of oaths and their relation to *vassi*, *fideles*, and military service has been vigorously debated but remains unresolved. Some of the more important works have been listed below for the convenience of the reader: P. Petot, "L'hommage servile: Essai sur la nature juridique de l'hommage," *Revue historique de droit français et étranger*, series 4, VI (1927), 68–107, but see esp. 96–106; F. Lot, "Le serment de fidélité à l'époque franque," *Revue belge de l'philologie et d'histoire*, 14 (1935), 405–426; Odegaard, "Carolingian Oaths of Fidelity"; and Ganshof, "Charlemagne's Use of the Oath."

Concerning various types of specialized troops, e.g., *laeti* and *milites*, see Bachrach, *Merovingian Military Organization*, 70–73; 78–80, for the former and for the latter 71–73, 78–80, 88–89. Regarding the specialized nature of Basque troops see Rouche, *L'Aquitaine*, 358–361.

32. See the very useful list compiled by Gabriel Fournier, "Les campagnes de Pépin le Bref en Auvergne et la question des fortifications rurales au VIIIe siècle," *Francia*, 2 (1974), 123–135. See also Gabriel Fournier, *Le peuplement rural en Basse Auvergne durant le haut moyen âge* (Paris, 1962), 343–351.

33. Fredegar Cont., ch. 25.

34. Fredegar Cont., chs. 25, 43, 45; Bachrach, *Merovingian Military Organization*, 50–51, for *custodes* at Tours.

35. Fredegar Cont., ch. 25. See the important study by Michel Rouche, "Les survivances antiques dans trois cartulaires du sud-ouest de la France aux X–XI siècles," *Cahiers de Civilisation Médiévales* 23 (1980), 93–108, who follows up these "Roman" elements.

36. Fredegar Cont., ch. 42; Bachrach, *Merovingian Military Organization*, 66–67.

37. Rouche, *L'Aquitaine*, 49, 350–352.

38. Fredegar Cont., ch. 42. For the sixth-century development of the levies of Bourges and the Auvergne, see Bachrach, *Merovingian Military Organization*, 37, 38, 43, 54–55, 60–61, 66–67, 70–71, 76; see the same work, 50, 51, 62, 71, 78, 88, 89, 96, 106, for *custodes* in general.

39. Cf. Rouche, *L'Aquitaine*, 350–361.

40. Fredegar Cont., ch. 47.

41. Fredegar Cont., ch. 10.

42. Fredegar Cont., chs. 45, 46, 50, 51. See also Bachrach, "Charles Martel," and Rouche, *L'Aquitaine*, 113–132, passim.

43. Fredegar Cont., ch. 45.

44. *Cartulaire de S. Victor de Marseille*, I, ed. M. Guérard (Paris, 1857), no. 31; and the discussion in Bachrach, "Charles Martel," 67.

45. Fredegar Cont., ch. 44.

46. For the Gascon levy, see *Annales Anianenses*, cols. 3–4, and *Chronicon Ucenense*, col. 25; also *Chronicon Moissacense*, p. 290. Cf. *Annales mettenses priores*, ann. 718, 761, and esp. 765. The textbook by Roger Collins, *The Basques*, 2nd ed. (Oxford, 1990), 109, is structured in much too general a format to be of value here.

47. Bachrach, *Merovingian Military Organization*, 47, 60, 66, 68, 76, 83, 125.

48. Bachrach, *Merovingian Military Organization*, 32, 71–72. The basic work on the *centena* is now Alexander C. Murray, "From Roman to Frankish Gaul: 'Centenarii' and 'Centenae' in the Administration of the Merovingian Kingdom," *Traditio*, 44 (1988), 60–100, who, however, may not give sufficient weight to the military role of this institutional structure.

49. *Annales Anianenses*, cols. 3–4, and *Annales Ucenense*, col. 25.

50. Bachrach, *Merovingian Military Organization*, 96.

51. The basic work on Merovingian and early Carolingian Frankish military colonies in Aquitaine remains M. Broëns, "Le peuplement germaniques de la Gaule entre la Méditerranée et l'océan," *Annals du Midi*, 65 (1955), 17–38. Some of Broën's more extreme claims have been justly criticized by Edward James, *The Merovingian Archaeology of South-West Gaul*, 2 vols. (Oxford, 1977), I, 202–207. The treatment of the toponomy by Rouche, *L'Aquitaine*, 144–150, is important, as are the observations by Ernst Gamillschag, *Romania-Germania*, 2nd ed. (Berlin, 1970), 228–238, concerning the place-name Guerche, which likely is derived from Frankish *Werki*. However, *Werki* does not always mean a "fortification" and in more general terms means a built-up place. Salin, *La civilisation merovingienne*, I, 383, has pointed out that the places called Guerche generally do not seem to have been fortified or at least whatever fortifications may have been there are less than obvious. The Guerche place-name, nevertheless, would appear to be evidence for settlement in which at least some Frankish words survived.

52. Fredegar Cont., chs. 25, 42, 43, 46, and *Annales regni Francorum*, ann. 742, 761, 762, 766, 767. Bachrach, "Charles Martel," 55–57; and Donald Bullough, "*Europae Pater*: Charlemagne and His Achievement in Light of Recent Scholarship," *English Historical Review*, 75 (1970), 89–90.

53. Cf. Fournier, "Les campagnes de Pépin le Bref," 123–135; and *Le peuplement rural*, 343–351.

54. Bachrach, *Merovingian Military Organization*, 17, 20, 21, 37–38, 101, 105.

55. Fredegar Cont., ch. 43; and Bullough, "*Europae Pater*," 89–90, and 89 n. 2.

56. Fredegar Cont., ch. 46; and Bachrach, "Charles Martel," 57.

57. Fredegar Cont., chs. 43, 46, 50; *Annales regni Francorum*, an. 766; and *Annales mettenses priores*, an. 766. To date, archaeologists can demonstrate that certain rural fortifications of the eighth century are still standing, but it is not yet possible to ascertain whether these strongholds withstood a drubbing by Pippin's forces. See Fournier, "Les campagnes de Pépin le Bref," 123–135; and *Le peuplement*, 343–351.

58. Bernard S. Bachrach, "Early Medieval Fortifications," 531–569.

59. Eugen Ewig, "L'Aquitaine et les Pays Rhénans au haut moyen âge," *Cahiers de civilisation mediévalé*, 1 (1958), 50, and reprinted in Eugen Ewig, *Spätantikes un fränkisches Gallien: Gesammelte Schriften (1952–1973)*, 2 vols., ed. Hartmut Atsma (Munich, 1976), I, 553–572.

60. Fredegar Cont., chs. 44, 45.

61. Frank, *Scholae Palatinae*, 118, 169, 198, 226; Jones, *The Later Roman Empire*, I, 666; and Bachrach, *Merovingian Military Organization*, 16, 23, 44.

62. Bachrach, *Merovingian Military Organization*, 79, 82.

63. Fredegar Cont., chs. 43, 45.

64. Fredegar Cont., chs. 45, 49, 51.

65. Fredegar Cont., chs. 44, 45, 51. Cf. the remark that before the capture of Remistanius, Chunibert was count, but after the capture of the former, a certain Gislarius is styled count.

66. Fredegar Cont., ch. 46. The term *castrum* was a synonym for *arx* or *praetorium*, the usual military designations for the main fortification located within a *civitas*.

67. *Annales regni Francorum, an.* 766, and Fredegar Cont., ch. 46, for the *scara*. There is as yet no adequate study of the *scara* in Carolingian times, but a useful start on the problem is provided by Verbruggen, "L'armée et la stratétegie de Charlemagne," 420–434. For the definition of *centena* quoted above, see Wallace-Hadrill, *The Long-Haired Kings and Other Studies in Frankish History*, 193; and also Bachrach, *Merovingian Military Organization*, 81, 87–88, 109, for *scara* in Merovingian times, and 25, 32, 34, 46, 71–72, 97, 108, 109, 124 for the *centena*. For a general overview of the *centena* see Murray, "From Roman to Frankish Gaul," 60–100.

68. Fredegar Cont., chs. 46, 50, and *Annales regni Francorum, ann,* 766, 769.

69. See note 38 for *custodes*, and Fredegar Cont., chs. 25, 42, 43, for the terms used to describe the garrisons of the independent dukes of Aquitaine.

70. See the interesting observations regarding the problems of the southern magnates and rural fortifications by Fournier, "Les campagnes de Pépin le Bref," 123–135; and Fournier, *Le peuplement*, 343–351.

71. Fredegar Cont., chs. 45–46.

72. Fredegar Cont., chs. 43, 48, 51, 52.

73. *Cap. reg. Fr.*, I, no. 18, ch. 10.

74. *Cap. reg. Fr.*, no. 1; and Gregory, *Hist.*, bk. II, ch. 37, with the discussion by Bachrach, *Merovingian Military Organization*, 11; for further background see Brühl, "Das Fränkische *Fodrum*," 54–56, 73.

75. *Cap. reg. Fr.*, I, no. 18, ch. 6; and the discussion by Bachrach, "Military Organization in Aquitaine," 12. See Clovis' order reported by Gregory of Tours (*Hist.*, bk. II, ch. 37). Cf. Weidemann, *Kulturgeschichte*, II, 278–279.

76. Astronomer, *V. Hludowici*, ch. 7. A great deal more work needs to be done on the supply system for the Carolingian armies. However, important insights are to be found in Magnou-Nortier, "The Enemies of the Peace," 58–79. With regard to this text see Carlrichard Brühl, "Das Fränkische *Fodrum*," *Zeitschrift der Savigny Stiftung für Rechtsgeschichte, Germanistische Abteilung*, 76 (1959), 73.

77. Concerning the etymology of the term see Brühl, "Das Fränkische *Fodrum*," 54–56.

78. Astronomer, *V. Hludowici*, ch. 7.

79. Astronomer, *V. Hludowici*, ch. 7, which, however, may have been a topos regarding the suffering of the poor. Cf. above, Chapter 2, concerning the complaints made by Lupus of Ferriers and Benedict of Aniane concerning the costs of war.

80. See the general observation by Bachrach, "Military Organization in Aquitaine," 1–33.

81. This Saxon campaign is dated in the *Annales regni Francorum, an.* 758, but it should be dated to 757 so that the two years without war prior to the first invasion of Aquitaine, which is mentioned by Fredegar Cont., ch. 41, can be accommodated.

82. Fredegar Cont., ch. 40, for these diplomatic exchanges between Pippin and Constantine, and *Annales regni Francorum, an.* 758, for Pippin's campaign against the Saxons. N.b. this round of diplomatic exchanges followed hard upon the legation of 757, which brought an organ as one of many presents to Pippin. See *Annales regni Francorum, an.* 757.

83. See *Annales regni Francorum, an.* 757, for the previous embassy. Constantine's offer in 763 to have his son marry Pippin's daughter, Gisla, adumbrates the emperor's thinking in these matters. Regarding the marriage negotiations see Peter Classen, "Karl der Grosse, das Papsttum und Byzanz: Die Begründung des karolingischen Kaisertums," in *Karl der Grosse*, ed. Braunfels, I, 555, with the literature cited in n. 68.

84. A detailed study of Byzantine interests in the western Mediterranean is well beyond the scope of the present work. See, however, Classen, "Karl der Grosse, das Papsttum und Byzanz," 537–608, for an overview.

85. For background see David C. Braund, *Rome and the Friendly King: The Character of Client Kingship* (London, 1984). The matter of relative equality of the two parties engaged in *amicitia* is discussed by Wolfgang H. Fritze, *Untersuchungen zur frühslawischen und frühfränkischen Geschichte bis ins 7. Jahrhundert* (Frankfurt a.M. and Berlin, 1994), 102, and fits very well with the discussion above of the arrangement made between Charles Martel and Duke Eudo.

86. Fredegar Cont., ch. 40, for the gifts and oaths.

87. *Cod. Carol.*, no. 45, regarding Gisla. The pope's observation concerning an earlier initiative by Pippin to "put away" his wife Bertha, discussed briefly, as well, in the above-mentioned letter, was connected with his interest in an alliance with the Byzantines.

88. *Cod. Carol.*, nos. 14–21; Cf. Noble, *The Republic of St. Peter*, 108–109, who believes that Pope Paul overestimated the Lombard and Byzantine threat. At one point (108) Noble labels Paul's anxiety "papal paranoia."

89. Cf. Murray, "Immunity, Nobility, and the Edict of Paris," 18–39.

90. Fredegar Cont., ch. 41. N.b. F. L. Ganshof, "Les relations exterieures de la monarchie franque sous les premiers souverains carolingiens," *Annali di Storia del Diritto, Rassegna Internationale*, 6–7 (1961–62), 1–53; and translated as "The Frankish Monarchy and Its External Relations, from Pippin III to Louis the Pious," in *The Carolingians*, 172, classifies Pippin's communication as an ultimatum.

91. Vegetius, *De re Militari*, bk. III, *prol.* Wallace-Hadrill, "War and Peace in the Early Middle Ages," 20, points out: "it was significant that the goddess of peace was iconographically very like the goddess of victory."

92. Augustine, *De civ. Dei*, XIX, cap. 7, as elaborated by Wallace-Hadrill, "War and Peace in the Early Middle Ages," 23.

93. Fredegar Cont., ch. 41.

94. Fredegar Cont., ch. 41; and for useful background on the *mandatum* see Olivier Guillot, "La droit romain classique et la lexicographie de termes du latin médiéval impliquant délégation de pouvoir," *La lexicographie du latin médiéval et ses rapports avec les recherches actuelles sur la civilisation du moyen-âge: Paris 1978* (Paris, 1981), 153–166.

95. Fredegar Cont., ch. 41.

96. *Annales regnum Francorum, an.* 759, for the year-ending celebration of Easter at Jupille. Attigny is most propitiously positioned with regard to the Roman road system south from Liège to Troyes through which Pippin's army marched on the way to Aquitaine. See Rouche, *L'Aquitaine*, 252–253, with regard to the roads, and with regard to Attigny see Brühl, *Fodrum, gistum, servitium regis*, I, 18.

97. Bernard S. Bachrach, "Was the Marchfield Part of the Frankish Constitution?" *Medieval Studies*, 36 (1974), 78–85. Reprinted in *Armies and Politics in the Early Medieval West* (London, 1993), with the literature cited there and the same pagination.

98. Fredegar Cont., ch. 41. Although the early medieval sources and even the military handbooks of the later Roman and early Byzantine empires do not discuss the problem, a first week or so at the beginning of a campaign serves as a necessary "shakedown" phase for the checking out of equipment.

99. Fredegar Cont., ch. 41. Wallace-Hadrill, *The Fourth Book*, 110, translates the term *exercitus*, which Fredegar's Continuator uses to describe the force originally levied as a "general force" and translates the phrase "omni exercitu Francorum," with which Pippin is described by the Continuator as crossing the Loire, as "the whole Frankish army." The different terminology used by the Continuator may indicate that two somewhat differently composed forces are being discussed in this chapter, and perhaps Wallace-Hadrill intuited this when he translated *exercitus* as a "general force."

100. Fredegar Cont., ch. 42.

101. Fredegar Cont., ch. 46, portrays Waiofar as considering Bourges "caput Aquitaniae."

102. The carrying of boats for crossing rivers and the use of pontoon bridges are well attested in the late antique and early medieval tradition: Anon., *De rebus Bellicis*, ch. 16; Vegetius, *De re Militari*, bk. III, ch. 7; Anon., *Strategy*, ch. 19; Maurice, *Strategikon*, bk. IX, ch. 1. For the Carolingians see Haywood, *Dark Age Naval Power*, 90, 101–103.

103. Vegetius, *De re Militari*, bk. III, ch. 7; Anon., *Strategy*, ch. 19; and Maurice, *Strategikon*, bk. XI, ch. 4; bk. XII, B, ch. 21.

104. Regarding Pippin's prudent military behavior see Bachrach, "Charles Martel," 54–57.

105. Fredegar Cont., ch. 41; *Annales q.d. Einhardi, an.* 760, provides the key information here, when Pippin arrived "in loco, qui Tedoad vocatur, positis castris, consedisset." For the identification of Doyet see Rouche, *L'Aquitaine*, 123, and the discussion 523 n. 76.

106. Bachrach, "Animals and Warfare," 716–725.

107. It is common to underestimate the exceptional effort required to train a warhorse. See on this point the outstanding study by Gillmore, "Practical Chivalry," 7–29.

108. Fredegar Cont., ch. 41; *Annales q.d. Einhardi, an.* 760.

109. *Annales regni Francorum, an.* 760; Fredegar Cont., ch. 41. Waiofar's *missi* may have had the duke's *mandatum* to negotiate with Pippin.

110. Fredegar Cont., ch. 42. For background material on such embassies see Ganshof, "The Frankish Monarchy and Its External Relations," 289–302.

111. A detailed examination of the early medieval history of *supplicatio* is needed to complement Geoffrey Koziol, *Begging Pardon and Favor: Ritual and Political Order in Early Medieval France* (Ithaca, N.Y., 1992).

112. See Rouche, *L'Aquitaine*, 122.

113. Regarding the manipulation of diplomatic interchanges see Ganshof, "The Frankish Monarchy and Its External Relations," 289–302.

114. Fredegar Cont., ch. 42.

115. See Russell, *The Just War in the Middle Ages*, for background which permits the judgment that contemporaries were unlikely to have judged Pippin to have been engaged in a war of aggression.

116. According to Fredegar Cont., ch. 42, Pippin may have heard the news as early as 1 May and not much later. This means that Waiofar mustered his troops in April and likely completed operations in the *regnum Francorum* before the end of the first week in May, if not earlier.

117. Fredegar Cont., ch. 42, provides a good description of Waiofar's military objectives.

118. Bachrach, "Animals and Warfare," 716–725.

119. Fredegar Cont., ch. 42, for Waiofar's operations. N.b. both the *Annales regni Francorum, an.* 761, and the *Annales q.d. Einhardi, an.* 761.

120. Fredegar Cont., ch. 42.

121. Both the *Annales regni Francorum, an.* 761, and the *Annales q.d. Einhardi, an.* 761, emphasize revenge as a motive for Waiofar's actions, suggesting that the Carolingian court heard something of Waiofar's argument in this context. Revenge was a legitimate reason to go to war as emphasized by Isidore, *Etymol.*, bk. 18, ch. 1.

122. Fredegar Cont., ch. 42, asserts that Waiofar's army was successful "because there was no one to stop them."

123. F. L. Ganshof, "La Tractoria," 69–91.

124. Fredegar Cont., ch. 42, indicates that Pippin had a large force available in the area around Düren and southward toward the Loire.

125. Fredegar Cont., ch. 42, "iubet omnes Francos ut hostiliter placito instituto ad Ligerem venissent." See Chapter 2, above, regarding the selection of troops for *expeditio*.

126. Concerning the structure of the royal military household see Chapter 2, above.

127. Fredegar Cont., ch. 42.

128. Fredegar Cont., ch. 42.

129. Fredegar Cont., ch. 42.

130. See the helpful list compiled by Fournier, "Les campagnes de Pépin le Bref," 123–135; and also his *Le peuplement*, 343–351.

131. Fredegar Cont., ch. 42; and Longnon, *Géographie de la Gaule au VIe siècle*, 481, regarding the topography.

132. Fredegar Cont., ch. 42. Regarding the treatment of prisoners, in general, see below.

133. *Annales regni Francorum, an.* 762; *Annales q. d. Einhardi, an.* 762; and Fredegar Cont., ch. 42. Phrases such as "cum praeda vel spolia multa" have a formulaic ring to them and are discussed above, as is division of booty.

134. Fredegar Cont., ch. 47, indicates that even after almost four years of war, Waiofar thought that Pippin might accept his submission on terms that would leave him as *dux*.

135. Fredegar Cont., ch. 48, provides what would appear to have been *fragmenta* of a now lost communique from Waiofar to Pippin offering to behave in an appropriate manner.

136. *Annales regni Francorum, ann.* 761, 762, for Pippin's winter headquarters.

137. Fredegar Cont., ch. 46.

138. *Annales regni Francorum, an. 762, Annales mettenses priores, an. 762,* and Fredegar Cont., ch. 43, all make clear that both major strongholds were attacked and taken in the same year. Indeed, Fredegar Cont., ch. 43, claims that the army which took Bourges in the late summer of 762 then took Thouars. This is probably an error insofar as it provides a vastly oversimplified account of what actually took place (see below).

139. Bachrach, *Merovingian Military Organization,* 108–111.

140. See Bachrach, *The Anatomy of a Little War,* 80–81, 102, 161–167, regarding the strategic position of Bourges in the Merovingian era. A more general picture is to be found in Claude, *Topographie und Verfassung der Städte Bourges und Poitiers,* 40–47, 64–75, 104–110.

141. Dietrich Claude, *Topographie und Verfassung der Städte Bourges und Poitiers bis in das 11. Jahrhundert* (Historische Studien, 380, Lübeck-Hamburg, 1960). 40–47, remains the basic work. There is some controversy regarding the length of the walls. See the discussion by Brühl, *Palatium und Civitas,* I, 163–164, with the additional literature cited there.

142. Fredegar Cont., ch. 43, provides information regarding the composition of the forces at Bourges. See the discussion by Bachrach, "Military Organization in Aquitaine," 11–12; Claude, *Topographie und Verfassung der Städte Bourges und Poitiers,* 66 n. 634, indicates that the account by Fredegar's Continuator is particularly detailed.

143. Fredegar Cont., ch. 43. Claude, *Topographie und Verfassung der Städte Bourges und Poitiers,* 66.

144. See, for example, Vegetius, *De re Militari,* bk. I, ch. 24, and bk. III, ch. 8.

145. Regarding the education of the officer corps in the late antique world and the early Middle Ages, see Bachrach, "Some Observations Concerning the Education of the 'Officer Corps,'" 7–13.

146. Concerning Byzantine standard operating procedure in this context see Maurice, *Strategikon,* bk. X; Anon., *Strategy,* ch. 29; and Anon., *Book on Tactics,* ch. 1.

147. Bachrach, "Charles Martel," 54–54. Concerning the two sieges of Avignon see Fredegar Cont., ch. 14; and with regard to the particular difficulties entailed in attacking this fortress city see Bachrach, *Anatomy of a Little War,* 74–77, with the literature cited there.

148. Fredegar Cont., chs. 37, 38. The basic work on the topography of Pavia remains Donald Bullough, "Urban Change in Early Medieval Italy: The Example of Pavia," *Papers of the British School at Rome,* 34 (1966), 82–130.

149. Fredegar Cont., ch. 37. The nature of Lombard military organization is very controversial and it is well beyond the scope of this study to examine it in detail. However, see Giovanni Tabacco, *I Liberi del Re nell'italia carolingia e post-carolingia* (Spoleto, 1966), and the critique by Pierre Toubert, "La liberté au haut Moyen Age et le problème de *arimanni," Le moyen âge,* 63 (1967), 127–144.

150. Fredegar Cont., ch. 37.

151. Fredegar Cont., ch. 38.

152. Fredegar Cont., ch. 20.

153. The traditional view that this fortification was originally built by the Romans is accepted by Claude, *Topographie und Verfassung der Städte Bourges und Poitiers,* 47, who provides references to earlier literature. By contrast, Brühl, *Palatium und Civitas,* I, 165, though he recognizes that Fredegar's Continuator, ch. 43, provides the only references to external fortifications, argues by analogy with *castra* constructed at Arras and

Tours for a date sometime between the ninth and eleventh centuries. Until an exhaustive archaeological examination of the site is undertaken the original date of construction and subsequent level of military use cannot be known.

154. Fredegar Cont., ch. 43, for Chunibert in command at Bourges.

155. Claude, *Topographie und Verfassung der Städte Bourges und Poitiers*, 47; and Brühl, *Palatium und Civitas*, I, 165.

156. Claude, *Topographie und Verfassung der Städte Bourges und Poitiers*, 43.

157. Fredegar Cont., ch. 43.

158. For further discussion see Bachrach, *Anatomy of a Little War*, 161–167.

159. Fredegar Cont., ch. 43. Claude, *Topographie und Verfassung der Städte Bourges und Poitiers*, 66.

160. Victor D. Hanson, *Warfare and Argiculture in Classical Greece* (Pisa, 1983), passim, demonstrates this point in great detail from a technical perspective. The relatively similar nature of the equipment used for destructive purposes and the vines and trees makes Hanson's observations acceptable for medieval Europe.

161. Fredegar Cont., ch. 47, does make such distinctions, and clearly Pippin was not ripping up the vineyards in 762. Concerning the traditional view on these matters see, for example, Alexander the Great, who kept his soldiers from ravaging Asia and is reported to have told them "they ought not destroy what they were fighting to possess." The emperor Julian took a similar position, as did Clovis. Regarding Alexander see J. F. C. Fuller, *The Generalship of Alexander the Great* (London, 1958), 285, where the work of Justin is discussed and quoted. For Julian see Eunapius, *fr.* 18; and regarding Clovis see Bachrach, *The Anatomy of a Little War*, xvii–xviii.

162. Fredegar Cont., ch. 43. Claude, *Topographie und Verfassung der Städte Bourges und Poitiers*, 66.

163. Fredegar Cont., ch. 43.

164. Fredegar Cont., chs. 43, 46. The emplacement of catapults on the wall likely could not have been accomplished without the use of wooden revetments to hold the earth in place.

165. Graham-Campbell, *The Viking World*, 208–209.

166. Patrick Wormald, "The Age of Offa and Alcuin," in *The Anglo-Saxons*, gen. ed. James Campbell (Ithaca, N.Y., 1982), 120–121, provides a brief but useful introduction.

167. The basic work on Charlemagne's canal project is Hofmann, "*Fossa Carolina*: Versuch einer Zussammenschau."

168. See, for example, the brief survey by M. D. Reeve, "Agrimensores," in *Texts and Transmission: A Survey of the Latin Classics*, ed. L. D. Reynolds and P. K. Marshall (Oxford, 1983), 1–6; and O. A. W. Dilke, *The Roman Land Surveyors* (Newton Abbot, 1971).

169. *Cap. reg. Fr.*, I, no. 75; see Vegetius, *De re Militari*, bk. I, ch. 24, bk. III, ch. 8.

170. Vegetius, *De re Militari*, bk. I, ch. 24.

171. Vegetius, *De re Militari*, bk. III, ch. 8.

172. Vegetius, *De re Militari*, bk. III, ch. 8. I have omitted above the simple ditch without a wall (bk. I, ch. 24), which Vegetius suggests could be "nine feet wide and seven feet deep."

173. Vegetius, *De re Militari*, bk. I, ch. 24.

174. Vegetius, *De re Militari*, bk. III, ch. 8.

175. See, for example, Anon., *Strategy*, ch. 29.

176. Regarding Fulrad, in general, see Alain J. Stoclet, *Autour de Fulrad de Saint-Denis (v. 710–784)* (Paris, 1993).

177. Bachrach, "Logistics in Pre-Crusade Europe," 65–72.

178. Bachrach, "Some Observations on the Military Administration of the Norman Conquest," 1–25, and Bachrach, "The Cost of Castle-Building," 46–62 (four plates).

179. Bachrach, "Medieval Siege Warfare: A Reconnaissance," 119–133.

180. Bachrach and Aris, "Military Technology and Garrison Organization," 1–17.

181. Fredegar Cont., ch. 43.

182. See Bachrach, *The Anatomy of a Little War*, 166–167, for background.

183. For the background on Carolingian military demography see Werner, "Heeresorganization und Kriegsführung," 791–843.

184. Bachrach and Aris, "Military Technology and Garrison Organization," 1–17.

185. Fredegar Cont., chs. 37, 38, regarding the large Carolingian army at Pavia.

186. See the discussion by Hodgkin, *Italy and Her Invaders*, V, 161–162.

187. Werner, "Heeresorganization und Kriegsführung," 791–843.

188. *Annales q.d. Einhardi, an.* 762, calls attention to the large size of Pippin's army, although no numbers are provided.

189. Bachrach, "Was the Marchfield Part of the Frankish Constitution?" 78–85; and Bachrach, "Animals and Warfare," 716–729.

190. See the discussion by Bachrach, "Was the Marchfield Part of the Frankish Constitution?" 78–85, with the literature discussed there.

191. See regarding the river and its floods Roger Dion, *Histoire des levées de la Loire* (Paris, 1961).

192. Concerning rations and their transportation see Engels, *Alexander the Great and the Logistics of the Macedonian Army*, 14–16, 120–121, who deals with the problems of foraging from a logistic perspective; and Bachrach, "Animals and Warfare," 716–729. See also the key work by Jonathan P. Roth, *The Logistics of the Roman Army at War (264 B.C.–A.D. 235)* (Leiden, 1999).

193. Engels, *Alexander the Great and the Logistics of the Macedonian Army*, 14–16, 120–121. These are worst-case models which, if kept in place over a considerable period of time, would hurt troop morale. For more realistic evaluations of troop needs see Goldsworthy, *The Roman Army at War*, 287–296.

194. Bachrach, "Animals and Warfare," 716–729. However, as indicated by Ober, "Hoplites and Obstacles," 193 n. 5, that about 10 percent of pack animals on average will be "lame or sore" at any one time. The same ratio may be assumed for horses used to pull wagons and even for riding horses. For additional information regarding pack animals see also N. G. L. Hammond, "Army Transport in the Fifth and Fourth Centuries," *Greek, Roman, and Byzantine Studies*, 24 (1983), 27–31.

195. Durliat, "La polyptyque d'Irminon pour l'armée," 183–208, discusses these taxes in kind, including live animals for the army.

196. See the logistic reconstruction by Bachrach, *Anatomy of a Little War*, 131–132.

197. Fredegar Cont., ch. 43.

198. Fredegar Cont., chs. 34, 43.

199. Fredegar Cont., chs. 34, 43.

200. Fredegar Cont., ch. 43.

201. Regarding urban storehouses see Bachrach, *Anatomy of a Little War*, 24–25.

202. See the discussion in Chapter 5, above.

203. Fredegar Cont., ch. 43; and the discussion by Bachrach, "Military Organization in Aquitaine," 11–12.

204. Fredegar Cont., ch. 43.

205. Bachrach, "Animals and Warfare," 716–729.

206. Fredegar Cont., ch. 43.

207. Fredegar Cont., ch. 43.

208. Although Fredegar Cont., ch. 46, uses the phrase "omnes muros eorum in terra prostravit," this is such an exaggeration that the extent of the damage must be rejected as inaccurate. Likely, Waiofar ordered breaches to be made in the walls, and perhaps he ordered the gates to be taken down and burned. Concerning preservation of these fortifications into the High Middle Ages and beyond, see Bachrach, "Early Medieval Fortifications," 531–569.

209. Fredegar Cont., chs. 44–53, and the discussion by Bachrach, "Military Organization in Aquitaine," 9–13.

Appendix. The Organization of Naval Assets

1. For background, see Michel Reddé, *Mare Nostrum: Les infrastructures, le dispositif, et l'histoire de la marine militaire sous l'empire Romain* (Rome, 1986); Y. Le Bohec, Review of Reddé, *Mare Nostrum*, in *Journal of Roman Archaeology*, 2 (1989), 326–331; Lionel Casson, *Ships and Seamanship in the Ancient World*, 2nd ed. (Baltimore, 1995); and Dietmar Kienast, *Untersuchuingen zu den Kriegsflotten der römischen Kaiserzeit* (Bonn, 1966). With regard to specific matters of interest here, see J. R. Moss, "The Effects of the Policy of Aetius on the History of Western Europe," *Historia*, 22 (1973), 711–731; W. W. Gauld, "Vegetius on Roman Scout-Boats," *Antiquity*, 64 (1990), 402–406; and O. Höckmann, "Rheinschiffe aus der Zeit Ammianus: Neue Funde in Mainz," *Antike Welt*, 133 (1982), 40–47.

2. With regard to Gaul, which is the focus here, see Reddé, *Mare Nostrum*, 307–308, 317–319.

3. Casson, *Ships and Seamanship*, provides the general background.

4. Sidonius Appollinaris, *Epit.*, VIII, 8; and the discussion by Bachrach, "Grand Strategy in the Germanic Kingdoms," 59.

5. *V. Genovefae*, chs. 35, 39; with the discussion by Bachrach, *Merovingian Military Organization*, 4; Martin Heinzelmann and Jean-Claude Poulin, *Les vies anciennes de sainte Geneviève de Paris* (Paris, 1986), 44–45. Haywood, *Dark Age Naval Power*, 90, is forced to admit that Clovis' inability to blockade Paris early in his reign indicates that "On the inland waterways, the early Merovingians appear to have been impotent." He makes no effort to explain this major problem with his thesis regarding Frankish naval power (see below).

6. For background, see Bachrach, *Merovingian Military Organization*, 3–17, concerning the armies of Clovis and their acculturation. But now see Bachrach, "Quelques observations sur la composition et les caractéristiques des armées de Clovis," I, 689–703, for a more nuanced view of certain aspects of the early Merovingian military.

7. Bachrach, *Merovingian Military Organization*, 18. Cf. Haywood, *Dark Age Naval Power*, 84, 183 n. 38, who inaccurately states that on p. 34 of the above-mentioned work, "Bachrach also justifies his view that the fleet was not Frankish by an unsupported statement, one which is highly inaccurate into the bargain: 'there is no record . . . of the

Franks as an ethnic group taking part in any noteworthy naval activity either before or after this event.'"

Haywood's claim (p. 1) that Frankish naval activity during the later Roman empire rivaled that of Vikings in the ninth century is risible. So too are his claims (p. 91) that there were "warships which the Franks used in the Merovingian period" and (p. 93) that there was a strategic reality in the Merovingian period that reasonably might be labeled "Frankish naval power," i.e., ethnically Frankish ships and sailors.

Indeed, for all of the putative prowess of ethnic Franks as a naval power during the later Roman empire, Haywood adduces only three written sources, none of which is contemporary with the events they purport to recount. These texts are Aurelius Victor, *De Caesaribus*, XXXIII, 3; *Incerti Panegyricus Constantio Caesari*, VIII (V), 18, 3; and Eutropius, *Breviarium ab urbe condita*, IX, 21. Even Haywood recognizes that his citations of the works of Zosimus and Orosius, regarding the above, are derivative fifth-century borrowings from much earlier written sources and have no evidentiary value.

Aurelius Victor, writing ca. 360, tells a bizarre story about a group of *Franci* who, ca. 260, after participating in the pillaging of Gaul, occupied Spain and almost destroyed Tarraconensis on the eastern coast. He then indicates that some of these Franks, after acquiring ships (presumably in Tarraconensis), penetrated as far as Africa. What this century-old story of ships hijacked in Spain has to do with ethnic Frankish naval prowess is hardly self-evident. Haywood would seem to imagine that these *Franci*, presumably from the swamps of northwestern Germany, who found themselves in a Spanish port, had expert knowledge concerning the handling of ships built for operations in the Mediterranean, whether galleys or sailing rigs or both. If the story contains even a grain of truth, we must believe that the indigenous crews were kept on board to sail or row and navigate these craft, while the *Franci* were merely a very nasty lot of "passengers" who disembarked on occasion to loot one or another village along the seacoast.

In the second text, the anonymous author of the above-cited panegyric for Constantius, who wrote in ca. 298, penned an even more bizarre tale that putatively took place during the reign of the Emperor Probus (276–282). In this story, Frankish prisoners who had been exiled to Pontus escaped and seized some ships. Then, according to the panegyric, these craft were sailed from the Black Sea "directly to Greece and Asia," and from there they went to the Libyan shore, then to Syracuse, and finally through the Straits of Gibraltar, around the Atlantic coast of Spain and through the English Channel and on to the Frankish homeland in northwestern Germany. Whatever one may think of the quality of ships built to sail the Mediterranean and of the skill of the sailors in these waters, this tale is not to be taken seriously and provides no evidence for the prowess of ethnic *Franci* in the world of seamanship. In this case, as in the hijacking at Tarraconensis, whatever seamanship that was involved was that of the Mediterranean crews, pilots, and navigators.

Finally, we come to a rather laconic and problematic account by Eutropius, a high official in the East Roman government, who completed his *Brevarium* in 369. Eutropius tells his readers about a Roman general named Carausius, who commanded a fleet and an army in the English Channel ca. 285–286. According to this account, Carausius crushed a group of *Franci* and *Saxones* who infested the Channel. Whether this single and unsupported account, written more than eighty years after the fact, should be taken as strong evidence for ethnic Frankish "naval power," much less naval power rivaling that of the Vikings, is problematic.

Indeed, Aurelius Victor, *De Caesaribus*, XXXIX, 20, a contemporary of Eutropius, who, as contrasted to the latter lived in the West and was far better informed concerning matters there, recounts the activities of Carausius but refers to men whom he defeated in the Channel merely as *Germani*. Whether the putative sea power of ethnic *Franci* was involved seems not to have been of much interest to Aurelius Victor. In addition, even if the Franks and Saxons infested the Channel there is no basis to suggest that the former were sailors or shipbuilders. As will be seen below, there is no reason to believe that the Franks, if they operated on the water, sailed on "Frankish" ships.

Haywood seems to be following and expanding upon the serious misuse of these same Roman sources by Ian Wood, "The Channel from the Fourth to the Seventh Centuries A.D.," in *Maritime Celts, Frisians and Saxons*, ed. Seán McGrail (London, 1990), 93–94. N.b. Stéphane Lebecq, "On the Use of the Word 'Frisian' in the Sixth-Tenth Centuries Written Sources: Some Interpretations," in *Maritime Celts, Frisians and Saxons*, ed. McGrail, 86, after being seriously misled by Wood's "treatment" of the Roman sources, wonders what happened to these Frankish seafarers and guesses "possibly they became Frisians?" It is not clear whether Lebecq is being ironic.

Whatever one chooses to make of ethnic Frankish "sea power" during the later Roman empire, and I suggest not very much, Haywood admits (77): "After the 'barbarian conspiracy' of 367, Frankish piracy disappears, at least from the sources, and it is not until the reign of Charlemagne that there is again plentiful evidence for Frankish naval activity." It is doubtful that there is compelling evidence for ethnic Frankish naval power prior to 367 in any of the sources cited by Haywood. However, in a more important vein, the notion that Haywood believes, for example, that the crews of Charlemagne's Mediterranean fleets were ethnically Frankish casts serious doubt on his understanding of ethnicity.

8. In the *Notitia Dignitatum*, for example, there is no evidence for *Franci* serving in Roman fleets while, as we have seen above, they were recruited both for mounted units and for infantry units.

9. Haywood, *Dark Age Naval Power*, 45–50, has not been able to adduce from any written source a description of a ship designed by or built by ethnic Franks. Indeed, the accounts by Aurelius Victor, *De Caesaribus*, XXXIII, 3; and in *Incerti Panegyricus Constantio Caesari*, VIII (V), 18, 3; describe, as seen above, *Franci* hijacking ships in the Mediterranean.

10. For various "ethnic" types of ships see Casson, *Ships and Seamanship*, 340–341. In general regarding the early medieval North, see Michael E. Jones, "The Logistics of the Anglo-Saxon invasions," ed. M. Daniel, *Papers of the Sixth Naval History Symposium Held at the U. S. Naval Academy on 29–30 September 1983* (Wilmington, Del., 1987), 62–69.

11. See for an exhaustive collection of material, Horst Zettel, *Das Bild der Normannen und der Normanneneinfälle in westfränkischen, ostfränkischen und angelsächsischen Quellen des 8. bis 11. Jahrhunderts* (Munich, 1977).

12. *Anglo-Saxon Chronicle*, an. 896. See the discussion by Richard Abels, *Lordship and Military Obligation in Anglo-Saxon England* (Berkeley, 1988), pp. 109–110.

13. Notker, *Gesta Karoli*, bk. II, ch. 14.

14. Haywood, *Dark Age Naval Power*, 93, admits that "It would probably be a mistake to look for a specifically Frankish shipbuilding tradition," and (p. 91) he avers that the "Merovingians . . . continued to use ship-types based upon them [Romano-Celtic types]." At least in the matter of ship design and ship building, Haywood seems will-

ing to recognize, if only obliquely, that the Franks, as an ethnic group, did not rival the Vikings in these pursuits.

15. Bachrach, *Merovingian Military Organization*, 3–35; Bachrach, "The Imperial Roots of Merovingian Military Organization," 25–30; and Bachrach, "Quelques observations sur la composition et les caractéristiques des armées de Clovis," 1690–703.

16. This campaign, concerning which there is but one source that has any overall claim to historical consideration (Gregory, *Hist.*, bk. III, ch. 3), has been the subject of much speculation. For the basic treatment of this operation in its historical context, see Bachrach, *Merovingian Military Organization*, 18–19, 34–35. Cf. the dating suggested by G. Storms, "The Significance of Hygelac's Raid," *Nottingham Medieval Studies*, 14 (1970), 9–10. For a useful deflation of much of this speculation, see Walter Goffart, "Hetware and Hugas: Datable Anachronisms in *Beowulf*," in *The Dating of Beowulf*, ed. C. Chase (Toronto, 1981), 83–101. Unfortunately, Haywood, *Dark Age Naval Power*, 78–85, speculates even more egregiously on the basis of ninth- and tenth-century fables.

17. *Notitia Dignitatum*, oc., XXXVIII, 8; and the discussion by Grenier, *Manuel d'archéologie*, V, 390 ff. The *Liber Historiae Francorum*, ch. 19, places this campaign in the Chattuarian region (*pagus*); and Storms, "The Significance of Hygelac's Raid," 9–10, may be correct in seeing this *pagus* in the lower Rhine area, which on the basis of place-name evidence, would seem to have its administrative center at Nijmegen on the Waal, about four kilometers south-southeast of its confluence with the Rhine. However, Nijmegen during this period was at least 160 kilometers from the blue water of the North Sea at the mouth of the Old Rhine where the sea battle, itself, would seem to have taken place, if the location of the Chattuarian *pagus* is correct.

18. See, for example, J. Rougé, "Ports et escales dans l'empire tardif," and Giulio Schmiedt, "I porti Italiani nell'alto medioevo," both in *Settimane di Studio del Centro Italiano di Studi sull'alto Medioevo*, 25 (Spoleto, 1978), 67–124 and 128–254, respectively.

19. Bachrach, "On the Origins of William the Conqueror's Horse Transports," 516.

20. See the basic work by Hans Jankuhn, "Der Fränkische-friesische Handel zur Ostsee im frühen Mittelalter," *Vierteljahrschrift für Sozial- und Wertschaftsgeschichte* 40, (1953), 193–243, who collects a vast corpus of data; and some of the nuances introduced by Stéphane Lebecq, "Dans l'Europe du Nord des VIIè-IXè siècles: Commerce frison ou commerce franco/frison?" *Annales. Economies. Sociétés. Civilisations*, 41 (1986), 361–377.

21. *Annales S. Amandi, an.* 773, refers only to "Karolus cum exercitu" and makes no mention of ships. However, the *Annales* do make clear that Charles' force penetrated as far as Westergo, which could be accomplished only with the help of ships. See Walthar Vogel, *Geschichte der deutschen Seeschiffsfahrt* (Berlin, 1915), I, 75; who is followed by Haywood, *Dark Age Naval Power*, 89.

22. *Annales mettenses priores*, p. 27, misses the correct date by a year and, p. 28, indicates that the "gens Frisionum fidem . . . promiserat."

23. *Annales mettenses priores*, p. 27; and n.b. Fredegar Cont., ch. 17, indicates when discussing the revolt of 734, see below, that the Frisians were in rebellion "again." However, he did not speak of their previous revolt.

24. Fredegar Cont., ch. 17.

25. Fredegar Cont., ch. 17.

26. Fredegar Cont., ch. 17; who is closely followed by *Annales mettenses priores*, p. 28, but with a two-year error in the dating.

27. Fredegar Cont., ch. 17; *Annales mettenses priores*, pp. 27, 28, read together.

28. Fredegar Cont., ch. 17.

29. Fredegar Cont., ch. 17. For the *fossa Drusiana* see Colin M. Wells, *The German Policy of Augustus: An Examination of the Archaeological Evidence* (Oxford, 1972), 111–116; and regarding the continued use of the Vecht canal see Willibaldus, *V. Bonifatii*, ch. 8; and the discussion by Lebecq, *Marchands et navigateurs*, I, 124.

30. Fredegar Cont., ch. 17; and *Annales mettenses priores*, p. 28.

31. Fredegar Cont., ch. 17; *Annales mettenses priores*, p. 28.

32. See Lebecq, *Marchands et navigateurs*, II, 206; and followed by Haywood, *Dark Age Naval Power*, 185.

33. Fredegar Cont., ch. 17; and *Annales mettenses priores*, p. 28.

34. Fredegar Cont., ch. 17; and *Annales mettenses priores*, p. 28.

35. For a review of the evidence see Bachrach, "On William the Conqueror's Horse Transports," 506–512.

36. *Cap. reg. Fr.*, no. 49, ch. 3.

37. Fredegar Cont., ch. 17; and *Annales mettenses priores*, p. 28. Cf. Haywood, *Dark Age Naval Power*, 89, who claims that Charles ravaged Westergo.

38. Even Haywood, *Dark Age Naval Power*, 88–89, who is obsessed by putative Frankish naval power and considers this operation "one of the outstanding naval campaigns of the early Middle Ages," does not conclude that the battle of the Boorne was fought on the water.

39. See, for example, *Annales mettenses priores*, p. 28.

40. For the date of the Carolingian conquest of Durstede, see Halbertsma, "The Frisian Kingdom," 73–75.

41. Regarding the vast size of the Durstede harbor, see W. A. Van Es, and W. J. Verwers, *Excavations at Dorestad 1. The Harbour Hoogstraat 1* (Amersfoort, 1980).

42. For a good review, see Gillian Hutchinson, *Medieval Ships and Shipping* (London, 1994), 10–15, where both the archaeological and pictorial evidence are discussed.

43. Concerning the etymology, see Siegfried Fliedner, " 'Kogge' und 'Hulk' Ein Beitrag zur Schiffstypengeschichte," in *Die Bremer Hanse-Kogge Fund Konservierung Forschung* (Bremen, 1969), 54–62; and he is followed by Detlev Ellmers, *Frühmittelalterliche Handelsschiffahrt in Mittel- und Nordeuropa* (Neumünster, 1972), 59; and Detlev Ellmers, "The Frisian Monopoly of Coastal Transport in the Sixth-Eighth Centuries A.D.," in *Maritime Celts, Frisians and Saxons*, ed. Seán McGrail (London, 1990), 91.

44. The basic study for the date is now Robert Vlek, *The Medieval Utrecht Boat: The History and Evaluation of the First Nautical Archaeological Excavations and Reconstructions in the Low Countries* (Oxford, 1987), 65–67, 103, 162, who reexamined the old dendrochronological and C14 dating of the timbers, presents new information from new samples, and concludes that the ship was built during the early eleventh century rather than in the later eighth century, as previously had been thought. I remain unconvinced by the arguments for either date. Ellmers, "The Frisian Monopoly," 92, retains his previous adherence to the older date; Hutchinson, *Medieval Ships and Shipping*, 12, seems convinced by the newer dating; while Haywood, *Dark Age Naval Power*, 130–133, accepts the earlier date but does not cite Vlek's publication.

45. For drawings of coins that depict various ships, see Lebecq, *Marchands et navigateurs*, I, 182; and Haywood, *Dark Age Naval Power*, 133.

46. The basic work is now Vlek, *The Medieval Utrecht Boat*, but it is controversial

on many points of detail. For easily available descriptions, see Johannes P. W. Philipsen, "The Utrecht Ship," *Mariners Mirror*, 51 (1965), 35–46; Basil Greenhill, *The Archaeology of the Boat* (London, 1976), 190–192; and P. Johnstone, *The Seacraft of Prehistory* (London, 1980), 119–120. It seems clear that as archaeologists have reconstructed the Utrecht boat, its mast was poorly supported for operation on the open sea. However, this may be the fault of the reconstruction. The lack of material surviving from the deck area makes it impossible to reconstruct the seat for the mast. The Utrecht boat had two "steering" oars.

47. It is curious that Haywood, *Dark Age Naval Power*, 130–133, whose primary interest is in naval power, does not contemplate how military force could have been projected from a so-called proto-*hulc*.

48. Hutchinson, *Medieval Ships and Shipping*, 5.

49. Philipsen, "The Utrecht Ship," 45; and Richard Unger, *The Ship in the Medieval Economy, 600–1600* (London, 1980), 60, for the estimation of cargo weight.

50. Detlev Ellmers, "Frisian and Hanseatic Merchants Sailed the Cog," in *The North Sea*, ed. A. Bang Anderson (Oslo, 1985), 79–95; Unger, *The Ship in the Medieval Economy*, 60–61; and Hutchinson, *Medieval Ships and Shipbuilding*, 15–20.

51. Haywood, *Dark Age Naval Power*, 133.

52. Ellmers, "Frisian and Hanseatic Merchants," 79–95; Unger, *The Ship in the Medieval Economy*, 60–61.

53. There is no evidence prior to the later reign of Charlemagne that the Carolingian government sought to develop regular naval forces in the north. Until these efforts were undertaken, the Carolingians, who were ostensibly on the offensive for the previous two generations, could commandeer ships when needed. When the development of a defensive strategy was at issue, however, a government fleet was needed. To rely upon the commandeering of merchant and fishing vessels on a regular basis for defensive operations would have cut deeply into the maritime aspects of the Carolingian economy. Perhaps even more important militarily, Charlemagne could not rely on having the proper number of ships at the right time in the right place for responding to the enemy. Planning offensive operations and responding to enemy attacks are very different strategic and tactical matters. Indeed, Alfred the Great followed a policy very similar to that developed by Charlemagne for defensive purposes. Concerning Charlemagne's efforts to build a fleet, see the very brief summary by Haywood, *Dark Age Naval Power*, 118–124; and regarding Alfred, see Abels, *Lordship and Military Obligation*, 109–110.

54. Regarding comparatively small-oared craft see Vegetius, *De re Militari*, bk. IV, ch. 37; and the discussion by C. E. Dove, "The First British Navy," *Antiquity*, 45 (1971), 17–19; the arguments by O. Höckman, *Antike Seefahrt* (Munich, 1985), 133–134; and Haywood, *Dark Age Naval Power*, 45–49.

55. These *scarfa*, depending on their size, could be used for a wide variety of non-military purposes, e.g., as lighters to unload large sailing vessels and as "tugs" to help maneuver these same large sailing vessels in tight places.

56. See, for example, Hollister, *Anglo Saxon Military Institutions on the Eve of the Norman Conquest*, 103–126.

57. Fredegar Cont., ch. 17.

58. Zosimus, bk. III, ch. 5.2; and cf. the discussion by Erich Zöllner, *Geschichte der Franken bis zur Mitte des 6. Jahrhunderts* (Munich, 1970), 19–20.

59. Fredegar Cont., ch. 20. N.b. *Annales mettenses priores*, p. 29, uses the phrase

"Machinisque compositis." This may leave the impression either that the machines were being transported in pieces and were subsequently assembled for the siege or that the assembled machines were merely being deployed. Or the Metz annalist intended both meanings.

60. Carolingian capacity in the area of bridge building is discussed in Chapter 4.

61. Bachrach, *The Anatomy of a Little War*, 75–77.

62. *Annales mettenses priores*, p. 29, does not speak of "Machinisque compositis" when discussing their use at the siege of Narbonne.

63. Fredegar Cont., ch. 20; *Annales mettenses priores*, p. 29.

64. Fredegar Cont., ch. 20, and for the geography Wallace-Hadrill, *Fredegar*, p. 95, n. 2. Regarding the *Via Domitia*, see Raymond Chevallier, *Roman Roads*, 160.

65. Fredegar Cont., ch. 20. Wallace-Hadrill, *Fredegar*, 95 n. 1, incorrectly identifies the bay as the Étang de Leucate. The Berre River, however, runs into the Étang de Sigean. At present the most northerly reaches of the Étang de Leucate are twelve kilometers from the most southerly reaches of the Étang de Sigean, with a considerable amount of dry land between the two. Haywood, *Dark Age Naval Power*, 186 n. 82, follows Wallace-Hadrill, above, in indicating the wrong body of water.

66. Fredegar Cont., ch. 20. The battle had to be fought on the north or left bank of the Berre because the chronicler gives us no reason to believe that Charles' army had crossed the river. The Muslims, however, landed on the left bank of the river, which gave them a direct land route to Narbonne and thus saved them the trouble of crossing the Berre.

67. Fredegar Cont., ch. 20; and cf. the translation by Wallace-Hadrill: "The survivors, with some idea of escaping in boats (navale evectione evadere), swam out into the sea lagoons. They fought among themselves in their struggle to get aboard." Cf. Fredegar Cont., ch. 17, where Wallace-Hadrill translates "navale evectione praeparat" as "prepared a naval expedition."

68. Fredegar Cont., ch. 20. The account, misdated in the *Annales Fuldenses, an.* 734, clearly refers to this battle.

69. Haywood, *Dark Age Naval Power*, 90, rather tendentiously refers to this as an example of "the Franks using ships on inland waterways in military operations."

70. Fredegar Cont., ch. 32.

71. Cf. Haywood, *Dark Age Naval Power*, 90, who simply asserts, "Pippin III prepared a naval force to launch an assault on Bavarian rebels."

72. Astronomer, *V. Hludowici*, ch. 15.

73. For background on such vessels see *De rebus bellicis*, ch. XVI, 1, 2; and Ammianus Marcellinus, *Hist.*, 24.3.1. More generally see the discussion by Homell, "Floats and Buoyed Rafts in Military Operations," 73–79.

74. *Cap. reg. Fr.*, no. 32, ch. 64.

75. *De Procinctu romanae Miliciae*, ch. VI.

76. See, for example, Gregory of Tours, *Hist.*, bk. IV, ch. 23, which owes something to Virgil.

Bibliography

Abbreviations

The citation of classical sources follows the system utilized by the *Oxford Classical Dictionary*, 2nd ed. (Oxford, 1970), ix–xxii, where complete references are to be found.

CC, SL = *Corpus christianorum*, series latina

CLA = *Chartae Latinae Antiquiores*, vols. 13, 14, ed. Hartmut Atsma and Jean Vezin (Zurich, 1981, 1982).

CSEL = *Corpus Scriptorum Ecclesiasticorum Latinorum*

HGL = *Histoire générale du Languedoc*, ed. C. DeVic and J. Vaissette, 15 vols. (Toulouse, 1872–1893)

IRMA = *Ius Romanum Medii Aevi*

MGH = *Monumenta Germaniae Historica*

    AA = *Auctores antiquissimi*

    Cap. = *Legum sectio II. Capitularia*

    Epist. = *Epistolae*

    FIGA = *Fontes iuris germanici antiqui*

    LL = *Leges nationum Germanicarum*

    Poet. = *Poetae latini medii aevi*

    SRL = *Scriptores rerum Langobardicarum et Italicarum saec. VI–IX.*

    SSRM = *Scriptores rerum Merovingicarum*

    SS. = *Scriptores*

    SS in Us. Schol. = *Scriptores in Usum Scholarum*

PL = *Patrologia cursus completus, series Latina*, ed. J.-P. Migne (Paris, 1844–1864).

Sources

Abbo, *De bello Parisiaco*, ed. and trans. Henri Waquet. *Le siège de Paris par les Normands: Poème du IXe siècle* (Paris, 1942).

Abbo, *Testamentum*, ed. P. Geary, *Aristocracy in Provence* (Stuttgart, 1985).

Adalhard, *De ordine palatii*. See Hincmar.

Agathias, *Hist.* = *Historia*, ed. R. Keydell (Berlin, 1967); *Agathias, The Histories*, trans. Joseph D. Frendo (Berlin, 1975).

Alcuin, *Propositiones ad acuendos juvenes* (PL. 101, pp 1143–1160).

———, *De Virtutibus et Vitiis* (*PL*, 101, cols. 613–638).

———, *Epist.*= *Epistolae*, ed. E. Dümmler. *MGH Epist.* IV; Epist. Karolini aevi 2 (Hannover, 1895).

———, *V. S. Willibrordi* = *V. Willibrodi*, ed. W. Levison. *MGH. SRM* VII (Hannover, 1919).

Aldhelm, *Epist.* = Aldhelmi Opera Omnia, ed. R. Ehwald in *MGH. AA*, XV (Berlin, 1919).

Angelbert, *Versus de Bella quae fuit acta fontaneto*, ed. Dümmler; Peter Godman, *Poetry of the Carolingian Renaissance* (London, 1985), 48–50, provides a text and translation, 262–265, as does Helen Waddell, *Mediaeval Latin Lyrics*, 4th ed. (New York, 1933), 102–105.

Anglo-Saxon Chronicle, trans. and ed. M. J. Swanton (London, 1996). *Anglo-Saxon Chronicle: A Collaborative Edition*, ed. David Dumville and Simon Keynes (Cambridge and Totowa, N.J., 1983–1996).

Annales Alamannici, MGH, SS, vol. I (Hannover, 1826); and *Annales Alamannici*, ed. Lendi = Walter Lendi, *Untersuchungen zur frühalemannischen Annalistik: Die Murbacher Annalen* (Freiburg, Switzerland, 1971).

Annales Anianenses, *HGL*, vol. II.

Annales de Saint Bertin, ed. Félix Grat et al. (Paris, 1964).

Annales Fuldenses, ed. and trans. Reinhold Rau. *Ausgewählte Quellen zur deutschen Geschichte des Mittelalters*, pt. 3 (Berlin, 1960).

Annales Guelferbytani, MGH, SS, vol. I (Hannover, 1826); and *Annales Guelferbytani*, ed. Lendi = Walter Lendi, *Untersuchungen zur frühalemannischen Annalistik: Die Murbacher Annalen* (Freiburg, Switzerland, 1971).

Annales Laubacenses cont., MGH, SS, vol. I (Hannover, 1826).

Annales Laureshamenses, MGH, SS, vol. I (Hannover, 1826).

Annales mettenses priores, ed. B. von Simson, *MGH. SS in Us. Schol.* vol. X (Hannover, 1895).

Annales Mosellani, MGH, SS, vol. I (Hannover, 1826).

Annales Nazariani, MGH. SS. vol. I (Hannover, 1826); and *Annales Nazariani*, ed. Lendi = Walter Lendi, *Untersuchungen zur frühalemannischen Annalistik: Die Murbacher Annalen* (Freiburg, Switzerland, 1971).

Annales Petaviani, MGH. SS. vol. I (Hannover, 1826).

Annales qui dicitur Einhardi, ed. F. Kurze, *MGH, SS in Us. Schol.* vol. VI (Hannover, 1895).

Annales regni Francorum, ed. F. Kurze, *MGH, SS in Us. Schol.* vol. VI (Hannover, 1895).

Annales Sancti Amandi, MGH, SS, vol. I (Hannover, 1826).

Annales Tiliani, MGH, SS, vol. I (Hannover, 1826).

Anon., *Ab ore verbum prolatum*, ed. C. Blume and G. Dreves. *Historiae Rythmicae: liturgische Reimofficien des Mittelalters* (Leipzig, 1889–1904).

Anon., *Book on Tactics*, ed. Dennis = *Three Byzantine Military Treatises*, text, translation, and notes by G. Dennis (Washington, D.C., 1985).

Anon., *Epist. consol. ad pergantes bellum*, ed. Hermann Schmitz, *Miscellanea Tironiana* (Leipzig, 1896).

Anon., *De rebus Bellicis*. Part 2: De rebus bellicis: *The Text*, ed. Robert Ireland (Oxford, 1979).

Anon., *Strategy*, ed. Dennis = *Three Byzantine Military Treatises*, text, translation, and notes by G. Dennis (Washington, D.C., 1985).

Ardo, *Vita Benedicti*, ed. W. Wattenbach, *MGH, SS*, vol. 15.1.

Astronomer, *V. Hludowici* = Reinhold Rau, ed., *Ausgewählte Quellen zur deutschen Geschichte des Mittelalters* (Berlin, 1960).

Augustine, *De civitate Dei*, ed. Bernard Dombart and Alphonse Kalb. *Aurelli Augustini Opera*, pt. 14, *CC, SL*, vols. 47–48. 2 vols. (Turnhout, 1955).

Bede, *Historia ecclesiastica gentis anglorum*, ed. and trans. Bertram Colgrave and R. A. B. Mynors. Oxford Medieval Texts (Oxford, 1969).

Beowulf, ed. F. Klaeber, 3rd ed. (Lexington, Mass., 1950).

Bobbio Missal = *The Bobbio Missal: A Gallican Mass-Book. Facsimile*, ed. J. W. Legg, Henry Bradshaw Society, 53 (London, 1917); and *The Bobbio Missal: A Gallican Mass-Book*, ed. E. A. Lowe, Henry Bradshaw Society, 53 (London, 1924).

Boniface, *Epist.* = *S. Bonifatti et Lulli epistolae*, ed. M. Tangl. *MGH, Epist.* vol. I (Hannover, 1916).

Cap. reg. Fr. = *Capitularia regum Francorum*, I, ed. A. Boretius. *MGH. Cap.* (Hannover, 1883).

Carmen de Conversione Saxonum, ed. Kaul Hauck, in "Karolingische Taufpfalzen, Pfalzen und Reichsklöstern," *Nachrichten der Akademie der Wissenschaften, Göttingen*, I. *Philologisch-historische Klasse* (1985), 3–95.

Carmen de Hastingae Proelio of Guy Bishop of Amiens, eds. Catherine Morton and Hope Munz (Oxford, 1972).

Cartulaire de. S. Victor de Marseille, ed. M. Guérard (Paris, 1857).

Cathwulfus, *Epist.* = *Epistolae Karolini aevi*, ed. E. Dümmler. *MGH, Epist.* vol. IV (Hannover, 1895).

Chronicon Laurissense breve, ed. H. Schnorr von Carolsfeld, *Neues Archiv*, 36 (1911), 15–39.

Chronicon Laurissense Breve, MGH, SS, vol. I (Hannover, 1826).

Chronicon Moissacense, MGH. SS. I (Hannover, 1826).

Chronicon Ucenense, HGL, vol. II.

Codex Carolinus, ed. W. Gundlach, *MGH. Epist.* (Berlin, 1892), I, 469–657.

CTh. = *Theodosiani Libri cum constitutionibus Sirmondianis et Leges Novellae*, ed. T. Mommsen and P. Meyer (Berlin, 1905), 2 vols. *The Theodosian Code and Novels and the Sirmondian Constitutions*, trans. with commentary by Clyde Pharr et al. (Princeton, 1952).

Consuetudines Corbeienses, ed. Josef Semmler. In *Corpus Consuetudinum Monasticorum*, ed. K. Hallinger; 5 vols. (Sieburg, 1963), I, 355–422. English translation in Walter Horn and E. Born, *The Plan of St. Gall*, trans. Charles W. Horn; 3 vols. (Berkeley, 1979), III, 93–123.

De remediis peccatorum, ed. H. Schmitz. *Die Bussbucher und die Bussdisciplin der Kirche*, 2 vols. (Düsseldorf, 1898, rpt. Graz, 1958).

Dhuoda, *Manuel pour mons fils*, ed. and trans. Pierre Riché (Paris, 1975).

Echternach, ed. Wampach = *Geschichte der Grudnherrschaft Echternach im Frühmittelalter*, II *Quellenband* (Luxemburg, 1936).

Einhard, *V. Karoli* = *Éginhard, Vie de Charlemagne*, ed. and trans. Louis Halphen (Paris, 1923).

Erchanberti Breviarium, MGH SS. vol. I (Hannover, 1826).

Eunapius, *fr.* = *The Fragmentary Classicising Historians of the Later Roman Empire: Eunapius, Olympiodorus, Priscus and Malchus*, ed. and trans. R. C. Blockley (Liverpool, 1981), 2 vols.

Exeter Book, ed. and trans. I. Gollancz and W. S. Mackie, 2 vols. Early English Text Society (London, 1895–1934).

Flodoard, *Annales* = *Les Annales de Flodoard*, ed. Ph. Lauer (Paris, 1905).

Form. Andecav. = *Formulae Merowingici et Karolini aevi*, ed. Karl Zeumer. *MGH, Formulae* vol. V (Hannover, 1886).

Form. Bituricenses = *Formulae Merowingici et Karolini aevi*, ed. Karl Zeumer. *MGH, Formulae* vol. V (Hannover, 1886).

Fortunatus, *Carm.* = Venantius Fortunatus, *Opera poetica*, MGH, AA, 4.1 (Hannover, 1881).

——, *Pange lingua gloriosi*, ed. Bulst. *Hymni latini antiquissimi LXXV* (Heidelberg, 1956).

——, *Vexilla regis prodeunt*, ed. Bulst. *Hymni latini antiquissimi LXXV* (Heidelberg, 1956).

Fredegar, *Chron.* = *Fredegarii Chronicorum Liber Quartus cum Continuationibus*, ed. and trans. J. M. Wallace-Hadrill (London, 1960). The references to *The Fourth Book* are to the introduction to this work or to Wallace-Hadrill's translation.

Fredegar Cont. = *Fredegarii Chronicorum Liber Quartus cum Continuationibus*, ed. and trans. J. M. Wallace-Hadrill (London, 1960).

Gesta Abbatum Fontanellensium, ed. F. Lohier and J. Laport (Rouen, 1936).

Gesta Consulum = *Chronica de Gestis Consulum Andegavorum* in *Chroniques des comtes d'Anjou et des seigneurs d'Amboise*, eds. Louis Halphen and René Poupardin (Paris, 1913).

Gesta episcoporum Autissiodorensium, ed. G. H. Pertz, *MGH, SS*, 13.

Gregory, *Liber gloria confessorum* = ed. B. Krusch, *MGH. SSRM* 1.

——, *Hist.* = *Liberi Historiarum X*, ed. B. Krusch and W. Levison, *MGH. SSRM*. (Hannover, 1937–1951) I.1.

Hariulf, *Chron.* = *Hariulf, Chronique de l'abbaye de Saint-Riquier (Ve siècle-1104)*, ed. Ferdinand Lot (Paris, 1894).

Hermoldus Nigellus, *Elegia*, ed. and trans. Edmond Faral. *Poème sur Louis le Pieux au roi Pepin* (Paris, 1964).

——, *Poème* = *Poème sur Louis le Pieux au roi Pepin*, ed. and trans. Edmond Faral. (Paris, 1964).

Hincmar, *Epist.* = *PL*, vol. 126.

——, *De ordine palatii*, ed. Thomas Gross and Rudolf Schieffer in *MGH. Fontes Iuris germanici Antiqui in usum scholarum separatim editi*, (Hannover, 1980); and Hincmar, *De Ordine Palatii*, ed. and trans. Maurice Prou (Paris, 1884).

——, *Ad Carolum Calvum*, = *PL*, vol. 126.

——, *Collectio de Ecclesiis et Capellis*, *MGH. Fontes Germanici Anqtiqui in usum scholarum separatim editi*, ed. Martina Stratmann (Hannover, 1990).

Isidore, *Etymol.* = *Isidori Hispalensis episcopi Etymologiarum sive Originum libri xx*, ed. W. M. Lindsey, 2 vols. (Oxford, 1911).

John, *Mirac. S. Demetrii*, ed. Lemerle = Paul Lemerle, *Les plus anciens recueils des miracles de Saint Démétrius*, 2 vols. (Paris, 1979).

Julian of Toledo, *Historia Wambae Regis*, *MGH, SSRM*, V (Hannover, 1910), 486–535.

Letaldus, *Miracula Martini Abbatis Vertavenis*, ed. Bruno Krusch, *MGH, SSRM*, vol. III.

Lex Alamannorum, rev. ed. K. A. Eckhardt *MGH, LL* II (1966).

Lex Baiuvariorum, ed. K. A. Eckhardt. *Germanenrechte* II (1934), 88–91.

Lex Gundobada, ed. L. de Salis. *MGH, LL* II, 1 (Hannover, 1892).

Lex Ribuaria, ed. F. Beyerle and R. Buchner. *MGH, LL* I, 3/2 (Hannover, 1954).

Lex Salica = *Pactus legis Salicae*, ed. Eckhardt, Karl August. *MGH, LL*, I, 4.1 (Hannover, 1962).

Liber Historiae Francorum, ed. Bruno Krusch, *MGH, SSRM*, II.

Lib. Pont. = *Le Liber Pontificalis, Texte, introduction et commentaire*, 3 vols., ed. L. Duchesne and revised Cyrille Vogel (Paris, 1955–1957).

Mappae Clavicula: A Little Key to the World of Medieval Techniques, ed. and trans. Cyril Smith and John Hawthorne (Philadelphia, 1974).

Marculfi Formulae, ed. K. Zeumer. *MGH, Formulae Merowingici et Karolini aevi* V (Hannover, 1886).

Maurice, *Strategikon = Das Strategikon de Maurikios*, ed. G. Dennis (Vienna, 1981); and *Maurice's Strategikon: Handbook of Byzantine Military Strategy*, trans. G. Dennis (Philadelphia, 1984).

Miracula S. Austregisili, ed. B. Krusch, *MGH, SSRM*, 4.

Monumenta Novelsa vetustioria, ed. C. Cipolla (Rome, 1998). Theophylact Simocatta, *History*, ed. C. De Boor and re-ed. P. Wirth (Stuttgart, 1972).

Nithard, *Hist. = Historiarum libri IV*, ed. R. Rau. *Quellen zur Karolingischen Reichsgeschichte* I (Darmstadt, 1955).

Notitia Dignitatum, ed. Otto Seeck (Berlin, 1876).

Notker, *Gesta Karoli*, ed. and trans. Reinhold Rau. *Ausgewählte Quellen zur deutschen Geschichte des Mittelalters* (Berlin, 1960).

Ordo quando rex cum exercitu ad prelium egreditur = Le Liber ordinum en usage dans l'église wisigothique et mozarabe d'Espagne du cinquième au onzième siècle, ed. Marius Férotin. *Monumenta ecclesiae liturgica*, 5 (Paris, 1904).

Das Palimpsestsakramentar im Cod. Aug. CII, ein Messbuch altester Structur aus dem Alpengebiet Texte und Arbeiten, II, ed. Alban Dold and Anton Baumstark (Beuron, 1925).

Paschasius Radbertus, *V. S. Adalhardi = Ex vita s. Adalhardi*, ed. G. H. Pertz. *MGH, SS* II (Hannover, 1829).

Passio Kiliani, W. Levison, *MGH, SSRM*, 5.

Passio Praejecti episcopi Arvernensis, ed. B. Krusch, *MGH, SRM*, V.

Paul, *Hist.* = Paulus Diaconus, *Historia Langobardorum*, *MGH, SRL*.

Poenitentiale Bedae, ed. Schmitz. *Die Bussbucher und die Bussdisciplin der Kirche*, 2 vols. (Düsseldorf, 1898, rpt. Graz, 1958).

Poenitentiale Cummeani, ed. Schmitz. *Die Bussbucher und die Bussdisciplin der Kirche*, 2 vols. (Düsseldorf, 1898, rpt. Graz, 1958).

Poenitentiale Parisiense II, ed. Schmitz. *Die Bussbucher und die Bussdisciplin der Kirche*, 2 vols. (Düsseldorf, 1898, rpt. Graz, 1958).

Poenitentiale Valicellanum II, ed. Schmitz. *Die Bussbucher und die Bussdisciplin der Kirche*, 2 vols. (Düsseldorf, 1898, rpt. Graz, 1958).

Procopius = *BG* = Procopius Caesariensis, *Opera omnia*, ed. J. Haury and G. Wirth, 4 vols., 2nd ed. (Leipzig, 1962–64).

Recapitulatio legis salicae, ed. I. H. Hessels. *Lex Salica. The Ten Texts* (London, 1880).

Rhabanus Maurus, *De Procinctu romanae Miliciae*, ed. Ernst Dümmler in *Zeitschrift für deutsches Alterthum*, 15 (1872), 413–451.

———, *De Universo = PL*, vol. 111.

———, *Epist.* = *Epistolae*, E. Dümmler. *MGH*, vol. V; *Epist. Karolini aevi* 3 (Hannover, 1898–99).

———, *Poenitentiale = PL* vol. 110.

Le sacramentaire gélasien d'Angoulême, ed. P. Cagin (Angoulême, n.d. [1919]).

Sacramentary of Gellone = Sacramenatarium Gellonense, ed. A. Dumas and J. Deshusses, *CCL*, 159–159A (1983).

Servatus Lupus, *Epist.* = *Epistolae*, ed. L. Levillain, 2 vols. (Paris, 1927–35).

Sidonius Apollinaris, *Epistulae et Carmina*, ed. Christian Lütjohann *MGH, AA*, vol. VIII (Berlin, 1887).

Urkundenbuch S. Gallen, ed. Hermann Wartmann (Saint Gall, 1863; rpt. 1931).

Die Urkunden der Karolinger, MGH, Dip. Karol, vol. I.

Vegetius, *De re Militari = Epitoma rei militaris*, ed. Carl Lang (Leipzig, 1885).

V. Amandi, ed. B. Krusch, *MGH, SSRM*, 5.

V. Ansberti, ed. W. Levison, *MGH, SSRM*, 5.

V. Arnulfi, ed. B. Krusch, *MGH, SSRM*, 2.

V. Audoini, ed. W. Levison, *MGH, SSRM*, 5.

V. Eucherii, ed. W. Levison, *MGH, SSRM*, 7.

V. Genovefae, ed. Martin Heinzelmann and Jean-Claude Poulin, *Les vies anciennes de sainte Geneviève de Paris* (Paris, 1986).

V. Hadriani = See *Lib. Pont.*

V. Landiberti episcopi Traeiectensis vetussima, W. Levison, *MGH, SSRM*, 5.

V. Pardulfi, ed. W. Levison, *MGH, SSRM*, 7.

V. Rigoberti, ed. W. Levison, *MGH, SSRM*, 7.

V. Stephani II = See *Lib. Pont.*

V. Wilfridi = ed. B. Colgrave, *The Life of Wilfrid by Eddius Stephanus* (Cambridge, 1927).

Walahfrid, *De exord.* = Walafrid Strabo, *Carmina*, ed. E. Dümmler, *MGH, Poet.*

Waltharius, ed. Strecker = *Waltharius*, ed. K. Strecker, with a German translation by P. Vossen (Berlin, 1947).

Willibaldus, *V. S. Bonifatii*, ed. W. Levison, *MGH, SRG in Us. Schol.*

Zacharius, *Epist.* See Boniface, *Epist.* re *fragmentum*.

Scholarly Works

Abel, Siguard, and Bernhard Simson, *Jährbucher des fränkischen Reiches unter Karl dem Grossen*, 2 vols., 2nd ed. (Leipzig, 1883–1888).

Abels, Richard, *Lordship and Military Obligation in Anglo-Saxon England* (Berkeley, 1988).

Adams, Simon, "Tactics or Politics? 'The Military Revolution' and the Hapsburg Hegemony, 1525–1648," in *Tools of War: Instruments, Idea, and Institutions of Warfare, 1445–1871*, ed. John A. Lynn (Urbana, Ill., 1990), 28–52.

Affeldt, Werner, "Untersuchungen zur Königserhebung Pippins," *Frühmittelalterliche Studien*, 14 (1980), 112–126.

Alföldi-Rosenbaum, E., "The Finger Calculus in Antiquity and in the Middle Ages: Studies on Roman Game Counters I," *Frühmittelalterliche Studien*, 5 (1971), 1–9.

Althof, Herman, *Waltharii Poesis. Das Walthariuslied Ekkehards I. von St. Gallen*, 2 vols. (Leipzig, 1899, 1905).

Anderson, J. K., *Ancient Greek Horsemanship* (Berkeley, 1961).

———, *Hunting in the Ancient World* (Berkeley, 1985).

———, "Hoplite Weapons and Offensive Arms," in *Hoplites: The Classical Greek Battle Experience*, ed. Victor Hanson (London, 1989), 15–37.

Anderson, Thomas, Jr., "Roman Military Colonies in Gaul: Salian Ethnogenesis and the Forgotten Meaning of *Pactus Legis Salicae* 59.5," *Early Medieval Europe* 4 (1995), 129–144.

Aris, Rutherford, and Bernard S. Bachrach, "*De Motu Arietum* (On the Motion of Battering Rams)," in *Differential Equations, Dynamical Systems, and Control Science: A Festschrift in Honor of Lawrence Markus*, ed. K.D. Elworthy, W. Norrie Everitt, and E. Bruce Lee (New York and Hong Kong, 1993), 1–13.

Arnold, Benjamin, *German Knighthood, 1050–1300* (Oxford, 1985).

Arnzt, Ludwig, "Der Feldaltar in Vergangenheit und Gegenwart," *Zeitschrift für Christliche Kunst*, 28 (1915), 89–105.

Arwindsson, Greta, "A New Scandinavian Helmet from the Vendel-Time," *Acta Archaeologica*, 3 (Copenhagen, 1932), 21–46.

———, "A New Form of Scandinavian Helmet from the Vendel Time," *Acta Archaeologica* 5, (Copenhagen, 1934), 31–59.

Auer, Leopold, "Formen des Krieges im abendländischen Mittelalter," in *Formen des Krieges vom Mittelalter zum "Low-Intensity-Conflict,"* ed. Manfried Rauchensteiner and Erwin A. Schmid (Graz, 1991), 17–43.

Aymard, J., *Essai sur les chasses romaines des origines à la fin du siècle des Antonins* (Paris, 1951).

Baatz, Dietwulf, "Die römische Jagdarmbrust," *Archäologisches Korrespondenzblatt*, 21 (1991), 283–299.

Bachrach, Bernard S., "The Origin of Armorican Chivalry," *Technology and Culture*, 10 (1969), 166–171; and reprinted in Bernard S. Bachrach, *Armies and Politics in the Early Medieval West* (London, 1993), with the same pagination.

———, "Charles Martel, Mounted Shock Combat, the Stirrup, and Feudalism," *Studies in Medieval and Renaissance History*, 7 (1970), 49–75, and reprinted in Bernard S. Bachrach, *Armies and Politics in the Early Medieval West* (London, 1993), with the same pagination.

———, "Procopius and the Chronology of Clovis's Reign," *Viator*, 1 (1970), 21–31. Reprinted in Bernard S. Bachrach, *Armies and Politics in the Early Medieval West* (London, 1993), with the same pagination.

———, "Procopius, Agathias and the Frankish Military," *Speculum*, 45 (1970), 435–441. Reprinted in Bernard S. Bachrach, *Armies and Politics in the Early Medieval West* (London, 1993), with the same pagination.

———, "The Feigned Retreat at Hastings," *Medieval Studies*, 33 (1971), 344–347.

———, *Merovingian Military Organization: 481–751* (Minneapolis, 1972).

———, *A History of the Alans in the West* (Minneapolis, 1973).

———, "Was the Marchfield Part of the Frankish Constitution?" *Mediaeval Studies*, 36 (1974), 78–85. Reprinted in Bernard S. Bachrach, *Armies and Politics in the Early Medieval West* (London, 1993), with the same pagination.

———, "Military Organization in Aquitaine Under the Early Carolingians," *Speculum*, 49 (1974), 1–33: reprinted in Bernard S. Bachrach, *Armies and Politics in the Early Medieval West* (London, 1993), with the same pagination.

———, "Early Medieval Fortifications in the 'West' of France: A Technical Vocabulary," *Technology and Culture*, 16 (1975), 531–569.

———, *Early Medieval Jewish Policy in Western Europe* (Minneapolis, 1977).

———, "Charlemagne's Cavalry: Myth and Reality," *Military Affairs*, 47 (1983): 181–187, in quarto, and reprinted in Bernard S. Bachrach, *Armies and Politics in the Early Medieval West* (London, 1993), 1–20.

———, "A Picture of Avar-Frankish Warfare from a Carolingian Psalter of the Early

Ninth Century in Light of the *Strategicon*," *Archivum Eurasiae Medii Aevi*, 4 (1984), 5–27 (appeared in 1986) and reprinted in Bernard S. Bachrach, *Armies and Politics in the Early Medieval West* (London, 1993).

———, "The Cost of Castle-Building: The Case of the Tower at Langeais, 992–994," in *The Medieval Castle: Romance and Reality*, ed. K. Reyerson and F. Powe (Dubuque, Iowa, 1984), 46–62 (four plates).

———, "The Practical Use of Vegetius' *De re Militari* During the Early Middle Ages," *The Historian*, 47 (1985), 239–255.

———, "Animals and Warfare in Early Medieval Europe," *Settimane di Studio del Centro Italiano di Studi sull'alto Medioevo*, 31 (Spoleto, 1985), 1, 707–764. Reprinted in Bernard S. Bachrach, *Armies and Politics in the Early Medieval West* (London, 1993), with the same pagination.

———, "On the Origins of William the Conqueror's Horse Transports," *Technology and Culture*, 26 (1985), 505–531.

———, Review—J. M. Wallace-Hadrill, *The Frankish Church* (Oxford, 1983), in *The Historian*, 48 (1986), 280–281.

———, "Some Observations on the Military Administration of the Norman Conquest," 1–25, in *Anglo Norman Studies VIII*, ed. R. Allen Brown (Woodbridge, 1986).

———, "Some Observations on the Bayeux Tapestry," *Cithara*, 27 (1987), 5–28.

———, Review: *Domesday Studies: Papers Read at the Novocentenary Conference of the Royal Historical Society and the Institute of British Geographers: Winchester, 1989*, ed. J. C. Holt (Woodbridge, Suffolk, 1987) in *Albion*, 20 (1988), 450–455.

———, "*Caballus et Caballarius* in Medieval Warfare," in *The Study of Chivalry*, ed. Howell Chickering and Thomas H. Seiler (Kalalmazoo, 1988), 173–211.

———, "Gildas, Vortigern and Constitutionality in Sub-Roman Britain," *Nottingham Medieval Studies*, 32 (1988) 126–140; and reprinted in Bernard S. Bachrach, *Armies and Politics in the Early Medieval West* (London, 1993), with the same pagination.

———, Review: Rosamond McKitterick, *The Carolingians and the Written Word* (Cambridge, 1989) in *Journal of Interdisciplinary History*, 21 (1990), 321–323.

———, "Fulk Nerra's Exploitation of the *facultates monarchorum*, ca. 1000," in *Law, Custom, and the Social Fabric in Medieval Europe: Essays in Honor of Bryce Lyon*, ed. Bernard S. Bachrach and David M. Nicholas (Kalamazoo, 1990), 29–49.

———, Review of Julia M. H. Smith, *Province and Empire: Brittany and the Carolingians* (Cambridge, 1992) in *Choice* (November 1992), 491.

———, *Armies and Politics in the Early Medieval West* (London, 1993).

———, Review: M. M. Hildebrandt, *The External School in Carolingian Society* (Leiden, 1992) in *History of Education Quarterly*, 33 (1993), 99–101.

———, "Logistics in Pre-Crusade Europe," in *Feeding Mars: Logistics in Western Warfare from the Middle Ages to the Present*, ed. John A. Lynn (Boulder, 1993), 57–78.

———, "Grand Strategy in the Germanic Kingdoms: Recruitment of the Rank and File," *L'Armée romaine et les chefs barbares du IIIe au VIIe siècle*, ed. Françoise Vallet and Michel Kazanski (Paris, 1993), 55–63.

———, "Anthropology and Early Medieval History: Some Problems," *Cithara*, 34 (1994), 3–10.

———, "Medieval Siege Warfare: A Reconnaissance," *Journal of Military History*, 58 (1994), 119–133.

———, *The Anatomy of a Little War: A Diplomatic and Military History of the Gundovald Affair: 568–586* (Boulder, 1994).

————, "On Roman Ramparts," in *Cambridge Illustrated History of Warfare*, ed. Geoffrey Parker (Cambridge, 1995), 64–91.

————, "Some Observations Concerning the Education of the 'Officer Corps' in the Fifth and Sixth Centuries," in *La noblesse romaine et les chefs barbares du IIIe au VIII siècle*, in quarto, ed. Françoise Vallet and Michel Kazanski (Paris, 1995), 7–13.

————, "Medieval Military Historiography," *Companion to History*, ed. Michael Bentley (London, 1997), 203–220.

————, "The Imperial Roots of Merovingian Military Organization," in *Military Aspects of Scandinavian Society in a European Perspective, A.D. 1–1300*, ed. Anne Norgard Jorgensen and Birthe L. Clausen (Copenhagen, 1997), 25–31 (in quarto).

————, "Quelques observations sur la composition et les caractéristiques des armées de Clovis," *Clovis, histoire et mémoire*, 2 vols., ed. Michel Rouche (Paris, 1997), 1: 689–703.

————, "The Siege of Antioch: A Study in Military Demography," *War in History*, 6 (1999), 127–146.

————, "Early Medieval Military Demography: Some Observations on the Methods of Hans Delbrück," in *The Circle of War*, ed. Donald Kagay and L. J. Andrew Villalon (Woodbridge, Suffolk, 1999), 3–20.

————, "Early Medieval Europe," in *War and Society in the Ancient and Medieval Worlds: Asia, The Mediterranean, Europe, and Mesoamerica*, ed. Kurt Raaflaub and Nathan Rosenstein (Cambridge, Mass., 1999), 271–307.

————, "Gregory of Tours as a Military Historian," in *The World of Gregory of Tours*, ed. Kathleen Mitchell and Ian Wood (Leiden, 2000), forthcoming.

————, "Imperial Walled Cities in the West and Their Early Medieval *Nachleben*," in *City Walls: The Urban Enceinte in Global Perspective*, ed. James D. Tracy (Cambridge, 2000).

————, "Military Lands in Historical Perspective," *Haskins Society Journal*, 9 (2001), forthcoming.

Bachrach, Bernard S., and Rutherford Aris, "Military Technology and Garrison Organization: Some Observations on Anglo-Saxon Military Thinking in Light of the Burghal Hidage," *Technology and Culture*, 31 (1990), 1–17.

Bachrach, Bernard S., and Jerome Kroll, "Justin's Madness: Weakmindedness or Organic Psychosis?" *Journal of the History of Medicine and Allied Sciences*, 48 (1993), 40–67.

Bauters, Paul, *Adalhard van Huise (750–826) abt von Corbie en Corvey* (Oudenaarde, 1964).

Baynes, J. C. M., *Morale* (London, 1967).

Beare, William, *Latin Verse and European Song* (London, 1957).

Becher, Matthias, "Der sogenannte Staatsstreich Grimoalds," in *Karl Martell in Seiner Zeit*, ed. Jörg Jarnut, Ulrich Nonn, and Michael Richter (Sigmaringen, 1994), 119–147.

Beck, H. G. J., *Pastoral Care of Souls in Southeast France in the Sixth Century*, Analecta Gregoriana, 51 (1950).

Behr, Bruno, *Das alemannische Herzogtum bis 750* (Frankfurt am Main, 1975).

Bennett, Matthew, "*La Règle du Temple* as a Military Manual, or How to Deliver a Cavalry Charge," *Studies in Medieval History Presented to R. Allen Brown*, ed. C. Harper-Bill, C. J. Holdsworth, and J. L. Nelson (Wolfeboro, N.H., 1989), 7–19.

Bergengruen, Alexander, *Adel und Grundherrschaft im Merowingerreich* (Wiesbaden, 1958).

Berger, Adolf, *Encyclopedic Dictionary of Roman Law* (Philadelphia, 1953).

Berlière, Ursmer, "Le nombre des moines dans les anciens monastères," *Revue Bénédictine*, 41 (1929), 231–261; 42 (1930), 19–42.

Birley, Eric, "The Religion of the Roman Army, 1895–1977," *Aufstieg und Niedergang der Römischen Welt*, ii *Die Principat*, II 16.2, ed. Hildegard Temporini (Berlin, 1978), 1506–1541.

Bischoff, Bernhard, *Manuscripts and Libraries in the Age of Charlemagne*, trans. and ed. Michael Gorman (Cambridge, 1994).

Bishop, Edmund, *Liturgica Historica: Papers on the Liturgy and Religious Life of the Western Church* (Oxford, 1918).

Bishop, M. C., "The Military *fabrica* and the Production of Arms in the Early Principate," in *The Production and Distribution of Roman Military Equipment*, ed. M. C. Bishop (Oxford, 1986), 1–42.

Bivar, A. D. H., "Cavalry Equipment and Tactics on the Euphrates Frontier," *Dumbarton Oaks Papers*, 26 (1972), 273–291.

Blackburn, Mark, "Money and Coinage," in *The New Cambridge Medieval History: c. 700–c. 900*, ed. Rosamond McKitterick, II (Cambridge, 1995), 538–559, with the bibliographies, 984–987.

Blanchet, Adrien, *Les enceintes romaines de la Gaule* (Paris, 1907).

Bliese, John, "Aelred of Rievaulx's Rhetoric and Morale at the Battle of the Standard, 1138," *Albion* 20 (1988), 543–556.

——, "The Battle Rhetoric of Aelred of Rievaulx," *Haskins Society Journal*, 1 (1989), 99–107.

——, "Rhetoric and Morale: A Study of Battle Orations from the Central Middle Ages," *Journal of Medieval History*, 15 (1989), 201–226.

——, "When Knightly Courage May Fail: Battle Orations in Medieval Europe," *The Historian*, 53 (1991), 489–504.

——, "The Just War as Concept and Motive in the Central Middle Ages," *Medievalia et Humanistica*, new series, 17 (1991), 1–26.

——, "The Courage of the Normans—A Comparative Study of Battle Rhetoric," *Nottingham Medieval Studies*, 35 (1991), 1–16.

——, "Deliberative Oratory in the Middle Ages: The Missing Millenium in the Study of Public Address," *Southern Communication Journal*, 59 (1994), 273–282.

——, "Rhetoric Goes to War: The Doctrine of Ancient and Medieval Military Manuals," *Rhetoric Society Quarterly*, 24 (1994), 105–130.

——, "Fighting Spirit and Literary Genre," *Neuphilologische Mitteilungen*, 96 (1995), 417–436.

Bloch, Marc, *Feudal Society*, trans. L. A. Manyon (London, 1962).

——, "The Problem of Gold in the Middle Ages," *Land and Work in Medieval Europe*, trans. J. E. Anderson (Berkeley, 1967), 186–229.

Böhme, H., *Germanische Grabfunde des 4 bis 5 Jahrhunderts zwischen unterer Elbe und Loire* (Munich, 1974).

Böhmer, J. F., and Engelbert Mühlbacher, *Resgesta Imperii: Die Regesten des Kaiserreichs unter den Karolingern, 751–918*, vol. I (Innsbruck, 1908).

Bond, Brian, *Liddell Hart: A Study of His Military Thought* (London, 1973).

Borst, Arno, "Das Karlsbild in der Geschichtswissenschaft von Humanismus bis Heute," in *Karl der Grosse: Lebenswerk und Nachleben*, ed. W. Braunfels, 4 vols. (Düsseldorf, 1965), IV, 364–402.

Bosch, Johannes van den, *Cappa, Basilica, Monasterium et le culte de Saint Martin de Tours, Etude lexicologique et sémasiologique*, Latinitas Christianorum primaeva, 13 (Nijmegen, 1957).

Bosl, Karl, *Franken um 800: Structureanalyse einer fränkischen Königsprovinz*, 2nd ed. (Munich, 1969).

Bosworth, A. B., "Arrian and the Alani," *Harvard Studies in Classical Philology*, 81 (1977), 217–255.

Bowlus, Charles R., *Franks, Moravians, and Magyars: The Struggle for the Middle Danube, 788–907* (Philadelphia, 1995).

Boyer, Marjorie Nice, *Medieval French Bridges: A History* (Cambridge, Mass., 1976).

Bradbury, Jim, *The Medieval Archer* (New York, 1985).

———, *The Medieval Siege* (Woodbridge, 1992).

Bradley, Omar N., and Clay Blair, *A General's Life: An Autobiography* (New York, 1983).

Braund, David C., *Rome and the Friendly King: The Character of Client Kingship* (London, 1984).

Braunfels, W., and Helmut Beumann, ed., *Karl des Grosse: Lebenswerk und Nachleben*, 5 vols. (Düsseldorf, 1965).

Breysig, Theodor, *Jahrbücher des fränkischen Reiches, 714–741* (Leipzig, 1869).

Broëns, M., "Le peuplement germanique de la Gaule entre la Mediterranée et l'océan," *Annales du Midi*, 65 (1955), 17–38.

Brooks, Nicholas, "The Development of Military Obligations in Eighth- and Ninth-Century England," in *England Before the Conquest: Studies in Primary Sources Presented to Dorothy Whitelock*, ed. Peter Clemoes and Kathleen Hughes (Cambridge, 1971), 69–84.

Brown, Giles, "Introduction: the Carolingian Renaissance," in *Carolingian Culture: Emulation and Innovation*, ed. Rosamond McKitterick (Cambridge, 1994), 1–51.

Brown, T. S., *Gentlemen and Officers: Imperial Administration and Aristocratic Power in Byzantine Italy A.D. 554–800* (Rome, 1984).

Bruce-Mitford, Rupert, et al., *The Sutton Hoo Ship Burial*, 3 vols. in 4 (London, 1978).

Brühl, Carlrichard, "Königpfalz und Bischofsstadt in fränkischer Zeit," *Rheinische Vierteljahrsblätter*, 23 (1958), 161–274.

———, "Das fränkische *Fodrum*," *Zeitschrift der Savigny Stiftung für Rechtsgeschichte, Germanistische Abteilung*, 76 (1959), 53–81.

———, *Fodrum, gistum, servitium regis: Studien zu den wirtschafts Grundlagen des Königtums im Frankenreich und in den fränkischen Nachfolgestaaten Deutschland, Fränkreich, Italien vom 6 bis zur Mitte des 14 Jahrhunderts*, 2 vols. (Cologne, 1968).

———, *Palatium und Civitas: Studien zur Profantopographie spätantiker Civitates vom 3. bis zum 13 Jahrhundert*, I *Gallien* (Cologne, 1975).

Brunner, Karl, "Continuity and Discontinuity of Roman Agricultural Knowledge in the Early Middle Ages," in *Agriculture in the Middle Ages*, ed. Del Sweeney (Philadelphia, 1995), 21–40.

Brunterc'h, J.-P., "Le duché du Maine et la marche de Bretagne," in *La Neustrie: Les Pays au Nord de la Loire, 650 à 850*, ed. Hartmut Atsma, 2 vols. (Sigmaringen, 1989), I, 29–127.

Buchner, Rudolf, *Die Rechtsquellen* (Weimar, 1953).

Bucholz, Arden, *Hans Delbrück and the German Military Establishment* (Iowa City, 1985).

Bullough, Donald, "Urban Change in Early Medieval Italy: The Example of Pavia," *Papers of the British School at Rome*, 34 (1966), 82–130.

————, "*Europae Pater*: Charlemagne and His Achievement in Light of Recent Scholarship," *English Historical Review*, 75 (1970), 89–90.

————, "Roman Books and Carolingian *renovatio*," *Church History*, 14 (1977), and republished with corrections in Bullough, *Carolingian Renewal: Sources and Heritage* (Manchester, 1991), 1–38.

————, "*Aula Renovata*: The Carolingian Court Before the Aachen Palace," *Proceedings of the British Academy*, 71 (1985), 267–301.

————, *Carolingian Renewal: Sources and Heritage* (Manchester, 1991).

Butler, R. M., "Late Roman Town Walls in Gaul," *Archaeological Journal*, 116 (1959), 25–50.

Butzen, Reiner, *Die merowinger östlich des mittleren Rheins* (Würzburg, 1987).

Cam, Helen Maud, *Local Government in "Francia" and England* (London, 1912).

Cameron, Avril, "Agathias on the Early Merovingians," *Annali della Scuola Normale Superiore di Pisa*, ser. 2, 37 (1968), 95–140.

————, *Agathias* (Oxford, 1970).

Campbell, Duncan B., "Auxiliary Artillery Revisited," *Bonner Jahrbücher*, 186 (1986), 117–132.

Campbell, J. Brian, *The Emperor and the Roman Army, 31 B.C.-A.D. 235* (Oxford, 1984).

————, "Teach Yourself How to Be a General," *Journal of Roman Studies*, 77 (1987), 13–29.

Casson, Lionel, *Ships and Seamanship in the Ancient World*, 2nd ed. (Baltimore, 1995).

Chelini, Jean, *L'Aube du Moyen Age: Naissance de la chrétienté occidentale. La vie religieuse des laïcs dans l'Europe carolingienne (750–900)* (Paris, 1991).

Chevallier, Raymond, *Roman Roads*, trans. N. H. Field (Berkeley, 1976).

Chevedden, Paul E., "Artillery in Late Antiquity: Prelude to the Middle Ages," in *The Medieval City Under Siege*, ed. Ivy A. Corfis and Michael Wolfe (Woodbridge, 1995), 131–173.

Childs, W. P. A., *The City Reliefs of Lycia* (Princeton, 1978).

Classen, Peter, "Karl der Grosse, das Papsttum und Byzanz: Die Begründung des karolingischen Kaisertums," in *Karl der Grosse: Lebenswerk und Nachleben*, ed. W. Braunfels and Helmut Beumann, 5 vols. (Düsseldorf, 1965), I, 537–608.

————, "Karl der Grosse und die Thronfolge im Frankenreich," *Festschrift für Hermann Heimpel*, 3 vols. (Göttingen, 1972), III, 109–134.

Claude, Dietrich, *Topographie und Verfassung der Städte Bourges und Poitiers bis in das 11. Jahrhundert (Historische Studien*, 380, Lübeck-Hamburg, 1960).

Clausewitz, Karl von, *On War*, trans. Michael Howard and Peter Paret (Princeton, 1976).

Coale, Ansley, and Paul Demeny, *Regional Model Life Tables and Stable Populations* (Princeton, 1966).

Coleman, C. B., *Constantine the Great and Christianity* (New York, 1914).

Collins, Roger, *Early Medieval Spain: Unity in Diversity, 400–1000* (New York, 1983).

————, *The Arab Conquest of Spain: 710–797* (Oxford, 1989).

————, *The Basques*, 2nd ed. (Oxford, 1990).

————, "Deception and Misrepresentation in Early Eighth Century Frankish Historiography," in *Karl Martell in seiner Zeit*, ed. Jörg Jarnut, Ulrich Nonn, and Michael Richter (Sigmaringen, 1994), 235–247.

Contamine, Philippe, *La Guerre au Moyen Age*, 4th ed. (Paris, 1994).

————. *War in the Middle Ages*, trans. Michael Jones (Oxford, 1984).

Contreni, John, "The Carolingian Renaissance: Education and Literary Culture," in *The New Cambridge Medieval History: c. 700–c. 900*, ed. Rosamond McKitterick (Cambridge, 1995), II, 709–747.

Costambeys, Marios, "An Aristocratic Community on the Northern Frankish Frontier, 690–726," *Early Medieval Europe*, 3 (1994), 39–61.

Coulston, J. C., "Roman Archery Equipment," in *The Production and Distribution of Roman Military Equipment*, ed. M. C. Bishop (Oxford, 1985), 220–336.

———, "Late Roman Armour, Third-Sixth Centuries A.D.," *Journal of Roman Military Equipment Studies*, 1 (1990), 139–160. London, 1992.

Coupland, Simon, "Charles the Bald and the Defence of the West Frankish Kingdom Against the Viking Invasions: 840–877" (Ph.D. diss., Cambridge, 1987).

———, "Carolingian Arms and Armor in the Ninth Century," *Viator*, 21 (1990), 29–50.

Craig, G. A., "Delbrück: The Military Historian," in *Makers of Modern Strategy from Machiavelli to the Nuclear Age*, ed. Peter Paret et al. (Princeton, 1986), 326–353.

Crépin, André, "Les dépouilles des tués sur le champ de bataille dans l'histoire, les arts et la pensée du haut moyen âge," in *La guerre, la violence et les gens au moyen âge*, ed. Philippe Contamine and Olivier Guyotjeannin, 2 vols. (Paris, 1996), I, 15–24.

Crone, Patricia, *Slaves on Horses: The Evolution of the Islamic Polity* (Cambridge, 1980).

Davidson, Hilda Ellis, "The Training of Warriors," in *Weapons and Warfare in Anglo-Saxon England*, ed. Sonia Chadwick Hawkes (Oxford, 1989), 11–23.

Davies, Roy W., *Service in the Roman Army* (New York, 1989).

Davis, R. H. C. "Domesday Book: Continental Parallels," in *Domesday Studies: Papers Read at the Novocentenary Conference of the Royal Historical Society and the Institute of British Geographers: Winchester, 1989*, ed. J. C. Holt (Woodbridge, Suffolk, 1987), 15–39.

———, *The Medieval War Horse: Origin, Development and Redevelopment* (London, 1994).

Dawson, Doyne, *The Origins of Western Warfare: Militarism and Morality in the Ancient World* (Boulder, 1996).

Deichmann, F. W., *Frühchristliche Bauten und Mosaike von Ravenna* (Baden-Baden, 1958).

Delaruelle, Etienne, "Essai sur la formation de l'idée de Croisade," *Bulletin de littérature ecclésiastique*, 42 (1941), 24–45.

Delbrück, Hans, *History of the Art of War Within the Framework of Political History*, vol. 3: *The Middle Ages*, trans. Walter J. Renfroe, Jr. (Westport, Conn., 1982). Originally published as *Geschichte der Kriegskunst im Rahmen der politischen Geschichte*, III, 2nd ed. (Berlin, 1907).

Delbrück, Richard, *Spätantike Kaiserprotraits* (Berlin, 1935).

Deloche, M. *La trustis et l'antrustion royal sous les deux premières races* (Paris, 1873).

Dennis, George, "Flies, Mice and the Byzantine Crossbow," *Byzantine and Modern Greek Studies*, 7 (1981), 1–5.

Deviosse, Jean, *Charles Martel* (Paris, 1978).

DeVries, Kelly, *Medieval Military Technology* (Peterborough, Ont., 1992).

———, *Infantry Warfare in the Early Fourteenth Century: Discipline, Tactics, and Technology* (Suffolk, 1996).

Diaz y Diaz, M. C. "La historiografía hispana desde la invasíon hasta el año 1000," *Settimane di Studio del Centro Italiano di Studi sull'alto Medioevo*, 16 (Spoleto, 1970),

I. 313–355, and reprinted in M. C. Diaz y Diaz, *De Isidoro al siglo XI* (Barcelona, 1976), 205–234.

Diels, H., *Antike Technik*, 3rd. ed. (Leipzig, 1924).

Dilke, O. A. W., *The Roman Land Surveyors: An Introduction to the Agrimensores* (Devon, 1971).

Dion, Roger, *Histoire des levées de la Loire* (Paris, 1961).

Domaszewski, Alfred von, *Das Fahnen im römischen Heere* (Vienna, 1885).

———, *Die religion des römischen Heeres* (Linz, 1895).

Donner, Fred McGraw, *The Early Islamic Conquests* (Princeton, 1981).

Dove, C. E., "The First British Navy," *Antiquity*, 45 (1971), 17–19.

Duby, Georges, *The Legend of Bouvines: War, Religion, and Culture in the Middle Ages*, trans. Catherine Tihanyi (Berkeley, 1990).

Durliat, Jean, "La polyptyque d'Irminon pour l'Armée," *Bibliothéque de l'École des Chartes*, 141 (1983), 183–208.

———, *Les finances publiques de Diocletien aux Carolingiens (284–889)* (Sigmaringen, 1990).

Dutton, Edward, *The Politics of Dreaming in the Carolingian Empire* (Lincoln, Neb., 1994).

Earle, Edward Mead, "Introduction," in *Makers of Modern Strategy*, ed. Edward Mead Earle (Princeton, 1943), vii–xi.

Ebling, Horst, *Prosopographie der Amsträger des Merowingerreiches von Chlothar II. (613) bis Karl Martell (741)* (Munich, 1974).

Ellmers, Detlev, *Frühmittelalterliche Handelsschiffahrt in Mittel-und Nordeuropa* (Neumünster, 1972).

———, "Frisian and Hanseatic Merchants Sailed the Cog," in *The North Sea*, ed. A. Bang Anderson (Oslo, 1985), 79–95.

———, "The Frisian Monopoly of Coastal Transport in the Sixth-Eighth Centuries A.D.," in *Maritime Celts, Frisians and Saxons*, ed. Sean McGrail (London, 1990).

Elton, Hugh, *Warfare in Roman Europe, A.D. 350–425* (Oxford, 1996).

Engels, Donald, *Alexander the Great and the Logistics of the Macedonian Army* (Berkeley, 1978).

Enright, Michael I., *Lady with a Mead Cup: Ritual, Prophecy and Lordship in the European Warband from La Tène to the Viking Age* (Portland, Ore., 1996).

Erdmann, Carl, *The Origin of the Idea of Crusade*, trans. M. W. Baldwin and Walter Goffart with a foreword and additional notes by M. W. Baldwin (Princeton, 1977).

Espérandieu, Emile, *Recueil général des bas-reliefs de Gaule romaine*, 2 vols. (Paris, 1908).

Essentials of Fire Fighting, ed. Michael A. Wieder, Carol Smith, Cinthia Brackage, 3rd ed. (Stillwater, Okla., 1992).

Evergates, Theodore, "Historiography and Sociology in Early Feudal Society: The Case of Hariulf and the 'Milites' of Saint-Riquier," *Viator*, 6 (1975), 35–49.

Ewig, Eugen, "Die fränkischen Teilreiche im 7. Jahrhundert (613–714)," *Trierer Zeitschrift*, 22 (1954), 85–144, and reprinted in Eugen Ewig, *Spätantikes und fränkisches Gallien: Gesammelte Schriften (1952–1973)*, 2 vols., ed. Hartmut Atsma (Munich 1976, 1979), I, 85–144.

———, "L'Aquitaine et les Pays Rhénans au haut moyen âge," *Cahiers de civilisation médiévale*, 1 (1958), 37–54 and reprinted in Eugen Ewig, *Spätantikes und fränkisches Gallien: Gesammelte Schriften*, I, 553–572.

———, "Zum christlichen Königsgedanken im Frühmittelalter," in *Das Königtum. Seine geistigen und rechtlichen Grundlagen, Vorträge und Forschungen*, 3 (1956), 7–73; and reprinted in Eugen Ewig, *Spätantikes und fränkisches Gallien: Gesammelte Schriften*, I, 3–71.

———, *Spatantikes und fränkisches Gallien: Gesammelte Schriften (1952–1973)*, 2 vols., ed. Hartmut Atsma (Munich, 1976–1979).

Fahmy, Aly Mohamed, *Muslim Sea Power in the Eastern Mediterranean from the Seventh to the Tenth Century A.D.* (London, 1980).

Fanning, Steven C., "Tacitus, Beowulf and the Comitatus," *Haskins Society Journal*, (2001), forthcoming.

Ferrill, Arther, "The Grand Strategy of the Roman Empire," in *Grand Strategies in War and Peace*, ed. Paul Kennedy (New Haven, 1991), 71–85.

Fleckenstein, Josef, *Die Hofkapelle der deutschen Könige*, 2 vols. (Stuttgart, 1959).

———, "Die Struktur des Hofes Karls des Grossen im Spiegel von Hinkmars *De ordine palatii*," *Zeitschrift des Aachener Geschichtsvereins*, 83 (1976), 5–22.

Fliedner, Siegfried, " 'Kogge' und 'Hulk' Ein Beitrag sur Schiffstypengeschichte," in *Die Bremer Hanse-Kogge Fund Konservierung Forschung* (Bremen, 1969), 54–62.

Fontaine, Jacques, *Isidore de Séville et la culture classique dans l'Espagne wisigothique* (Paris, 1959).

Fossier, Robert, *La Terre et les hommes en Picardie*, 2 vols. (Paris, 1968).

———, *Polyptyques et Censiers* (Brepols, 1978).

Fouracre, Paul J., "Observations on the Outgrowth of Pippinid Influence in the 'Regnum Francorum' After the Battle of Tertry (687–715)," *Medieval Prosopography*, 5.2 (1984), 1–31.

———, "Frankish Gaul to 814," in *The New Cambridge Medieval History: c. 700–c. 900*, II, ed. Rosamond McKitterick (Cambridge, 1995), 85–109.

Fournier, Gabriel, "Les campagnes de Pépin le Bref en Auvergne et la question des fortifications rurales au VIIIe siècle," *Francia*, 2 (1974), 123–135.

———, *Le peuplement rural en Basse Auvergne durant le haut moyen âge* (Paris, 1962).

France, John, "The Military History of the Carolingian Period," *Revue belge d'histoire militaire*, 26 (1985), 81–100.

———, *Victory in the East: A Military History of the First Crusade* (Cambridge, 1994).

Frank, Richard I., *Scholae Palatinae: The Palace Guards of the Later Roman Empire* (Rome, 1969).

Franke, H., "Siege and Defense of Towns in Medieval China," ed. F. Kierman, *Chinese Ways in Warfare* (Cambridge, Mass., 1974), 167–174.

Fritze, Wolfgang, "Zur Enstehungsgeschichte des Bistums Utrecht: Franken und Friesen 690–734," *Rheinische Vierteljahrsblätter*, 35 (1971), 107–151.

———, *Papst und Frankenkönig. Studien zu den papstlich-frankischen Rechtsbeziehungen von 754 bis 824* (Sigmaringen, 1973).

———, *Untersuchungen zur frühslawischen und frühfränkischen Geschichte bis ins 7. Jahrundert* (Frankfurt am Main and Berlin, 1994).

Fuchs, S., "Bronzebeschläge des Langobardenzeit aus Italien," *Mitteilungen der deutschen archaeologischen Instituts, römische Abteilung*, 55 (1950), 100–113.

Fuller, J. F. C., *The Generalship of Alexander the Great* (London, 1958).

Gale, D. A., "The Seax," *Weapons and Warfare in Anglo-Saxon England*, ed. Sonia Chadwick Hawkes (Oxford, 1989), 49–62.

Gamillschag, Ernst, *Romania-Germania*, 2nd ed. (Berlin, 1970).

Ganshof, F. L., "*La Tractoria*: Contribution à l'étude des origines du droit de gîte," *Tijdschrift voor rechtsgeschiedenis*, 8 (1928), 69–91.

——, "Benefice and Vassalage in the Age of Charlemagne," *The Cambridge Historical Journal*, 6 (1939), 147–175.

——, "Une crise dans le règne de Charlemagne, les années 778 et 779," in *Mélanges d'histoire et de littérature offerts à Monsieur Charles Gilliard* (Lausanne, 1944), 132–144.

——, "Die uitrusting van de lijfwachters der Karolingische koningen en keizers," *Genste bijdragen tot de kunstgeschiedenis*, 12 (1949–1950), 122–126.

——, "Notes sur les origines byzantines du titre 'Patricius Romanorum,'" *Annuaire de l'institut de philologie et d'histoire orientales et slaves*, 10 (1950), 261–282.

——, *Recherches sur les Capitulaires* (Paris, 1958).

——, "Charlemagne et le serment," *Mélanges d'histoire du Moyen Age dédiés à la mémoire de Louis Halphen* (Paris, 1951), 259–290; translated as "Charlemagne's Use of the Oath," in F. L. Ganshof, *The Carolingians and the Frankish Monarchy: Studies in Carolingian History*, trans. Janet Sondheimer (London, 1971), 111–124.

——, "Charlemagne et l'usage de l'écrit en matière administrative," *Le Moyen Age*, 57 (1951), 1–25; and translated as "The Use of the Written Word in Charlemagne's Administration," in F. L. Ganshof, *The Carolingians and the Frankish Monarchy*, trans. Janet Sondheimer (London, 1971), 125–142.

——, "A propos de la cavalerie dans les armées de Charlemagne," *Académie des Inscriptions et Belles-Lettres: Comptes rendus des séances* (1952), 531–537.

——, "Zur Entstehungsgeschichte und Beduetung des Vertrages von Verdun (843)," *Deutsches Archiv für Erforschung des Mittelalters*, 12 (1956), 313–330; translated as "The Genesis and Significance of the Treaty of Verdun (843)," in F. L. Ganshof, *The Carolingians and the Frankish Monarchy*, trans. Janet Sondheimer (London, 1971), 289–302.

——, "L'Eglise et le pouvoir royal dans la monarchie franque sous Pépin III at Charlemagne," *SSCI*, 7 (Spoleto, 1960), 95–141; translated as "The Church and the Royal Power Under Pippin III and Charlemagne," in *The Carolingians and the Frankish Monarchy*, trans Janet Sondheimer (London, 1971), 205–239.

——, "Les relations exterieures de la monarchie franque sous les premiers souverains carolingiens," *Annali di Storia del Diritto, Rassegna Internationale*, 5–6 (1961–62), 1–53; translated as "The Frankish Monarchy and Its External Relations: From Peppin III to Louis the Pious," in F. L. Ganshof, *The Carolingians and the Frankish Monarchy*, trans. Janet Sondheimer (London, 1971), 162–204.

——, *Feudalism*, trans. Philip Grierson, 3rd Eng. ed. (New York, 1964).

——, "Charlemagne's Army," in *Frankish Institutions Under Charlemagne*, trans. B. and M. Lyon (Providence, R.I., 1968), 59–68, 151–161.

——, "L'Armée sous les Carolingiens," *Settimane di Studio de Centro Italiano di Studi sull'alto medioevo*, 2 vols. (Spoleto, 1968), I, 109–130.

——, *The Carolingians and the Frankish Monarchy*, trans. Janet Sondheimer (London, 1971).

García Moreno, Louis, A., "Covadonga, Realidad y Leyenda," *Boletín de la Real Academia de la Historia*, 194 (1996), 353–380.

Garlan, Yvon, "De la poliorcétique dans les 'Phéniciennes' d'Euripide," *Revue des etudes anciennes*, 68 (1966), 264–277.

——, *Recherches de poliorcétique grecque* (Athens, 1974).

Gauld, W. W., "Vegetius on Roman Scout-boats," *Antiquity*, 64 (1990), 402–406.

Geary, Patrick, *Aristocracy in Provence: The Rhône Basin at the Dawn of the Carolingian Age* (Stuttgart, 1985).

Gensen, Rolf, "Christenberg, Burgwald und Amöneburger Becken in der Merowinger- und Karolingerzeit," in *Althessen im Frankreich*, ed. Walter Schlesinger (Sigmaringen, 1975), 121–172.

——, "Frühmittelalterliche Burgen und Siedlungen in Nordhessen," in *Ausgrabungen in Deutschland*, 2 vols. (Mainz, 1975), II, 313–337.

Gerberding, Richard, *The Rise of the Carolingians and the Liber Historiae Francorum* (Oxford, 1987).

——, "716: A Crucial Year for Charles Martel," in *Karl Martel in Seiner Zeit*, ed. Jörg Jarnut, Ulrich Nonn, and Michael Richter (Sigmaringen, 1994), 205–216.

Gessler, E. A., *Die Trutzwaffen der Karolingerzeit vom VIII. bis zum XI Jahrhundert* (Basel, 1908).

Gilbert, J. M., "Crossbows on Pictish Stones," *Proceedings of the Society of Antiquaries of Scotland*, 107 (1975–1976), 316–317.

Gillmore, Carroll, "Practical Chivalry: The Training of Horses for Tournaments and Warfare," *Studies in Medieval and Renaissance History*, n.s., 13 (1992), 7–29.

——, "The Introduction of the Traction Trebuchet into the West," *Viator*, 12 (1981), 1–8.

Glubb, J. B., *The Great Arab Conquests* (London, 1963).

Godman, Peter, *Poetry of the Carolingian Renaissance* (London, 1985).

——, *Poets and Emperors: Frankish Politics and Carolingian Poetry* (Oxford, 1987).

Goetz, Hans-Werner, *Life in the Middle Ages from the Seventh to the Thirteenth Century*, trans. Albert Wimmer and ed. Steven Rowan (Notre Dame, Ind., 1993).

——, "Social and Military Institutions," *The New Cambridge Medieval History: c. 700– c. 900*, II, ed. Rosamond McKitterick (Cambridge, 1995), 471–480.

Goffart, Walter, *Barbarians and Romans, A.D. 418–584: The Techniques of Accommodation* (Princeton, 1980).

——, *The Narrators of Barbarian History (550–800): Jordanes, Gregory of Tours, Bede, and Paul the Deacon* (Princeton, 1988).

——, "From Roman Taxation to Medieval Seigneurie: Three Notes: 1. The *Iugum* in Ostrogothic Italy; 2. The Ambulatory Hide; 3. Flodoard and the Frankish Polyptych," *Speculum*, 47 (1972), 165–187, 373–394; and reprinted in Walter Goffart, *Rome's Fall and After* (London, 1989), 167–211.

——, "Hetware and Hugas: Datable Anachronisms in *Beowulf*," *The Dating of Beowulf*, ed. C. Chase (Toronto, 1981), 83–101.

——, "Old and New Merovingian Taxation," *Past and Present*, 96 (1982), 3–32, and reprinted in Goffart, *Rome's Fall and After* (London, 1989), 213–231.

——, "Paul the Deacon's 'Gesta episcoporum Mettensium' and the Early Design of Charlemagne's Succession," *Traditio*, 42 (1986), 59–93.

——, "From *Historiae* to *Historia Francorum* and Back Again: Aspects of the Textual History of Gregory of Tours," in *Religion, Culture, and Society in the Early Middle Ages: Studies in Honor of Richard E. Sullivan*, ed. Thomas F. X. Noble and John J.

Contreni (Kalamazoo, 1987), 55–76; and reprinted in Walter Goffart, *Rome's Fall and After* (London, 1989), 255–274.

——, "Merovingian Polyptychs: Reflections on Two Recent Publications," in *Rome's Fall and After* (London, 1989), 233–253.

——, *Rome's Fall and After* (London, 1989).

——, "Two Notes on Germanic Antiquity Today," *Traditio*, 50 (1995), 9–30.

Goldsworthy, Adrian K., *The Roman Army at War 100 B.C.-A.D. 200* (Oxford, 1996).

Goubert, Paul, "Religion et superstitions dans l'armée byzantine à la fin du VIe siècle," *Orientalia Christiana Periodica*, 13 (1947), 495–500.

Graham-Campbell, James, *The Viking World* (London, 1980).

Greenhill, Basil, *The Archaeology of the Boat* (London, 1976).

Grenier, Albert, *Manuel d'archéologie gallo-romaine* (Paris, 1934), vol. 6:1.

Grierson, Philip, and M. Blackburn, *Medieval European Coinage* I, *The Early Middle Ages (5th-10th Centuries)* (Cambridge, 1986), 81–154.

Griffiths, W. B., "The Sling and Its Place in the Roman Imperial Army," in *Roman Military Equipment: The Sources of Evidence. Proceedings of the Fifth Roman Military Equipment Conference, 1988*, ed. C. van Driel-Murray (Oxford, 1989), 255–279.

Guilhiermoz, Paul, *Essai sur l'origine de la noblesse en France au moyen âge* (Paris, 1902).

Guillot, Olivier, "La droit romain classique et la lexicographie de termes du latin médiéval impliquant délégation de pouvoir," *La lexicographie du latin médiéval et ses rapports avec les recherches actuelles sur la civilisation du moyen-âge: Paris 1978* (Paris, 1981), 153–166.

Guterman, Simeon L., *From Personal to Territorial Law: Aspects of the History and Structure of the Western Legal-Constitutional Tradition* (Metuchen, N.J., 1972).

——, *The Principle of the Personality of Law in the Germanic Kingdoms of Western Europe from the Fifth to the Eleventh Century* (New York, 1990).

Hahn, Heinrich, *Jahrbücher des fränkischen Reiches, 741–752* (Berlin, 1863).

Halbedel, A., "Fränkische Studien: Kleine Beiträge zur Geschichte und Sage des deutschen Altertums," *Historische Studien* 132 (Berlin, 1915).

Halbertsma, H., "The Frisian Kingdom," *Berichten van de Rijksdienst voor het Oudheidkundig Bodemonderzoek*, 15–16 (1965–1966), 69–108.

Haldon, John F., *Recruitment and Conscription in the Byzantine Army, c. 550–950* (Vienna, 1979).

——, "Solenarion—The Byzantine Crossbow," *Historical Journal of the University of Birmingham*, 12 (1970), 155–157.

——, "Some Aspects of Byzantine Military Technology from the Sixth to the Tenth Centuries," *Byzantine and Modern Greek Studies*, 1 (1975), 15–16.

Hall, Bert S., "Crossbows and Crosswords," *Isis*, 64 (1973), 527–533.

Halphen, Louis, "La conquête de la Saxe," *Revue historique*, 130 (1919), 252–278, and 132 (1919), 257–305, and reprinted in Louis Halphen, *Études critiques sur l'histoire de Charlemagne* (Paris, 1921).

——, *Études critiques sur l'histoire de Charlemagne* (Paris, 1921).

——, "*De ordine palatii* d'Hincmar," *Revue historique* 183 (1938), 1–9, and reprinted in Louis Halphen, *A travers l'histoire du moyen âge* (Paris, 1950), 83–91.

——, *Charlemagne et l'empire carolingien* (Paris, 1949).

——, *A travers l'histoire du moyen âge* (Paris, 1950).

Halsall, Guy, "The Origins of the *Reihengräberzivilisation*: Forty Years on," in *Fifth-*

Century Gaul: A Crisis of Identity? ed. J. Drinkwater and H. Elton (Cambridge, 1992), 196–207.

——, *Settlement and Social Organization: The Merovingian Region of Metz* (Cambridge, 1995).

Hammond, N. G. L., "Army Transport in the Fifth and Fourth Centuries," *Greek, Roman, and Byzantine Studies,* 24 (1983), 27–31.

Hanson, Victor, *Warfare and Argiculture in Classical Greece* (Pisa, 1983).

——, *The Western Way of War: Infantry Battle in Classical Greece* (New York, 1989).

——, "Hoplite Technology in Phalanx Battle," in *Hoplites: The Classical Greek Battle Experience,* ed. Victor Hanson (London and New York, 1991), 63–84.

Hardy, Robert, *Longbow: A Social and Military History,* 3rd ed. (London, 1992).

Härke, Heinrich, "Early Saxon Weapon Burials: Frequencies, Distributions and Weapon Combinations," in *Weapons and Warfare in Anglo-Saxon England,* ed. Sonia Chadwick Hawkes (Oxford, 1989), 49–62.

Harmuth, Egon, "Die Armbrustbilder des Haimo von Auxerre," *Zeitschrift der Gesellschaft für historische Waffen- und Kostümkunde,* n.s. 12 (1970) 127–130.

——, *Die Armbrust* (Graz, 1975).

——, "Ein arabische Armbrust," *Zeitschrift der Gesellschaft für historische Waffen- und Kostümkunde,* n.s. 25 (1983), 141–144.

Harrison, Dick, *The Early State and the Towns: Forms of Integration in Lombard Italy (A.D. 568–774)* (Lund, 1993).

Hartmann, Wilfried, *Die synoden der Karolingerzeit im Frankenreich und in Italian* (Paderborn, 1989).

Haselbach, Irene, "Aufstieg und Herrschaft der Karolinger in der Darstellung der sogenannten *Annalen Mettenses priores,*" *Historische Studien,* 412 (1970), 1–208.

Hatto, A. T., "Archery and Chivalry: A Noble Prejudice," *Modern Language Review,* 35 (1940), 40–55.

Haywood, John, *Dark Age Naval Power: A Reassessment of Frankish and Anglo-Saxon Seafaring Activity* (London, 1991).

Head, Thomas, *Hagiography and the Cult of the Saints* (Cambridge, 1990).

Heer, Joseph Michael, *Ein karolingische Missionskatechismus* (Freiburg, 1911).

Helgeland, J., "Roman Army Religion," *Aufstieg und Niedergang der Römischen Welt,* ii *Die Principat,* II 16.2, ed. Hildegard Temporini (Berlin, 1978), 1470–1505.

Herlihy, David, "Demography," in *Dictionary of the Middle Ages,* ed. J. R. Strayer, 12 vols. (New York, 1984), IV, 136–148.

——, "The Carolingian mansus," *Economic History Review,* 13 (1960), 79–89.

Higounet, Charles, *Bordeaux pendant le haut moyen âge* (Bordeaux, 1963).

Hildesheimer, Ernest, "Les clercs et l'exemption du service militaire à l'époque franque," *Revue d'histoire ecclésiastique de France,* 29 (1943), 5–18.

Hill, Donald R., "Trebuchets," *Viator,* 4 (1973), 99–116.

——, "The Camel and the Horse in the Early Arab Conquests," in *War, Technology and Society in the Middle East,* ed. W. J. Parry and M. E. Yapp (Oxford, 1975), 32–43.

——, "Siege-Craft from the Sixth to the Tenth Century," in *De Rebus Bellicis.* Part I, *Aspects of the* De Rebus Bellicis: *Papers Presented to Professor E. A. Thompson,* ed. M. W. C. Hassal (Oxford, 1979), 111–17.

Hlawitschka, Eduard, *Vom Frankenreich zur Formierung der europäischen Staaten- und Völkergemeinschaft, 840–1046* (Darmstadt, 1986).

Höckmann, O., "Rheinschiffe aus der Zeit Ammianus: Neue Funde in Mainz," *Antike Welt*, 133 (1982), 40–47.

———, *Antike Seefahrt* (Munich, 1985).

Hodgkin, Thomas, *Italy and Her Invaders*, 8 vols. (Oxford, 1880–1899).

Hoffmann, Hartmut, *Untersuchung zur karolingian Annalistik* (Bonn, 1958).

Hofmann, Hans Hubert, "*Fossa Carolina*: Versuch einer Zussammenschau," in *Karl der Grosse: Lebenswerk und Nachleben*, ed. W. Braunfels and Helmut Beumann, 5 vols. (Düsseldorf, 1965), I, 437–53.

Hollister, C. Warren, *Anglo-Saxon Military Institutions on the Eve of the Norman Conquest* (Oxford, 1962).

Holt, James, *Robin Hood* (London, 1982).

Holtzmann, Robert, "Die Italienpolitik der Merowinger und des Königs Pippin," in *Das Reich: Idee und Gestalt. Festschrift für Johannes Haller*, ed. H. Dannenbauer and F. Ernst (Stuttgart, 1940), 95–132.

Homell, J., "Floats and Buoyed Rafts in Military Operations," *Antiquity*, 19 (1945), 73–79.

Horn, Walter, and E. Born, *The Plan of St. Gall*, 3 vols. (Berkeley, 1979).

Hubert, Jean, "Les routes du moyen âge," in *Les Routes de France, depuis les origines jusqu'à nos jours* (Paris, 1979), 25–56.

Huuri, K. K., *Zur Geschichte des mittelalterlichen Geschützwesens aus orientalischen Quellen* (Helsinki, 1941).

Hutchinson, Gillian, *Medieval Ships and Shipping* (London, 1994).

Hyland, Ann, *The Medieval Warhorse from Byzantium to the Crusades* (Dover, N.H., 1994).

———, *Training the Roman Cavalry from Arrian's "Ars Tactica"* (Dover, N.H., 1993).

Isaac, Benjamin, *The Limits of Empire* (Oxford, 1990).

Jackson, A. H., "Hoplites and the Gods: The Dedication of Captured Arms and Armour," in *Hoplites: The Classical Greek Battle Experience*, ed. Victor Hanson (London and New York, 1991), 228–249.

Jahn, Joachim, "Hausmeier und Herzöge: Bemerkungen zur agilolfingisch-karolingischen Rivalität bis zum tode Karl Martells," in *Karl Martell in Seiner Zeit*, ed. Jörg Jarnut, Ulrich Nonn, and Michael Richter (Sigmaringen, 1994), 317–344.

James, Edward, "Cemeteries and the Problem of Frankish Settlement in Gaul," in *Names, Words and Graves*, ed. Peter H. Sawyer, (Leeds, 1979), 55–89.

———, *The Merovingian Archaeology of South-West Gaul*, 2 vols. (Oxford, 1977).

James, S. T., "The *fabricae*: State Arms Factories of the Later Roman Empire," in *Military Equipment and the Identity of Roman Soldiers: Proceedings of the Fourth Roman Military Equipment Conference, 1986*, ed. J. C. Coulston (Oxford, 1988), 257–331.

Jänichen, Hans, "Warin, Rudhard und Scrot," *Zeitschrift für Würtembergische Landesgeschichte*, 14 (1955), 372–384.

Jankuhn, Hans, "Der Fränkische-friesische Handel zur Ostsee im frühen Mittelalter," *Vierteljahrschrift für Sozial- und Wirtschaftsgeschichte* 40 (1953), 193–243.

Janssen, Walter, "Some Major Aspects of Frankish and Medieval Settlement in the Rhineland," in *Medieval Settlement: Continuity and Change*, ed. Peter Sawyer (London, 1976), 41–60.

Jarnut, Jörg, "Untersuchungen zur Herkunft Swanahilds, der Gattin Karl Martells" *Zeitschrift für bayerische Landesgeschichte*, 40 (1977), 345–349.

———, "Die frümittelalterliche Jagd unter Rechts-und Sozialgeschichtlichen Aspekten," *Settimane di studio del Centro Italiano di studi sull'alto medioevo*, 31 (Spoleto, 1985), 746–798.

———, *Agilolfingerstudien. Untersuchungen zur Geschichte einer adligen Familie im 6. und 7. Jahrhudnert* (Stuttgart, 1986).

———, "Die Adoption Pippins durch König Liutprand und die Italienpolitik Karl Martells," in *Karl Martell in Seiner Zeit*, ed. Jörg Jarnut, Ulrich Nonn, and Michael Richter (Sigmaringen, 1994), 217–226.

Joch, Waltraud, "Karl Martell – ein Minderberechtigter Erbe Pippins?" in *Karl Martel in Seiner Zeit*, ed. Jörg Jarnut, Ulrich Nonn, and Michael Richter (Sigmaringen, 1994), 149–169.

Johnson, Stephen, *Late Roman Fortifications* (Totowa, N.J., 1983).

Johnstone, P., *The Seacraft of Prehistory* (London, 1980).

Jones, A. H. M., *The Later Roman Empire, 284–602: A Social, Economic, and Administrative Survey*, 2 vols. (Norman, Okla., 1964).

———, "Military Chaplains in the Roman Army," *Harvard Theological Review*, 46 (1953), 239–240.

Jones, Charles H., "Bede and Vegetius," *Classical Review*, 46 (1932), 248–249.

Jones, Michael E., "The Logistics of the Anglo-Saxon Invasions," *Papers of the Sixth Naval History Symposium held at the U.S. Naval Academy on 29–30 September 1983*, ed. M. Daniel (Wilmington, Del., 1987), 62–69.

Joranson, Einar, *The Danegeld in France* (Rock Island, Ill., 1923).

Kaegi, Walter E., Jr., "The Crisis in Military Historiography," *Armed Forces and Society*, 7 (1980), 299–316.

Keegan, John, *The Face of Battle* (New York, 1976).

Kennedy, Paul, "Grand Strategy in War and Peace: Toward a Broader Definition," in *Grand Strategies in War and Peace*, ed. Paul Kennedy (New Haven, 1991), 1–7.

Kern, Paul B., *Ancient Siege Warfare* (Bloomington, Ind., 1999).

Keutgen, Friedrich, "Die Entstehung der Deutschen Ministerialität," *Vierteljahrschrift für Sozial- und Wirtschaftsgeschichte*, 8 (1910), 1–16, 169–195, 481–547.

Keyser, Erich, *Bevölkerungsgeschichte Deutschlands*, 2nd ed. (Leipzig, 1941).

Kienast, Dietmar, *Untersuchuhngen zu den Kriegsflotten der römischen Kaiserzeit* (Bonn, 1966).

Kleinclausz, Arthur, *Charlemagne* (Paris, 1934).

Klumbach, H., ed., "Spätrömische Gardehelme," *Münchner Beiträge zur Vor- und Frühgeschichte*, 15 (Munich, 1973).

Knüll, Bodo, *Historische-Geographie Deutschlands im Mittelalter* (Breslau, 1903).

Köhler, G., *Die Entwicklung des Kriegwesens und der Kriegführurng in der Ritterzeit von Mitte des 11. Jahrhunderts bis zu den Hussitenkriegen*, 3 vols. (Breslau, 1886–1909).

Koeniger, Albert Michael, *Die Militärseelsorge der Karolingerzeit: Ihr Recht und ihre Praxis* (Munich, 1918).

Kolias, Taxiarchis, *Byzantinische Waffen: ein Beitrag zur byzantinischen Waffenkunde von den Anfangen bis zur der lateinischen Eroberung* (Vienna, 1988).

Korfmann, M., "The Sling as a Weapon," *Scientific American*, 229 (1973), 35–42.

Kottje, Raymund, *Die Tötung im Kriege: Ein moralisches und rechtliches Problem im frühen Mittelalter* (Barsbüttel, 1991).

Koziol, Geoffrey, *Begging Pardon and Favor: Ritual and Political Order in Early Medieval France* (Ithaca, N.Y., 1992).

Krawinkel, Hermann, *Untersuchungen zum fränkischen Benefizialrecht* (Weimar, 1937).

Kroeber, A., "Partage du royaume des Francs entre Charlemagne et Carlomann Ier," *Bibliothèque des Chartes*, 20 (1856), 341–350.

Kroell, M., *L'immunité franque* (Paris, 1910).

Krüger, Karl Heinrich, "Königskonversionen im 8. Jahrhundert," *Frühmittelalterliche Studien*, 7 (1973), 169–222.

Künstle, Karl, "Zwei Dokumente zur altchristlichen Militärseelsorge," *Der Katholik*, 3rd ser., 22 (1900), 122.

Laistner, M. L. W., *Thought and Letters in Western Europe*, rev. ed. (Ithaca, N.Y., 1956).

Lambert, A. M., *The Making of the Dutch Landscape*, 2nd ed. (London, 1985).

Landes, Richard, *Relics, Apocalypse, and the Deceits of History: Ademar of Chabannes, 989–1034* (Cambridge, Mass., 1995).

Last, Martin, "Die Bewaffnung der Karolingerzeit," *Nachrichten aus Niedersachens*, 41 (1972), 77–93.

Latouche, Robert, *The Birth of Western Economy: Economic Aspects of the Dark Ages*, trans. E. M. Wilkinson (London, 1961).

Lazenby, John, "The Killing Zone," in *Hoplites: The Classical Greek Battle Experience*, ed. Victor Hanson (London and New York, 1991), 87–109.

Lebecq, Stéphane, *Marchands et navigateurs frisons du haut moyen âge*, 2 vols. (Lille, 1983).

———, "Dans l'Europe du Nord des VIIe–IXe siècles: commerce frison ou commerce franco/frison?" *Annales. Economies. Sociétés. Civilisations*, 41 (1986), 361–377.

———, "On the Use of the Word 'Frisian' in the Sixth–Tenth Centuries Written Sources: Some Interpretations," in *Maritime Celts, Frisians and Saxons*, ed. Seán McGrail (London, 1990), 85–92.

Le Bohec, Y., Review of Reddé, *Mare Nostrum*, in *Journal of Roman Archaeology*, 2 (1989), 326–331.

Leighton, Albert, *Transport and Communication in Early Medieval Europe* (Newton Charles, England, 1972).

Le Jan-Hennebicque, Régine, "Satellites et bandes armées dans le monde franc (VIIe–Xe siècles)," in *La combattant au moyen âge* (Nantes, 1990), 97–109.

Lemerle, Paul, "La composition et le chronologie des deux premiers livres des Miracula S. Demetrii," *Byzantinische Zeitschrift*, 46 (1953), 354.

———, *Les plus anciens recueils des miracles de Saint Démétrius*, 2 vols. (Paris 1979).

Lendels, J. G., *Engineering in the Ancient World* (Berkeley, 1978).

Lendi, Walter, *Untersuchungen zur frühalemannischen Annalistik: Die Murbacher Annalen* (Freiburg, Switzerland, 1971).

Lendle, Otto, *Text und Untersuchungen zum technischen Bereich der antiken Poliorketik* (Wiesbaden, 1983).

Lesne, Emile, *Histoire de la propriété ecclésiastique en France*, 6 vols. (Lille, 1910–1943).

———, "Les diverses acceptions du terme 'beneficium' du VIIIe au IXe siècle," *Revue historique de droit français et étranger*, ser. 4, 3 (1924), 5–56.

Levison, Wilhelm, "Konstantinische Schenkung et Silvesterlegende," in *Miscellanea Francesco Ehrle* (Rome, 1924), II, 159–247.

———, "A Propos du Calendrier de S. Willibrord," in *Revue Bénédictine*, 50 (1938), 37–41, and reprinted in Wilhelm Levison, *Aus rheinischer und fränkischer Frühzeit* (Düsseldorf, 1948),, 342–346.

————, *England and the Continent in the Eighth Century* (Oxford, 1946).

————, "St. Willibrord and His Place in History," in Wilhelm Levison, *Aus rheinischer und fränkischer Frühzeit* (Düsseldorf, 1948), 314–329.

————, *Aus rheinischer und fränkischer Frühzeit* (Düsseldorf, 1948).

Lewis, Archibald R., "The Dukes in the *Regnum Francorum*, A.D. 550–751," *Speculum*, 51 (1976), 381–410.

Lewis, Archibald R., and Timothy J. Runyan, *European Naval and Maritime History, 300–1500* (Bloomington, Ind., 1985).

Lewis, Bernard, *Islam from the Prophet Muhammad to the Capture of Constantinople*, 2 vols. (New York, 1974).

Leyser, Karl, "Early Medieval Warfare," in *The Battle of Maldon*, ed. Janet Cooper (London, 1993), 87–108, and reprinted in Karl Leyser, *Communications and Power in Medieval Europe: The Carolingian and Ottonian Centuries*, ed. Timothy Reuter (London and Rio Grande, 1994), 29–50.

————, *Communications and Power in Medieval Europe: The Carolingian and Ottonian Centuries*, ed. Timothy Reuter (London, 1994).

Liddell Hart, Basil Henry, *Strategy*, 2nd rev. ed. (New York, 1974).

Lintzel, Martin, "Gau, Provinz und Stammesverband in der altsächsischen Verfassung," *Sachsen und Anhalt*, 5 (1929), 1–37, and reprinted in Lintzel, *Ausgewählte Schriften*, 2 vols. (Berlin 1961), 262–292.

————, "Karl der Grosse und Karlmann," *Historische Zeitschrift*, 140 (1929), 1–22, and reprinted in Lintzel, *Ausgewälte Schriften*, II, 10–26.

————, "Die Unterwerfung Sachsens durch Karl den Grossen und der sächsische Adel," *Sachsen und Anhalt*, 10 (1934), 30–70, and reprinted in Lintzel, *Ausgewälte Schriften*, I, 96–127.

————, "De Sachsen und die Zerstörung des Thüringerreiches," *Sachsen und Anhalt*, 13 (1937), 51–58; reprinted in Lintzel, *Ausgewählte Schriften*, I, 58–63.

————, "Karl Martells Sachsenkrieg im Jahre 738 und die Missionstätigkeit des Bonifatius," *Sachsen und Anhalt*, 13 (1937), 59–65; and reprinted in Lintzel, *Ausgewählte Schriften*, I, 87–92.

————, "Die Vorgänge in Verden im Jahre 782," *Niedersachs. Jahrbuch*, 15 (1938), 1–37 and reprinted in Lintzel, *Ausgewälte Schriften*, I, 147–173.

————, "Karl der Grosse und Widukind," reprinted in Lintzel, "Die Schlacht am Süntel," *Gesammalte Werke*, I, 199–224.

————, "Die Sachsenkrieg Chlothars I," *Sachsen und Anhalt*, 4 (1928), 1–13; and reprinted in Lintzel, *Ausgewählte Schriften*, I, 64–73.

————, "Die Tributzahlungen der Sachsen an die Franken zur Zeit der Merowinger und König Pippins," *Sachsen und Anhalt*, 4 (1928), 13–28, and reprinted in Lintzel, *Ausgewählte Schriften*, I, 74–86.

————, *Ausgewählte Schriften*, 2 vols. (Berlin, 1961).

Loewe, Raphael, "Jewish Evidence for the History of the Crossbow," in *Les Juifs au regard de l'histoire: Mélanges en l'honneur de Bernhard Blumenkranz*, ed. Gilbert Dahan (Paris, 1985), 87–107.

Löhlein, Georg, *Die Alpen- und Italienpolitik der Merowinger im VI. Jahrhundert* in *Erlanger Abhandlungen zu mittleren und neuen Geschichte*, ed. B. Schniedler and O. Brandt (Erlangen, 1932), 1–81.

Long, Pamela O., and Alex Roland, "Military Secrecy in Antiquity and Early Medieval Europe: A Critical Reassessment," *History and Technology*, 11 (1994), 259–290.

Longnon, Auguste, *Géographie de la Gaule au VIe siècle* (Paris, 1878).

López Pereira, José Eduardo, *Estudio crítico sobre la crónica mozárabe de 754* (Zaragoza, 1980).

Lot, F., "Le serment de fidélité à l'époque franque," *Revue belge de l'philologie et d'histoire*, 14 (1935), 405–426.

———, *L'art militaire et les armées au moyen âge Europe et dans le Prôche-Orient*, 2 vols. (Paris, 1946).

Löwe, Heinz, "Hinkmar von Reims und der Apocrisiar," in *Festschrift für Hermann Heimpel*, 3 vols. (Gottingen, 1972), III, 197–225.

Lundquist, Sune, "Vendelhjälmarna Uesprung," *Fornvännen*, 20 (1925), 181–207.

———, "Sköld och svärd ur Vendel," *Fornvännen*, 45 (1950), 1–24.

Luttwak, Edward N., *The Grand Strategy of the Roman Empire: From the First Century A.D. to the Third* (Baltimore, 1976).

MacGregor, A. M., "Two Antler Crossbow Nuts and Some Notes on the Early Development of Crossbow," *Proceedings of the Society of Antiquaries of Scotland*, 107 (1975–1976), 317–321.

MacKurdy, J. T., *The Structure of Morale* (Cambridge, 1943).

MacMullen, Ramsey, "Inscriptions on Armor and the Supply of Arms in the Roman Empire," *American Journal of Archaeology*, 64 (1960), 23–40.

———, *Soldier and Civilian in the Later Empire* (Cambridge, Mass., 1967).

Maenchen-Helfen, Otto, *The World of the Huns: Studies in Their History and Culture* (Berkeley, 1973).

Magnou-Nortier, Elisabeth, "The Enemies of the Peace: Reflections on a Vocabulary, 500–1100," in *The Peace of God: Social Violence and Religious Response in France Around the Year 1000*, ed. Thomas Head and Richard Landes (Ithaca, 1992), 58–79.

Mangoldt-Gaudlitz, H. von, *Die Reiterei in den germansichen und frankischen Herren bis zum Ausgang der deuschen Karolinger* (Berlin, 1922).

Markus, Lawrence, "Saint Augustine's Views on the 'Just War'," in *Studies in Church History*, 20 (1983), 1–13.

Marsden, E. W., *Greek and Roman Artillery: Historical Development* (Oxford, 1969).

———, *Greek and Roman Artillery: Technical Treatises* (Oxford, 1971).

Marshall, P. K., "Florus," in *Texts and Transmission: A Survey of the Latin Classics*, ed. L. D. Reynolds and P. K. Marshall (Oxford, 1983), 164–166.

———, "Scriptores Historiae Augustae," in *Texts and Transmission: A Survey of the Latin Classics*, ed. L. D. Reynolds and P. K. Marshall (Oxford, 1983), 354–356.

———, "Valerius Maximus," in *Texts and Transmission: A Survey of the Latin Classics*, ed. L. D. Reynolds and P. K. Marshall (Oxford, 1983), 428–430.

Mathisen, Ralph W., "Barbarian Bishops and the Churches 'in barbaricis gentibus' During Late Antiquity," *Speculum*, 72 (1997), 664–697.

McCleod, W., "The Range of the Ancient Bow," *Phoenix*, 19 (1965), 1–14.

McClusky, S., "Gregory of Tours, Monastic Timekeeping, and Early Christian Attitudes to Astronomy," *Isis*, 81 (1990), 8–22.

McCormick, Michael, "The Liturgy of War in the Early Middle Ages: Crisis, Litanies, and the Carolingian Monarchy," *Viator*, 15 (1984), 1–23.

————, *Eternal Victory: Triumphal Rulership in Late Antiquity, Byzantium and the Early Medieval West* (Cambridge, 1986).

McKitterick, Rosamond, *The Frankish Kingdoms Under the Carolingians: 751–987* (London, 1983).

————, *The Carolingians and the Written Word* (Cambridge, 1989).

————, "England and the Continent," in *The New Cambridge Medieval History: c. 700–c. 900*, II, ed. Rosamond McKitterick (Cambridge, 1995), 64–84.

McLaughlin, R. Emmet, "The Word Eclipsed: Preaching in the Early Middle Ages," *Traditio*, 46 (1991), 77–122.

Menghin, Wilfried, *Das Schwert im frühen Mittelalter: chronologische-typologischen Gräbern des 5. bis 7. Jahrhunderts* (Stuttgart, 1983).

Mercier, Marcel, and André Seguin, *Charles Martel et la bataille de Poitiers* (Paris, 1944).

Miller, David Harry, "Ethnogenesis and Religious Revitalization Beyond the Roman Frontier: The Case of Frankish Origins," *Journal of World History*, 4 (1993), 277–285.

Millett, Allan R., Williamson Murray, and Kenneth H. Watman, "The Effectiveness of Military Organizations," in *Military Effectiveness*, ed. Allan R. Millett and Williamson Murray, 3 vols. (London and Boston, 1988), I, 1–30.

Mohr, Walter, *Studien zur Charakteristik des karolingischen Königtums im 8. Jahrhundert* (Saarlouis, 1955).

Mordek, Hubert, "Die Hedenen als politische Kraft im austrasischen Frankenreich," in *Karl Martell in Seiner Zeit*, ed. Jörg Jarnut, Ulrich Nonn, and Michael Richter (Sigmaringen, 1994), 345–366.

Moreton, Bernard, *The Eighth-Century Gelasian Sacramentary: A Study in Tradition* (Oxford, 1976).

Morillo, Stephen, *Warfare Under the Anglo-Norman Kings, 1066–1135* (Woodbridge, 1994).

————, *The Battle of Hastings* (Woodbridge, 1996), 190–193.

Morony, Michael G., *Iraq After the Muslim Conquest* (Princeton, 1984).

Mortet, Victor, "Un formulaire du VIIIe siècle pour les fondations des édifices et de ponts d'après des sources d'origine antique. Nouvelle édition critique," *Bulletin Monumentale*, 71 (1907), 422–465.

Mortimer, R. C., *The Origin of Private Penance in the Western Church* (Oxford, 1939).

Moss, J. R., "The Effects of the Policy of Aetius on the History of Western Europe," *Historia*, 22 (1973), 711–731.

Müller-Mertens, Eckhard, *Karl der Grosse, Ludwig der Fromme und die Freien* (Berlin, 1963).

Murray, Alexander, *Reason and Society in the Middle Ages* (corr. ed. Oxford, 1985).

Murray, Alexander C., *Germanic Kinship Structure; Studies in Law and Society in Antiquity and the Early Middle Ages* (Toronto, 1983).

————, "From Roman to Frankish Gaul: 'Centenarii' and 'Centenae' in the Administration of the Merovingian Kingdom," *Traditio*, 44 (1988), 60–100.

————, "Immunity, Nobility, and the Edict of Paris," *Speculum*, 69 (1994), 18–39.

Murray, Oswyn, "The Idea of the Shepherd King from Cyrus to Charlemagne," in *Latin Poetry and the Classical Tradition: Essays in Medieval and Renaissance Literature*, ed. Peter Godman and Oswyn Murray (Oxford, 1990), 1–13.

Needham, Joseph, "China's Trebuchets, Manned and Counterweighted," in *On Pre-*

Modern Technology and Science: Studies in Honor of Lynn White, Jr., ed. Bert S. Hall and Delno C. West (Malibu, Calif., 1976), 107–145.

Nees, Lawrence, "The Originality of Early Medieval Artists," in *Literacy, Politics, and Artistic Innovation in the Early Medieval West: Papers Delivered at "A Symposium on Early Medieval Culture," Bryn Mawr College, Bryn Mawr, Pa.*, ed. Celia M. Chazelle (New York, 1992), 77–133.

Nelson, Janet, "The Church's Military Service in the Ninth Century: A Contemporary View?" *Studies in Church History*, 20 (1983), 15–30, and reprinted in Janet Nelson, *Politics and Ritual in Early Medieval Europe* (London, 1986), 117–132.

——, "Public *Histories* and Private History in the Work of Nithard," *Speculum*, 60 (1985), 251–293, and reprinted in Janet Nelson, *Politics and Ritual in Early Medieval Europe* (London, 1986), 195–237.

Nicolle, David, *Medieval Warfare Source Book*, vol. I, *Warfare in Western Christendom* (London, 1996).

Nishimura, David, "Crossbows, Arrow Guides, and the *Solenarion*," *Byzantion*, 58 (1988), 422–435.

Nitz, Hans-Jürgen, "The Church as Colonist: The Benedictine Abbey of Lorsch and Planned Waldhufen Colonization in the Odenwald," *Journal of Historical Geography*, 9 (1983), 105–126.

Noble, Thomas F. X., *The Republic of St. Peter: The Birth of the Papal State, 680–825* (Philadelphia, 1984).

Nonn, Ulrich, "Merowingische Testamente. Studien zum Fortleben einer römische Urkundenform im Frankenreich," *Archiv für Diplomatik*, 18 (1972), 1–129.

——, "Das Bild Karl Martells in mittelalterlichen Quellen," in *Karl Martel in Seiner Zeit*, ed. Jörg Jarnut, Ulrich Nonn, and Michael Richter (Sigmaringen, 1994), 9–21.

Ober, Josiah, "Hoplites and Obstacles," in *Hoplites: The Classical Greek Battle Experience*, ed. Victor Hanson (London, 1989), 173–196.

Odegaard, Charles E., "Carolingian Oaths of Fidelity," *Speculum*, 14 (1941), 284–296.

——, *Vassi and Fideles in the Carolingian Empire* (Cambridge, Mass., 1945).

Oelsner, Ludwig, *Jahrbücher des fränkischen Reiches unter König Pippin* (Leipzig, 1871).

Ohler, Norbert, *Krieg und Frieden im Mittelalter* (Munich, 1997).

Oman, Charles, *A History of the Art of War in the Middle Ages*, 2 vols., 2nd ed. (London, 1924).

——, *On the Writing of History* (New York, 1939).

Önnerfors, Alf, *Die Verfasserschaft des Waltharius-Epos aus sprachlicher Sicht* (Düsseldorf, 1978).

Oulton. J. E. L., "Rufinus's Translation of the Church History of Eusebius," *Journal of Theological Studies*, 30 (1929), 164–168.

Parrott, David, "Strategy and Tactics in the Thirty Years' War: The 'Military Revolution'," *Militärgeschichtliche Mitteilungen*, 18 (1985), 8–21.

Parsons, David, "Sites and Monuments of the Anglo-Saxon Mission in Central Germany," *Archaeological Journal*, 140 (1983), 280–321.

Partington, J. R., *A History of Greek Fire and Gunpowder* (Cambridge, 1960).

Partner, Nancy, "The New Cornificius: Medieval History and the Artifice of Words," in *Classical Rhetoric and Medieval Historiography*, ed. Ernst Breisach (Kalamazoo, 1985), 5–59.

Paulsen, Peter, *Alamanische Adelsgräber von Niederstotzingen* (Stuttgart, 1967).

————, "Flugellanzen: Zum archäologischen Horizont der Wiener *Sancta lancea*," *Frümittelalterliche Studien*, 3 (1969), 289–312.

Paxton, Frederick S., *Christianizing Death: The Creation of a Ritual Process in Early Medieval Europe* (Ithaca and London, 1990).

Payne-Gallwey, R. W. F., *The Crossbow, Mediaeval and Modern, Military and Sporting*, 2nd ed. (London, 1958).

Peltier, Henri, *Adalhard, Abbé de Corbie* (Amiens, 1969).

Percival, John, "The Precursors of Domesday: Roman and Carolingian Land Registers," in *Domesday Book: A Reassessment*, ed. Peter Sawyer (London, 1985), 5–27.

Périn, Patrick, and Laure-Charlotte Feffer, *Les Francs*, 2 vols. (Paris, 1987).

Périn, Patrick, and R. Legoux, *La datation des tombes mérovingiennes. Historique, méthodes, applications* (Geneva, 1980).

Petot, P., "L'hommage servile: Essai sur la nature juridique de l'hommage," *Revue historique de droit français et étranger*, series 4, 6 (1927), 68–107.

Petrikovits, H. von, "Fortifications in the North-Western Roman Empire from the Third to the Fifth Centuries A.D.," *Journal of Roman Studies*, 61 (1971), 178–218.

Pétrin, Nicole, "Philological Notes on the Crossbow and Related Missile Weapons," *Greek, Roman and Byzantine Studies*, 33 (1992), 265–291.

Philipsen, J. P. W., "The Utrecht Ship," *Mariners Mirror*, 51 (1965), 35–46.

Pierce (McKitterick), Rosamond, "The 'Frankish' Penitentials," *Studies in Church History*, 11, ed. Derek Baker (Oxford, 1975), 31–39.

Poly, Jean-Pierre, "La corde au cou: les Franks, la France, et la Loi Salique," *Genèse de l'état moderne en Méditerranée. Paris, 287–320* (Paris, 1993), 287–320.

Poulin, Jean-Claude, *Les vies anciennes de sainte Geneviève de Paris* (Paris, 1986).

Poschmann, Bernhard, *Die abendländische Kirchenbusse im frühen Mittelalter* (Breslau, 1930).

Prestwich, J. O., "The Military Household of the Norman Kings," *English Historical Review*, 96 (1981), 1–35.

Prinz, Friedrich E., "Herzog und Adel im agilulfingischen Bayern. Herzogsgut und Konsensschenkungen vor 788," *Zeitschrift für bayerische Landesgeschichte*, 25 (1962), 283–311.

————, "King, Clergy and War at the Time of the Carolingians," in *Saints, Scholars and Heroes: Studies in Medieval Culture in Honour of Charles W. Jones*, ed. M. King and W. Stevens (Collegeville, Minn., 1979), II, 301–329.

Pritchett, W. K., *The Greek State at War*, 4 vols. (Berkeley, 1971–1985).

Rabe, Susan A., *Faith, Art, and Politics at Saint-Riquier: The Symbolic Vision of Angilbert* (Philadelphia, 1995).

Raddatz, Karl, "Die Bewaffnung der Germanen vom letzten jahrhundert vor Chr. Geb. bis zur Völkerwanderungzeit," in *Aufsteig und Niedergang der romanische Welt; Geschichte und Kultur Roms im Spiegel der neueren Forchung*, 2. 12.3, ed. Hilda Temporini (Berlin, 1985), 281–361.

Randsbourg, Klavs, *Hjortspring: Warfare and Sacrifice in Early Europe* (Aarhus, 1995).

Rathgen, Bernard, *Das Geschütz im Mittelalter* (Berlin, 1928).

Ray, Roger, "Rhetorical Scepticism and Verisimilar Narrative in John of Salisbury's *Historia Pontificalis*," in *Classical Rhetoric and Medieval Historiography*, ed. Ernst Breisach (Kalamazoo, 1985), 61–102.

Reddé, Michel, *Mare Nostrum: Les infrastructures, le dispositif, et l'histoire de la marine militaire sous l'empire Romain* (Rome, 1986).

Reeve, M. D., "Agrimensores," in *Texts and Transmission: A Survey of the Latin Classics*, ed. L. D. Reynolds and P. K. Marshall (Oxford, 1983), 1–6.

———, "Notitia Dignitatum," in *Texts and Transmission: A Survey of the Latin Classics*, ed. L. D. Reynolds and P. K. Marshall (Oxford, 1983), 253–257.

———, "Suetonius," in *Texts and Transmission*, 399–406.

Reuter, Timothy, "Plunder and Tribute in the Carolingian Empire," *Transactions of the Royal Historical Society*, 5th ser., 35 (1985), 75–94.

———, "The End of Carolingian Military Expansion," in *Charlemagne's Heir: New Perspectives on the Reign of Louis the Pious (814–840)*, ed. Peter Godman and Roger Collins (Oxford, 1990), 391–405.

———, *The Annals of Fulda* (Manchester, 1992).

Reynolds, L. D., "Ammianus Marcellinus," in *Texts and Transmission: A Survey of the Latin Classics*, ed. L. D. Reynolds and P. K. Marshall (Oxford, 1983), 6–8.

———, "Apuleius," *Texts and Transmission*, 15–16.

———, "Eutropius," *Texts and Transmission*, 159–162.

———, "Frontinus," *Texts and Transmission: A Survey of the Latin Classics*, ed. L. D. Reynolds and P. K. Marshall (Oxford, 1983), 167–172.

———, "Justinus," in *Texts and Transmission*, 197–199.

———, "Livy," in *Texts and Transmission*, 205–214.

———, "Sallust," in *Texts and Transmission*, 341–349.

———, "Velleius Paterculus," in *Texts and Transmission*, 431–433.

Reynolds, Susan, *Fiefs and Vassals: The Medieval Evidence Reinterpreted* (Oxford, 1994).

Richardson, F. M., *Fighting Spirit: A Study of Psychological Factors in War* (London, 1978).

Riché, Pierre, *Education and Culture in the Barbarian West: Sixth Through Eighth Centuries*, trans. John Contreni (Columbia, S.C., 1976).

———, *Écoles et enseignement dans le haut moyen âge* (Paris, 1979).

———, *The Carolingians: A Family Who Forged Europe*, trans. M. I. Allen (Philadelphia, 1993).

Riesch, Holger, " 'Quod nullus in hostem habeat baculum sed arcum' Pfeil und Bogen als Beispiel für technologische Innovationen der Karolingerzeit," *Technikgeschichte*, 61 (1994), 209–226.

Riesenberger, Dieter, "Zur Geschichte des Hausmeiers Karlmann," *Westfalische Zeitschrift*, 120 (1970), 271–286.

Robinson, H. Russell, *Oriental Armour* (London, 1968).

———, *The Armour of Imperial Rome* (London, 1975).

Rogers, R., *Latin Siege Warfare in the Twelfth Century* (Oxford, 1992).

Roloff, Gustav, "Die Umwandlung des fränkischen Herrs von Chlodowig bis Karl den Grossen," *Neue Jahrbucher für das klassische Altertum*, 9 (1902), 389–399.

Rosenwein, Barbara H., *Negotiating Space: Power, Restraint, and Privileges of Immunity in Early Medieval Europe* (Ithaca, N.Y., 1999).

Roth, Jonathan P., *The Logistics of the Roman Army at War (264 B.C.–A.D. 235)* (Leiden, 1999).

Roth, Paul, *Geschichte des Beneficialwesens von den ältesten Zeiten bis ins zehnte Jahrhundert* (Erlangen, 1850).

———, *Feudalität und Unterthanverband* (Weimar, 1863).

Rouche, Michel, *L'Aquitaine des Wisigoths aux Arabes, 418–781: Naissance d'une région* (Paris, 1979).

———, "Les survivances antiques dans trois cartulaires du sud-ouest de la France aux X–XI siècles," *Cahiers de civilisation médiévales* 23 (1980), 93–108.

———, "Les Aquitains ont-ils trahi avant la bataille de Poitiers?" *Le moyen âge*, 74 (1968), 5–26.

Rougé, J., "Ports et escales dans l'empire tardif," *Settimane di Studio del Centro Italiano di Studi sull'alto Medioevo*, 25 (Spoleto, 1978), 67–124.

Rübel, Karl, "Frankisches und spätrömisches Kriegswesen," *Bonner Jahrbücher*, 114 (1906), 136–142.

Russell, Frederick, *The Just War in the Middle Ages* (Cambridge, 1975).

Sackur, W., *Vitruv und die Poliorketiker. Vitruv und die christliche Antike. Bautechnisches aus der Literatur des Alterums* (Berlin, 1925).

Salin, Eduard, *La civilisation mérovingienne*, 4 vols. (Paris, 1957).

Sánchez-Albornoz, Claudio, *Entorno a los orígenes del feudalismo*, 3 vols. (Mendoza, 1942).

Sawyer, Peter H., *The Age of the Vikings* (London, 1962).

Schieffer, Rudolf, "Karl Martell und seine Familie," in *Karl Martel in seiner Zeit*, ed. Jörg Jarnut, Ulrich Nonn, and Michael Richter (Sigmaringen, 1994), 305–315.

Schieffer, Theodor, *Winfrid-Bonifatius und die Grundlegung von Europas* (Freiburg, 1954).

———, "Early Medieval Fortification in Hesse: A General Historical Report," *World Archaeology*, 7 (1976), 243–260.

Schlesinger, Walter, "Kaisertum und Reichsteilung. Zur *divisio regnorum* von 806," in *Forschung zu Staat und Verfassung, Festgabe für Fritz Hartung*, ed. R. Dietrich and G. Oestreich (Berlin, 1958), 9–51, and reprinted in Walter Schlesinger, *Beiträge zur deutschen Verfassungsgeschichte des Mittelalters*, 2 vols. (Göttingen, 1963).

———, "Early Medieval Fortification in Hesse: A General Historical Report," *World Archaeology*, 7 (1976), 243–260.

Schlight, John, *Monarchs and Mercenaries; A Reappraisal of the Importance of Knight Service in Norman and Early Angevin England* (Bridgeport, Conn., 1968).

Schmidlin, Joseph, *Review* of Joseph Michael Heer, *Ein karolingische Missionskatechismus* (Freiburg, 1911), in *Zeitschrift für Missionwissenschaft*, 2 (1912), 258.

Schmiedt, Giulio, "I porti Italiani nell'alto medioevo," *Settimane di Studio del Centro Italiano di Studi sull'alto Medioevo*, 25 (Spoleto, 1978), 128–254.

Schmitz, Hermann, *Miscellanea Tironiana* (Leipzig, 1896).

Schneider, R., *Die Artillerie des Mittelalters* (Berlin, 1910).

Schneider, Reinhard, *Das Frankenreich* (Munich, 1982).

———, "Fränkische Alpenpolitik," in *Die Transalpinen Verbindungen der Bayern, Alemannen und Franken bis zum 10. Jahrhundert*, ed. Helmut Beumann and Werner Schröder (Sigmaringen, 1987), 23–49.

Schramm, E., *Die antiken Geschütze der Saalburg* (Berlin, 1918).

Schubert, H. von, *Die Unterwerfung der Alemannen unter die Franken* (Strassburg, 1984).

Schwarzlose, Friedrich Wilhelm, *Die Waffen der alten Araber aus ihren Dichtern dargestellt* (Leipzig, 1886).

Secrétan, Henri F. "Le christianisme de premiers siècles et le service militaire," *Revue de théologie et de philosophie*, n.s. 2 (1914), 345–365.

See, Klaus von, "Exkurs zum Haraldskvaedhi: Beserker," in *Edda, Saga, Skaldendichtung: Aufsätze zur skandinavischen Litaratur des Mittelalters* (Heidelberg, 1981), 311–317.

Shanzer, Danuta, "Dating the Baptism of Clovis: The Bishop of Vienne vs. the Bishop of Tours," *Early Medieval Europe*, 7 (1998), 29–57.

Shay, Jonathan, *Achilles in Vietnam: Combat Trauma and the Undoing of Character* (New York, 1994).

Smail, R. C., *Crusading Warfare, 1097–1193*, 2nd ed. (Cambridge, 1995).

Smith, Julia M. H., *Province and Empire: Brittany and the Carolingians* (Cambridge, 1992).

——, "The Sack of Vannes by Peppin III," *Cambridge Medieval Celtic Studies*, 11 (1986), 17–27.

Spencer, Mark, "Dating the Baptism of Clovis, 1886–1993," *Early Medieval Europe* 3 (1994), 97–116.

Sprandel, Rolf, *Der merovingische Adel und die Gebiete östlich des Rheins*, in *Forschung zur oberrheinischen Landesgeschichte*, V (Freiburg im Breisgau, 1957).

Springer, M, "Vegetius im Mittelalter," *Philologus*, 123 (1979), 85–90.

Sproemberg, H., "Die Seepolitik Karls des Grossen," in H. Sproemberg, *Beitrage zur belgisch-niederländerischen Geschichte* (Berlin, 1959), 1–29.

Staab, Franz, "A Reconsideration of the Ancestry of Modern Political Liberty: The Problem of the So-Called 'King's Freemen' (*Königsfreie*)," *Viator*, 11 (1980), 51–69.

Starr, Chester, G., *The Roman Imperial Navy*, 2nd ed. (Cambridge, 1960).

——, *The Influence of Sea Power on Ancient History* (New York, 1989).

Staudte-Lauber, Annalena, "Carlus Princeps Regionem Burgundie Sagiciter Penetravit. Zur Schlacht von Tours und Poitiers und dem Eingreifen Karl Martells in Burgund," in *Karl Martell in Seiner Zeit*, ed. Jörg Jarnut, Ulrich Nonn, and Michael Richter (Sigmaringen, 1994), 79–100.

Stein, Frauke, *Die Adelsgräber des achten Jahrhunderts in Deutschland*, 2 vols. (1967).

Stephenson, Carl, "The Origin and Significance of Feudalism," *American Historical Review*, 46 (1941), 788–812; and reprinted in Carl Stephenson, *Medieval Institutions: Selected Essays*, ed. Bryce D. Lyon (Ithaca, N.Y., 1954), 205–233.

Steuer, Heiko, "Archaeology and History: Proposals on the Social Structure of the Merovingian Kingdom," in *The Birth of Europe: Archaeology and Social Development in the first Millennium A.D.* ed. Klaves Ransbourg (Rome, 1989), 100–122.

——, *Frühgeschichtliche Sozialstrukturen im Mittleuropa. Eine Analyse der Auswertungsmethod des archäologischen Quellen* (Göttingen, 1982).

——, "Historische Phasen der Bewaffnung nach Aussagen der Archäologischen Quellen Mittel- und Nordeuropas im ersten Jahrtausend n. Chr.," *Frühmittelalterliche Studien*, (1970), 348–383.

Stevens, Wesley M., *Bede's Scientific Achievement: Jarrow Lecture, 1985* (Jarrow, Durham, England, 1985).

——, "Cycles of Time: Calendrical and Astronomical Reckonings in Early Science," *Time and Process: Interdisciplinary Issues, The Study of Time VII*, ed. J. T. Fraser and Lewis Rowell (Madison, Conn., 1993), 27–51.

Stevenson, W. H., "Trinoda Necessitas," *English Historical Review*, 29 (1914), 689–703.

Stoclet, Alain J., *Autour de Fulrad de Saint-Denis (v. 710–784)* (Paris, 1993).

Stork, Ingo, "Friedhof und Dorf, Herrenhof und Adelsgräber," *Die Alamannen* (Stuttgart, 1996), 270–310.

Störmer, Wilhelm, "Zur Frage der Functkion des kirchlichen Fernbesitzes im Gebiet der Ostalpen vom 8. bis zum 10 Jahrhundert," in *Die Transalpinen Verbindungen der Bayern, Alemannen und Franken bis zum 10 Jahrhundert,* ed. H. Beumann (Sigmaringen, 1987), 379–403.

Storms, G., "The Significance of Hygelac's Raid," *Nottingham Medieval Studies,* 14 (1970), 3–26.

Strickland, Matthew, "Military Technology and Conquest:" The Anomaly of Anglo-Saxon England," *Anglo-Norman Studies,* 19 (1996), 353–382.

———, *War and Chivalry: The Conduct and Perception of War in England and Normandy, 1066–1217* (Cambridge, 1996).

Swanton, J., *Spearheads of the Anglo-Saxon Settlements* (London, 1983).

Syme, Ronald, *The Roman Revolution,* 2nd ed. (Oxford, 1951).

Szövérffy, Joseph, "Venantius Fortunatus and the Earliest Hymns to the Holy Cross," *Classical Folia,* 20 (1966), 107–22.

Tabacco, Giovanni, *I Liberi del Re nell'italia carolingia e post-carolingia* (Spoleto, 1966).

Tackenberg, Kurt, "Über die Schutzwaffen der Karolingerzeit un ihre Wiedergabe in Handschriften und auf Elfenbeinschnitzereien," *Frühmittelalterliche Studien* 3 (1969), 227–288.

Tarrant, R. J., "Lucan," in *Texts and Transmission,* 215–218.

———, "Tacitus," in *Texts and Transmission,* 406–409.

Tarver, W. T. S., "The Traction Trebuchet: A Reconstruction of an Early Medieval Siege Engine," *Technology and Culture,* 36 (1995), 136–168.

TeBrake, William H., *Medieval Frontier: Culture and Ecology in Rijnland* (College Station, Tex., 1985).

Thompson, James Westfall, "The Statistical Sources of Frankish History," *American Historical Review,* 40 (1935), 625–645.

Thordeman, Bengt, *Armour from the Battle of Wisby, 1361,* 2 vols. (Uppsala, 1939).

Toubert, Pierre, "La liberté au haut moyen âge et le problème de *arimanni,*" *Le moyen âge,* 53 (1967), 127–144.

Treadgold, Warren, *Byzantium and Its Army; 284–1081* (Stanford, 1995).

Unger, Richard, *The Ship in the Medieval Economy, 600–1600* (London, 1980).

Van Dam, Raymond, "Images of Saint Martin in Late Roman and Early Merovingian Gaul," *Viator,* 19 (1988), 1–27.

Van Es, W. A., and W. J. Verwers, *Excavations at Dorestad 1. The Harbour Hoogstraat 1* (Amersfoort, 1980).

Verbruggen, J. F., *The Art of Warfare in Western Europe During the Middle Ages, from the Eighth Century to 1340,* trans. Sumner Willard and S. C. M. Southern, 2nd ed. (Woodbridge, Suffolk, 1997).

———, "L'armée et la stratégie de Charlemagne," in *Karl der Grosse: Lebenswerk und Nachleben,* I, ed. W. Braunfels and Helmut Beumann 5 vols. (Düsseldorf, 1965), 420–434.

———, "L'art militaire dans l'empire carolingien (714–1000)," *Revue belge d'histoire militaire,* 23 (1979), 299–310; 24 (1980), 393–411.

Verkamp, Bernard J., "Moral Treatment of Returning Warriors in the Early Middle Ages," *Journal of Religious Ethics,* 16.2 (1988), 223–249.

Verhulst, Adriaan, "An Aspect of the Question of Continuity Between Antiquity and the Middle Ages," *Journal of Medieval History,* 3 (1977), 175–206.

————, "Economic Organisation," in *The New Cambridge Medieval History*, ed. Rosamond McKitterick, II (Cambridge, 1995), 481–509.

Vieillefond, J.-R., "Les Pratiques religieuses dans l'armée byzantine d'après les traités militaires," *Revue des Etudes Anciennes*, 37 (1935), 322–330.

Villain, M., "Rufin d'Aquilée et l'histoire ecclésiastique," *Recherches de science religieuse*, 33 (1946), 188–199.

Vlek, Robert, *The Medieval Utrecht Boat: The History and Evaluation of the First Nautical Archaeological Excavations and Reconstructions in the Low Countries* (Oxford, 1987).

Vogel, Cyrille, *La discipline pénitentielle en Gaule des origines à fin du VIIe siècle* (Paris, 1952).

————, *Les "Libri paenitentiales"* (Brepols, 1978).

————, "Les rituels de la pénitence tarrifée," in *Liturgia opera divina e umana, Studi offerti à S. E. Mons. A. Bugnini, biblioteca Ephemerides Liturgicae*, Subsidia 26 (Rome, 1992), 419–427.

Vogel, Walthar, *Geschichte der deutschen Seeschiffsfahrt* (Berlin, 1915).

Vryonis, Speros, Jr., "The Evolution of Slavic Society and the Slavic Invasions in Greece: The First Major Slavic Attack on Thessaloniki, A.D. 597," *Hesperia*, 50 (1981), 378–390.

Waddell, Helen, *Mediaeval Latin Lyrics*, 4th ed. (New York, 1933).

Waitz, Georg, *Deutsche Verfgassungsgeschichte*, 8 vols., 2nd ed. (Berlin, 1893–1896).

Wallace-Hadrill, J. M., *The Long-Haired Kings and Other Studies in Frankish History* (London, 1962).

————, "Charlemagne and England," in *Karl der Grosse: Lebenswerk und Nachleben*, I, ed. W. Braunfels and Helmut Beumann (Düsseldorf, 1965), I, 683–698.

————, "War and Peace in the Early Middle Ages," *Transactions of the Royal Historical Society*, 5th ser., 25 (1975), and reprinted in J. M. Wallace-Hadrill, *Early Medieval History* (Oxford, 1975), 19–38.

————, "A Background to St. Boniface's Mission," in *England Before the Conquest: Studies in Primary Sources Presented to Dorothy Whitelock*, ed. P. Clemoes and K. Hughes (Cambridge, 1971), and reprinted in J. M. Wallace-Hadrill, *Early Medieval History* (Oxford, 1975), 138–154.

————, *Early Medieval History* (Oxford, 1975).

————, *Bede's Ecclesiastical History of the English People: A Historical Commentary* (Oxford, 1988).

————, *The Frankish Church* (Oxford, 1983).

Wallach, Luitpold, "Alcuin on Virtues and Vices: A Manual for a Carolingian Soldier," *Harvard Theological Review*, 48 (1955), 175–195.

Walters, Dafydd, "From Benedict to Gratian: The Code in Medieval Ecclesiastical Authors," in *The Theodosian Code*, ed. Jill Harries and Ian Wood (Ithaca, N.Y., 1993), 200–216.

Wand, Norbert, "Die Büraburg und das Fritzlar-Waberner Becken der merowingisch-karolingischen Zeit," in *Althessen im Frankreich*, ed. Walter Schlesinger (Sigmaringen, 1974), 173–210.

Watkins, Oscar D., *A History of Penance*, 2 vols. (London, 1920).

Watson, Andrew M., "Toward Denser and More Continuous Settlement: New Crops and

Farming Techniques in the Early Middle Ages," in *Pathways to Medieval Peasants*, ed. J. A. Raftis (Toronto, 1981), 65–82.

Weidemann, Konrad, "Archäologische Zeugnisse zur Eingliederung Hessens un Mainfrankens," in *Althessen im Frankreich*, ed. Walter Schlesinger (Sigmaringen, 1975), 95–119.

Weidemann, Margarete, *Kulturgeschichte der Merowingerzeit nach den Werken Gregors von Tours*, 2 vols. (Mainz, 1982).

Weigel, H., "Studien zur Eingliederung Ostfrankens in das merowingish-karolingische Reich," *Historische Vierteljahresschrift*, 28 (1934), 449–502.

Wells, Colin, M., *The German Policy of Augustus: An Examination of the Archaeological Evidence* (Oxford, 1972).

Wemple, Suzanne, *Women in Frankish Society: Marriage and the Cloister, 500–900* (Philadelphia, 1981).

Werner, Joachim, "Zur Herkunft der frühmittelaltliche Spangenhelm," *Praehistorische Zeitschrift*, 33–34 (1949–1950), 178–193.

———, "Zur Entstehung der *Reihengräberzivilisation*: ein Beitrag sur Methode unde frügeschichtliche Archäologie," *Archaeolgoia Geographia*, 1 (1950), 139–167.

———, "Ein langobarischen Schild von Ischl an der Als," *Bayerische Vorgeschichtsblätter*, 18–19 (1952), 45–58.

———, "Bewaffnung und Waffenbeigabe in der Merowingerzeit," *Settimane di Studio del Centro Italiano sull'alto Medioevo*, 15.1 (Spoleto, 1968), 95–108.

Werner, Karl Ferdinand, "Heeresorganization und Kriegsführung im deutschen Königreich des 10. und 11. Jahrhunderts," *Settimane di Studio del Centro Italiano sull'alto Medioevo*, 15 (Spoleto, 1968), 791–843.

———, "Les principautés périphériques dans le monde franc du VIIIe siècle," *Settimane di Studio del Centro Italiano di studi sull'alto medioevo*, 20 (1972), 483–532.

———, "*Missus-Marchio-Comes*. Entre l'administration centrale et l'administration locale de l'Empire carolingien," *Histoire comparée de l'administration (IVe–XVIIe siècles)*, ed. Werner Paravicini et Karl Ferdinand Werner (Munich, 1980), 191–239.

———, "*Hludovicus Augustus*: Gouverneur l'empire chrétien—Idées et réalités," in *Charlemagne's Heir: New Perspectives on the Reign of Louis the Pious (814–840)*, ed. Peter Godman and Roger Collins (Oxford, 1990), 3–123.

Werner, Matthias, *Der Lütticher Raum in früfrankischer Zeit* (Göttingen, 1980).

Wheeler, Everett L., "Methodological Limits and the Mirage of Roman Strategy," *Journal of Military History*, 57 (1993), 7–41, 215–240.

Whitby, Michael, *The Emperor Maurice and His Historian: Theophylact Simocatta on Persian and Balkan Warfare* (Oxford, 1988).

White, Lynn T., Jr., *Medieval Technology and Social Change* (Oxford, 1962).

Wieland, Gernot. *Waltharius* (Philadelphia, 1986).

Wilson, David, "Trade Between England and Scandinavia and the Continent," *Untersuchungen zu Handel und Verkehr der vor- und frühgeschichtlichen Zeit in Mittel- und Nordeuropa*, III, *Der Handel des frühen Mittelalters*, ed. Kalus Düwel, Herbert Jahnkuhn, Harald Siems, and Dieter Timpe (Göttingen, 1983), 225–246.

Winterbottom, M., "Caesar," *Texts and Transmission*, ed. L. D. Reynolds (corrected rpt. Oxford, 1986), 35–36.

———, "Curtius Rufus," *Texts and Transmission*, 148–149.

Wolff, Philippe, "L'Aquitaine et ses marges," in *Karl der Grosse: Lebenswerk und Nach-leben*, I, ed. W. Braunfels H. Beumann, 5 vols. (Düsseldorf, 1965), 269–306.

Wolfram, Herwig, *History of the Goths*, trans. Thomas J. Dunlap (Berkeley, 1979).

———, *Die Geburt Mitteleuropas: Geschichte Österreichs vor seiner Entstehung, 378–907* (Berlin, 1987).

———, "Baiern und das Frankenreich," *Die Bajuwaren*, ed. Hermann Dannheimer and Heinz Dopsch (Salzberg, 1988), 130–135.

———, "Tassilo III. und Karl der Grosse—Das Ende der Agilolfinger," *Die Bajuwaren*, ed. Hermann Dannheimer and Heinz Dopsch (Salzberg, 1988), 160–166.

———, "Karl Martell und das fränkische Lehenswesen. Aufnahme eines Nichtbe-standes," in *Karl Martel in Seiner Zeit*, ed. Jörg Jarnut, Ulrich Nonn, and Michael Richter (Sigmaringen, 1994), 61–78.

Wood, Ian, *The Merovingian North Sea* (Alingas, Sweeden, 1983).

———, Review—Geary, Patrick, *Aristocracy in Provence: The Rhône Basin at the Dawn of the Carolingian Age* (Stuttgart, 1985), in *French History*, 1 (1987), 118–119.

———, "The Channel from the Fourth to the Seventh Centuries AD," in *Maritime Celts, Frisians and Saxons*, ed. Seán McGrail (London, 1990), 93–97.

———, "Saint Wandrille and Its Hagiography," in *Church and Chronicle in the Middle Ages: Essays Presented to John Taylor* ed. Ian Wood and Graham Laud (London, 1991), 11–12.

———, "Frankish Hegemony in England," in *The Age of Sutton Hoo: The Seventh Century in North-Western Europe*, ed. M. O. H. Carver (Woodbridge, Suffolk, 1992), 234–241.

———, "The Code in Merovingian Gaul," in *The Theodosian Code*, ed. Jill Harries and Ian Wood (Ithaca, N.Y., 1993), 159–177.

———, *The Merovingian Kingdoms, 450–751* (London, 1994).

Wormald, Patrick, "The Age of Offa and Alcuin," in *The Anglo-Saxons*, ed. James Camp-bell (Ithaca, N.Y., 1982), 101–128.

Wright, Roger, "Review Article: Michael Banniard, *Viva voce: Communication écrit et communication orale du IVe au IX siècle en occident latin* (Paris, 1992)," *Journal of Medieval Latin*, 3 (1993), 78–94.

Zeki Validi, A., "Die Schwerter der Germanen nach arabishcen Berichten des 9–11. Jahr-hunderts," *Zeitschrift der Deutschen Morgenländischen Gesellschaft*, 90 (1936), 19–36.

Zettel, Horst, *Das Bild der Normannen und der Normanneneinfälle in westfränkischen, ostfränkischen und angelsächsischen Quellen des 8. bis 11. Jahrhunderts* (Munich, 1977).

Zöllner, Erich, *Geschichte der Franken bis zur Mitte des 6. Jahrhunderts* (Munich, 1970).

Index